FISCHLERS' HOCKEY ENCYCLOPEDIA

FISCHLERS'

HOC

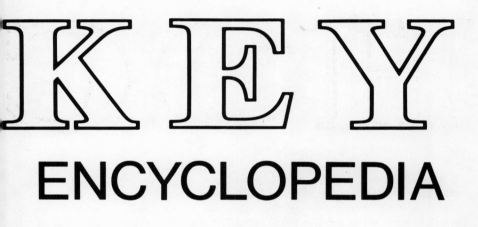

KEY

ENCYCLOPEDIA

STAN AND SHIRLEY FISCHLER

THOMAS Y. CROWELL COMPANY   NEW YORK
ESTABLISHED 1834

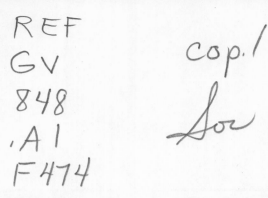

Photo Credits
Daniel S. Baliotti: page 49, 496, 511; David Bier: 498; Vincent P. Claps: 317, 454, 524, 575; Terry Foley: 20, 108, 217, 238, 328, 463; New York Rangers: 122, 259, 330; United Press International: 13, 67, 74, 309, 539.

Library of Congress Cataloging in Publication Data
Fischler, Stan.
  Fischlers' hockey encyclopedia.

  1. Hockey. I. Fischler, Shirley, joint author.
II. Title.
GV847.F45   796.9'62   75-12749

ISBN 0-690-00297-1

10 9 8 7 6 5 4 3 2 1

To Mom and Dad, and most of all to Stan, without whom this love affair with hockey would never have begun.

Shirley Walton Fischler
Boiceville, New York
May 1975

To Mom and Dad, and most of all to Shirley and Ben, without whom this love affair with hockey would never have reached such fruition.

Stan Fischler
Boiceville, New York
May 1975

ACKNOWLEDGMENTS

The authors wish to thank the following for their valuable help in the preparation of this book: Nancy Demmon, Helene Elliot, Jim Finkenstaedt, Richard Friedman, Jeff Goldsmith, Ida Gross, Howard Hyman, Ira Lacher, Melinda Muniz, Pat Muniz, Karen Robertson, Mike Rubin, Roy Schecter, Roy Urrico, and Barry Wilner; Jay Acton, Sheila LaLima, Linnea Leedham, and Buddy Skydell of the Thomas Y. Crowell Company; as well as Bob Casey and Judy Epstein of National Hockey League Services, Walt Marlow at World Hockey Association Headquarters, Lefty Reid, Curator of the Hockey Hall of Fame, and the publicists of all NHL and WHA teams.

INTRODUCTION

A man's reach should exceed his grasp, Robert Browning once suggested, or what's a heaven for? Obviously, Robert Browning never tried to compile a hockey encyclopedia from A to Z.

Reach we did, from Taffy Abel to Larry Zeidel. After years of collecting, filing, collating, and writing—lo and behold—our grasp, unlike Browning's experience, *exceeded our reach*.

We had so many names, so many subjects, that volumes would have been required to find room for everyone. As a result a lot of good men, funny subjects and, perhaps, favorites of yours, made their exit on the cutting-room floor. It was as painful as telling a rookie or an aging veteran in training camp that he wasn't good enough to make the team; even though the reject believed otherwise.

Our objective, nevertheless, was to produce the most comprehensive A to Z listing of hockey subjects, from players to teams to riots, ever attempted. We believe we succeeded.

Producing detail was the biggest obstacle. Because of space limitations we omitted minor statistical matter on owners and managers but provided it, as thoroughly as possible, on players. The All-Star statistics used in this book were based on the National Hockey League's official year-end All-Star listings.

In some cases, especially, the turn-of-the-century players and other pre-NHL aces, statistical information was at best limited. All available sources, from the NHL office to the Hockey Hall of Fame in Toronto, were combed for detail.

More than anything, we have attempted to make this project as entertaining, readable, and fun as it is comprehensive. In that sense we sincerely hope that our reach equalled our grasp.

FISCHLERS' HOCKEY ENCYCLOPEDIA

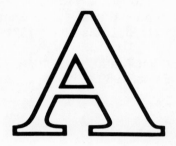

CLARENCE JOHN "TAFFY" ABEL

BORN: Sault Ste. Marie, Michigan, May 28, 1900
POSITION: Defenseman, New York Rangers, 1926–29; Chicago
    Black Hawks, 1929–34

Bunyanesque Taffy Abel, imported from Minneapolis' minor league club in 1926 along with Ivan "Ching" Johnson, was one of the original members of the New York Rangers who fielded their first team that year.

Abel and Johnson teamed on the Rangers' backline to give the Blueshirts' defense a fortification that averaged 225 pounds and menaced enemy forwards at every turn. Built like a skating dirigible, Taffy played three full seasons with the Rangers, including the 1928 Stanley Cup-winning sextet, before being traded to Chicago. He was the first U.S.-born skater in the N.H.L.

The native of Sault Ste. Marie, Michigan, played five full seasons with the Black Hawks, all of them alongside Lilliputian Harold "Mush" March with whom he developed an astonishing Mutt-and-Jeff goal-scoring routine.

It worked this way: Abel would carry the puck over the enemy blue line with the tiny March following close behind. Once Taffy was about ten feet inside the opponent's defensive zone, he would pass the puck to March and skate toward the net, "spreading himself out as wide as possible." March would then fire the puck through an opening in Abel's legs. Never has such a screened shot been seen before or since.

SIDNEY GERALD ABEL

BORN: Melville, Saskatchewan, February 22, 1918

POSITION: Center, Detroit Red Wings, 1938–43, 1945–52; Chicago Black Hawks, 1952–53; Coach, Chicago Black Hawks, 1952–54; Detroit Red Wings, 1958–68; St. Louis Blues, 1971; General Manager, Detroit Red Wings, 1962–71; St. Louis Blues, 1971–73; Kansas City Scouts, 1973–

AWARDS: Hart Trophy, 1949; All-Star (First Team), 1949, 1950; (Second Team), 1951; Hockey Hall of Fame, 1969

There may have been better centers in the National Hockey League than Sid Abel (alias "Ole Bootnose" because of his prominent proboscis), but few were more productive in all the vital areas. He was a dogged and creative playmaker, the balance wheel between Gordie Howe and Ted Lindsay on Detroit's Production Line. He could score as well as develop goal-making plays for others.

Reared in the wheat fields of Melville, Saskatchewan, Abel became a member of the Red Wings in 1938–39, remaining in the Motor City until 1952 when he was released to become player-coach of the Chicago Black Hawks in 1952–53. Curiously, that season has been overlooked by hockey historians, although it underlined Abel's insatiable drive.

Sid inherited one of the worst collections of ragtag major leaguers in NHL history, a team that had finished last in five out of the previous six seasons, and somehow he made them a winner. The difference was his spirited play at center coupled with the extraordinary goaltending of angular Al Rollins, who emerged with the Hart (MVP) Trophy at season's end.

Abel not only drove his charges into the playoffs but very nearly scored a stunning semifinal Stanley Cup playoff victory over the Montreal Canadiens. The Black Hawks lost the series in the seventh and final game when rookie goalie Jacques Plante, imported from Buffalo, bailed out the Canadiens.

However, Abel is best remembered for his exploits in Detroit. "Sid," said hockey historian Ed Fitkin, "will go down in the Red Wings' history as the greatest competitor and inspirational force the Red Wings ever had." Few would have bet on that when he arrived in Detroit as a nineteen-year-old in the fall of 1937.

A six-footer who weighed in at only 155 pounds, Abel was greeted by manager-coach Jack Adams. "You got a future, kid," Adams told him, "but you have to build yourself up."

After watching Abel dazzle in workouts, Adams suggested he stick around Detroit and play in the Michigan–Ontario League, which then was flourishing. Abel demurred and returned to western Canada to play with the Flin Flon (Manitoba) Bombers, one of the better senior division clubs in the Dominion.

The year of seasoning was just what Abel needed. When he returned to the Red Wings' camp in the fall of 1938, Adams beamed over Sid's play. "I don't know how he'll stand up in pro hockey," said Adams, "but Abel's got class written all over him."

Detroit signed him to an NHL contract in 1938–39, but injuries delayed his development as a major leaguer. The Red Wings tried him at left wing for a while, but he didn't achieve meaningful recognition until 1941–42, playing on a line with Eddie Wares and Don "the Count" Grosso.

Abel was named alternate All-Star left wing for 1941–42, but he was a thoroughly distraught young man in April 1942. His Red Wings took on the Toronto Maple Leafs in the Stanley Cup finals. The Red Wings were a distinct underdog, yet Detroit won the first three games of the best-of-seven series and appeared certain to win the Cup. When it appeared the Red Wings would wrap up the series at Detroit's Olympia Stadium, Toronto rallied for a victory and then won the next three games and the championship. "To Abel," said a friend, "it was the greatest disappointment of his life."

The balm was administered the following autumn when manager-coach Adams named Sid captain of the Red Wings. Detroit finished first and won the Stanley Cup. Significantly, Detroit defeated Boston, 6–2, in the opening game of the finals, and Abel enjoyed the most productive night of his career to that point with a goal and three assists. He finished the playoffs with 5 goals and 8 assists for 13 points in 10 games.

Prior to the 1943–44 campaign, Abel enlisted in the Royal Canadian Air Force, but not before marrying Red Wings' secretary Gloria Morandy. He was away from hockey for almost three years, serving as physical training instructor for the RCAF both in Canada and overseas.

Sid returned to the Red Wings in February 1946. He was twenty-eight years old and there were suspicions that he, like many returning war veterans, was too old and had been away too long. Still, he stayed with the Red Wings and survived the training camp cuts in 1946–47, scoring 19 goals that season.

At the start of the 1947–48 race, Abel was installed as the center between galloping youngsters Gordie Howe (right wing) and Ted Lindsay (left wing), a pair he had worked with only occasionally in previous years.

"I don't know where I'd be without Sid," said Howe. "He just has to whack me with his stick when I'm not playing well and say 'Get going' and that's all I ever need."

Lindsay, who was to develop into one of hockey's best left wingers under Abel's guidance, swore by his veteran center. "Sid is the greatest of them all," said Lindsay. "He seems to know more about what I'm doing than I do myself, and he's always in the right spot."

It wasn't until the 1948–49 season, at age thirty-one, that Abel realized his dream of a 20-goal season. He scored 28 that year, with a little help from his friends, Lindsay and Howe. "It just seemed," said Sid, "that every time I shot, I scored. I kept telling my wife to pinch me. I felt sure that one day I'd wake up and find that I was just dreaming."

The Lindsay-Abel-Howe combine developed into the dreadnoughts of the ice lanes. Abel had the savvy, and both Howe and Lindsay percolated along with a mixture of style, explosiveness, and aggression that terrorized opposing teams. With the Production Line orchestrating the wins, Detroit captured the first of seven consecutive Prince of Wales trophies (first place) in 1949. The Red Wings won the Stanley Cup in 1950 and again in 1952 whereupon Abel decided to try coaching—and playing—with the Black Hawks.

Abel eventually returned to Detroit, becoming coach of the Red Wings in January 1958 when Jimmy Skinner was forced by illness to retire. He remained coach until 1962–63 when he became the Red Wings' general manager. Despite friction between Abel and the aging Jack Adams, Sid remained in command and stayed on the Detroit payroll in one way or another through part of the 1970–71 season, although it was clear that his power base had eroded with the arrival of Ned Harkness.

Despite his age, Abel signed as coach of the St. Louis Blues in 1971–72, a move that was a mistake from the start. He was named general manager of the Blues in October 1971 and remained in that position until April 17, 1973, when he was appointed general manager of the Kansas City Scouts.

Clearly, Abel's major contribution to hockey was as a player, and he was named to the Hockey Hall of Fame in June 1969. As a coach and manager, he frequently was lauded for his relaxed style, although the assignment in Kansas City was one to severely try his patience.

EUGENE EDWARD (GENE) ACHTYMICHUK

BORN: Lamont, Alberta, September 7, 1932
POSITION: Forward, Montreal Canadiens, 1956–58; Detroit Red Wings, 1958–59

Of all players to reach the National Hockey League (1956–59) from Lamont, Alberta, Gene Achtymichuk (Atch-ti-mi-chook) owned the most difficult name to pronounce.

CHARLES F. ADAMS

The Boston Bruins' franchise was conceived as the result of a Stanley Cup playoff in Montreal! After Charles Adams saw his first playoff, this former grocery boy solicited the help of Art Ross, and in 1924 the Beantown Bruisers were born.

Desperately in need of strong players, Adams purchased the entire Western Canada League from the Patrick family in 1926, and followed this move by guaranteeing $500,000 to help build Boston Garden, which has been the home of the Bruins ever since. Adams was inducted into the Hockey Hall of Fame prior to his death in 1947.

JOHN J. (JACK) ADAMS

BORN: Fort William, Ontario, June 14, 1895
DIED: May 1, 1968
POSITION: Forward, Toronto Arenas, 1917–19; Toronto St. Pats, 1922–26; Ottawa Senators, 1926–27; Coach, Detroit Red Wings, 1927–47; General Manager, Detroit Red Wings, 1927–63; President, Central League, 1963–68
AWARDS: Lester Patrick Trophy, 1966; Hockey Hall of Fame, 1959

Without Jack "Jovial Jawn" Adams there might never be a Detroit Red Wings franchise today. A native of Fort William, Ontario, Adams had played NHL hockey with the Toronto Arenas, the Toronto St. Patricks, and the Ottawa Senators, as manager-coach. He was an exceptionally galvanic personality who would do anything to win and rarely concerned himself with the consequences.

NHL president Frank Calder must certainly have admired Adams when Jack walked into the NHL office prior to the 1927–28 season and asserted that he was the man for the vacant Detroit NHL coaching job. Calder agreed and telephoned club president Charlie Hughes to set up an appointment.

Adams then met Hughes and revealed the same brashness, a characteristic for which he was renowned. "I'd been involved in winning the Stanley Cup for Ottawa," said Adams, "so I told Hughes that he needed me more than I needed him."

Hughes must have agreed, because he signed Adams to a contract and told him to get started building a winner. A year later Hughes knew he had taken the right course. From a dismal 12–28–4 record, the Detroiters climbed to the .500 mark, winning 19, losing 19, and tying 6 games. It wasn't a good enough record for a Stanley Cup berth, but there was no question that the road to the Cup had opened for Detroit's then Cougars. The following season Detroit, with a new nickname, the Falcons, finished third in the American Division.

Adams soon discovered that building a winner required more than native enthusiasm. Money was necessary to buy and sign players, but the depression had hit the motor industry and loose cash was as distant as the Stanley Cup.

The turning point toward better times for the teams was reached in 1933, when the franchise was bought by James Norris, Sr., a grain millionaire with a fervent love of hockey. Norris had played hockey for the Montreal Amateur Athletic Association's famous Winged Wheelers. He suggested a new team name, the Red Wings, and an insignia symbolic of the industry which dominates the city.

A no-nonsense type, Norris was even brasher than Adams. He laid it on the line with the manager. "I'll give you a year on probation," Norris warned, "with no contract."

Adams may not have had a written pact with Norris, but he quickly gained the millionaire's confidence as well as access to his bankroll to sign superior players. He bought Syd Howe (no relation to Gordie) from the St. Louis Flyers for $35,000. Howe was soon playing the brand of hockey that eventually put him in the Hall of Fame. Hec Kilrea was purchased from Toronto for $17,000 and the Wings were off, flying toward the top.

By the 1935–36 season, the Adams-Norris combine was the best in hockey. The manager was not only off probation but had become so friendly with his awesome boss that he referred to Norris as "Pops."

By March 22, 1936, the final day of the 1935–36 season, Detroit was perched atop the American Division with a record of 24 wins, 16 losses, and 8 ties for 56 points, the best record in either division.

To win the Cup in 1936 first required that the Red Wings dispatch the strong Montreal Maroons in the opening playoff round that began March 24, 1936 at the Forum in Montreal. To this day, the game remains a classic among classics. It was the longest hockey match ever played in the NHL. Exactly 116 minutes and 30 seconds of sudden-death overtime was required, almost two additional full games. The winning goal was scored by Modere "Mud" Bruneteau of the Red Wings at 16:30 of the sixth overtime.

The Red Wings plummeted in 1937–38. Not only did they fail to retain their hold on first place but they didn't even gain a playoff berth. It took six years for Adams's Red Wings to win another Stanley Cup. That was accomplished in the 1942–43 season when they finished first.

Without any question, 1946 was the most important year in the history of

Adams and his Detroit hockey club. It was then that a muscular youngster with a Saskatchewan drawl arrived in Detroit. His name was Gordie Howe. He was accompanied by another young player, Ted Lindsay, who had joined the Red Wings two years before. After juggling combinations of players, Adams eventually placed captain Sid Abel, the center, on a line with Howe on right wing and the truculent Lindsay on left. No three forwards ever jelled more firmly, and as they began to pump goal after goal into the enemy nets it was rather appropriate that the city which developed the motor production line should name the Abel, Lindsay, and Howe trio *the* "Production Line."

However, they weren't the only stars. The defense was replete with talented skaters, such as "Black" Jack Stewart, Bill Quackenbush, and Leonard "Red" Kelly, who guarded rosy-cheeked Harry Lumley in goal.

To reach the top, however, they would have to cope with the dynastic Toronto Maple Leafs sextet, which from 1947 through 1949 was to win a then record three straight Stanley Cups. It wasn't until 1949–50 that the Red Wings were ready once again for a serious assault on the championship. After finishing first, for the second year in a row, the Wings' first objective was the Maple Leafs, whom they defeated in seven games, but only after Howe had sustained a near-fatal head injury in the opening match. That put Detroit in the finals against the New York Rangers, whom they beat in seven games.

Adams's clubs went on to win three more Stanley Cups, and finished first six more times until Jack stepped down in 1962–63 to become president of the Central League.

Since Detroit was admitted to the NHL in 1926, they have finished in first place thirteen times and have won the Stanley Cup seven times, a record unsurpassed by any other American team in the league. Adams had reason to be proud.

JOHN F. "BUNNY" AHEARNE

As president of the International Ice Hockey Federation, J. F. "Bunny" Ahearne has ruled European hockey with an iron fist for more than a decade. A onetime travel agent, Ahearne has remained a thorn in the side of North American professionals who have attempted to circumvent his jurisdiction in order to arrange matches between NHL and Russian teams as well as other European powers. Until the early seventies, Ahearne was able to thwart such attempts by strict interpretations of the amateur rules. Bunny insisted that the Europeans, who technically if not actually were amateurs, could not compete with the professionals from North America. At least not without his special sanction. Ahearne's first major setback occurred in 1972 when a Canadian professional All-Star team (Team Canada) played an eight-game series with the allegedly amateur Russians. A similar series—this time with WHA All-Stars—was played in 1974.

ANDREW AITKENHEAD

BORN: Glasgow, Scotland, March 6, 1904
POSITION: Goalie, New York Rangers, 1932–35

Blond, blue-eyed goaltender Andrew Aitkenhead of Glasgow, Scotland, was hired by New York Rangers' manager-coach Lester Patrick in the 1932–33 season as a replacement for John Ross Roach. Aitkenhead's addition to the New York sextet was a pivotal one at the time, particularly since Roach had played mediocre goal for the Rangers during the previous season.

With Andy starring in the nets, the Rangers defeated Toronto three games to one in the best-of-five Stanley Cup final in April 1933 to win the world championship. That, however, was the acme of Andy's success. He played one more full season and only ten games of the 1934–35 campaign before making his exit from the major leagues.

ALLAN CUP

Symbol of senior amateur hockey supremacy in Canada, this trophy was originally given to the Montreal Victorias in 1908 by Sir Montague Allan, C.V.O., after the Stanley Cup had become a professional trophy.

The Cliffsides of Ottawa were the first league winners that year, but were challenged and defeated by Queen's University, who thus became the first winners of the Allan Cup.

In 1928 the Allan Cup was given outright to the Canadian Amateur Hockey Association.

SIR MONTAGUE ALLAN, C.V.O.

Known primarily as the donor of the Allan Cup, Montague Allan was a Montreal sportsman and financier. In 1908, at the urging of one of amateur hockey's major builders, William Northey, Allan put up the trophy, then valued at about $300. For this gesture, Allan was ultimately inducted into the Hockey Hall of Fame.

THE AMERICAN HOCKEY LEAGUE

The present American Hockey League actually stems from three leagues—the Canadian Professional League, the International League, and the Canadian–American League. The Canadian Professional and the Can–Am had their beginnings the same season, that of 1926–27—but the former gave way to the

International after three years of operation, while Can–Am was a going concern when the International took it over in 1936–37 to form the International–American League. Soon after it became known simply as the American Hockey League.

There was an element of trial and error as the American Hockey League went through more than two dozen cities to arrive at its fluctuating lineup. Only one city, Providence, Rhode Island, has had continuous representation since professional hockey started branching out in 1926–27. Before that, the Rhode Island Reds were charter members of the Canadian–American League.

As the name implies, the Canadian Professional League was composed entirely of clubs located in Dominion cities. Stratford, London, Hamilton, Windsor, and Niagara Falls, all in the Province of Ontario, made up the circuit. The Canadian–American League got its name because of the inclusion of Quebec City with the original four United States cities—New Haven, Springfield, Boston, and Providence.

While the Canadian Professional League started with five clubs, it didn't remain at that strength long. Two years after first making its bid for public attention, it became an eight-club league, this being accomplished by the addition of Detroit, Kitchener, and Toronto. However, the lineup lasted only one season as Stratford, winner of two championships, dropped out and its place was taken by Buffalo for the 1928–29 season.

The inclusion of three United States teams in 1929–30 brought about a change of name and the circuit became known as the International League. Cleveland replaced Kitchener and finished in first place.

Three withdrawals in 1930–31 brought more changes in the International League. Toronto, Niagara Falls, and Hamilton dropped out and in came Pittsburgh and Syracuse, to form a seven-club league which remained unchanged through 1931–32. In the following campaign Pittsburgh withdrew, reducing the circuit to six clubs and for the three following seasons, the alignment read London, Windsor, Detroit, Buffalo, Cleveland, and Syracuse.

Expansion was in the wind in 1935–36 and the league again became an eight-club circuit. Syracuse, Buffalo, London, and Rochester made up the Eastern section with Rochester appearing for the first time. In the West, Pittsburgh returned with Detroit, Cleveland, and Windsor.

All told, the Canadian Professional League, later becoming the International League, operated with thirteen clubs in the ten-year period. In the Canadian–American League there were fewer changes over the same stretch and the league never fielded more than a half-dozen clubs at any one time.

To the original Can–Am League of New Haven, Springfield, Quebec, Boston, and Providence, Philadelphia was added in 1927–28, but the next year Quebec folded and Newark came in for a single season. Newark withdrew before 1929–30, and for two seasons the league had only five clubs. The Bronx joined for 1931–32, and again the league was five teams strong.

Springfield was replaced by Quebec in 1932–33, but in 1935–36 Springfield returned and Quebec was gone again.

Then, in 1936–37, sweeping changes came with the organization of the International–American League, which soon abandoned the International designation and became known simply as the American Hockey League. Buffalo, Cleveland, Pittsburgh, and Syracuse made up the Western group and Philadelphia, Springfield, New Haven, and Providence went into the Eastern division. Buffalo was unable to complete the 1936–37 campaign, when its arena was destroyed by fire.

Buffalo was out for three years, but returned for the campaign of 1940–41 when the Municipal Auditorium was completed. Springfield was in for six seasons before becoming a war casualty in 1942–43, the same year that Philadelphia dropped out. New Haven went through part of the 1942–43 campaign, withdrew, then returned to competition again.

Hershey came in for the season of 1938–39 and Indianapolis joined up the following year. Washington was a newcomer in 1941–42, remained active for two seasons and then withdrew. No fewer than ten clubs were in action in 1941–42.

The American League, like its big league counterpart, the National Hockey League, survived World War II and thrived thereafter, although it occasionally lost franchises. Former AHL franchises such as Buffalo, Philadelphia, Washington, St. Louis, Indianapolis, and Baltimore eventually moved on to major leagues, some to the NHL and others to the World Hockey Association.

By 1975 the league consisted of a lopsided nine teams, including a Canadian entry: Providence, Rochester, Nova Scotia, Springfield, and New Haven in the North Division; and Virginia, Richmond, Hershey, and Syracuse in the South Division.

LORNE ANDERSON

BORN: Renfrew, Ontario, July 26, 1931
POSITION: Goalie, New York Rangers, 1951–52

Hockey's answer to "Wrong Way" Riegels, Lorne Anderson was a third-string New York Rangers' goaltender in the early fifties when Chuck Rayner was number one goalie and Emile Francis number two. As a result, Anderson did his job for the New York Rovers of the Eastern League and played only three NHL games, all in the 1951–52 season. His notorious "wrong way" routine took place on the night of March 23, 1952, during the final game of the regular season between the Rangers and the Chicago Black Hawks. With the score 6–2 in New York's favor, and only 15 minutes remaining, Bill Mosienko of Chicago had Anderson going the wrong way on three shots within 21 seconds.

Mosienko's record-breaking goals did to Anderson what Bobby Thomson's 1951 home run did to Ralph Branca. Needless to say, Anderson never played a big-league game again in his life.

THOMAS LINTON (TOMMY) ANDERSON

BORN: Edinburgh, Scotland, July 9, 1911
POSITION: Defenseman, Detroit Red Wings, 1934–35; New York
    Americans, 1935–42
AWARDS: Hart Trophy, 1942; All-Star (First Team), 1942

Playing for the perennially weak New York Americans from 1935 through 1942, when the star-crossed club finally folded, Tommy Anderson shone as one of the NHL's highest scoring defensemen. Curiously, his best year was his last, 1941–42, when he scored 12 goals and 29 assists for 41 points in 48 games. A native of Edinburgh, Scotland, Anderson broke in with the Red Wings (1934–35) before being dealt to New York a year later.

LOUIS FREDERICK (LOU) ANGOTTI

BORN: Toronto, Ontario, January 16, 1938
POSITION: Center, New York Rangers, 1964–65; Chicago Black
    Hawks, 1966–67, 1969–73; Philadelphia Flyers, 1967–68; Pitts-
    burgh Penguins, 1968–69; St. Louis Blues, 1973–74; Coach, St.
    Louis Blues, 1974

The small (5'8") centerman from Toronto saw action with five NHL clubs since turning pro with the Rochester Americans of the American Hockey League back in 1962–63. After some bouncing around between the minors and the Rangers, Angotti was sold to the cellar-dwelling Chicago Black Hawks, where he gained a solid chunk of fan appreciation. The honeymoon was short-lived, however, as the Hawks put Lou in the expansion pool in 1967, where he was gobbled up by the new Philadelphia Flyers. He lasted one season with the Flyers, then after a couple of whirlwind trades finally landed in Pittsburgh.

Lou was then traded to St. Louis, but the Hawks picked him up in the intraleague draft. For the next four years, from 1969–70 to 1972–73, Angotti was a favorite once again in the Chicago Stadium, as the fans roared their appreciation of the little man with the whirling dervish moves and the persistent checking. He did an especially good job in the 1972–73 semifinal Stanley Cup playoffs against the Rangers, as he successfully bottled up the potent Ranger centers.

The much-traveled Lou was selected by the St. Louis Blues in the 1973 intraleague draft, and for a while the fans in the St. Louis Arena appreciated his skills as much as those in Chicago did. The cry of "Lou" could be heard whenever he touched the puck. Lou briefly tried coaching with the sagging Blues, but gave it up early in the 1974–75 season.

ANNOUNCERS

Not all hockey stars appear on the ice. The world's fastest sport has some of the fastest announcers presenting hockey fans with concise, colorful, and sometimes controversial descriptions of the action.

Millions of Canadians have grown up listening to the voice of Foster Hewitt, the only radio broadcaster in the Hockey Hall of Fame. Hewitt captured the nation with his Saturday night broadcasts of the Toronto Maple Leafs, and his introduction—"from the gondola, high atop Maple Leaf Gardens"—is known to just about every Canadian hockey fan.

So too is the voice of the Montreal Canadiens' Danny Gallivan. Gallivan has been broadcasting the Canadiens for more than twenty years on the English radio stations in Montreal. In French, it's the popular duo of René Lecavalier and Lionel Duval, along with former Canadien Gilles Tremblay.

Outstanding hockey broadcasters abound on both sides of the border. They include Bill Hewitt, Bob Cole, and Brian McFarlane of the Canadian Broadcasting Company, all operating "up North." In the United States are quite a few transplanted Canadians and a number of homebreds, including Dan Kelly, Marv Albert, Al Albert, Steve Albert, Don Earle, Bob Wilson, Ken McDonald, and Lloyd Pettit, to name just a few.

On television, the most popular Canadian series is "Hockey Night in Canada," which nationally televises the games of the Toronto Maple Leafs, Montreal Canadiens, and Vancouver Canucks. Besides the regular play-by-play men doing the broadcasts, the color analysts are former NHL greats, such as John Ferguson and Jean Beliveau.

In 1967, the Columbia Broadcasting System in the United States began its weekly telecasts of National Hockey League games. The original men behind the "mike" were Jim Gordon and Stu Nahan. In 1968, Dan Kelly, the voice of the St. Louis Blues, replaced Nahan, and in 1970, Bill Mazer replaced Jim Gordon who then began doing play-by-play for the Rangers.

In 1972, the National Broadcasting Company signed a four-year agreement to televise the "Game of the Week in the NHL," when CBS and the league could not agree on terms. The new faces and voices were Tim Ryan, who used to broadcast the New York Rangers' games, Ted Lindsay, former Detroit great and member of the Hockey Hall of Fame, and, a familiar face to Canadians, Brian MacFarlane.

JOSEPH SYLVANUS (SYL) APPS

BORN: Paris, Ontario, January 18, 1915
POSITION: Center, Toronto Maple Leafs, 1936–43, 1945–48
AWARDS: Calder Trophy, 1937; Lady Byng Trophy, 1942; All-Star
   (First Team), 1939, 1942; (Second Team), 1938, 1941, 1943;
   Hockey Hall of Fame, 1961

Syl Apps was the Bobby Orr of the pre-World War II era, and for some time
beyond. The original "All-Canadian boy," Apps was born in the tiny town of
Paris, Ontario. His father believed he should become well educated and proficient in sports, and he helped young Syl on both counts. The name Apps soon
became prominent in both the classroom and the athletic field. In fact, Syl
could handle every sport better than any youngster his age.

Long and lean, Syl had developed a graceful skating style, which later was
to inspire Montreal author Vincent D. Lunny to call him "a Rembrandt on the
ice, a Nijinsky at the goalmouth." By the time Syl was fourteen years old, the
village team found a center ice spot for him, and his hockey career had begun.

"His dazzling bursts of speed," wrote Ron McAllister, "and great sweeping
strides made him an exciting player to watch, and he soon discovered that he
was gaining quite a reputation among sports fans in his hometown."

Apps betrayed one "weakness" which alarmed his coach Russell Sander-
cock of the Paris Juniors. He showed no inclination to retaliate when fouled by

the opposition; and since he was easily the best player on his team, the enemy constantly tried to reef him along the boards or behind the net. Syl would always take his blows and return to action as if nothing had happened.

Later other "obstacles" blocked Apps's climb to the NHL—pole-vaulting and football. At the age of seventeen, Syl entered McMaster University in Hamilton, Ontario, on a scholarship, majoring in political economy, and he turned out for the track team. His specialty was pole-vaulting, and he became so adept at it that in 1934 he was invited to represent the Dominion of Canada at the British Empire Games in London, England.

Apps won his event and returned home, this time to try out for football. He became captain of the McMaster football team and spearheaded its march to the Intercollegiate Championship. Syl also had been playing for McMaster's hockey team and was as impressive among the collegians as he had been in junior hockey. Syl was so impressive that Bill Marsden, a former Toronto hockey coach who had moved to the University of Western Ontario, told his friend Conn Smythe about the big kid with the long strides.

When Smythe and Apps finally met, Syl made it clear that before he considered the NHL he wanted to complete his college education and compete in the Olympic Games, to which he had been invited. He also wasn't quite sure that he was capable of playing big-league hockey. Smythe nursed some doubts, too, and they agreed that a year in the tough Ontario Hockey Association Senior A League would provide a good indication of Syl's NHL potential.

The answer was supplied at the end of the season. Apps had led the league in scoring. He then headed for Berlin, Germany, and the Eleventh Olympiade, where before 100,000 spectators, including Adolf Hitler, Syl vaulted to a sixth-place tie for Canada.

He returned to Canada, 6'0", 180 pounds, with the world at his feet. He could move on to graduate school, or he could accept Smythe's offer to attend the Maple Leafs' training camp. Throughout the late summer and early autumn speculation mounted about Syl's decision between hockey and advanced education. A September meeting with Smythe sealed his fate with the Maple Leafs.

Coach Dick Irvin put Apps at center between Busher Jackson and Gordie Drillon. Although veteran Jackson no longer was noted for his diligence, the two younger players would remain on the ice for long hours after regular workouts, perfecting Drillon's "secret weapon," the tip-in shot. Apps was vital to the play since he was required to deliver the pass. Drillon, of course, was to get credit for the goals, but as Toronto *Globe and Mail* reporter Bill Roche pointed out, "The serious-minded Apps was the one who proposed that they do the experimenting."

The results came immediately, and by midseason Apps was hailed as a shoo-in for Rookie of the Year. "He's a better player than Howie Morenz was at the same age," said Detroit manager Jack Adams, who always was grudging in his acclaim for a Toronto player.

Smythe, who from time to time remarked that he didn't want any Lady Byng (good conduct) hockey players on his team, tried to inspire Apps into some form of belligerence.

Apparently Smythe did little to encourage Syl's truculence. Syl finished the season with only 10 minutes in penalties, but, more important, he scored 16 goals and 29 assists for 45 points, second to Dave "Sweeney" Schriner of the Americans. Apps had missed the scoring championship by only one point. In the balloting for the Calder Trophy, given to the season's top rookie, Apps polled 79 out of a possible 81 votes and easily won the award.

The aging Busher Jackson didn't last very long on the Apps line. Irvin replaced him the following season with Bob Davidson, a husky, hard-checking winger, and the D-A-D (Drillon-Apps-Davidson) Line was born.

Norfield M. Stephen, a subscriber to Maple Leaf Gardens' games for many years, once described Apps's significance to the line. "Syl," wrote Stephen, "was a terrific skater, stickhandler, and had speed to burn at all times on the ice. He possessed the faculty of breaking fast from a standing stop, which left his opposition flat-footed. He took great pride in having one of his linemates score from a play set up by him. In fact, I think that he enjoyed that better than if he had bulged the twine himself. Every time Apps touched the puck, the crowds would let out a deafening and dramatic roar, because they sensed something spectacular, and in most cases he did not disappoint them."

Thanks to Syl's crisp passes, Drillon led the NHL in scoring during the 1937–38 season, with 26 goals and 26 assists for 52 points. The unselfish Apps finished second again, having scored 21 goals and 29 assists for 50 points. Injuries began taking their toll in the next season, especially torn shoulder muscles, yet he still managed to lead the Maple Leafs in scoring and was improving with every month.

While he was earning his place among hockey greats, Syl also managed to take his first turn in the political arena. He was nominated as the conservative candidate for the federal election in North Brant. He was defeated in the election, however, and once again he concentrated full time on his hockey campaign. In 1948, he led the Leafs to first place and the Stanley Cup.

Apps retired from pro hockey in 1948 and went on to become a member of the Ontario Legislature for Kingston and a member of the Cabinet.

SYLVANUS MARSHALL (SYL) APPS

BORN: Toronto, Ontario, August 1, 1947
POSITION: Center, New York Rangers, 1970–71; Pittsburgh
    Penguins, 1971–

Bromidic as it may sound, there is no question that Syl Apps is a chip off the old block. The son of the Toronto Maple Leafs Hall of Famer, young Syl has gradually developed into one of the gems of National Hockey League expansion, and the Pittsburgh Penguins acknowledged this by signing him on June 21, 1973, to a five-year pact for an estimated $750,000. He then proved his value by leading Pittsburgh in scoring with 24 goals and 61 assists for 85 points, seventh best in the league. It was the brand of play that inevitably led to an assortment of raves.

"He reminds me of his old man." That is the highest compliment any hockey fan could ever deliver to Syl. Toronto coach Red Kelly, who had played against the elder Apps, agreed that father and son have a lot in common. "Young Syl's dad was a great guy and a great player," said Kelly. "He went so fast I looked like a post on the ice by comparison. His son shows similar qualities. He's strong and he hits and he has a good fake. This is something that has to be born in a hockey player. It comes from breeding. Young Syl has the breeding, and I've always said that bloodlines are a wonderful thing."

But in Apps's case, breeding also meant pressure—the onus of having to live up to a father's reputation. In Syl's case it was an awesome burden to bear.

Young Syl climbed from the Junior ranks to the Kingston Frontenacs Senior club and then to the New York Rangers' farm system. He played two games for Buffalo in the American League during 1968–69, scored one goal and two assists and promptly was given a "watch-carefully" tag by the New York scouts.

A season later he was transferred to Omaha of the Central Pro League and scored 16 goals and 38 assists for 54 points in 68 games.

During the 1970 CHL playoffs he scored a league-leading 10 goals and 9 assists for 19 points in 12 games. He also played seven playoff games for Buffalo and managed a commendable 2 goals and 3 assists.

The Rangers promoted him to the big team in 1970–71 and then traded him to Pittsburgh in January 1971. The Penguins' fans were not exactly delirious with joy. Pittsburgh general manager Jack Riley sent the popular—if not productive—Glen "Slats" Sather to New York. One irate Penguins fan hung a sign in the home rink: "Why Slats?"

Ironically, it was in a game against Toronto—his dad's former team—that Syl was architect on a goal that brought Penguins fans to his side. First, he faked Ron Ellis and then dispatched a pass to teammate Greg Polis who went in for the score. Not long after that, Syl himself executed a breakaway goal which left then-coach Red Kelly dancing in the aisles. To this day Kelly considers it a gem of offensive hockey.

"Jacques Plante was in the Toronto nets," Kelly recalled. "Syl first gave him a lunge to his right and then a lunge to his left. I could see Plante thinking 'I've got him' and put his stick out for the puck. But then Syl deked him again and it made bubbles inside me. It was the most beautiful goal I've seen in a long time."

Soon after that the "Why Slats?" sign came down. And Syl's scoring went up and up.

ALGER (AL) ARBOUR

BORN: Sudbury, Ontario, November 1, 1932
POSITION: Defenseman, Detroit Red Wings, 1953–54, 1956–58; Chicago Black Hawks, 1958–61; Toronto Maple Leafs, 1961–66; St. Louis Blues, 1967–71; Coach, St. Louis Blues, 1970–72; Coach, New York Islanders, 1973–

A defenseman, Al Arbour generally performed his job in an unspectacular fashion. He did not make those rink-length dashes, nor did he bash oncoming forwards with board-rattling checks. He simply frustrated the opposition with timely stick checks by blocking shots and by continually foiling good scoring opportunities. He totally epitomized what is called the "defensive defenseman," scoring a mere 12 goals in a career spanning twelve seasons in the NHL.

Alger Arbour first turned pro in 1953 in the Detroit Red Wing organization at the age of twenty, playing for their Western Hockey League club in Edmonton. The following season he was given a brief trial with the parent club, but by season's end he found himself in Sherbrooke.

In fact, it wasn't until the 1956–57 season that Arbour took a regular turn on defense with Detroit. After being drafted by the Chicago Black Hawks in the intraleague draft in June 1958, he finally began to come into his own. In June 1961, the Toronto Maple Leafs claimed him in the draft and from then until 1967 he alternated, playing with the Leafs and their Rochester Americans farm club in the AHL, where he won the Eddie Shore Award as the AHL's top rearguard in the 1964–65 season.

When the AHL expanded to twelve teams in 1967, Arbour, who was one of the few players to wear glasses, was the second defenseman chosen by the new St. Louis Blues. For three years the tall defenseman played brilliantly, qualifying for the West Division All-Star team each year and playing an important role in the club's early success. Each season the Blues competed in the Stanley Cup finals, touching off a love affair with their fans unparalleled in contemporary sports.

In June 1970, Arbour was named coach of the St. Louis Blues, a position he held for 50 games before returning to the bench as a player. The following season he was appointed assistant general manager, but once again took over the coaching reins on Christmas Day, 1971. He then held that position until November 8, 1972, when, unable to tolerate front office interference, he relinquished his coaching responsibilities to become a scout with the new Atlanta Flames.

On June 11, 1973, Arbour was named the third coach of the New York Islanders, a club which had set virtually every record for futility in its maiden season. Before coming to New York, he had never missed qualifying for the playoffs as a player or a coach, and only one year into his Islanders' coaching stint he had his team competing for first place in the Lester Patrick Division.

In 1975 the Islanders made the playoffs, then defeated the Rangers and Penguins before being ousted in seven games by the Flyers.

GEORGE EDWARD "CHIEF" ARMSTRONG

BORN: Skead, Ontario, July 6, 1930
POSITION: Center, Toronto Maple Leafs, 1949–50, 1951–71
AWARDS: Hockey Hall of Fame, 1975

George Armstrong, an Indian lad from Skead, Ontario, was the choice to be groomed by the Toronto Maple Leafs' owner Conn Smythe as a replacement at pivot once Syl Apps retired in April 1948. Tall and awkward, Armstrong had climbed through the Leafs' minor hockey system playing for the Toronto Marlboros in both the Ontario Hockey Association's Junior and Senior divisions. He had a two-game trial with the Leafs in 1949–50 and played twenty NHL games with them in 1951–52 after which he was signed on as a regular.

It was clear, despite Armstrong's relentless improvement, that he'd never be another Syl Apps, Max Bentley, or Ted Kennedy, the best of the NHL centers in the late forties, although he most resembled the latter. Like Kennedy, Armstrong—nicknamed "Chief"—was a plodding skater with a bland shot. But he played a persistent two-way game and eventually was named Leafs' captain after Kennedy's retirement. However, it wasn't until Punch Imlach's reign as Toronto coach that Armstrong reached his apex as a player. During his captaincy, the Leafs won four Stanley Cups and finished first once.

The Chief remained with Toronto throughout his career, ultimately retiring at the conclusion of the 1970–71 season after playing 1,187 games for the Maple Leafs. He then became coach of the Toronto Marlboros of the OHA Junior A League. In June 1975 he was elected to the Hall of Fame.

MURRAY ALEXANDER ARMSTRONG

BORN: Manor, Saskatchewan, January 1, 1916
POSITION: Forward, Toronto Maple Leafs, 1938–39; New York Americans, 1940–42; Detroit Red Wings, 1943–46

Murray Armstrong was a mediocre forward who broke into the NHL with the Toronto Maple Leafs in 1938–39 and was traded to the New York Americans a year later. In 1943–44, after the Amerks folded, Armstrong became a Red Wing and stayed with the Detroiters until his NHL career ended in 1945–46. After he left the professionals, Murray became head hockey coach at Denver

University which, in turn, became one of the most successful collegiate hockey empires. Big-leaguers such as the Black Hawks' Keith Magnuson and Cliff Koroll were among the more successful Denver products. A winner of the NCAA Coach of the Year Award, Armstrong remained a controversial figure in American collegiate hockey because of his use of Canadian-born skaters as opposed to homebred stickhandlers.

ROBERT RICHARD (BOB) ARMSTRONG

BORN: Toronto, Ontario, April 7, 1931
POSITION: Defenseman, Boston Bruins, 1950–51, 1952–62

Long before Ted Green and Derek Sanderson came along to vent their fury with the big, bad Boston Bruins, Bob Armstrong was terrorizing opponents on the Bruins' blue line. A big, balding "defensive defenseman," Armstrong scored only 13 goals in ten full seasons in Boston from 1952 through 1962, but he could hit. In those days when the huskier Bruins were intimidating the smaller New York Rangers, Armstrong engaged tiny Wally Hergesheimer of New York in a tussle at Boston Garden. Before any serious blows could be struck the pair wound up in a knotty clinch. After the game, Hergesheimer told newsmen that Armstrong was very fortunate that no further blows were struck. "If there were," Hergesheimer quipped, "I would have bled all over him!"

WILLIAM BARRY ASHBEE

BORN: Weston, Ontario, July 28, 1939
POSITION: Defenseman, Boston Bruins, 1965–66; Philadelphia Flyers, 1970–74; Assistant Coach, Philadelphia Flyers, 1974–

One of the genuinely tragic figures of hockey, Barry Ashbee was struck down by a blazing slapshot during the 1974 Stanley Cup semifinals between the New York Rangers and Philadelphia Flyers. Ashbee, who had spent most of his fifteen-year career in the minors, didn't gain a regular NHL berth until 1970–71 when the Flyers signed him to a contract. He was the linchpin of Philadelphia's solid defense during the 1973–74 campaign when the Flyers finished first in the West Division and guided Philadelphia to an opening round triumph over Atlanta in the 1974 playoffs.

But on April 28, 1974 at Madison Square Garden his career suddenly ended when Rangers' defenseman Dale Rolfe shot at the Flyers' net. The puck hit Ashbee's right eye with all its force. He lost nearly all sight in the eye and retired to become a Flyers' scout. "I'm not bitter," Ashbee insisted. "Some people strive for sixty years and they can't make it. I got what I wanted when I was thirty-four—a Stanley Cup win for the Flyers. I had thought about being on a Cup winner since I was seven."

Barry Ashbee

ATLANTA FLAMES

The Atlanta Flames franchise was born in 1972–73, the same season the WHA started operation. This proved to their advantage, while it decimated the other freshman, the New York Islanders.

Bill Putnam, instrumental in forming a strong Philadelphia Flyer organization, was brought in as president of the Flames. He chose an excellent ex-scout named Cliff Fletcher to be his manager. While the Islanders watched a huge chunk of their players march over to the WHA, Fletcher lost no one to the new league.

Putnam named Bernie "Boom Boom" Geoffrion coach of the infant team, and at first look, this seemed unwise, since Geoffrion's only other coaching had been a half-season with the New York Rangers, which led to a bleeding ulcer. A member of the Hockey Hall of Fame, Boom Boom was known for his explosive and erratic temper.

Instead, Geoffrion's thick Gallic accent and joie de vivre, coupled with a winning start to the first season, went over like hot cakes, and the new 15,078-seat Omni saw many a full house. By midseason the Flames were astoundingly in the midst of a West Division pennant race.

The Flames didn't make it to the playoffs that first season, but the fans didn't seem to mind. They cheered the team even when they lost, which is a miracle among hockey audiences—just ask them in Toronto!

The goaltending Atlanta had in its first season was truly superior; Don Bouchard and Phil Myre, both Quebec natives, were outplayed in the nets of the West Division only by superstar Tony Esposito of Chicago.

The club's high scorer of the year was a nobody named Bob Leiter, while their number one draft choice, Jacques Richard, was a disappointing ninth among club scorers. They were bolstered by the midseason acquisition of brawny Curt Bennett at center. On defense Atlanta began with such veteran journeymen as Noel Price and Pat Quinn and youthful Randy Manery.

The Flames went so far on what they had that they made the Stanley Cup playoffs their sophomore year. They had also acquired more talent in the form of rookie Tom Lysiak at center, who ran a close race against Islanders' Denis Potvin for the Calder Trophy.

Ironically, Atlanta faced another expansion baby in its first playoff episode— the Philadelphia Flyers. This team was to become the first child of modern expansion to win the Stanley Cup, and in the spring of 1974 the Flames were swept aside in four straight games.

In February 1975, Boom Boom stepped down, stating obscurely that his reasons would never be known by "anyone but me and my wife," and Fred Creighton became coach while Fletcher remained manager.

HARRY LAWRENCE (LARRY) AURIE

BORN: Sudbury, Ontario, February 8, 1905
POSITION: Right Wing, Detroit Cougars, 1927–30; Detroit Falcons, 1930–33; Detroit Red Wings, 1933–39
AWARDS: All-Star, 1937

The Detroit Red Wings' first Stanley Cup championship in 1935–36 was accomplished in large part because of the work of Larry Aurie, dynamo of the Wings' first line, consisting of Aurie, Herbie Lewis, and Marty Barry. Aurie had been a member of the Detroit sextet since 1927–28 and remained with the club through 1938–39. Aurie, Barry, and Lewis sparked the Red Wings to first place again in 1936–37 and to another Stanley Cup triumph. Detroit thus became the first NHL team ever to finish first and win the Cup in two straight seasons. Aurie, however, had reached the end of his hockey rope and the Red Wings sagged terribly in seasons to come. Detroit manager Jack Adams always regretted not trading Aurie after the 1936–37 season. "Instead of standing pat," said Adams, "I should have traded. I'll never hesitate to bust up a champion team again."

AVCO WORLD TROPHY

The World Hockey Association's version of the National Hockey League's Stanley Cup is the Avco World Trophy. It was presented to the WHA in the league's first season, 1972–73, by Avco Financial Services. The company provides financial counseling and cash loans through more than 1,500 offices in the United States, Canada, Australia, and the United Kingdom. The Avco World Trophy has been awarded to every WHA league champion since the

1972–73 campaign. Since then, two clubs won the trophy—the New England Whalers in 1972–73, and the Houston Aeros in 1973–74 and 1974–75.

DONALD WILLIAM "ELBOWS" AWREY

BORN: Kitchener, Ontario, July 18, 1943
POSITION: Defenseman, Boston Bruins, 1963–73; St. Louis Blues, 1973–74; Montreal Canadiens, 1974–

Around the NHL he's known as "Elbows," which tells you something about Don Awrey's style of defending. He puts everything he has (200 pounds) into playing defense, partly because he enjoys that aspect of the game and, more probably, because his scoring packs as much punch as a glass of warm milk. In sixteen seasons of professional hockey, including stops in the CPHL and AHL Don has never scored more than a handful of goals in a single winter. Although he's one of the NHL's fastest skaters, he's never been tempted to concentrate on offense.

Defense may be boring as a rule, but not the way Awrey plays it. Crowds have become accustomed to his full-speed bodychecks, and it's a common sight to see him dive into the path of a speeding slapshot. It's a reckless, yet highly efficient style, and one which has endeared him to the fans.

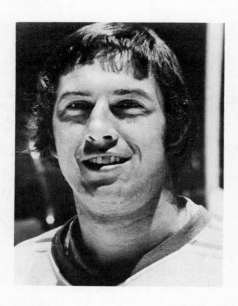

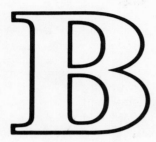

PETER JOSEPH BABANDO

BORN: Braeburn, Pennsylvania, May 10, 1925
POSITION: Left Wing, Boston Bruins, 1947–49; Detroit Red Wings,
1949–50; Chicago Black Hawks 1950–52; New York Rangers,
1952–53

Like Dusty Rhodes of baseball fame, Pete Babando was a journeyman who might never have achieved acclaim except that he came through, as did Rhodes, in a clutch situation.

At Olympia Stadium in Detroit on April 23, 1950, the Rangers and Red Wings were tied at three games apiece and the scored tied, 3–3, in the Stanley Cup final. Babando, a short, chunky skater who had played two seasons with the Bruins (1947–48, 1948–49) before being traded to Detroit, took a face-off pass from George Gee and beat New York goalie Chuck Rayner with a screened shot at 8:31 of the second overtime. Babando's reward was a ticket to the lowly Chicago Black Hawks the following season. He played two seasons in the Windy City before being traded, ironically, to the Rangers during the 1952–53 season, his last in the majors.

RALPH GERALD BACKSTROM

BORN: Kirkland Lake, Ontario, September 18, 1937
POSITION: Center, Montreal Canadiens, 1956–70; Los Angeles
   Kings, 1971–73; Chicago Black Hawks, 1973; Chicago Cougars
   (WHA), 1973–75
AWARDS: Calder Trophy, 1959; Most Sportsmanlike Player (WHA),
   1974; All-Star (WHA), 1974

The hockey history of Ralph Backstrom reads like the proverbial good news–bad news story. Fortunate to become a part of the mighty Montreal Canadiens' organization in 1958–59, when he won the Calder Memorial Trophy as Rookie of the Year, and a member of six Stanley Cup championship winners, Backstrom was also unfortunate enough to play third-string center behind two of the game's finest, Jean Beliveau and Henri Richard.

After playing third fiddle for twelve seasons, Backstrom decided to retire in 1970, but was talked into returning, whereupon he was promptly traded to the Los Angeles Kings for Gord Labossiere and Ray Fortin. Switched to left wing, which he had played in Juniors, Ralph wound up MVP with the Los Angeles fans in 1972.

In February 1973 Backstrom was traded to the Chicago Black Hawks for young blood in the guise of Dan Maloney. Disgruntled with a return to the background behind the likes of Stan Mikita, he signed with the Chicago Cougars of the WHA in August 1973.

Backstrom's style has always been an expression of his Canadiens' background—classy skating and excellent stickhandling. These talents helped the Cougars to an upset spot in the WHA playoff finals in 1974, and the rest of his story has been nothing but good news: Most Sportsmanlike Player in the WHA, MVP, and Most Popular Player of the Cougars (1973–74), 1974 All-Star, team leader in goals and total points (33 goals and 50 assists for 83 points in 1973–74), and uncontested star of the 1974 WHA Canada–Russia series.

A symbol of Backstrom's hard-earned success was a letter he received from one of hockey's living legends, Conn Smythe: "I have never believed in the statement that it doesn't matter whether you win or lose, but how you play the game. However, with your example in the Russian series, I have to say that it has some merit."

IRVINE WALLACE "ACE" BAILEY

BORN: Bracebridge, Ontario, July 3, 1903
POSITION: Left Wing, Toronto Maple Leafs, 1926–34
AWARDS: Art Ross Trophy, 1929; Hockey Hall of Fame, 1975

Ace Bailey, a superb puck carrier and penalty killer, was one of the few skaters ever to come very close to getting killed during a hockey game. On the night of December 12, 1933, Bailey was skating for the Maple Leafs against the Bruins at Boston Garden. As Toronto nursed a lead in the fateful match, the Bruins grew more and more frustrated, especially when Bailey expertly killed a penalty against the Leafs. It was during that sequence that Boston defenseman Eddie Shore was tripped by King Clancy of the Leafs.

Many observers insist that Shore mistakenly believed that Bailey had tripped him. They assert that Shore then pursued Bailey to get even. At the time Bailey had his back to Shore who was skating fiercely at the Toronto forward. The Boston defenseman struck Bailey across the kidneys, sending him head over heels until he landed on his head with terrifying force.

Bailey was badly hurt and was removed to a hospital where he was given little hope of surviving. Doctors performed two brain operations to save his life. Eventually he recovered enough to return to a normal life although he never played pro hockey again. Weeks later Bailey minimized Shore's role in the fracas. "We didn't see each other coming," Ace said graciously.

Shore, who had been suspended by the NHL, was sent on a recuperative vacation by the Bruins. A month later the governors ruled that since the Bruin had never before suffered a match penalty for injuring an opponent he would be reinstated. He returned to the Boston lineup in January 1934, and later shook hands with Bailey at a special All-Star game benefit in Ace's behalf. In later years Bailey became a minor NHL official at Maple Leaf Gardens in Toronto.

ROBERT ALLEN (BOB) BAILEY

BORN: Kenora, Ontario, May 29, 1931
POSITION: Forward, Toronto Maple Leafs, 1953–56; Chicago Black
    Hawks, 1957; Detroit Red Wings, 1958

In two full seasons with the Toronto Maple Leafs, (1953–54 and 1954–55) Bob Bailey's only contribution to the game was a deliberate collision with Maurice "Rocket" Richard after which the Rocket attempted to end Bailey's career on the spot. Bob barely escaped with his life and inflicted his inferior play on the NHL two more seasons, finishing up in 1957–58 with Chicago and Detroit. He later bounced around the minors and did a short stint as coach of the Eastern League's Philadelphia Ramblers. He lost that job after complaining that the team bus wasn't fit for pigs, let alone hockey players. "I told them to get rid of it," said Bailey, "but they wouldn't. That's when I resigned."

DONALD H. (DAN) BAIN

BORN: Belleville, Ontario, 1874
DIED: August 15, 1962
POSITION: Forward, Winnipeg Victorias, (MHL), 1896, 1899–1902
AWARDS: Hockey Hall of Fame, 1945

Before this Hall of Fame member made his mark in hockey, he had won the three-mile Manitoba title on roller skates, become Winnipeg's champion gymnast at the age of seventeen, and captured the Dominion trapshooting title in Toronto.

At the age of twenty-one he began playing hockey as a center with the Winnipeg Victorias. They won the Stanley Cup that year (1896) and again in 1901, when they defeated the Montreal Shamrocks.

Bain never played professional hockey and, in fact, he retired from the game after a remarkably short seven-year career.

HOBART (HOBEY) BAKER

BORN: Wissahickon, Pennsylvania, January, 1892
DIED: 1918
POSITION: Rover, played entirely on amateur teams in the United States (Princeton, New Jersey, and St. Nicholas Club, New York City)
AWARDS: Hockey Hall of Fame, 1945

Improbable as it may seem, one of the most respected hockey players in Canada before World War I was Hobey Baker, an American, who never played professionally and never played for a Canadian team.

Born in a small Pennsylvania town, Baker learned to skate effortlessly and stickhandle with remarkable finesse. Hobey first played organized hockey in Concord, New Hampshire, at St. Paul's School. By 1910 he was at Princeton where he captained his team to two intercollegiate titles. He also kicked a field goal in football which earned the Tigers a tie with Yale.

In the Ross Cup series in Montreal against the Montreal Stars, he led his amateur St. Nicholas (New York City) team to victory and the press commented in astonishment: "Uncle Sam has the cheek to develop a first class hockey player—who wasn't born in Montreal!"

Baker died in 1918, testing a plane as a combat pilot in the United States Armed Forces. He was posthumously inducted into the Hockey Hall of Fame.

MURRAY BALFOUR

BORN: Regina, Saskatchewan, August 24, 1936
DIED: 1965
POSITION: Right Wing, Montreal Canadiens, 1956–58; Chicago Black Hawks, 1959–64; Boston Bruins, 1964–65

Regina-born Murray Balfour died of lung cancer at the age of thirty in 1965. Reared in the Montreal Canadiens' farm system, Balfour was obtained by the Black Hawks in 1959–60 and played right wing on a line with Bobby Hull and Red Hay. A rugged skater, Balfour helped Chicago to the 1961 Stanley Cup championship by scoring a sudden-death goal against Montreal in the third overtime of the semifinals. Balfour scored 5 goals and 5 assists for 10 points in 11 playoff games that spring for the Hawks.

HAROLD BALLARD

Harold Ballard, the outspoken president of Maple Leaf Gardens, has had more than his share of headaches since assuming control of the venerable Ontario arena in 1961.

In July 1969, Ballard and his sidekick on the Maple Leaf franchise, Stafford Smythe, were charged with income tax evasion. If that wasn't enough, less than two years later the duo was arrested, this time charged with fraud, theft, and mismanagement of Maple Leaf Gardens funds. Ballard served time for his sins at a minimum security prison in Ontario, but Smythe died unexpectedly before his trial was completed.

Ballard, evidently, didn't mellow one bit in his approach to his hired help either. When asked to explain his team's lack of oomph in the early going of the 1974–75 season, Ballard wasn't a bit hesitant to name names. "Inge Hammarstrom," he spouted, "could go into the corner with six eggs in his hip pocket and not break one of them."

Ballard's acid tongue wasn't restricted to the players either. "Red Kelly," he observed, "is too nice a guy to coach."

Kelly responded to his boss's needle the next night by patrolling the Leafs' bench brandishing an imposing-looking bullwhip.

A cynical view of Ballard was taken in December 1974 by Montreal *Gazette* columnist John Robertson who said of the Leaf boss: "I can't remember the exact crime Harold Ballard was convicted of—theft, fraud, tax evasion or a combination of all three—but whatever it was shapes up as a simple misdemeanor when compared to the $13 he's charging for 'gold seats' at the Gardens for Toronto Maple Leaf hockey games."

BALTIMORE BLADES

There have been two Baltimore Blades, a wartime (1944–45) club that won the Eastern League Mayor Walker Trophy in 1945, and a more recent World Hockey Association club that made its debut and also folded in 1975. The original Blades, playing out of the old Carlin Ice Rink, were a colorful club with characters such as defenseman Paul "Boxcar" Waldner, goalie Nick Pidsodny, the only netminder ever to lead a league in penalties, and blond forward Arlie Carlson. The Blades' name was changed to Clippers and in 1947–48 the Clippers won the Walker Cup. When the Carlin Rink burned down the Clippers were moved to Charlotte, North Carolina.

The latter-day Blades originally were the WHA Los Angeles Sharks that were moved to Detroit as the Michigan Stags at the start of the 1974–75 season. Weak attendance in Detroit and deep financial difficulties compelled the WHA to move the Stags to Baltimore where they became the Blades before folding at the end of the 1974–75 season.

WILLIAM (BILL) BARBER

BORN: Callander, Ontario, July 11, 1952
POSITION: Left Wing, Philadelphia Flyers, 1972–

Bill was Philadelphia's first choice in the 1972 NHL amateur draft. A native of Callander, Ontario, and one of five brothers, Bill was encouraged to play hockey by his father, who hoped that at least one of his sons would make it to the NHL.

"Just to make sure we had everything going for us, Dad built us a rink that was almost regulation size, had hydro poles put up, and lights strung out."

Barber was selected by the Flyers after he had spent three years with the Kitchener Juniors in the OHA. During that time he had 127 goals and 171 assists, while playing both the center and forward spots. He expected to make the Flyers without any trouble, but was farmed out to Richmond before the start of the 1972–73 season because his checking was not up to NHL standards. A month later he was back and on his way to a fine major league career, although he is disparagingly considered the most outrageous "swan-diver" in the NHL.

Bill Barber's 30 goals and 34 assists did not win him the Calder Trophy in 1972–73. But he did win the hearts of Flyer fans.

WILLIAM (BILL) BARILKO

BORN: Timmins, Ontario, March 25, 1927
DIED: August 1951
POSITION: Defenseman, Toronto Maple Leafs, 1946–51

Bill Barilko died at the height of his career in a plane crash just after he had scored the winning goal in sudden-death overtime to clinch the Stanley Cup for the Toronto Maple Leafs in April 1951.

Although Barilko never was an All-Star, he had gained total respect around the NHL for his fearsome "snake-hip" bodychecks and his ability to block dangerous enemy shots on goal along with his partner Garth Boesch. Barilko became a Maple Leaf during the 1946–47 season, elevated from the Hollywood Wolves of the Pacific Coast League. It was no coincidence that he played on four Stanley Cup championship teams in five years prior to his untimely death at the age of twenty-four.

DOUGLAS BARKLEY

BORN: Lethbridge, Alberta, January 6, 1937
POSITION: Defenseman, Chicago Black Hawks, 1957–60; Detroit
    Red Wings, 1962–66; Coach, Detroit Red Wings, 1971–72, 1975–

After toiling in the minors for years, Barkley was brought up to the Detroit Red Wings as a defenseman in 1962. During the 1963–64 season he led NHL defensemen in scoring (with 11 goals), but on January 30, 1966, Doug Mohns, the Chicago Black Hawks' left wing, accidentally struck Barkley in the right eye with his stick. Barkley lost the sight of that eye and a promising hockey career, but returned to the Red Wings as coach in the 1971–72 season. Unfortunately for Barkley the Red Wings were in serious trouble and tried to solve their problems by playing musical coaches. Barkley went out the revolving door, but returned to the Red Wings' job in June 1975.

MARTIN A. (MARTY) BARRY

BORN: St. Gabriel, Quebec, December 8, 1905
DIED: Unknown
POSITION: Center, New York Americans, 1928; Boston Bruins,
    1930–35; Detroit Red Wings, 1936–39; Montreal Canadiens,
    1940–41
AWARDS: Lady Byng Trophy, 1937; All-Star (First Team), 1937;
    Hockey Hall of Fame, 1965

What Tinker-to-Evers-to-Chance was to baseball, Marty Barry-to-Larry Aurie-to-Herb Lewis was to hockey in the midthirties. The Detroit Red Wings' best forward combination, the Barry-Aurie-Lewis line, led the Wings to the top of the American Division of the NHL in 1935–36 and, ultimately, to the Stanley Cup.

A native of Quebec City, Barry broke into the NHL with the New York Americans in 1927–28, then moved on to the Boston Bruins in 1929–30 where he remained through the 1934–35 season. By baseball standards he would have been regarded as a consistent .300-plus hitter, having scored 20-or-more-goal seasons each year in Boston. Prior to the 1935–36 campaign, Marty was traded to Detroit. His skills blended with Aurie and Lewis. A year later Barry achieved a personal scoring high of 44 points (17 goals, 27 assists) as the Wings finished first in the American Division again. In the final game of the Stanley Cup playoffs, Barry scored two key goals against the Rangers to pace Detroit to their second consecutive world championship. Marty skated for the Wings through the 1938–39 season before being traded to the Montreal Canadiens.

JAMES BAKER (JIMMY) BARTLETT

BORN: Verdun, Quebec, May 27, 1932
POSITION: Forward, Montreal Canadiens, 1954–55; New York Rangers, 1955–60; Boston Bruins, 1960–61

Some hockey players achieve eminence for their off-ice accomplishments. Jimmy Bartlett was one of them. He played three full NHL seasons—two with the Rangers (1958–59, 1959–60) and one with Boston (1960–61)—and merely started a few fights and scored a few goals. Off-ice, he had a loosy-goosy attitude toward life and enjoyed a practical joke. "I'll always remember him," said ex-Rangers' teammate Aldo Guidolin, "as the guy who stood on the roof of my house one day, and tossed a shovelful of snow on my head as I walked out the door on my way to a practice."

HENRY (HANK) BASSEN

BORN: Calgary, Alberta, December 6, 1932
POSITION: Goalie, Chicago Black Hawks, 1954–56; Detroit Red Wings, 1960–67; Pittsburgh Penguins, 1967–68

If the NHL record book set aside a section on the most consistently lousy goalies, year in and year out, Hank Bassen would have to have a niche. A truculent redhead who often seemed more pleased bouncing his stick off an enemy shin than stopping a puck, Bassen was the goalie Andy Bathgate nearly faked out of Madison Square Garden while scoring on a penalty shot in 1962. Bassen also was the Red Wings' goalie in April 1961 when the Black Hawks beat Detroit at Olympia Stadium to win their last Stanley Cup. Mercifully, he left the NHL after playing twenty-two games for the Pittsburgh Penguins in 1967–68.

ALDEGE (BAZ) BASTIEN

BORN, Timmins, Ontario, August 29, 1920
POSITION: Goalie, Toronto Maple Leafs, 1945–46

There was only one thing that prevented Baz Bastien from becoming one of the NHL's foremost goaltenders and that was Turk Broda. Bastien was the second-ranked Toronto Maple Leafs' goalie behind Broda who was in his prime during the late forties when Bastien also happened to be in *his* prime. As a result, Baz played most of his hockey for the Leafs' American League farm team in Pittsburgh where he compiled an admirable record. Whatever chance he had for big-league stardom was ended during the 1949–50 season when a puck hit him in the eye. Although he lost sight in the eye, Baz attempted a comeback, wearing a special plastic mask. But, as Bastien explained, "the mask kept fogging up." He spent the next eighteen years coaching and managing in the AHL and later moved to the Red Wings' front office. When the Kansas City Scouts were admitted to the NHL for the 1974–75 season, Bastien joined his old pal Sid Abel in the front office.

ANDREW JAMES (ANDY) BATHGATE

BORN: Winnipeg, Manitoba, August 28, 1932
POSITION: Right Wing, New York Rangers, 1953–63; Toronto Maple
    Leafs, 1963–65; Detroit Red Wings, 1965–67; Pittsburgh
    Penguins, 1967–68, 1970–71; Vancouver Blazers (WHA), 1974
AWARDS: Hart Trophy, 1959; All-Star (First Team) 1959, 1962; (Second Team), 1958, 1963

Bathgate at first appeared too much the pacifist for the NHL jungle. But he put up his dukes when necessary, licking such notorious hockey cops as Howie Young, then of the Red Wings, and Vic Stasiuk of the Bruins. By 1954–55 Andy was in the NHL to stay, and soon was being favorably compared with the greatest Ranger right wing, Bill Cook.

While it's never been firmly established who invented the slapshot—Bernie Geoffrion and Bobby Hull often are mentioned—Bathgate was among the earliest practitioners. It was Andy's shot at Madison Square Garden in November 1959 that smashed Montreal goalie Jacques Plante's face and inspired Plante to don a face mask *permanently,* thus ushering in the era of the goalie mask. Bathgate also was among the first to develop a curved "banana" blade.

By the end of the 1961–62 season during which Andy scored 84 points in 70 games, he had become the most popular Ranger, team captain, and seemingly a permanent fixture on Broadway. He also was prime trade bait, and in February 1964 he was dealt to Toronto in a huge trade. Don McKenney accompanied Bathgate to Toronto. In exchange, the Leafs sent Dick Duff, Bob Nevin, Rod Seiling, Arnie Brown, and Bill Collins to New York.

As a result of the trade, the Leafs won the 1964 Stanley Cup. Bathgate scored five important playoff goals and said getting traded to the Leafs was the biggest break in his life. But just a season later Bathgate had a falling out with manager-coach Punch Imlach. "There's a limit to an athlete's endurance," said Bathgate. "Imlach has pushed a few of the players past that limit physically and mentally."

Furious, Imlach snapped back at his ace: "There's no limit to what you can do," Imlach told Bathgate. "Who says there's a limit? Only you! I live by the creed that you can always be better than you are."

Imlach unloaded Bathgate to Detroit in 1965–66. His play declined sharply and in 1967–68 he was dealt to the expansion Pittsburgh Penguins. He returned to form in Pittsburgh, but appeared more and more disenchanted and departed the NHL in 1968. Andy played briefly in Switzerland, returning to Canada to become coach of the Vancouver Blazers in the WHA in 1974. An eye injury suffered in a home accident in 1973 limited vision by 80 percent in Andy's right eye. Despite the impaired vision, Bathgate returned temporarily to active play in December 1974 with the Blazers.

ROBERT THEODORE (BOBBY) BAUER

BORN: Waterloo, Ontario, February 16, 1915
DIED: September 16, 1964
POSITION: Right Wing, Boston Bruins, 1936–42, 1945–52
AWARDS: Lady Byng Trophy, 1940, 1941, 1947; All-Star (Second Team), 1939–41, 1947

Although moderns may think of Bobby Bauer as the man who helped devise a hockey skate of the same name, Bauer the hockey player gained early stardom in the early thirties while attending St. Michael's College in Toronto. In 1934–35 Bauer graduated to Kitchener of the Ontario Hockey League, a junior league for players under twenty-one. He teamed with Milt Schmidt and Woody Dumart, both pals from Kitchener, and the "Sauerkraut Line" was born.

A right winger, Bauer was signed by the Boston Bruins in the spring of 1935. The NHL got its first look at the Krauts in 1937–38 as the Bruins began to maraud over opponents. Thanks to Bauer, Schmidt, and Dumart, Boston finished first four successive times and won the Stanley Cup twice. In 1942 Bauer enlisted along with his buddies in the Royal Canadian Air Force. He returned to the NHL in 1945–46 and retired after the following season, although

Bobby made one more appearance, in 1951–52, to play at Boston Garden in a "night" in honor of the Kraut Line. He scored a goal and an assist on that occasion and then permanently retired.

ROBERT T. (BOBBY) BAUN

BORN: Lanigan, Saskatchewan, September 9, 1936
POSITION: Defenseman, Toronto Maple Leafs, 1956–67, 1971–73;
    Oakland Seals, 1967–68; Detroit Red Wings, 1968–71; Coach,
    Toronto Toros (WHA), 1975–

Among hockey pros Bob Baun was recognized as one of the hardest—and cleanest—bodycheckers in the game. Players respected Baun for his respect of the rulebook. Billy Harris, Baun's teammate at Toronto and later at Oakland (Seals), once put it this way: "His duels with Bobby Hull are legend now. And the respect they showed each other was evident every time they collided. You seldom saw an elbow or a raised stick. Just a brutal test of strength between two fine athletes."

When Baun was sitting on the bench, or when he was shelved with an injury, opponents took a completely different view of the Oakland team. "The night Baun missed a game in Chicago, we started taking liberties," said then Black Hawk Bobby Hull. "We realized he wasn't in town, so we could get away with a lot more. When Baun's around, that right side is like an obstacle course."

Sometimes Baun got caught in his own obstacles as he did in March 1961, in New York. Camille Henry of the Rangers ran into Baun and in the entanglement Henry's skate sliced through the skin of Baun's neck. It appeared to be a routine injury and Bobby returned in the third period. But seconds after he boarded the team bus following the game, he began to gasp desperately. He attempted to yell for help but couldn't squeeze out a sound. Neck muscles cut by the skate had started to hemorrhage. Bobby gagged as his tongue slipped down his throat.

Baun waved his arms, groping for attention. When his teammates realized the trouble, they rushed him to a hospital, where doctors performed an emergency operation to permit breathing. Less than a week later Bobby was taking a regular turn on the Leaf defense in the Cup playoffs.

"Baun was a marvel," said Leaf trainer Bobby Haggert. "I remember one weekend when he hurt his ankle on a Saturday night, kept an ice pack strapped to it for twenty-four hours, then played a game on Sunday. On his first shift he stepped into Reg Fleming with a check that rattled Reggie's wishbone. Next minute he stopped a shot on the same foot. Instead of crying 'uncle' he stayed out there, didn't miss a shift and handed Fleming two more bruising checks."

Among all his notable achievements, Baun's most stirring heroics came in the 1964 Cup finale. The Leafs trailed Detroit in games, 3–2, and were clinging to a 3–3 tie in the sixth game. With ten minutes remaining, Baun threw his leg in front of a Gordie Howe shot. The rocklike rubber disk cracked a bone in

Baun's ankle and he had to be carried from the ice. The period ended with the score still tied. As the players left the ice to prepare for a sudden-death over-time, the team doctor stuck a needle in Baun's foot, pressed the painkiller into his veins, then swathed the ankle with bulging bandages.

Baun buried his head in his hands as the other players trooped back to the ice. He waited and waited and then he lifted himself up and followed them. "When I saw him come out, I sent him over the boards," said Punch Imlach who was coaching the Leafs. "It was a great show of courage, but you expect those things from a guy like Baun."

As the time clock's hands approached the two-minute mark, the puck slith-ered to Baun at center ice. He took a stride and golfed a shot that struck de-fenseman Bill Gadsby's stick and ricocheted crazily up in the air like a clay pigeon. Before goalie Terry Sawchuk could move, the puck flew over his shoulder and into the net for the winning goal.

With the series tied, 3–3, the Leafs ordered Baun to a doctor for X rays of his broken ankle, but he refused them. "If there was anything wrong, I didn't want to know the details," Baun remarked. Riddled with painkiller, Baun took a regular turn throughout the final game. Toronto won, 4–0, for its third straight Stanley Cup. Baun was selected one of the playoff's three outstanding stars, although his inconsistency prevented him from being named a First Team All-Star. With or without All-Star recognition, Bobby more than made his pres-ence felt in the NHL.

"He was one of the roughest players in the league," said Chicago's coach Billy Reay. In June 1975 he was named coach of the Toronto Toros.

JEAN "LE GROS BILL" BELIVEAU

BORN: Trois Rivieres, Quebec, August 31, 1931
POSITION: Center, Montreal Canadiens, 1951–71
AWARDS: Hart Trophy, 1956, 1964; Art Ross Trophy, 1956; Conn
    Smythe Trophy, 1965; All-Star (First Team), 1955–57, 1958–61,
    (Second Team), 1958, 1964, 1966, 1969

A day after the Montreal Canadiens clinched first place in the National Hockey League in March 1968, Sid Abel, general manager-coach of the Detroit Red Wings, made it quite clear how important captain Jean Beliveau was to the Canadiens. "If Beliveau stays healthy," Abel predicted, "the Canadiens are a cinch to win the Stanley Cup, too."

Two months later, Abel's forecast was realized. The Flying Frenchmen of Montreal defeated the Boston Bruins in four straight games; the Chicago Black Hawks in five; and finally, the St. Louis Blues in four. Beliveau, known in the French-speaking province of Quebec as *Le Gros Bill* (Big Bill), as always, led the team to victory.

Remaining injury-free was never easy for Beliveau. Throughout his eighteen-year National Hockey League career, the princely, 6'3", 205-pound center was hobbled by an assortment of problems. One of the worst occurred during the 1966–67 season when he was hit in the eye by a wildly swung stick and his sight was imperiled.

"The pressure on my nerves bothered me more than the pain," said Beliveau. "The first thing I did, naturally, was to open my eye to see if I had vision. I couldn't even see the big, bright lights. The next day, I could see a little bit. I'm a lucky man. But all the time I kept wondering how I would react when I started playing again. Would I instinctively pull back when a stick was raised in a corner? If I did, it would be the end for me."

But the moment he rejoined the team, the fear reflex evaporated and he was the Beliveau of old. This facet of Beliveau was never more evident than during the 1967–68 season when the Canadiens were lodged in the subterranean depths of last place in the East Division as late as December 27, 1967. On that night, the Canadiens trailed the Red Wings by two goals with four minutes remaining in the game. Then rookie Jacques Lemaire scored and Beliveau tied the contest. According to former Montreal coach Toe Blake, Beliveau's goal turned the tide for the Canadiens.

But that goal was more symbolic. The following highlights are significant of Beliveau's contribution to Montreal's 1967–68 championship:

●Only 10 of his 31 goals were scored against the weaker teams in the NHL's Western Division, demonstrating that Beliveau played more solidly in the clutch games than the likes of Gordie Howe and Bobby Hull.

●He went over the 1,000-point mark—was presented a European sports car as a memento—and is the only player in the NHL to do it, with the exception of Howe.

●He totaled 68 points (31 goals, 37 assists) in only 59 games, scoring on 15.1 percent of his shots, surpassing NHL scoring champion Stan Mikita's 13.2 average.

●He scored 9 of the 50 goals compiled by the Canadiens' effective power play.

●His wingmen enjoyed productive seasons: Yvan Cournoyer scored 28 goals and Gilles Tremblay 23.

At midseason when votes were tabulated for the Hart Memorial Trophy (MVP), Mikita accumulated 34 points to Beliveau's 4. But in the second-half poll, Beliveau outscored Mikita, 39–18, which gave the Chicago center the overall prize, 52–43—a decision that, incidentally, did not wear well with all critics. "To me," said Red Sullivan, then the Pittsburgh Penguins' coach, summing up the case for Beliveau, "Big Jean was more important to the Canadiens than Mikita was to the Hawks."

Mustard-tongued George "Punch" Imlach, the Buffalo Sabres' general manager, who is given to quick criticism, said of Beliveau: "It's practically impossible for anyone who knows him well to have any ill feeling toward him. He would go on the ice, play one heckuva game, change, and leave without saying much. He was one player all the fellows liked.''

A typical Beliveau team-first gesture, which endeared him to his colleagues, occurred late in December 1967, when the Canadiens were playing Imlach's Leafs at Maple Leaf Gardens in Toronto. The Leafs were carefully guarding a 2–1 lead with less than three minutes remaining in the game when Beliveau tied the score after teammate John Ferguson had relayed the puck to Claude Provost who, in turn, passed to Beliveau. Instead of accepting congratulations for his effort, Beliveau lamented the fact that Ferguson was not given an assist on the play. ''What's wrong with the official scorer here?'' Beliveau asked. ''Fergy made the big play on our goal and they refuse to give him an assist. I was shocked when I didn't hear a correction after I had brought the matter to the attention of referee Art Skov and the fellows at the timer's bench. But for Fergy we would have lost the game. All I had to do was put the puck in.''

As a captain, Beliveau was surprisingly diffident. He rarely, if ever, shouted to his teammates on the bench and he was hardly the rah-rah type in the dressing room. Yet, somehow, he managed to inspire grand efforts from the men who wore the red, white, and blue uniforms of the Canadiens. More than anything it seemed to come from Beliveau's quiet charisma, inspired by how he acted more than what he said. ''It's hard to put into words how we felt about Jean,'' former teammate Ralph Backstrom once explained. ''It's just that . . . well, we were so damned proud to have him as our captain.''

''It was his quiet dignity,'' added ex-teammate Dick Duff. ''He was so unassuming for a guy of his stature. . . . He was a very unselfish player. He had great moves—that great range—and anybody playing on a line with him was certain to wind up with a lot of goals. If you got there, the puck would be there.

''I remember when I was with Toronto. We knew we had to stop Beliveau, so Bob Pulford would be assigned to him. Pully was supposed to bump him all night to slow him down. But the guy kept going. He had so much courage, so much determination.'' The results are all there in the record book.

Beliveau retired from the ice in 1971, and his jersey number, 4, was retired with him. He now is a public relations man for the Canadiens.

GORDON (GORDIE) BELL

BORN: Portage La Prairie, Manitoba, March 13, 1925
POSITION: Goalie, Toronto Maple Leafs, 1945–46; New York
    Rangers, 1956

From time to time journeymen goaltenders are handed a big-league baton and sprint with it successfully to the finish line. Gordie Bell (along with Alfie

Moore, Joe Miller, et. al.) was one such goalie. For years Bell bounced around the minors, playing everywhere from Buffalo to Washington. He got his NHL chance in 1955–56 when regular Rangers' goalie Gump Worsley was injured during the Stanley Cup semifinal round with the heavily favored Montreal Canadiens. Playing at the hostile Montreal Forum, Bell thwarted the Flying Frenchmen in a splendid display of goalkeeping while his Rangers triumphed, 4–2. In time the Rangers were wiped out, Worsley returned to the nets, and Gordie Bell never was heard from again in the NHL.

HARRY "HUDDIE" BELL

BORN: Regina, Saskatchewan, October 31, 1925
POSITION: Defenseman, New York Rangers, 1946–47

Nicknamed "Huddie" by New York writer Sam B. Gunst, defenseman Harry Bell played briefly for the New York Rangers, but mostly for the Eastern League New York Rovers. In a spectacular farewell to the Atlantic City Sea Gulls, Bell beat the Jersey team with a last second (19:59) goal in the third period of the final match played by the Sea Gulls at Convention Hall in Atlantic City. Bell, who owned a wicked shot, previously had scored twice in the third period of that memorable game. However, the Rangers were unimpressed and "Huddie" remained a minor leaguer for the rest of his life.

CLINTON BENEDICT

BORN: Ottawa, Ontario, 1894
POSITION: Goalie, Ottawa Senators (NHA and NHL), 1913–24; Montreal Maroons, 1924–30
AWARDS: Hockey Hall of Fame, 1965

While the consensus down through the years points to the legendary Georges Vezina as the first great goalkeeper of pro hockey, a bit more investigation reveals that Clint Benedict had a better overall goals-against average and was also singularly responsible for introducing the practice of flopping to the ice to stop a shot. He also was one of the first goalies to use a face mask.

Believe it or not, prior to 1918, it was a penalty for the goalie to leave his feet in order to block the puck. Benedict would have none of this nonsense and, rather than call a penalty on the maverick netminder every few minutes, the league capitulated and changed the rule.

Benedict was in goal on four Stanley Cup winners during his eighteen-year career, winning the centerpiece three times with the Ottawa Senators and once with the Montreal sextet near the end of his playing days. A flamboyant showman, Benedict is a member of the Hockey Hall of Fame.

CURT BENNETT

BORN: Regina, Saskatchewan, March 27, 1948
POSITION: Center, St. Louis Blues, 1970–72; New York Rangers, 1972; Atlanta Flames, 1973–

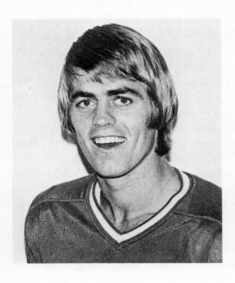

Probably the best hockey player ever to come out of Brown University, Curt Bennett has plied his trade at every position except goal in his NHL tenure. Curt began in St. Louis, moved on to the New York Rangers before joining Atlanta in exchange for Ron Harris. Bennett is one of hockey's better penalty killers, a shifty skater with tricky moves, and, in short, a jack-of-all-trades.

HARVEY BENNETT

BORN: Edington, Saskatchewan, July 23, 1925
POSITION: Goalie, Boston Bruins, 1944–45

The father of Atlanta Flames' forward Curt Bennett, Harvey Bennett was an angular goaltender from Edington, Saskatchewan, who played one season for the Boston Bruins (1944–45) and allowed 103 goals in 24 games for a 4.29 goals-against average. It has been said that Bennett's spreadeagle split saves were among the most spectacular prior to the return of Charlie Rayner of the Rangers from the armed forces. Bennett played his best goal for the Boston Olympics of the Eastern League and later for the American League Providence Reds.

BILL BENTLEY

Bill Bentley fathered more professional hockey players than any other man. His sons Max and Doug, both Hall of Famers, were the most famous, but there was also Wyatt, Roy, Reg, and Jack—not to mention seven daughters who comprised a Bentley women's team, which was as good as the men's squad, if not better. "The girls," said Papa Bill, "could beat the blisters off the boys nine times out of ten."

The trademark of Max and Doug Bentley was speed and deadly accurate wrist-shooting. They learned both techniques from their dad. "Milkin' them damn cows," said Bill, a homesteader in Saskatchewan, "is what built up their wrists. That's how they could snap the puck into the net so fast."

Max and Doug also inherited their swift skating ability from Bill who claimed that he once beat Norval Baptie, one of the greatest speed-skaters and figure skaters in the United States. "Norval Baptie," said Bill, "was born in a blizzard and raised in our town. He was a pretty good speed-skater until I beat him and then he threw away his speed skates and became a figure skater."

When Max and Doug had become established pros they became skeptical of their dad's story about knowing Baptie. Then, one day in the forties, Doug came across a photo of Baptie in a Chicago Stadium hockey program. He brought it back to Delisle, covered Baptie's name, and asked his dad to identify the picture.

"Well, hell, Doug," Bill Bentley chuckled, "that's the old former speed-skater, Norval Baptie. Did I ever tell you why that fella turned to figure-skatin'?"

DOUGLAS WAGNER BENTLEY

BORN: Delisle, Saskatchewan, September 3, 1916
DIED: November 24, 1972
POSITION: Left Wing, Chicago Black Hawks, 1939–44, 1945–51; New York Rangers, 1953–54
AWARDS: Art Ross Trophy, 1943; All-Star (First Team), 1943–44, (Second Team), 1949; Hockey Hall of Fame, 1964

It is amazing how alike the Bentley brothers were on the ice. Max, a center for his twelve-year career, finished with 544 points, while, Doug, a left wing and center who often teamed with his sibling on the same line in Chicago and New York, totaled 543.

After three failures in attempts to make NHL squads, Doug finally made it to the big leagues with the Black Hawks. He teamed with Max in 1942–43, and both reached stardom.

Doug led the NHL in scoring with 73 points that year. The next season he scored the most goals, 38, and was second in league scoring. He then joined his younger brother in the army and missed the 1944–45 campaign.

The brother act was broken up in 1947 when Max was dealt to Toronto. "I thought of quitting," Doug stated about his feelings concerning the deal. "But I felt I still had a good year left in me."

He was wrong. Bentley had four seasons remaining as an NHLer. He quit the Hawks in 1951 to coach Saskatoon of the Western League.

Doug was coaxed out of retirement to help the Rangers, and brother Max, in their drive toward a playoff spot in 1954. In his first game with New York after two years in retirement, Doug registered a goal and three assists, Max had two goals and a pair of setups, and the Rangers won, 8–3. Doug stayed with New York for the rest of the season as the Rangers fell short in their playoff bid.

Doug went back to coaching Saskatoon the next year. Max joined him there in 1954. Doug made a brief comeback in 1962 with the Los Angeles Blades of the WHL.

MAXWELL HERBERT LLOYD (MAX) BENTLEY

BORN: Delisle, Saskatchewan, March 1, 1920
POSITION: Center, Chicago Black Hawks, 1940–43, 1945–47; Toronto Maple Leafs, 1947–53; New York Rangers, 1953–54
AWARDS: Hart Trophy, 1946; Art Ross Trophy, 1946–47; Lady Byng Trophy, 1943; All-Star (First Team), 1946, (Second Team), 1947; Hockey Hall of Fame, 1966

The original "Dipsy Doodle Dandy from Delisle," Max Bentley is regarded by some purists as the most exciting—if not the best—center who ever lived. Kid brother of Doug Bentley, Max originally starred on the Pony Line with Doug and Bill Mosienko at Chicago. All lightweights, the pony boys were extraordinary stickhandlers and playmakers who could only be thwarted by rough play.

Max won the NHL scoring championship in 1946 and 1947 before being involved in one of the NHL's biggest trades. Despite the Bentleys' prolific scoring, the Black Hawks were a hopelessly weak team, short on goalkeeping and equally weak on defense.

After being traded to Toronto, it took a while for Max to adjust to his new surroundings. He went ten straight games without a goal, but once he got going, there was no stopping him.

With Bentley in the lineup, the Leafs became the supreme NHL power. They finished first in 1948 and then went on to win their second consecutive Stanley Cup. Never before had a team won three straight world championships, but Max led the Leafs to the third Cup in a row in April 1949, and a fourth in five years in April 1951.

After that, age began to erode Max's talents, and the Leafs began losing more and more frequently. In the 1952 Cup semifinals against Detroit, Toronto was routed in four straight games.

Rangers' general manager Frank Boucher had his eye on Max and in the summer of 1953 he persuaded him to make a comeback. Max drove a hard bargain. In addition to his $15,000 contract—extraordinary for those days—Max persuaded Boucher to bring his wife and kids and his nephew, Bev, as spare goaltender, *and* Bev's wife and a family friend, who was a companion and baby-sitter, to New York.

Boucher was delighted because with Max in the fold he believed he could persuade brother Doug to come out of retirement. That took a bit longer, but in midseason Doug agreed and he flew to Manhattan amid the fuss and fanfare normally accorded a conquering hero.

At last the Bentleys were reunited for the first time since November 1947 when Max had been traded to the Maple Leafs. In their first game as a team again, Max and Doug played on a line with Edgar Laprade, whose unique stickhandling and skating talents melded perfectly with the Bentleys'. The Rangers played the Bruins, routing them, 8–3, mostly because of the Bentleys and Laprade. "It was one of those wonderful moments in sports," said Boucher, "when everything comes together, when the juices truly flow, and in this fleeting moment, late in their careers, Doug and Max shed the years as they piled up eight scoring points between them."

Max was a hypochondriac of the first order, important ammunition for enemy skaters during the homestretch of the 1953–54 season. "Before one game," said former Bruins' coach Lynn Patrick, "I told my center, Cal Gardner, who had once played with Max, to strike up a conversation with Bentley on the ice before the game started. I wanted Cal to tell Max how terrible he looked and that he should see a doctor immediately after the game."

Gardner fulfilled his mission. By the opening face-off, Max had become terribly concerned about his health. He played a poor game; the Bruins won and gained a playoff berth while the Rangers finished fifth. Max and Doug returned to Delisle; this time to stay. Doug died of cancer in 1972 while Max continued to operate the family wheat farm and tell stories about the great days of long ago.

REGINALD BENTLEY

BORN: Delisle, Saskatchewan, May 3, 1914
POSITION: Forward, Chicago Black Hawks, 1942–43

The third, and least proficient, of the Chicago Black Hawks' Bentley brothers, Reg skated on a line with brothers Max and Doug in the 1942–43 National Hockey League season. Although the others appeared capable of "carrying"

Reg, he lasted only eleven games in the majors and scored a goal and an assist. His place on the line eventually was taken by Bill "Wee Willie" Mosienko. The Bentleys and Mosienko comprised Chicago's Pony Line, one of the most productive in NHL history. Reg enjoyed them vicariously as he bounced around from one minor league team to another.

GORDON "RED" BERENSON

BORN: Regina, Saskatchewan, December 8, 1939
POSITION: Center, Montreal Canadiens, 1961–66; New York Rangers, 1966–67; St. Louis Blues, 1967–71, 1974– ; Detroit Red Wings, 1971–74

When Red Berenson, the scholarly center with the educated stick, was traded by the New York Rangers to the St. Louis Blues in November 1967, the deal was largely ignored. But when Berenson was dealt from St. Louis to the Detroit Red Wings early in February 1971, the news resounded with the impact of a thunderclap. In less than four years the anonymous redhead from Regina, Saskatchewan, emerged as the Babe Ruth of St. Louis hockey, the man who put the Blues on the ice map—and into the Stanley Cup finals.

It was Berenson who scored six goals in a single game against the Philadelphia Flyers and who became the first superstar of the National Hockey

League's expansion West Division. "The Red Baron" of the Blues, as he came to be known, was in a class with Bobby Hull, Gordie Howe, and Jean Beliveau.

Then, without warning, he was traded away by the very team which coveted him so dearly. It was the shot heard round the hockey world. The precise reasons for the trade may never be known, but its repercussions lasted for years. Berenson claimed the deal was simply a union-busting move on the part of the Blues' front office. "I think the Blues traded me because I was president of the NHL Players' Association," said Berenson. "I don't know why the Blues should be uptight about the association, but I'm convinced I was dealt because of that. Needless to say, I was shocked and disappointed."

So were the hockey fans in St. Louis. They were hardly ecstatic to learn that the Blues obtained Garry Unger and Wayne Connolly in exchange for Berenson and Tim Ecclestone. Even the Blues' front office acknowledged the flak.

"I don't blame the fans," said Sid Salomon III, executive vice-president of the Blues. "If I were on their side of the fence, I'd probably be writing or phoning my criticism. But we weren't trading for today, tomorrow, or the next NHL season. We were dealing for the next ten years. We believed Unger was the kind of man we needed to build a Stanley Cup winner."

Red found himself at home in Detroit in more ways than one. He had B.A. and M.A. degrees from the University of Michigan and, of course, played much of his college hockey in that area.

When Berenson made All-America at Michigan the late Jack Adams, Detroit's vitriolic manager, attempted to lure him to Detroit. But the Montreal Canadiens owned his rights at the time and had no intention of parting with them. Curiously, the Canadiens often seemed indifferent to Berenson once he moved up to the NHL in 1961–62.

Berenson's hockey smarts weren't always appreciated. Montreal's Toe Blake underplayed Red and Berenson insists he never got a good chance to prove himself. "I was a different kind of player compared with the ones Blake was accustomed to. He knew I was a college man—not that I consider myself an intellectual, I don't—and I don't think he believed I could make it. When your coach is thinking that way, your chances are not too good."

But Berenson hardly saw more ice when he was traded to the Rangers. At first it seemed he'd be the number one center, but an injury sidelined him and his place was taken by Orland Kurtenbach; every time he made a comeback he'd suffer another injury and the word—unfairly—made the rounds that he was brittle.

Red was traded to St. Louis by the Rangers in 1967, where he became an instant star. But by the 1970–71 season, Berenson had worn out his welcome with St. Louis and the Salomon family owners—probably because of his deep involvement in the burgeoning players' association. He was traded to Detroit with Tim Ecclestone. Again he came temporarily to life and productivity, but by January 1975 he was back in St. Louis, perhaps near the end of his best playing years, although he rallied and seemed capable of another renaissance.

GARY GUNNAR BERGMAN

BORN: Kenora, Ontario, October 7, 1938
POSITION: Defenseman, Detroit Red Wings, 1964–73, 1974–   ; Minnesota North Stars, 1974
AWARDS: Team Canada, 1972

The fact that defenseman Gary Bergman played nine straight seasons for the Detroit Red Wings and they made the playoffs only three times should not be construed as a reflection on the bald backliner. He played a workmanlike, if not spectacular, game; good enough to be invited to play for Team Canada 1972 against the Soviet National Team. Bergman was unusually petulant—and also unusually competent—against the Russians. It was the very highest point in his career which began a rapid descent thereafter, in Detroit and then for the Minnesota North Stars, but ended up back in Detroit by October 1974.

LOUIS BERLINQUETTE

BORN: Unknown
DIED: June 2, 1959
POSITION: Left Wing, Montreal Canadiens (NHA and NHL), 1912–25;
   Pittsburgh Pirates, 1925–26

Probably the original utility forward, left winger Louis Berlinquette played on almost every offensive conglomeration the early Montreal Canadiens could produce. Consequently, Louis was considered a "sub" throughout most of his twenty-six-year career. But despite his embarrassing "spare" status in the program lineups, Berlinquette managed to appear in more games than any skater of his day.

SERGE BERNIER

BORN: Padoue, Quebec, April 29, 1947
POSITION: Center, Philadelphia Flyers, 1968–72; Los Angeles Kings,
   1972–73; Quebec Nordiques (WHA), 1973–
AWARDS: All-Star (WHA, Second Team), 1975; Team Canada (WHA),
   1974

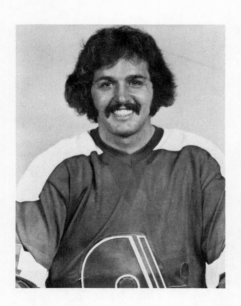

Serge Bernier was not one of the original Philadelphia Flyers, but he came close. The first choice of the Flyers in the 1967 amateur draft, Bernier spent a few seasons with the AHL Quebec Aces before being brought up to the parent club to stay in 1970.

Bernier impressed the club right from the start, garnering 23 goals in his first NHL campaign, along with 28 assists for 51 points, respectable for a first-year player.

However, after a couple of subpar seasons for the Flyers, Bernier was traded to the Los Angeles Kings in a massive six-player deal that also saw Bill Lesuk and Jim Johnson travel West and brought Bill Flett, Ed Joyal, Jean Potvin, and Ross Lonsberry to the City of Brotherly Love.

When the World Hockey Association beckoned in 1973–74, Bernier headed back north to Quebec City, where he turned in his best season ever, with 37 goals and 49 assists for the Quebec Nordiques.

As a further tribute to his fine play, Serge was invited to play for Team Canada '74 against the Soviet Union and turned in a fine performance despite the WHA squad's defeat by the sophisticated Russian team.

ROBERT VICTOR (BOB) BERRY

BORN: Montreal, Quebec, November 29, 1943
POSITION: Left Wing, Montreal Canadiens, 1968–69; Los Angeles
    Kings, 1970–

Bob Berry, a steady, opportunistic portsider, broke into pro hockey in 1968–69 with the Montreal Canadiens' organization. Sold to the Los Angeles Kings in 1970, Bob has emerged as the Hollywood sextet's all-time leading lamplighter. A Rock of Gibraltar around the opposition's net, most of Bob's goals are scored on rebounds, deflections, and goalmouth scrambles. With most of Berry's scoring shots traveling a distance of slightly over two feet, Bob has ranked in the top ten among the NHL's most accurate sharpshooters and is one of the league intellects, too.

A versatile athlete who spurned offers from pro baseball and semipro football, Berry toured the USSR in 1967–68 as a member of Canada's National Hockey Team.

WILLIAM S. (BILL) BEVERIDGE

BORN: Ottawa, Ontario, July 1,1909
POSITION: Goalie, Detroit Red Wings, 1929–30; Ottawa Senators,
    1930–34; St. Louis Eagles, 1934–35; Montreal Maroons, 1935–38;
    New York Rangers, 1942–43

Bill Beveridge was a goalie who had always had the misfortune to be on the receiving end of a poor defensive team's night out. His efforts, however, contradicted the stats, and despite playing for a number of defensively horrendous clubs, he still managed to finish a nine-year career with a lifetime goals-against average of 2.98.

NICHOLAS GERALD (NICK) BEVERLEY

BORN: Toronto, Ontario, April 21, 1947
POSITION: Defenseman, Boston Bruins, 1965–66, 1969–70, 1971–73; Pittsburgh Penguins, 1973–74; New York Rangers, 1974–

When Nick Beverley was traded to the New York Rangers in 1974 by Pittsburgh, for Vic Hadfield, New York City was somewhat shocked. Granted, Hadfield, once a fluke 50-goal scorer, was edging over the hill, but to trade a fighting, scoring left wing for a quiet, unobtrusive defenseman?

Without delving further into the kinky minds of hockey management and their motives, suffice it to say that the Gotham press corps responded by labeling Nick steady, smooth, reliable, and other adjectives which would cover up for the fact that he wasn't really the world's toughest defenseman.

Beverley had plied his trade in the NHL for the Bruins from 1972 until midseason 1973, when he was dealt to the Pittsburgh Penguins—probably because he wasn't Boston's cup of tea—too "nice." When Rod Seiling, the butt of Ranger fans' bad feelings for years, left the New York sextet, it looked certain that if nothing else, Nick Beverley might well become the new rearguard scapegoat.

PAUL BIBEAULT

BORN: Montreal, Quebec, April 13, 1919
POSITION: Goalie, Montreal Canadiens, 1940–43; Toronto Maple Leafs, 1943–44; Boston Bruins, 1944–45; Chicago Back Hawks, 1946–47
AWARDS: All-Star (Second Team), 1944

A French-Canadian goalie with modest talents, Paul Bibeault nevertheless figured in a history-making experiment in his rookie NHL season (1940–41) with the Canadiens. Coach Dick Irvin had two goalies, Bert Gardiner and Bibeault, at the time. During a game against the Americans, Irvin alternated Gardiner and Bibeault at seven-minute intervals and came up with a 6–0 victory. Bibeault became the Canadiens' regular goalie the following season, but was bombed one time too many. In a game against Detroit, he allowed 10 goals in a 10–0 humiliation. In 1943–44 Paul played for the Maple Leafs, then with Boston a year later. He split the next two seasons between Boston, Montreal, and Chicago before leaving the NHL for good.

LESLIE JOHN (LES) BINKLEY

BORN: Owen Sound, Ontario, June 6, 1936
POSITION: Goalie, Pittsburgh Penguins, 1967–72; Ottawa Nationals
(WHA), 1972–73; Toronto Toros (WHA), 1973–

When goalie Les Binkley played in Philadelphia, Hugh Brown of *The Evening Bulletin* observed: "Binkley looks somewhat like he sounds, meaning he could pass for a near-sighted, narrow-chested bird watcher." After nine seasons in the minors, Les was plucked by the Pittsburgh Penguins to be second-string goalie behind Hank Bassen in the NHL's first big expansion in 1967–68. But as soon as the campaign got underway, it became apparent that Binkley not only was better than Bassen but he was better than a lot of other goaltenders in the National Hockey League.

"I know of only one man who had the edge on Binkley," said Red Sullivan in the middle of that season, "and that was Johnny Bower of Toronto. There are one or two others who were Bink's equal. There are several who get more publicity. But there is no one outside of Bower who had more ability as a goaltender than Binkley."

But if Binkley was so good, what kept the NHL bosses from finding him? One factor was the six-team league which was already loaded with good goalies. When expansion came six openings developed, and goaltenders were sought by every new club. According to Les, another problem had been his eyesight. "The contact lenses, that's what kept me back," he said. "They [the managers] knew I had good reflexes, but they were afraid I couldn't see."

Binkley jumped to the WHA in 1972, joining the Ottawa Nationals and remained active through 1974–75 with the Toronto Toros.

JACK ARTHUR BIONDA

BORN: Huntsville, Ontario, September 18, 1933
POSITION: Defenseman, Toronto Maple Leafs, 1955–56; Boston Bruins, 1956–59

Jack Bionda is living proof that a very good lacrosse player can be given a pair of skates, a stick, and a puck and will *not* be a very good hockey player. The Bruins hoped otherwise in 1956–57 after the Maple Leafs had failed in experimenting with Bionda. Then Bruins' manager Lynn Patrick predicted that Bionda would be an NHL All-Star. "He has those necessary instincts which make stars," said Patrick. That turned out to be the overstatement of the half-century. Bionda played for Boston in 1957–58 and three games in the 1958–59 campaign before the Bruins' front office saw the light. Bionda was, in fact, one of Canada's foremost lacrosse players—not to be confused with big league hockey.

CECIL BLACHFORD

BORN: June 24, 1880
DIED: May 10, 1965
POSITION: Forward, Montreal (CAHL), 1903; Montreal Wanderers (FAHL, ECAHA, NHA), 1904–08, 1910

The first captain of the pre-NHL Montreal Wanderers, Blachford led his team to three successive Stanley Cup championships despite a medical chart that should have had him convalescing on the sunny shores of the Riviera. Cecil missed much of the 1906 and 1907 campaigns, due to a serious case of blood poisoning and later a fierce stick duel with Charlie Spittal of Ottawa. But Cecil shrugged off these minor disturbances and brought his team the championship in both seasons.

Blachford retired in 1909, but that old itch was back again the following year. He returned to the Wanderers in 1910, and again helped them collect Lord Stanley's Cup, and then he hung 'em up for keeps.

BLACKS

Quite a fuss was made when the Washington Capitals of the NHL signed a black, Mike Marson, to a 1974–75 contract. Only one black man had ever reached the NHL before Marson. Willie O'Ree was the first black to break the color barrier, with the Boston Bruins in 1960–61 after a two-game trial in 1957–58. Now too old for another crack at the majors, there are those who believe that with a break or two O'Ree could have lasted longer than one season.

"I never got a chance in my first tryout in Boston," said O'Ree, who played six years with San Diego of the Western League. "The second time around I had nobody to blame but myself. I had plenty of chances but I was uptight, rushed things, and didn't get the goals I might have if I wasn't so overanxious."

Another who made it temporarily was Alton White, with the WHA. Like O'Ree, White wasn't naive enough to believe his color was ignored by those who played against or watched him on the ice.

"Over the years," said O'Ree, "a fan here, a player there slurred me, but there wasn't much of it. In the NHL they rode me, but just like they would any other player. Sure, I've heard things. I've been booed a lot, but I like to think it's because I was one of the stars of a rival team, not because of my color."

By contrast, White insists he had few problems because of his color. "Once in a while," Alton said, "I heard some wisecracks from people in the stands. But at least they knew I was out there working. I was very well accepted in Providence and had no problems whatsoever. I got along well with all the people; the fans treated me exceptionally well."

If White had been owned outright by a club such as Pittsburgh, Buffalo, Los Angeles, or Philadelphia the chances are that he'd have been in the NHL. "It was tough for me to go up," he said, "because I was owned by Providence. So, in order for me to go up I'd have had to be sold. I got a little bit down when I saw guys go up when I knew I was a better hockey player. And they went up because they were owned by a different organization. Then along came the WHA and my big chance. The reason there are so few blacks in pro hockey is that there are relatively few Negroes in Canada."

Although there is no apparent discrimination against blacks in hockey today, this was not always the case. During the mid- and late forties, an entire black line consisting of the Carnegie brothers, Ossie and Herbie, and Manny McIntyre starred for Sherbrooke in the Quebec Senior Hockey League. Herbie, regarded as the best of the three, was believed to be the equal of most NHL stars, but couldn't crack the majors. Herbie hinted that his skin color had more than a little to do with it. Certainly, if the line was in its playing prime today it would be an instant hit in the NHL.

Now that the NHL and WHA have expanded, and more American-born players are being groomed for major league hockey, the inevitable question is whether a black skater from the United States will ever reach the big time. If the question had been asked five to ten years ago the answer would be an emphatic no! But recently more and more black youngsters have taken up hockey and with very positive results. The municipally operated ice-skating rink in Harlem currently has a full-scale hockey program and, judging by current production, should be sending a few boys to Canadian Junior leagues within a few years.

THOMAS (TOM) BLADON

BORN: Edmonton, Alberta, December 29, 1952
POSITION: Defenseman, Philadelphia Flyers, 1972–

Tom Bladon's greatest claim to fame to date is replacing injured Flyer defenseman Barry Ashbee in the 1974 Stanley Cup semifinals. Bladon filled in nicely, hardly a surprise to Philly fans. Bladon was a Flyer second-round amateur draft choice in 1972, and "Sparky" was immediately placed on the "point" for the power play. In 1973–74 Bladon set a club record for goals by a defenseman with 12, and the six-foot, one-inch native of Edmonton, Alberta, continues as the club's leading offensive defenseman.

ANDREW DRYDEN (ANDY) BLAIR

BORN: Winnipeg, Manitoba, February 27, 1908
POSITION: Center, Toronto Maple Leafs, 1928–36; Chicago Black Hawks, 1936–37

Because of his experience as manager of the hockey squad at the University of Toronto, Maple Leafs' general manager Conn Smythe kept his scouting radar trained on Canadian universities. In 1928 Smythe zeroed in on Andy Blair, a beanpole center who played for St. John's College in Winnipeg. Blair signed with Toronto in 1928–29 and found himself right at home with another university player, Hap Day. "Andy," Day recalled, "even wore a 'Joe College' moustache and, believe it or not, played the game with a handkerchief stuck up the sleeve of his uniform."

Blair lasted eight full seasons in the Queen City and proved to be a capable, if not spectacular, performer. One of his most notable performances came in his rookie season when the Maple Leafs played the Senators of Ottawa.

As a coach Smythe had stressed the expression "strategy" in discussions with his players. During the game against the Senators, Blair borrowed

Smythe's fetish after finding himself in a near-impossible situation. The score was 0–0 in the third period. For the Maple Leafs this was a commendable accomplishment since they rarely won, let alone tied, a game. This time, however, the Leafs appeared to be heading for a tie at the very least until they ran into an unusual spate of penalties. First, Art Duncan, then Red Horner were banished, leaving Toronto with only two defensemen, Art Smith and Hap Day. Suddenly, both Day *and* Smith were penalized. The Maple Leafs were out of defenseman (this was before the NHL instituted the delayed penalty ruling). Smythe was able to send out only goalie Chabot and center Blair! The referee dropped the puck, and Blair managed to win the face-off. With his long arms and expert stickhandling ability, Andy gave Ottawa the impression that he was a skating octopus. "Every time an Ottawa player lunged for the puck," said Day, "Blair seemed to pull it away from him."

At last the puck was frozen, and a face-off was called. Blair realized he seemed to be skating against the hockey world, and he wondered just how he could survive the ordeal. Andy, who occasionally suffered from a mild stutter when he was under severe pressure, skated over to the bench, where Smythe was leaning over the boards. The nervous rookie pulled off his gauntlets, yanked the handkerchief from his jersey, blew his nose, and repeated Smythe's favorite word.

"Okay, C. C. C. . . . . Conn," Blair sputtered, "tell me what the *strategy* is now."

WREN BLAIR

Wren Blair, otherwise known as the Bird of hockey, was a milkman who made it big in the NHL. Blair became disenchanted with his Ontario milk route at an early age and turned to coaching and managing amateur teams. He is one of a dozen hockey people who have taken personal credit for discovering Bobby Orr when the *wunderkind* was a twelve-year-old playing Junior C level amateur hockey in the Ontario Association. (Lynn Patrick, Milt Schmidt, and God are among the others who have taken bows for finding Orr and signing him to a Bruins' contract.) When the NHL expanded from six to twelve teams in 1967–68, Blair was named general manager and coach of the Minnesota North Stars. He frequently relinquished the coaching because of ill health, but retained the managerial post. In 1970–71, the Blair-developed North Stars reached a high point in their young life by reaching the semifinal round of the Stanley Cup playoffs before being eliminated by Montreal in six games. From there it was all downhill for the Bird. The North Stars aged rapidly while their young aces failed to mature quickly enough. In 1973–74 Minnesota missed a playoff berth and Blair left the NHL, returning to minor league hockey.

HECTOR "TOE" BLAKE

BORN: Victoria Mines, Ontario, August 21, 1912
POSITION: Left Wing, Montreal Maroons, 1934–35, Montreal Cana-
diens, 1935–48; Coach, Montreal Canadiens, 1955–68
AWARDS: Hart Trophy, 1939; Art Ross Trophy, 1939; Lady Byng
Trophy, 1946; All-Star (First Team), 1939, 1940, 1945, (Second
Team), 1938, 1946; Hockey Hall of Fame, 1966

A hard-nosed left wing who scored enough goals to be nicknamed "the Old
Lamplighter," Hector "Toe" Blake remained a Montreal hockey player from
his rookie year—and only season—with the Maroons (1934–35) to his retirement following the 1947–48 campaign with the Canadiens for whom he played
during all his other NHL years.

Blake played hard and talked loud, something that didn't endear him to referees around the NHL. That's why to this day it remains a mystery how Blake
won the Lady Byng Trophy for good sportsmanship in the 1945–46 season.

But Toe had been a trophy winner long before that. While the Canadiens
were finishing sixth in 1938–39, Blake led the league in scoring. His awards included the Hart Trophy as the most valuable player, not to mention an All-Star
nomination. "When Dick Irvin became Canadiens' coach in 1941," wrote
hockey historian Charles L. Coleman, "his rebuilding job was done around
Blake."

At the start of the forties, Blake was used on a line with Johnny Quilty and
Joe Benoit, but Irvin was soon to change that with the insertion of Elmer Lach
at center. The Canadiens were improving, with Blake leading the way, but they
didn't reach maturity as a championship club until the 1943–44 season when
Irvin inserted young, fiery Maurice "Rocket" Richard on right wing on the line
with Blake and Lach.

The trio, which was named the Punch Line, finished one-two-three (Lach,
Blake, Richard) in scoring on the team, the Canadiens finished first and won
the Stanley Cup. The Punch Line became one of the classiest units in league
annals and helped the Canadiens to another Stanley Cup in 1946. Blake scored
29 regular season goals that year, but then began a decline in his playing for-
tunes. He scored only nine goals in 1947–48, a year in which the Canadiens
missed the playoffs, and then made his exit from the NHL.

Regarded as sure-fire coaching timber, Toe broke in as a bench boss in the
minors with stints in such unlikely places as Houston, Buffalo, and Valleyfield,
Quebec. When Dick Irvin resigned as Canadiens' coach after the 1954–55
season several names were tossed in the hopper, but the only serious contender
was Blake.

The Old Lamplighter had studied coaching well in the Quebec Senior
League. He was partially French Canadian, and he was admired by all the
players, particularly Maurice Richard. Kenny Reardon, who had moved up to a

key front-office position with the Canadiens, was a strong advocate of Blake, and ultimately the opinions of manager Frank Selke and Reardon prevailed. On June 8 the signing of Blake was officially announced before a standing-room crowd at the Forum, and Les Canadiens were ready to become the greatest team in hockey history.

Toe Blake wielded a dictator's baton over Les Canadiens, but at first he ruled them like a benevolent despot. This was easy because the players, to a man, respected Blake, and vice versa. The pivotal personality on the team was the Rocket. He went out of his way to assure the Canadiens' hierarchy that he backed Blake to the hilt, and he meant every word of it.

Now it was up to the Old Lamplighter to produce. All the ingredients were there: a young competent goaltender, a strong, intelligent defense, and the most explosive collection of scorers in history. It was simply a matter of stirring them to the proper boil without creating the fire hazard of previous years. Richard riots were to be avoided at all costs.

"Blake and Selke were trying to give the Rocket all they had by way of a tranquilizing program," says author Josh Greenfeld. "They started giving him de-pep talks long before the season began. They pointed out to him that he was thirty-five years old, that he did not have to carry the emotional burden of victory alone, that he still would be treated with sufficient respect by the other players around the league even if he went a little easier on the roughhouse, and that the important thing was not one game, not one fight, but to lead the team to a Stanley Cup victory."

His scrubs, such as defenseman Jean-Guy Talbot and Bob Turner, were good enough to be first-liners on almost any other team, which was a credit to Selke's superb farm system. It was, indeed, a galaxy that dazzled nobody more than it did Blake. "I couldn't help be amazed once we started holding our first workouts," said Toe. "I was glad I was as young as I was. Otherwise I would have been killed. All those great shots. The puck was flying around with such speed I thought I was in a shooting gallery."

Blake's success at Valleyfield in the Quebec Senior League was well known to management, but it hardly made an impression on the rank-and-file fan who had as many doubts about Blake as Toe himself. "I was nervous," the rookie coach allowed. "I felt I had to produce with a club like that. So much potential. And it was a big test for me. But the Rocket went out of his way to help me. So did Kenny Mosdell and Floyd Curry and Butch Bouchard.

"Sometimes it's tough to coach players you once had as teammates. But these fellas went out of their way to make it easy for me. Even from the beginning we were like one big happy family."

Blake was so successful with his "happy family" that he helped to engineer the arrival of eight Stanley Cups in his thirteen-year tenure.

The pilot of Les Canadiens' dynasty, Blake had finished first nine times and was regarded by many experts as the finest all-round coach the NHL has known. "Under Toe's stabling influence," said Toronto *Star* sports editor Jim Proudfoot, "the Rocket earned the stature he surely would have missed otherwise. This might have been Blake's finest achievement as a coach. Another would be the rehabilitation of the Montreal club after it came apart in 1961 and 1962. In two years the Canadiens were back in first place and, a year after that, they won the Stanley Cup again."

But with each triumph Blake became more and more irritable, more difficult on his players and, perhaps more important, on himself. After the Canadiens had finished first in the NHL's East Division and won the 1968 Stanley Cup Blake finally gave in to his better judgment and his nerves and retired.

"Toe Blake," said Rocket Richard in a succinct analysis, "was probably the best coach who ever stepped behind the bench in the NHL; and his record proves it."

AUGUST (GUS) BODNAR

BORN: Fort William, Ontario, August 24, 1925
POSITION: Center, Toronto Maple Leafs, 1943–47; Chicago Black
    Hawks, 1947–54; Boston Bruins, 1954–55
AWARDS: Calder Trophy, 1944

When Gus Bodnar was promoted to the Toronto Maple Leafs in the fall of 1943 at age twenty, coach Hap Day quipped: "It appears that we have reached the Children's Hour in the NHL." But Bodnar, a slick center, immediately proved that he was a winner. In his first NHL game, October 30, 1943, against the Rangers, Bodnar scored 15 seconds after the opening face-off against goalie Ken McAuley. Gus thus set a record for "fastest goal scored by a rookie." He finished his first season with 22 goals and 40 assists for 62 points in 50 games. His total set a league record for rookies and he was named the outstanding freshman in the league. Surprisingly, his play never again quite reached that standard, although he played on Stanley Cup winners in 1945 and 1947 with the Leafs.

A native of Fort William, Ontario, Gus worked for a while with Bud Poile and Gaye Stewart, also from the same city. Their unit, "the Flying Forts," went *en masse* along with Ernie Dickens and Bob Goldham to the Chicago Black Hawks in a trade for Max Bentley and Cy Thomas in November 1947. Bodnar played capably for Chicago and assisted Bill Mosienko when Bill broke a scoring record with three goals in 21 seconds on March 23, 1952.

Gus was traded to the Bruins in 1953–54 and finished his NHL career in Boston in 1954–55.

GARTH VERNON BOESCH

BORN: Millestone, Saskatchewan, October 7, 1920
POSITION: Defenseman, Toronto Maple Leafs, 1946–50

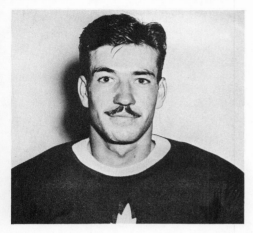

Only two players wore moustaches in the NHL during the forties—Don "Bones" Raleigh of the Rangers and Garth Boesch of the Maple Leafs. Raleigh's was only a temporary fixture; Boesch's remained permanent and complimented his cool defensive style. A Saskatchewan wheat farmer, Boesch was a cog in the Toronto dynasty launched by Conn Smythe in 1946. From the 1947 playoffs through April 1949, the Leafs won three Stanley Cups in three tries, aided by the superb play of Boesch. His defense partner was Bill Barilko and together, they perfected the Maginot Line knee drop, in which they would simultaneously fall to their knees to block enemy shots, as if they were connected by invisible rods. During the 1949–50 season when Smythe conducted his notorious fight against fat on his team, Boesch was one of the few Leafs to check in on the scale *under* his established weight. As defensemen go, Boesch was one of the most underrated quality backliners ever to play in the majors.

MARC BOILEAU

BORN: Pointe Claire, Quebec, September 3, 1932
POSITION: Forward, Detroit Red Wings, 1961–62; Coach, Pittsburgh
    Penguins, 1974–

Marc Boileau was named coach of the Pittsburgh Penguins on February 6, 1974, following the dismissal of Ken Schinkel. He thus became the fourth coach of the Pens in their seven-year history.

Boileau sharpened his coaching skills for his NHL debut by serving as player-pilot for the Fort Wayne Komets of the International Hockey League for three seasons, guiding them to IHL titles in 1972 and 1973.

Part of Boileau's coaching influence is toughness. He possesses the pugilistic talents of Bob "Battleship" Kelly and Steve Durbano, the former Blues toughy who once spent 402 minutes in the sin bin for the Omaha Knights of the Central Hockey League. "When I took over," recalls Boileau, "These guys had stopped believing in themselves. They were expecting to lose and that was one of the reasons they were losing."

Boileau did not distinguish himself as a player, toiling only for fifty-four games in one season for the Detroit Red Wings, despite playing professionally for eleven seasons.

LEO JOSEPH BOIVIN

BORN: Prescott, Ontario, August 2, 1932
POSITION: Defenseman, Toronto Maple Leafs, 1951–55; Boston Bruins, 1955–65; Detroit Red Wings, 1966–67; Pittsburgh Penguins, 1967–69; Minnesota North Stars, 1969–70

Gravity and beef were Leo Boivin's major assets. Standing 5'7", Boivin weighed in at anywhere from 190 to 200 pounds. He broke into the NHL with Toronto in 1951–52, was traded to Boston in 1954–55, and spent nine colorful seasons with the Bruins before being traded to Detroit. In the twilight of his career, Boivin skated for Pittsburgh and Minnesota before closing his NHL work in 1970.

IVAN BOLDIREV

BORN: Zrenjanin, Yugoslavia, August 15, 1949
POSITION: Center, Boston Bruins, 1970–72; California Seals, 1972–74; Chicago Black Hawks, 1974–

Ivan Boldirev has the distinction of coming from Zrenjanin, Yugoslavia, which is something no one else in the NHL can say . . . or pronounce.

On May 24, 1974, Boldirev was traded from the California Seals to the Chicago Black Hawks for Len Frig and Mike Christie, where he joined another East European center, Stan Mikita. Other than their respective backgrounds and position, the two players have little in common. Mikita is small and classy; Boldirev is big and scores more by brawn than finesse.

FRANK THURMAN "BUZZ" BOLL

BORN: Fillmore, Saskatchewan, March 6, 1911
POSITION: Forward, Toronto Maple Leafs, 1933–39; New York Americans, 1939–42; Boston Bruins, 1942–44

Buzz Boll worked his way from the ground up to make it in the NHL—literally. While waiting for an opening on the Toronto Maple Leafs in the early thirties, Boll took a job as night watchman at the excavation site of Maple Leaf Gardens in Toronto in 1931. His boss was Conn Smythe, the club manager, who provided Boll with a cord of wood, a shack, a stove, and a baseball bat to ward off intruders. After the Gardens was completed, Boll became a full-fledged Leaf regular during the 1933–34 season and played forward in Toronto until he was traded to the Americans in 1939–40. After the Amerks folded in 1942, Boll joined the Bruins and starred for them in 1942–43 when he scored 52 points in 43 games. He played another season in Boston before retiring.

HUGH EDWARD BOLTON

BORN: Toronto, Ontario, April 15, 1929
POSITION: Defenseman, Toronto Maple Leafs, 1949–57

When Bill Barilko, the Toronto Maple Leafs' ace defenseman, was killed in a plane crash following the 1951 Stanley Cup victory, the Toronto management hoped that scholarly Hugh Bolton—a rare college grad who later became a teacher—could fill Barilko's skates. Bolton couldn't although he was a regular from 1951–57.

MARCEL BONIN

BORN: Montreal, Quebec, September 12, 1932
POSITION: Forward, Detroit Red Wings, 1952–55; Boston Bruins, 1955–57; Montreal Canadiens, 1957–62

Absolutely the one and only NHL skater ever to have wrestled a bear and eaten glass—with no serious aftereffects on either count—Marcel Bonin was one of hockey's more colorful characters from his debut in 1952–53 with the Red Wings to his final season, 1961–62, with the Canadiens. In between his wild sorties, Bonin was an effective forward whose most productive season was 1959–60, when he scored 17 goals and 34 assists for 51 points in 59 games. He played on three Montreal Stanley Cup winners (1958, 1959, 1960) and contributed mightily to each. During the 1959 Cup march, Marcel scored 10 goals and 5 assists for 15 points in 11 playoff games. Having toughened up by wrestling bears in northern Quebec lumber camps, Bonin was not afraid to take on the biggest and toughest of NHL foes.

Hall of Fame defenseman Bill Gadsby said the most painful injury he suffered was at the hands of Bonin. "Marcel followed through on a shot," said Gadsby, "and jammed his stick up my nostril. They were the sorest stitches I ever had."

RICHARD R. (DICKIE) BOON

BORN: January 10, 1878
DIED: May 3, 1961
POSITION: Defenseman, Montreal (CAHL), 1900–03; Montreal Wanderers (FAHL), 1904–05
AWARDS: Hockey Hall of Fame, 1952

Hall of Famer who never played professional hockey, Dickie Boon played his junior hockey with the talented Mike Grant on the Young Crystals team of Montreal.

In 1897 he played with the Monarch Hockey Club, followed by a two-year stint with the Montreal A.A.A. Juniors. In 1901 Boon made the senior club, which went on to win the Stanley Cup against the Winnipeg Victorias in 1902. Boon and his teammates were so small that they became known as "the Little Iron Men."

In 1903 Boon became manager of the Montreal Wanderers and, until his retirement in 1916, piloted the Wanderers to three Stanley Cups.

CARL GEORGE "BUDDY" BOONE

BORN: Kirkland Lake, Ontario, September 11, 1932
POSITION: Forward, Boston Bruins, 1957–58

Carl "Buddy" Boone played only one full season (1957–58) in the NHL with Boston, but he gained notoriety as a marauding forward. "Boone," said ex-Ranger Camille Henry, "was one of the dirtiest players I ever went up against." Because of his jowls, Boone was often called "Buddy Balloon."

CHRISTIAN GERARD (CHRIS) BORDELEAU

BORN: Noranda, Quebec, September 23, 1947
POSITION: Center, Montreal Canadiens, 1968–70; St. Louis Blues, 1970–72; Chicago Black Hawks, 1972; Winnipeg Jets (WHA), 1972–74; Quebec Nordiques (WHA), 1974–

The oldest of three hockey-playing Bordeleau brothers, Chris Bordeleau bounced around the NHL for four seasons, mostly as a penalty killer and odd-line centerman. His best NHL season was 1970–71 in St. Louis, when Bordeleau scored 21 goals and 53 points.

Chris' measly NHL totals were a thing of the past in August 1972 when he jumped to the newly founded Winnipeg Jets of the World Hockey Association. Often skating on a line with Bobby Hull, Chris racked up 47 goals and 101 total points in his first WHA season, almost matching his entire four-year NHL output.

BOSTON BRUINS

Ostensibly, the Boston Bruins were born in a Montreal hotel room in 1924, when the National Hockey League governors voted to grant the first American franchise to New England grocery magnate Charles F. Adams. But, practically, the Bruins were born in the wheat fields of Saskatchewan, where Eddie Shore grew up and learned to play hockey. It was Eddie Shore who gave the Bruins life when they were struggling for existence in those uncertain early days in the NHL. Without Shore, the Bruins might well have collapsed.

Adams had become enamored of hockey after watching amateur games around Boston. He sponsored a team, but soon became disenchanted upon discovering that some of his rivals were spreading rather large gratuities among their players, even going so far as to lure several lads down from Canada. This breach of the good-fellowship code didn't wear well with Adams, and he seemed ripe, as well as ready, to switch his interest to professional hockey.

A group headed by Tom Duggan, Frank Sullivan, and Russ Layton began hammering away at Adams to obtain a big league franchise.

"In 1924," Adam's son, Weston, explained, "he went to Montreal to attend the Stanley Cup final. That did it. When he returned home, he told us this was the greatest hockey he ever had seen. He wouldn't be happy until he had a franchise. Shore made hockey in Boston, but Montreal got us started."

Adams wasted little time organizing his new enterprise. During his Canadian excursion he had met a crusty, dour Scot by the name of Art Ross who had had a successful career as a player. He liked the man and promptly named him coach, general manager, and scout of the new team. Ross signed a number of qualified players, including goalie Alex Connell and Clarence "Hap" Day, who was later to be a star defenseman with Toronto and one of the NHL's most successful coaches. Other first-year Bruins were Carson Cooper, Hooley Smith, Ed Gorman, and Bert McCaffrey.

When the 1924–25 season ended, the Bruins' only claim to fame was that they were America's first NHL team. They barely held up the bottom of the six-team league; with a feeble record of six wins and twenty-four losses, the Boston group lagged far behind the Montreal Maroons, Ottawa Senators, Montreal Canadiens, Toronto Maple Leafs, and Hamilton Tigers.

"We had three teams that year," said Adams, "one coming, one going, and one playing."

The Bruins won their first Stanley Cup in the spring of 1929, sparked by Eddie Shore, who became known as the "Edmonton Express" and "Mr. Hockey" on his way to hockey's Hall of Fame. They went on to win three Cups in two decades.

Besides Shore, there were such stars as goalie Tiny Thompson; the famed "Dynamite Line" of Cooney Weiland, Dit Clapper, and Dutch Gainor; right wing Harry Oliver; and defensemen Lionel Hitchman and George Owen.

With Shore, now in the Hall of Fame from that team are Thompson, Clapper, and Oliver.

The Bruins' vaunted Kraut Line of Milt Schmidt, Bobby Bauer, and Woody Dumart, along with other new stars, goalie Frank Brimsek, John Crawford, Bill Cowley, Mel Hill, Roy Conacher, together with holdover Dit Clapper, gave the Bruins Stanley Cup teams in 1939 and 1941.

The Kraut Line enlisted in the Royal Canadian Air Force as a unit early in 1942. Brimsek and Conacher followed them into the service at the end of the season and that broke up the powerhouse.

Ross retired to the front office in 1942 to concentrate on his duties as general manager. Clapper, the only member of the three Stanley Cup champions and an All-Star both as right wing and defenseman, succeeded him as coach.

Clapper, the first NHL player to be active for twenty years, was a playing coach until he retired to the bench during the 1946–47 season. With his retirement, he was honored with election to the Hall of Fame.

George Boucher had a one-year term as coach in 1949–50.

Lynn Patrick succeeded Boucher and was the Bruins' bench boss for four and a half years before he relinquished the coaching reins to Milt Schmidt just before Christmas, 1954. Patrick had taken over as general manager from Ross in 1953 and he remained with the club in that capacity until the spring of 1967 when Leighton "Hap" Emms replaced him.

Schmidt coached a year and a half before moving into the front office as assistant to the general manager, while Phil Watson took over as coach. But Milt returned to the bench in 1962–63 and remained there until Harry Sinden was hired in 1966.

Schmidt, meanwhile, became general manager and in his first year, 1967–68, made a multi-player trade with Chicago that transformed the Bruins into a playoff team for the first time in nine years. He acquired Phil Esposito, Ken Hodge, and Fred Stanfield for Pit Martin, Gilles Marotte, and Jack Norris.

Esposito, Hodge, and Stanfield all hit the 20-goal plateau and Esposito lost out to Stan Mikita for the individual scoring title on the final night of the season.

In 1968–69, the Bruins finished second to the Canadiens in league play and lost out in a thrilling six-game semifinal Stanley Cup playoff series.

That season Esposito became the first player in history to score more than 100 points in a season, collecting 126 in all, including 49 goals. He won the Hart Trophy as most valuable player as well as the Art Ross Memorial Trophy as the top scorer. He was named to the All-Star team along with Bobby Orr.

Orr won the Calder Trophy as the outstanding rookie in 1966–67 and Derek Sanderson repeated the following year. Boston won the Stanley Cup in 1970 and 1972.

A third generation of the Adams family took over at the helm of the Bruins when Weston W. Adams, Jr. was named president to succeed his father on March 31, 1969. Milt Schmidt was succeeded as general manager by Harry Sinden and the coaching slot has been nervously occupied by Bep Guidolin (1972—73), and, most recently, Don Cherry (1974—).

HENRY CHARLES BOUCHA

BORN: Warroad, Minnesota, June 1, 1951
POSITION: Center, Detroit Red Wings, 1971–74; Minnesota North
    Stars, 1974–75; Minnesota Fighting Saints (WHA), 1975–

While not the most talented player to arrive in the NHL in recent years, Henry Boucha has managed to attract a lot of attention. When Boucha began with Detroit in 1971, he was that rare player, an American, who also happened to be part Chippewa Indian. His chippy style and the fact that he instituted the use of a sweatband to contain his flowing locks, endeared him to Red Wing fans.

Once a member of the U.S. Olympic team, which captured a silver medal at the 1972 Olympics in Sapporo, Japan, Boucha set an NHL record on January 28, 1973, by scoring a goal a mere six seconds after the opening face-off.

Boucha was traded to Minnesota for Danny Grant on August 24, 1974, and it wasn't long before he made the headlines again, in a near-tragic incident. On January 4, 1975, the Bruins were in Bloomington, Minnesota, playing the North Stars, when Henry was brutally butt-ended by Bruin center Dave Forbes, as the two players left their respective penalty boxes. After two bouts of surgery to correct double vision, Boucha returned to the ice within two months, while Forbes was slapped with a ten-game suspension, the second highest punishment ever meted out by league president Clarence Campbell (Maurice Richard received a record 15-game suspension in 1955), and was also reprimanded by a Minnesota district attorney. Boucha "jumped" to the WHA Minnesota Fighting Saints in June 1975.

EMILE "BUTCH" BOUCHARD

BORN: Montreal, Quebec, September 11, 1920
POSITION: Defenseman, Montreal Canadiens, 1942–56
AWARDS: All-Star (First Team), 1945, 1946, 1947; (Second Team), 1944; Hockey Hall of Fame, 1960

A tall French-Canadian defenseman, Emile "Butch" Bouchard learned his hockey on the sidewalks of Montreal not far from the Forum during the early thirties. At first, Bouchard was considered too awkward to be an effective hockey player. His long arms and legs suggested an octopus trying to maneuver on the ice, and when young Butch had tried out for the team at Académie Roussin, he literally fell on his face.

The Bouchard family moved and Butch enrolled at St. Francis Xavier School where he easily won a berth on the team. His style continued to improve, and before long, Paul Stuart, a Montreal sports commentator, invited Bouchard to join his amateur team. In time, Bouchard was signed to play for the Verdun Maple Leafs, along with another promising young man named Joseph Henri Maurice Richard.

From the Maple Leafs Butch graduated to senior hockey where Dick Irvin spotted him and assigned Bouchard to Providence of the American Hockey League. "He wants to play in the NHL so badly," said Irvin, "he'd probably do it for nothing if we asked him."

After a season at Providence, Bouchard was signed to a Canadiens contract, although some members of the Montreal front office weren't as enthusiastic about the gangly defenseman as their coach. At least one official of the Canadian Arena Company urged Irvin to demote Bouchard, but he replied succinctly: "That kid will be with the Canadiens as long as I am." Which is precisely what happened. Not only did he become a mainstay of the Canadiens, he ultimately achieved Hall of Fame status.

In his first game against the Toronto Maple Leafs, Butch was confronted by the slick-skating Sweeney Schriner. The Leaf forward tried an assortment of head and stick feints, but Bouchard held his ground like a seasoned pro. The one-on-one challenge became an obsession with Schriner, but each time Butch stopped him cold. With each rebuff, Toronto coach Hap Day became more and more frustrated. "Listen, Sweeney," he demanded, "next time you get into Canadiens territory, go around the *other* side."

Schriner accepted the advice and on his next expedition toward the Montreal goal he skated face to face with the veteran Red Goupille. The Leaf ace faked to the left, went to the right, left Goupille standing in his tracks, and scored easily. "At that time," noted a Toronto observer, "Bouchard became a marked man."

When Butch and the Canadiens visited Boston Garden, Bouchard so emphatically mauled the Bruin forwards that an irate female fan jabbed him in the derrière with a hatpin that felt like a harpoon. "Please don't do that!" pleaded Butch. To Bouchard's amazement a collection of Boston policemen moved in and attempted to arrest *him* for bothering the lady. But before they could reach Butch, his teammates pushed him back onto the ice.

After the game Irvin charged Bruin manager Art Ross with fomenting "the plot" to get Bouchard, although it was later established that Ross was ill in bed at the time and nowhere near the scene of the "crime." Butch's son, Pierre, became a Canadiens' defenseman in the midseventies.

FRANK BOUCHER

BORN: Ottawa, Ontario, October 7, 1901
POSITION: Center, Ottawa Senators, 1921–22; New York Rangers, 1926–38, 1943–44; Coach, New York Rangers, 1939–48; General Manager, New York Rangers, 1948–55
AWARDS: Lady Byng Trophy, 1928, 1929, 1930, 1931, 1933, 1934, 1935 (trophy awarded to him in perpetuity, 1935, and second trophy donated); All-Star (First Team), 1933, 1934, 1935; (Second Team), 1931; Hockey Hall of Fame, 1958

One of the classiest players in NHL history, Frank Boucher gained acclaim first as a member of the Royal Canadian Mounted Police, then as a sparkling Ranger on the "A" Line with the Cook brothers, Bill and Bun.

There were many scintillating skaters on that first Ranger team, but none captured the imagination of the Garden crowd like the brothers Cook and Frank Boucher. They moved with the grace of figure skaters and passed the puck with radarlike accuracy. Bill was the crackerjack shot, Bun had the brawn, and Boucher had all the class in the world.

"Boucher became a center such as the league seldom has known," wrote

Dink Carroll of the Montreal *Gazette,* "and a darling of the gallery gods and of the rich folk in the promenade seats as well. He would take the puck away from the enemy with the guile and smoothness of a con man picking the pockets of yokels at a country fair, then whisking it past the enemy goaltender or slipping it to Bill or Bun."

Without question Boucher was the cleanest player ever to lace on a pair of skates in the NHL. He won the Lady Byng Trophy so many times—seven times in eight seasons—the league finally *gave* it to him in perpetuity and a new Lady Byng Trophy was struck.

Oddly enough the one fight Boucher had in his entire NHL career took place in the Rangers' very first game in Madison Square Garden, November 16, 1926, against the Montreal Maroons, the Stanley Cup champions. "They were big," wrote New York *Times* columnist Arthur Daley, "and they were rough. Every Maroon carried a chip on his shoulder."

The chips became heavier when Bill Cook took a pass from brother Bun and scored what proved to be the only goal of the night. Fortified with a one-goal lead, the Rangers began counterattacking with their bodies and fists. Balding Ching Johnson would drop a Maroon to the ice and then grin his very special trademark smile that delighted the Garden crowd. Huge Taffy Abel hit every Montreal skater in sight, and soon the rink was on the verge of a riot.

Up until then the gentlemanly Boucher had minded his business and stayed out of trouble. But "Bad" Bill Phillips, one of the most boisterous of the visitors, worked Boucher over with his elbows, knees, and stick at every opportunity. "The patient Boucher," wrote Daley, "endured the outrages until a free-for-all broke out."

At that point Boucher very discreetly dropped his stick, peeled off his gloves, and caved in Phillips's face with a right jab. The Maroon badman slumped to the ice, whereupon Boucher politely lifted him to his feet and belted him again. When Boucher lifted Phillips for the second time, the Montrealer grabbed his stick and bounced it off Boucher's head, whereupon referee Lou Marsh interceded. Miraculously, both men escaped injury, acquiring only five-minute majors for scrapping.

GEORGE "BUCK" BOUCHER

BORN: Ottawa, Ontario, 1896
DIED: October 17, 1960
POSITION: Defenseman, Ottawa Senators, 1917–28; Montreal Maroons, 1929–31; Chicago Black Hawks, 1931–32; Coach, Boston Bruins, 1949–50

Frank Boucher's older brother, George "Buck" Boucher, starred as a defenseman for the Ottawa Senators in the NHL from 1917–28. During the 1928–29 season he was traded to the Montreal Maroons and finished his NHL career with Chicago in 1931–32. He coached the Boston Bruins briefly in 1949–50, leaving rather abruptly after a front-office tiff.

ROBERT (BOB) BOUCHER

BORN: Ottawa, Ontario
POSITION: Forward, Montreal Canadiens, 1923–24

A forward like brothers Frank and Bill, Bob Boucher skated but one season (1923–24) in the NHL with the Montreal Canadiens. He lacked his brothers' productivity; he didn't get a point the entire season.

WILLIAM (BILLY) BOUCHER

BORN: Ottawa, Ontario
POSITION: Forward, Montreal Canadiens, 1921–27, Boston Bruins, 1927; New York Americans, 1927–28

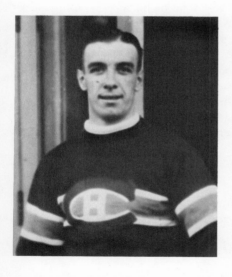

Brother of Frank, George, and Bob Boucher, Bill also was an excellent forward. Unlike Frank who played all his NHL hockey for the Rangers, Bill played mostly for the Canadiens (1921–22 until mid-1926–27 when he was traded to Boston) and finally the Americans in 1927–28 when his NHL career ended. As a Canadien, Bill played on a line with a young Howie Morenz and Aurel Joliat. In 1924, Bill and Bob—both Canadiens—skated against Frank in the Stanley Cup playoffs. At the time Frank skated for the old Vancouver Maroons in the Pacific Coast League, which challenged NHL titlists for the Stanley Cup. In one game the Boucher family scored all the goals. When Bill walked downtown in Montreal after the game that night he saw an illuminated sign on which the game result was posted: It read: BILLY BOUCHER 2; FRANK BOUCHER 2.

LEO A. BOURGAULT

BORN: Sturgeon Falls, Ontario, January 17, 1903
POSITION: Defenseman, Toronto Maple Leafs, 1926; New York Rangers, 1927–31; Ottawa Senators, 1931–33; Montreal Canadiens, 1933–35

A teammate of Ching Johnson and Frank Boucher on the original Rangers, defenseman Leo Bourgault was obtained by the Rangers from Toronto halfway through the Blueshirts' first season (1926–27). "Leo," said teammate Boucher, "was a French-Canadian with a broken nose and a heart of gold. He was only about five-foot-six, but built like a backhouse, and for so small a fellow he had the guts of a second-story man. He was very light on his feet and a fine puck carrier."

Bourgault was a member of the Rangers' first Stanley Cup-winning team (1928) and teamed with huge Taffy Abel when Ching was injured early in the 1928–29 campaign. Bourgault was so good that when Johnson returned, manager Lester Patrick had no compunctions about trading Abel to Chicago. Leo played for the Rangers until 1930–31 when he was traded to Ottawa. He split the following season between the Canadiens and Black Hawks, finishing his NHL career in 1934–35 with the Canadiens.

JOHNNY WILLIAM BOWER

BORN: Prince Albert, Saskatchewan, November 8, 1924
POSITION: Goalie, New York Rangers, 1953–55, 1956–57; Toronto Maple Leafs, 1958–70
AWARDS: Vezina Trophy, 1965 (shared with Terry Sawchuk); All-Star (First Team), 1961

Goaltending was the Toronto Maple Leafs' big weakness before manager Punch Imlach arrived. When the club finished last in 1957–58, Ed Chadwick, goaltender in all seventy games, finished the season with a 3.23 goals-against average, worst of all the league regulars. Billy Reay, Imlach's predecessor, scouted the minors for a replacement. Reay's first choice was Al Rollins, who had starred for the last Leaf Cup winner. Rollins was playing for Calgary in the Western League, but he played poorly the night Reay was scouting him and

Johnny Bower

lost his return ticket to the NHL. Reay's second choice was Johnny Bower, a veteran who had bounced around the minors for years and had a brief stint (1953–55) with the New York Rangers before returning to the bushes.

Cynical about past treatment and uncertain about his NHL future, Bower rejected Reay's first offer. "I was happy in Cleveland," he said. "I'd had my fling at the NHL, and besides, I didn't think I could help Toronto."

Another consideration was that he was almost thirty-four years old, ancient for a goaltender in those days. Then something changed Bower's mind, and he decided to sign with the Leafs. Bower's play during the 1958–59 season made him the Leafs' regular goaltender. He was a glutton for punishment, especially during practice sessions, during which he performed as diligently as the rawest of rookies. "I've always had to work hard," Bower explained. "I don't know any other way to play the game."

Johnny hung up his skates and pads for the last time in 1969–70 and became head scout for the Leafs.

RUSSELL BOWIE

BORN: August 24, 1880
DIED: April 8, 1959
POSITION: Center and Rover, Winnipeg Victorias (CAHL, ECAHA),
   1899–1908
AWARDS: Hockey Hall of Fame, 1945

Russell Bowie, who toiled at center ice for the turn-of-the-century Victorias, has been called, by hard-line oldtimers, the greatest pivotman to play the game. A quick glance at Bowie's stats shows that he was indeed the Phil Esposito of his day. Throughout his ten seasons with Winnipeg, from 1899–1908, he amassed 234 goals in eighty games, almost three goals per game!

He led the league in scoring for five years, and was a perpetual All-Star.

Oddly, Bowie remained an amateur throughout his career, although there were allegations that he had accepted a retainer from the professional Montreal Wanderers in 1907. However, he was finally cleared. While the Wanderers went on to win a string of championships, the Victorias, starring Russell Bowie, never drank Stanley Cup champagne.

WILLIAM SCOTT (SCOTTY) BOWMAN

BORN: Montreal, Quebec, September 18, 1933
POSITION: Coach, St. Louis Blues, 1967–71; Montreal Canadiens, 1971–

While playing junior hockey, Scotty Bowman suffered a severe head injury which completely altered his career. The mishap, in 1951–52, inspired Bowman to become a coach. He joined the Montreal Canadiens' system, moving up the ladder coaching both on the junior and minor professional levels. Scotty was hired as coach of the St. Louis Blues during its formative years and guided the club when it entered the NHL in 1967–68. He coached St. Louis to the Stanley Cup finals in each of his first three seasons, but suffered a worsening of relations with the Salomon family, owner of the Blues. He left St. Louis after the 1970–71 season to become coach of the Montreal Canadiens, succeeding Al MacNeil. His club finished first and won the Stanley Cup in 1973. Once a severe taskmaster, Bowman unwound during the 1974–75 season. "It was," said one Canadiens watcher, "as if the realization struck him that he was dealing with human beings—not machines. And to deal productively with human beings, it is necessary to act like one." However, his Canadiens were ousted by Buffalo in the 1975 Stanley Cup semifinals.

ANDREW JOHN (ANDY) BRANIGAN

BORN: Winnipeg, Manitoba, April 11, 1922
POSITION: Defenseman, New York Americans, 1940–42

Every hockey fan who's up on his ancient history has heard the inspiring story of Lester "the Silver Fox" Patrick and how the feeble, forty-five-year-old manager dramatically took over in goal for his New York Rangers during the 1928 Stanley Cup playoffs when the regular Blueshirt netminder was knocked cold. But Andy Branigan, an otherwise undistinguished defenseman with the New York Americans, was the last forward or defenseman to ever don the pads in a similar crisis situation.

On February 28, 1941, the Americans were straining to overcome a 5–4 disadvantage against the host Detroit Red Wings when the Amerks goaltender, Chuck Rayner, suffered a serious leg injury, forcing him to the sidelines. This was before the NHL required teams to dress two goalkeepers for each game, so after ten minutes of wrestling with his better judgment, Branigan volunteered to fill in for the hobbling Rayner.

Branigan performed more than adequately, slamming the door on the Wings for the remaining seven minutes of the game, but the New Yorkers couldn't get the equalizer and the contest ended, a 5–4 Red Wing victory.

CARL THOMAS BREWER

BORN: Toronto, Ontario, October 21, 1938
POSITION: Defenseman, Toronto Maple Leafs, 1957–65; Detroit Red
    Wings, 1969–70; St. Louis Blues, 1970–72; Toronto Toros (WHA),
    1973–74
AWARDS: All-Star (First Team), 1963; (Second Team), 1962, 1965,
    1970

Carl Brewer had an unusual hockey career, to say the least. At the age of twenty-six, in the prime of his ice life, Brewer quit the Maple Leafs to study at the University of Toronto. He campaigned successfully to regain his amateur status, then performed with the Canadian National Team. Carl coached in the International Hockey League and also the Helsinki IFK sextet in Finland. "The funny part of it," he says, "is that I didn't have any master plan in mind when I made the changes."

His professional tenure included ten NHL seasons with the Leafs, Red Wings, and Blues, and a year in the WHA with the Toronto Toros. He was a four-time All-Star, and an all-time philosopher. "The game of hockey itself is very easy," he professes. "It's the thinking about it that makes it hard."

Brewer retired in 1974 to do TV color commentary for the Toros.

FRANCIS CHARLES (FRANK) "MR. ZERO" BRIMSEK

BORN: Eveleth, Minnesota, September 26, 1915
POSITION: Goalie, Boston Bruins, 1938–43, 1945–49; Chicago Black
    Hawks, 1949–50
AWARDS: Calder Trophy, 1939; Vezina Trophy, 1939, 1942; All-Star
    (First Team), 1939, 1942; (Second Team), 1940–41, 1943,
    1946–48; Hockey Hall of Fame, 1966

For years Bruins' manager Art Ross had received excellent service from goalie Tiny Thompson, and so it was no surprise when Tiny started the 1938–39 campaign in the Boston nets. But Ross was unhappy, not so much about Thompson as about a young goalkeeper, Frank Brimsek, who was impressing scouts at nearby Providence in the International American League. Brimsek was not only

Frank Brimsek

a good hockey player but he was that rare breed—a good American-born, American-developed player, who had learned the game in the cold wastes of Eveleth, Minnesota. Also, the Detroit Red Wings had revealed their willingness to spend $15,000, at that time a respectable sum, for Thompson.

Ross put one and one together. Thompson was aging; Brimsek was ready. Late in November 1938, the Bruins announced that their veteran goalie had been sold to Detroit. Brimsek would henceforth start in the Boston goal. Neither Thompson, his teammates, nor most of the Bruin fans could believe the news. After all, Tiny had won the Vezina Trophy four times and was still considered one of the finest goalies around even after playing ten years in the NHL.

"The team took it pretty badly," former Bruin Milt Schmidt noted. "Dit Clapper was Tiny's roommate, and he was ready to quit. We just couldn't understand Mr. Ross replacing a sure thing with a rookie." Nothing about Brimsek altered the prevailing opinion that he could be a flop. One critic immediately denounced his potential on the grounds of his Slavic background. "Slavs," the man said, "don't have the temperament to be goalies." Those who remembered him in Providence recalled that he had a habit of not really appearing to be "in" the game when the action picked up. Others decided that an American kid just couldn't make it in the Canadian-dominated NHL.

Brimsek did nothing to enhance his image. He had an idiosyncrasy of wearing a pair of old red hockey pants instead of the then traditional gold, brown, and white Bruins' outfit, and his footwork was less than sparkling. But his glove hand was amazingly fast and his confidence enormous. "He's as quick as a cat," said Rangers' manager Lester Patrick, who would be among the last to laud a rival Bruin. "Trying to get him to make a first move is like pushing over the Washington Monument."

The doubts about Brimsek's potential were eliminated within his first dozen games. In a stretch of three weeks he scored six shutouts in seven games, was immediately dubbed "Mister Zero," and went on to win both the Calder Trophy as rookie of the year and the Vezina Trophy as top goalie.

Brimsek permanently secured the affection of Bruins' fans after his first two shutouts. When Boston faced Montreal in the next game at the Garden, the kid goalie appeared destined for still another superb goalless game, as the second period ticked to a close. But the visitors organized a two-on-one rush late in the period. Herb Cain, who was later to star for the Boston club, broke free and beat Brimsek from directly in front of the net. Once the home fans had digested the momentary tragedy, they suddenly broke into an unremitting chorus of applause for "Mister Zero," whose record had reached 231 minutes and 54 seconds of shutout goaltending.

HARRY "PUNCH" BROADBENT

BORN: Ottawa, Ontario, 1893
DIED: March 6, 1971
POSITION: Right Wing, Ottawa Senators (NHA and NHL), 1913–15, 1919–24, 1927–28; Montreal Maroons, 1924–27; New York Americans, 1928–29
AWARDS: Art Ross Trophy, 1922; Hockey Hall of Fame, 1962

Right winger Harry Broadbent rightfully deserved his nickname Punch, because he packed plenty of it with his fists as well as his scoring prowess. In fact, Punch holds a scoring record that still stands today. In 1922, a year that saw Harry lead all NHL scorers, Broadbent lit the red lamp in sixteen consecutive contests. This feat has never been duplicated, even in today's faster, higher scoring games.

A Hall of Famer, Broadbent played on four Stanley Cup winners, three with the Ottawa Senators and one with the 1926 Montreal Maroons. Punch finished up his career in 1929 with the New York Americans.

WALTER "TURK" BRODA

BORN: Brandon, Manitoba, May 15, 1914
DIED: October 17, 1972
POSITION: Goalie, Toronto Maple Leafs, 1936–43, 1945–52
AWARDS: Vezina Trophy, 1941, 1948; All-Star (First Team), 1941,
   1948; (Second Team), 1942; Hockey Hall of Fame, 1967

Any similarity between Walter "Turk" Broda and a big-league goaltender was
a mirage. Pudgy and slow on his feet, Broda seemed to be the antithesis of a
goaltender.

   They called him "Turkey Egg" in the wheat country that surrounds Brandon, Manitoba. During a history lesson an instructor told his class that an English king was given that nickname because of the huge freckles covering his
face. Since nobody had more freckles than Broda, after the history lesson
Walter was immediately hailed as Turkey Egg. Eventually he was called just
plain "Turk."

Although his skating was poor, Broda earned a spot on the school team by default. Luckily his principal noticed that Turk betrayed an unusual enthusiasm. The principal began working privately with his student, teaching him the finer points of goaltending, until Broda's game began to improve. He soon caught on with a local club called the Brandon North Stars, and played goal for them in a one-game playoff with the Elmwood Millionaires. Broda's club lost 11–1!

One spring the Red Wings were on an exhibition tour of western Canada. One of their stops was Winnipeg, and it was there that Broda made his presence known. He discovered that Detroit manager Jack Adams was staying at a downtown hotel. He learned Adams's room number and, accompanied by his teammate Modere "Mud" Bruneteau, nervously went up to see the boss of the Red Wings. Adams was surprisingly hospitable, and after some mental gymnastics he finally remembered the name Broda. When Turk asked if he could meet some of the Red Wings, Adams was impressed with his enthusiasm and provided him with a ticket for the exhibition game that night.

"They were like two kids on a picnic," said Adams after watching Broda and Bruneteau at the Winnipeg Amphitheater that night. "They took in every move. Once in a while they would excitedly talk to each other, pointing out some particularly good play. I figured if two kids were that interested in becoming hockey players, they would certainly be worth a look."

Minutes after the game ended, Adams invited Broda and Bruneteau to the Detroit Red Wings' training camp the following autumn. Turk was twenty years old when he showed up at the Red Wings' base, an exuberant, naive hayseed who immediately became the butt of the veterans' jokes. Detroit boasted two splendid goalkeepers at the time, John Ross Roach, a veteran, and Normie Smith, a young and gifted goalie destined to start in the minors with the Detroit Olympics. Broda was around strictly for laughs.

There were plenty of laughs. One afternoon Roach and Smith approached Turk with a sheaf full of papers. "Broda," said Roach, "don't you think it's time you joined the union?"

Turk was baffled, a not uncommon reaction for him in those days. "What union?"

"Are you kidding?" snapped Roach. "Don't you know that we goalies have our own association—the Goaltenders' Union? You should become a member."

Oozing with pride, impressed that so distinguished a player as John Ross Roach had invited him to join the association, Turk quickly peeled off the $25 "dues" requested by his elder. The ploy ended when veteran goalie Alex Connell, who was looking on, nearly fell over backwards with laughter.

Turk was returned to the minors. Conn Smythe bought his contract from the Detroit organization in 1936. Leaf fans wondered who Broda was, but they soon found out.

Turk finished his critical rookie year as a Maple Leaf with a 2.32 goals-against average, fifth best in the eight-team league, but so close to pacesetters Davey Kerr, Norm Smith, Wilf Cude, and Tiny Thompson that Broda had proved that he belonged with the best, at least for the moment.

The Maple Leafs' accent-on-offense style of play made it enormously difficult for Broda to win the Vezina Trophy, but carefree Turk didn't seem to mind. ''Sure those goal-hungry forwards can make life tough for me,'' he said, ''but I don't mind as long as Mr. Smythe and the fans don't expect me to lead the league in shutouts.''

Broda did win the goaltender's acme, however; in fact, he won the Vezina twice (1941 and 1948), helped the Leafs to six Stanley Cups, and eventually earned shinny immortality in the Hall of Fame.

ADAM BROWN

BORN: Johnstone, Scotland, February 4, 1920
DIED: August 9, 1960
POSITION: Forward, Detroit Red Wings, 1941–42, 1943–44, 1945–47;
    Chicago Black Hawks, 1947–51; Boston Bruins, 1951–52

Hard-hitting Bill Gadsby was one of the fiercest board-checkers in hockey. Gadsby's personal favorite bodycheck was administered by Adam Brown, who played for both Chicago and Detroit.

Brown hit Montreal's little Norm Dussault about one-third of the way in from the boards. ''Dussault's stick flew into the crowd,'' Gadsby said. ''So did one of his gloves. And the other glove flew about 30 feet down the ice.

''The best thing about it was the way Brown stood over him with his chest out, looking like Tarzan, and Dussault lying flat on the ice.'' Adam's son, Andy, became a big league goalie in the seventies.

ANDREW CONRAD (ANDY) BROWN

BORN: Hamilton, Ontario, February 15, 1944
POSITION: Goalie, Detroit Red Wings, 1971–73; Pittsburgh Penguins, 1973–74; Indianapolis Racers (WHA), 1974–

Andy Brown came up to the Detroit Red Wings for ten games in 1971–72 and seven games in 1972–73. He was then sold to the Pittsburgh Penguins for cash and future considerations (a low blow for any player), but was most recently seen (yes, seen, for he's the only goalie left in hockey who wears no mask) in Indianapolis with the WHA Racers, which is appropriate, since his second crazy occupation is car racing.

GEORGE V. BROWN

George Brown is one of the few Hockey Hall of Fame "builders" from the United States. In 1910, after the building of the old Boston Arena, he organized the Boston Athletic Association hockey team. The BAA developed into a power in international hockey (amateur), competing with top ranking college and club teams from Canada.

When the old arena burned down in 1918, Brown formed a corporation which built the new Boston Arena. Although he was never involved with the Bruins or Boston Garden, it was Brown who created the base of interest in the sport that enabled professional hockey to thrive in Beantown. Before his death in 1937, he had helped form the old Canadian-American League and the now-defunct Boston Tigers.

STEWART ARNOLD (ARNIE) BROWN

BORN: Oshawa, Ontario, January 28, 1942
POSITION: Defenseman, Toronto Maple Leafs, 1961–62, 1963–64; New York Rangers, 1964–71; Detroit Red Wings, 1971–72; New York Islanders, 1972–73; Atlanta Flames, 1973–74; Michigan Stags (WHA), 1974; Vancouver Blazers (WHA), 1975

Arnie Brown was considered a defenseman with real potential when he was traded to the New York Rangers by the Toronto Maple Leafs in February 1964, along with Dick Duff, Bob Nevin, Rod Seiling, and Bill Collins for Andy Bathgate and Don McKenney. Unfortunately he never lived up to those advance notices. Brown loved to make rushes up-ice, getting himself caught constantly. When he wasn't making rushes at the wrong time, he wasn't hitting, either. He was traded to Detroit, then Atlanta, and in the fall of 1974 he was placed on waivers. He then drifted into the WHA, via the Michigan Stags who became the Baltimore Blades in midseason before they, too, placed poor Arnie on waivers.

EDWARD ERNEST HENRY (ED) BRUNETEAU

BORN: St. Boniface, Manitoba, August 1, 1919
POSITION: Forward, Detroit Red Wings, 1940–41, 1943–49

Often confused with brother Modere "Mud" Bruneteau who scored the winning goal in the NHL's longest game (March 24, 1936), Ed Bruneteau was a solid forward for the Detroit Red Wings alternately from 1940–41 through 1948–49. Ed's problem was that he never scored a Stanley Cup sudden-death goal; hence, obscurity as opposed to Mud's eternal niche as a Cup hero.

MODERE "MUD" BRUNETEAU

BORN: St. Boniface, Manitoba, November 28, 1914
POSITION: Right Wing, Detroit Red Wings, 1935–46

On March 24, 1936, the Detroit Red Wings and the Montreal Maroons played the longest NHL game ever. By the time the Maroons and Red Wings had played through the second overtime without a goal, the crowd began to get restless. The players, of course, were laboring on badly chopped ice that didn't have the benefit of modern resurfacing machines. Nevertheless, they plodded on past midnight with no end in sight.

When the sixth period began, a cascade of cheers went up from the previously numbed crowd. Perhaps they hoped to inspire the Maroons to a spirited rush and a score, but this didn't happen.

Despite the hour, the majority of spectators remained in their seats. The monumental contest had become an obsession with both players and fans. Everyone seemed determined to see it through to a conclusion.

Four minutes and 46 seconds after the ninth period began, the teams had broken the longest-game record set by Toronto and Boston and, still, there was no end in sight. It was past 2 A.M. and many of the spectators were fighting to keep their eyes open, not wanting to miss the decisive goal if it ever was to be scored.

By this time the veterans of both teams were fatigued beyond recovery. It was essential to employ the players with the most stamina left, and, naturally, those were the inexperienced younger skaters. One of them was Modere "Mud" Bruneteau, a native of St. Boniface, Manitoba, who had played the previous season for the Wings' minor league team, the Detroit Olympics. He was the youngest man in the longest game, equipped, Jack Adams believed, with the strongest legs. Adams, then the Detroit coach, once remembered, "The game settled into an endurance test, hour after hour. One o'clock came, and then 2 A.M., and by now the ice was a chipped, brutal mess. At 2:25 I looked along our bench for the strongest legs, and I scrambled the lines to send out Syd Howe, Hec Kilrea, and Bruneteau."

As a rookie on a loaded first-place club, Bruneteau had seen very little action. But he was young, and at the twelve-minute mark of the ninth period, Mud Bruneteau was in a lot better shape than most of his teammates or opponents.

Adams's instructions were typically explicit. "Boys, let's get some sleep. It's now or never!"

Bruneteau surrounded the puck in the Detroit zone and passed it to Kilrea. They challenged the Montreal defense, Kilrea faking a return pass, then sliding it across the blueline. Bruneteau cut behind the defense and retrieved the puck. "Thank God," he says, "Chabot fell down as I drove it in the net. It was the funniest thing. The puck just stuck there in the twine and didn't fall on the ice."

There was a dispute when the goal judge neglected to flash his red light, but referee Nels Stewart arbitrated. "Your bloody right it's a goal!" Stewart announced, and put up his hand as a signal. After 116 minutes and 30 seconds of overtime the Red Wings had defeated the Maroons, 1–0.

Bruneteau continued to be a second-stringer with Detroit, after his big night in the longest game, and it wasn't until the war years, 1941–46, with the Red Wings depleted, that he began to see regular action.

BRUNO AND BLYTHE

The very first press agents for the New York Rangers, when they made their debut on Broadway in November 1926, were a couple of delightfully weird characters named Bruno and Blythe; no more, no less! Before the Blueshirts took the ice at Madison Square Garden, Bruno and Blythe believed that the Rangers would never draw fans unless they appealed to New York's ethnic population. "The Rangers," said Bruno, "need a Jewish player." To which Blythe added: "And an Italian player, too." But, alas, the Rangers had neither a Jew nor an Italian in their lineup in 1926. That being the case, Bruno and Blythe *put* a Jew and an Italian *in* the lineup. They decided that the Jew would be the Rangers' French-Canadian goalie, Lorne Chabot. Bruno changed his name to *Chabotsky*. Blythe then went to work on forward Oliver Reinikka and converted him to Ollie *Rocco*. Poof! You're Italian! Unfortunately, neither player enjoyed his *nom de glace*. What's more the Canadian hockey writers knew Chabot and Reinikka for what they really were and lampooned Bruno and Blythe. As a result the two press agents became *ex*-press agents faster than Chabot could shoot the puck to Rocco . . . rather Reinikka.

JOHN PAUL "CHIEF" BUCYK

BORN: Edmonton, Alberta, May 12, 1935
POSITION: Left Wing, Detroit Red Wings, 1955–57; Boston Bruins, 1957–
AWARDS: Lady Byng Trophy, 1971, 1974; All-Star (First Team), 1971; (Second Team), 1968

John Bucyk, one of the most unobtrusive players on a strong and flashy Bruin squad, spanned two decades of Boston hockey history, performing his tasks on left wing through some of the best and the worst years that team ever witnessed.

Bucyk played Junior with the Edmonton (Alberta) Oil Kings, came to the NHL with the Detroit Red Wings in 1955, and two years later was traded to Boston for Terry Sawchuk.

In Boston, Johnny was reunited with Bronco Horvath and feisty Vic Stasiuk,

John Bucyk

with whom he had played in Edmonton, and the Uke Line (for Ukrainian) came into being. The world looked rosy that season, with the Bruins making the Stanley Cup finals in 1958. It was Horvath who coined Bucyk's nickname, "the Chief," after his straight ebony hair, swarthy complexion, and stoic visage.

In 1958–59, Bucyk was so good at digging the puck out of the corners for linemate Horvath that Bronco came within two points of winning the scoring title, behind Bobby Hull.

"I always work the corners and get the puck out," Bucyk explained. "You can't score from the corners. If you pass off and the other guy scores, what's the difference? A goal is a goal."

But the goals of the Uke Line were to no avail, for Boston dropped to fifth place that year, and when Horvath was drafted by Chicago and Stasiuk traded to Detroit, the Uke Line became a thing of the past.

Bucyk continued his efficient ways, but the Bruins mopped up the basement for six years, and were next-to-last another two. It wasn't until 1967–68 that Boston, with Orr, Esposito, Hodge, Cashman, and, of course, John Bucyk, once again climbed to the top of the NHL.

Bucyk's life then became one of setting records while his more spectacular teammates, Orr and Esposito, broke bigger ones or more of them, leaving the Chief in the shadows, which he seems to prefer.

Bucyk surpassed Milt Schmidt's old Bruin point record of 576 in 1968–69. That season he also became the first Bruin to score 250 goals. Bucyk also won the Lady Byng Trophy twice, in 1971 and 1974, for his gentlemanly conduct.

BUFFALO SABRES

Hockey is no new arrival to the scene in Buffalo, New York. For many years a strong minor league hockey town, Buffalo attempted to enter the NHL with the 1967–68 expansion. They were foiled by the Toronto Maple Leafs' influence, largely because Toronto feared loss of revenue from the market they had developed themselves in the Buffalo area. When the asking price for a franchise jumped to a fat $6 million, Maple Leaf interests figured they could let Buffalo in with no loss in revenue.

Big league hockey promoters in Buffalo were led by Seymour H. Knox III, a regional vice-president of Domenick and Domenick, a New York Stock Exchange member, and his brother, Northrup R. Knox, once a fine goaltender at Yale. The Knox brothers and their backers won their drive for NHL hockey in 1970.

In a brilliant and ironic move, the Knoxes hired Punch Imlach as general manager-coach. Imlach had for many years performed these functions for the Maple Leafs, and was known, depending upon whom you spoke to, as the builder/destroyer of the once-mighty Leafs.

General opinion had it, though, that hiring Imlach couldn't produce a miracle: Imlach was far past his feisty, tyrannical prime, and there was such a dearth of talent that even a younger Imlach couldn't produce the proverbial silk purse out of a sow's ear.

General opinion was wrong! If not a silk purse, the freshmen Sabres were far from a sow's ear, and it was Imlach's ingenuity and the NHL draft that created a fair starting team, instead of a hodge-podge of leftovers.

Imlach drafted Gilbert Perreault, for several years the scourge of junior hockey. The six-foot, 195-pound French-Canadian could do everything offensively, and well. He naturally evoked the inevitable comparisons to a Jean Beliveau.

Youth was the theme for the Sabres, and by the last month of their sophomore season, the oldest hand on the team was center and captain Gerry Meehan. Meehan was twenty-five!

By the Sabres' third season Imlach's work bore fruit—the team made the Stanley Cup playoffs. Buffalo was ecstatic and the arena had become the scene for regular sellouts. Unfortunately the team had to face a powerful Montreal Canadiens outfit in the first round, but they forced Montreal to six games—not bad for an expansion baby.

In 1973–74 veteran Tim Horton was tragically killed in an automobile accident and Buffalo mourned. The team finished fifth in the East Division and out of the playoffs.

The Sabres were a powerhouse in 1974–75, however, and with their blistering offense they went to the Stanley Cup finals against the Philadelphia Flyers, losing in six games.

HYMAN (HY) BULLER

BORN: Montreal, Quebec, March 15, 1926
DIED: August 3, 1968
POSITION: Defenseman, Detroit Red Wings, 1943–45; New York Rangers, 1951–54
AWARDS: All-Star (Second Team), 1952

During the six-team era of the NHL, several outstanding skaters remained buried in the minors. When Rangers' manager Frank Boucher finally acquired Hy Buller—one of the few Jewish skaters in the NHL—in 1951 from the Cleveland Barons' farm club, he was a seasoned pro who could play a solid defense yet bolster the attack with his hard shots from the blue line. His value was proven in his rookie season with election to the second All-Star team. He retired prematurely after the 1953–54 campaign. The reasons behind Buller's retirement always have remained enshrouded in mystery. One theory had it that a series of debilitating injuries had caused Buller to lose his playing edge and rather than play mediocre defense, he chose to gracefully leave the NHL. Another theory was that Buller had become disenchanted with the game's violence and was depressed over a series of dangerous collisions with some NHL headhunters that he decided to retire rather than risk serious injury.

WILLIAM (BILLY) BURCH

BORN: Yonkers, New York, November 20, 1900
DIED: December 1950
POSITION: Defenseman/Forward, Hamilton Tigers, 1922–25; New York Americans, 1925–32; Boston Bruins, 1932; Chicago Black Hawks, 1932–33
AWARDS: Hart Trophy, 1925; Lady Byng Trophy, 1927; Hockey Hall of Fame, 1974

A star with Hamilton of the National Hockey League, Billy Burch led a revolt of players against management in the spring of 1925. When the Hamilton sextet was transferred to New York to become the Americans, Burch and teammate Jackie Forbes each got $20,000 for three-year contracts. Burch starred for the Amerks through the 1931–32 season. The following season he split between

Boston and Chicago. That was his last season in the NHL. Despite his lengthy NHL career (eleven years), Burch appeared in only one playoff, 1928–29, but scored neither a goal nor an assist.

CHARLES FREDERIC (CHARLIE) BURNS

BORN: Detroit, Michigan, February 14, 1936
POSITION: Center, Detroit Red Wings, 1958–59; Boston Bruins, 1959–63; Oakland Seals, 1967–68; Pittsburgh Penguins, 1968–69; Minnesota North Stars, 1969–73; Coach, Minnesota North Stars, 1974–75

The utility players' utility player, Charlie Burns skated for Detroit (1958–59), Boston (1959–60 through 1962–63), Oakland (1967–68), Pittsburgh (1968–69), and finally Minnesota (1969–70 through 1972–73). He became notorious as one of the few players to wear a plate in his head because of a head injury. This inspired Burns to wear a protective helmet as well. He was most adept at defensive play and later became the man the North Stars rushed down to the bench whenever their coach began losing too many games. This happened again during the 1974–75 season when Burns replaced general manager-coach Jack Gordon behind the bench. In June 1975 Burns was replaced by Ted Harris.

ROBERT ARTHUR (ROBIN) BURNS

BORN: Montreal, Quebec, August 27, 1946
POSITION: Left Wing, Pittsburgh Penguins 1970–73; Kansas City Scouts, 1974–

In 1974–75, Robin Burns became the second player in hockey history to wear the infamous 13 on his jersey. Jack (Two-Season) Stoddard wore it for the Rangers in the early fifties.

The Kansas City Scouts selected Burns from the Pittsburgh Penguins' roster after his impressive Calder Cup (American League playoffs) showing in 1974. The aggressive left winger led the Hershey Bears in scoring with ten goals in fourteen playoff games.

WALTER L. BUSH, JR.

After years of work as an amateur hockey executive in Minnesota, Walter Bush emerged on the professional circuit holding the presidency of the Minnesota North Stars. In 1973 Bush was awarded the Lester Patrick Trophy and in 1975 he was rumored as a potential successor to NHL president Clarence Campbell, but problems with his own faltering team were believed to have swayed him to remain in Minnesota.

STEVE BUZINSKI

BORN: Dunblane, Saskatchewan, October 15, 1917
POSITION: Goalie, New York Rangers, 1942–43

No player receives as much physical abuse as a goaltender, and no goaltender in Ranger history was so bombarded by rubber as Steve Buzinski, a youthful wartime replacement in 1942–43. It was said that Steve had a sunburn on his neck caused by the perennial glow of the red goal light behind him.

Despite the fact that his average (6.11) was abominable, Steve had a delightful way about him and even fancied himself a pretty fair goalie. Asked how it felt to stop big-league shots after jumping straight from the Swift Current (Saskatchewan) Intermediates, Buzinski replied, "Same as back home. It's easy as pickin' cherries off a tree." Shortly after that deathless remark Steve stopped a high backhander and nonchalantly tossed the puck to the side of the net. Unfortunately it was the wrong side, the red light pointing out his error to thousands of exasperated fans. Before very long Buzinski was back in Swift Current.

MICHAEL ARTHUR (MIKE) BYERS

BORN: Toronto, Ontario, September 11, 1946
POSITION: Right Wing, Toronto Maple Leafs, 1967–68; Philadelphia
    Flyers, 1968–69; Los Angeles Kings, 1970–71; Buffalo Sabres,
    1971–72; Los Angeles Sharks (WHA), 1972; New England
    Whalers (WHA), 1972–

Not only did this Toronto-born winger for the New England Whalers score 25
or more goals in 1972–73 and 1973–74 but off-ice he's a connoisseur of wine,
art, and oceanography. How's that for an unusual hockey player? Mike, who
looks like a professor in his civvies and glasses, played several years in the
NHL with Los Angeles and Buffalo, before settling down with the Whalers.

LADY BYNG TROPHY

In 1925, Lady Byng, wife of Canada's governor-general at the time, presented
a trophy "to the player adjudged to have exhibited the best type of sportsmanship and gentlemanly conduct combined with a high standard of playing
ability." The first recipient was Frank Nighbor of Ottawa who won the trophy
two years in a row. After Frank Boucher of the Rangers won the award seven
times in the next eight seasons he was given the trophy to keep and Lady Byng
donated another trophy in 1936. Lady Byng died in 1949 after which the NHL
presented a new trophy, changing the name to Lady Byng Memorial Trophy.

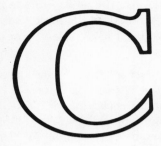

TERRANCE MICHAEL (TERRY) CAFFERY

BORN: Toronto, Ontario, April 1, 1949
POSITION: Center, Chicago Black Hawks, 1969–70; Minnesota North
   Stars, 1971–72; New England Whalers (WHA), 1972–
AWARDS: WHA Rookie of the Year, 1973

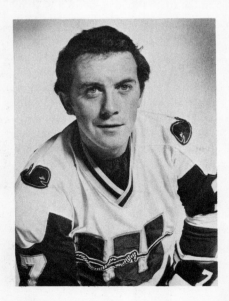

In 1972 Terry Caffery won Rookie of the Year Award in the American Hockey
League. In 1973, after he signed with the New England Whalers of the WHA,

he scored 39 goals and 61 assists for 100 points, which earned him the same award in the WHA. Then disaster struck in the form of a knee injury. Caffery had multiple operations, suffered through an infection in the knee, and missed the entire 1973–74 season. By October 1974 this former Toronto Marlies junior ace had recovered enough ability to lead his team in scoring. Caffery is small (5'9") and *looks* slow, but is deceptive. His playmaking ability and classy stickhandling are pleasing to the eye and more pleasing to the Whalers' scoreboard.

LAWRENCE LOUIS (LARRY) CAHAN

BORN: Fort William, Ontario, December 25, 1933
POSITION: Defenseman, Toronto Maple Leafs, 1954–56; New York Rangers, 1956–59, 1961–65; Oakland Seals, 1967–68; Los Angeles Kings, 1968–71; Chicago Cougars (WHA), 1972–73

Never a smoothie, Larry Cahan was a behemoth defenseman who broke into the NHL with Toronto in 1954–55 and eventually spread his limited talents over the Rangers (1956–57 through 1964–65), Oakland (1967–68), and Los Angeles (1968–71), before closing his career in the WHA with the Chicago Cougars (1972–73). Totally fearless, Cahan is best remembered by New York fans for a pair of decisions over Bruins' badman Ted Green.

It was Cahan, teaming with partner Ron Harris, who put the crunch on Minnesota North Stars forward Bill Masterton in January 1968. Masterton was catapulted to the ice by the legal check and never regained consciousness. Tragically, he died a day later.

HERBERT CAIN

BORN: Newmarket, Ontario, December 24, 1912
POSITION: Left Wing, Montreal Maroons, 1933–38; Montreal Canadiens, 1938–39; Boston Bruins, 1939–46
AWARDS: Art Ross Trophy, 1944; All-Star (Second Team), 1944

Herb Cain is best remembered for leading the NHL in scoring with Boston during the 1943–44 season (82 points in 48 games), and least remembered for nearly killing himself accidentally during a practice one afternoon when he played for the Canadiens (1938–39) while ebullient Tommy Gorman was Montreal's creative manager. At the time, Gorman was obsessed with the idea that too many of his veterans were lugging the puck behind the net before heading for enemy territory. His lectures on the subject proved fruitless, and finally Tommy decided that more drastic measures had to be taken. So, just prior to a practice session, he walked out onto the ice armed with a couple of hundred yards of thick rope. With the help of some rink attendants, Gorman attached the rope to the goal net and then extended it to each of the sideboards, thereby creating what amounted to a roadblock from the goal line to the end boards. The players were not to skate behind the net before starting a rush.

Unfortunately, Gorman neglected to inform all his players of the scheme, and Herb Cain, who was the first on the ice, had no idea a barricade had been erected. Typical of an enthusiastic skater, Cain leaped on the ice and pursued the puck, which happened to be sitting a few feet behind the rope. Herb's interest was so consumed with the puck he completely ignored the rope. By this time Cain had picked up speed and was hurtling at about twenty miles an hour when he started what was to be a circling of the net with the puck.

Before the startled rinksiders could shout a warning, Cain struck the rope at neck level, became enmeshed in the twine, and, with the momentum behind him, began whirling upside down like a miniature Ferris wheel. He ultimately landed on his back and was knocked unconconscious when his head struck the hard ice. Luckily, his injuries proved not to be serious. The rope was never seen again at the Forum.

FRANK CALDER

Originally secretary of the old National Hockey Association, Frank Calder was named first president of the National Hockey League when it was formed in 1917.

A nonplayer, it may well have been the fact that Calder was a calm Scotsman that helped form the solvent, strong base that is today's wealthy NHL.

The league presented the Calder Trophy and later the Calder Memorial trophy for rookie-of-the-year honors to commemorate the service of this avid hockey fan. Calder, a member of the Hall of Fame, died February 4, 1943.

CALGARY COWBOYS. See VANCOUVER BLAZERS.

CALIFORNIA SEALS

If it can be said that there is a hockey team whose history might well be retitled "Orphans of the Storm," that team is the California (alias Oakland, alias Golden) Seals.

The Seals joined the NHL for the 1967–68 season. Before they had played a game, press pundits predicted that the Seals would be one of the first expansion teams to make the playoffs. They were dead wrong.

That first season was a debacle, and the Seals ended up 20 points in the cellar. Worse yet, they were on their way to setting nonwinning records, with stretches of eleven and fourteen games without a win.

The team's problems began at the top. A feisty coach-general manager, Bert Olmstead couldn't stand losing, and he let his team and the press know it. One night in Boston, he was seen waving a hockey stick at a Bruin fan. He locked the dressing room door to reporters and withheld his phone number, and he publicly scolded his players. One player remarked: "If Olmstead did public relations for Santa Claus, there wouldn't be any Christmas."

Another problem was attendance—there wasn't any. The team was playing in the new Oakland–Alameda County Coliseum Arena because the Cow Palace in San Francisco had been rejected for poor sight lines. It seemed no one wanted to cross the bridge from San Francisco, nor were there great hordes of Oaklanders scrambling to see games.

Prior to the 1970–71 season, the Seals were acquired by the notorious Charlie Finley, who changed the color of their jerseys and skates, and still they had the worst record in the league.

Garry Young was then made general manager of the sorry crew, and one of his first acts was a big trade with the Boston Bruins. Young sent Carol Vadnais and winger Don O'Donoghue to Boston for Reg Leach and defensemen Bob Stewart and Rick Smith. The Seals improved only slightly and Young got the gate.

In 1972–73 when the WHA arrived, the Seals lost Paul Shmyr, Tom Webster, Gerry Pinder, Norm Ferguson, Bobby Sheehan, and Wayne Carleton. They finished the season in the cellar with a mere eleven wins.

In February 1974 the NHL purchased the the Seals from Charlie Finley and everyone breathed a big sigh of relief. A longtime friend of hockey, Munson Campbell was made president of the franchise. Campbell, an old crony of Bruce Norris in Detroit, brought in Bill McCreary as g.m. and appointed Marshall Johnston coach. Johnston, then the youngest coach in the NHL at thirty-three, was fired midway through the 1974–75 campaign. The Seals were purchased in 1975 by San Francisco hotelier Mel Swig, and ex-NHL defenseman Jack Evans was named coach.

HAROLD HUGH (HARRY) CAMERON

BORN: Pembroke, Ontario, February 6, 1890
DIED: October 20, 1953
POSITION: Defenseman, Toronto Blueshirts (NHA), 1913–17; Montreal Wanderers (NHA), 1917; Toronto Arenas, 1918–19, 1920, 1921–24; Ottawa Senators, 1919; Montreal Canadiens, 1920
AWARDS: Hockey Hall of Fame, 1962

One of the first "offensive defensemen," Harry Cameron was a scoring legend in his own time during the formative years of the NHL. Cameron also was one of the first tempermental stars, his antics forcing the management of his team, Toronto, to heap many fines and, finally, suspensions on their star blue liner.

But despite his run-ins with the establishment, Cameron was instrumental in bringing three Stanley Cups to Toronto during his eleven-year career there. In 1924 Harry was allowed to quit the Toronto team and journey to Saskatoon where he chipped in three more solid seasons before retiring.

CLARENCE SOUTHERLAND CAMPBELL

BORN: Fleming, Saskatchewan, July 7, 1905
POSITION: Referee, 1929–1940; President of NHL, 1946–
AWARDS: Lester Patrick Trophy, 1972; Clarence S. Campbell Bowl
    in his honor, 1973

President of the National Hockey League since 1946, Clarence Campbell has been one of sport's more maligned figures. He has also brought his game into the public eye on both sides of the border, led the league through numerous expansions, and survived many an owner's and player's tirade.

Campbell returned from World War II and immediately went to work for Red Dutton, then head man of the NHL. Campbell had been close to the sport, "although I wasn't ever much good at hockey, I was good enough to play in Europe when a Rhodes scholar." He had refereed in the NHL, and Dutton had a specific job in mind for the forty-one-year-old bachelor.

"As we were walking out of the office, Red turned to me and said, 'By the way, when we get to the meeting, I'm going to resign and recommend you for president of the league.' That was the first I heard of it, or anybody did for that matter. The owners voted on it and they gave me a raise to $10,000 and put me in charge.

"Being a referee has been enormously valuable to me here. As a referee, you condition yourself to accept criticism. You learn to live in an atmosphere of hostility. As a commissioner, you are almost like an official. From the start everything is against you, and you'd better understand that."

The NHL has undergone many changes under Campbell. It went from a solid, six-team organization to twice that size in one swoop.

Hockey has become a faster, more violent sport in recent times. The advent of the slapshot and the increase of fighting brawls have been big revisions from the game Campbell used to officiate.

"I'm pretty adaptable, pretty pragmatic," he says. "There's nothing romantic about me."

It has been Campbell's misfortune to be best remembered for suspending Maurice Richard just before the 1955 playoffs. Richard had just been the instigator (or victim, as the Rocket claimed) in a bloody ruckus in Boston.

"I had warned him after an almost identical incident in Toronto," the commissioner says, "that I would suspend him if it ever happened again. He had been making a profit out of every fine I laid on him. If I fined him $250, he would get $2,500 in donations. You can't tolerate such a frustration of league authority.

"The violence in the league then had reached an alarming stage. The blood had to stop. I'd drive to games with the owners, and they were petrified at what might happen on the ice. But they were also frightened that I would monkey with a good product."

Richard was suspended for the remainder of the season and the playoffs, and Montreal fans erupted. "You've got to remember," Campbell remembers, "this was the time of an enormous sociological upheaval. It was just the beginning of the French movement, and the only man in Quebec better known than Richard was the prime minister."

Campbell claims he never thought twice about attending the next Canadiens' game at the Forum. Escorting his secretary, Phyllis King, who later became his wife, and two other women, the league president calmly strode to his seat, despite the hatred and ugly catcalls emanating from the Forum fans. Bottles and vegetables were hurled at the NHL boss during the opening period. In the inter-mission, a fan threw a punch at him. Eventually, the Forum erupted into a riot and the game was forfeited.

Perhaps Campbell could have avoided much of the uproar at the Forum that night by simply staying home. But his presence at that contest, and his firmness in the Richard decision, established his authority once and for all.

"It's funny," he says, "but until I made that decision, I was never really ac-knowledged as the head of the NHL."

There is no argument that the NHL has progressed under him to major sports status, and despite errors in judgment, such as that night in the Montreal Forum, Campbell has enjoyed his stay atop hockey's Mount Olympus.

KENNETH WAYNE CARLETON

BORN: Sudbury, Ontario, August 4, 1946
POSITION: Left Wing, Toronto Maple Leafs, 1965–69; Boston Bruins, 1969–71; California Seals, 1971–72; Toronto Toros (WHA), 1972–74; New England Whalers (WHA), 1974–
AWARDS: All-Star (WHA, Second Team), 1974

One of the greatest junior players ever, Wayne Carleton came to the NHL briefly in 1965–66 with Toronto, bounced back and forth between the Maple Leafs and the minors until 1969–70 when he was traded to Boston. Carleton suffered a series of injuries during those years, but more importantly, never seemed to live up to his junior press notices. Carleton didn't play the tough brand of hockey Boston fans had expected because of his size (6'3", 215 lbs.).

Wayne Carleton

He was drafted by the California Seals in 1971 and then signed with Ottawa of the WHA in 1972. Suddenly, Carleton began making like a star, scoring 42 goals and 49 assists for 91 points that year and tallying 92 points in 1973–74, after Ottawa had become the Toronto Toros. Nicknamed ''Swoop'' because of his deceptively fast skating style and booming shot, Carleton was traded to the New England Whalers in the fall of 1974 for future considerations and a second-round draft choice.

EUGENE WILLIAM (GENE) CARR

BORN: Nanaimo, British Columbia, September 17, 1951
POSITION: Center and Left Wing, St. Louis Blues, 1971; New York
Rangers, 1971–74; Los Angeles Kings, 1974–

Gene Carr has had an erratic career in the National Hockey League, until he finally settled in Los Angeles, where he began to play as if he wanted to stay.

Carr, a speed skater who hails from Nanaimo, British Columbia, was drafted in the first round of the amateur pickings in 1971 by the St. Louis Blues. That same year, Gene was the subject of a big trade between the Blues and the New York Rangers, which saw Andre Dupont and Jack Egers, along with current Kings' linemate Mike Murphy, go to St. Louis for Carr, Jim Lorentz, and Wayne Connelly.

Although the Rangers front office was extremely high on Carr, he was somewhat of a disapointment to the critical New York fans. His speed seemed a handicap to him. He would often overskate the puck, breaking up a good rush.

Injuries too, gave Carr trouble. One particularly crippling blow—a broken collarbone—came right after he had scored a hat trick at Madison Square Garden, turning the boos of the fans into cheers.

The Rangers gave up on Carr, however, in the middle of the 1973–74 season, and swapped him, to L.A. for "future considerations." Carr has admitted he's more relaxed with the Kings than with the more rigid life-style of the Rangers.

LORNE BELL CARR

BORN: Stoughton, Saskatchewan, July 2, 1910
POSITION: Right Wing, New York Rangers, 1933–34; New York Americans, 1934–41; Toronto Maple Leafs, 1941–46
AWARDS: All-Star (First Team), 1943, 1944

You never would have figured Lorne Carr as an NHL star by his rookie season (1933–34) with the Rangers. In fourteen games he scored no goals and no assists and was traded to the New York Americans in the following campaign. It was then that the native of Stoughton, Saskatchewan, emerged as a star. Carr played excellently for the Amerks until 1941–42, when he was traded to the Toronto Maple Leafs. In his first season with Toronto, Lorne was a vital factor in the Leafs' conquest of the Stanley Cup, as he was again in 1944–45.

Carr completed his career in 1945–46 with the Maple Leafs, retiring with a total of 204 goals at a time when that was considered a very big total. He was twice voted First Team All-Star right wing.

JOSEPH GORDON CARVETH

BORN: Regina, Saskatchewan, March 21, 1918
POSITION: Forward, Detroit Red Wings, 1940–46, 1950–51; Boston Bruins, 1946–48; Montreal Canadiens, 1948–50

The advent of World War II spelled the end of several big-league careers as stickhandlers joined the armed forces and returned with their skills dimmed beyond redemption. On the other hand, the war provided opportunities to lesser-skilled skaters who blossomed in the diluted brand of wartime hockey. One such player was Detroit Red Wings' right wing Joe Carveth, a native of Regina, Saskatchewan, who, after several trials, played his first full season with the Red Wings in 1942–43 and remained in the Motor City through the 1945–46 season. His best year was 1943–44 when he scored 21 goals and 35 assists for 56 points. A year later he compiled 54 points. He was traded to Boston in 1946–47 for Roy Conacher and in 1947–48 dealt to Montreal for Jimmy Peters. He finished his NHL career back in Detroit, after being traded back to the Wings in the 1949–50 season for Calum MacKay. Carveth helped the Detroiters to a Stanley Cup championship in his NHL swan song.

WAYNE JOHN CASHMAN

BORN: Kingston, Ontario, June 24, 1945
POSITION: Left Wing, Boston Bruins, 1964–65, 1966–
AWARDS: All-Star (Second Team), 1974

Wayne Cashman comes as close to being *the* big, bad Bruin as anybody else on the Boston roster. No one pushes him around. What's more, no one pushes the other Bruins around whenever Wayne is on the ice. Wayne's temperament often resembles that of an aroused loan shark, but he insists the rough stuff was a strategy, not a vendetta. "If you can get a guy to alter his game by half a step, then you've created an advantage for your team," he said.

During the second half of the 1972–73 season, a back injury prohibited him from playing his customary hard-hitting brand of hockey. Before each game and practice he was taped "like a mummy." But he never considered sitting it out. "We had won the Stanley Cup the year before," he explained. "Once you win it, you don't ever want to let it get away. I wanted to keep playing. I wasn't going to sit back and watch some other team take it away from us."

Montreal, of course, did eventually take it away, and Cashman began a summer of extensive medical therapy for his injury. Perhaps he hadn't won the Stanley Cup. But he certainly won his private battle, not to mention added respect from a roomful of guys who had watched him win so many fights before.

LORNE CHABOT

BORN: Montreal, Quebec, October 5, 1900
DIED: October 10, 1946
POSITION: Goalie, New York Rangers, 1926–28; Toronto Maple
    Leafs, 1928–33; Montreal Canadiens, 1933–34; Chicago Black
    Hawks, 1934–35; Montreal Maroons, 1935–36; New York Ameri-
    cans, 1936–37
AWARDS: Vezina Trophy, 1935; All-Star (First Team), 1935

In the midtwenties it was fashionable to sign goaltenders who were small in stature on the theory that a half-pint goalie was more agile than a taller man. Montreal-born Chabot was the exception. He stood 6′1″, weighed 185 pounds, and joined the original Rangers after playing for the Port Arthur (Ontario) Allan Cup champions. His averages in two seasons with New York were 1.56 and 1.79. In his second year (1928) Chabot and the Rangers won the Stanley Cup, although he suffered a serious eye injury and was replaced by Lester Patrick halfway through the series.

WILLIAM (BILL) "THE BIG WHISTLE" CHADWICK

BORN: New York, October 10, 1915
POSITION: NHL Referee, 1940–55
AWARDS: Lester Patrick Trophy, 1975; Hockey Hall of Fame, 1964

Bill Chadwick spent sixteen years refereeing in the NHL and throughout that time *he was blind in his right eye*. "It wasn't until recently that I actually started talking about it," Chadwick said not long ago. "During my refereeing career I didn't think it would be smart to think about it, because I might not have been as effective."

A native New Yorker, Chadwick was a New York Rangers' prospect when he suffered the hockey mishap that changed his career. It was March 1935 and he was going to play in an all-star game at Madison Square Garden. As Chadwick stepped on the ice to start the game, he was hit in the eye by a puck accidentally fired by an opponent. After hospitalization, Chadwick was informed he now had only one good eye.

Amazingly, he returned *to play* the following season with the Rangers' farm club, the New York Rovers, and this time was hit in the good eye. At that point he quit playing although he recovered full vision in his left eye.

A few weeks later he was pressed into emergency service as an Eastern League referee, when the regular official was snowbound. He soon became a regular arbiter, then an NHL linesman, and finally an NHL referee.

Now a prosperous businessman and "color" man for Ranger telecasts, Chadwick refereed through the World War II years and then the turbulent postwar period against such irksome characters as Ted Lindsay and Gordie Howe. According to Chadwick, his disability turned out to be useful in its own way. "Because *I* knew about my problem," he explained, "I made it a point to be on top of the play. I skated harder and was involved in the game at all times.

"Having only one good eye didn't hamper me at all. In those days I had 20–20 vision in my left eye, so it was no problem. I was never far away when there was a play on the net.

"I really don't know if any of the players really knew about it," said Chadwick. "But this much I do know; in all my years I refereed and was an NHL linesman nobody said anything to me about my eye. If anybody had done it, I certainly would have remembered because I was very sensitive about it.

"On the other hand, I know that the NHL governors knew about it and I'm pretty damn sure that some of the managers like Conn Smythe, Art Ross, and Jack Adams knew."

Over the years, Chadwick was regarded as one of the most competent referees ever to skate in the NHL, although some fans might take exception to that statement as they took exception to his calls.

Once in a game between Toronto and the Bruins at Boston, Chadwick called a misconduct penalty against Jimmy Thomson of the Maple Leafs. A period later he called a similar penalty against a Bruin. A Boston Garden fan was so angry he wrapped up several newspapers and swung at Chadwick.

"He knocked me cold," Chadwick recalled. "When I finally came to my senses Thomson was standing next to me and pointed out the guy who had hit me. I had him ejected from the building. A week later I got a letter from the fan apologizing for hitting me.

"I really liked what Thomson did. It proved what I already knew—that players can disagree with you all the way, but they won't let anyone interfere with your game."

Although he believed he had a few years left in his legs, Chadwick retired at the age of thirty-nine. A year later, an amazing thing happened; Bill Chadwick, a referee, was given a "night" in his honor at Madison Square Garden, probably the first and only time a referee was so honored in the NHL.

Naturally, when Chadwick stepped out on the Garden ice to receive his plaque a cascade of boos poured down on him. "If there weren't boos from the gallery," Chadwick concluded, "I'd have known that they didn't appreciate me!"

LUDE CHECK

BORN: Brandon, Manitoba, May 22, 1919
POSITION: Forward, Detroit Red Wings, 1943–44; Chicago Black
    Hawks, 1944–45

A native of Brandon, Manitoba, Lude Check was a forward who played briefly in the NHL for Detroit (1943–44) and Chicago (1944–45). He later starred in the minors, always causing confusion with coaches and broadcasters. When Lude was remiss in guarding his wingman, his coach inevitably would scream "Check, check [as in Lude], check!" As a checker, he was a bit Lude but never obscene.

GERALD MICHAEL (GERRY) CHEEVERS

BORN: St. Catharines, Ontario, December 7, 1940
POSITION: Goalie, Toronto Maple Leafs, 1961–62; Boston Bruins,
    1965–72; Cleveland Crusaders (WHA), 1972–
AWARDS: All-Star (WHA, First Team), 1973, (Second Team), 1974,
    1975; Best Goaltender (WHA), 1973; Team Canada (WHA), 1974

Many years ago Cheevers developed a knack for doing the unlikely—a trait that reached a point of perfection during the summer of 1972 when he walked out on the Boston Bruins after winning the Stanley Cup for them and signed with the Cleveland Crusaders of the brand new World Hockey Association.

The move proved Cheevers was one of the best goaltenders in hockey (the Bruins suffered mightily without him) and that Cheevers had plenty of nerve, gambling with the new circuit. When Cheevers returned to Boston Garden on

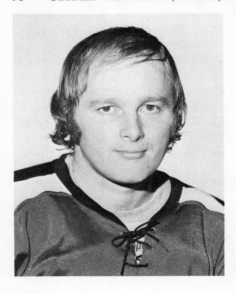

Gerry Cheevers

November 27, 1972 with the Cleveland Crusaders, the 9,000 spectators knew immediately that the Bruins would never be the same without the man they called "Cheesie." Veteran Boston hockey writer Tom Fitzgerald of *The Globe* observed: "Those who profess allegiance to the Bruins must have had cause for renewed regrets. They could hark back to Gerry's record of 32 unbeaten games (1971–72) as they marvelled at some of his clutch moves."

Cheevers further proved his superiority while playing for Team Canada against the Russians in an eight-game series in September 1974. NHL scoring ace Phil Esposito who knows all there is to know about goaltending, is another Cheevers booster. "With us," said Esposito, "Gerry was a winner. He used to tell me the average didn't matter, that he didn't care if we won 8–7. I didn't believe him. We'd talk about it and I'd say, 'C'mon, Gerry, admit it. You'd like a great average.' But he insisted that it didn't matter. After a while I believed him. And I found out that he was one of the all-time greats when it came down to the money games."

Money was what lured Cheevers to the WHA. He received an estimated $1 million deal to switch to Cleveland for seven years. It was double what the Bruins had to offer. "At first," Cheevers recalled, "I thought of 999 reasons why I should stay in Boston. Then I thought of 999 reasons why I should go. Reason number 1,000 was the turning point: the money."

One reason why it's more possible for Cheevers to relax than for other goal-tenders is that he has several safety valves. For one thing, Gerry takes himself a little less seriously than other goalies. For another, he has an excellent outlet for his emotions in horse racing. "I've been around the track for years," he explained. "First it was Fort Erie, Ontario, then Woodbine, near Toronto. I like racing because of the people and the thoroughbred racehorse. I think it's the greatest thing in the world."

Perhaps the highest compliment one could pay Cheevers was delivered by Boston attorney Bob Woolf, who likened Cheevers to former basketball ace Bill Russell. "Except for Russell," said Woolf, himself a former crack basketeer, "I don't know any other athlete who got up for a game like Cheevers.

"He psyches himself to the degree that you feel nobody can touch him. And he believes this. He's an easy-going fellow who makes up his mind to do something—and then he goes ahead and does it, whatever it is."

DON CHERRY

BORN: Kingston, Ontario, February 5, 1934
POSITION: Defenseman, Boston Bruins, 1954–55; Coach, Boston
    Bruins, 1974–

Don Cherry earned the opportunity to coach the Boston Bruins after two seasons as Coach of the Year in the American Hockey League. His Rochester clubs, with no major league affiliations, still managed to challenge for the Calder Cup, and finished first in 1973–74 in the divisional race.

His job with the Bruins was a difficult one, especially for a man who played in only one NHL game. He led men like Bobby Orr and Phil Esposito, top stars for years, with only a minor league background. But it is a background that included four minor league championships in his last five years as a player.

REAL CHEVREFILS

BORN: Timmins, Ontario, May 2, 1932
POSITION: Forward, Boston Bruins, 1951–55, 1956–59; Detroit Red
    Wings, 1955–56

Chevrefils was one of the most gifted skaters to grace the NHL in the fifties. A Boston rookie in 1951–52, Chevrefils teamed with Leo Labine to give the Bruins a vibrant one-two punch that threatened at one point to dominate the league. But somehow, Chevrefils never could live up to his billing, and in 1955–56 was dealt to the Detroit Red Wings. He returned to the Bruins the following season and completed his NHL career in 1958–59, washed up before his thirtieth birthday.

CHICAGO BLACK HAWKS

No team, in any sport, in any place, at any time, has rivaled the Chicago Black Hawks' history, a history replete with a rollicking gashouse spirit and blended with a zany air suggestive of a Marx brothers' comedy. From its inception in 1926, Chicago's hockey team has won often and big, always exuding a unique quality that has characterized its image.

Major Frederic McLaughlin, a rather unpredictable gentleman, to say the least, was founding father, guiding light, general factotum, and first governor of the Chicago Black Hawks. About the same time that Chicago received a National Hockey League franchise in 1926, the Western Hockey League folded. Players of the Portland Rosebuds were made available to the National Hockey League in general, and more specifically to the Black Hawks.

Coached by Pete Muldoon, who as manager-coach of the Seattle Metropolitans had led them to a 1917 Stanley Cup victory, the Hawks finished third in the five-team American Division, ahead of Pittsburgh and Detroit, and only four points behind second-place Boston. Babe Dye wound up fourth in scoring in the American Division, hard on the heels of league-leading Bill Cook of the Rangers. All in all, it was a more impressive debut than the other new entry, Detroit, which finished fifth in the American Division.

Unfortunately for coach Muldoon, his first-round opponents in the Stanley Cup playoffs were the Boston Bruins, who had the benefit of two-years' big league play behind them. Even worse, arena-leasing problems made it impossible for the Black Hawks to play their first game in Chicago; so the series opened in New York, and the Bruins romped to a 6–1 victory. In those days the semifinals were decided on the basis of total goals scored in two games. To win, the Black Hawks would have to make up the five-goal deficit on unfriendly Boston Garden ice. The challenge was too much for the men of Muldoon. They bravely fought Boston to a 4–4 tie, thereby losing the series ten goals to five.

Although impartial observers regarded this as a not too disgraceful turn of events for the Black Hawks, the perfectionist Major McLaughlin was not at all pleased. Hockey legend has it that McLaughlin summoned coach Muldoon to his office and reprimanded him for allowing the Black Hawks to go to pot. The Major is supposed to have said, "This club is good enough to finish in first place."

"You're crazy," the infuriated Muldoon reportedly shot back.

"You're fired!" shouted the offended Major.

Muldoon, walking out of McLaughlin's office, wheeled and looked his former boss in the eye. "I'm not through with you. I'll hoodoo you. This club will *never* finish in first place." Thus was a hockey fable born.

Major McLaughlin laughed contemptuously as his former coach stalked out. But with the passing years the laugh turned to a frown, and the Muldoon declaration became known as the "Muldoon Jinx." For try as they might, the Black Hawks could not get past second place until 1966–67.

Still, the Hawks appeared to be in grand shape. They had a respected coach in Dick Irvin, and his orchestration of the Chicago players gave every indication that better things were to come. Perhaps this was too much to expect from the Black Hawk franchise. Irvin left the team during the summer to accept a similar job with the Maple Leafs. It was also too much to expect Major McLaughlin to follow Irvin with an equally competent coach. Instead, the Major chose a chap named Godfrey Matheson who had absolutely no big league hockey coaching experience.

Following Matheson's early "retirement," the Major now had an opportunity to select any one of several qualified professional coaches to handle the promising team. Instead, he succumbed to one of his quirks, a desire to have Americans rather than Canadians associated with the Hawks. When he had bought the Hawks, McLaughlin had been determined that he would someday staff his team with American skaters, although it was well known that the best players were Canadians. The Major wasn't ready to put an all-American team on the ice for the 1931–32 season, but he decided to solve his existing problem by selecting a coach born in the United States.

His choice as Matheson's successor was Emil Iverson, who seemed to qualify for the job on the basis of one factor alone—he was an American. His other credentials included a stint as a figure skater and experience as a physical culturist. There was no indication that Iverson had ever coached a hockey club. "The fact is," said a player, "he was the Black Hawks' trainer and had never coached a day in his life."

With Matheson gone and Iverson at the helm, the Black Hawks headed for Toronto to open the brand-new Maple Leaf Gardens on November 12, 1931.

When it was over, Iverson's ill-trained, perplexed men were the most surprised people in the building. They had beaten the Maple Leafs, 2–1.

Yet nothing the Black Hawks did seemed to alter the Muldoon Curse. They finished seven points behind the American Division leaders, the Rangers, and were eliminated by the New Yorkers in the opening playoff round. By this time, Major McLaughlin must have wished that Pete Muldoon had never entered his life. However, there was little he could do now but continue to experiment with new personnel and hope for the best.

The Black Hawks finally gained league-wide respectability in 1934 when they won their first Stanley Cup with Tommy Gorman orchestrating the club as manager and coach. Their second Cup win, a more zany experience, occurred in 1938 when baseball umpire Bill Stewart coached the Hawks in an upset win over the Toronto Maple Leafs. Stewart was fired the next season in a dispute with Major McLaughlin.

Another golden era of sorts for Windy City fans emerged when the brothers, Max and Doug Bentley, arrived on the Chicago scene in the early forties. Doug led the NHL in scoring in 1943 while Max won the scoring championship in 1946 and 1947. But between 1947 and 1958 Chicago suffered its worst hockey depression. The Hawks in that span made the playoffs only once (1952–53) in twelve tries. By the 1954 season there were fears that the franchise might fold, but owners Arthur Wirtz and Jim Norris decided to bail out the club with an infusion of new money, and with manager Tommy Ivan, imported from Detroit, as the architect. Ivan developed the Chicago farm system which soon sent the likes of Bobby Hull, Stan Mikita, and Dennis Hull to the Windy City, and in 1961 the Hawks won the Stanley Cup.

The toughest body-blow suffered by the Chicago front office occurred in June 1972 when Bobby Hull quit the Black Hawks to sign a $2.75 million contract with the Winnipeg Jets of the World Hockey Association. Despite Hull's jump, the Black Hawks finished first in the NHL's West Division in 1973 and second in the West Division a season later. In the 1975 Stanley Cup playoffs, they upset the Bruins in the opening round before losing to Buffalo.

CHICAGO COUGARS

If Chicago Cougars' defenseman Pat Stapleton had any kind of complaint, he could always go to coach Pat Stapleton, or if that didn't get results, he could always go over his head to owner Pat Stapleton in the 1974–75 season. Center Ralph Backstrom also was owner Ralph Backstrom of the WHA team, and goalie Dave Dryden was also owner Dave Dryden. The three players joined to buy the team during the 1974–75 season, saving the Chicago franchise from oblivion.

Stapleton and Backstrom, who jumped to the Cougars from their crosstown rivals, the Black Hawks, in the second season of the WHA, revitalized a team which had finished out of the playoffs in its first year. Under the guidance of the two NHL veterans, the Cougars were fourth in the East Division in 1973–74. Backstrom, the team's leading scorer with 33 goals and 50 assists for 83 points, added 19 more points in the playoffs. Chicago beat New England, four games to three, in the opening round, defeated Toronto four games to three in the semifinal round, and lost four straight to the Houston Aeros in the final round for the Avco World Trophy. The Cougars were forced to play their playoff games in a suburban shopping center's ice rink, as their home rink, the Amphitheater, was hosting the circus, and the Black Hawks management refused to let the homeless Cougars use Chicago Stadium.

The Cougars slipped into deep financial trouble right from their very inception when the brothers, Jordan and Walter Kaiser, who owned extensive real estate in the Chicago area, launched the team. They had hoped to build a new arena in suburban Chicago rather than remain at the old International Amphitheater near the Stockyards. When plans for the new rink evaporated in 1974–75 the Kaisers relinquished control of the team and Backstrom, Stapleton, and Dryden took over. They seriously considered moving the Cougars out of Chicago if fan support remained low, but by May 1975 the team dissolved, with the players dispersed among the rest of the league.

HENRY EDWARD (HANK) CIESLA

BORN: St. Catharines, Ontario, October 15, 1934
POSITION: Forward, Chicago Black Hawks, 1955–57; New York Rangers, 1957–59

Fewer skaters entered the NHL with more promise and departed with less accomplished than tall, gangly Hank Ciesla of St. Catharines, Ontario. A star with St. Catharines' Junior A team, Ciesla was believed to be sure-fire big-league material when he graduated to the Black Hawks in 1955–56. But the qualities that worked so well for him in amateur hockey failed in the majors. After two full seasons in the Windy City, after which Hank scored only 18 goals in 140 games, he was dealt to the Rangers where his performance was equally disappointing (11 goals in 129 games). He was dropped to the minors a season later, never to return. A truly nice guy who finished last.

CINCINNATI STINGERS

Admitted to the World Hockey Association for the 1975–76 season, the Cincinnati Stingers' home ice is the $20 million Riverfront Coliseum with 16,500 seats. The Stingers' roots lie in an abortive attempt by Cincinnati to gain entrance into the National Hockey League. After several bids by the Ohio city were rejected by the NHL, Stingers' chairman William O. DeWitt, a former baseball owner, turned to the WHA. The Stingers actually were organized in 1972 with Brian E. Heekin as president and Terry Slater, former coach of the Los Angeles Sharks, as the team's first mentor. Cincinnati signed several promising players well in advance of 1975–76 and placed them on other WHA teams during the 1974–75 season. These included Mike Pelyk, Steve Andrascik, Ron Plumb, and Dennis Sobchuk. William O. DeWitt's son, William O. DeWitt, Jr., was named executive vice-president and chief executive officer.

FRANCIS MICHAEL (KING) CLANCY

BORN: Ottawa, Ontario, February 25, 1903
POSITION: Defenseman, Ottawa Senators, 1921–30; Toronto Maple
    Leafs, 1930–37; Referee (NHL), 1937–49, Coach, Toronto Maple
    Leafs, 1953–56, Vice President, Toronto Maple Leafs, 1967–
AWARDS: All-Star (First Team), 1931, 1934; (Second Team), 1932,
    1933; Hockey Hall of Fame, 1958

Some good old Irish luck intruded to help Maple Leafs' manager Conn Smythe obtain one of the most genuinely colorful characters hockey has known, Francis "King" Clancy, whose ancestors lived among the peat bogs and rich grassy fields of Ireland.

The son of Thomas Clancy, Frank was born in Ottawa and was practically pushed into sports by his burly father. Unfortunately, young Frank was slightly built and it was not uncommon to hear a despairing neighbor complain:

"Tom's youngster will never be the athlete his father is; he's just too small."

But Frank developed an indefatigable spirit, which was embellished by his natural hockey talent. Despite his size, he joined the best amateur club in Ottawa, and, according to one observer, "His courage and speed and nervy play began to gain him a reputation among fans and players alike." When young Clancy was only eighteen, he decided that he was ready for the NHL.

So did Thomas Gorman, manager of the NHL Ottawa Senators, who had heard about Clancy's exploits in the city league. He sent an invitation to Clancy to visit the Senators' office for a conference. But Gorman had difficulty suppressing his laughter when he saw the 125-pound Clancy. "And you want to play *defense?*" chortled Gorman with amazement. Gradually the Senators' boss realized that his deprecating manner did not faze Clancy. Gorman soon got the message. "Okay," he said, "put on your skates and come out to practice. If you make the team, I'll sign you for three years at $800 per season."

The Ottawa skaters were not merely good; they represented the cream of Canada's hockey players, Stanley Cup champions in 1920 and 1921, with such now-legendary stickhandlers as George Boucher, Eddie Gerard, Sprague Cleghorn, and Frank Nighbor. When they realized what a surplus of gutsiness Clancy required even to dare to skate with them, they obliged by passing him the puck to see what the kid could do.

Ron McAllister wrote in *Hockey Heroes:* "Everyone who watched his debut marveled at the confidence of the Irish lad as he sailed into the Stanley Cuppers as though they were all kids together playing shinny on a local rink!"

When the practice had concluded, Clancy received the equivalent of a standing ovation; the veteran Senators patted him generously on the back and wished him well. Gorman was among the first to congratulate Clancy, but he remarked that his size was more suited to the library than the hockey rink. He handed Clancy a contract as a substitute player and said: "We'll put 50 pounds of rock salt in your shirt to weigh you down!"

When they got down to business, Clancy put in his two cents worth: "If you think I'm that good, and you want to give me $800—I'll certainly accept."

The two shook hands, and Clancy became a Senator substitute, collecting splinters on the bench during his rookie season. But irrepressible Frank Clancy was destined to crack the big team, and soon he was pressed into service as a utility skater, even playing goal. His weight had leaped to 147 pounds, and before Gorman could shake his head in disbelief, Clancy had earned a spot on the first team. As a member of the Ottawa club, Clancy played on four Stanley Cup winners and appeared to be a fixture in the capital city. Then the depression began, and the Senators' attendance dropped off at an alarming rate. By the time the 1930–31 season approached, the Ottawa management needed money fast. There was only one thing to do: peddle a star to a wealthier club. And the most attractive star on the club was none other than King Clancy.

Thus the Senators played right into Conn Smythe's hands. Conn was looking for a colorful superstar, and the moment he heard about Clancy's availability, he decided to get him. There was only one problem—Smythe didn't have the money. He knew he would lose Clancy to the Rangers or Black Hawks if he didn't find the cash somehow. Always a gambler, Smythe pulled off yet another daring move.

Smythe had become a horse racing buff, and he owned a colt named Rare Jewel, who just happened to be running at Woodbine Racetrack in Toronto at that time. The odds were 100–1 against Rare Jewel (optimistic odds at that), yet Smythe put his bankroll on his horse and then cheered him on to an astonishing victory. With the winnings he had enough money to purchase Clancy.

Smythe bought Clancy from Ottawa for $35,000 and threw in two extra players, Art Smith and Eric Pettinger, who were worth a total of $15,000 on the NHL market. Clancy cost Smythe $50,000 but he proved to be worth every penny of it. He later became an NHL referee and ultimately a vice-president of the Maple Leafs.

AUBREY VICTOR "DIT" CLAPPER

BORN: Newmarket, Ontario, February 9, 1907
POSITION: Defenseman and Right Wing, Boston Bruins, 1927–47
AWARDS: All-Star (First Team), 1939, 1940, 1941, (Second Team), 1931, 1935, 1944; Hockey Hall of Fame, 1945

Dit Clapper, a tower of strength whether playing right wing or defense, labored for the Boston Bruins for twenty consecutive seasons. During his long and distinguished career with the powerhouse Bruins, he helped them to six championships and three Stanley Cups. Clapper scored well over 200 goals and was named to the All-Star team six times.

Clapper's most memorable seasons as a forward came when he, Cooney Weiland, and Dutch Gainor combined to form the feared Dynamite Line. This trio swept the Beantowners to the 1929 Stanley Cup. With Dit's aid the Bruins lost only five games in the entire 1930 season, but they were defeated in the playoffs by the Montreal Canadiens.

In 1939, after ten years as one of the premier forwards in the league, Clapper made the switch to defense. Paired with the legendary Eddie Shore, Dit made First Team All-Star and the Bruins again won the Stanley Cup.

Clapper saw double duty as a player-coach during his last three years with the Bruins until his retirement as a player in 1947. He continued on as coach of the Bostonians for a few more seasons and was elected to the Hall of Fame.

ROBERT EARLE (BOBBY) CLARKE

BORN: Flin Flon, Manitoba, August 13, 1949
POSITION: Center, Philadelphia Flyers, 1969–
AWARDS: Hart Trophy, 1973, 1975; Bill Masterton Trophy, 1972; All-Star (First Team), 1975, (Second Team), 1973, 1974, 1975; Team Canada, 1972

In a roundabout way it can be said that the Philadelphia Flyers' 1974 Stanley Cup was won on the ice of Moscow's Sports Palace in September 1972. That was when Team Canada defeated the Soviet National Hockey Club, and Bobby Clarke, the diabetic kid from northerly Flin Flon, Manitoba, emerged as the most sought-after player in the eyes of Russian hockey experts.

"Clarke is the one NHL player we like watching most," said a Soviet hockey official. "We have rarely seen anyone work so hard on the ice."

The Russian bigwig merely echoed a sentiment being repeated more and more on the North American continent where Clarke was becoming renowned as the heir apparent to Phil Esposito of Boston as the best center in big-league hockey. Bolstered by the experience against the Russians, Clarke returned to his Philadelphia Flyers and completed the 1972–73 campaign with the most coveted individual prize in the NHL—the Hart Trophy as the league's most valuable player.

"I've been lucky," said the twenty-four-year-old pivot. "I've gotten some good breaks and I was able to take advantage of them." One of those breaks was growing up in the hockey-mad town of Flin Flon, one of the coldest spots in Canada—not surprisingly, since it's not all that far from the Arctic Circle.

"Flin Flon," kidded Clarke's teammate Orest Kindrachuk, "is five miles north of where civilization ends."

Actually, Flin Flon is a major mining area in the province of Manitoba and

Bobby Clarke

one of the foremost producers of young hockey talent. Like so many crack stickhandlers, Clarke played junior hockey there for the Flin Flon Bombers. "My father was a miner," Bobby recalled, "and spent a lot of years underground. He wanted me, first of all, to get a good education. He wanted me to have a better life than he had. Now, Dad's a mine foreman, so he's doing okay."

All professional scouts were aware that Bobby was a diabetic and, not surprisingly, scorned him as a potential NHL prospect. Even the Flyers overlooked him at first, but, under the prodding of bird dog Gerry Melnyk, they decided to take a gamble.

Three years after Melnyk's recommendation, Bobby was voted Flyers' captain, the youngest leader in the NHL. He was also a prime architect in the ascendency of Philadelphia as a hockey power. In the spring of 1973 the Flyers reached the Stanley Cup semifinals for the first time, before being eliminated by Montreal in five tough games. It was during this series that Clarke first gained attention as a less-than-dainty combatant.

The Canadiens said he was downright dirty. The Flyers countered that he was tough—not dirty. Whatever the description, this much was clear: Clarke played the game extraordinarily hard, and by 1973–74 everybody knew it.

"Forget the baby face," said Philadelphia *Inquirer* columnist Frank Dolson, "the easy smile, the refreshing modesty. When the game begins, the face grows hard, the young man grows mean. For a couple of hours a night, 78 nights a year—plus playoffs—the sweet, lovable guy who scores all those goals and kills all those penalties and wins all those games for the Flyers turns into one of the meanest so-and-so's in the NHL.'' And that from a hometown critic.

As for the opponents? ''I say the guy is a mean hockey player,'' snapped Canadiens' coach Scotty Bowman. ''I think the guy tries every way to win for his team.''

As for his own coach? ''What makes Bowman so mad,'' said Philadelphia's Fred Shero, ''is that Bobby's like a leech. Check, check, check. What Bowman was trying to say was that Bobby's the ultimate competitor. He'll fight everybody and beat 'em.''

As for Clarke, here's what Bobby has to say about himself: ''I'm afraid that I've acquired a bad image. But show me one player who doesn't throw the odd elbow.''

Clarke, like the other Flyers, has grown to resent accusations that his club reached the top at the point of a hockey stick. Quite the contrary. ''You don't have to be a genius to figure out what we do on the ice,'' said Clarke. ''We take the shortest route to the puck, and arrive in ill humor!''

Such was Clarke's deportment during the regular 1973–74 season as he captained his troops to the Clarence Campbell Bowl, emblematic of the West Division championship. And such was his act during the astonishing 1974 Stanley Cup playoffs. He was a tower of strength as Philadelphia breezed past Atlanta in four straight games and knocked out tough Rangers' center Walt Tkaczuk in the opening game of the semifinals. ''My defenseman, Moose Dupont, pushed me,'' said Clarke, ''and my shoulder accidentally hit Tkaczuk in the head.''

Throughout the series the Rangers tried to retaliate, mostly with verbal barbs like those tossed by New York humorist Peter Stemkowski. ''If there were still only six teams in this league,'' cracked Stemkowski at Clarke one night, ''you wouldn't be around.''

Clarke shrugged off the insults and went about the business of knocking the Rangers out of the playoffs. Against Boston in the finals, he went head-to-head with his rival, center Phil Esposito, and won so many face-offs from the Boston ace that Beantown papers wondered if Phil had actually lost his touch.

That, of course, was not the case; it was merely that Clarke had become so much better. Likewise, his Flyers had become so strong that they eliminated Boston in six games, capped by a stirring 1–0 victory at the Spectrum. When the game ended, Clarke, who figured the Flyers could do it all along, cradled the Stanley Cup to his chest and skated proudly around the ice with hockey's number one prize.

''People didn't think we could beat New York,'' he chortled. ''Then they didn't think we'd beat the Bruins. They say we're hungry and we hustle. But the fact is we're a good hockey club with good ability.'' Mostly because Bobby Clarke is captain.

OGILVIE (ODIE) CLEGHORN

BORN: Montreal, Quebec, 1891
DIED: July 13, 1956
POSITION: Forward/Goalie, Montreal Canadiens, 1918–25; Pittsburgh Pirates, 1925–26, 1927–28; NHL Referee, 1930s

Few big leaguers can make Odie Cleghorn's claim of having been a forward, goaltender, *and* referee in the National Hockey League. The Montreal-born skater played for the Canadiens from 1918–19 through 1924–25 and completed his NHL career spending the next two seasons with the Pittsburgh Pirates.

Cleghorn attained notoriety of sorts in Boston as the culprit in a strange Stanley Cup episode between the Maple Leafs and Bruins in the midthirties. The clubs were matched in a short two-game series, total goals to count. Boston won the opener, 3–0, in Boston Garden. The second match, at Maple Leaf Gardens in Toronto, saw Boston lead, 1–0, in the first period. Toronto now was behind four goals to none and the Leafs' ace Charlie Conacher was being effectively checked by Boston's Red Beattie. Toronto defenseman King Clancy suggested a strategy to help turn things around:

"Why don't you go out and belt Beattie?" Clancy asked. "Give it good to the sneaky bastard."

"I'd get a penalty," Conacher said.

"So what's a penalty?" asked Clancy, who later became a referee. "Look, I'll get the puck and pass it to you just when Beattie's near you. When he gets close, whack him!"

Conacher obeyed the instructions of his Irish playmate. He jammed an elbow into Beattie's flushed features, but Odie Cleghorn, a tolerant referee, overlooked the foul.

A few minutes later Clancy tripped Eddie Shore, the meat and sinew of the Boston team. Cleghorn also missed that infraction, to Shore's very vocal chagrin: "Trip, Odie! I was tripped!"

Clancy, skating in malicious circles, stimulated Shore's wrath. "The man's blind, Eddie! He's robbin' you, sure as hell! Look how he blew the call on Beattie!"

Then Red Horner, a few minutes later, deflected a shot from Art Jackson past Tiny Thompson in the Boston goal. The Bruins, led by Shore, clamored around Cleghorn, vehement in their insistence that Horner had been illegally standing inside the goal crease.

Clancy's urchin sense of opportunity stoked the turmoil. "Eddie," he bawled at Shore, "what a lousy decision! You're bein' robbed blind. Blind!"

Shore's temper came untied. He shot the puck at Cleghorn, hitting that distinguished gentleman in the middle of his ample rear.

"You're gone!" the referee hollered. "That'll cost you a two-minute penalty!"

Injustice fanned Shore's indignation. He picked up the puck and pitched it into a delighted Toronto crowd.

"And that'll be 10 minutes more!" the referee said, as he added a misconduct penalty to the minor.

While Shore was gone, fuming, the Leafs scored four goals to grab a 5–4 lead on the round. They kept scoring after he returned, finally winning the game, 8–3, and the series, 8–6. Conacher scored three goals and assisted on two others, but on most scorecards Clancy and Cleghorn were responsible for needling the Bruins into elimination.

SPRAGUE CLEGHORN

BORN: Montreal, Quebec, 1890
DIED: July 11, 1956
POSITION: Defenseman, Ottawa Senators, 1919–21; Toronto St.
    Pats, 1921; Montreal Canadiens, 1922–25; Boston Bruins, 1926
AWARDS: Hockey Hall of Fame, 1958

Sprague Cleghorn was a Montreal native and a big, capable leader. "He was a product of a rough neighborhood," said the late Bobby Hewitson, then curator of hockey's Hall of Fame, "where everything you got you had to fight for. And he played hockey the same way. You could be sure that Sprague was well fitted for it."

Anyone who had any doubts about Cleghorn's toughness should have been in the Ottawa rink on the night of February 1, 1922. Sprague had played three years for the Senators and saw no reason why the Ottawa sextet had dealt him to Montreal. He made no effort to conceal his hatred for the Senators' management, and on this night he took out his hostility on any member of the opposition who happened to get in his way. A sequence of events involving Cleghorn and the Senators is vividly described in *The Trail of the Stanley Cup* by Charles L. Coleman:

"A vicious swing at Eddie Gerard cut him over the eye for five stitches. Nighbor was charged and in falling damaged his elbow. A butt end for Cy Denneny required several stitches over the eye and some in his nose. This worked out to a match foul and a fifteen-dollar fine for Sprague. The Ottawa police offered to arrest Cleghorn for assault. Referee Lou Marsh said in his report that he considered Sprague and his brother Odie a disgrace to the game."

BILL CLEMENT

BORN: Buckingham, Quebec, December 20, 1950
POSITION: Center, Philadelphia Flyers, 1971–75; Washington Capitals,
  1975–

The most cerebral member of the Philadelphia Flyers' notorious "Broad Street
Bullies," center Bill Clement has remained in the shadow of more ostentatious
teammates. He was Philadelphia's first choice (eighteenth overall) in the 1970
amateur draft, becoming a Flyers' regular in 1971–72. He ripened to stardom in
the 1974 Stanley Cup finals against the Boston Bruins, coolly helping Philadelphia to the championship. A year later he set his personal points high mark
with 37 in the 1974–75 season. Shortly after the 1974–75 season he was traded
to the Washington Capitals in exchange for their first pick in the amateur draft.

CLEVELAND BARONS

During the forties and early fifties the city of Cleveland was considered the best minor league hockey center in North America. Playing out of the 10,000-seat Cleveland Arena, the American League Barons were directed by popular hockey entrepreneur Jim Hendy. It was Hendy's hope—and expectation—that Cleveland would become the NHL's first post-World War II expansion team. In 1952 it appeared that the Barons would, in fact, be admitted to the NHL. Newspapers prematurely suggested that Cleveland had won the big-league hockey franchise. Actually, the Barons had been given verbal approval by NHL governors. However, a rechecking of the Cleveland team's financial structure caused a turnabout in the NHL thinking and the Baron's big-league bid was rejected. The reversal stunned Hendy—not to mention Cleveland fans—to the core. Charges that the NHL's reappraisal was unfair were taken quite seriously by objective critics—but *not* by the NHL. The Barons remained a viable AHL franchise until Cleveland entered the World Hockey Association in 1972.

CLEVELAND CRUSADERS

Cleveland's Nick Mileti may have gotten the last of the WHA's original franchises in June 1972, but he wasted no time catching up to the league's other teams. A month after acquiring the Crusaders, Mileti pulled off a coup by signing goalie Gerry Cheevers, who had just led the Boston Bruins to their second Stanley Cup championship in three years. Cheevers became the foundation of the Crusaders' team. He was the First Team All-Star goaltender in the NHL in 1972–73, and made the Second Team in 1973–74. Defenseman Paul Shmyr, who was a First Team All-Star both years, joined Cheevers to make the Crusaders a solid East Division contender. The club lost to the New England Whalers in the semifinal round of the playoffs in its first year, and lost to Toronto four games to one in the quarterfinal round in its second year. Cheevers was the leading goalie in the playoffs in the league's maiden season, as he posted a goals-against average of 2.40 after 548 minutes of play.

For the first two seasons of their existence the Crusaders played in the old Cleveland Arena. They moved to the $20 million Coliseum in Richfield, Ohio, for the 1974–75 season. Seating 18,500, the Coliseum was, however, roundly criticized for its distant location from downtown Cleveland and poor access facilities—not to mention a $2.50 car-parking fee. Meanwhile, Mileti, who ran the team from the outset, began to relinquish control over the team during the 1974–75 campaign as Crusaders' crowds remained lower than originally expected in the vast new arena. One nationally read columnist wrote that the Crusaders never should have left Cleveland and the old Arena in the first place. On February 4, 1975, Jay P. Moore, a Cleveland area industrialist and civic leader, obtained controlling interest in the Crusaders and became its president, succeeding Mileti who remained a major stockholder in the franchise.

MATTHEW LAMONT (MAC) COLVILLE

BORN: Edmonton, Alberta, January 8, 1916
POSITION: Right Wing and Defenseman, New York Rangers, 1935–42, 1945–47

With his brother Neil at center and Alex Shibicky on left wing, Mac Colville rounded out one of the top NHL lines of the late thirties. At 5' 8", Mac was a blocky forward who played 18 games for the Rangers in 1935–36 and became a regular the following season. Called "the dour Scot" because a frown was his normal expression, Mac was reserved and remote. A tireless worker, he was reaching the peak of his career when World War II arrived. Mac enlisted after the 1941–42 season and returned in 1945–46 when he played 39 games and scored 7 goals and 6 assists for 13 points. The handwriting was on the wall, but Mac didn't read it right until the following year when he retired after fourteen games with no goals and no assists.

NEIL MacNEIL COLVILLE

BORN: Edmonton, Alberta, August 4, 1914
POSITION: Defenseman and Center, New York Rangers, 1935–49; Coach, New York Rangers, 1950–51
AWARDS: All-Star (Second Team), 1939, 1940, 1948

Although he was the elder Colville (older than Mac by two years), Neil Colville remained in the NHL longer than his kid brother. After a one game trial in 1935–36, Neil became a regular in 1936–37 and a star with Mac and Alex Shibicky, giving the Rangers one of the NHL's strongest lines until the linemates enlisted in the Canadian Armed Forces. When the war ended, the Colvilles reacted differently to the competition, in 1946–47. Mac played fourteen games and then retired. Neil scored four goals in sixty games but did not retire. He was switched to defense, teaming with Frankie Eddolls. The change worked out so well that Neil won a spot on the NHL's Second All-Star team. He remained a Ranger until 1948–49, playing fourteen games and then calling it quits. In the fall of 1950 he became the Rangers' coach, but failed to deliver a playoff team, and soon his ulcer caught up with him and Colville retired.

BRIAN CONACHER

BORN: Toronto, Ontario, August 31, 1941
POSITION: Forward, Toronto Maple Leafs, 1961–62, 1965–68; Detroit
    Red Wings, 1971–72; Ottawa Nationals (WHA), 1972

Last of the famed Conacher family to skate in the majors, Brian turned regular with the Toronto Maple Leafs in the 1966–67 season. A defensive forward, he scored 14 goals and 13 assists in 66 impressive games and then starred in the 1967 Stanley Cup playoffs. In twelve playoff games, Conacher scored three goals and two assists as the Leafs marched to the Stanley Cup. However, Brian began feuding with Leafs' boss Punch Imlach and continued to do so in the 1967–68 season when his production slipped. Conacher eventually quit hockey and wrote a book, *Hockey in Canada, The Way It Is,* in which he criticized Imlach, the Boston Bruins, and several other hockey subjects. When the WHA appeared, Brian played briefly with the Ottawa Nationals before turning to coaching.

CHARLES WILLIAM (PETE) CONACHER, JR.

BORN: Toronto, Ontario, July 29, 1932
POSITION: Left Wing, Chicago Black Hawks, 1951–54; New York
    Rangers, 1954–56

The son of Hall of Famer Charlie Conacher, Pete Conacher was an athlete who had too many press clippings to carry (mostly his dad's). Peter made his debut in 1951–52, playing two games for the Black Hawks. A year later he was a full-time NHL player, but not a very good one, promoted before he was ready by a desperately poor hockey club. A day before Thanksgiving, 1954, Conacher and Bill Gadsby were dealt to the New York Rangers. The Broadway press agents, familiar with the Conacher name, gave Pete a big buildup, but all he could produce was a handful of goals. He finished off his career in the obscurity of the American League.

CHARLES WILLIAM (CHARLIE) CONACHER, SR.

BORN: Toronto, Ontario, December 10, 1909
DIED: December 30, 1967
POSITION: Right Wing, Toronto Maple Leafs, 1929–38; Detroit Red Wings, 1938–39; New York Americans, 1939–41; Coach, Chicago Black Hawks, 1948–50
AWARDS: Art Ross Trophy, 1934, 1935; All-Star (First Team), 1934, 1935, 1936; (Second Team), 1932, 1933; Hockey Hall of Fame, 1961

There are those who insist today that Charlie Conacher was the most exciting player they have ever seen and his shot was the hardest of its day, when slapshots were unheard of and a player beat a goaltender with a quick snap of his wrist.

Scouting Conacher was easy. Charlie learned his hockey on Toronto's Jesse Ketchum Public School rink, and he learned all other sports from his older brother, Lionel, who was to be voted Canada's athlete of the half-century. Charlie broke in as a goalie, but soon he moved to the front line. However, his career was nearly ended at the age of ten when he developed a passion for mountain-climbing, a rather illogical choice in Toronto, where the elevation rarely climbs much above sea level.

To overcome this problem Charlie would find bridges on which to practice his mountaineering techniques. One day in 1920 he challenged the Huntley Street span in Toronto, which crossed a ravine. Young Conacher was proceeding smartly through the iron supports on the underside of the bridge when he missed a steel stepping area, lost his balance, and plummeted some 35 feet to the ground below.

At this point fate intervened, and Charlie was intercepted by a pine tree, which cushioned his blow so perfectly that he escaped with only minor scratches, or so it seemed. Unknown to him at the time, his kidney was damaged, but that injury was not to affect him until much later in his life.

When autumn came, Conacher was able to play hockey, and he continued to improve each winter. He eventually became captain of Selke's Marlboros in 1926, a club that won the Memorial Cup for Canada's Junior championship. Conacher's booming shot was his forte, but his skating still left something to be desired. Thus, when Smythe announced that Charlie had made the team for 1929–30, straight out of Juniors, there was considerable surprise.

Charlie made his NHL debut on November 14, 1929, at the Mutual Street Arena. Chicago's Black Hawks, with the redoubtable Charlie Gardiner in goal, were the opponents, and the fans filling the old Toronto ice palace were frankly skeptical of Conacher's ability to skate and shoot with the pros, especially since he had never had basic hockey training in the minor leagues.

The game was close, but Charlie was never out of place. At one point the puck came to him as he skated over the blue line. Conacher caught it on the blade of his stick and in the same motion flung the rubber in Gardiner's direction. Before the Chicago goalie could move, the red light had flashed, and Charlie Conacher was a Leaf to stay.

Not long after that he once again proved himself, this time against his brother Lionel, who skated on defense for the New York Americans. In no time Charlie left his brother befuddled with a series of "dekes," skated past Lionel's belated attempt at a bodycheck, and fired the puck past goalie Roy Worters.

At first Smythe used Conacher on a line with Joe Primeau at center and Harold Cotton on left wing; but despite Conacher's instant success, Primeau still failed to click. Just before Christmas, 1929, Smythe made the move that would alter hockey history. He pulled Cotton off the line and inserted Busher Jackson in his place on right wing. Hockey's first and most renowned Kid Line was born. Success was as dramatic as a volcanic eruption. Toronto defeated the Black Hawks, the Canadiens, and the Maroons right after Christmas and went undefeated until January 23 of the new year. Charlie went on to become one of the most dynamic of NHL forwards. He later took a turn at coaching the Chicago Black Hawks with little success.

LIONEL PRETORIA "BIG TRAIN" CONACHER

BORN: Toronto, Ontario, May 24, 1901
DIED: May 26, 1954
POSITION: Defenseman, Pittsburgh Pirates, 1925–26; New York Americans, 1926–30; Montreal Maroons, 1930–33, 1934–37; Chicago Black Hawks, 1933–34
AWARDS: All-Star (First Team), 1934, (Second Team), 1933, 1937

An amazing specimen of a man, Lionel Conacher was chosen Canada's Athlete of the Half-Century (1900–1950). He was a superstar in hockey even before that word was invented, despite the fact that shinny was only his third or fourth best game.

Lionel "Big Train" Conacher turned pro in 1926 as a defenseman with the Pittsburgh Pirates of the NHL. During his second season in the steel city, Lionel was traded to the New York Americans where he shuttled back and forth from defense to the forward line for the next three seasons. Conacher developed into a dangerous scoring threat with the Amerks, but really preferred blue line duty.

In 1931, Conacher was traded to the Montreal Maroons for Red Dutton, but he couldn't shake the bad habits he had picked up on the Gay White Way. After three seasons with Montreal, Conacher was again traded, this time to the Chicago Black Hawks and the watchful eyes of coach Tommy Gorman.

Lionel settled down to some serious hockey playing with the Hawks and led them to the 1934 Stanley Cup while making First Team All-Star. Through a complex, three-cornered deal, Big Train found himself back with the Maroons the following season where he was on another cup winning squad.

Conacher played two more years with the Maroons, making the All-Star team in 1937, his last year as a player. Later in life he was elected to a seat in Parliament where he died of a heart attack during his term of office.

ROY GORDON CONACHER

BORN: Toronto, Ontario, October 5, 1916
POSITION: Left Wing, Boston Bruins, 1938–42, 1945–46; Detroit Red Wings, 1946–47; Chicago Black Hawks, 1947–52
AWARDS: Art Ross Trophy, 1949; All-Star (First Team), 1949

There were five boys—and five girls—in the famed Ben Conacher clan in Toronto as the Roarin' Twenties unfolded. Some of them became bywords in Canadian sport. Lionel was the best-rounded of the group and Charlie was the most exciting on ice. Dermott was a fine football player, but later gave up sports for a regular job. Roy and Bert were younger twin brothers and both appeared destined for NHL stardom. But Bert was blinded in his left eye when he was sixteen and never had a pro career.

Roy did, however, make it to the top. He first starred for the Bruins from 1938–39 through 1945–46. Boston traded him to Detroit in 1946–47. Roy had a productive season scoring 30 goals in 60 games for the Red Wings, but was always considered a rather unpredictable athlete. He was especially close with brother Bert, and when Detroit traded Roy to Chicago in 1947 he refused to join the Black Hawks unless Bert moved with him to Chicago. Roy paid the rent and Bert agreed. Roy's wife, Fran, was philosophical. "When I married Roy," she said, "I married them both." Roy finished his career in the middle of the 1951–52 season with Chicago.

ALEX CONNELL

BORN: Ottawa, Ontario, February 8, 1902
DIED: May 10, 1958
POSITION: Goalie, Ottawa Senators, 1924–31, 1932–33; Detroit Falcons, 1931–32; Montreal Canadiens, 1934–37
AWARDS: Hockey Hall of Fame, 1958

An excellent goaltender with Ottawa, then Detroit, Ottawa again, and finally the Montreal Maroons, Alex Connell played in the National Hockey League from 1924–25 through 1936–37. During the 1931–32 season he had an unusual brush with death. Playing for Detroit, Connell tended goal at Madison Square Garden against the New York Americans. Then, the Americans were owned by notorious Prohibition rumlord William "Big Bill" Dwyer, one of the richest bootleggers in the country. During the game Connell engaged in a keen argument with the goal judge and tried to hit the judge with his large goalie stick. Unknown to Connell, the goal judge was a "hit man" for Dwyer. Members of the gang tried unsuccessfully to rub out Connell after the game and only quick-thinking by a cordon of police saved the goaltender's life.

WAYNE CONNELLY

BORN: Rouyn, Quebec, December 16, 1939
POSITION: Right Wing, Montreal Canadiens, 1960–61; Boston Bruins, 1961–64, 1966–67; Minnesota North Stars, 1967–69; Detroit Red Wings, 1969–71; St. Louis Blues, 1971; Vancouver Canucks, 1971–72; Minnesota Fighting Saints (WHA), 1972–

Wayne Connelly traveled around the National Hockey League more than any other active player, seeing action with six teams in eleven years—Montreal, Boston, Minnesota, St. Louis, Detroit, and Vancouver.

Wayne Connelly

His best season came in 1967–68, when he scored 35 goals for the expansion Minnesota North Stars, plus eight more in the playoffs. But Connelly considers his best season to be 1969–70, when he accumulated 23 goals and 36 assists for 59 points.

Connelly, however, jumped at the chance to go to the World Hockey Association, signing with the Minnesota Fighting Saints for a no-cut, three-year contract, estimated to be worth somewhere between $250,000 and $300,000.

One of the mainstays of the Saints, Connelly scored 40 goals in 1972–73. The following year, Connelly upped his scoring marks to 42 goals and 53 assists for 95 points.

Wayne was the first player to join the WHA, when he jumped from the Vancouver Canucks.

EDWARD (EDDIE) "COWBOY" CONVEY

BORN: Toronto, Ontario
POSITION: Left Wing, New York Americans, 1930–32

King Clancy and his Toronto Maple Leafs' teammates tried to make a star out of Eddie "Cowboy" Convey, a journeyman foward who was Clancy's team-mate before being sent to the New York Americans.

When Convey came to Toronto with the New York sextet, after being traded to the Americans, word spread around the Maple Leafs' dressing room that Cowboy was on the brink of demotion to the minors. This concerned the sensitive Clancy, who told his Toronto colleagues that *something* had to be done for Convey. "Look," King said, "if we get a few goals up, let's make it easy for Cowboy and help him score a couple."

Sure enough, the Leafs sped to a 4–0 lead and had the game well in hand when Convey skated on to the ice against Toronto's Kid Line with Clancy on defense and Lorne Chabot in goal. King winked at Conacher to be sure that Charlie got the message, and in the next moment Convey skated past Conacher, who was kind enough not to check him. Cowboy was one-on-one with Clancy, and King fell backward on his skates, allowing Convey to break in on the goal-tender.

Chabot was aware of Convey's scoring drought, and he believed that his best move to allow Cowboy to score was to make no move at all. He simply remained inert in the nets as Convey sized up the situation. There was plenty of air to the left and plenty to the right; Cowboy had a delectable choice, and he promptly fired the puck considerably wide of the target—and so high that it flew directly into the grandstand.

Uncertain whether to be furious or amused with Convey, the Leafs eventually returned to the bench and agreed that their former teammate deserved one more chance. The same group of Toronto players was on the ice a few minutes later when Cowboy galloped toward Chabot.

In what amounted to an almost precision maneuver, Conacher permitted Convey to pass him, and Clancy artfully faked a bodycheck that missed. "Eddie went cruising in on Chabot," Clancy remembered, "who was ready to step aside and, in fact, fell to the ice, giving Convey a whole goal to shoot at. Bam! Eddie shot the puck, and don't you think he hit Chabot right in the Adam's apple with the darn puck. Chabot went down, choking and gagging."

For a change the Leafs stopped worrying about Convey and rushed to their injured goaltender. Chabot looked up and snapped, "Cut this nonsense out or that guy'll kill me!" It was then that Clancy realized his altruism had gone too far. He looked at Chabot, perhaps thinking that one more try might be in order, when the wounded goalie stared back at King and shouted: "Screw Convey!"

FREDERICK JOSEPH "BUN" COOK

BORN: Kingston, Ontario, September 18, 1903
POSITION: Left Wing, New York Rangers, 1926–36
AWARDS: All-Star (Second Team), 1931

The rugged member of the famed Cooks-Boucher Line, Bun Cook was frequently overshadowed by his more spectacular older brother, Bill, and the smoothy, Frank Boucher. But Bun himself was a deft passer who could muck his way in the corners with the best of them. He was an original Ranger, playing on two Cup-winning teams. He was forced out of the lineup during the 1935–36 season by a recurring throat problem.

LLOYD COOK

BORN: Unknown
POSITION: Defenseman, Vancouver Millionaires (PCHA), 1915–16, 1918–24; Boston Bruins, 1924–25

A fixture on defense in the old Pacific Coast League, Lloyd Cook was as slick a stickhandler and scorer as any forward of the day. Cook started his career with the Vancouver Millionaires in 1915, a year that saw his team skate away with the Stanley Cup.

After a brief trial with the Spokane franchise in 1917, Cook returned home to British Columbia and teamed with Art Duncan to form one of the most feared defensive duos in all of hockey. This pair dominated Pacific Coast blue lines for the next seven seasons, three of which saw the Millionaires in the thick of the battle for the Stanley Cup.

In 1924 Cook went east for a trial with the Boston Bruins of the NHL, but his heart wasn't in it. After four games, Lloyd Cook retired from hockey.

WILLIAM OSSER (BILL) COOK

BORN: Brantford, Ontario, October 9, 1896
POSITION: Right Wing, New York Rangers, 1926–37; Coach, New York Rangers, 1951–53
AWARDS: Art Ross Trophy, 1927, 1933; All-Star (First Team), 1931, 1932, 1933, (Second Team), 1934; Hockey Hall of Fame, 1952

Many oldtimers regard Bill Cook as the finest right winger of all time. Certainly, he ranks among the greatest, past or present, including Gordie Howe, Bernie Geoffrion, and any number of other old goldies. What set Cook apart from the others, ironically, was his unseparability from brother Bun and Frank Boucher. Together, the Cook brothers and Boucher were the cornerstones of the sensational Ranger teams, starting in 1926–27, when the Blueshirts opened on Broadway, and through the midthirties. It was impossible to talk of Bill Cook without mentioning brother Bun, or their close friend and linemate, Boucher.

When the Rangers won the Stanley Cup in 1928 and again in 1933 it was Bill Cook leading the way with Bun and Boucher right there to supply, or receive, the passes. Although he originally had made his mark in Canadian pro hockey, Bill became part of the woof and warp of the New York sporting scene and remained a Ranger until his retirement after the 1936–37 season. With Boucher as manager, he returned to New York as coach for a brief term from December 1951 through the 1952–53 season. Bill is best remembered as a player, and nobody remembers him better than his old pal Boucher, who described him this way:

"Bill would do most of the talking. He'd say, 'Now look, Bunny (and I knew that although he was addressing his words to Bunny he damned well meant me too), when I want that puck, I'll yell for it, and you get that damn puck to me when I yell.' On the ice, Bill's cry was the most amazing half-grunt, half-moan, half-yell that I ever heard. He'd let this weird sound out of him, meaning that he was in the clear. And he'd say in these skull sessions of ours, 'When I yell, I want the puck then; don't look up to see where I am; just put it there and I'll be there.' So I'd be carrying the puck and hear that goddamned crazy noise from Bill, and I'd be sure to put the puck at an angle, in advance of the sound, sort of leading him because I knew he'd be cutting in on the goal, going like hell, and I'd angle the pass, not fast or it would lead him too far, but slow so he would take it in full stride, and a lot of times I'd be lying on my back, knocked down by a defenseman just as I released the puck, and although I couldn't see anything, I'd hear the roar of the crowd and know that he'd banged it pass the goaltender. Bill didn't have a bullet shot, or at least not a long bullet like the golf-style slapshot Bobby Hull perfected. But he had a very hard wrist-shot from close-in, and could score equally well backhand or forehand."

JACK KENT COOKE

They all laughed at Christopher Columbus when he said the world was round. And they all laughed at Jack Kent Cooke when he said the hockey world would revolve around his Los Angeles Kings. Cooke expected the laughter. Given to braggadocio under normal circumstances, Cooke was up against a conservative board of governors when he first applied for a franchise in the expanded National Hockey League. But his salesmanship worked. The owners took his $2 million and then, almost as an afterthought, asked Cooke where he proposed to have his team play its games during 1967–68.

"I'm going to build the most beautiful arena in the world," Cooke told them, "and it'll be ready sometime in the opening season."

Armed with a franchise and plans for an arena, Cooke then went about the business of building a hockey team. He hired Leonard "Red" Kelly, the former Detroit Red Wing and Toronto Maple Leaf star, as his coach. Then, he and Kelly attended the NHL draft meeting at Montreal in June 1967, and came away with a collection of players who were conspicuous by their lack of big-league credentials. The fact that Cooke also had purchased the Springfield Indians of the American League didn't really seem to impress his critics. All that the Kelly-Cooke combine appeared to have in its favor was Terry Sawchuk, the onetime leading goaltender in hockey, but who, in his twilight years, was, at best, a question mark.

The Kings ended their first season in the new expansion West Division only one point out of first place. Needless to say, Cooke was voted Top Executive of the Year by *The Hockey News*. "The flamboyant owner not only put a winning team on the ice," explained *Hockey News* publisher Ken McKenzie, "but he completed construction of one of the sport's most glamorous enterprises with the opening of the $20,000,000 Forum despite heavy opposition."

The irrepressible Cooke always has been less concerned with his opponents than opponents were with him. But the onetime orchestra leader and radio-station owner managed to capture more newspaper space than all eleven of his NHL owner colleagues combined; a feat that delighted him no end. "What's the fun of laying out five million dollars," demanded Cooke, "if you can't get excited about what you've bought."

Cooke had been excited as a team owner before. He had a good chunk of the Toronto Maple Leafs baseball club in the International League, until it became apparent the Leafs were losing their grasp on the public. Besides, the Leafs were minor league and Cooke was never satisfied with anything less than the top drawer. Eventually he moved on to buy a quarter share of the Washington Redskins football team, and he paid $5,175,000 for the Los Angeles Lakers of the National Basketball Association.

By January 1968 the apologies began flowing into Cooke's office. Obviously, he had pulled a coup. Whereas the Pittsburgh Penguins had gone with jaded veterans who appeared to be "playing their last two years to entitle them to full pensions," as Cooke pointed out, the Kings' youngsters were outsprinting their rivals and just about any established team that chose to match them in speed.

Cooke was also shrewd in purchasing the Springfield team. Many of the minor-league players proved good enough to move into the NHL. Better still for the Kings, they had played together before and meshed cleanly together, while other expansion teams were having trouble getting their players accustomed to one another.

On top of that was Cooke's real frosting, his monument to himself, the Los Angeles Forum. "It must be seen to be believed," commented Eric Hutton in *Maclean's* magazine of Canada, "and maybe not even then. It is the gaudiest sports palace this side of the heyday of the Colosseum of Ancient Rome, of which the Forum is, in fact, a modernized copy."

JOSEPH (JOE) COOPER

BORN: Winnipeg, Manitoba, December 14, 1914
POSITION: Defenseman, New York Rangers, 1935–38, 1946–47; Chicago Black Hawks, 1938–46

Joe Cooper began and ended his major league career with the New York Rangers. The lantern-jawed defenseman broke in during the 1935–36 season and remained a Ranger until he was dealt to Chicago prior to the 1938–39 season. He remained with the Black Hawks until 1946–47, returning for one more season on Broadway. A quiet, competent worker, Cooper was inadvertently credited with the hardest punch in hockey. It happened in March 1947 as a result of a mass brawl between the Rangers and Canadiens at Madison Square Garden. Cooper delivered a terrific punch to Murph Chamberlain, knocking him into the timekeeper's booth. However, a photo of the punch mistakenly reported that Cooper had knocked Chamberlain into the Garden *press box*. The press box actually was located 50 feet above the timekeeper's booth. Until the mistake was corrected weeks later, Cooper was believed to be the strongest man in the world.

BERT CORBEAU

BORN: Unknown
DIED: September 22, 1942
POSITION: Defenseman, Montreal Canadiens, 1915–22; Hamilton Tigers, 1922–23; Toronto St. Pats, 1923–26; Toronto Maple Leafs, 1926–27

A tough defenseman who spent his first five National Hockey League seasons (1917–18 through 1921–22) with the Montreal Canadiens, Corbeau frequently teamed with the more notorious Edouard "Newsy" Lalonde to bulldoze opponents. Typical was a playoff game between the Canadiens and the Toronto Arenas on March 11, 1918. In that one Corbeau and Lalonde seemed more intent on decapitating the Queen City boys than on scoring. Bert spent the 1922–23 season with Hamilton and then, ironically, wound up playing for the Toronto St. Pats. He remained in Toronto through the 1926–27 season when the St. Pats changed their name to the Maple Leafs, whereupon Corbeau exited from the big time.

LESTER JOHN THOMAS (LES) COSTELLO

BORN: South Porcupine, Ontario, February 16, 1928
POSITION: Left Wing, Toronto Maple Leafs, 1947–49

Just when it appeared that Les Costello would make it as a hockey pro, he abruptly quit to become a Roman Catholic priest. "I could have continued to play professionally," said Costello, a native of South Porcupine, Ontario, "but I had a strong inclination to go into the priesthood. It was my call in life."

In the late forties, Costello was a highly regarded Toronto Maple Leafs' prospect who played briefly on a line with Hall of Famer Max Bentley and Fleming Mackell. "Cos played the game hard," said Mackell, "He had more than his share of fights and always came to my aid when I got into one. Once, when we were playing in Pittsburgh, Cos made a point getting even with the veteran defenseman Ott Heller, who was with Indianapolis. Well, that night Cos really gave Heller a taste of his own medicine and Heller didn't bother us much after that."

Costello also had a good sense of humor on ice. "Once in Cleveland," Mackell recalled, "Cos was belted six times and each time fell flat on his back. After a while I skated over and asked him what the trouble was. 'I'm just testing these big guys to see how strong they are,' he told me. And then he laughed."

Costello played fifteen games for the Maple Leafs in 1948–49 and scored two goals and three assists. He played on Toronto's 1948 Stanley Cup winners. "There may have been better players," said Mackell, "but none with more fire and determination."

MURRAY COSTELLO

BORN: South Porcupine, Ontario, February 24, 1934
POSITION: Forward, Chicago Black Hawks, 1953–54; Boston Bruins, 1954–55; Detroit Red Wings, 1956–57

Kid brother of Les Costello, Murray Costello bounced around the National League between 1953–54 and 1956—57, skating for Chicago, Boston, and Detroit and failing with each. He later turned executive of the old Western Hockey League and co-publisher of *The Western Hockey League News,* a weekly that temporarily threatened to compete with *The Hockey News*. Costello remained a minor league executive and many observers insisted that he was too smart to become involved with the NHL.

HAROLD "BALDY" COTTON

BORN: Nanticoke, Ontario, November 5, 1902
POSITION: Left Wing, Pittsburgh Pirates, 1925–28; Toronto Maple
    Leafs, 1928–35; New York Americans, 1935–37

A competent left winger, Harold "Baldy" Cotton broke into the National Hockey League with the Pittsburgh Pirates in 1925–26, but gained fame years later as a member of the "Gashouse Gang" Toronto Maple Leafs of the early thirties. Toronto manager Conn Smythe bought Cotton from Pittsburgh for the 1928–29 season and used him on a number of lines.

Cotton inadvertently played a part in the formation of one of the NHL's most spectacular units—the Kid Line of Joe Primeau, Busher Jackson, and Charlie Conacher—when Smythe placed Baldy alongside Primeau and Conacher. Just before Christmas 1929, Smythe made the move that would alter hockey history. He pulled Cotton off the line and inserted Jackson. Immediately, the line dazzled the hockey world.

Undaunted, Cotton played capably wherever he was asked. He also was a chief protagonist in the endless practical jokery that was part of the woof and warp of that Maple Leaf club.

During the 1932–33 campaign, Cotton fell victim to a prank that has since gone down in the annals of superb but dangerous hockey lessons. The prank had its origins in a Saturday night game at Maple Leaf Gardens. Cotton had been playing an especially competent game for Toronto that night, diligently working himself into scoring position. But whenever it was time for him to receive the puck, his teammates failed to deliver. It appeared that Hal was not going to reap dividends no matter what he did, and he became more and more unhappy about the turn of events.

By the time the game had ended and the Maple Leafs returned to their dressing room, Cotton had reached a high state of pique, which continued to grow in intensity as the players headed for the railroad station and the overnight trip to New York City for a match against the Rangers.

Eventually Cotton got his frustration out of his system and began belaboring his linemates with assorted adjectives regarding their failure to pass the puck. The only trouble was that Hal didn't know when to stop. His peroration continued through the night and extended to the next day, when the hockey club checked into the Hotel Lincoln, now called the Royal Manhattan. Cotton and his roommate, Charlie Conacher, took the elevator up to their suite on the twentieth floor. Charlie was tired, and he went right to bed. Still mulling over his misfortune, Cotton walked back and forth in the room, berating each of his teammates who had failed to deliver the puck to him.

During the first minutes of the diatribe Conacher pretended not to hear a word. But when Cotton suddenly announced in a fit of rage that he would obtain retribution by refusing to pass the puck to any of his teammates who were in scoring position, Conacher rose from his pillow and wondered whether he had heard Cotton correctly. Hal repeated his threat.

That did it. Conacher, a man with a physique reminiscent of Paul Bunyan, leaped out of bed and grabbed Cotton. Charlie knew—as did all the Leafs—that Cotton had an obsessive fear of high places. Out of the corner of his eyes Conacher noticed an open window. He carried Cotton to the window sill, gripped him firmly about the ankles, and held Cotton out the open window. Head down, screaming frantically, Cotton could do nothing but stare at the sidewalk twenty floors below.

While all this was going on, Conacher delivered his ultimatum by asking Cotton whether he was or was not going to pass the puck. Without waiting for an answer, Charlie carefully lowered Cotton another inch toward the street below. Sheer terror brought Hal to his senses, and he hurriedly canceled his earlier threats. Whereupon Conacher calmly lifted him up and back into the room. It was the last time Cotton ever threatened to be a one-man team.

After his retirement from hockey in 1937, following a season with the New York Americans, Cotton drifted into scouting and broadcasting. He became a regular fixture on the Canadian Broadcasting Corporation's Hot Stove League programs between periods of the Toronto Maple Leafs' Saturday night games. Cotton soon became renowned as a storyteller.

ARTHUR EDMUND (ART) "TRAPPER" COULTER

BORN: Winnipeg, Manitoba, May 31, 1909
POSITION: Defenseman, Chicago Black Hawks, 1931–35; New York
    Rangers, 1935–42
AWARDS: All-Star (Second Team), 1938–40; Hockey Hall of Fame,
    1974

Considering the little ink he received it's amazing that Art Coulter, the former Black Hawks' (1931–32 through 1935) and then Rangers' defenseman ever made it to the Hall of Fame. But Coulter was a quiet gem, a man who became the Rangers' captain during their second golden era at the end of the thirties. "He was a superb ice general," said his coach Frank Boucher. "He lent strength to our smaller players, always on the spot if opposing players tried to intimidate them, responding beautifully to new responsibilities. He was a well set up fellow, quite tall, very muscular without an ounce of fat."

Art was nicknamed "the Trapper" because he would talk fishing and hunting by the hour. Coulter teamed with Muzz Patrick to give the Rangers a fearless, bruising defense. He also was the linchpin of the Rangers' offensive penalty-killing team, an innovation the New Yorkers introduced in 1939. Coulter was the anchor man, working with forwards Alex Shibicky, Neil and Mac Colville. Over the season the Rangers outscored their opponents almost two to one when they were shorthanded. Coulter remained a Ranger through the 1941–42 campaign.

YVAN SERGE "ROADRUNNER" COURNOYER

BORN: Drummondville, Quebec, November 22, 1943
POSITION: Right Wing, Montreal Canadiens, 1963–
AWARDS: Conn Smythe Trophy, 1973; All-Star (Second Team), 1969,
    1971–73

Montreal's Canadiens are known as "the Flying Frenchmen" and nobody wearing the *"bleu* [blue], *blanc* [white], *et rouge* [red]" uniform flies faster than Yvan Cournoyer, the compact right wing.

Shooting and skating have been Cournoyer's main interest in life since he was a kid in the French-speaking town of Drummondville, Quebec. When he was fourteen, his family moved to Montreal and he quickly climbed hockey's sandlot ladder, winding up with Lachine, a powerful team in the Canadien-sponsored Metropolitan Junior League.

NHL scouts had heard good things about the little kid with the big part in his hair, but they really took notice after the final game of a Lachine-Verdun series. Yvan's club was trailing by one goal with less than a minute remaining when he captured the puck behind his own net. Bobbing and weaving, he skated around the opposition and shot the puck past the Verdun goalie. Then he scored the winning goal in sudden-death overtime.

Cournoyer soon graduated to the Junior Canadiens, a regal teen-age version of the parent club. Claude Ruel was his coach then as he was later with the NHL Canadiens. "I could tell right away," says Ruel, "that he had the same scoring knack as the Rocket. I told him to shoot even more, to strengthen his shot."

Yvan went home to his father's machine shop, probed around for some scrap steel, and designed some shot-improvers. "I made a couple of steel pucks," he recalls, "about two pounds each. Then I went down to the basement and shot them at heavy carpets lined up against the wall." The exercise may have weakened the foundations of the house, but it strengthened his wrists. By the following winter he had a much better shot.

This improvement was well timed. The Canadiens were scanning the junior hockey horizon for future heirs to Henri Richard and Jean Beliveau, the reigning French-Canadian scoring titans. They called Yvan up for a five-game tryout in the 1963–64 season and he scored in his first game. "He pounced on the puck like a cat," said Beliveau. However, coach Toe Blake was less enthused. He gave Yvan part-time work during his rookie year, 1964–65, and Cournoyer scored only seven goals. "But I never let down," says Yvan, "because when you let down you're finished.'' In time he became one of the most productive Canadiens scorers.

WILLIAM (BILLY) COUTURE (COUTU)

BORN: Sault Ste. Marie, Ontario, (date unknown)
POSITION: Defenseman, Montreal Canadiens, 1917–20, 1921–26; Hamilton Tigers, 1920–21; Boston Bruins, 1926–27

Who was the most vicious hockey player of all time? Some critics suggest that it was ''Bad'' Joe Hall who played for the Montreal Canadiens from 1917–19. Others mention Eddie Shore who starred for the Boston Bruins in the late twenties and thirties. But a prime candidate has to be Billy Coutu (pronounced Coo-chou), a defenseman from Sault Ste. Marie, Ontario, whose real moniker was Couture, and who was one of only three players expelled from the NHL.

Originally with the Canadiens from 1917 through 1926—with a brief stop in 1920–21 with Hamilton—Coutu became a Bruin in 1926–27 and was brutal with friend and foe alike. During a Bruins' practice Coutu once punched Shore in the mouth. Later, after Shore had retailated, Coutu delivered a pulverizing bodycheck that dispatched Shore to the ice, his ear soaked with blood and hanging loose as if it had been sliced with a razor. Coutu was a Bruin when he put the slug on a referee and thereby earned his permanent exit from pro hockey. Coutu smashed referee Gerry LaFlamme in the final game of the 1927 Stanley Cup final against Ottawa. NHL president Frank Calder then leveled the explusion.

Coutu insisted he was only following instructions the night he was permanently excused from the NHL. ''Art Ross,'' he said, ''started the whole thing.'' Ross was the Boston manager in 1927 and not unknown for defiance of authority. Coutu claimed he didn't blame Ross at the time because he didn't want to hurt Ross while he lived. ''He's dead now, bless his soul,'' Coutu said. ''So I guess I can talk—tell it how it was, like they say.

''Anyway, we're getting a raw deal in Ottawa this night, so Art called us together. 'Start a commotion,' he told us, 'and make sure the referee is in the middle.'

''Well, we had one dandy fight. Players on both teams were in on it. I was nearest the referee, so I let him have it. LaFlamme was his name. He's dead now, too, poor fellow.''

Remorse was not one of Coutu's emotions when he played, on the testimony of Maple Leafs' vice-president King Clancy, who opposed him with Ottawa in the 1926–27 playoffs. ''Coutu'd wield his stick like a razor,'' Clancy maintained. ''He'd just as soon cut your heart out with it.''

BILL COWLEY

BORN: Bristol, Quebec, June 12, 1912
POSITION: Center, St. Louis Eagles, 1934–35; Boston Bruins, 1935–47
AWARDS: Hart Trophy, 1941, 1943; Art Ross Trophy, 1941; All-Star (First Team), 1938, 1941, 1943, 1944, (Second Team), 1945; Hockey Hall of Fame, 1968

Overshadowed during most of his National Hockey League career by team-mate-center Milt Schmidt, Bill Cowley nevertheless has been regarded as one of the classiest playmakers. He entered the NHL during the 1934–35 season with the St. Louis Eagles, but became a Bruin to stay the following year. He starred for the Boston sextet through the 1946–47 season. Smaller than Schmidt, Cowley relied on guile more than strength, emphasizing subtlety over Schmidt's accent on sock. Many critics believe that if Cowley had been blessed with linemates such as Woody Dumart and Bobby Bauer, who complemented Schmidt on the Kraut Line, then Cowley would have been by far the most productive Bruin.

JOHN SHEA (JACK) CRAWFORD

BORN: Dublin, Ontario, October 26, 1918
POSITION: Defenseman, Boston Bruins, 1938–50
AWARDS: All-Star (First Team), 1946; (Second Team), 1943

A defenseman's defenseman, Jack Crawford was a Boston Bruins' mainstay from 1938–39 until his retirement at the conclusion of the 1949–50 season. Crawford played for both the 1939 and 1941 Stanley Cup winners as well as the Prince of Wales Trophy winners in 1938, 1939, 1940, and 1941. For a decade Crawford was unique among NHL regulars as being the only skater to wear a helmet. Curiously, Crawford's helmet was worn not so much for reasons of health, but rather for cosmetic purposes. Jack was very, very bald. The helmet did a very, very good job concealing his pate.

SAMUEL RUSSELL "RUSTY" CRAWFORD

BORN: Cardinal, Ontario, November 7, 1885
DIED: Unknown
POSITION: Left Wing, Quebec Bulldogs (NHA), 1913–17; Ottawa Senators/Toronto Arenas, 1917–18; Toronto Arenas, 1918–19
AWARDS: Hockey Hall of Fame, 1962

Portsider Crawford broke into the big-league wars in 1913 with Quebec of the NHA. The rookie left winger found himself in the thick of Stanley Cup competition, and chipped in three key goals as Quebec's sextet copped the storied silverware.

Five years later, Crawford skated for another Cup winner. This time it was Toronto of the NHL with the scrappy winger potting two goals in as many playoff games.

Crawford moved out west in 1922, skating for Saskatoon of the WCHL before moving on to Calgary and finally Vancouver. Said to be one of the best backcheckers and most spirited team players ever to play the game, Rusty Crawford earned his niche in hockey's Hall of Fame.

DAVE CREIGHTON

BORN: Port Arthur, Ontario, June 24, 1930
POSITION: Center, Boston Bruins, 1948–54; Toronto Maple Leafs, 1954, 1958–60; Chicago Black Hawks, 1955; New York Rangers, 1955–58

One of Canada's top-rated junior stars in the late forties, Dave Creighton was a teammate of the equally starry Danny Lewicki for the Port Arthur (Ontario) West End Bruins, a team which won the Memorial Cup, emblematic of Canada's junior championship. But like Lewicki, Creighton never quite made it big as a major leaguer. He broke in with the Boston Bruins in 1948–49 and skated in the Hub through the 1953–54 season. A year later his playing time was split between the Toronto Maple Leafs and Chicago Black Hawks. The New York Rangers acquired Creighton in 1955–56 and he played his best hockey on Broadway, centering for Camille Henry on left wing and Andy Hebenton on the right. In 1957–58 Creighton scored 17 goals and 35 assists for 52 points in 70 games, his best NHL season. His production slipped thereafter. He was dealt to Toronto for the 1958–59 campaign, scored only three goals in thirty-four games and completed his NHL career in 1959–60 when he scored but once in fourteen games for the Maple Leafs.

TERRANCE ARTHUR (TERRY) CRISP

BORN: Parry Sound, Ontario, May 28, 1943
POSITION: Center, Boston Bruins, 1965–66; St. Louis Blues, 1967–72; New York Islanders, 1972–73; Philadelphia Flyers, 1973–

"The other guy from Parry Sound," Bobby Orr's hometown, is Terry Crisp. The Flyer utilityman was obtained from the New York Islanders in 1973, and he has been digging into the corners and toward the net for the Flyers ever since. Terry is one of the more heady players in the game, and Fred Shero has dubbed Crisp "a coach on the ice."

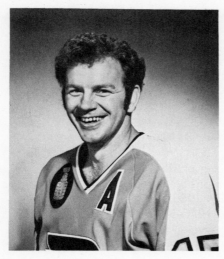

Terry Crisp

STANLEY CROSSETT

BORN: Port Hope, Ontario, (date unknown)
POSITION: Defenseman, Philadelphia Quakers, 1930–31

Stan Crossett was a towering defenseman from Port Hope, Ontario. Crosset's experience in the NHL—and one episode in particular—symbolized more than anything the ill-starred life of the Philadelphia Quakers. The Quakers were in Detroit for a game against the Falcons (later the Red Wings) and coach Cooper Smeaton gathered his men together for a pregame skull session. He addressed himself mainly to Crossett, warning him against trying to split the vaunted Detroit defense of Reg Noble and Harvey "Rocky" Rockburn.

"These two guys have perfected the art of sandwiching attackers," said Smeaton. "Noble steers people into Rockburn and then Rockburn creams you. If you try to split them you can get hurt. And I mean hurt!"

Crossett appeared to be listening, but then in the second period Crossett stole the puck from a Detroit skater and did precisely what Smeaton had told him not to do. Archie Campbell, the Quakers' trainer, watched the play in awe from the Philadelphia bench. "Noble got him first," Campbell remembers, "then Rockburn sent him flying off his feet. It was no ordinary hoist either. The big fellow seemed to take off like an airplane. Then he made a perfect three-point landing on elbows and stomach and started to skid along the ice. The wind had probably been knocked out of him before he ever touched the ice."

Many professional hockey players have mastered the art of the "swan dive," a maneuver designed to capture the referee's attention and obtain a penalty against the opposition. But everyone in the arena knew this time that Crossett was in trouble before he even landed.

"He was helpless," says Campbell. "He slid on his stomach from mid-ice right over to the boards with his stick extended in front of him. When the stick hit the boards, it jabbed Crosset's chin and knocked him out cold."

Unknown to Crossett, he had accidentally committed a foul on the play while he was in midair. It seems that his stick had snagged Rockburn, opening a bloody wound over Rocky's eye. While Crossett was stretched out unconscious on the ice he was given a five-minute major penalty by the referee for drawing blood!

Meanwhile, trainer Campbell dashed out on the ice to care for the injured Crossett. He waved smelling salts in front of the still Quaker until Stan came to his senses. Campbell then escorted him to the penalty box, helped place him on the bench, and then dangled more smelling salts until Crossett realized that he was neither in the dressing room nor on the Quakers' bench.

"What in Heaven's name am I doing here?" he asked of Campbell.

And calmly as possible, Archie tried to explain.

JOSEPH RICHARD (JOE) CROZIER

BORN: Winnipeg, Manitoba, February 9, 1929
POSITION: Defenseman, Toronto Maple Leafs, 1959–60; Coach, Buf-. falo Sabres, 1972–74, Vancouver Blazers (WHA), 1974–75

Joe Crozier has gone through almost every possible job for anyone connected with hockey. He served as a player in minor pro and senior hockey, and had a one-year tryout with the Toronto Maple Leafs in 1959–60. He has been a coach and general manager, holding those positions with the Rochester Americans of the AHL and the old Vancouver Canucks of the WHL. Crozier was dismissed from that position only minutes before the Canucks entered the NHL in the 1970–71 expansion, and was replaced by Bud Poile.

The 1970–71 season was spent as a broadcaster for the Canucks. Next season, Buffalo Sabres' general manager and coach George "Punch" Imlach hired Crozier to be the coach and GM of their AHL affiliate, Cincinnati Swords.

When Imlach suffered a heart attack midway through that year, Crozier was called up to fill in for Imlach. Crozier filled the bill extremely well, as he led the Sabres to a playoff berth and a tough series with the Montreal Canadiens, before finally losing in six games.

When the Sabres chose not to rehire Crozier after the 1973–74 season, Crozier was asked to coach the World Hockey Association Vancouver Blazers which he agreed to do, rather poorly, in 1974–75.

ROGER ALLAN CROZIER

BORN: Bracebridge, Ontario, March 16, 1942
POSITION: Goalie, Detroit Red Wings, 1963–70; Buffalo Sabres, 1970–
AWARDS: Calder Memorial Trophy, 1965; Conn Smythe Trophy, 1966; All-Star (First Team), 1965

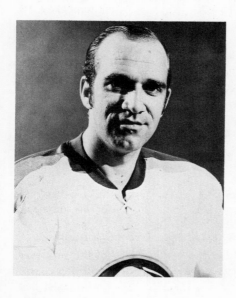

Coaxing Roger Crozier out of retirement is never an easy thing, although it has been accomplished more than once, the latest convincing being done by Punch Imlach in 1974. When Roger is sharp, he is among the best in hockey, but stomach and pancreas problems have hindered ''the Dodger'' since he captured the Calder Trophy in 1964–65 and the Conn Smythe the following season. His lifetime goals-against average is a hair over 3.00, despite playing with mediocre teams through most of his NHL tenure.

NELSON (NELS) CRUTCHFIELD

BORN: Knowlton, Quebec, July 12, 1911
POSITION: Defenseman/Forward, Montreal Canadiens, 1934–35

One season (1934–35) was all Nels Crutchfield could manage in the National Hockey League, but it was enough for him to gain notoriety. A utility defenseman-forward for the Montreal Canadiens, Crutchfield made the mistake of crossing the path of New York Rangers' right wing ace Bill Cook one night in March 1935.

It happened in a playoff game between the Rangers and the Montreal Canadiens. Bill Cook, the greatest right winger in Ranger history, couldn't untrack himself this night, and Nels, a Montreal rookie, wasn't exactly helping him. First, Crutchfield, who had made the jump to the NHL from McGill University, deposited Cook to the ice with an assortment of checks. Cook, who normally would have gone directly to war with the rookie, stuck to hockey. "I told the referee about it several times," Cook said, "but he wouldn't do anything about it."

Finally, Cook cornered the puck and wheeled for a rush toward the Montreal goal when who should appear on the horizon but Crutchfield. This time the crafty Cook was ready. He shoved the top of his stick through his gloves and into Crutchfield's body, a routine counterattack. "The next thing I saw," Cook remembered, "was a million stars."

Crutchfield axed Cook across the face with his stick, opening a deep cut. Before the Ranger ace could regain his equilibrium, the referee separated the two, sending them to the penalty box, almost. Instead, Crutchfield went mildly berserk.

Cook managed to avert catastrophe by deflecting the first of Nel's wild blows with his arm, but two blows were enough to defuse him for the moment. "When I finally came around," he said, "all I saw was the stockings of players scrappin'. I never saw so many people getting belted on the ice."

What he hadn't seen was his brother Bun leading a charge of Rangers over the boards. Bun carried his stick over his shoulder, racing on a collision course with Crutchfield who didn't see him coming. There are those who insist that Crutchfield would have been dead in less than a minute were it not for a thoughtful gesture on the part of the Cooks' linemate, Frank Boucher, who deftly stuck his skate out and tripped Bun just in front of his intended victim. "Frank told me," Cook added, "that he had to stop my brother, or Bun would have killed Crutchfield."

Just what persuaded the rookie to go on the rampage in the first place baffled observers for many years. It wasn't until eighteen years later that Aurel Joliat, Crutchfield's teammate, offered the explanation. "I had dinner that night," Joliat explained. "Nels ordered a great big steak. They must have given him a side of leather, because he had to saw away at it. After he'd eaten half of it, he made them take it back and bring him another. He ate all of that. I've always figured that meat made him kind of loco."

Cook required eight stitches to close the wound. "I was kinda groggy for the rest of the game." He returned to the lineup in the third period wearing a football helmet. Late in the game he captured the puck, stickhandled through the Canadiens' defense, and scored the winning goal. When the series was over, he vaulted the boards and churned his way toward Crutchfield. This time Boucher wasn't around to intervene, but it wasn't necessary. Cook removed his gloves and shook hands with the rookie.

WILFRED (WILF) CUDE

BORN: Barry, Wales, Great Britain, July 4, 1910
DIED: May 5, 1968
POSITION: Goalie, Philadelphia Quakers, 1930–31; Boston Bruins, 1931–32; Detroit Red Wings, 1933–34; Montreal Canadiens, 1934–41
AWARDS: All-Star (Second Team), 1936–37

Wilf Cude was a solid NHL goaltender who had his best years with the Montreal Canadiens of 1935–38. He was the Second Team All-Star goalie in 1936 and 1937 and provided living proof of the frustrations that can consume a goaltender.

It happened one night while the Canadiens were playing their neighboring rivals, the Montreal Maroons. Maroon forward Dave Trottier had the puck at center ice and was bearing down on Wilf in the Habitant nets. Suddenly, Trottier snapped off an unexpected long shot that whizzed past the startled Cude and into the cage.

With his stick raised triumphantly in the traditional "I just scored a goal" pose, Trottier circled the net, paused at the goal mouth and laughed in Cude's ever-reddening face. That did it. Swinging his heavy goalie's lumber like a medieval mace, Cude chased the still giggling Trottier all the way to center ice until the frenzied netminder was forcibly restrained by his teammates and led back to the confines of his goal crease.

BRIAN JOSEPH CULLEN

BORN: Ottawa, Ontario, November 11, 1933
POSITION: Center, Toronto Maple Leafs, 1954–59; New York Rangers, 1959–61

One of the chief reasons why the Toronto Maple Leafs aimed high but finished low in the midfifties was the mistaken hopes placed in Brian Cullen, a gifted high-scoring junior ace who was too slow and clumsy to become the superstar that Toronto scouts had predicted. In Brian's finest year, 1957–58 (43 points in 67 games), the Leafs finished dead last. The Leafs unloaded Brian to the Rangers in 1959–60. He played two terrible years on Broadway and then left the NHL for good; Toronto's answer to baseball's Clint Hartung.

CHARLES FRANCIS (BARRY) CULLEN

BORN: Ottawa, Ontario, June 16, 1935
POSITION: Forward, Toronto Maple Leafs, 1955–59; Detroit Red Wings, 1959–60

Second of the three Cullen brothers, Barry generated a bit less enthusiasm than Brian and produced somewhat less in three full seasons with the Maple Leafs (1956 through 1959) and one more with the Red Wings. Taller and huskier than Brian, Barry nevertheless was afflicted with the same problem—he wasn't as good as his junior hockey clippings.

RAYMOND MURRAY CULLEN

BORN: Ottawa, Ontario, September 20, 1941
POSITION: Center, New York Rangers, 1965–66; Detroit Red Wings, 1966–67; Minnesota North Stars, 1967–70; Vancouver Canucks, 1970–71

Like his brothers, Brian and Barry, Ray Cullen played barely passable NHL hockey for four teams. And like his older brothers, Ray simply didn't have enough of the goods to stick. He broke in with the Rangers in 1965–66, then touched ice for the Red Wings (1966–67), and North Stars (1967–68, 1968–69, 1969–70) before closing out his career in Vancouver (1970–71).

LES ROY CUNNINGHAM

BORN: Calgary, Alberta, October 4, 1913
POSITION: Center, New York Americans, 1936–37; Chicago Black Hawks, 1939–40

An absolute whiz in the minors—when the minors were virtually major league—Les Cunningham played briefly in the bigs for the Americans (1936–37) and Black Hawks (1939–40). He starred for years with the Cleveland Barons and eventually coached in the minors. During his stint in San Francisco of the old Pacific Coast Hockey League, Les started several youngsters to the top, including Wally Hergesheimer whom he taught to shift (to fake, or "deke" another player by moving quickly from side to side). Cunningham currently is western Canadian scout for the WHA's Cleveland Crusaders.

FLOYD JAMES "BUSHER" CURRY

BORN: Chapleau, Ontario, August 11, 1925
POSITION: Forward, Montreal Canadiens, 1947–48; 1949–58

A solid, workmanlike winger was Floyd "Busher" Curry. One of the lesser lights on the power-packed Montreal Canadien squad of the midfifties, Curry's specialty was stopping the opposing teams' big scorers.

Busher went about his task without complaint, forsaking the offensive duties and backchecking like a demon to blunt his opposite number. Called a coach's "dream player" during his days in the NHL, Busher went on to coach and generally assist in the Habs' system.

IAN ROBERTSON "CRASH" CUSHENAN

BORN: Hamilton, Ontario, November 29, 1933
POSITION: Defenseman, Chicago Black Hawks, 1956–58; Montreal
    Canadiens, 1958–59; New York Rangers 1959–60; Detroit Red
    Wings, 1963–64

Ian Cushenan was a mountainous defenseman with Chicago (1956–57, 1957–58), Montreal (1958–59), New York (1959–60), and finally Detroit (1963–64). Few opponents dared to cross Cushenan's path, but one who did was Doug Mohns, most recently with Washington, but who, at the time, was skating for the Boston Bruins. Trouble started when Cushenan accidentally dropped his stick. As he leaned over to pick it up, Mohns shot it away from him. Once again Cushenan went to retrieve it and again Mohns used his own stick to shove it further away. Then Doug skated blithely up ice, figuring that Ian would be occupied for a while.

This time the enraged Cushenan ignored the stick. Instead he took off after Mohns, drew abreast of him, and, without bothering to remove his gloves in the time-honored tradition, proceeded to crash his large, leather-armored hand against the side of Mohns's jaw with bone-shattering results.

Cushenan received a match misconduct, but only a $50 fine. President Campbell ruled that under ordinary circumstances the fine would have been higher, but that in this case Mohns had provoked the attack.

PETE CUSIMANO

Pete Cusimano never scored a goal in professional hockey. He never made a save, got an assist, or even served a two-minute bench penalty. Yet, Pete Cusimano is one of the most colorful and infamous characters hockey has ever known—Pete Cusimano threw octopi!

Pete and his brother Jerry were diehard Detroit Red Wing fans. During the 1952 playoffs the Wings were hot—they had already won seven consecutive contests and the two brothers felt that some symbolic sacrifice was in order.

"My dad was in the fish and poultry business," Pete explained, ". . . anyway, before the eighth game in '52, my brother suggested, 'Why don't we throw an octopus on the ice for good luck? It's got eight legs and that might be a good omen for eight straight wins." It was a stroke of pure genius.

April 15, 1952 marked the first time Pete Cusimano heaved a half-boiled denizen of the deep over the protective glass and onto the ice of the Detroit Olympia. With one loud *splaaat!* the fate of the Wings' opponents was sealed. Yes hockey fans, Detroit won the Cup in 1952 and Cusimano, knowing a good thing when he saw one, continued to sling the slimy creatures in every Detroit playoff series for the next fifteen years.

The Red Wings have not fared as well in the playoffs as Cusimano would like, but then, there's throwing the octopus just for the sake of throwing it.

"You ever smelt a half-boiled octopus?" asks Pete. "It ain't exactly Chanel No.5 y'know." And with a maniacal gleam in his eye, he added, "You should see how the refs jumped."

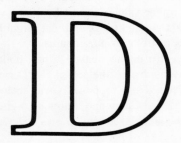

CARL "CULLY" DAHLSTROM

BORN: Minneapolis, Minnesota, July 3, 1913
POSITION: Center, Chicago Black Hawks, 1937–45
AWARDS: Calder Trophy, 1938

A native of Minneapolis, Minnesota, Cully Dahlstrom was one of the American-born players Major Frederic McLaughlin signed with the Black Hawks in his quest during the thirties for an All-American team. The major wasn't all that crazy about Dahlstrom and, in fact, preferred Oscar Hanson, but American-born coach Bill Stewart (the baseball umpire) preferred Dahlstrom. It turned out that Stewart was right. Dahlstrom underlined his coach's faith in him by winning the Calder Trophy as the NHL's rookie of the year. Dahlstrom later emerged as the Black Hawks' playoff hero in March and April 1938, when Chicago upset Toronto for the Stanley Cup. Dahlstrom remained a Black Hawk his entire career, retiring after the 1944–45 season.

HENRY (HANK) DAMORE

BORN: Niagara Falls, Ontario, July 17, 1918
POSITION: Forward, New York Rangers, 1943–44

During World War II, when the comedians Abbott and Costello were the hit of Hollywood, theatrical producers and sports promoters frequently tried to find Lou Costello lookalikes. By far the closest Lou Costello lookalike in pro sports was short, pudgy Hank Damore, a genuinely artistic and speedy—despite his girth—center who starred for the New York Rovers of the old Eastern League.

142

Because of his resemblance to Lou Costello, not to mention his artistry, Damore became a favorite of Sunday afternoon crowds at Madison Square Garden where the Rovers played. In 1943–44 Damore received a four-game tryout with the big-league Rangers and scored one goal. It was his one and only shot at the majors.

NICHOLAS (NICK) DAMORE

BORN : Niagara Falls, Ontario, July 10, 1916
POSITION: Goalie, Boston Bruins, 1941–42

Older brother of Hank Damore, Nick Damore was a goaltender who was born too soon. He made his National Hockey League debut in 1941–42 with the Boston Bruins when Frankie Brimsek was the darling of Beantown. Damore played only one game, allowed three goals and then starred for years in the minors. Had he been around for expansion hockey of the 1970s, he would have been considered a superstar.

JOSEPH "LEO" DANDURAND

It is quite possible that there would not be a Montreal Canadiens hockey club today were it not for the efforts of Leo Dandurand. A French-Canadian sportsman, Dandurand was a partner with Joe Cattarinich and Louis Letourneau in a Cleveland, Ohio, racetrack when the Canadiens were put on the auction block in October 1921. Since the Musketeers, as the trio was known, were occupied with their thoroughbred venture, they were unable to be in Montreal at the time of the sale, but Dandurand was consumed with a desire to obtain the hockey team. He phoned a friend, Cecil Hart, in Montreal and asked if he would stand in and bid as high as possible for the Canadiens.

Hart agreed and went to the auction where he found himself in competition with Tom Duggan, who was representing both himself and the Mount Royal Arena Company. Duggan opened with a bid of $8,000 and Hart countered with $8,500. The auction was abruptly halted when NHL president Frank Calder revealed that he was representing an Ottawa group intent on purchasing Les Canadiens. Calder said he wanted to contact his party for further instructions. At that point the bidding was postponed for a week.

When the auction was reopened, Duggan startled the audience by placing ten $1,000 bills on the table. Calder said he would top that. Now it was Hart's turn. He asked for time and dashed into the next room where he phoned Leo in Cleveland. Unfortunately, neither Letourneau nor Cattarinich was around when Hart called Dandurand. Leo decided to gamble and instructed Hart to go the limit.

The emissary returned to the room and raised the bid to $11,000, catching both Duggan and Calder unawares. The two adversaries looked at each other and conceded the decision to Hart who, in turn, ran out and phoned back Dandurand with the news. Leo didn't know whether to be jubilant or crestfallen, but he had no choice but to tell his partners they had just acquired a professional hockey team. The investment paid off immediately because Les Canadiens collected a $20,000 profit the first year they owned it.

JOHN PROCTOR (JACK) DARRAGH

BORN: Cornwall, Ontario, December 4, 1890
DIED: June 25, 1924
POSITION: Forward, Ottawa Senators, 1911–24
AWARDS: Hockey Hall of Fame, 1962

Jack Darragh, a steady, unspectacular and unselfish hockey player, toiled faithfully for his team, the Ottawa Senators, for thirteen seasons until his untimely death in 1924.

Only one other player, Harvey Pulford, skated for Ottawa longer than Darragh. Never a big star, Darragh chipped in amazingly consistent goal totals for the Senators in all but two of his thirteen campaigns.

But it was the playoffs where Jack really shone. Over eight Cup competitions, Darragh's totals read twenty goals in thirty games.

Jack saw four Stanley Cups come to Ottawa during his years of service there, although the last one, won in 1923, was captured without his services. Tired and weak after the grind of the regular season, Darragh chose not to make the trip west for the 1923 Cup competition. A year later he died of peritonitis.

ALLAN "SCOTTY" DAVIDSON

BORN: Kingston, Ontario, 1892
DIED: World War I
POSITION: Forward, Toronto Blueshirts (NHA), 1912–14
AWARDS: Hockey Hall of Fame, 1950

Allan Davidson learned his hockey in Kingston, Ontario, under the Father of Hockey, James T. Sutherland. Under Davidson's leadership, the Kingston Frontenacs won the OHA championship, overcoming a three-goal deficit to squelch Preston in the series. They repeated this performance in 1911.

Scotty turned pro with the Torontos the following year, and in 1912–13 he scored 19 goals in 20 games. Sometimes compared to New York Ranger immortal Bill Cook, Davidson scored 24 goals in his last season, as the Torontos won the Stanley Cup. Davidson was killed in action during World War I and was posthumously elected to the Hockey Hall of Fame.

GARY L. DAVIDSON

Gary Davidson and Dennis Murphy were the founders of the World Hockey Association in 1972. Davidson was no newcomer to the professional sports rivalry, having been instrumental in the formation of the American Basketball Association in 1967.

"It has been conclusively proved by the players themselves that there is room in hockey for a second major league," declared Davidson, explaining the philosophy for the birth of the WHA. "That those players had the courage to follow the leadership of the WHA's equally courageous owners is ample testimony to our credibility."

Davidson was the creator of the non-reserve clause in the standard player contract of the league, something unique in professional sports. This, plus the innovations in the new league's rules, gave the southern Californian cause for optimism concerning the future of the WHA, which had gotten off to a somewhat rocky start.

"You measure an enterprise by its growth," stated Davidson. "WHA franchises rose in value from $25,000 to $2 million within 18 months."

Davidson's active involvement with the league consisted mostly of assembling the financial packages needed to put a league in business. He slackened off in his private law practice to put more energy in the league.

Davidson retired as president of the WHA in 1974, succeeded as WHA president by his crony, Dennis Murphy.

JOHN DAVIDSON

BORN: Ottawa, Ontario, February 27, 1953
POSITION: Goalie, St. Louis Blues, 1973–75; New York Rangers, 1975–

Like his pop-singing namesake, John Davidson made the big time as a youngster. Unlike the show-biz celebrity, who only occasionally faces a hostile gathering, St. Louis goalie Davidson goes up against harsh opponents every night.

Davidson, the first draft pick of the Blues in 1973, became a regular netminder immediately, at the tender age of twenty. The 6′3″ goaltender was dealt to the New York Rangers in June 1975.

ROBERT (BOB) DAVIDSON

BORN: Toronto, Ontario, February 10, 1912
POSITION: Left Wing, Toronto Maple Leafs, 1934–46

A member of the Toronto Maple Leafs' organization nearly all his adult life, Bob Davidson most recently was known as the club's chief scout. However, during his playing days, which spanned 1934–46 (all with the Leafs), Davidson was a peerless defensive forward who also knew how to score. He managed a career total of 94 goals and 160 assists.

Davidson played for four Stanley Cup winners, but he's more often remembered for what he did *not* do—that is, guard Maurice Richard one night. During a game between the Leafs and Montreal Canadiens on March 23, 1944, Richard scored all five goals in a 5–1 Canadiens' win over Toronto, while Davidson supposedly was checking him.

"Midway through the second period," Davidson recalled, "I was checking Richard along the boards. Up to this point he hadn't scored and I was feeling pretty good. While I'm keeping him in against the boards a fan reaches over and grabs my stick. Naturally, I presumed the referee saw it and there would be a whistle. There was no whistle. While I'm held up by the fan, Richard slips away and scores. After that we couldn't get him stopped. He scored five, and I was on the ice for them all!"

CLARENCE HENRY "HAP" DAY

BORN: Owen Sound, Ontario, June 14, 1901
POSITION: Defenseman, Toronto St. Pats, 1924–26; Toronto Maple
   Leafs, 1926–37; New York Americans, 1937–38; Coach, Toronto
   Maple Leafs, 1940–50
AWARDS: All-Star (Coach, Second Team), 1944; Hockey Hall of
   Fame, 1961

Clarence "Hap" Day learned his hockey in a small Ontario village near Owen Sound. At times he would plod miles through the snow to find a place to play hockey, and he eventually became a leader with the Midland Juniors.

He proved his mettle one day on an outdoor rink, playing against bigger boys. The afternoon was bitter cold, heightened by an icy wind cutting across the hockey rink. In order to protect himself Day mistakenly donned a second sweater, which was considerably longer than the one he should have worn. Drooping down his body, the sweater gave Day the look of a larger skater and encouraged the enemy to take hefty charges at him from every angle. Day was constantly being smashed to the ice.

To the amazement of his foes, Day clambered back to his feet over and over again until a blow late in the game left him lying in a state of semiconsciousness along the sideboards. By then even the enemy had grown to respect young Day, and a group of players skated over to the fallen defenseman. "Y'know, kid," one of the bigger players on the opposition remarked, "you must be a lot lighter than you look." Day had come to his senses. He quickly dusted the ice shavings off his jersey. "Oh, no," he replied, "I'm really quite heavy. I must have slipped!"

Hap Day's courage and ability enabled him to climb the long, hard hockey ladder in Ontario. He moved from the Midland Juniors to the Intermediate sextet and then to Hamilton's Tigers. Hockey was not the only subject on his mind; Day wanted very much to be a pharmacist, and he enrolled at the University of Toronto, where he eventually obtained a degree. While attending the university he played for the varsity club. It was then that Charlie Querrie spotted Day and persuaded him—not without a considerable battle—to turn pro instead of applying for a job in the nearest drugstore.

When Querrie signed him, Day was a left winger. However, Conn Smythe believed that Hap's potential was more suited to defense, and he moved him back to the blue line when he took control of the Maple Leafs. Day was right at home in the defense slot and emerged as a superb, hard-checking defenseman who specialized in skating opponents out of the play. Later, as Leaf coach, he won Stanley Cups in 1942, 1947, 1948, and 1949.

DENIS DeJORDY

BORN: St. Hyacinthe, Quebec, November 12, 1938
POSITION: Goalie, Chicago Black Hawks, 1962–70; Los Angeles
    Kings, 1970–72; Montreal Canadiens, 1972; Detroit Red Wings,
    1972–74
AWARDS: Vezina Trophy (shared with Glenn Hall), 1967

Denis DeJordy was born a decade too soon. By the time expansion arrived DeJordy was approaching thirty and past his prime as a major league goaltender, which was a pity because Denis was the seventh best goalie in all hockey when the NHL was a six-team league. DeJordy's problem was that he belonged to the Chicago Black Hawks, and the Hawks' first-string goaler was "Mister Goalie" himself, Glenn Hall. As a result Denis played only small parts of the 1962–63, 1963–64, and 1964–65 campaigns at a time when he should have been honing his skills to sharpness. Two things happened—DeJordy played his best hockey with Buffalo of the American League and when he finally did get his NHL chance on a full-time basis in 1968–69 he was over the hill.

He was dealt to Los Angeles in 1969–70 and played equally poor hockey for the Kings and later (1971–72) Montreal (1972–73) and Detroit. He made a one-period return with the Red Wings in 1973–74, allowing four goals and confirming suspicions that DeJordy's beautiful-career-that-never-was had finally ended.

ALEX PETER "FATS" DELVECCHIO

BORN: Fort William, Ontario, December 4, 1931
POSITION: Center, Detroit Red Wings 1950–73; Coach, Detroit Red
   Wings, 1973–75; General Manager, Detroit Red Wings, 1974–
AWARDS: Lady Byng Trophy, 1959, 1966, 1969; Lester Patrick Tro-
   phy, 1974; All-Star (Second Team), 1953

"He's not the brawniest hockey player I ever saw—but he is one of the brain-iest." Those were veteran Red Wings' trainer Ross "Lefty" Wilson's words in describing his long time teammate, friend, and now boss as he presented Alexander Peter Delvecchio for the Lester Patrick Award in New York on March 18, 1974.

No one is better qualified to assess the talents of the former Red Wing than the irrepressible Mr. Wilson who watched Alex through twenty-two seasons as a player with the red and white machine.

Then, in the 1973–74 season, Lefty and all of hockey watched as the likeable and well-respected "Fats" moved from the role of team captain and highest scoring active player (Detroit and NHL totals: 1,549 games played; 456 goals; 825 assists; 1,281 points; and 383 penalty minutes) to coach and general manager of the team he skated for so long and so well.

Taking over as coach on November 7, 1973, Delvecchio quietly replaced turmoil and uncertainty with harmony and new spirit. The change was so evident that owner Bruce A. Norris tapped the former number 10 to be number one in shaping the future of the Red Wings. On May 21, 1974, Alex Delvecchio became general manager and coach with full authority in every phase of the club's operation. In June 1975, he gave up the coaching reigns to Doug Barkley and concentrated on managing.

ALBERT (AB) DeMARCO, SR.

BORN: North Bay, Ontario, May 10, 1916
POSITION: Center, Chicago Black Hawks, 1938–40; Toronto Maple Leafs, 1942; Boston Bruins, 1943–44; New York Rangers, 1944–47

A hawk-nosed forward who did time with Chicago, Toronto, Boston, and New York from 1938 through 1947, Ab DeMarco, Sr., had excellent puck sense that more than compensated for his frail physique. His best season was 1944–45 when he scored 24 goals and 30 assists for 54 points in 50 NHL games. He frequently starred on postgame radio shows conducted in the Rangers' dressing room by color commentator Ward Wilson. "Gee, Ward," DeMarco would say after every one of the frequent Rangers' losses, "we just didn't get the breaks tonight."

ALBERT THOMAS (AB) DeMARCO, JR.

BORN: Cleveland, Ohio, February 27, 1949
POSITION: Defenseman, New York Rangers, 1969–73; St. Louis Blues, 1973–74; Pittsburgh Penguins, 1974; Vancouver Canucks, 1974–

The son of former NHLer Ab DeMarco, Sr., Ab Jr. has been beset by an incredible string of injuries since breaking into the NHL in 1969. Originally a promising blue liner with the New York Rangers, Abbie started to bounce around the league as he gained a hard-luck reputation as a brittle player.

Possessing a deceptive skating style and one of the best point shots in the NHL, Ab has yet to put together a completely injury-free major league campaign.

CORBETT DENNENY

BORN: 1894
DIED: January 16, 1963
POSITION: Left Wing and Center, Toronto Shamrocks, (NHA), 1915; Toronto Arenas (NHA), 1916–17, 1918–19; Ottawa Senators (NHA), 1917; Toronto St. Pats, 1919–23; Vancouver Millionaires (PCHA), 1923; Hamilton Tigers, 1924; Toronto Maple Leafs, 1926–27; Chicago Black Hawks, 1927–28

Corbett and his brother Cy both started their hockey careers with the Toronto Shamrocks back in 1915. After the Shams folded, Cy settled down with the Ottawa Senators, but Corbett roamed around the ice-hockey world, getting in on two Stanley Cup acts with Toronto in 1918 and 1922.

A forward who could play either center or left wing, Corbett's best years were with Toronto when he pivoted a line with Reg Noble and Babe Dye. In 1923 he was traded to Vancouver and never truly regained his scoring touch. He helped Saskatoon reach the playoffs in 1925 and 1926, but never was on a Cup winner again. He finished out his career with Chicago in 1928.

CYRIL (CY) DENNENY

BORN: Farrans Point, Ontario, 1897
POSITION: Left Wing, Toronto Shamrocks, (NHA), 1915–16; Ottawa Senators, 1917–28; Boston Bruins, 1928–29
AWARDS: Scoring leader (prior to NHL's Art Ross Trophy), 1924; Hockey Hall of Fame, 1959

After the Toronto Shamrocks caved in financially, the Denneny brothers were signed by the Toronto Arenas where they skated together on a line centered by Duke Keats. This awesome threesome accounted for 66 goals during the 1916 season, tops in the league for scoring by a single line. There was only one problem though, the Arenas finished dead last.

Happily, Cy was rescued when the Ottawa Senators pulled off the coup of the season by sending $750 and a player named Sammy Herbert to Toronto in return for Denneny's services. It took only one season for Cyril to establish himself as the regular left winger on the powerful Senator squad—no one would unseat him for the next nine years.

A rough 'n tumble type player despite his small stature, Denneny was sometimes cast into an enforcer's role when looking out for smaller, mild-mannered linemates. The rugged Harry Broadbent was a tough cop on the beat as well, and when this duo was paired together, they were gleefully referred to as "The Gold Dust Twins" by the delirious Senator faithful.

Cy skated for five Stanley Cup teams in his long and illustrious career, four with the Senators and the fifth with the 1929 Bruins. He was a fantastic scoring machine, and although he only led the league once in total points—he never dropped below fourth in the standings for ten consecutive years.

After retiring in 1929, Cy saw service as a referee and hockey coach. He is a member of the Hockey Hall of Fame.

GERARD FERDINAND (GERRY) DESJARDINS

BORN: Sudbury, Ontario, July 22, 1944
POSITION: Goalie, Los Angeles Kings, 1968–70; Chicago Black Hawks, 1970–72; New York Islanders, 1972–74; Michigan Stags (WHA), 1974–75; Baltimore Blades (WHA), 1975; Buffalo Sabres, 1975–

Gerry Desjardins is a good goaltender who must be a masochist! After six seasons in the NHL, mostly getting bombed behind terrible teams, he decided in 1974 to bolt to the WHA. On the surface that might look smart, except that he went to the Michigan Stags, which eventually became the Baltimore Blades, during the 1974–75 season. By March 1975, he was on his way back to the NHL, with the Buffalo Sabres.

Desjardins began the pros as a Montreal property, but was traded to the needy Los Angeles Kings for two first-round draft choices in 1968. He played one and a half seasons in Los Angeles, compiling a respectable average despite the sorry state of the team. He made it well known, however, that he didn't want to spend his life in California being shelled, and was traded to the Black

Hawks in 1970 for Gilles Marotte, Jim Stanfield, and Denis DeJordy. He was in Chicago for more than two seasons, but played infrequently behind the flashy Tony Esposito.

Drafted by the newborn New York Islanders in 1972, he then received two years of shell shock behind the then terrible Islanders—it was either feast or famine! In May 1975 he helped Buffalo to the Stanley Cup finals.

DETROIT RED WINGS

Professional hockey in the Detroit area dates back to 1926 when a Detroit syndicate purchased the Victoria (British Columbia) Cougars of the Western Hockey League and moved the club to the Motor City. Playing their home games in nearby Windsor, the team finished in the league cellar.

But in the 1927 season things showed improvement. Ten-year NHL star Jack Adams began his illustrious thirty-five-year career with Detroit as manager and coach. The team moved into the gleaming new Olympia Stadium on the night of November 22, 1927. With a new leader and a new home, the Cougars played .500 hockey and finished in fourth place. But success in the late twenties was only moderate. In the 1930–31 season a change of nickname to Falcons failed to improve their fourth place finish.

Meanwhile in Chicago, industrialist James Norris was operating the semipro Chicago Shamrocks. He was itching to own an NHL franchise. Despite owning the Chicago Stadium, Norris was frustrated in his attempts to buy the Black Hawks, Major Fred McLaughlin's entry into hockey's premiere league.

Informed that, despite their second-place finish in the depression year of 1932–33, the Detroit franchise was on shaky ground financially, the patriarch of the Norris family successfully bid on and purchased both the hockey team and Olympia Stadium.

The name Falcons was supplanted by Red Wings, with the insignia of a winged automobile wheel, similar to that of a team called the Winged Wheelers with whom Mr. Norris had played in his earlier years in Montreal. The 1933–34 season saw the "new look" Norris franchise under Jack Adams win the league championship—the first of thirteen such triumphs for the red and white team. In 1935–36 they won it all—the NHL championship and their first of seven Stanley Cups.

Over the years, some of the most illustrious names in hockey have been identified with the Red Wings. Twenty-nine Red Wings are enshrined in the NHL Hall of Fame. More then eighty Red Wings have enjoyed All-Star status. Detroit players have captured upwards of forty individual league trophies.

The most amazing string of titles in NHL history was recorded from 1948–49 to 1954–55, when the Red Wings won a record seven consecutive league championships. In that span they captured four Stanley Cups.

The team and the Stadium have remained in the Norris family continuously. Following the death of the elder Norris in 1952, his daughter, Marguerite Riker, became president and is the only woman ever to hold that position with an NHL team. During her tenure the Red Wings finished in first place for three seasons and won the Stanley Cup twice (1954–55). In 1955, Marguerite relinquished the presidency to her brother, the current president, Bruce A. Norris.

ERNEST LESLIE (ERNIE) DICKENS

BORN: Winnipeg, Manitoba, June 25, 1921
POSITION: Defenseman, Toronto Maple Leafs, 1941–42, 1945–46; Chicago Black Hawks, 1948–51

A heavily bearded defenseman, Ernie Dickens was lionized as a rookie, whom the Toronto Maple Leafs inserted in their lineup while down three games to none to the Detroit Red Wings in the 1942 Stanley Cup finals. Dickens played capably and the Leafs won four straight and the Cup. During the 1947–48 season he was one of five players the Leafs traded to Chicago for Max Bentley and Cy Thomas in one of the NHL's biggest trades. His last big-league season was 1950–51.

JOHN HERBERT (HERB) DICKENSON

BORN: Mount Hope, Ontario, June 11, 1931
POSITION: Forward, New York Rangers, 1951–53.

There have been few more promising or more tragic figures than Herb Dickenson, a glittering New York Rangers' left winger who reached the NHL in 1951–52, scoring 14 goals and 13 assists for 27 points in 37 games. Skating on a line with Wally Hergesheimer and Paul Ronty, Dickenson was off to an excellent start in 1952–53 (4 goals and 4 assists for 8 points in 11 games) when an eye injury abruptly ended his hockey career.

ROBERT (BOB) DILL

BORN: St. Paul, Minnesota, April 25, 1920
POSITION: Defenseman, New York Rangers, 1943–45

Nobody epitomized the spirit of the Curtis Bay (Maryland) Coast Guard Cutters Eastern League team more than Bob Dill, a husky defenseman. The Cutters were known as "Hooligan's Navy," and Dill was one of the happiest and heaviest-hitting hooligans of them all. Dill played two NHL seasons (1943–44 and 1944–45) with the Rangers, leaving two memories. One was a

caption over a New York *Daily News* photo after Bob had scored a goal—DILL
PICKLES CLINCHER. The other was a fight with Maurice Richard in which the
Montreal ace twice flattened Dill in a matter of a few minutes.

CECIL GRAHAM (CEC) DILLON

BORN: Toledo, Ohio, April 26, 1908
POSITION: Right Wing, New York Rangers, 1930–39; Detroit Red
   Wings, 1939–40
AWARDS: All-Star (First Team), 1938 (tied with Gordie Drillon of
   Toronto); (Second Team), 1936, 1937

Cecil Dillon is one of the few natives of Toledo, Ohio, to star in the NHL. He
joined the Rangers in 1930–31 where he became a close friend of Frank Boucher. A lithe, handsome, black-haired forward, Dillon loved western stories
and longed to visit the plains states and the Canadian prairies. He had a quick,
accurate shot and skated on one Stanley Cup–winning team.

WAYNE DILLON

BORN: Toronto, Ontario, May 25, 1955
POSITION: Center, Toronto Toros (WHA), 1973–75; New York
   Rangers, 1975–

In their search for talent, World Hockey Association teams began signing
eighteen-year-old junior players prior to the 1973–74 season. One of the outstanding prospects obtained by the WHA's Toronto Toros was forward Wayne
Dillon, an eighteen-year-old who successfully made the jump from junior
hockey to the majors, becoming an instant star of great poise and maturity for
the Toros of Toronto.

   Dillon "jumped" the WHA in June 1975 and signed with the NHL's New
York Rangers.

BILL DINEEN

BORN: Arvida, Quebec, September 18, 1932
POSITION: Forward, Detroit Red Wings, 1953–57; Chicago Black
   Hawks, 1957–58; Coach, Houston Aeros (WHA), 1972– ; General
   Manager, Houston Aeros (WHA), 1975–

A solid journeyman forward, Bill Dineen became coach of the WHA's
Houston Aeros and led them to the Avco World Cup in 1974 and 1975.
During an NHL career that spanned 1953–58, Dineen played for Detroit and
then Chicago. In his rookie season, 1953–54, Bill scored an impressive 17

goals in 70 games. His manager Jack ''Jolly Jawn'' Adams promised Dineen a bonus in his contract from $6,000 to $6,500 for the 1954–55 season. ''I thought I was getting a raise of $500,'' Dineen recalled. ''What I didn't know at the time was that the NHL had raised its minimum salary from $6,000 to $6,500. So all Adams did was give me the minimum once again!''

MARCEL DIONNE

BORN: Drummondville, Quebec, August 3, 1951
POSITION: Center, Detroit Red Wings, 1971–75; Los Angeles Kings, 1975–
AWARDS: Lady Byng Trophy, 1975

Marcel Dionne of the Detroit Red Wings, a developing superstar, has been almost as confused as his beleaguered team in recent seasons. The Detroiters suffered with six coaches in a half-dozen years while searching in vain for a playoff combination. It isn't that Dionne played bad hockey. In 1973–74 his 78 points (24 goals and 54 assists) led the team. In 1971–72, his 77 points as a rookie set a mark for National Hockey League freshmen, and the next season he upped the total to 90, with 40 goals and 50 assists.

The problem has been that Dionne and the Red Wings became entangled in the totally disorganized Ned Harkness regime in Detroit, as did ''Mister

Hockey'' himself, Gordie Howe, who quit the Wings and signed with the WHA's Houston Aeros in 1973–74.

Dionne's dilemma began midway through the 1972–73 campaign when Johnny Wilson was the Red Wings' coach, and before the dispute was over, Marcel and Harkness were to have their falling out. The boiling point was reached when Harkness accused the 5' 8", 175-pound Dionne of not giving "the old 100 percent" in practice.

"I'm not going to give 100 percent in practice," snapped Dionne. "I don't believe practice makes perfect. I think it can only hurt a player if he skates his very best in practice." This sentiment put him on a collision course with Wilson and a suspension followed.

But Wilson soon was fired by Harkness and into the maelstrom stepped Ted Garvin, a tough, "old-school" coach who strictly policed facial hair and shaggy heads, and ran his practices with heavy emphasis on fundamentals. Only days after Garvin took over, a major clash erupted between Garvin and Dionne. Before November 1973 was gone, so was Garvin, fired by Harkness, who replaced him with easy-going Alex Delvecchio. Even with Delvecchio piloting the club, Dionne was in trouble. General Manager Harkness felt that Dionne symbolized the pampered young hockey player.

Harkness got his walking papers late in the 1973–74 season and into the breach stepped Delvecchio, a sophisticated, laissez faire operator who became both coach and general manager.

In a dramatic departure from Garvin's rigid authoritarianism, Delvecchio took a soft-sell attitude toward his skaters. In 1974–75 Dionne responded with 47 goals and 74 assists for 121 points. Still unhappy Marcel became a free agent in June 1975 and was obtained by the Los Angeles Kings.

KENNETH EDWARD (KEN) DORATY

BORN: Stittsville, Ontario, June 23, 1906
POSITION: Forward, Chicago Black Hawks, 1926–27; Toronto Maple
    Leafs, 1932–35; Detroit Red Wings, 1937–38

Even the severest of hockey critics acknowledged that the Toronto–Boston playoff confrontation on April 3, 1933, remains one of the classic sports events of all time. It was marked by robust bodychecks, superlative goaltending by Lorne Chabot of Toronto and Tiny Thompson of Boston—and not a single goal in regulation time.

One by one the clubs battled through period after period of sudden-death overtime and the game went on into the early morning. Early in the sixth overtime Bruins' defenseman Eddie Shore attempted a clearing pass which was intercepted by Andy Blair of Toronto. Blair spotted Ken Doraty and slipped a pass to the little forward, who raced in and scored the winning goal, at 4:46 of the sixth overtime—164:46 of the game, the longest game played in the NHL up until that time.

ROBERT JAMES (JIM) "FLIPPER" DOREY

BORN: Kingston, Ontario, August 17, 1947
POSITION: Defenseman, Toronto Maple Leafs, 1968–72; New York Rangers, 1972; New England Whalers (WHA), 1972–75; Toronto Toros (WHA), 1975–
AWARDS: All-Star (WHA) Second Team, 1973

A product of the Toronto Maple Leafs' organization, "Flipper" Dorey was once best known for his wild checking and excessive penalties, and once held the record for most penalty minutes in one game (48). Dorey was traded to the New York Rangers for Pierre Jarry in 1972, and the Rangers' docile defensive corps could have used the beef, but Dorey was injured in his first game.

Jim jumped to the WHA in 1972–73, playing for the New England Whalers. A physical fitness nut, Dorey was dealt in 1974–75 to the Toronto Toros.

GERHARDT (GARY) DORNHOEFER

BORN: Kitchener, Ontario, February 2, 1943
POSITION: Right Wing, Boston Bruins, 1963–67; Philadelphia Flyers,
    1967–

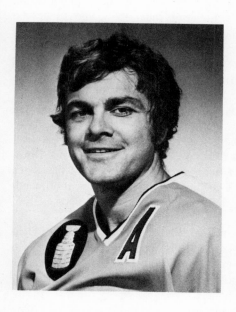

It is amazing that Gary Dornhoefer missed only twenty-five contests in the
Flyers' Stanley Cup season of 1973–74. The big right winger was plagued by
torn knee ligaments and a broken wrist during the regular campaign, yet still
managed to total 50 points. His best season was 1972–73, when Dorny accounted for 30 goals and 49 assists. Originally the property of the Boston
Bruins, Gary derived as much pleasure as anyone in beating the Bruins for the
Cup in 1974, even though he was sidelined in game three of the final series
with a shoulder separation.

EDDIE DOROHOY

BORN: Medicine Hat, Alberta, March 13, 1929
POSITION: Forward, Montreal Canadiens, 1948–49

Eddie Dorohoy, who played for the Montreal Canadiens in post-World War II
years, could probably be called the most outspoken player ever to hit the big
time. Unfortunately, his gift for gab was greater than his hockey ability.

Dorohoy was only nineteen years old when the Montreal Canadiens promoted him to the NHL. Normally, a rookie would be awed in the hallowed surroundings of the Canadiens' dressing room, with immortals such as Maurice "Rocket" Richard and Elmer Lach around him. But not Eddie "the Pistol" Dorohoy.

The moment coach Dick Irvin placed the rookie on a line with Lach and Richard, Dorohoy began telling the old masters how the game should be played. On one occasion the three of them were launching a rush during an intrasquad scrimmage when Dorohoy abruptly skidded to a halt and demanded a conference. It was like Jimmy Durante telling the New York Philharmonic to "Stop the music!"—in the middle of Beethoven's Fifth.

Dorohoy somberly called Richard and Lach over to him. "Listen," he said, glaring at the pair as if he was the coach, "the trouble with you guys is that you're out of position."

Irvin, who was watching the episode from the sidelines, nearly fell over backward with laughter at the sight of Dorohoy lecturing his stars. But Dorohoy noticed Irvin out of the corner of his eye and demanded that the coach cease and desist immediately. "What's so funny?" said Dorohoy, reprimanding the senior coach in the league. "Richard and Lach can make mistakes, too. I'm only trying to help them."

Dorohoy wasn't much help to the Canadiens that season. They slumped terribly and Irvin soon became disenchanted with his funnyman. Dick suggested that the 150-pound Dorohoy go on a crash diet to increase his weight on the theory that it would help his scoring potential. Eddie managed to stuff himself enough so that he finally reached 162 pounds.

"Now," said Irvin, "you're too fat and soft!"

"The only thing soft," countered Eddie, "is your head."

"Maybe," snapped the coach, "but you're benched."

Even with Dorohoy on the sidelines the Canadiens lost. Irvin was beside himself with rage and wished that he could persuade his gabby forward to learn how to score goals. "Why can't you put that puck in the net?" demanded the exasperated Irvin.

"From the angle on the bench I'm sitting on," quipped Dorohoy with unimpeachable logic, "I'm lucky to touch the puck."

That did it as far as Irvin was concerned. He demoted Dorohoy to the Canadiens' farm team in Dallas, Texas, which was about as far away from Montreal as Irvin could send a player, although Dick thought he could still hear Dorohoy's voice echoing clear across the United States. "Sure, I pop off," Dorohoy agreed, "but I don't say anything malicious. What's the use of living if you can't say what you think?"

Dorohoy eventually wound up playing for Victoria in the Western Hockey League and, if anything, his filibustering increased. "I must be the only hockey player in history," he boasted, "who was ever fined in the summer. Hell, I just took it out of my unemployment insurance."

KENT DOUGLAS

BORN: Cobalt, Ontario, February 6, 1936
POSITION: Defenseman, Toronto Maple Leafs, 1962–67; Oakland
    Seals, 1967; Detroit Red Wings, 1968–69; New York Raiders
    (WHA), 1972–73; New Jersey Knights (WHA), 1973–74
AWARDS: Calder Trophy, 1963

Rescued from the wilds of Eddie Shore's Springfield Indians by Toronto Maple Leafs' mastermind Punch Imlach, Kent Douglas won the Calder Trophy as NHL rookie of the year in 1962–63. One of the NHL's brainiest defensemen, Douglas remained a Toronto iceman until the 1967–68 season when he was signed by the expansion Oakland Seals. The Seals dealt him to Detroit that same year and Douglas finished his NHL career the following season with the Red Wings. However, the advent of the World Hockey Association was a bonanza for Douglas. He was signed by the New York Raiders in 1972–73 and though he never regained his proper playing weight, played commendably enough in the WHA for two seasons before returning to the minors to stay.

GORDIE DRILLON

BORN: Moncton, New Brunswick, October 23, 1914
POSITION: Right Wing, Toronto Maple Leafs, 1936–42; Montreal
    Canadiens, 1942–43
AWARDS: Art Ross Trophy, 1938; All-Star (First Team), 1938, 1939;
    (Second Team), 1942; Hockey Hall of Fame, 1975

One of the best NHL scorers was a 6'2", 178-pound right winger from Moncton, New Brunswick. Hefty and handsome, Drillon alarmed Leaf manager Conn Smythe in one way: He seemed disinclined to fight, and that left Conn wondering whether Gordie could fill Charlie Conacher's skates. In his rookie year, 1936–37, Drillon scored 16 goals and 17 assists for 33 points in 41 games. A season later he had established himself as a first-rate forward with 26 goals, 26 assists, and 52 points. He led the league in goals and points.

Unfortunately, Drillon had two raps against him: He was following the beloved Conacher, and he had a habit of scoring the kinds of goals that lacked spectator appeal. The public considered Drillon more lucky than skillful and tended to label his efforts "garbage goals."

Those who followed Drillon and studied his craft soon realized that there was a subtle secret to Gordie's goal-scoring. Drillon would park himself in front of the net, angle his stick, and allow passes to ricochet off the stick blade and into the cage before the goalie could move. This skill was accomplished after long weeks of practice with Broda, his goaltender.

"Drillon's stick," said Bill Roche of the *Globe and Mail*, "was pressed to the ice with all the right winger's power. Broda was kept jumping from one goalpost to another as the puck bounced sharply off Drillon's blade.''

Although Roche appreciated the genius behind Drillon's seemingly simple play, opponents kept ribbing Gordie about his ''luck.'' Once he was severely withered by veteran players on the New York Americans, who happened to steal a look at Drillon in a private workout with Broda and a teammate.

Just then Red Dutton, manager and coach of the Americans, drifted by and heard the carping. He admonished his athletes that they'd do better to study Drillon than to scorn him. That night Gordie scored two of his ''garbage goals,'' the Maple Leafs won, and Dutton lost not only the game but a hat he had thrown on the ice in utter disgust after his players had allowed Gordie's second goal.

Drillon was named to the Hockey Hall of Fame in 1975.

CHARLES GRAHAM DRINKWATER

BORN: Unknown
POSITION: Defenseman and Forward, Montreal Victorias, 1893, 1895–99
AWARDS: Hockey Hall of Fame, 1950

Hall of Fame member Charles Drinkwater played not only for championship teams while he attended McGill University (football as well as hockey) but he went on to play for the Montreal Victorias who copped the Stanley Cup in 1895, 1897, 1898, and 1899—this, of course, was when the Cup was strictly an amateur contest.

JUDE DROUIN

BORN: Mont-Louis, Quebec, October 28, 1948
POSITION: Center, Montreal Canadiens, 1968–70; Minnesota North Stars, 1970–1975; New York Islanders, 1975–

Like many Quebeçois youngsters, Jude Drouin dreamed of someday playing center for the Montreal Canadiens. Unlike most French-Canadian boys, Drouin got the chance to do precisely that—for twelve games—in which he registered one assist. Drouin's break came when he was dealt to Minnesota in 1970, a year in which he set a mark for rookies with 52 assists. Despite his size—or lack of it—Drouin, one of the best stickhandlers in the game, became an important cog in the North Star machinery.

In the middle of the 1974–75 season he was traded to the Islanders, where he starred in the Isles' miracle playoff performances, before they succumbed to the Flyers in a seventh semifinal game.

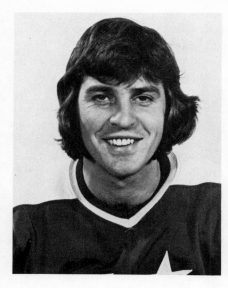

Jude Drouin

DAVID MURRAY (DAVE) DRYDEN

BORN: Hamilton, Ontario, September 5, 1941
POSITION: Goalie, New York Rangers, 1961; Chicago Black Hawks, 1965–70; Buffalo Sabres, 1970–74; Chicago Cougars (WHA), 1974–75; Edmonton Oilers (WHA), 1975–

Dave Dryden, who is one-half of a goaltending brother act, toiled for the Chicago Cougars in 1974–75. He joined the Cougars after several good seasons for the Buffalo Sabres of the NHL, and before that, the Chicago Black Hawks. He is Ken Dryden's older brother.

In 1973–74, Dryden enjoyed his best season, as he played in 53 games for the Sabres, posting a very admirable 2.97 goals-against average, plus a starting spot on the East Division All-Star team.

After the Cougars folded in the spring of 1975, Dave signed with Edmonton of the WHA.

In a game against the Montreal Canadiens in early 1971, Dave played goal at one end of the ice for Buffalo, while down at the other end, his brother Ken played for the Canadiens. It was the first time that two brothers faced each other in goal in an NHL game.

Dave Dryden

KENNETH WAYNE (KEN) DRYDEN

BORN: Hamilton, Ontario, August 8, 1947
POSITION: Goalie, Montreal Canadiens, 1970–73, 1974–
AWARDS: Calder Trophy, 1972; Vezina Trophy, 1973; Conn Smythe
   Trophy, 1971; All-Star (First Team), 1973; (Second Team), 1972

The bombshell of September 1973—"Ken Dryden quits hockey for the law books"—was obliterated by the bombshell of May 1974, when the elongated goaltender signed a record contract with the Montreal Canadiens, returning to the nets after a season that saw the Canadiens collapse in his absence.

Dryden began his National Hockey League career in the NHL limelight. Elevated by the Canadiens late in the 1970–71 season, from the Montreal Voyageurs of the American Hockey League, Dryden played in only six regular-season games. Then, as the Canadiens captured the Stanley Cup under coach Al MacNeil, Dryden won the Conn Smythe Trophy as the most valuable player in the playoffs. Dryden posted a 2.24 goals-against average in 1971–72, his official rookie season (he was still considered a rookie because he had played less than 26 games in the previous season) and was awarded the Calder Trophy as the best NHL freshman. The next season, his average climbed a hair to 2.26, as he played in 54 games, 10 less than his rookie year. Dryden carted home the Vezina Trophy for this effort.

It was then that Ken dropped the big verbal bomb. He announced he was quitting pro hockey to take a $7,000-a-year job as a law clerk in Toronto.

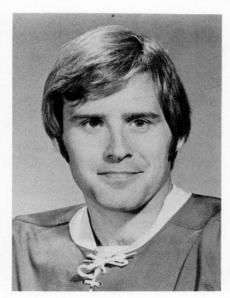

Ken Dryden

Money was—and wasn't—his object. He was willing to work for peanuts as a law clerk because the Habs weren't willing to meet his financial terms. ''If you want to have an ongoing relationship,'' said Dryden about Sam Pollock (Canadiens' general manager) and the Canadiens, ''you've got to be reasonable about money. This contract was going to upset me and the relationship couldn't be maintained.''

Dryden's replacements were three relative novices—Wayne Thomas, Michel Plasse, and Michel ''Bunny'' Larocque. Many observers felt the Canadiens would fold without extra competence between the crossbars. Ultimately, they were right. Meanwhile, Ken enjoyed several activities, among them, playing defense in a Toronto industrial league. He also did television commentary for the Toronto Toros of the World Hockey Association.

Naturally, the rumor mill flourished. Would Dryden jump to the WHA in 1974–75? It was no secret that he and Pollock had had their differences. Toros' president John Bassett wanted to build a new arena and would need a drawing card. Evidently Dryden would be able to choose between a five-year, $1,000,000 WHA contract and a three-year $450,000 Canadiens' contract. All was resolved on May 24, 1974, when Dryden returned to Montreal to sign his new NHL contract. The McGill Law School graduate employed an old Cornell classmate, Arthur Kaminsky, as his agent. The contract was one of the highest ever for goalies, estimated at well over $100,000 a year. But Ken had a mediocre year in 1974–75 as the Canadiens were wiped out of the Stanley Cup playoffs by Buffalo.

RICHARD CLARENCE (RICK) DUDLEY

BORN: Toronto, Ontario, January 31, 1949
POSITION: Left Wing, Buffalo Sabres, 1972–75; Cincinnati Stingers
    (WHA), 1975–

Rick Dudley developed into one of those rare professional athletes who excelled at two sports, ice hockey and lacrosse. He turned hockey pro with the
Minnesota North Stars' organization, but was shelved by a leg injury in less
than two seasons. Buffalo obtained the rights to Dudley after a tip from an old
lacrosse coach. Dudley made his NHL debut in 1972–73 with the Sabres, but
didn't achieve eminence until the 1974–75 season, when he became the team's
fifth leading scorer with 31 goals. He hurt his knee during the 1975 Stanley
Cup playoffs against Montreal and missed the first two contests of the Cup
finals against Philadelphia. When he returned, the Sabres won the next two.

Following the Sabres' elimination in six games, Dudley announced he had
joined Cincinnati's new team in the rival WHA.

DICK DUFF

BORN: Kirkland Lake, Ontario, February 18, 1936
POSITION: Left Wing, Toronto Maple Leafs, 1954–63; New York
Rangers, 1964; Montreal Canadiens, 1965–69; Los Angeles
Kings, 1970; Buffalo Sabres, 1971–72

A smallish but tough left wing, Dick Duff skated exclusively for the Toronto
Maple Leafs from 1955–56 until February 1964 when he was traded to the New
York Rangers in a major deal involving four other Leafs and two Rangers.
Moody and unpredictable, Duff scored his highest number of goals (29) in
1958–59. But his finest moment in the NHL occurred in April 1962 at Chicago
Stadium when he beat Black Hawks' goalie Glenn Hall to give the Stanley Cup
to Toronto for the first time since 1951. As a Ranger, Duff was useless, but in
1964–65 he was traded to Montreal for Bill Hicke and suddenly came to life
again. In 1967–68 he scored 46 points in 66 regular games for the Canadiens
and Montreal won the Stanley Cup. He was equally effective the following year
and once again the Canadiens took the championship. Duff was traded to Los
Angeles in 1969–70 and then to Buffalo in 1970–71. He played eight games for
Buffalo in 1971–72 before permanently leaving the NHL.

WOODROW WILSON CLARENCE "WOODY" AND "PORKY" DUMART

BORN: Kitchener, Ontario, December 23, 1916
POSITION: Left Wing, Boston Bruins, 1936–54
AWARDS: All-Star (Second Team), 1940–41, 1947

The Boston Bruins' crack Kraut Line usually spotlighted center Milt Schmidt or
right winger Bobby Bauer. But its left winger, Woody Dumart, packed a hard
shot and did the less flashy checking that kept him more in the shadows than
his pals. Dumart and Schmidt originally played together—without Bauer—for
Kitchener in the Ontario Hockey League, a junior league for players under
twenty-one. Dumart made his debut with the Bruins in 1936–37 and played his
entire career in Boston, culminating with the 1953–54 campaign. One of Dumart's least-publicized but most effective performances occurred during the
1953 Stanley Cup semifinals against the first-place Detroit Red Wings. Woody,
an aging veteran, was asked to shadow the inimitable Gordie Howe, Detroit's
crack right wing. Dumart accomplished his task so well that the Bruins upset
the Red Wings in six games and Howe was limited to only two goals.

ARTHUR (ART) DUNCAN

BORN: 1892
DIED: April 13, 1975
POSITION: Defenseman, Vancouver Millionaires, 1916, 1919–25;
     Toronto, 228th Battn., 1917; Detroit Cougars, 1926–27; Toronto
     Maple Leafs, 1927–30; Coach, Toronto Maple Leafs, 1931–32

A big broth of a defenseman, Art Duncan spent most of his professional hockey career minding blue lines for the Vancouver Millionaires of the old PCHA. Paired with his partner, the artful Lloyd Cook, this defensive duo guided Vancouver to four consecutive league championships from 1921 to 1924.

Sadly, the spell was broken the following season when Cook departed for Boston of the NHL. Several replacements were matched with big Art, but it just wasn't the same.

Traded to Calgary the following season, Duncan finally finished out his playing career with Toronto of the NHL. Art went on to serve as coach of the Maple Leafs. He died in 1975.

THOMAS (TOMMY) DUNDERDALE

BORN: Unknown
POSITION: Center, Toronto Shamrocks (NHA), 1910; Quebec Bulldogs (NHA), 1911; Victoria Aristocrats (PCHA), 1912–15, 1919–23; Portland Rosebuds (PCHA), 1916–18
AWARDS: Leading Scorer (PCHA), 1913, 1914; Hockey Hall of Fame, 1974

Tommy Dunderdale, a high-scoring pivot man, began his pro hockey career with the NHA's Shamrocks in 1910. He scored 14 goals in 12 games with the Irish—it was an omen of bigger and better things to come.

After a season-long stint with Quebec, Dunderdale moved out to Victoria of the newly formed PCHA. Pacific Coast goalies regretted his itch to move out west for the next 12 seasons.

During that time, Dunderdale became the all-time leading lamplighter in PCHA history. Surprisingly, Tommy led the league in scoring for only two seasons during this splurge, losing out on 1920 honors by but one goal.

Tommy's lifetime stats show 225 goals scored in 290 games over a span of seventeen seasons. But a more startling barometer of Dundy's effectiveness around the net are his numbers for the eleven campaigns which saw him at the top of his game—they read an amazing 190 goals scored in 185 contests.

Dunderdale began to slacken off in 1921, however, and he finished out his career with Saskatoon and Edmonton in 1924.

ANDRE "MOOSE" DUPONT

BORN: Three Rivers, Quebec, July 27, 1949
POSITION: Defenseman, New York Rangers 1970–71; St. Louis Blues, 1971–73; Philadelphia Flyers, 1973–

Rejected by the Rangers and Blues, Andre Dupont is a boisterous defenseman reclaimed by Flyers' coach Fred Shero during the 1972–73 season and turned into a first-rate defenseman. "Dupont," said Philadelphia *Bulletin* writer Jack Chevalier, "is one of a handful of players who give the fans $8 worth of entertainment every night." The rap against the French-Canadian toughie in New York and St. Louis was that he turned overemotional in many games, took foolish penalties, and hurt rather than helped his team.

"Andre is learning," said Shero, "but he still drives me crazy sometimes." Dupont was a Flyers' hero in their 1974 Stanley Cup triumph over the Bruins and could very well turn into an All-Star by 1980. The man they call "Moose," had been carefully tutored by Flyers' assistant coach Mike Nykoluk. "Moose," said Nykoluk, "has to learn to think." However, Chevalier probably said it best: "It's possible that thinking could spoil Dupont's game!"

HARRY STEVEN (STEVE) DURBANO

BORN: Toronto, Ontario, December 12, 1951
POSITION: Defenseman, St. Louis Blues, 1972–74; Pittsburgh Penguins, 1974–

"Steven Durbano," Toronto *Star* columnist Milt Dunnell once said, "has been described as vicious, vindictive, hot-tempered and irresponsible." Certainly, Steve's record as a brawler in Canadian junior hockey supports the latter description. Playing and alternately brawling for the Toronto Marlboros in the Ontario Hockey Association, Durbano amassed 371 penalty minutes in the 1968–69 season and 324 minutes the following year.

In the NHL, he immediately sold tickets and impressed opponents. "One night we played against him in his rookie NHL year," said then Vancouver coach Vic Stasiuk, "and he handled the puck like Bobby Orr. He's big and now he's finding out that no one wants any part of him. He's handling the puck with confidence because nobody wants to touch him."

The New York Rangers, a traditionally nonbelligerent club, owned Durbano, but the St. Louis Blues, who preferred a little more mustard on the ice, wanted Steve and dealt goalie Peter McDuffe and center Curt Bennett to New York for Durbano in June 1972.

Already armed with the hot-tempered Plager brothers, Bob and Barclay, St. Louis was now overflowing with fast punchers. And, almost immediately, Steven began swinging away. During a five-game stretch in February 1973, Durbano logged seventy-six penalty minutes and sat out a two-game sentence for allegedly throwing a glove at referee Ron Wicks.

In January 1974, St. Louis traded Durbano to Pittsburgh with Ab DeMarco and J. Bob Kelly for Bryan Watson, Greg Polis, and a draft choice. He continued his pounding ways there until early in the 1974–75 season when he suffered a compound fracture of his wrist, leaving him a great deal of time to ponder the wages of his sins on ice.

WILLIAM ARNOLD (BILL) DURNAN

BORN: Toronto, Ontario, January 22, 1915
DIED: Toronto, Ontario, October 31, 1972
POSITION: Goalie, Montreal Canadiens, 1943–50
AWARDS: Vezina Trophy, 1944 through 1947, 1949, 1950; All-Star (First Team), 1944 through 47, 1949, 1950; Hockey Hall of Fame, 1964

Bill Durnan's approach to goaltending suggested Georges Vezina. Like Vezina, Durnan played without a pair of skates until his teens, when a friend

Bill Durnan

"borrowed" his father's unused blades and urged Bill to wear them. Durnan protested that it made little sense wearing the blades even if he was playing goal because he really couldn't skate. In time he made it to Montreal.

"We weren't impressed with Durnan at first," said Canadiens' manager Tommy Gorman, "but he seemed to get better with every game. As goaltenders go he was big and hefty, but nimble as a cat and a great holler guy."

Les Canadiens assumed that Durnan would fit right into the lineup for the 1943–44 season, especially when it was learned that Paul Bibeault had received his call from the Canadian army. Gorman invited Bill to the Canadiens' training camp at Ste. Hyacinthe, Quebec, and the elderly "rookie" quickly impressed Irvin with his ability to glove shots.

"Sign him up," Irvin urged, "and we'll open the season with Durnan in the nets." They did and Les Habitants were off and running to one of the most extraordinary seasons that any team ever enjoyed in the NHL. Durnan, in turn, developed into one of the NHL's finest goaltenders.

NORM DUSSAULT

BORN: Springfield, Massachusetts, September 26, 1925
POSITION: Forward, Montreal Canadiens, 1947–51

Little Norm Dussault was living proof that speed alone could not make a successful major leaguer. A native of Springfield, Mass., Dussault played for the Montreal Canadiens from the 1947–48 season through the 1950–51 campaign, dazzling opponents with his footwork and little else. In 206 regular NHL games, Dussault scored 31 goals and 62 assists and soon sped his way through the minors.

MERVYN A. "RED" DUTTON

BORN: Russell, Manitoba, July 23, 1898
POSITION: Defenseman, Montreal Maroons, 1926–31; New York
     Americans, 1931–36; President of NHL, 1943–46
AWARDS: Hockey Hall of Fame, 1958

Red Dutton, a great defenseman of the early NHL, broke into pro hockey with Calgary of the old WCHL. After five years with the Tigers, Dutton signed with the Montreal Maroons where he spent four years gleefully bouncing opposing forwards off the boards.

In 1931, Red was traded to the New York Americans in exchange for the great Lionel Conacher. Red was one of the leading badmen of the day, but the Americans were basically a hapless bunch of skaters with no real leadership to speak of.

It was not until 1936, when Red became player-manager of the Americans that they began to approach respectability. Dutton's leadership got the Amerks into the playoffs, but he suffered a painful back injury and was forced to watch from the sidelines as the Toronto sextet bounced the Americans back to Broadway in the semifinal round.

After Dutton retired as a player, he served as manager for six more seasons. The Redhead remained very active on the pro hockey scene and was president of the NHL for three years from 1943 to 1946. Dutton is a member of the Hockey Hall of Fame.

CECIL HENRY "BABE" DYE

BORN: Hamilton, Ontario, May 13, 1898
DIED: January 3, 1962
POSITION: Right Wing, Toronto St. Pats, 1919–21, 1921–26; Hamil-
     ton Tigers, 1921; Chicago Black Hawks, 1926–27; New York
     Americans, 1928–29
AWARDS: Art Ross Trophy, 1923, 1925; Hockey Hall of Fame, 1970

A right winger with limitless potential, Cecil "Babe" Dye was unique among young athletes who learned their trade in the renowned Jesse Ketchum School playground in Toronto. Raised by his mother on Boswell Avenue, Babe had lost his father only a year after he was born. Esther Dye vowed that her son would not lack athletic instruction and proceeded to help her son. "Essie" Dye was an exceptional woman, and nobody appreciated her more than her son. "Mom knew more about hockey than I ever did," Babe once remarked, "and she could throw a baseball right out of the park. She could even cook—as a pinch-hitter!"

Esther Dye's first order of business when the first winter frost arrived was to flood the backyard rink adjacent to their house; then she would lace on the skates with Cecil. She taught her son until Babe knew everything there was to know about handling a puck, especially the art of shooting it at blinding speed.

"Babe could shoot the puck from any length or from any spot on the rink," said Canadian author Ron McAllister. "He could score with his back turned, or from any side at all. In time, he played with the older boys of the neighborhood, who were forced to welcome him, in spite of his size, for young Dye had a shot like a thunderclap and an astounding accuracy. His light weight became only secondary for Dye because he could snap a two-inch plank with one of his drives." Babe could pitch and hit a baseball as well as he could manipulate a puck. In 1919 he was invited to sign with the Baltimore Orioles, but he refused in favor of a contract with the Toronto baseball club. Babe's heart was torn between baseball and hockey. His compromise was to play both sports, but his name was to be parlayed into a household word because of his exploits on the ice, starting with the 1921–22 season, when he donned the Toronto colors.

The Babe played magnificently, scoring 30 goals in 24 games to tie for the league lead with Harry Broadbent of Ottawa. In the playoffs Babe Dye didn't assert himself to the utmost until the Stanley Cup finals reached the second game. Vancouver, with Lester Patrick behind the bench, edged the St. Pats 4–3 in the first contest, but a goal by the Babe at 4:30 of sudden-death overtime gave Toronto a 2–1 win in the second game. Vancouver went ahead for the last time in the series with a 3–0 triumph in the third match.

Dye continued to sparkle in the Toronto colors. He scored 17 goals in 19 games during 1923–24 and still hadn't reached his peak. Thanks to the Babe's 38 goals in 29 games, Toronto finished a close second to Hamilton in the 1924–25 race. League arrangements called for the second-place Toronto team to meet the third-place Canadiens for the right to play Hamilton in the NHL finals. However, the Hamilton players staged a surprise strike, demanding more money. League president Frank Calder angrily rejected their demands and ordered the winner of the Montreal-Toronto series be declared league champions.

This time Dye was overshadowed by a new star on the NHL horizon. Howie Morenz outshone Dye, leading Montreal to a 3–2 victory in the opening playoff game in Montreal and a 2–0 return match at Toronto. The Babe, meanwhile, was held scoreless and the St. Pats lost possession of the Stanley Cup.

Dye played one more season, 1925–26, with Toronto and scored 18 goals.

However, he was traded to Chicago the following year, scoring 25 goals for the Black Hawks. His swan song was played in 1928–29 when the Babe played briefly and ingloriously for the New York Americans. That ended his illustrious NHL career.

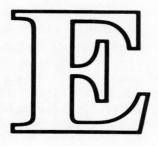

ALAN EAGLESON

Alan Eagleson, a bespectacled Toronto attorney, has had as much impact on the game of professional ice hockey as Clarence Campbell or Bobby Orr.

It was through Orr, hockey's version of the Messiah, that Eagleson first burst brashly into the public eye. When Orr was only a teen-ager, he was a million-dollar commodity in the eyes of the lords of ice hockey, and Orr's father, a sensible enough chap, figured that if his son was properly represented, he could swing the best possible financial deal for himself. How right he was.

Under the eagle eye of none other than Eagleson, Orr negotiated an absolutely unheard of contract for a first-year player—$40,000 per year for two years—almost four times the original figure offered him by the Boston Bruins.

A new day had finally dawned on the world of professional hockey. In short order, Eagleson's crusades led to the reinstatement of Carl Brewer's amateur status, the formation of the NHL players' association, the classic 1972 Team Canada–USSR series, and the removal of Eddie Shore as coach of the AHL's Springfield Indians because of "highly unorthodox" coaching techniques. Add to that list the scores of skaters under Eagleson's tender loving care and the man whom Bobby Hull said "did more for hockey in two years than anybody else did in twenty, as head of the NHL Players' Association."

FRANK HERBERT EDDOLLS

BORN: Lachine, Quebec, July 5, 1921
DIED: August 13, 1961
POSITION: Defenseman, Montreal Canadiens, 1944–47; New York
    Rangers, 1947–52

He didn't know it at the time, but defenseman Frank Eddolls was the cause of a breakup between two old friends and associates—Lester Patrick, the Rangers' vice-president and Frank Boucher, the club manager. In trying to rebuild the Rangers during the summer of 1947, Boucher dealt youngsters Hal Laycoe, Joe Bell, and George Robertson to Montreal for Eddolls and center Buddy O'Connor. Patrick, who was being phased out of the Madison Square Garden hierarchy, opposed the deal, but Boucher overruled him. "Lester," said Boucher, "stopped speaking to me."

The deal was a beauty for Boucher. Eddolls became one of the NHL's best defensemen and O'Connor won the Hart and Lady Byng trophies. Thanks to Eddolls, the Rangers made the playoffs in 1947–48 for the first time in six years. Frankie played for the Rangers through the 1951–52 season and starred for the New Yorkers in the 1950 playoffs when the Rangers took the Red Wings to the seventh game of the finals before losing. He later became a popular and successful minor league coach before his untimely death of a heart attack in the middle of a round of golf on August 13, 1961.

EDMONTON OILERS

Hockey fans on the Canadian prairie got their first taste of major league hockey with the formation of the Edmonton (then Alberta) Oilers. Soon after the World Hockey Association was organized, Bill Hunter, a prominent Edmonton entrepreneur, investigated the possibility of a franchise in that city, and the Oilers' franchise was among the ten original teams in the league. Hunter took the post of vice-president and general manager of the team.

Led by goalie Jack Norris and center Jim Harrison, the Oilers tied for fourth place in the Western Division their first season. They missed a playoff spot when they lost a playdown game to the Minnesota Fighting Saints, 4–2. The Oilers finished third behind Houston and Minnesota in 1973–74, and lost to the Saints four games to one in the opening round of the playoffs. Oiler defenseman Allan Hamilton, who had jumped to the WHA from the Buffalo Sabres, was named to the WHA's Second All-Star Team.

Hunter, who managed the WHA's Team Canada against Russia in 1974, has been responsible for many changes in Edmonton. Among them was the opening of the $13 million Coliseum replacing the team's old rink, which had a seating capacity of only 5,200. The new sports palace has a capacity of 16,000, with provision for an additional 4,000 spectators.

Hunter also brought the great Jacques Plante to Edmonton. At age forty-six, Plante made his second big league comeback, after a year as coach and general manager of the Quebec Nordiques, Limited to occasional appearances in the nets, he shared the netminding duties with Ken Brown and Chris Worthy.

Before the 1974–75 season, the Oilers moved into the WHA's Canadian Division, along with Quebec, Toronto, Vancouver, and Winnipeg.

MARTIN JOSEPH (PAT) "BOXCAR" EGAN

BORN: Blackie, Alberta, April 25, 1918
POSITION: Defenseman, New York Americans, 1939–43; Detroit Red Wings, 1943–44; Boston Bruins, 1944–49; New York Rangers, 1949–51
AWARDS: All-Star (Second Team), 1942

One of two players—the other being Paul Waldner of the Baltimore Blades—nicknamed "Boxcar," Pat Egan played defense for the New York Americans (1939–43), Detroit Red Wings (1943–44), and Boston Bruins (1944–49) before finishing his hard-hitting career with the Rangers. Although his last two seasons were on Broadway, they were among Egan's best. His thumping body-checks complemented the smooth style of defensemate Frankie Eddolls. As a result, Rangers' goalie Chuck Rayner came up with the best season of his career and won the Hart Trophy. The Rangers, in turn, went all the way to the seventh game of the Stanley Cup finals before losing to Detroit in a second sudden-death overtime. Pat left the NHL after the 1950–51 campaign.

EICHLER AUTOMATIC GOAL JUDGE

The Eichler Automatic Goal Judge was neither a goal judge nor automatic. When Eichler Beer was popular in New York City during World War II its theme was "You're the Tops" as in the Cole Porter tune of the same name. Eichler sponsored the New York Rangers' broadcasts on radio station WHN. The announcers were Bert Lee, Sr., and Ward Wilson, both waggish fellows with a creative bent. They persuaded Eichler officials that it would help sell beer if they devised horns which beeped out the opening notes to "You're the Tops." Eichler agreed and a series of three horns were strapped into the broadcasting cage overhanging Madison Square Garden whenever the Rangers played. Seconds after the Rangers scored, Lee would shout, "And now for the Eichler Automatic Goal Judge," and he'd beep the three horns to the tune of "You're the Tops." When Schaefer succeeded Eichler as the Rangers' sponsor, Lee trotted out a Schaefer Automatic Goal Judge, but it was very hard to beep out the theme "Our hand has never lost its skill."

CHAUCER ELLIOTT

BORN: Kingston, Ontario, 1879
DIED: March 14, 1913
POSITION: Forward (amateur only), 1899–1905; Referee (OHA), 1903–13
AWARDS: Hockey Hall of Fame, 1961

Playing "point" for the Kingston Granites in 1899, Hall of Fame member Chaucer Elliott led the team to a league title. He also coached the Hamilton Tigers, the Argonauts, the Montreal AAA, and even organized a semiprofessional baseball league that included Kingston. He later owned, organized, and managed St. Thomas in the old Canadian Baseball League.

In 1903 he became a hockey referee and was generally considered one of the best officials in the OHA. He officiated for some ten seasons.

RONALD JOHN EDWARD (RON) ELLIS

BORN: Lindsay, Ontario, January 8, 1945
POSITION: Right Wing, Toronto Maple Leafs, 1963–
AWARDS: Team Canada, 1972

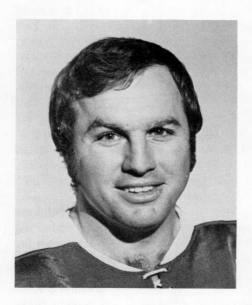

Perhaps the greatest compliment ever paid Ron Ellis, the steady, unspectacular winger for the Toronto Maple Leafs, was afforded by Ace Bailey, the legendary Leaf of years past. It seems that Ron wore jersey number eight for his first four seasons with the Leafs until Bailey himself suggested that Ellis be given number six. Six, by the way, happened to be Ace's very own numeral that was retired along with him when Bailey hung up his skates in 1934.

Ellis has been a model of consistency and unselfishness with the Leafs ever since he broke in as a regular in 1964. An honest, two-way hockey player, Ellis was one of the unsung heroes of the 1972 Team Canada–Soviet Union series. While linemate Paul Henderson deservedly got all the ink, Ellis's superb defensive work and positional play nullified the awesome scoring power of his opposite wingers in all eight games of the classic series.

EQUIPMENT

The shot came high from the stick of forward Larry Mickey and it had a murderous look about it. Like a guided missile on high, it appeared innocent enough from a distance. The hockey puck, six ounces of hard vulcanized rubber, blurred through the air. It was meant to go into the net, behind Gilles Villemure, the New York Rangers' goaltender. For a split-second Villemure lost sight of the hard piece of rubber. It was too late. Like a chunk of flak the puck slammed at about 95 mph into his neck and all 5′ 8″ and 170 pounds of Villemure crashed limply to the ice. "At first," said a teammate, "I thought he was dead."

Villemure survived, but the episode dramatized the vulnerability of hockey players—especially goaltenders—to injury in what is the world's fastest major sport. It is a vulnerability so great that on a goaltender, for example, a piece of protective equipment has been designed for every portion of the body—except the neck.

"What we really need," says WHA goalie Gerry Cheevers, "is something like an armored diver's helmet which would cover *everything* from the top of our head down to our neck." Eventually this may happen, because the design of new hockey equipment follows demand. It also may explain why hockey players are the most armored men in sports.

It wasn't always this way.

In fact, up until the midtwenties, goaltenders were frighteningly ill-protected from the missiles headed their way. For leg protection they wore nothing but borrowed cricket pads, and might still be wearing them today were it not for Pop Kenesky, an inventive Hamilton, Ontario, harness-maker who designed a pad which was wider and stuck out at the sides instead of going around the leg.

Pretty soon the National Hockey League goaltenders heard about Pop Kenesky's invention and they began buying them. Until his death in early 1975, ninety-eight-year-old tobacco-spitting Pop Kenesky was still hand-making the pads for nearly every goaltender in professional hockey and for several players in Europe. His design has been somewhat modified by the Gerry Cosby Sporting Goods firm in New York City.

Amazingly, the contemporary goalie pad differs little from the original model. Its width has been trimmed from 12 to 10 inches by league rule and some minor modifications have been made to suit particular goalies. But Pop, who made 300 pairs a year—charging approximately $140 a set—warned against tampering with his basic design.

Once Harvey Teno, a capable American League goalie, warned Pop that he was putting too much padding in the pads. Kenesky said he wasn't, but to please Teno he made a lighter pad. "Next thing I knew," said Pop, "he got hit in one of the weak spots and the poor guy quit hockey."

The Kenesky pad contains three pieces of cream-colored horsehide, felt, rubberized canvas, and special stuffing. The sides are stuffed with deer hair, and the front with kapok. According to Kenesky, the deer hair is light and provides top protection when stuffed hard. "On account of the slapshot, which comes so fast," said Pop, "I stuff the pads harder than I did years ago."

Pop didn't care to fool with unorthodox requests if he could help it, but he had some dandies in his day. When Earl Robertson tended goal for the old New York Americans he made a rare request of Kenesky, and Pop obliged. Robertson wanted a rabbit's foot stuffed into each pad. Another time, Pop put together a set of pads made out of goatskin for Johnny Bower of the Toronto Maple Leafs, but the process turned out to be too costly.

A more practical suggestion was made by Harry Lumley, then with the Detroit Red Wings. He disliked the straight up-and-down quality of the pads and asked Pop to build in a pocket at the shins—goalies call it a "scoop"—so that the puck drops straight to the ice when hitting it instead of rebounding to an opponent. Lumley's idea has been built into almost every pad since then.

Some goaltenders became so enamored with their Kenesky pads they refused to obtain new ones, although the team would foot the bill. Bill Durnan of the Montreal Canadiens won six Vezina trophies before he even *thought* about a new set of pads. Each spring he'd send his old set to the Kenesky shop in Hamilton, Ontario, and have them repaired. One year Pop's son, Frank, who now owns the business, suggested that Durnan try a new pair. "Y'know," the goalie shot back, "it's a good idea—but I'm quitting after this season. It would take me a whole year to break in a new set of pads."

Next to the goal pads the most personalized piece of hockey equipment is the goalie's face mask, which now is worn by all but one (Andy Brown of the WHA's Indianapolis Racers) regular big league netminder. A Massachusetts manufacturer as well as several NHL trainers have become known for their mask design, but nobody has cornered the market like Pop Kenesky.

The goalie mask still remains a contentious piece of equipment, on the grounds that it cuts off an all-important angle at the skate level. Jacques Plante is the man who introduced the mask to regular goaltending use while he was playing for Montreal. A shot by Andy Bathgate nearly decapitated Plante at Madison Square Garden and he left the ice smeared with blood.

"I never saw the shot that smashed into my face," said Plante. "When they stitched me up, Toe Blake, the Canadiens' coach, asked me if I would go back in. I said only if I could wear the mask which I had worn in our workouts. He okayed it and I played. I must have been a sight. The mask was crude. I was patched up, and there was just enough blood on my face to complete the picture.

"Later in the season I was in a slump and Blake asked if I'd mind taking off the mask, to regain my touch. I took it off one night in Detroit and they got three goals. After the game, Blake came over to me and said: 'Put the mask back on. I don't want to shoulder the blame if you get injured without it.' We began to roll after that game and went on to win the Stanley Cup in eight straight games. Since then the mask has been refined. It's stronger and lighter. A few years ago in the playoffs a shot by Fred Stanfield of Boston hit me right smack in the mask. If it wasn't for that protection I'd be dead today."

In addition to the mask and pads, goaltenders also are unique among hockey players in that they wear a thick, baseball-catcher's-like chest protector under their jerseys. Their gloves also differ, one being similar to a first-baseman's mitt—the better to nab the shots—and the other a rectangular piece of leather designed to deflect pucks out of danger.

Besides using his skates to block shots primarily, and doing little actual free-skating in comparison with his teammates, the goalie uses a decidedly different skate than his forwards or defensemen.

The traditional hockey skate blade is supported by two tubes at each end, connecting with the tubular blade. The goalie's skates are tubeless, consisting of one long blade—reminiscent of an old-fashioned skate—stretching from in front of the boot to the back. The upper side of the blade has several tongues of steel extending upward from the bottom to prevent pucks from slipping through the opening between the blade and the bottom of the skate boot. Since the pucks often strike the goalie's boot at speeds of upwards of 120 mph, a thick fiber covering protects each boot from the steel reinforced boxed toe back to the heel.

More and more forwards and defensemen are wearing helmets. Since the death of Minnesota's Bill Masterton in 1968 following a collision on the ice at Metropolitan Sports Center, a clamor has persisted to make helmets mandatory. Yet owners and managers—who believe players appear more glamorous and appealing without a helmet—insist that the choice should be a personal one made by the players themselves.

As a result, many players refuse to wear the helmets, which is curious since helmets have been a vital part of football equipment since Pudge Hefflefinger, the last of the bareheaded breed, retired in 1898. The complaint about hockey helmets is that they (a) are too cumbersome, (b) too hot, (c) too loose, and (d) curb one's hearing potential. In addition there is a certain psychological masculine element involved. However, helmets are now mandatory at the amateur, college, and junior levels, a portent of the future.

Larry Zeidel, who played pro hockey for more than twenty years, accumulated two fractured skulls and more than 200 stitches in his head alone, yet he never accepted a helmet as a regular piece of equipment. "Nobody else wore one," said Zeidel, now a Philadelphia stockbroker, "so, naturally, I didn't want to be the first!"

Gloves, however, are always worn. For a goaltender, the glove may be the most important baggage he carries to the crease with him. In order to stop the bullets shot at him from opposing slapshooters, cage guardians use the same glove as a baseball first baseman. Having a "quick glove hand" is as necessary to a goalie as a mask these days. It is illegal to play with a damaged glove, and few players would be caught at such a disadvantage.

Hockey sticks are made from northern white ash trees, hard wood sufficiently strong to take a lot of punishment. No stick can exceed 55 inches in length or be more than 12½ inches thick from the heel to the top of the shaft.

The blade of the stick is between two and three inches in width and all edges must be bevelled. The curve of a blade can vary; the NHL forbids curves greater than half an inch, the WHA allows curves up to an inch and half.

The rule limiting the curve of a stick came as a result of loud complaints by goaltenders, who were justifiably concerned that shooters could get the puck off at speeds in excess of 100 miles an hour. The WHA, trying to promote action and scoring, allows the more pronounced curve.

The puck itself hasn't changed much. The slabs of vulcanized rubber an inch thick and three inches in diameter are frozen before the game to make them slide easier over the frozen surface. The home team is responsible for keeping an adequate supply on hand and for freezing them. Aside from its bevelled edges the puck looks the same as it did when hockey was first played—only it is harder to see now!

AUTRY ERICKSON

BORN: Lethbridge, Alberta, January 25, 1938
POSITION: Defenseman, Boston Bruins, 1959–61; Chicago Black Hawks, 1962–64; Toronto Maple Leafs, 1966–67; Oakland Seals, 1967–68, 1969–70

The only National Hockey League player ever named after oldtime cowboy star Gene "I'm Back in the Saddle Again" Autry, Aut Erickson alternately skated for Boston, Chicago, and Oakland between 1959–60 and 1969–70. In 1966–67, while a Toronto Maple Leafs' farmhand, he was called to the NHL to skate in one playoff game. When the New York Islanders entered the NHL in 1972–73, he was named an aide to general manager Bill Torrey. Erickson made headlines in a somewhat unusual manner during the June 1974 hockey meetings in Montreal when Hall of Famer Eddie Shore unloaded a punch that sent Erickson careening across the press suite after Aut allegedly pestered the former NHL star.

ANTHONY JAMES (TONY) ESPOSITO

BORN: Sault Ste. Marie, Ontario, April 23, 1943
POSITION: Goalie, Montreal Canadiens, 1968–69; Chicago Black Hawks, 1969–
AWARDS: Calder Trophy, 1970; Vezina Trophy, 1970, 1972 (with Gary Smith), 1974 (with Bernie Parent); All-Star (First Team), 1970, 1972; (Second Team), 1973, 1974

One thing the National Hockey League has never lacked is brother acts—the Bentley boys, Rocket and Pocket Rocket Richard, and the high-scoring Hulls, to name a few, all of them first-rate forwards and stars of their day. So when Tony Esposito, fourteen months the junior of brother Phil, made his big-league debut in goal against the Oakland Seals on November 29, 1968, hockey followers did not take special notice. No fanfare, no big buildup—Phil's "kid brother" was just another rookie netminder about to be painfully indoctrinated into the frozen world of ricocheting rubber.

Just before the Thanksgiving holiday in 1968, thirty-nine-year-old Gump

Worsley suddenly walked out on the Montreal Canadiens during a trip to the West Coast. Tony, then playing for the Houston Apollos, was instructed to join the parent club in Los Angeles. "I'll never forget that night," the 5'11", 185-pounder recollected with a smile. "What a thrill it was to climb into a Montreal uniform, even if it was only to sit on the bench."

Tony played sparingly for the Habs. In June 1969 the Canadiens left him unprotected in the intraleague draft and he was picked up by Chicago.

Tony fitted right into the Hawks' scheme. Coach Billy Reay displayed a lot of confidence in him by starting Espo in the 1969–70 season opener at St. Louis. Tony was bombed, 7–2, but Reay continued to give him the lion's share of the work while veteran goalie Denis DeJordy was relegated to a backup role.

Although the Hawks and Bruins finished in a virtual tie for first place in the East with identical point totals, Chicago was awarded that honor on the basis of most wins. That meant the Black Hawks would face the Detroit Red Wings in the opening round of the 1970 Stanley Cup playoffs, while Boston drew the New York Rangers.

Both the Hawks and the Bruins advanced to the semifinal round with relatively little trouble. The stage was set for one of the all-time classic grudge matches. The Boston players felt that they deserved first place since they had finished with the best won-lost percentage, while Chicago was determined to prove that they were the rightful heirs to the Prince of Wales Trophy, emblematic of first place in the NHL's East Division.

And needless to say, the Espositos had their own personal affair to settle. Tony was determined to keep his older brother off the scoresheet. But Phil put his seven-year NHL savvy to use and led the Bruins to the Stanley Cup by way of a four-game sweep of the Hawks. Poor Tony manned the goal in each game.

Even with Tony's outstanding goaltending the Hawks have been unable to nail down the big prize. Is Tony doomed to a career as an also-ran? Not according to brother Phil. He claims it's just a matter of time before his younger brother becomes the second member of the family to have his name inscribed on the Stanley Cup.

PHILIP ANTHONY (PHIL) ESPOSITO

BORN: Sault Ste. Marie, Ontario, February 20, 1942
POSITION: Center, Chicago Black Hawks, 1963–67; Boston Bruins, 1967–
AWARDS: Hart Trophy, 1969, 1974; Art Ross Trophy, 1969, 1971–74; All-Star (First-Team), 1969–75, (Second Team), 1968, 1975

There are some critics who unequivocally believe that Phil Esposito is the finest center ever to skate in the National Hockey League. They point to the indisputable fact that he regularly leads the NHL in scoring; that he is consistently voted to the First All-Star Team and that the Boston Bruins' renaissance di-

Phil Esposito

rectly coincided with his arrival in Beantown at the start of the 1967–68 season. For further emphasis the Esposito Marching and Chowder Society is quick to point out that Phil was chief architect of Team Canada's pulsating four-games-to-three (one tie) victory over the Russian National Team in September 1972.

"That series," said Toronto *Globe and Mail* columnist Dick Beddoes, "would not have been won without Esposito's big rough, relentless leadership. I saw him make what will become a hockey heirloom, passing down through the generations." However, there are others who insist that when you discuss Esposito it must be in the past perfect tense; that something left the hulking centerman in 1973 never to return. Phil-knockers mention that he was knocked out of the 1973 Stanley Cup playoffs with a bodycheck from Ron Harris, a third-string New York Rangers defenseman. The anti-Esposito clan then emphasizes that Phil seemed to have lost his scoring touch in the clutch when Boston skated in the 1974 and 1975 playoffs.

Which proves, more than anything, that there are at least two sides to the Esposito controversy. There is, however, absolutely no doubt that he is a superstar. Just the fact that he was able to recover from the near-crippling 1973 knee injury to win the 1973–74 scoring title—his fifth in six years—is testimony to the man's superiority and gumption.

Because he has worked with two burly and gifted wingmen, Ken Hodge and Wayne Cashman, Esposito has been virtually unstoppable in his favorite camping ground outside the face-off circle about 15 feet from the net. One scouting report on Esposito analyzed him this way:

"Esposito combines reach, strength, intelligence, and competitiveness to the degree that the only way he can be countered is with superbly coordinated defensive play.'' As a result, Esposito is the surest bet among active players with a chance of surpassing Gordie Howe's all-time record of 786 NHL goals. This proves that Phil can score equally as well in the NHL as he could against the Europeans. In fact, he was the one member of Team Canada in 1972 who could not be handled by the Soviet defensemen.

''I'll tell you how good Phil Esposito is,'' said Buffalo Sabres' manager Punch Imlach. ''When you're playing against Espo, you start at least one goal down.'' There's nothing vague about that; yet many experts have a considerable problem defining the Esposito style. Unlike teammate Bobby Orr and the flamboyant Bobby Hull, Esposito relies more on subtle skills.

''You can't compare Orr and me or Hull and me,'' said Phil. ''They bring people to their feet. They are spectacular players. Orr is the best player in the game; I know it and I admit it. I also know that my role is to score goals, to pick up loose pucks and put them behind the goaltender any way I can. So that's what I try to do—and the people still call me a garbage collector.''

While Phil's ex-teammate, Bobby Hull, built his reputation on a booming slapshot, Esposito concentrates on a quick wrist drive that is deadly accurate, though Phil rarely looks directly at the net. ''I've developed a feel for where it is, just as John Havlicek of the Celtics has a knack for knowing where the basket is. Besides, taking even the quickest look wastes precious time.''

Two big plusses for Esposito have been linemates Hodge and Cashman, both tough and remarkably adept at finding loose pucks in corners—partly because the enemy doesn't like to challenge them—from where they deposit them on Phil's waiting stick. ''Without Cashman and Hodge,'' Esposito freely acknowledges, ''I wouldn't score half as many goals.''

As life would have it, nearly all of Esposito's goals were forgotten when the Philadelphia Flyers knocked off the Bruins in six games in May 1974 to become the first expansion team to win the Stanley Cup.

Unlike most opponents, the rambunctious Flyers completely manacled Esposito, who was topped in every department—especially face-offs—by the tenacious Bobby Clarke. Even more grating were the words of Bruins' coach Bep Guidolin who singled out Esposito and other Boston skaters for lack of effort. ''Determination and second effort is what beat us,'' said Guidolin. ''Our big players should have worked harder and put out more. Too much money is being paid to some individuals.''

It was a stinging rebuke, perhaps deserved, perhaps not. Certainly, those who have revered Esposito through the years believed that Guidolin had verbally skated on thin ice. ''How do any of us,'' snapped Dick Beddoes, ''justify defacing Phil Esposito? Guidolin exhibited a sort of graceless taste considering that Esposito's sweat, through a prolonged schedule, was a major factor in making Guidolin resemble a genius.'' Guidolin was replaced for 1974–75, but Phil went on, finishing second in scoring behind Orr, with 61 goals and 66 assists in regular season play, for 127 points.

CLAUDE EVANS

BORN: Longueuil, Quebec, April 28, 1933
POSITION: Goalie, Montreal Canadiens, 1954–55; Boston Bruins, 1957–58

Although it never could be definitively proven, Claude Evans is believed to be the inventor of the "latter-day upright goaltending position." According to this theory, most shooters don't know where they are shooting the puck; and, more often than not, if given both corners of the net to shoot at, the forwards will inevitably either shoot wide or into the upright goaltender. As a result, Evans accomplished more with less physical activity than most goaltenders. However, most of his accomplishments took place in the minors.

A native of Longueuil, Quebec, Evans played three NHL games for the Montreal Canadiens in 1954–55, allowing 12 goals in three games for a 4.00 goals-against average. The Boston Bruins invited Evans up for one game in 1957–58. This time he allowed four goals. It has been said that Evans rarely went down to the ice to block a shot. He merely stood in the middle of the goal crease and let the shooters either fire wide, hit the post, hit him—or score!

WILLIAM JOHN (JACK) AND "TEX" EVANS

BORN: Garnant, South Wales, Great Britain, April 21, 1928
POSITION: Defenseman, New York Rangers, 1948–58; Chicago Black Hawks, 1958–63; Coach, California Seals, 1975–

There have been few players with more raw strength than Jack "Tex" Evans who split his NHL career between the Rangers (1948 through 1958) and the Black Hawks (1958 through 1963). Tex also was renowned for his "lantern jaw" and his reluctance to speak. When Evans roomed with the equally shy Andy Hebenton, their entire day-long conversation went as follows:

"Tex, do you wanna see a movie today?"

"Yup!"

End of twelve-hour Evans–Hebenton dialogue.

Evans was named coach of the California Seals in May 1975.

WILLIAM "WILD BILL" EZINICKI

BORN: Winnipeg, Manitoba, March 11, 1924
POSITION: Right Wing, Toronto Maple Leafs, 1944–50; Boston Bruins, 1950–52; New York Rangers, 1954–55

"Wild Bill" Ezinicki had sinewy arms and a body that bulged from daily weightlifting. A right winger for the grand Toronto Cup winners (1947–48, 1948–49), he had a passion for free-skating that was outdone only by his passion for bodychecking. He also had a passion for tape, winding reams of it around his stick and around his knees and legs until they bulged grotesquely.

Once Wild Bill had four teeth knocked out in a key homestretch game, but despite pain and nervous shock, he returned to score the winning goal. He would collide with opponents—usually bigger opponents—from any direction. Sometimes he would wait for an opponent to speed in his path, and then he would bend forward, swing his hips, and send his foe flying over him. If Ezzie got the worst of a fracas—which did not happen often—he could still get consolation from his insurance policy; the policy paid him $5 for every stitch resulting from a hockey injury. "It's just like double indemnity," he'd say.

Ezinicki was adored in Toronto and despised everywhere else. The Red Wings charged him with deliberately injuring goalie Harry Lumley. Boston *Globe* writer Herb Ralby said, "Toronto has the leading candidate for the most hated opponent in Ezinicki." In New York a woman in a front row seat jammed a long hatpin in Ezinicki's derriére as he bent over to take a face-off. On November 8, 1947, Ezinicki crumpled Ranger center Edgar Laprade to the ice with a bodycheck. Laprade suffered a concussion, and Ranger coach Frank Boucher protested to league president Clarence Campbell with a scathing telegram:

LAPRADE IN HOSPITAL WITH CONCUSSION FROM CHARGE BY EZINICKI AFTER WHISTLE ON AN OFFSIDE PLAY. REFEREE GEORGE GRĀVEL CLAIMS HE DID NOT SEE OFFENSE. HOW MUCH LONGER IS EZINICKI GOING TO GET AWAY WITH EL-BOWING, HIGH-STICKING, AND DELIBERATE INJURIES TO OPPONENTS? BELIEVE CURB MUST BE PUT ON THIS PLAYER IMMEDIATELY.

Smythe counterattacked the charge by urging Campbell to fine Boucher $1,000 for "acting in a manner prejudicial to the league." Smythe's trump card was a movie of the action. He offered to have a special screening for Boucher and six New York writers who were visiting Toronto. Boucher refused, and Smythe chortled: "They don't want to see a legal bodycheck. It might give their players a bad habit."

Eleven days after the incident Campbell completed his investigation and said, "Reports of the officials show that the check by Ezinicki was perfectly legal and not a charge. The injury to Laprade was not caused by Ezinicki's stick but by Laprade striking the ice as he fell."

Soon after Campbell's decision Smythe was named president of Maple Leaf Gardens, and Ezinicki was toasted by some of his most fearsome opponents. "He's a tough little guy," said Montreal's equally tough Ken Reardon, "but he's definitely not dirty. He can check and pester you and sometimes hurt you, and he can make you mad, but he's not dirty. Because he's short, he can hurt. Those low bodychecks of his enable him to throw his shoulder into your stomach." Ezinicki played on Toronto Cup winners in 1947, 1948 and 1949. He later was traded to Boston. After retiring from hockey he became a successful golf pro in Massachusetts.

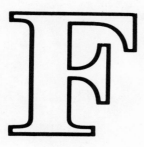

FACE-OFF

The face-off became a part of hockey thanks to referee Fred Waghorne. Waghorne knew from personal experience that many a referee was dissatisfied with the old manner of facing off, when the puck was placed on ice by the arbiter, who then had to make certain each center was lined up correctly and fairly. This often led to sticks in tender areas of the ref's anatomy.

Waghorne claims it was 1900 when he decided that dropping the puck, then "allowing them to do as they darn well pleased," was the best method of beginning play. So he did exactly that in a contest in "southwestern Ontario" and "didn't receive a single squawk from either players or fans."

The next winter, Waghorne was allowed to use the innovation in a National Hockey Association game at Almonte, and it has been a part of hockey ever since.

WILLIAM JOHN (BILLY) FAIRBAIRN

BORN: Brandon, Manitoba, January 7, 1947
POSITION: Right Wing, New York Rangers, 1968–

When Billy Fairbairn came up to the big leagues with the New York Rangers in 1968, he was so excruciatingly shy that the mere approach of a reporter would cause him to blush to his hair roots. Although he can now handle after-game repartee with less pain, reticence has remained his forte.

Fairbairn was almost immediately paired with center Walt Tkaczuk, forming one of the most formidable penalty-killing teams in the NHL. Billy is also ex-

Bill Fairbairn

cellent at digging the puck out of the corners fearlessly, although he is not one to fight unless goaded.

After a lengthy bout of mononucleosis in 1970, Fairbairn remained virtually injury-free through the 1974–75 season, practically a miracle for the perpetually decimated Rangers.

FANS

There are times when the people who pay to watch hockey games put on a better show than the players themselves. Observers differ as to which city has the wildest spectators in the NHL, but those from Boston, Chicago, and St. Louis rank at the top of the list.

For many years Bruin followers suffered through some of the worst hockey ever seen in any NHL city. Nevertheless, they still kept coming and, somehow, managed to retain their sense of humor. During the early sixties, when the

Bruins were at their lowest ebb, the Boston sextet received "help" from an unexpected source.

On a Monday morning following the usual Sunday night Boston defeat, a fan named Sandy turned up at the then coach Milt Schmidt's office. "I want a tryout with the Bruins," he insisted. "I've seen your team play and I think I can make the club."

Schmidt wasn't about to dismiss a philanthropist without a hearing. "How old are you? Who have you played for? What makes you think you can play in the NHL?"

Sandy listened intently and then replied, "I can skate faster than anyone on the Bruins and I'll bet $10 I can."

Intrigued by the man's gall, Schmidt suggested that Sandy return home and pick up his skates. Yes, he was willing to accept the challenge.

Sandy showed up the following morning with a pair of skates that had not been sharpened in two years. Bruins trainer Dan Canney took care of that and then Sandy was ready to take the ice. "What's your position?" asked Schmidt.

"Wing," said Sandy. So Schmidt decided to go along with the gag.

Murray Oliver, then a Bruins center, started a rush toward goalie Ed John-ston. Johnny Bucyk was on the left and Sandy on the right. When they arrived to within ten feet of the goalie Oliver slipped a perfect pass to Sandy. Precisely at that moment, Johnston stepped aside, leaving nothing but an open net for the skating fan. Sandy took a swipe at it but missed the puck and crashed into the endboards.

"I guess I'm really a defenseman," Sandy advised Schmidt. The coach obliged and decided to pair him with the veteran Leo Boivin.

Their first challenge was a three-man rush by the Oliver line. As Bucyk and Oliver picked up speed, Boivin began shouting at Sandy. "Back up, boy, back up!"

"For what?" demanded Sandy. But before he could finish his question the Oliver line had skated past them and scored a goal.

Schmidt wasn't about to give up on his prospect. "Now's your chance," said Schmidt, "pick a player and he'll race you for the ten-dollar bill."

"Never mind a player," said Sandy, "I'll race you instead."

Suddenly, the exuberant rooter reconsidered. "Ah, never mind," he insisted. "I don't want to embarrass anyone."

By contrast, Chicago fans would think nothing of embarrassing their own. "There was a fellow in the balcony," recalled ex-Black Hawk publicist Johnny Gottselig, "with a fedora on the end of a fishing line. He'd fire it onto the ice and then he'd haul it back up. One night he blew the whole thing. As he reeled in the hat, Frank Mahovlich, when he was with the Maple Leafs, swiped it with his stick and snapped it off the line."

At the time Gottselig also was handling the radio play-by-play for the Black

Hawks. "In those days," said Gottselig, "the broadcasts were sponsored by White Owl cigars. One night I was doing the game when right in front of me, dangling from a line, were half-a-dozen Phillie's cigars. Well, I knew that most of those people brought transistor radios to the game so they can listen as well as watch, so I made a point of saying 'make sure you get your White Owls on the way home.' The next game the line came down from above with a whole box of White Owls."

Gottselig remembered when a fan showed up at Chicago Stadium with a six-foot-six dummy of Mahovlich with a hangman's rope around his neck. "He wanted to hang Big M in effigy from the top balcony," said Gottselig. "We had to take it away from him. From that height it could have been dangerous if it fell on anybody."

It is generally conceded that hockey fans in Montreal and Toronto are the most decorous in the NHL. "They go to a game as if they're going to the opera," said Weston Adams, Jr., president of the Bruins. "Our fans can be a little rougher."

Others consider that an understatement. Pat Jordan, an author who had never been to Boston until the 1969–70 season, was astonished at the behavior of Bruins fans. "They do not come to their Garden for comfort," said Jordan. "Nor do they come after a fine dinner and cocktails like New York Rangers fans go to at their Garden. Boston fans come after an argument with their wives, their dinners pushed aside in anger. They come not to complement a good day, but in one last angry attempt to 'get even' with another in a long line of very bad days."

During the early fifties the "gallery gods" in New York hurled so much abuse at defenseman Allan Stanley that manager Frank Boucher felt obliged to trade him to Chicago; he played excellent hockey there and later continued to do so at Toronto.

Montreal's fans have been equally harsh on some of their own players. "They generally are more patient with a French-Canadian player," said former Canadiens' managing director Frank Selke, Sr. "But they show much less tolerance towards Anglo-Saxons."

As a result, Selke once was forced to do to his left wing Ab McDonald what Boucher did to Stanley. McDonald was dealt to the Black Hawks where he, too, became a star. "If Ab had stayed here," said Selke, "the fans would have ruined his morale. He would have been no good to anybody, including himself."

When McDonald returned to the Montreal Forum in a Chicago uniform a few weeks later he scored the winning goal for the Black Hawks and the Montreal fans hailed him with a hefty round of applause. "First they chase him out of Montreal," Selke lamented, "and now they applaud him!"

DOUGLAS ROBERT (DOUG) FAVELL

BORN: St. Catharines, Ontario, April 5, 1945
POSITION: Goalie, Philadelphia Flyers, 1967–73; Toronto Maple
Leafs, 1973–

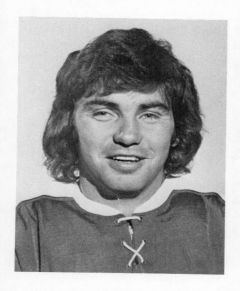

Doug Favell, a cherubic, slightly off-the-wall netminder, was traded to the Toronto Maple Leafs in 1973 in a deal that saw Bernie Parent's NHL playing rights transferred to the Philadelphia Flyers. A talented and acrobatic goaltender, Doug received his professional tutelage in the Boston Bruin organization before being picked by the Flyers in the 1967 expansion draft.

Favell labored for five years with the Flyers shouldering the bulk of the work over his last three seasons. Doug teamed with Ed Johnston and Dunc Wilson in a three-goalie rotation during his first season with Toronto. When Johnston was traded to St. Louis in 1974, the Leafs' number one spot went to the buoyant Favell. Doug is an indoor lacrosse professional in the off-season.

JOHN BOWIE (JOHNNY) FERGUSON

BORN: Vancouver, British Columbia, September 5, 1938
POSITION: Right Wing, Montreal Canadiens, 1963–71

When the third-place Boston Bruins took on the first-place Montreal Canadiens in the opening round of the Eastern Division's Stanley Cup playoffs in April 1968, there were whispers that the Canadiens were in for an upset. "You watch

John Ferguson

the Bruins' tough guys go after the smaller Montrealers early in the game, soften 'em up, and then you'll see the game turn in Boston's favor," one newsman prophesied.

In the first game of the series Canadien "policeman" Johnny Ferguson detected the Bruins' strategy on his radarscope and went after Ted Green. With one hand he grabbed Green's jersey and lifted it high over the Boston player's head so that Green was both blinded and partly handcuffed. And with the other hand, Ferguson pummeled Green about the head until there was little doubt that the Montrealer had scored a decisive victory over a man who rarely lost fights.

Just how decisive the victory was soon became evident. The Bruins turned pussycats and, with their tails between their legs, lost the series in four straight games. While Ferguson didn't exactly win the round for Montreal, he turned the psychological lever in their direction and the Canadiens roared on to win the Stanley Cup.

When Ferguson was playing for Cleveland in the American League, it was not uncommon for him to take on more than one opponent. Once, he was confronted by Gary Collins of Pittsburgh. "I suppose you think you're tough," Collins challenged Ferguson.

"Tough enough to handle you," Ferguson replied and then hauled off and belted Collins. The force of the blow sent both men sprawling through an open door, whereupon Bob Bailey, another Pittsburgh player, threw himself on Ferguson. Soon both benches cleared and a gala brawl took place that eventually resulted in a total of $610 in fines.

Respect was the key prize that Ferguson earned after joining Montreal in the 1963–64 season, and not merely for his fighting ability. During the Stanley Cup semifinal with the Rangers in 1967, it was Fergy who lifted the Canadiens into the finals by scoring the winning goal in sudden-death overtime for the fourth game. But scoring certainly was not his forte. A lumbering skater, he often suggested a rhinoceros galumphing up and down the rink. His shot was just average at best, and he was not exactly known for his stickhandling ability.

Fergie's intense hatred for the opposition extended beyond the ice, and he was known to snub his rivals even during the off-season, when he indulged his other great love, horse racing.

Johnny's involvement with hockey and the horses began in British Columbia where as a youngster he became both an exercise boy at the local stable and a "rink rat" for the arena.

But with the seventies came the era of the high-salaried player and Ferguson's fanatic intensity seemed out of place. Somewhat bitter about the blasé attitude of young pros, he retired from hockey to write a column on racing and manage a retail business.

GUYLE FIELDER

BORN: Potlatch, Idaho, November 21, 1930
POSITION: Center, Chicago Black Hawks, 1950–51; Detroit Red
    Wings, 1957–58

Although he is remembered by few outside of the Western League, Guyle Fielder became pro hockey's all-time leading scorer, totaling more than 2,000 points in a career that began in 1950–51 with the Chicago Black Hawks and concluded with the Portland Buckaroos of the Western League in 1972–73. With such impressive credentials it is difficult to believe that the smallish center couldn't make it in the NHL. He did have his big league chances.

Although playing for a minor league farm club, he was in four Stanley Cup playoff games with Detroit in 1953, in two playoff games with Boston in 1954, and started six games with Detroit in 1957. The Red Wings placed Fielder on a line with Gordie Howe and Guyle failed. "It might have been different if I'd been able to play on a line without Howe," he explained. "Gordie was the same type of player that I was. He liked to have control of the puck, make the plays, set up the others to score. There wasn't much point in having both of us out there on the same line." Guyle played six games, scored no points and then was released. "I said I'd rather play in the minors than sit on the bench in the NHL," said Fielder. And he did. Guyle never got another chance in the majors; but he won nine WHL scoring championships, led in assists for 13 years and was most valuable player three times.

J. A. FINDLAY

J. A. Findlay, an otherwise undistinguished referee, left his indelible mark on the annals of hockey officiating on the frozen Montreal afternoon of February 18, 1899. The Montreal Victorias were defending the Stanley Cup against the Winnipeg Victorias in a two-game, total-goals-scored series. Montreal had prevailed, 2–1, in the first contest and now, with time running out in the second game, was clinging to a 3–2 lead.

As a Winnipeg skater desperately lugged the puck out of his end in a last-ditch attempt to knot the score, a somewhat overzealous Montreal defender whacked him across the legs with a vicious two-hander. Referee Findlay, after assessing the damage, banished the offender for two minutes.

Winnipeg's bench exploded. Surely, they argued, this was a deliberate attempt to injure and merited at least a match penalty. Findlay disagreed and ordered the teams to line up for the ensuing face-off. Winnipeg refused to take the ice. Findlay took this bit of obstinance as a personal affront and, highly insulted, he huffily climbed into his horse-drawn sleigh and went home. With over 8,000 spectators not knowing what in blazes was going on, two arbitrators hastily arrived at Findlay's door and finally persuaded him to return to the rink and finish the game. More than an hour after his dramatic exit, Findlay finally returned and ordered both squads be ready to resume play in fifteen minutes. After the allotted time had passed and Winnipeg still refused to take the ice, Findlay awarded the game and the Cup to the defending Montreal Victorias and was never heard from again.

CHARLES O. FINLEY

A baseball entrepreneur, Charles O. Finley believed that it would be good business to own a hockey team in Oakland, as a companion to his Athletics' baseball club. The Oakland Seals, which had been suffering financially ever since the opening game in 1967–68, became available to Finley prior to the 1970–71 season. The flamboyant "Charlie O" bought the hockey club and promptly changed its name to the California Golden Seals. He added colored skates, new jerseys, and several other gimmicks, but the Seals finished with the worst record in either division. Matters actually worsened under Finley's regime. He claimed that his manager, Garry Young, had signed players to exorbitant contracts without his knowledge and Young was fired. The Seals continued to flounder and Finley became more and more of an outcast among his colleagues on the NHL Board of Governors. Finley's aide, Munson Campbell, quit in disgust and soon Charlie O began shopping for potential purchasers of the Seals. Finally, after four years of ownership, Finley sold the Seals back to the NHL and quit hockey.

FERDINAND CHARLES (FERNIE) FLAMAN

BORN: Dysart, Saskatchewan, January 25, 1927
POSITION: Defenseman, Boston Bruins, 1944–51, 1954–61; Toronto
    Maple Leafs, 1951–54
AWARDS: All-Star (Second Team), 1955, 1957, 1958

Long before Bobby Orr and the Big Bad Bruins came along in the late sixties, the Boston hockey club had become notorious as a bashing sextet. From 1954 through 1961 its chief violent basher was defenseman Fernie Flaman, a smooth-skating defenseman who broke into pro hockey as a teen-ager during World War II.

Flaman developed his hard-hitting style with the Eastern League Boston Olympics, playing briefly with the Bruins in 1944–45 and 1945–46. A year later he became a permanent NHL skater with Boston. In 1950–51 he was traded to the Maple Leafs where his style was less appreciated than in Beantown. He returned to the Bruins at the start of the 1954–55 campaign.

"Fernie was a solid bodychecker," said Hall of Famer Milt Schmidt who coached Flaman in Boston, "and was at his best when things were rough."

Rare was the night when Flaman lost a fight. He decisioned Rangers' badman Lou Fontinato at Madison Square Garden and once nearly killed Montreal's Henri Richard with a devastating but legal bodycheck during a game at Boston Garden. Following his playing days, Flaman became a coach, first with the pros, later in the collegiate ranks.

REGINALD STEPHEN (REGGIE) FLEMING

BORN: Montreal, Quebec, April 21, 1936
POSITION: Left Wing, Montreal Canadiens, 1959–60; Chicago Black
    Hawks, 1960–64; Boston Bruins, 1964–66; New York Rangers,
    1966–69; Philadelphia Flyers, 1969–70; Buffalo Sabres, 1970–71;
    Chicago Cougars (WHA), 1973–74

A likeable, boisterous forward, Reg Fleming fought as many one-on-one fistfights as any player in hockey history during a career that began in 1959–60 in Montreal with the Canadiens and ended in 1973–74 with the WHA's Chicago Cougars. Fleming first achieved notoriety during the 1960–61 season when, as a member of the Chicago Black Hawks, he punched out New York Rangers'

Reg Fleming

goaltender (and U.S. Olympic hero) Jack McCartan at center ice in Madison Square Garden. But Fleming could do more than fight. After a short stint with the Bruins in 1965–66 and part of 1966–67, Reg was dealt to New York where he was lionized as a Rangers' hero. One of his most significant decisions came against Canadiens policeman John Ferguson. In 1969–70 Fleming moved on to Philadelphia and then to Buffalo the following year before jumping to the WHA where his big league career came to a close.

WILLIAM MEYER "COWBOY" (BILL) FLETT

BORN: Vermillion, Alberta, July 21, 1943
POSITION: Right Wing, Los Angeles Kings, 1967–71; Philadelphia Flyers, 1971–74; Toronto Maple Leafs 1974–75; Atlanta Flames, 1975–

"Cowboy" Bill Flett, a powerful right winger with a blistering shot, was traded to the Toronto Maple Leafs from the 1974 Stanley Cup-winning Philadelphia Flyers before the victory champagne had fizzed out of his bushy beard. Once called the strongest player in hockey, Flett has been accused of dogging it on occasion, a cardinal sin in the eyes of Fred Shero, the Flyer mentor. A prod-

Bill Flett

uct of the Maple Leaf farm system, Cowboy, who once roped steers in Alberta, was snapped up by the Los Angeles Kings in the 1967 expansion draft. After four and a half seasons on the West Coast, Flett was shipped to the Flyers in a seven-player deal. Bill chipped in his best performance in 1972–73 when he scored 43 goals and 31 assists for the Flyers. By May 1975 Flett was placed on waivers and picked up by the Atlanta Flames.

LOUIS (LOU) FONTINATO

BORN: Guelph, Ontario, January 20, 1932
POSITION: Defenseman, New York Rangers, 1954–61; Montreal Canadiens, 1961–63

In many ways Lou Fontinato portrayed the best and worst aspects of pro hockey. He was lionized as a Broadway hero during most of his Ranger career and was feared throughout the league from his rookie season 1954–55 until the day Gordie Howe destroyed his effectiveness with a flurry of lethal punches at Madison Square Garden.

On the day in question, Fontinato had a couple of scores to settle with Howe. For one thing, the Detroit superman had nearly sliced Fontinato's ear off with his stick in an earlier game, and for another Fontinato was anxious to erase any doubts about who was the toughest man in the league. Besides, he felt obliged

Lou Fontinato

to assist Eddie Shack who got into a fracas and seemed to be losing his bout with Howe on points.

Fontinato moved swiftly from his outpost at the blue line. The distance from the blue line to the bout was about seventy feet, which the Ranger policeman negotiated in a few seconds. The circumstances were perfect for Fontinato. In most of his fights he would defeat opponents by a surprise attack, raining blows on them before they could muster a defense. Howe, who was concentrating on Shack, didn't see Fontinato coming. The Ranger knocked him off-balance and discharged a flurry of punches that normally would have sent an opponent reeling for cover. Howe stared down the blows without flinching. He seemed to be sizing up Fontinato. Then, the counterattack began. Howe's short jabs moved like locomotive pistons, striking the Ranger around the nose and eyes. *Clop! Clop! Clop!* At about this time the linesmen moved in to halt the bout, but nobody wanted to get near the punches. Fontinato returned with a few drives to Howe's midsection, but Howe ignored them. The once fearsome Ranger had been mashed almost beyond recognition. His nose was broken at a right angle to his face which was dripping with blood. Only one factor saved him from complete disaster—he wasn't knocked down.

The defeat ruined Fontinato. His air of braggadocio vanished. His play deteriorated and so did the Rangers. Coach Phil Watson traced the team's amazing end-of-season collapse and last-day ouster from a playoff berth to the Fontinato disaster.

Fontinato was traded by New York to the Montreal Canadiens prior to the 1961–62 campaign and was playing his second season in Montreal when he nearly was killed in a freak accident during a game, ironically, with the Rangers at the Montreal Forum. Racing with New York's Vic Hadfield for a loose puck at the end boards, Fontinato got there first. The Canadiens' defenseman then attempted to upend Hadfield by crouching low as his foe was about to hit Lou into the boards. Fontinato did manage to crouch, but Hadfield bodied Lou in such a way that the defenseman's neck was broken. His career ended on the same violent note which it began.

Prior to the accident Lou had built a reputation on hard checks and fast fists. He once bloodied Maurice Richard in New York, inspiring columnist Red Smith to describe the game as a "Roman circus." Fontinato had rarely lost a bout although he took on the NHL's toughest skaters; then Howe came along!

DAVID STEPHEN (DAVE) FORBES

BORN: Montreal, Quebec, November 16, 1948
POSITION: Left Wing, Boston Bruins, 1973–

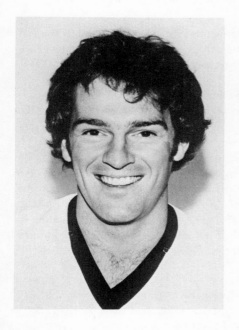

An obscure young forward with modest skills, Dave Forbes no doubt would have remained in the shadows of teammates Bobby Orr and Phil Esposito had he not become involved in one of hockey's uglier clashes during an NHL game on January 4, 1975 at Bloomington, Minnesota. In a battle with Henry Boucha of the North Stars, Forbes of the Bruins struck the Minnesota skater near the right eye. Thirty stitches were required to close the wounds and Boucha's eye underwent surgery to correct double vision apparently caused by a small fracture in a bone under the eye. In an unprecedented action, Hennepin (Minnesota) County attorney Gary Flakne indicted Forbes, charging him with aggravated assault in connection with the fight with Boucha. Flakne said the hockey stick wielded by Forbes was considered a dangerous weapon. Thus, Forbes, who had difficulty scoring a goal, became an overnight celebrity because of Flakne's indictment.

FRANK FOYSTON

BORN: Minesing, Ontario, February 2, 1891
DIED: January 24, 1966
POSITION: Center, Toronto Arenas (NHA), 1913–16; Seattle Metropolitans (PCHA), 1916–25; Detroit Cougars, 1927–28
AWARDS: Scoring Leader (PCHA), 1920, 1921; Hockey Hall of Fame, 1958

Frank Foyston was a high-scoring centerman on the powerful Toronto team of the early NHA. Foyston, centering a line with wingers Alan Davidson and Jack Walker, helped catapult the Ontarians to the coveted Stanley Cup in 1914, Toronto's second year of operation.

Foyston labored for one more season with Toronto before jumping leagues to play for Seattle of the PCHA. Frank terrorized Pacific Coast goaltenders for the next nine years at Seattle, winning the league scoring title twice and directing his newly found sextet to the 1917 Stanley Cup.

Frank was a fixture at center for Seattle until 1925 when the Washington franchise dropped out of the league. Foyston signed on with the Victoria club and adapted beautifully to his new surroundings, helping his new team to the Stanley Cup in his very first season there. Frank played one more season with Victoria before the entire western league collapsed from under him. Skating in the twilight of his career, Foyston finished out his playing days with Detroit of the NHL. One of the great scorers of all time, Foyston is a member of hockey's Hall of Fame.

EMILE PERCY "THE CAT" FRANCIS

BORN: North Battleford, Saskatchewan, September 13, 1926
POSITION: Goalie, Chicago Black Hawks, 1946–48; New York Rangers, 1948–52; General Manager, New York Rangers, 1964–   ; Coach, New York Rangers, 1965–68, 1969–73, 1974–75

Emile Francis, the man who was to become the winningest coach in Rangers' history (but without ever winning the Stanley Cup!), was also a much-traveled goaltender who got his first break in 1943–44, playing in the old Eastern League for Redvers MacKenzie and the Philadelphia Falcons. Francis was as

Emile Francis

happy about playing in Philadelphia as the Philadelphians were delighted to have him on their side. Decades later, as general manager and coach of the Rangers, Francis reminisced about his Eastern League stint with the Falcons.

"The thing that I remember most," he said, "was my first trip to New York with the Falcons. We took the train into Penn Station and then Red MacKenzie hurried off the platform. I thought we were going first class and would take cabs to Madison Square Garden.

"Instead, MacKenzie said, 'Alright, you guys, everybody into the subway.' We wound up taking the subway two stops to Fiftieth Street where the old Garden used to be. That was probably the only time in my life I regretted being a goaltender. It was murder riding the subway of New York with the huge goal bag on my shoulder."

As a member of the Falcons, Francis was paid $50 a week. But because of a curious Canadian–American monetary agreement, the young goalie only got half that amount. "I received $25," he recalls, "and the other $25 was deposited in my account in Canada. So I actually had to manage on $25 a week."

Francis only played one season for the Falcons. A year later he tended goal for the Washington Lions of the Eastern League.

Francis made it to the NHL in 1946–47, appearing in nineteen games for the Chicago Black Hawks. The following season he guarded the cage fifty-four times. At best, "the Cat" (nicknamed for his catlike moves in the cage) was a mediocre netminder for a rather poor Chicago outfit.

Emile eventually found his way to New York, where he occasionally tended goal for Frank Boucher's Rangers.

"On a few occasions when Chuck Rayner was sidelined," Boucher said, "we got some excellent work from Francis, whom we'd acquired from Chicago. Mostly, Emile worked up at New Haven, but he had fourteen games with us in 1951–52. I had been in the stands one night at Providence watching the New Haven club, looking for players who might help the Rangers, when Emile took a terrible cut. He was just a little fellow, 5'7" or so, and weighing maybe 155, and his view was blocked by a big defenseman named Jerry Claude, 6'2" and burly. He didn't see a shot from the point which Claude could have blocked but which he ducked at the last instant. The puck hit the Cat in the mouth and nose. It knocked six teeth loose and cut his nose badly. I went down to the dressing room to see how he was. He was the only New Haven goaltender so he knew he'd have to go back into the net when the doctor finished patching him up.

" 'Has anybody got any brandy?' I asked.

"Somebody produced a bottle and I poured a stiff slug for Emile. He downed it, shook his head, climbed to his feet, and went back to the padded cell.

"There was another night, in New York, when the puck tore his lip real badly so that it curled around his nose. Our club doctor, Vincent Nardiello, did the stitching, with Emile sprawled on his back in the dressing room. I know from experience that the most painful part of the body for stitching is around the nose and lips. Emile kept saying, 'Doc, doc, for the love of Mike, hurry up!' He was really suffering, but he just lay there telling the doctor to get the damned job done.

"Emile had more guts than most. He lost eighteen teeth during his career, had his nose broken five times, and needed something like 250 stitches to close up the cuts. He had ligaments torn in both knees, and required surgery on his right ankle. Dr. Kazuo Yanagisawa, another Ranger doctor, operated on his shoulder, in 1951, because of chronic pain after a shoulder separation. It's not any wonder that Cat Francis was a success as a coach and general manager of the team in later years; he'd been through it all. My friend, Gene Ward, columnist for the New York *Daily News,* once remarked to me that he'd never seen anyone in sports with courage to match that of the goaltenders.

"Emile went to Vancouver," Boucher concluded, "for the 1952–53 season, a club I'd arranged a working agreement with, and he was named the league's most valuable player."

The Cat ended his playing career at Spokane of the Western League, after having "dislocated both shoulders," in 1960. He immediately began coaching at Guelph, Ontario, a junior team with Rod Gilbert and Jean Ratelle, who went on to star for Francis with the Rangers.

"I wanted to the start at the bottom," he said.

The road to the top of the Ranger organization was quickly traversed, and by 1964 he was New York's general manager. The next season, he took over as coach, and his career was the most successful of any Ranger mentor. Although his teams never captured a Stanley Cup, Francis coached more Ranger games than anyone, and his NHL winning percentage was second only to Toe Blake.

Francis the coach was known as a strict disciplinarian while eliciting fierce loyalty from his players. Often criticized for his trading of many fine young prospects (Syl Apps, Curt Bennett, and Juha Widing, to name a few), Francis defended himself on the grounds that he acquired experience (Glen Sather, Dale Rolfe, Peter Stemkowski) that would better the team's run to the Stanley Cup. Unfortunately, they never got there, and by the end of the 1974–75 season the Rangers were demoralized and former Ranger Ron Stewart was selected as the new coach as Francis retained the g.m. post.

FRANK FREDERICKSON

BORN: Winnipeg, Manitoba, 1895
POSITION: Forward, Detroit Cougars, 1926; Boston Bruins, 1927–28;
    Pittsburgh Pirates, 1929–30; Detroit Falcons, 1930–31
AWARDS: Hockey Hall of Fame, 1958

One of the few National Hockey League players of Icelandic extraction to gain a niche in the Hockey Hall of Fame, Frank Frederickson had been a World War I pilot and hero before making a name for himself in professional hockey. Frederickson's NHL career spanned 1926–27 through 1930–31 during which time he skated for Detroit, Boston, Pittsburgh, and Detroit again.

BILL FRIDAY

BORN: Hamilton, Ontario, January 23, 1933
POSITION: Referee (NHL), 1963–72; Senior Referee (WHA), 1972–

When the World Hockey Association came along to challenge the National Hockey League, it listed as a top priority the signing of reputable, experienced referees. Several raids of NHL officials were conducted and one of the prize WHA catches was Bill Friday who emerged as the number one WHA referee. As an official, Friday has generally been competent, although he once infuriated Detroit's notorious Pete Cusimano, the octopus-pitching fan. During the game Cusimano let fly, directing the octopus at Friday. It missed, but not by much. Cusimano said he would have hit Friday, except that a priest was sitting next to him. "I'd have hit him, Father," said Cusimano, "if you had blessed the octopus." The priest, obviously a Friday-admirer, replied: "No; not necessarily."

WILLIAM ALEXANDER (BILL) GADSBY

BORN: Calgary, Alberta, August 8, 1927
POSITION: Defenseman, Chicago Black Hawks, 1946–54; New York
    Rangers, 1954–61; Detroit Red Wings, 1961–66; Coach, Detroit
    Red Wings, 1968–69
AWARDS: All-Star (First Team), 1956, 1958, 1959; All-Star (Second
    Team), 1953, 1954; Hockey Hall of Fame, 1970

Bill Gadsby broke in with the Black Hawks during the 1946–47 season and
remained in the big time until 1965–66 when he retired as a member of the Detroit Red Wings. During that span he was a three-time (1956, 1958, and 1959)
member of the NHL First All-Star Team and was equally comfortable as a
defensive or offensive defenseman. Gadsby played for Chicago until the
1954–55 season when he was traded to the Rangers a day before Thanksgiving
along with Pete Conacher for Al Stanley and Nick Mickoski. In his very first
game as a Ranger, Gadsby dove in front of a Bruins' shot, preventing a goal,
but breaking several bones in the process. The play symbolized the gutsy style
that made Bill a hit on Broadway until 1961–62 when the Rangers' general
manager Muzz Patrick dealt him to the Red Wings where he continued to
excel. Curiously, Gadsby in all his NHL years never played on a Stanley Cup
champion, although he came close in 1963–64 and 1965–66 with Detroit.

JOHN "BLACK CAT" GAGNON

BORN: Chicoutimi, Quebec, June 8, 1905
POSITION: Forward, Montreal Canadiens, 1930–34, 1935–39; Boston
Bruins, 1934–35; New York Rangers, 1939–40

In the early thirties, John "Black Cat" Gagnon had developed into one of the most formidable scorers on the Montreal Canadiens. One night, Toronto manager Conn Smythe decided that the Black Cat should be softened up, and he chose his husky forward, Harvey Busher Jackson, to handle the job. From the opening face-off, Jackson, for no apparent reason, would continually crash headlong into the surprised Gagnon. The Black Cat knew Jackson as a pleasant chap off the ice and asked him why he was battering him so violently.

"Sorry, Johnny," Busher replied, "that's orders."

Each time Jackson floored Gagnon, the Leaf would look down at the crumpled Canadien and repeat, "that's orders." Finally, in utter desperation, Gagnon shot back, "Hey, Busher, how long those goddamned orders for?"

Gagnon was nicknamed "the Black Cat" because of his swarthy complexion and jet black hair, which always seemed to be pasted down with a gluelike hair pomade, as well as the quick, darting moves and natural puck sense that earned him a place on the Canadiens' first line in 1931 with Howie Morenz and Aurel Joliat.

With the Gagnon-Morenz-Joliat line leading the way, the Canadiens finished first in the NHL's Canadian Division in 1930–31. Gagnon's two key goals in the fourth game of the Stanley Cup finals against the Chicago Black Hawks turned the series around for Montreal which then went on to win the Cup.

Gagnon's star began descending during the 1932–33 season when he clashed with coach Newsy Lalonde. At one point late in the campaign it was rumored that Gagnon had been fined $200 for indifferent play. But the most demoralizing blow occurred after the 1933–34 season when Gagnon's pal, Morenz, was traded to Chicago. In 1934–35 Gagnon himself was traded to the Boston Bruins, but then returned to the Canadiens until 1939–40 when he was traded to the Americans late in the season. He scored a goal for New York in the 1940 playoffs and then retired to become a scout in Providence, Rhode Island.

DON GALLINGER

BORN: Port Colborne, Ontario, April 10, 1925
POSITION: Center, Boston Bruins, 1942–44, 1945–48

Don Gallinger might have gone down in the annals of the NHL purely as a good-shooting, swift-skating forward of considerable respectability. Instead, he and teammate Billy Taylor were banished from hockey—the only players ever punished in that manner—for betting on games during the 1947–48 season.

According to league president Clarence Campbell, then in office for only two years, the two were given "life suspensions for conduct detrimental to hockey and for associating with a known gambler." Although Campbell kept the details of the scandal quiet, mostly in deference to Taylor's wishes, Gallinger tried in recent years to have the banishment lifted.

Gallinger once told his story to Toronto *Globe and Mail* reporter Scott Young, who published the revelations in a six-article series. Gallinger admitted in those articles that he had, in fact, bet on games, although when the original scandal reports broke in February 1948 Gallinger denied everything to Campbell and Bruin owner Art Ross. Eighteen months later, however, Gallinger confessed to the betting in an emotional meeting held in Campbell's office.

With the assistance of the Detroit police, the NHL was able to obtain evidence against Taylor and Gallinger through the use of illegal wiretaps. The records showed that the two had frequently talked with one James Tamer, a noted Detroit gambler and paroled bank robber.

Gallinger later admitted the details of the operation. "My bets varied from $250 to $1,000 a game," Gallinger said. "My instructions from the guy," he continued, meaning Tamer, "were to bet on what I knew of the team's attitude and our injuries." Gallinger insisted that while he began to bet three months before the scandal was disclosed, only eight or nine games were actually involved.

Although details of Gallinger's involvement were kept confidential in deference to his father, the ex-Bruin center made pleas for reinstatement after his father died in 1951, but his efforts only won him criticism.

The campaign by Young to get Taylor and Gallinger reinstated in 1963 was met with even harsher criticism by the NHL bosses and by Campbell. In fact, the celebrated Campbell cool went out the window, when he offered that "If Scott Young was on fire, I wouldn't spit on him!"

Both Taylor and Gallinger were finally reinstated in the summer of 1970. Taylor returned to hockey, coaching an amateur team in Ontario.

GAME OFFICIALS

At one time, a hockey game was run by two referees working together. They were their own linesmen. Now there is one referee and two linesmen.

The referee controls the game. He calls all the penalties and must decide the legality of the goals, though sometimes he will call a time-out and ask his linesmen for an opinion before he makes a final decision.

The duty of the linesmen is to determine off-sides and icings. They drop the puck for face-offs. They chase the pucks after stoppage of play. And it is their unenviable job to break up fights while the referee assesses the penalties.

CHARLES ROBERT (CHARLIE OR CHUCK) GARDINER

BORN: Edinburgh, Scotland, December 31,1904
DIED: June 13, 1934
POSITION: Goalie, Chicago Black Hawks, 1927–34
AWARDS: Vezina Trophy, 1932, 1934; All-Star (First Team), 1931, 1932, 1934; All-Star (Second Team), 1933; Hockey Hall of Fame, 1945

Chicago Black Hawk Charlie Gardiner developed into one of the finds of the 1930s. Whenever he stepped between the goal pipes, he usually wore a broad smile. At first this seemed the height of presumptuousness, since his goalkeeping was scarcely flawless. But he worked diligently at his trade.

"He would come far out of the nets and sprawl on the ice in an effort to stop a score," reported Canadian writer Ron McAllister. "And even when his own team had folded up, he fought on and tried to defend his goal."

By 1929, Gardiner had improved so much that he finished second to the immortal George Hainsworth of the Montreal Canadiens in the race for the Vezina Trophy (awarded annually to the goalie whose team has the fewest goals scored against it). In 1932, he finally won the coveted prize and was named to the All-Star team.

In 1932–33, the Hawks finished fourth—out of the playoffs. The following year they rallied and launched their most serious assault on first place. That they failed by seven points and finished second to Detroit was no fault of Gardiner's. His goaltending had reached new degrees of perfection. He allowed only 83 goals in 48 games and scored ten shutouts. In fourteen other games he permitted just one goal.

But astute Gardiner watchers perceived that there was something unusual about the goalie's deportment, and they couldn't quite figure out what it was. Gardiner had lost his jovial manner and appeared melancholy.

Unknown to everyone, Gardiner was suffering from a chronic tonsil infection. However, the goaltender pressed on. Winning the Stanley Cup became an obsession with him, and the Black Hawks responded by defeating first the Canadiens and then the Montreal Maroons. This put them in the Cup finals against the awesome Detroit Red Wings, whose firepower included Ebbie Goodfellow, Larry Aurie, and Cooney Weiland.

The best-of-five series opened in Detroit and the Black Hawks won the first game, 2–1, in double overtime. In the second, also at Detroit's Olympia Stadium, the Hawks ran away with the game, 4–1. When the teams returned to Chicago for the third, and what appeared to be the final game, all hands were prepared to concede the Stanley Cup to the Black Hawks.

But it was not to be Charlie Gardiner's night. His body was wracked with pain and he prayed that he might recapture his physical condition of seasons past. By this time coach Lionel Conacher and manager Tommy Gorman realized they had a weary and tormented player. "He's bad," said Gorman, turning to Conacher in the dressing room before the teams took the ice. "What do you think we should do?"

Gardiner knew the bosses were discussing him. With great effort, he lifted himself off the bench and walked over to them. "Listen," he insisted in tremulous tones, "I want to play. Let me play—for the Cup."

Gardiner took command at the Chicago fortress for two periods. But weariness and pain overcame him in the third, and he wilted before the Detroit attack. When the final buzzer sounded Detroit had won the game, 5–2.

When the team returned to the dressing room, Gardiner collapsed on a bench. But he wasn't totally done in. "Look," he said to his depressed teammates, "all I want is one goal next game. Just one goal and I'll take care of the other guys."

As he took his place in the goal crease on April 10, 1934, Gardiner's body was already numb with fatigue—self-hypnosis alone enabling him to overcome the challenge of his ailment. For two periods the game remained scoreless. Early into the third period he began shouting encouragement to his players, even though it cost him valuable energy. Then Detroit captured the momentum and the Red Wings seemed to be headed for victory. But Gardiner's flailing arms and jabbing legs held them at bay.

When the regulation time ended, the score remained tied, 0–0. Now the game would go into sudden-death overtime. But every minute more meant less chance for the disabled Gardiner to prevail against his well-conditioned foe, Wilf Cude, in the Detroit nets.

The referee finally whistled the teams back to the ice for the overtime. Gardiner's teammates feared that he might collapse at any moment under the strain, as he had in the preceding four periods. But when he tapped his pads in front of the net for the face-off, he was wearing a broad smile, as if he knew something. And as the players began swirling at center ice, he waved his stick to the crowd.

Red Wings and Black Hawks crunched against each other for another period, and still there was no result. Another intermission was called, and then they returned to the ice for the second sudden-death overtime period. By now Gardiner was beside himself with pain, but he would fight it as long as he could stand on his skates.

At the ten-minute mark, tiny "Mush" March of the Black Hawks moved the puck into Detroit territory and unleased a shot at Wilf Cude. Before the goalie could move, the puck sailed past him, the red light flashed, and the Black Hawks had won their first Stanley Cup. Gardiner hurled his stick in the air and then just barely made it back to the dressing room under the thick backslaps of his mates.

Less than two months later he died in a Winnipeg hospital.

HERBERT MARTIN (HERB) GARDINER

BORN: Winnipeg, Manitoba, May 8, 1891
DIED: January 11, 1972
POSITION: Defenseman, Montreal Canadiens, 1926–28, 1929; Chicago Black Hawks, 1928
AWARDS: Hart Trophy, 1927; Hockey Hall of Fame, 1958

Herb Gardiner, who was signed to manage the Philadelphia Arrows in October 1929, emerged as a minor league "Mister Hockey" in Philadelphia. He delivered a championship to the city of Brotherly Love in the 1932–33 season when the Arrows compiled a record of 29 victories, only 12 losses, and 7 ties to finish in first place seven points ahead of runner-up Providence.

Unfortunately, the depression had hit the United States and there was talk of folding Philadelphia's sextet prior to the 1934–35 season because of losses at the gate. But on October 15, 1934, the club was saved when the Arrows' receivers decided to run the team. Gardiner was retained as manager and members of the defunct NHL Philadelphia Quakers were lent to the Arrows.

This tenuous arrangement had its pitfalls—mostly on the ice where the Arrows stumbled around, looking more like the old Quaker team than anything else. Attendance at the Arena remained low and it was obvious that some transfusion of talent was necessary to save pro hockey in Philadelphia.

The SOS sign was detected in New York City where Rangers' manager Lester Patrick decided he would pump new life into Gardiner's club by making them a farm team of the New York NHL club. The Arrows name was changed to Ramblers and Gardiner did his usual competent job operating the club. In fact, Gardiner's 1935–36 Philadelphia sextet was one of the most accomplished teams ever assembled in professional hockey.

"Gardiner developed in that season what was probably the greatest team Philadelphia ever had on ice," said Tom Lockhart, the former Rangers' business manager.

Unfortunately for Herb, the advent of World War II caused a severe drain on minor league talent. Pro hockey was temporarily discontinued in Philadelphia and Gardiner's glory years came to an end.

CALVIN PEARLY "GINGER" GARDNER

BORN: Transcona, Manitoba, October 30, 1924
POSITION: Center, New York Rangers, 1945–48; Toronto Maple Leafs, 1948–52; Chicago Black Hawks, 1952–53; Boston Bruins, 1953–57

In their searches for *the* big, starry center, the New York Rangers, Boston Bruins, Toronto Maple Leafs, and Chicago Black Hawks each thought they had found him in Cal Gardner, a tall redhead who was quickly nicknamed "Ginger" in his amateur hockey days. Gardner learned his hockey in the Winnipeg area and was signed by the Rangers' Eastern League affiliate, the New York Rovers. Gardner played center on the Atomic Line with Rene Trudell and Church Russell on the wings. The trio devastated the Eastern League and was elevated en masse for the 1945–46 season. Of the three, Gardner prevailed longest. He was traded to Toronto for the 1948–49 season and was supposed to be the Leafs' replacement for their retired center, Syl Apps, but never quite cut the ice as well. In 1952–53 Gardner played for Chicago and in the next four seasons finished his major league career in Boston. His son, Dave Gardner, made his NHL debut in 1972–73 with the Montreal Canadiens and is regarded as bright an offensive prospect as his father had once been.

DAN GARE

BORN: Nelson, British Columbia, May 14, 1954
POSITION: Right Wing, Buffalo Sabres, 1974–

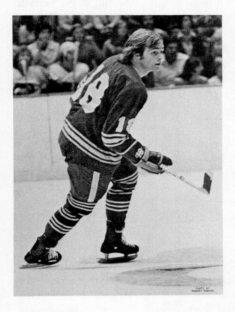

One of the most pleasant surprises of the Buffalo Sabres' 1974–75 season, right winger Dan Gare supplied pugnacity—despite his smallish stature—and goals (31) in the Sabres' march to the Stanley Cup finals. Because of his youthful appearance, Gare also was the butt of barbs in the Buffalo dressing room. Once, when he asked a teammate for shaving cream, the answer shot back was: "What would *you* want that for, Danny?" To which peach-faced Gare responded: "Oh, I have to shave regularly—every week!"

TED GARVIN

BORN: Sarnia, Ontario, August 30, 1920
POSITION: Coach, Detroit Red Wings, 1973

After an incredibly successful five-year coaching stint in the minor leagues with the Port Huron Wings, Ted Garvin, a portly, leather-lunged bench boss, was handed the unenviable task of leading the uninspired 1973–74 Detroit Red Wings. As Ted was soon to find out, life behind an NHL bench—and a losing bench at that—was no bed of roses.

Garvin, who came into the NHL with a reputation as a fiery, animated mentor, lasted only a few weeks with the hapless Wings before being replaced by Alex Delvecchio.

A high-scoring right winger during his minor league playing days, Garvin went on to serve as coach and general manager of the Red Wings' IHL Toledo Golddiggers after his brief stay in the Motor City.

GEORGE GEE

BORN: Stratford, Ontario, June 28, 1922
POSITION: Center, Chicago Black Hawks, 1945–48, 1951–54; Detroit
     Red Wings, 1949–51

If, as many critics have argued, the winning goal of the seventh game of the 1950 Stanley Cup finals between the Red Wings and Rangers was one of the biggest scores of all time, then the man who delivered the key pass on Pete Babando's shot rates credit. That man was George Gee.

A native of Stratford, Ontario (birthplace of legendary Howie Morenz), Gee played three and a half seasons for Chicago before being dealt to Detroit. Always reliable, Gee centered a line with Babando and Gerry "Doc" Couture against the Rangers until just past the eight-minute mark of the second sudden-death period of the seventh game in April 1950 at Detroit's Olympia Stadium. Opposing Gee at the face-off was the Rangers' center Buddy O'Connor. Gee made one vital move. He turned to Babando before the face-off. "Move over behind me," Gee instructed, "you're too far to the left." Gee then won the face-off and delivered the puck to Babando whose shot beat the Rangers' goalie Chuck Rayner to win the Stanley Cup for Detroit. Gee returned to the Black Hawks in 1951–52 and ended his career in Chicago after the 1953–54 season.

JEAN GUY "SMITTY" GENDRON

BORN: Montreal, Quebec, August 30, 1934
POSITION: Left Wing, New York Rangers, 1955–58, 1961–62; Boston
   Bruins, 1958–60, 1962–64; Montreal Canadiens, 1961; Philadel-
   phia Flyers, 1967–72; Quebec Nordiques (WHA), 1972–74;
   Coach, Quebec Nordiques (WHA), 1974–

While never quite fulfilling his pre-big league notices, Gendron became a solid
forward with the New York Rangers, Boston Bruins, Montreal Canadiens, and
Philadelphia Flyers during a big league career that spanned 1955–56 to
1973–74. Upon formation of the World Hockey Association, Gendron jumped
to the Quebec Nordiques and in 1974–75 became coach of the Quebec WHA
sextet. For no particular reason, he was nicknamed "Smitty" while still a
Ranger and the tag stuck with him throughout his hockey career.

BERNARD "BOOM-BOOM," "BOOMER" GEOFFRION

BORN: Montreal, Quebec, February 14, 1931
POSITION: Right Wing, Montreal Canadiens 1950–64; New York
   Rangers, 1966–68; Coach, New York Rangers, 1969; Atlanta
   Flames, 1972–75
AWARDS: Calder Memorial Trophy, 1952; Hart Trophy, 1961;
   Art Ross Trophy, 1955, 1961; All-Star (First Team), 1961; (Sec-
   ond Team), 1955, 1960; Hockey Hall of Fame, 1972

Nicknamed "Boom-Boom" because of the reverberation of his stick hitting the
puck and the puck hitting the endboards (although it often went directly into the

Bernie Geoffrion

net), Bernie Geoffrion had many of the incendiary qualities of Maurice "Rocket" Richard.

But the Geoffrion character had one ingredient that was missing in the Richard psyche—a flamboyant sense of humor. For the most part the Rocket was a quiet, introverted sort even when life was agreeable, but when Geoffrion was scoring easily he became an opera-singing clown who led the Canadiens' laugh parade. He began delighting teammates late in the 1950–51 season after scoring 103 goals in fifty-seven Montreal Junior League games. Geoffrion was under great pressure to turn pro with Les Canadiens and he resisted until there were only eighteen games remaining in the 1950–51 schedule. Geoffrion realized that the Calder Trophy for rookie of the year was given to players who had skated in twenty or more games. By waiting until there were fewer than twenty games in the 1950–51 schedule he thus became eligible to win it the following season.

The Boomer was no fool. He opened the 1951–52 season with two goals, including the winner, against Chicago in a 4–2 Montreal victory and immediately established himself as the newest Canadiens hero. For Geoffrion it was relatively easy. And not only was he an excellent young prospect but he had recently married figure skater Marlene Morenz, the attractive blonde daughter of the late Howie Morenz.

Soon after Geoffrion's opening scoring burst, Les Canadiens visited New York and Geoffrion was interviewed by New York *Daily News* sports columnist Jimmy Powers. The writer observed that the NHL had a prize crop of rookies and wondered just who the Boomer thought would win the prize.

"Me," said Geoffrion, in as candid a reply as Powers could hope for.

Geoffrion was right. He went into orbit in 1952 and remained one of the most flamboyant and productive right wingers in the NHL, playing right wing on a line with center Jean Beliveau and left winger Dickie Moore.

During the 1954–55 season Geoffrion became the center of controversy in the last week of the schedule when teammate Maurice "Rocket" Richard was suspended for the remainder of the season by NHL president Clarence Campbell.

Richard was leading the league in scoring at the time and appeared certain to win his first points title. But once the Rocket was suspended, Geoffrion—despite the wishes of pro-Richard fans—moved ahead of Richard and the Boomer won his first scoring championship. As a result of the triumph, Geoffrion was villified for several years by his hometown fans. However, he continued to play superbly and won the scoring championship and the most valuable player award (Hart Trophy) in 1960–61.

Geoffrion retired temporarily after the 1963–64 season to become coach of the American League Quebec Aces and coached them to two consecutive championships. Then he made a remarkable comeback with the New York Rangers, playing two full seasons on Broadway.

When he finally retired at the conclusion of the 1967–68 season Geoffrion had scored 393 career goals, placing him behind only a handful of players, including Gordie Howe, Maurice Richard, Bobby Hull, and Jean Beliveau. He was the second man—after Maurice Richard—ever to score 50 goals in one season, accomplishing that feat in 1960–61.

On August 24, 1972, Geoffrion reached another milestone when he was inducted into the NHL Hall of Fame. He was named coach of the newly organized Atlanta Flames of the NHL prior to the 1972–73 season and led them to the playoffs in 1973–74, their second full year in the league. However, he quit the team in the homestretch of the 1974–75 season under mysterious circumstances and became the president of an athlete representative concern.

EDWARD (EDDIE) GERARD

BORN: Ottawa, Ontario, February 22, 1890
DIED: December 8, 1937
POSITION: Left Wing and Defenseman, Ottawa Senators (NHA and NHL), 1914–22, 1923; Toronto St. Pats, 1922–23
AWARDS: Hockey Hall of Fame, 1945

Eddie Gerard, defensive player par excellence, was afforded his highest compliment as a player while skating for the 1922 Toronto St. Pats in their Stanley Cup series against Vancouver.

Normally Eddie was a brilliant forward/defenseman for the Ottawa Senators.

But when St. Pat ace defenseman Harry Cameron tore up his shoulder during the crucial series, an urgent SOS went out to Gerard to man Cameron's spot on the Toronto blue line.

Personnel loans such as these were commonplace in the early days of hockey, the one requirement being that you secure an okay from your opponents. As primitive as were the rules of the day, so must have been the sports media because Vancouver's usually wily Lester Patrick saw no harm in the eleventh hour replacement. After one game of Gerard's puck-hawking and bodychecks however, Lester gave the thumbs down to Gerard's stand-in act.

It was too late for Vancouver, however, and Toronto rolled to the Cup with no small thanks due to Gerard. Eddie played on three other Cup winners with his own Senators before retiring prematurely in 1923. He remained in hockey as a coach and manager and is a member of the Hockey Hall of Fame.

EDWARD (EDDIE) GIACOMIN

BORN: Sudbury, Ontario, June 6, 1939
POSITION: Goalie, New York Rangers, 1965–
AWARDS: Vezina Trophy (with Gilles Villemure), 1971; All-Star (First
    Team), 1967, 1971, (Second Team), 1968–70

When Rollie Giacomin was invited by Peanuts O'Flaherty, the coach of the Washington (Eastern League) Lions, to come down for a tryout, he was working a shift at the lumber mill, and asked his brother Eddie to stand in for him.

Upon Eddie's arrival in Washington, the coach looked at him, discovered he was not Rollie, and was unimpressed. The Lions, however, lost their next three games. With nothing to lose, and only six games left in the season, Eddie was given the go-ahead to play. The Lions won all six.

The following year, Giacomin was invited to the training camp of the American League Providence Reds and then spent the season playing for various minor league teams in the East.

In 1960–61, Giacomin was called back to the Reds in midseason and toiled over the next four years for them. Finally, on May 17, 1965, he was signed by the New York Rangers.

Eddie played thirty-six games for the dreadful Ranger team of 1964–65. He was hardly impressive and the Ranger management sent him to the Baltimore Clippers of the AHL, a Ranger farm club. Giacomin took his demotion as a competitor with equanimity, and determined to come back.

In 1966, the Ranger brass staked everything they had on Giacomin. The team had finished out of the playoffs for the previous five years, and weak goaltending and poor defense were big factors. General manager and coach Emile Francis was impressed with Giacomin despite his poor rookie showing. Giacomin got the assignment and finished the season with a 2.61 average and a league-leading total of nine shutouts. The Rangers made the playoffs and Giacomin was given a berth on the First Team All-Star squad.

In 1970, the Rangers lost the Stanley Cup quarterfinals for the fourth straight year. People said that the reason the Rangers wilted in May was because Giacomin was dog-tired, the result of playing in excess of sixty games in an era of coast-to-coast scheduling.

When Giacomin returned to the Rangers' training camp in Kitchener, Ontario, the following season, he learned that he would be sharing the goaltending chores with Gilles Villemure, a veteran of seven minor league seasons and a few stints with the Rangers. Giacomin disapproved of the two-goalie system. He insisted that he needed the extra work to stay at his sharpest. He vehemently denied charges that he was tired at season's end, and that he had failed in the playoffs. He had no choice, however, except to abide by Francis's decision. After eleven years of being the intrepid barefaced goalie, Giacomin also decided to wear a face mask.

The two-goalie system worked and by the end of the 1970–71 campaign, Giacomin had captured the coveted Vezina Trophy along with Villemure. Eddie Giacomin finished with an average of 2.15, the best of his professional career.

The Rangers clambered past the quarterfinals as they beat the Toronto Maple Leafs in a hard-fought six-game series. They then carried the Black Hawks to the full seven games before losing out in the semifinals. Giacomin was splendid.

A year later Giacomin's average was a respectable 2.70. He starred in the victorious quarterfinal series against the defending champion Montreal Canadiens. But he damaged his knee in the first game of the semifinals against the Black Hawks. Villemure replaced him, and played so well that the Rangers reached the finals for the first time in twenty years. Next came the classic confrontation between New York and Boston.

Giacomin couldn't stop the Bruins, but it was simply a case of too much Bobby Orr for the Blueshirts. The Rangers were eliminated in six games.

Eddie suffered early season problems in 1972–73, but midway through the year he found himself and played a stretch of several games in which he allowed less than a goal a game. He also recorded his forty-first career shutout, a Rangers record, surpassing that of Hall of Famer Chuck Rayner.

The Rangers cruised into the playoffs for the seventh straight year and once again were confronted by their arch foes from Boston.

Thanks to Giacomin's assorted splits and dives, the Rangers annihilated the Bruins in a surprisingly easy five-game series. They appeared to be sure winners in the Cup semifinals against Chicago, but a hot Hawk goalie, Tony Esposito, punctured the Rangers' balloon. But despite the playoff loss, Giacomin could be proud of his work.

It was after the 1972–73 season that Giacomin's performance began to seriously slip, and by 1974–75 his average was soaring dangerously, near the 3.50 mark, as the Rangers put on their worst playoff performance in years, losing a three-game opening round to the upstart New York Islanders.

GILLES JOSEPH GILBERT

BORN: Saint Esprit, Quebec, March 31, 1949
POSITION: Goalie, Minnesota North Stars, 1969–73; Boston Bruins, 1973–

Growing up in cosmopolitan Quebec meant that Gilles Gilbert had many diversions besides hockey. His friends played in pop music groups and sang, and he thought of joining them. In his spare time he took to writing and composed a full-length novel with a script to go with it, should anyone want to perform the play on stage. But Gilbert decided early to concentrate on hockey.

From the first-rate London Knights, a Junior A team in Western Ontario, Gilbert was drafted by the NHL Minnesota North Stars, where he was the understudy to veteran Gump Worsley. But Gilbert was given precious little ice time in Minnesota and grew to resent his wasted months there.

The Bruins obtained Gilbert in May 1973 by dealing veteran center Fred Stanfield to Minnesota. With Phil Esposito pumping goals and Bobby Orr defending, Gilbert gradually matured into a more than competent goalie. He played in fifty-four games during the 1973–74 season, allowing 158 goals for an average of 2.95. He also produced six shutouts while helping Boston to first place and the Prince of Wales Trophy.

In the 1974 playoffs Gilbert outgoaled Toronto's Doug Favell in the opening

Gilles Gilbert

round and then Tony Esposito of the Chicago Black Hawks in the semifinals. When Boston skated against Philadelphia in the Cup finals, Gilbert was regarded as the Bruins' soft underbelly, mostly because the Flyers boasted supergoalie Bernie Parent. But Gilles played superbly throughout the series, even in the Cup-clinching game won by the Flyers, 1–0. The winning goal was a deflection by Rick MacLeish of a blue line shot which Gilbert surely would have nabbed had it not changed direction.

RODRIGUE GABRIEL (ROD) GILBERT

BORN: Montreal, Quebec, July 1, 1941
POSITION: Right Wing, New York Rangers, 1960–
AWARDS: All-Star (First Team), 1972, (Second Team), 1968

Rod Gilbert's NHL career almost ended before it started. Playing for the Guelph Royals in the Ontario Hockey Association, he skidded on an ice-cream container top thrown to the ice by a fan and injured his back. A few days later an opponent leveled him with a strong check, and Gilbert fell to the ice, his back broken. The first operation on his spine was a near disaster; his left leg began to hemorrhage and amputation was seriously considered. During the summer of 1965 the bone grafts in his back weakened, and another operation

Rod Gilbert

was needed. Rod's career was in jeopardy; he played thirty-four games in a restrictive brace and then submitted to another operation. Happily, Rod's story has been all uphill to fame since then.

On February 24, 1968, at the Montreal Forum, Gilbert scored 4 goals against Rogatien Vachon, and also established an NHL record—sixteen shots on goal. In 1971–72 he hit for 43 goals, finished fifth in the NHL scoring race and was named right wing on the first All-Star team. He was the first Ranger in eight years to get a first team nomination. In 1974 Gilbert passed Andy Bathgate as the Rangers' all-time leading scorer. His milestone goal was celebrated by a five-minute, deafening ovation.

He teamed with Jean Ratelle and Vic Hadfield to form the Rangers' number one line. The GAG Line (goal-a-game) amassed 139 goals and 312 points in 1971–72. But Ratelle broke his ankle and Rod was hindered by pinched nerves in his neck; otherwise the Rangers might have taken the Cup from the Bruins that year.

In 1973–74 Gilbert scored 36 goals and 77 points despite the Rangers' problems. He showed his deep competitive spirit as he helped the Rangers in their upward spiral from sixth to third place. Rod's dramatic overtime goal in the semifinal playoff against the Philadelphia Flyers was one of his most spectacular plays. Rod again topped 30 goals in 1974–75, despite a sorry Ranger performance in the regular season.

FRANK "PUD" GLASS

BORN: 1884
DIED: March 2, 1965
POSITION: Forward, Montreal Wanderers (ECAHA), 1905–11; Montreal Canadiens (NHA), 1911–12

Pud Glass, a smallish but aggressive winger, skated for the Montreal Wanderers for seven of his eight seasons, from 1905–11. During that span, he helped the Wanderer sextet to four Stanley Cups, captaining his last championship team in 1910.

A slick playmaker as well as a proficient goal scorer, Pud is one of the true casualties of that era when no statistics were kept on assists. Had they been, he surely would rank as one of the great all-time scorers in hockey history.

Glass was traded to the Canadiens before the 1912 season and played one year with the Habs before retiring as a player. Pud didn't hang up his skates for good though; he continued on for many years as a referee in the NHL.

FREDERICK AUSTIN (FREDDIE) "NO KID" GLOVER

BORN: Toronto, Ontario, January 5, 1928
POSITION: Forward, Detroit Red Wings, 1949–50, 1951–52; Chicago Black Hawks, 1952–53; Coach, California Seals, 1968–71, 1972–74; Los Angeles Kings, 1971–72

During his sixteen seasons with the American League's Cleveland Barons, Fred Glover virtually rewrote the American Hockey League record book. During this time he set records for most career goals (522), most career assists (815), most total career points (1,337), and most career penalty minutes (2,402).

In six years as player-coach of the Barons he led the team to the American Hockey League's playoffs five times, winning the championship twice. He never quite clicked in the NHL despite trials with the Red Wings and Black Hawks and coaching stints with Oakland and Los Angeles.

GOAL JUDGE

In this modern era of great technological advances, why hasn't someone done something about the hockey goal judge?

Today's hockey players benefit immeasurably from improvements like the Fiberglas goalie mask, lighter, stronger sticks, and sturdier protective gear, but the men who hover behind the endboards with their forefingers primed and ready on the goal light buttons still operate under ice-age conditions.

Vested with the power of life or sudden-death, today's goal judges rely solely on the sharpness of their vision and steadiness of their hand. A blink of the eye could mean a missed goal; a sneeze or a hangnail could spell disaster.

When hockey was primarily an outdoor sport, played on the frozen ponds of North America, the goal was usually two upright posts protruding from the ice surface. The crossbar was "an imaginary line extending between the two posts" and netted cording was unheard of. Stationed behind the pipes, the goal judge, if he was smart, would try his best to hide behind the goalkeeper and pray that most shots were either wide or soft dribblers. If a shot did manage to find its mark, the goal judge would signify a tally by waving a white handkerchief. The absence of netting left quite a few shots to the imagination—depending on which side had the goal judge's sympathies.

There was also the added peril of avoiding the high speed skaters as they rounded the net in pursuit of the puck. One night, the immortal Howie Morenz was resting between periods during a game in Preston, Ontario, when there was a loud commotion outside the dressing room. It seems that on one of his lightning dashes around the cage, Morenz's skate blades had inadvertently sliced the toes from the goal judge's galoshes. The outraged official, after waiting for the period to end, had summoned the local gendarmes, charging Morenz with malicious damage to property.

After an extended period of arguing, the goal judge was reimbursed for his ruined rubbers and Morenz was allowed to continue in the game.

Goal judges have since been moved behind the arena's endboards and have even been encased in antiseptic Plexiglas enclosures to protect them from the wrath of fans and players alike. Instead of waving a white handkerchief, they now press the button for the red light, but it is still one of the loneliest jobs in hockey.

GOAL NETS

A goal net, or cage, is six feet wide and four feet high. The NHL's officially approved and adopted Art Ross Net is named after its inventor and former manager of the Boston Bruins. It is designed so that pucks entering the net will stay in, though occasionally a shot will rebound off a back post and carom out. The goal line itself is two inches wide.

In front of each goal is the goal crease, a rectangle designed to minimize traffic in front of the goalie. It is defined by a red line which runs a foot to the side of each goal post and four feet outward. Behind each goal sits a goal judge whose only responsibility is to decide whether the puck crosses the goal line in front of him. If it does, he pushes a button which lights up the red lamp overhead.

WARREN EDWARD "ROCKY" GODFREY

BORN: Toronto, Ontario, March 23, 1931
POSITION: Defenseman, Boston Bruins, 1952–55, 1962–63; Detroit
     Red Wings, 1955–62, 1963–68

When Warren Godfrey broke in with the Boston Bruins in 1952–53 as an NHL rookie defenseman, his manager Lynn Patrick was embarrassed by the youngster's clumsiness. "Godfrey," Patrick needled, "is the only player I've ever known in hockey who can trip over the blue line!" Perhaps. But Rocky lasted more than a decade in the bigs. After Boston, he played for Detroit (1955–56 through 1961–62), then back to the Bruins for one season before finishing his career in the Motor City from 1963–64 through 1967–68. By that time he was able to skate *over* the blue line without mishap.

ROBERT (BOB) GOLDHAM

BORN: Georgetown, Ontario, May 12, 1922
POSITION: Defenseman, Toronto Maple Leafs, 1941–42, 1945–47;
     Chicago Black Hawks, 1947–50; Detroit Red Wings, 1950–56

Bob Goldham turned hero immediately in his rookie NHL season (1941–42), playing defense for the Toronto Maple Leafs in the Stanley Cup finals against the Detroit Red Wings. Goldham, who had been elevated from the American League's Hershey Bears, was among several green, young players inserted into the Maple Leafs' lineup to replace such aging veterans as Bucko McDonald and Bingo Kampman as the Leafs fell behind three games to none. The Toronto sextet, sparked by the youthful Goldham, Ernie Dickens, Don Metz, and Wally Stanowski, rallied to win the next four games and the Cup. In time Goldham matured into an effective defenseman who was especially good at dropping to the ice to block enemy shots. During the 1947–48 season he was part of a package—including teammates Gus Bodnar, Bud Poile, Gaye Stewart, and Ernie Dickens—which the Leafs sent to Chicago for ace center Max Bentley and utility forward Cy Thomas. Goldham was dealt to Detroit in 1950–51 and finished his career with the Red Wings in 1955–56. More recently he has become a popular hockey commentator in Toronto.

WILLIAM ALFRED (BILL) GOLDSWORTHY

BORN: Kitchener, Ontario, August 24, 1944
POSITION: Right Wing, Boston Bruins, 1964–67; Minnesota North
  Stars, 1967–

In Minnesota there is a dance called the "Goldy Shuffle" which Minnesotans usually see performed thirty-five times or so through a hockey season by its inventor, Minnesota North Star Bill Goldsworthy.

Goldsworthy has been the backbone of the North Star offense since 1969. He played for Team Canada against the Soviets in 1972, and in 1973–74 was fifth among all NHL scorers with 48 goals.

EBENEZER RALSTON (EBBIE) GOODFELLOW

BORN: Ottawa, Ontario, April 9, 1907
POSITION: Center and Defenseman, Detroit Red Wings, 1930–43;
  Coach, Chicago Black Hawks, 1950–52
AWARDS: Hart Trophy, 1940; All-Star (First Team), 1937, 1940, (Second Team), 1936; Hockey Hall of Fame, 1963

Before Gordie Howe came along Ebbie Goodfellow marauded the ice lanes for Detroit's Red Wings. Ebbie was a native of Ottawa who played NHL hockey in

Detroit from 1929–30 until he retired in 1942–43. During that time he played on Stanley Cup winners in 1936 and 1937.

In his later years, Ebbie switched to defense and actually coached the Wings when regular coach Jack Adams was suspended following an outburst during the 1942 Stanley Cup finals with Toronto. At the time the Red Wings were leading the series three games to one, but the Leafs rallied and won the Cup four games to three. Ebbie took a turn at full-time coaching with the Chicago Black Hawks following World War II before quitting hockey altogether for business pursuits in Detroit.

JOHN (JACKIE) GORDON

BORN: Winnipeg, Manitoba, March 3, 1928
POSITION: Center, New York Rangers 1948–51; Coach, Minnesota
    North Stars, 1967–75

One of an endless line of Winnipeggers to reach the majors via the Rangers' farm system, Jack Gordon was a smallish center who skated for New York's 1950 Stanley Cup finalists. His big-league statistics (13 points in 36 games) were less impressive than his minor league record in Cleveland. Gordon later turned to coaching, converting a low-pressure style into several championship teams. Jack was signed by the Minnesota North Stars when expansion came in 1967. Some observers believe that young players failed to respond to him, citing the North Stars consistently lackluster records. When Wren Blair left Minnesota as general manager, Gordon assumed the general manager role in 1974–75.

THOMAS P. GORMAN

A rollicking Irishman, Tommy Gorman, managed the Chicago Black Hawks, Ottawa Senators, New York Americans, and Montreal Maroons before moving in as manager of the Montreal Canadiens. "He was," said Canadian author Bill Roche, "one of the hockey's all-time executives."

Tommy was one of the funniest men in sport and exceptionally creative. He was imported by New York bootleg baron William "Big Bill" Dwyer to manage Dwyer's brand new NHL club, the Americans, in 1925–26. To get the job, Gorman had to sell his interest in the Ottawa Senators of the NHL. Tommy signed a two-year contract with the Americans as manager and coach. After the Americans first season Gorman gave up coaching and hired Edouard "Newsy" Lalonde to run the bench. Meanwhile, Gorman wheeled and dealed to make the Amerks a colorful club. He obtained Lionel Conacher—Canada's athlete of the half-century—to play defense. He later obtained goalie Roy Worters, Conacher's diminutive drinking pal, from Pittsburgh.

Gorman must have wondered occasionally about his collection of zanies. For example, there was the time the Americans were training in New Haven in 1928. Their quarters were in the Garde Hotel, a hostel that the Americans' manager nearly saw destroyed before his eyes. "One night," Gorman later recalled, "Lionel Conacher was playing cards in a room with Billy Burch and others. All of a sudden Red Green threw an apple core and hit Conacher in the eye. Lionel leaped from his chair and chased Red down the hall. Green slammed a door behind him at the end of the hall only to have big Conacher draw back and make a shoulder lunge at the closed door. Conny missed the door but he crashed into the wall so hard that some of the back section of the building actually collapsed—with Conacher and Green beneath it. It cost the hockey club $500."

As manager of the Americans, Gorman was constantly harassed by the bosses of Madison Square Garden, which owned the rival New York Rangers. Once, during the 1928–29 season, Gorman was summoned to the Garden office by Rangers' president Col. John Hammond who was complaining about the Americans' off-ice conduct. He berated Gorman and insisted that at that very moment the American players were cavorting in a big party at a flat on Fifty-first Street around the corner from Madison Square Garden. Gorman dashed from the office, got the assistance of two detectives, and found the party. When they burst into the room they discovered not one of the Americans but nearly a dozen Rangers—celebrating the birthday of their defenseman, Ching Johnson!

In January 1933 Gorman was imported to manage the Chicago Black Hawks by owner Major Frederic McLaughlin. When Gorman arrived at Chicago Stadium he realized that all was not right with the team. During a workout he noted that goalie Charlie Gardiner was guarding the pipes at one end of the rink. When he glanced at the other end, a strange sight met his eyes. Instead of a substitute practice goalie, Gorman saw a full-sized scarecrow manning the nets as if it were a paid goaltender.

"The Major's idea," Gorman later related, "was that players would learn to shoot so they could score without hitting the dummy. It was supposed to increase their accuracy." As Gorman became acclimatized to the new job, he realized that it was but one of an endless list of eccentricities that permeated the franchise.

Like most Black Hawk employees of Major McLaughlin, Gorman soon had it up to his neck in hassling and departed for more pleasant surroundings. He eventually made his way to the Montreal Canadiens where he helped mold the marvelous Montreal dynasty of World War II days with Bill Durnan in goal, Butch Bouchard on defense, and Maurice "Rocket" Richard leading the attack. He was succeeded by Frank Selke, Sr., who, as Canadiens' managing director, guided the team from the late forties to the beginning of the sixties.

In his lengthy NHL career as manager and coach, Gorman had the distinction of winning the Stanley Cup for more different cities than any other individual, including the Ottawa Senators (1920, 1921, 1923) when Gorman was manager. In 1934 he managed and coached Chicago to the Cup championship. A year later Tommy did likewise with the Montreal Maroons. His last championship hurrahs occurred in 1944 and 1946 when he managed the Canadiens to Stanley Cup victories.

JOHN P. (JOHNNY) GOTTSELIG

BORN: Odessa, Russia, June 24, 1905
POSITION: Left Wing, Chicago Black Hawks, 1929–45; Coach, Chicago Black Hawks, 1945–48
AWARDS: All-Star (Second Team), 1939

The only NHL star to turn coach and then club press agent was Johnny Gottselig, born in Odessa, Russia. He became a Black Hawk in 1928–29 and remained one after he retired in 1944–45.

Gottselig was skating for the Hawks in 1933–34, their first championship year, and again when Chicago won its second Cup in 1938. Johnny coached Chicago in the midforties when tiny Max and Doug Bentley led the Hawks in scoring. "It's the same damn story every winter," Gottselig once lamented, "nobody is fast enough to catch the Bentleys, so they try to knock 'em out."

Gottselig solved that problem by having big defenseman John Mariucci beat up on anyone who beat up the Bentleys.

JOSEPH GEORGES PHILIPPE (PHIL) GOYETTE

BORN: Lachine, Quebec, October 31, 1933
POSITION: Center, Montreal Canadiens, 1956–63; New York Rangers, 1963–69, 1972; St. Louis Blues, 1969–70; Buffalo Sabres, 1970–72; Coach, New York Islanders, 1972–73
AWARDS: Lady Byng Trophy, 1970

A veteran of sixteen National Hockey League playing seasons, Phil Goyette made one key mistake—he agreed to coach the newborn New York Islanders in the 1972–73 season when the expansion club was one of the worst ever to skate in the majors. Goyette had become accustomed to class hockey since breaking in with the Montreal Canadiens in 1956–57. He played on four straight Stanley Cup championship teams before being traded to the New York Rangers after the 1962–63 season. Goyette continued to star on Broadway, spending six years with the New Yorkers before being traded to the St. Louis Blues before the start of the 1969–70 season. A slick, clean playmaker, Goyette enjoyed his single greatest year in St. Louis, scoring 29 goals and 49 assists for 78 points while winning the Lady Byng Trophy. He was drafted by the Buffalo Sabres the following summer and played for Buffalo for half a season before retiring as a player. But the Rangers persuaded him to return briefly that year for the homestretch. He then became the Islanders' coach and was fired in midseason.

ROBERT J. (BOB) GRACIE

BORN: North Bay, Ontario, November 8, 1911
POSITION: Forward, Toronto Maple Leafs, 1930–33; Boston Bruins, 1933–34; New York Americans, 1934–35; Montreal Maroons, 1935–38; Chicago Black Hawks, 1938–39

Self-confident to a fault, Bob Gracie joined the Toronto Maple Leafs in 1930–31 and played on the Stanley Cup winners a year later. Once, in a game against the Montreal Maroons, the match went into sudden-death overtime without a decision until the seventeen-minute mark when Toronto coach Dick Irvin dispatched Gracie to the ice. Gracie skated along the boards near the official scorer's bench. "Get a pencil," Gracie demanded of the scorer. "Write these words—'Goal by Gracie.' " The scorer smiled and ignored the kid. A minute later Gracie took a pass from Andy Blair and fired the winning goal. He was traded to Boston in 1933–34 and, that same year, to the Americans. A season later he was dealt to the Maroons and in 1938–39 to the Black Hawks, his last NHL team.

DANIEL FREDERICK (DANNY) GRANT

BORN: Fredericton, New Brunswick, February 21, 1946
POSITION: Left Wing, Montreal Canadiens, 1965–66, 1967–68; Minnesota North Stars, 1968–74; Detroit Red Wings, 1974–
AWARDS: Calder Trophy, 1969

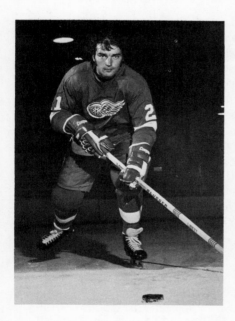

One of hockey's highest scoring left wingers today, Danny Grant became a Red Wing following the 1973–74 season. In six years with the North Stars Danny missed only five contests, averaged 29 tallies and won the Calder Trophy in 1969. His proficiency around the net and durability all over the ice make Danny one of hockey's prize possessions.

MICHAEL (MIKE) GRANT

BORN: 1870s
DIED: 1961
POSITION: Defenseman, Montreal Victorias (AHA), 1894–98; Montreal Victorias (CAHL), 1899–1900, 1902; Montreal Shamrocks, (CAHL), 1901
AWARDS: Hockey Hall of Fame, 1950

Some people actually have the audacity to say that Bobby Orr is *the* rushing defenseman. Well, back when an entire season consisted of seven or eight games, Mike Grant was an offensive-minded defenseman—the first such beast to be spotted in all of North America. Grant's spectacular end-to-end rushes were unheard of in a day when defensemen rarely, if ever, crossed center ice.

A huge, imposing man with a big, bushy moustache, Grant was instrumental in bringing four consecutive Stanley Cups to his team, the Victorias, from 1895–98. Grant retired as a player in 1902, but his flair for the flamboyant did not end with his playing days. Refereeing a Stanley Cup series some years later, Grant caused a minor uproar as he skated out to drop the puck wearing a dapper derby hat.

JOSEPH GERARD LEO "TIGER," "THE GAZELLE" GRAVELLE

BORN: Aylmer, Quebec, June 10, 1925
POSITION: Forward, Montreal Canadiens, 1946–50; Detroit Red Wings, 1950–51

Leo Gravelle, who played for the Montreal Canadiens from 1946 through 1950, was one of the fastest—if not *the* fastest—skater in NHL history, but he couldn't score worth a damn. But for the nickname and the speed Gravelle's play was otherwise undistinguished.

However, Leo did make headlines in November 1949 when he came to the aid of teammate Ken Reardon during a brawl at Chicago Stadium. It started when a fan yelled at Reardon: "You're a brave man with a hockey stick in your hand." The way it's been told, Reardon reached over with that same stick and opened up the fan's head. Leo Gravelle and Billy Reay skated over to help their teammate. A fan jumped on the ice, but referee Bill Chadwick repulsed this invasion. Others pressed up against the outside of the boards but were prevented from spilling on the rink's surface by the ushers.

Charges of assault were brought against Reardon, Gravelle, and Reay by four members of the crowd, and the three Canadiens were arrested at the end of the game. Black Hawk president Bill Tobin had to post bonds in order to prevent the trio from spending the night in jail.

EDWARD JOSEPH (TED) GREEN

BORN: Eriksdale, Manitoba, March 23, 1940
POSITION: Defenseman, Boston Bruins, 1960–72; New England
    Whalers (WHA), 1972–75; Winnipeg Jets (WHA), 1975–
AWARDS: All-Star (Second Team), 1969

For almost eight years, "Terrible Ted" Green epitomized the style of the Boston Bruins, bruising, roughhousing, and intimidating members of the opposing team every time he stepped out for a shift.

In the 1967–68 season, however, Green established himself as one of hockey's better rearguards, as he broke former Bruin Doug Mohns's records for assists by a defenseman, garnering a total of 36, along with 7 goals. The figures were even more amazing when you consider that Green was recovering from a knee injury.

Then came the infamous stick-swinging incident with the late Wayne Maki, then of the St. Louis Blues, on September 21, 1969.

Former teammate Derek Sanderson recalls that Maki hit Ted from behind as Green was clearing the puck from the Boston zone. Green turned to knock Maki down, but Maki speared him as he rose from the ice. Green swung his stick at Maki, again knocking him down, and fell off-balance. Maki then swung his stick and hit Green across the top of his head. Green went down in a heap, his brain embedded with chips from his skull. Two operations were required to save his life. Green's left side was paralyzed. It was a question of whether or not he could live a normal life, much less skate or play hockey.

The fallen Boston defenseman sat out the entire 1969–70 season, and watched from the privacy of his home as the Bruins fought and rumbled their way to their first Stanley Cup in thirty years. He could not accept the fact that his hockey career was behind him, however, and in the summer of 1970, he got his doctor's permission to try and play once again.

Gingerly, at first, then gaining more confidence with each day of training camp and the regular season, Ted Green worked his way back into the Bruins' scheme of things. There were noticeable differences; not the least of which was the death-black helmet Green was wearing and would continue to wear. He was also still a heavy hitter, but the brashness which had characterized his play of bygone years was long passed. Once a defenseman whom Ranger president William Jennings had placed a bounty on, Ted Green was now a good, tough hockey player, who refused to look for trouble, although he never backed down from it. His comeback reached its peak when the Bruins won the Stanley Cup in the 1971–72 season. Teddy Green was a key contributor.

With the formation of the World Hockey Association, in 1972, Ted Green accepted the offer of the New England Whalers and jumped to the new circuit. The members of the Whalers had so much faith in the rejuvenated Green that he was made captain of the team. His role with the new club was to serve as the veteran and leader of the team; he responded very well to the challenge, and showed that there was plenty of quality hockey player left in him. At the close of the 1974–75 season Green was traded to the Winnipeg Jets to finish his career in his hometown.

The story of Ted Green, the man who lived by the violence of hockey, and who nearly died by it, has to rank as one of the greatest comeback tales in the history of sport.

WILFRED "SHORTY" GREEN

BORN: Sudbury, Ontario, July 17, 1896
DIED: March 1960
POSITION: Forward, Hamilton Tigers, 1923–25; New York Americans, 1925–27; Coach, New York Americans, 1927–28
AWARDS: Hockey Hall of Fame, 1962

Shorty Green was a tiny, intense player whose zeal for the game was not lessened one bit by the fact that he was an epileptic. Sometimes the violent seizures would overtake the slight forward during a game and it took up to four players to restrain him.

After playing a few seasons for Hamilton, Shorty moved east with the New York Americans where he was one of the most popular players on a dismal conglomeration of losers. After one particularly violent game with the rival New York Rangers, Shorty was rushed to the hospital, suffering from internal bleeding.

The New York tabloids sadly announced that Green was dying and possibly wouldn't make it through to morning. As it turned out, reports of Green's untimely death were slightly exaggerated, but he was finished as a player. He did, however, inherit the Amerk coaching duties, but suffering through a losing season from the sidelines was too much for a fierce competitor like Green. After one season behind the American bench, he stepped aside. Shorty Green is a member of the Hockey Hall of Fame.

JIM GREGORY

The youngest of all the NHL general managers, the Toronto Maple Leafs' Jim Gregory began his administrative career as a trainer for the St. Michael's College junior club and gradually worked his way up the ladder from junior coach to manager to scout to head coach of the Vancouver Canucks of the Western Hockey League. Named the Leafs' general manager in 1969, Gregory has engineered some very successful trades and draft selections for rebuilding his team.

SILAS (SI) GRIFFIS

BORN: Kansas, 1883
DIED: 1950
POSITION: Rover and Defenseman, Rat Portage (Kenora) Thistles, 1903–07; Vancouver Millionaires (PCHA), 1912–18
AWARDS: Hockey Hall of Fame, 1950

Although born in the United States, Griffis moved with his family to Ontario in 1883, where they finally settled in Rat Portage—now called Kenora.

Griffis was unusually large for a hockey player of that bygone era (195 pounds), but fast, and he began his career with the Kenora amateur team as a rover (the seventh player who alternated between forward and defense). From 1900 to 1904 his team won the league championship. Si then went pro with the Kenora Thistles on defense and they won the Stanley Cup from the Montreal Wanderers in 1906.

Griffis retired shortly thereafter and moved to the West Coast. But when the Patricks started the Pacific Coast League, he returned to captain the Vancouver

Millionaires. In his first game out of retirement, he scored three goals and two assists. Before retiring again in 1918, he helped the Millionaires to a Cup win over Ottawa in 1915. He is a member of the Hockey Hall of Fame.

JOCELYN MARCEL GUEVREMONT

BORN: Montreal, Quebec, March 1, 1951
POSITION: Defenseman, Vancouver Canucks, 1971–74; Buffalo Sabres, 1974–

One of the wave of "offensive defensemen" coming out of junior hockey in the early seventies, Jocelyn Guevremont was the first choice of the Vancouver Canucks in the 1971 amateur draft. His credentials were impressive, as the young defenseman popped in 22 goals in his last year of junior play with the Montreal Junior Canadiens in 1970–71.

"Josh" was extremely impressive in his rookie campaign as he established a mark for most points in one season by a rookie defenseman (51), which was broken the following year by the New York Islanders' Denis Potvin. Although always regarded as an offensive specialist, Guevremont worked especially hard in training camp on shoring up his defensive game, which was sorely lacking on most of the Canucks until 1974–75.

But by that time Guevremont was also lacking on the Canucks, having been traded to Buffalo's Sabres at the beginning of that year's campaign.

ALDO RENO GUIDOLIN

BORN: Forks of Credit, Ontario, June 6, 1932
POSITION: Defenseman and Forward, New York Rangers, 1952–56

The first cousin of Armand "Bep" Guidolin, Aldo was an underrated defense-man-forward with the Rangers during the midfifties. However, he later became a successful coach in Baltimore and Omaha. His best minor league days were spent with Baltimore, Cleveland, and, briefly, with Springfield of the American League. At Springfield, Aldo became a close observer of boss Eddie Shore's bizarre coaching techniques. "He harped on three points," said Guidolin. "He wanted the hands two feet apart on the stick, the feet eleven inches apart on the ice, and he wanted you to skate in a sort of sitting position. You had to do it exactly right, or you were in big trouble."

Guidolin discovered this one morning during a practice. He had just com-pleted what he considered a perfect pass that resulted in a goal while skating at top speed. Then he heard the whistle and saw Shore motion to him. "Mister Guidolin," he said, "do you know what you did wrong?"

"The pass was perfect," said Guidolin. "I was in the sitting position. My two hands were on the stick. What more do you want?"

"Mis-ter Guidolin," Shore said, "your legs were two inches too far apart."

ARMAND (BEP) GUIDOLIN

BORN: Thorold, Ontario, December 9, 1925
POSITION: Forward, Boston Bruins, 1942–47; Detroit Red Wings, 1947–48; Chicago Black Hawks, 1948–52; Coach, Boston Bruins, 1973–74; Kansas City Scouts, 1974–

Through most of his adult life in hockey, Armand "Bep" Guidolin's chief claim to fame was that he had been the youngest player (sixteen) ever to perform in the NHL. But in the fall of 1971 the Boston Bruins brought all of their top farmhands to Boston and created the Braves, a new AHL team, installing Bep Guidolin as coach.

No team in the AHL was better conditioned, better disciplined, or more spirited. Bep's Braves won the eastern division title their first year in the AHL, leading the race from wire to wire. Midway through their second season, Bep got the call to replace Tom Johnson as coach of the parent Bruins. Immediately observers noted that the Bruins practices became much more exhausting, characterized by relentless drills and rink-length wind sprints. And their games became more conservative. "Other teams have been capitalizing on our mistakes," Bep complained. "We're going to start concentrating on little things again, like making at least two good passes in our own end."

Suddenly the Bruins, who had picked up just 12 points in the final fifteen games of Johnson's regime, began to flex their muscles again.

But then in the 1973–74 season, Guidolin feuded with Derek Sanderson and Phil Esposito and coached the first established NHL team (Boston) to ever lose to an expansion club in the Stanley Cup finals. As a result he was fired by the Bruins and hired to coach the New Kansas City Scouts, one of the two baby expansion clubs of 1974–75.

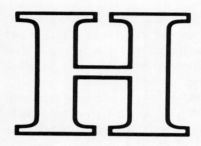

VICTOR EDWARD (VIC) HADFIELD

BORN: Oakville, Ontario, October 4, 1940
POSITION: Left Wing, New York Rangers, 1961–74; Pittsburgh
    Penguins, 1974–
AWARDS: All-Star (Second Team), 1972

A New York Ranger for thirteen seasons before being traded to the Pittsburgh Penguins for defenseman Nick Beverley, Vic Hadfield was the portsider on the Broadway Blueshirts' Goal-a-Game (G-A-G) Line.

Normally a plodding digger with a reputation as a tough guy, Vic scored 50 goals in 1971–72, an all-time New York Ranger record.

Named captain of the Broadway sextet in 1971, Hadfield was later beset by a series of nagging injuries that limited his potential as an enforcer as well as his ability to blast the puck past opposing netminders. After the Rangers' 1974 playoff defeat at the hands of the Philadelphia Flyers, Vic and his reported $100,000 salary were shipped to the Pens.

GEORGE HAINSWORTH

BORN: Toronto, Ontario, June 26, 1895
DIED: October 9, 1950
POSITION: Goalie, Montreal Canadiens, 1926–33, 1937; Toronto Maple Leafs, 1933–36
AWARDS: Vezina Trophy, 1927, 1928, 1929; Hockey Hall of Fame, 1961

Montreal Canadiens' goalie George Hainsworth was an English Canadian who measured only five-foot six inches, compared to his tall, distinguished French predecessor, Georges Vezina. Furthermore, at thirty-three years of age, Hainsworth seemed to be approaching the end, rather than the beginning, of his major league career.

His debut was something less than impressive. He was beaten, 4–1, in the season's opener at Boston and returned to Montreal where Ottawa outscored Les Canadiens, 2–1. This was followed by a 2–1 loss to the Maroons, thus confirming the suspicions of Canadien fans that Hainsworth was an unworthy successor to Vezina.

Hainsworth played every one of the forty-four games on the Canadiens' schedule, and finished the season with a goals-against average of 1.52, bettered only by Clint Benedict of the Maroons who registered a 1.51 mark.

Little by little the Canadiens' fans began warming up to Hainsworth. He won the Vezina Trophy first in 1926–27, again in the 1927–28 season with a remarkable 1.09 goals-against average, and managed to improve on that in 1928–29, this time allowing only 43 goals in 44 games for a 0.98 mark.

On the night of January 24, 1929, the Toronto Maple Leafs were visiting the Forum. As the Canadiens were peppering Hainsworth in the pregame warm-up, a practice shot caught the goaltender unawares and smashed into his nose, knocking him unconscious. A bloody mess, Hainsworth was carried into the dressing room and a call went over the Forum loudspeaker for the Canadiens' spare goalie. He couldn't be located.

The team physician worked over Hainsworth's broken nose, but the blow was so severe that within a matter of minutes the swelling had completely shut one eye. "Bandage me up," Hainsworth insisted, "I want to get out there."

Neither the doctor nor the Canadiens had much choice. Ten minutes later George skated out to his position for the opening face-off. The goal-hungry Maple Leafs immediately swarmed to the attack and bombarded Hainsworth with every variety of shot at their command.

Veteran reporters could hardly remember the fans sitting down throughout the game as Hainsworth portrayed a hockey version of Horatio at the bridge, and soon George himself was yelling and screaming along with his fans. "His face," wrote a critic, "one-sided and bulging, feverish and red from excitement and injury, loomed livid and macabre above the forest of sticks and whirling forms crowding close about him. This was his night of nights!"

The Maple Leafs managed to jam one shot behind him, but the inspired Canadiens scored a goal, too. The game ended in a 1–1 tie. From that point on Hainsworth was a Forum hero and played seven full seasons until he was forty years old.

Hainsworth seemed to improve with age. In 1928–29 he recorded 22 shutouts in 44 games and continued to excel for the Canadiens until the 1932–33 campaign. The entire Montreal team from Morenz to Hainsworth was in a slump that year. It hit its lowest point on February 21, 1933, when Les Canadiens visited Boston and were demolished, 10–0. His boss, Leo Dandurand was furious with Hainsworth, who had given up several "easy" goals and made up his mind to trade him at the earliest opportunity. One afternoon he picked up the telephone and called Conn Smythe, manager of the Maple Leafs. Within a few minutes it had been agreed that Smythe would trade the Toronto goalie Lorne Chabot for Hainsworth.

Chabot played only one season for Les Canadiens and registered a 2.15 goals-against average, whereas Hainsworth's mark was a less impressive 2.48. But Hainsworth lasted three full seasons in Toronto, during which the Leafs twice led the league, before returning briefly to Montreal in 1937, where he played several games before retiring.

GLENN HENRY "MR. GOALIE" HALL

BORN: Humboldt, Saskatchewan, October 3, 1931
POSITION: Goalie, Detroit Red Wings, 1952–57; Chicago Black Hawks, 1957–67; St. Louis Blues, 1967–71
AWARDS: Calder Trophy, 1956; Vezina Trophy, 1963, 1967 (with Denis DeJordy), 1969 (with Jacques Plante); Conn Smythe Trophy, 1968; All-Star (First Team), 1957, 1958, 1960, 1963, 1964, 1966, 1969, (Second Team), 1956, 1961, 1962, 1967; Hockey Hall of Fame, 1975

Glenn Hall, one of the greatest professional netminders of all time, managed to appear in an amazing 552 consecutive contests without missing a single game. Yet Hall was so fearful of his hazardous occupation, he would often get violently ill before games.

Over his eighteen-year big league career, Hall labored for three NHL clubs—the Detroit Red Wings, Chicago Black Hawks, and St. Louis Blues. He was named the First Team All-Star goalie seven times, three times having his name inscribed on the Vezina Trophy as the league's top goaltender.

Despite taking scores of painful stitches in his face, Hall did not don a goalie mask until the twilight of his career, claiming it restricted his vision when the puck was at his feet. One night, during the 1957 Stanley Cup playoffs, a screened shot suddenly flashed out of a tangle of bodies and smashed into Hall's maskless face. The game was delayed for a half hour while Hall took 23 stitches in his mouth before returning to finish the game.

Hall was named to the Hockey Hall of Fame in June 1975.

JOSEPH HENRY "BAD JOE" HALL

BORN: Stratfordshire, England, 1882
DIED: April 5, 1919
POSITION: Defenseman, Quebec (ECAHA), 1906; Montreal Canadiens and Shamrocks (ECAHA), 1908; Montreal Wanderers (ECAHA), 1909; Montreal Shamrocks, (NHA) 1910; Quebec Bulldogs (NHA) 1911–17; Montreal Canadiens, 1917–19

"Bad" Joe Hall was born in England but learned his hockey in western Canada. He first achieved distinction—or notoriety—playing for Houghton, Michigan, in the bloodthirsty International Pro League in 1905 and 1906. Those who became close friends of Hall's insist that he was the victim of a newspaperman's overzealous typewriter and really wasn't a bad fellow after all.

"He wasn't mean," said friend and teammate Joe Malone, "despite what a lot of people said about him. He certainly liked to deal out a heavy check and he was always ready to take it as well as dish it out. That in itself was remarkable when you consider that Joe weighed in at only a hundred fifty pounds. As far as I'm concerned he should have been known as 'Plain' Joe Hall and not 'Bad' Joe Hall. That always was a bum rap."

Whatever the case, Hall and Malone ignited the Canadiens to a successful first half of the 1917–18 season and by midpoint the Flying Frenchmen—by now dotted with English-speaking players—were in first place. Then on January 2, 1918, fire reduced the Montreal Arena to rubble. Both Les Canadiens and the Wanderers lost all their equipment and the arena damage was put at $150,000.

With the fall of the Montreal Arena, Les Canadiens lost their momentum until they adjusted to playing in the Jubilee Rink for the 1918–19 season. Les Canadiens then regained their winning ways and defeated Ottawa for the right to go west and challenge Seattle for the Cup.

The series opened on March 19. Seattle bombed Les Canadiens, 7–0, and appeared destined to sweep the series. But with Newsy Lalonde in command of his game, the visitors rebounded neatly to capture the second match, 4–2, and the teams settled down for what appeared to be a thrilling series. Seattle captured the third game, 7–2, setting the stage for what NHL historian Charles L. Coleman has described as "the greatest match ever played on the Pacific Coast."

Neither team scored in regulation time. One hour and forty minutes of sudden-death overtime were played before the game was called a draw. When the teams met again four nights later, the score was 3–3 going into overtime, but this time the Canadiens prevailed after 15:57 of extra play on a goal by Odie Cleghorn.

The game was significant in several respects. For one thing it made abundantly clear the fact that Les Canadiens had retained their flair for coming from behind, a trait that has remained with them into the present.

Equally meaningful was an incident that caught the eyes of some spectators as the teams battled for the winning goal. "Bad" Joe Hall, who in earlier games had battled vehemently with Seattle's Cully Wilson, appeared to lose his zest and finally left the ice and made his way to the dressing room. Unknown to all the onlookers, it was to the the last time Joe was ever to step on a rink.

Hall was rushed to the hospital, stricken with the flu bug that was causing an epidemic throughout North America. Immediately after the game several other Canadiens, including Lalonde and manager George Kennedy, were bedded with influenza but none as bad as Joe Hall.

With the series tied at two apiece an attempt was made to finish the playoff for the Stanley Cup. Kennedy requested permission to "borrow" players from Victoria to finish the series, but the hosts declined the bid and the playoff was canceled without a winner.

Six days after he had stumbled off the ice, Joe Hall died of influenza in a Seattle hospital. His friend and admirer, Joe Malone, was the most seriously affected by the news because he believed that Hall never had the opportunity to erase the bad name he had acquired. "There were plenty of huge, rough characters on the ice in Joe's time," said Malone, "and he was able to stay in there with them for more than eighteen years. His death was a tragic and shocking climax to one of the most surprising of all Stanley Cup series."

RED HAMILL

BORN: Toronto, Ontario, January 11, 1917
POSITION: Forward, Boston Bruins, 1937–41; Chicago Black Hawks, 1941–1951

A potent shooter with equally potent fists, Red Hamill split his NHL career between the Boston Bruins (1937–38 through 1940–41) and the Chicago Black Hawks (1941–42 through 1950–51). His most productive year was 1942–43 when he scored 28 goals and 16 assists for 44 points in 50 NHL games. Opponents insist that while there may have been fighters as powerful as Hamill, there have never been any more fearsome.

NED HARKNESS

BORN: Ottawa, Quebec, September 19, 1921
POSITION: Coach, Detroit Red Wings, 1970–71

Immensely successful as hockey coach at Cornell University, Ned Harkness was hardly a hit later as coach and then manager of the Detroit Red Wings.

Harkness was hired by owner Bruce Norris to run the Red Wings although Ned had never coached a day of big league hockey in his life. Harkness alienated many of the older Detroit players, especially Alex Delvecchio and Gordie Howe. In time he was to alienate young ones, such as Garry Unger, as well. Harkness believed in strict discipline—no cigar-smoking in the dressing room—whatever the cost. The results were disastrous for the Red Wings who plummeted to the bottom of the NHL and remained impotent long after Harkness was finally dismissed as coach in 1971. Out of the general manager slot by late 1973, he returned to his former milieu, having been named coach of the prenatal Union College hockey team in Schenectady, New York.

DAVID GLEN HARMON

BORN: Holland, Manitoba, January 2, 1921
POSITION: Defenseman, Montreal Canadiens, 1942–51
AWARDS: All-Star (Second Team), 1945, 1949

Obscured by teammates Maurice "Rocket" Richard, Bill Durnan, and Emile "Butch" Bouchard, Glen Harmon nevertheless was a mainstay of the Montreal Canadiens' defense during the Canadiens' Stanley Cup victories in 1944 and 1946. A Canadien throughout his career, the unobstrusive Harmon entered the NHL in 1942 and retired following the 1950–51 season. There have been few more honest competitors than this native of Holland, Manitoba.

TERRANCE VICTOR (TERRY) HARPER

BORN: Regina, Saskatchewan, January 27, 1940
POSITION: Defenseman, Montreal Canadiens, 1962–72; Los Angeles
    Kings, 1972–75; Detroit Red Wings, 1975–

When Terry Harper first came up to the NHL, he was one of the "hit men" on the artistic Montreal Canadiens. Les Habitants boasted a bevy of stickhandling virtuosos who could transform a game of shinny into an art form—but they also understood the need for a couple of not-so-subtle bodyguards to help protect the valuable merchandise.

Harper and forward John Ferguson became the awkward, but effective, heavies in the glittering Canadien troupe of players. Terry understood his role, and accepted it, and came to be known as the league's leading bleeder.

Over Terry's nine seasons as a regular Montreal blue liner, the Habs copped five Stanley Cups and failed but once to make the playoffs. Then in August 1972, Harper was traded to the Los Angeles Kings.

After a brief period of adjustment, Harper settled into his new surroundings nicely. Teamed with ex-Black Hawk Gilles Marotte, the duo formed one of the best "expansion" defensive pairings in the league until Marotte went to New York in 1973. Harper was named captain after one season with L.A., and improved the defense and team immensely before being traded to Detroit in June 1975.

EDWARD ALEXANDER (TED) HARRIS

BORN: Winnipeg, Manitoba, July 18, 1936
POSITION: Defenseman, Montreal Canadiens, 1963–70; Minnesota North Stars, 1970–73; Detroit Red Wings, 1973–74; St. Louis Blues, 1974; Philadelphia Flyers, 1974–75; Coach, Minnesota North Stars, 1975–

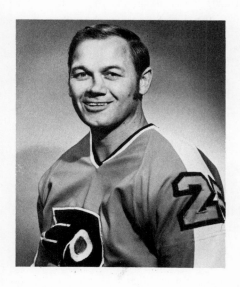

Ted Harris was a throwback defenseman to the days when crunching body-checks were more than the vogue than in contemporary hockey. He served a long minor league apprenticeship beginning with Philadelphia in the old Eastern League, then Springfield in 1956–59 where Hall of Famer Eddie Shore taught him how to skate effectively and bodycheck with authority. Harris reached the NHL in 1963–64 and spent six full seasons with the Canadiens before being acquired by the Minnesota North Stars in 1970. Harris had long been considered one of the NHL's three most effective fistfighters along with Johnny Ferguson and Orland Kurtenbach. Harris and Kurtenbach staged two classic one-on-one bouts in which each took a decision. Harris reached the Philadelphia Flyers in 1974–75 after briefly touching base in Detroit and St. Louis.

Harris announced his retirement as a player in the dressing room of the 1974–75 Stanley Cup Champion Philadelphia Flyers. Shortly thereafter he was named coach of the Minnesota North Stars.

RONALD THOMAS (RON) HARRIS

BORN: Verdun, Quebec, June 30, 1942
POSITION: Defenseman, Detroit Red Wings, 1962–64; Oakland
Seals, 1967–68; Detroit Red Wings, 1968–72; Atlanta Flames, 1972; New York Rangers, 1972–

Ron Harris became a New York Ranger by virtue of a ploy used by manager Emile Francis all too often: When the team gets hit with injuries in midseason or toward playoff time, Francis trades away talented young blood for emergency journeyman experience. The usual result is that the young blood goes on to glory with an expansion club, while the journeyman sours in New York after a season or two and gets traded, waivered, or drafted into oblivion.

Harris was needed in November 1972, and came to New York for Curt Bennett from Atlanta. His greatest use came inadvertently when he broke Phil Esposito's leg in the 1973 playoffs with a mean—but legal—check. He can, in a pinch, play forward, lugging the puck out well, and is popular with the crunch-loving fans.

WILLIAM EDWARD "HINKY" HARRIS

BORN: Toronto, Ontario, July 29, 1935
POSITION: Center, Toronto Maple Leafs, 1955–65; Detroit Red
Wings, 1965–66; California Seals, 1967–68; Pittsburgh Penguins, 1968–69; Coach, Ottawa Nationals/Toronto Toros (WHA), 1972–75

The story of Billy Harris's career as player and coach has been "close, but no cigar." Harris, a skinny, tall center, skated for the Toronto Maple Leafs from 1955 through 1965, never achieving the stardom originally expected of him. His playmaking was always adroit and he was adored by Toronto fans. But "Hinky" was less admired by Leafs' coach Punch Imlach who preferred more robust players. Harris was dealt to Detroit in 1965–66 and finally to Oakland in 1967–68.

A creative, cerebral type, Harris turned to coaching with the advent of the WHA and signed as coach of the Ottawa Nationals. When the Nats moved to Toronto and became the Toros, Harris went with them. In the summer of 1974 Hinky was named coach of Team Canada 1974 and was credited with a smooth, easy-going style as the WHA stars held the Russians even on Canadian ice. But Harris was blamed for being *too* soft on the players as they failed to win in Russia. He later was blamed for the Toros' failure to win big in the WHA and was fired in the middle of the 1974–75 season.

WILLIAM HENRY (BILLY) HARRIS

BORN: Toronto, Ontario, January 29, 1952
POSITION: Right Wing, New York Islanders, 1972–

When the time came for the baby New York Islanders to make the National Hockey League's number one junior draft pick in June 1972, they chose twenty-year-old Billy Harris.

Harris, 6′2″ and 195 pounds, like Yvan Cournoyer of the Canadiens, is a left-handed shooting right wing. Unlike Cournoyer, Harris played Junior A hockey with the Toronto Marlboros of the Ontario Hockey Association. In his final season with the Marlies he led the league in scoring with 57 goals and 72 assists for 129 points.

Harris's NHL contract was awesome, considering that he had not played a single game of pro hockey. It involved an estimated $300,000 for a three-year deal, with the last year of it renegotiable after two seasons.

Although he scored a healthy 28 goals, Harris's rookie season can best be described as miserable. He was expected to carry the full load for the fledgling club, and Billy lacked the maturity to handle the expectations, publicity, and general punishment a touted rookie gets from his opponents. After his freshman year Harris settled into his duties with respectability, largely because defensive phenom Denis Potvin had arrived to fill the vacuum as team leader and resident superstar.

GERALD WILLIAM (GERRY) HART

BORN: Flin Flon, Manitoba, January 1, 1948
POSITION: Defenseman, Detroit Red Wings, 1969–72; New York Islanders, 1972–

Burdened by knee injuries throughout his career, Gerry Hart was finally given regular playing time with the New York Islanders in 1974–75. Before being plucked by the Islanders in the 1972 expansion draft, the rugged but clumsy Hart had bounced up and down between the Detroit Red Wings and their minor league affiliates, the Fort Worth Wings of the Central League and the Tidewater Wings of the American League. Paired with Calder Trophy winner Denis Potvin over the last half of the 1973–74 season, Gerry played in the most games of his career (70) and performed solidly on a vastly improved Islander rearguard corps.

Injuries continued to bedevil Gerry in 1974–75. He suffered a concussion in a game with the Philadelphia Flyers at the Nassau Coliseum on November 5, 1974 which necessitated his wearing a helmet, but by spring, he was in superb form and contributed solidly against New York, Pittsburgh, and Philadelphia before the Islanders lost their semifinal playoff round.

THE HART TROPHY

The Hart Memorial Trophy is awarded annually to the NHL player "adjudged to be most valuable to his team." The winner, selected in a poll by the Professional Hockey Writers' Association in all NHL cities at the end of the regular season, receives $1,500; the runner-up receives $750.

The Hart Memorial was presented to the league in 1960, following the retirement of the original Hart Trophy to the Hockey Hall of Fame. That original award had been in turn donated to the NHL by Dr. David A. Hart, the father of former general manager and coach of the Montreal Canadiens, Cecil Hart.

With competition starting for the trophy in 1924, it is the second oldest award in the NHL. Frank Nighbor of the Ottawa Senators was the first winner of the trophy. The great Gordie Howe holds the record for winning it the most times—an incredible six occasions.

DOUGLAS NORMAN (DOUG) HARVEY

BORN: Montreal, Quebec, December 19, 1924

POSITION: Defenseman, Montreal Canadiens, 1947–61; New York Rangers, 1961–64; Detroit Red Wings, 1966–67; St. Louis Blues, 1968–69; Coach, New York Rangers, 1961–62

AWARDS: Norris Trophy, 1955–58, 1960–62; All-Star (First Team), 1952–58, 1960–62; (Second Team), 1959; Hockey Hall of Fame, 1973

Defenseman Douglas Harvey was so laconic in style, so calmly sure of himself, that he executed plays of extreme complication with consummate ease. Lacking the flamboyance of Eddie Shore or other Hall of Fame defensemen, Harvey was slow to receive the acclaim he deserved. "Often, Harvey's cool was mistaken for disinterest," said author Josh Greenfeld. "Actually it was the result of an always calculating concentration." But by 1955–56 Harvey's excellence had become apparent. "Doug Harvey was the greatest defenseman who ever played hockey—bar none," said Toe Blake. "Usually a defenseman specializes in one thing and builds a reputation on that, but Doug could do everything well."

Although Harvey was not known as an excessively dirty player, he was occasionally moved to violence when he was suitably provoked. Once, during a game with the Rangers in New York, Harvey planted the pointed blade of his stick in Red Sullivan's gut and sent the Ranger center to the hospital with a ruptured spleen. For a time Sullivan's condition was so grave he was given the last rites of the Catholic Church. Fortunately, he recovered completely and returned to play out his career in the NHL. Honest to a fault, Harvey never denied the attack, but he pointed out that Sullivan had developed an obnoxious, not to mention dangerous, habit of "kicking skates," so that when the two went into the corner of the rink Sullivan would kick Harvey's skates out from under him, making it very easy for the Montrealer to fall on his head. According to Doug, he warned Sullivan about his unfortunate proclivity and when the warning went unheeded the stick was plunged into Sullivan's stomach.

Harvey was a superb rusher but lacked the blazing shot that characterizes Bobby Orr's arsenal. There is little doubt that Orr has the advantage offensively, but not as much as current statistics would suggest. "Harvey," wrote author Josh Greenfeld, "could inaugurate a play from farther back and carry it farther than any other defenseman."

He was a consummate craftsman, perhaps unmatched among defensemen of our time for union of style, wisdom, and strength. He won the James Norris Memorial Trophy seven times as the best defenseman in the game; he was elected an All-Star eleven times.

Toe Blake coached Harvey in Montreal in the late fifties, during one tyrannical span from 1955 to 1960 when the Canadiens won the Stanley Cup for five successive seasons. Harvey was distinguished then as the hub of Montreal's smothering power play, associated with Boom-Boom Geoffrion, Jean Beliveau, Rocket Richard and Richard Winston "Dickie" Moore.

"No player put my heart in my mouth as often as Doug," Blake said. "But I learned to swallow in silence. His style was casual, but it worked. He made few mistakes, and, 99 percent of the time correctly anticipated the play or pass." Blake added the definitive estimate of the most imposing NHL defenseman since the immortal Eddie Shore: "Doug played defense in a rocking chair."

Harvey began playing professionally in 1947, after rejecting an offer from the Boston Braves to play baseball. He had used up two summers in the Border Baseball League at Ottawa, once leading all batsmen with an average of .351. Before that, in the last massive global war, he spent sixteen months as a gunner on a Canadian merchant ship in the North Atlantic.

The high time professionally for Harvey was the fifties—unhurried on the ice, popular off it, casually capable on a team where temperaments are not customarily cool. But when he hit the far slope of his career, and kept playing, hockey's rigid group-think suggested there was something not quite respectable in a player refusing to admit he has been caught by age. His persistence, the purists insisted, made a mockery of the Game.

Harvey became a nomad in 1964, when the NHL governors made him a free agent in return for his long service. Such gestures are rare because many sportsmen discard nothing as long as they suspect there is some wheat left in the husk.

He coached the New York Rangers to brief success for one season, sufficiently gifted at leadership to guide them into an uncommon appearance in the Stanley Cup playoffs. Critics wondered why he abandoned the executive end of the pastime for service among the yeomanry. "Aw, what the hell," he said. "When I was a coach, I couldn't be one of the boys. This way, if I want a beer with 'em, I get a beer."

It appeared that Harvey's NHL career had ended after his 1963—64 campaign with the Rangers, but he returned to the majors in 1966–67 with the Red Wings. Again he seemed to be through, but in the 1968 playoffs the St. Louis Blues inserted Doug into their lineup for the playoffs against Philadelphia and he helped the Blues oust the favored Flyers. He played the entire 1968–69 season for St. Louis and quite capably.

Harvey's playing career ended at this point, but he remained a factor in hockey, was inducted into the Hall of Fame, and when the WHA was organized was named an assistant manager of the Houston Aeros. Harvey's most significant move was advising the Aeros to sign Gordie Howe's sons, Mark and Marty, who have become WHA stars.

GEORGE HAY

BORN: Listowel, Ontario, January 10, 1898
POSITION: Left Wing, Regina Capitals (WCHL), 1922–25; Chicago
    Black Hawks, 1927; Detroit Cougars, 1928–30; Detroit Falcons,
    1931, 1933
AWARDS: Hockey Hall of Fame, 1958

George Hay was a high-scoring portsider on the original Regina Capitals team of the newly formed WCHL. Hay scored 23 goals in 25 games during the Caps' first season and was instrumental in their winning the league championship only to lose to Vancouver in their postseason playoff series.

Hay chipped in three more solid seasons with Regina and one more with Portland when the franchise was shifted before joining Chicago of the NHL in 1927. Traded to Detroit the following season, Hay continued scoring well until his retirement in 1933.

WILLIAM CHARLES "RED" HAY

BORN: Saskatoon, Saskatchewan, December 8, 1935
POSITION: Center, Chicago Black Hawks, 1959–67
AWARDS: Calder Trophy, 1960

Insightful and creative, Bill "Red" Hay was one of the earlier university graduates to skate successfully in the big time. He broke in with the Black Hawks in 1959–60 and remained with Chicago until his premature retirement in 1966–67 at the age of thirty-two. A center, Hay contributed mightily to the Black Hawks' last Stanley Cup triumph in 1961 and was one of the most effective skaters in Chicago's ice renaissance. His teammate, Stan Mikita, said it best about Bill: "The trick in making us a winner," said Mikita, "was getting the team working—this is where a leader comes in and Billy Hay was just such a leader." Hay teamed with Bobby Hull and the late Murray Balfour on what was dubbed "the Million-Dollar Line."

ANDREW ALEX (ANDY) HEBENTON

BORN: Winnipeg, Manitoba, October 3, 1929
POSITION: Right Wing, New York Rangers, 1955–63; Boston Bruins, 1963–64
AWARDS: Lady Byng Trophy, 1957

One of the most durable players of all time, right winger Andy Hebenton played nine consecutive seasons—seventy games each—in the NHL *without missing a single game*. His total was 630 matches—a record—without having been sidelined because of injury or incompetence. In 1956–57, Andy won the Lady Byng Trophy while playing for the Rangers, a club for whom he quietly excelled from 1955–56 through 1962–63. He was drafted by the Bruins and played in Boston for one season before being dropped to the Western League where he played superior hockey for several years thereafter.

Hebenton's finest hour as a scorer occurred in a 1957 Stanley Cup playoff when he scored a sudden-death goal at 13:38 in New York's Madison Square Garden against Montreal's Jacques Plante after eluding defenseman Bob Turner. It was the first overtime playoff game in Madison Square Garden since 1940, and the Rangers won, 4–3, although they ultimately lost the series.

EHRHARDT HENRY (OTT) HELLER

BORN: Kitchener, Ontario, June 2, 1910
POSITION: Defenseman, New York Rangers, 1931–46
AWARDS: All-Star (Second Team), 1941

Ott Heller was a smiling defenseman who played on two out of the three (1933, 1940) Stanley Cup victories for the Rangers. A six-footer who had just turned twenty-one, Heller joined the Rangers in the 1931–32 season, but began playing regularly the following year. He served out his full fifteen-year career with the Rangers and was one of the steadiest and sturdiest players of all time. After concluding his major league career in 1945–46, Ott continued for years to skate in the minors. During World War II, Ott and Bryan Hextall were the only bright spots on an otherwise bleak Rangers' roster.

PAUL GARNET HENDERSON

BORN: Kincardine, Ontario, January 28, 1943
POSITION: Left Wing, Detroit Red Wings, 1962–68; Toronto Maple
    Leafs, 1968–74; Toronto Toros (WHA), 1974–
AWARDS: Team Canada (NHL), 1972, (WHA), 1974

Nothing will ever dim the memory of Paul Henderson's breathtaking heroics in the classic 1972 series between Team Canada and the artful icemen of the Soviet Union.

Team Canada, or Team NHL, was rudely awakened to the harsh realities of world-class hockey by the fifth game of the series when the USSR held a seemingly insurmountable 3–1–1 edge. This meant Team Canada would have to win all of the three remaining games in order to eke out a victory—a shocking turn of events, since all but a few so-called shinny experts had proclaimed that anything less than an eight-game Canadian sweep would be tantamount to a national disgrace.

Then came Henderson. Like the fairy-tale knight in shining armor, the quick left winger proceeded to rescue his mates from the very jaws of defeat. Incredibly, in each of the three remaining games, Henderson personally dashed the Soviet hopes for victory with dramatic tie-breaking goals. The final game saw Henderson rap his own rebound past a fallen Soviet netminder with only 34 seconds remaining to win the series for Canada.

Suddenly, Henderson was a national hero. Had 1972 been an election year, the provinces surely would have had a new prime minister.

Paul inauspiciously broke into hockey in 1962 with the Detroit Red Wings organization. After a brief stay with Pittsburgh of the AHL, Paul was brought up to the big leagues for good. He chipped in four solid seasons for the Wings until he was shipped to Toronto in 1968 as part of a deal for Frank Mahovlich.

Paul seemed to mature as a hockey player while with the Maple Leafs, blossoming into a 30-goal scorer and tireless backchecker.

In 1974, after six seasons with the Maple Leafs, Paul skipped across town to the WHA's Toronto Toros—just in time for a rematch with the Russians. Paul was deservedly one of the most feared skaters on the 1974 Team Canada squad, but there was no way he could duplicate his act of two seasons earlier. A much stronger Soviet six demolished the WHA's all-star squad with the memory of Henderson's heroics burning in their minds.

CAMILLE "THE EEL" HENRY

BORN: Quebec City, Quebec, January 31, 1933
POSITION: Left Wing, New York Rangers, 1953–64, 1967–68; Chicago Black Hawks, 1964–65; St. Louis Blues, 1968–70; Coach, New York Raiders/Golden Blades/New Jersey Knights (WHA), 1972–74
AWARDS: Calder Memorial Trophy, 1954; Lady Byng Trophy, 1958; All-Star (Second Team), 1958

When Jean Beliveau graduated from the Quebec (Junior) Citadelles to the Quebec Aces (QSHL) in 1951, he already had become a hockey deity—the most talked-about young player in Canada. "Jean Beliveau in Quebec," wrote author Leonard Shecter, "is like Mickey Mantle and Joe DiMaggio in the United States."

When the majestic, 6' 2", 192-pound Beliveau left the Citadelles, the man picked to fill his skates was scrawny Camille "the Eel" Henry, a 5' 10", 140-pound weakling with an extraordinary puck sense and so beloved a disposition, Camille actually *was* able to follow Beliveau's act with the Citadelles. What Beliveau had in size, Henry had in brains. There never was a craftier forward who could thread a needle with a puck and stick if need be.

Inevitably, he reached the NHL and was an instant hit. However, his club, the Rangers, employed Henry mostly in power-play situations during his rookie year. The Eel not only scored 24 goals but also won the Calder Trophy as rookie of the year. Perhaps more amazing was the night Camille scored four goals in one game against Detroit goalie Terry Sawchuk, then believed the best in the game. It was one of hockey's most memorable moments, related here in Henry's own words:

"Sawchuk looked like he was a cinch for the Vezina Trophy. He was two or three goals ahead of Toronto's Harry Lumley going into that game. It looked like he'd beat out Lumley for the first All-Star team. While Detroit's Marty Pavelich was serving a penalty, I tipped a shot past Sawchuk for my twenty-first goal of the season to give us a 2–0 lead.

"I was right in front of the net when Harry Howell hit me with a pass. I flipped the puck past Sawchuk again for my second goal of the game, both on power plays. That gave us a 3–2 lead. I would have been happy with two goals but I got another chance in the third period.

"I don't even remember just how I got my third goal of the game on a power play. But I beat Sawchuk to get the hat trick and I can tell you I was feeling pretty good. We still had the power play going, so we went up the ice again. I had the puck and came in on Sawchuk. I faked him and he sprawled in front of the net, but instead of shooting I carried it behind. Then I looked and noticed that his stick was smack against the ice at just the right angle. So I shot the puck against his stick and it caromed back in the opposite direction into the net for my fourth goal.

"That four-goal night won the Calder Trophy for me as rookie of the year. It also knocked Sawchuk out of all the honors he practically had in his pocket. I ran into him a week or so later. 'You little French baboon,' he said to me. 'You cost me plenty.' I guess I cost him a couple of thousand dollars because Lumley beat him out for both the Vezina and the first All-Star team on the strength of my four goals that night."

Almost overnight Henry became one of the most popular hockey players ever to skate in New York. He starred for the Rangers until 1964–65 when manager Emile Francis dealt him to Chicago in a trade that caused considerable protest. However, Camille was returned to New York in 1967–68. He spent the next two seasons, his last as a player, in St. Louis and then turned to coaching. When the WHA was organized Henry became coach of the New York Raiders, later known as the Golden Blades. When the club left New York, Henry soon lost his job.

SAMUEL JAMES "SUGAR JIM" HENRY

BORN: Winnipeg, Manitoba, October 23, 1920
POSITION: Goalie, New York Rangers, 1941–42, 1945–48; Chicago
    Black Hawks, 1948–49; Boston Bruins, 1951–55
AWARDS: All-Star (Second Team), 1952

When goaltender Davey Kerr retired in 1941 after helping the Rangers to the Stanley Cup in 1940 manager Frank Boucher replaced him with Samuel James "Sugar Jim" Henry who had starred for the Regina (Saskatchewan) Rangers, a senior team. Henry was an instant hit and proved it by orchestrating the New Yorkers to first place. His 2.98 goals-against average in the 1941–42 season suggested Vezina trophies to come, but Henry immediately enlisted in the Canadian Armed Forces and didn't return until 1945–46, by which time he was a bit rusty. In addition, the Rangers now had Chuck Rayner (formerly with the

Americans) in the nets. Henry and Chuck split the Rangers' goaltending until Sugar Jim was dealt to Chicago in 1948–49. He played well for a lousy team but still better for the Bruins from 1951–52 until he left the NHL at the end of the 1954–55 season.

WALTER EDGAR "WALLY" HERGESHEIMER

BORN: Winnipeg, Manitoba, January 8, 1927
POSITION: Right Wing, New York Rangers, 1951–56, 1958–59; Chicago Black Hawks, 1956–57

During the New York Rangers darkest days in the early fifties, the most consistent bright light was smallish right winger Wally Hergesheimer, Phil's younger brother, who broke into the NHL with several handicaps. He was a relatively slow skater; he had lost two fingers on his right hand as a result of a punch press accident; and he lacked a particularly hard shot. But Wally had a surplus of good humor and guts. Dubbed a "garbage collector" because of his knack of scoring goals from rebounds near the crease, "Hergie," as he was known, led the Rangers in scoring during 1952–53.

He and fellow Winnipegger Nick Mickoski were the only Rangers to live in

Brooklyn. The two then bachelors had an apartment in Brooklyn Heights over-looking Lower New York Bay and the Statue of Liberty. Hergesheimer never-theless finished his career with the Chicago Black Hawks.

HERSHEY BEARS

The town of Hershey, Pennsylvania, home of the vast Hershey Chocolate Cor-poration holdings, has long been a hockey hotbed. This is due, in part, to the handsome, 7,200-seat arena built by Hershey Estates. The arena has been the showplace of this Pennsylvania Dutch community. The Hershey Chocolate Corporation displayed an interest in hockey starting in 1932, when it donated the Hershey Challenge Trophy in the fall of 1932 when the Tri-State League—forerunner of the Eastern Amateur Hockey League—was organized. The Atlan-tic City Sea Gulls were the first winners of the Hershey Trophy. When the Eastern League was organized the Hershey Cup came into possession of that league. Hershey remained an amateur hockey power through the thirties, finally inspiring the company to back a professional team. Thus, in 1938–39, the Hershey Bears entered the American League and have been one of the most powerful minor league hockey clubs, year in and year out, ever since. On April 7, 1945, a crowd of 8,285—a Hershey record—filled the arena to see a playoff game between the Bears and the Cleveland Barons.

FOSTER HEWITT

In 1922, Foster Hewitt, the son of W. A. Hewitt, sports editor of the Toronto *Daily Star,* went to work for his father's paper. He soon switched from the news beat to the *Star*'s new radio desk, and on March 22, 1923, radio editor Basil Lake assigned young Foster to broadcast a Senior League hockey match between Toronto's Parkdale Club and Kitchener. When Foster tried to shunt the job to a regular sports staffer, his boss held firm and prophetically replied, "Some thirty or forty years from now you may be proud to say: 'I was the first person in all the world ever to broadcast a hockey game.' "

How right Lake was. Foster Hewitt entered the hockey scene in a unique manner, and was to popularize the game more than any single person in the world. He began his career at the age of eighteen, and despite the most adverse conditions—his glass-enclosed booth fogged up, making it almost impossible to distinguish the players—public reaction was overwhelmingly positive. Radio station CFCA made hockey broadcasts a staple along with other sporting events, all covered by Hewitt. But best of all, Hewitt began to report NHL games from the rafters of Mutual Street Arena. In no time at all Foster devel-oped a play-by-play style that has never been duplicated.

His inimitably high-pitched voice entranced his listeners. It would reach a crescendo at the precisely correct time. Hewitt wasted few words, using such expressions as "It's a *scramble*," to describe frenzy in front of the net. Nothing in Foster's repertoire matched his description of a goal. The quick ascent began with the words *"He shoots!"* Inevitably a pause would follow. If the shot missed by an inch or two, Hewitt might bellow *"Ohhh!"* matching the sentiment of the audience. But if the puck went in, his voice would leap over the loudspeaker *"He scores!"* in such a manner that the listener could *feel* the red light go on. Hewitt's voice announcing a goal inevitably sent a tingle through the body of even the most insensitive fans and thrilled everyone who ever heard him. More than that, *"He shoots! He scores!"* soon became a trademark throughout Toronto, creating an unprecedented interest in hockey in an already hockey-crazed metropolis.

WILLIAM A. HEWITT

Elected to the Hockey Hall of Fame in 1957, William Hewitt became involved in hockey at the executive level by way of sportswriting. He became sports editor of the Toronto *News,* moved briefly to the Montreal *Herald,* then returned to Toronto as sports editor of the Toronto *Star*.

Hewitt, who beats Clarence Campbell easily in length of tenure, was secretary of the OHA for fifty-eight years, secretary of the CAHA from 1915 to 1919, and joined the Maple Leaf Gardens as attractions manager when it opened in 1931.

Born in 1875, Hewitt is credited, along with Frank Nelson, with introducing the goal net to hockey, a major change from the two poles bored into the frozen ground until then. Years later Art Ross developed the modern hockey goal net.

BRYAN ALDWYN HEXTALL

BORN: Grenfell, Saskatchewan, July 31, 1913
POSITION: Center, New York Rangers, 1936–48
AWARDS: Art Ross Trophy, 1942; All-Star (First Team), 1940–42;
　　　(Second Team), 1943; Hockey Hall of Fame, 1969

A hard-nosed native of Saskatchewan, Bryan Hextall twice led the NHL in goal-scoring and once in total points. He had a terrific burst of speed, was appropriately tough, and could stickhandle with the best of them. Like the Cooks-Boucher line, the Hextall-Watson-Patrick unit dazzled the enemy with their stickwork until the outbreak of World War II depleted their ranks.

Bryan Hextall

DENNIS HAROLD HEXTALL

BORN: Winnipeg, Manitoba, April 17, 1943
POSITION: Center, New York Rangers, 1968–69; Los Angeles Kings, 1969–70; California Golden Seals, 1970–71; Minnesota North Stars, 1971–

The name Hextall has been associated with hockey for decades. Bryan Hextall is a member of hockey's Hall of Fame. Bryan Hextall, Jr., was a rugged NHL performer for years. Dennis Hextall has been heard loudly and clearly in many an NHL rink.

A late bloomer, Dennis scratched out a living with three NHL teams before finding a home in Minnesota. He registered 82 points in two consecutive seasons (1972–73 and 1973–74) to finish in the top ten in league scoring. He has also averaged over 130 penalty minutes a year.

WILLIAM LAWRENCE (BILLY) HICKE

BORN: Regina, Saskatchewan, March 31, 1938
POSITION: Right Wing, Montreal Canadiens, 1959–64; New York Rangers, 1965–67; Oakland/California Seals, 1967–71; Pittsburgh Penguins, 1971–72; Alberta/Edmonton Oilers (WHA), 1972–73

It was Billy Hicke's misfortune to have been designated as heir apparent to Maurice "Rocket" Richard's right wing position on the Montreal Canadiens after the Rocket retired in 1960. A compact, fleet skater who could put the puck in the net—in junior hockey, at least—Hicke played mediocre hockey with the Canadiens through the 1964–65 season whereupon he was traded to the New York Rangers. He was ineffective in New York and eventually was dispatched to the Oakland Seals in 1967–68 and ultimately the Pittsburgh Penguins in 1971–72. His last major league experience was with the WHA's Alberta Oilers. Hicke's 38 points in 73 WHA games in 1972–73 clearly indicated that his productive professional days had ended. His younger brother, Ernie, meanwhile was experiencing a similar bedouin existence in the NHL.

JOHN MELVIN "SUDDEN DEATH" HILL

BORN: Glenboro, Manitoba, February 15, 1914
POSITION: Forward, Boston Bruins, 1937–41; Brooklyn Americans, 1941–42; Toronto Maple Leafs, 1942–46

The 1939 Stanley Cup finals' best-of-seven series opened at Madison Square Garden on March 21, and after three periods Boston and New York had battled to a 1–1 tie. Now the teams pushed into the perilous waters of sudden-death overtime, and again there was no score. A second sudden death also produced no goals, the players bone weary from skating.

By now the Rangers' strategy had become apparent to manager Art Ross. The home club was determined to stifle Bill Cowley's scoring with some blanket checking while keeping an eye on Roy Conacher as well. New York's hope was to force the Bruin attackers into an errant pass, snare the puck, and capitalize.

A few seconds before the third overtime, Ross summoned Cowley to his side. "We've got to fool them," he told his superb center. "They're watching Conacher so carefully it would be better to feed Hill."

There is no record of Cowley's response, but the chances are he was stunned. "Feed Hill?" This seemed a joke. Compared with Conacher, Mel Hill was a feeble shooter who had managed only ten goals over the entire season. Surely, Ross couldn't be serious. But the manager was never more concerned about a play in his life. By the time the teams took the ice Cowley realized Hill was going to get that puck if Ross had anything to say about it.

It took nearly an entire overtime period before Cowley could convert Ross's advice into action. Late in the third sudden death the Bruin center crossed into Ranger territory and lured Murray Patrick toward him. Patrick was a big, hulking skater, and the long game had slowed him down considerably. He didn't quite get to Cowley in time and the Bruin eluded him, skated into the corner and made a perfect pass to Hill who was camped in front of goalie Dave Kerr. Hill swung and Kerr missed, and at 1:10 A.M. the Bruins had won the game.

The Bruins went on to win the series, four games to three, and thereafter number eighteen on the Bruins was known as "Sudden Death" Hill throughout the NHL.

WILBERT CARL "DUTCH" HILLER

BORN: Kitchener, Ontario, May 11, 1915
POSITION: Forward, New York Rangers, 1937–41, 1943–44; Detroit
   Red Wings, 1941–42; Boston Bruins, 1942; Montreal Canadiens,
   1942–43, 1944–46

When the Rangers won the Stanley Cup in 1940 the New Yorkers had one of the speediest clubs the NHL has known. The fastest of this group was Wilbert Carl "Dutch" Hiller, one of many Kitchener, Ontario, natives to reach the majors. "Dutch wasn't too big," said his coach Frank Boucher, "but he simply glided with an unusual gait in which he seemed to lift himself above the ice with each stride."

Hiller became a Ranger in 1937–38, played on the Cup winner, and then was traded to Detroit in 1941. A year later he was dealt to the Bruins and in 1942–43 to the Canadiens. He returned to the Rangers in 1943–44, but finished his career in the following two seasons with the Montreal Canadiens.

HISTORY

The true origins of the game of hockey are buried in history; some say Indians invented the game, while others claim it was imported by the Dutch who skated with sticks on their frozen canals. The first recorded hockey games were played in Halifax, Nova Scotia, and Kingston, Ontario, in the 1850s. McGill University of Montreal is credited with devising the first hockey rules, about 1875, while Kingston was the site of the first league.

Canada is not due all the credit for developing hockey, for it was played in such American cities as St. Paul, Minnesota, New York City, and Baltimore, Maryland, at the same time, and professional hockey was played in northern Michigan before it was in Canada.

By the 1890s there were leagues galore—all amateur—and in 1893 the Stanley Cup was first presented and won by the Montreal Wheelers of the Amateur Hockey Association of Canada. It wasn't until after the turn of the century in Houghton, Michigan, that the first outright professional leagues were formed—nearly all manned by Canadians, of course—the United States–based International Professional League in 1904 and the Ontario Professional Hockey League (or "Trolley League") of Canada in 1908. In 1910 the National Hockey Association was formed, predecessor to the National Hockey League which was created in 1917.

In the earliest days of organized hockey, equipment and rules were minimal. Shoulder and elbow pads were unknown, and skaters wore knickers and long stockings. Goaltenders protected their legs with cricket pads, not unlike modern goalie pads, but considerably lighter. The goal was simply two sticks imbedded in the ice. (See also **Equipment.**)

The actual game differed from modern hockey in several important aspects. There were seven players (the seventh man was the "rover," an all-purpose player who did exactly what the name describes—roving from offense to defense as the case demanded) who usually played the entire game of two thirty-minute halves. Substitutions were granted only in case of serious injury that was determined solely by the referee. In case of a tie there was one ten-minute overtime, and if the contest was still a deadlock after the overtime, the game was rescheduled.

In 1910 the first major revision was instituted, and the game changed to three twenty-minute periods. The following season the position of rover was dropped (although maintained in the PCHL until 1922) and hockey became a six-man game. In 1918, a year after the NHL began operation, three playing zones were created, forward passing in the center area came into existence and the first assists were tabulated. No team would be forced to play with less than three skaters and a goaltender, as had happened often in earlier times.

During the twenties the forward passing rules were altered several times, until by 1930 forward passing was permitted in all zones as long as a player did not precede the puck into the attacking zone.

The thirties saw the introduction of the penalty shot and the rule prohibiting "icing" of the puck. In 1942 overtime periods, except during Stanley Cup playoffs, were discontinued and in 1943 the red center line was introduced by Frank Boucher, symbolizing the modern era of hockey. The current system of one referee and two linesmen began in 1945. In the last three decades there have been few major changes in the game: the goal crease and face-off circles were enlarged, the number of players allowed to dress for a game (sixteen and goaltenders) was decreased, officials devised a set of signals for penalties and infractions, and the third man to enter an altercation is assessed an automatic game misconduct penalty in the NHL.

LIONEL HITCHMAN

BORN: Toronto, Ontario, 1903
POSITION: Defenseman, Ottawa Senators, 1922–25; Boston Bruins, 1925–1934

Along with Eddie Shore, Lionel Hitchman gave the Boston Bruins one of the most fearsome defense combinations in National Hockey League history. The Toronto-born backliner broke into the majors with Ottawa in 1922–23, but was traded to Boston in 1924–25. He remained a Bruin until his retirement after the 1933–34 season. Defense-oriented to a fault, Hitchman scored more than ten points only once in his NHL career—11 points in 1925–26—but more than compensated for that deficiency with his superb backline hitting, stickchecking, and playmaking.

HOCKEY HALL OF FAME

Officially opened August 26, 1961, the Hockey Hall of Fame is located in Toronto. Funds for the Hall were provided by the six NHL teams in existence at the time—Canadiens, Rangers, Bruins, Red Wings, Maple Leafs, and Black Hawks.

The eligibility requirements are as follows:

Any person who has distinguished himself in the sport is eligible for election. This includes players, referees, and executives. Active careers for players and refs must be terminated for three years before admission can be granted; unless, of course, there are extenuating circumstances—such as the death of an outstanding participant before that period has passed.

Candidates are chosen by a selection committee (from the NHL, CAHA) on the basis of "playing ability, character, integrity and contribution to their team and the game of hockey in general," after nomination by the Hockey Hall of Fame Committee (also composed of representatives from the NHL, CAHA). (See also **UNITED STATES HOCKEY HALL OF FAME**.)

CHARLES EDWARD (CHARLIE) HODGE

BORN: Lachine, Quebec, July 28, 1933
POSITION: Goalie, Montreal Canadiens, 1954–67; Oakland Seals, 1967–70; Vancouver Canucks, 1970–72
AWARDS: Vezina Trophy, 1964, 1966 (with Lorne Worsley); All-Star (Second Team), 1964, 1965

At one point in his National Hockey League career, Charlie Hodge was so popular a Montreal Canadiens' goalie that enthused citizens named a street after him in the Canadian metropolis. Until 1963–64 Hodge had been the Canadiens' second fiddle to crack goalie Jacques Plante. Hodge became a regular goalie in 1963–64, turning a commendable 2.26 goals-against average, which won Hodge the Vezina Trophy. Charlie won the Vezina again, teaming with Lorne "Gump" Worsley in 1965–66. When Oakland joined the NHL in 1967–68, Hodge was drafted by the expansion franchise and played his last season with Vancouver in 1972.

KENNETH RAYMOND HODGE

BORN: Birmingham, England, June 25, 1944
POSITION: Right Wing, Chicago Black Hawks, 1964–67; Boston
    Bruins, 1967–
AWARDS: All-Star (First Team), 1971, 1974

Ken Hodge has been Phil Esposito's right-hand man, literally.

The 220-pound right winger has received more than 400 assists in the eight years he and Phil have been Boston teammates, many of which have been the result of his aggressive play along the boards and in the corners. Along with left winger Wayne Cashman, his first thought has been getting the puck to superscorer Esposito somewhere near the slot. If, as many observers claim, hockey games are won in the corners, Hodge has been one of the most valuable Bruins.

Sometimes it's dirty work, and usually it's a thankless assignment, but Hodge insists he never minded playing second fiddle to Phil. "Maybe I could have scored more if I just thought about myself personally," he said. "But in the years we've been together, each man on the Bruins has enjoyed his greatest season. So why change success? Especially when you've got a man in the slot who can score 76 goals one year and 66 the next?" Besides, Ken has had plenty of moments in the spotlight. In 1969–70 he netted 105 points and twice has gone over the 40-goal mark in a season.

Ironically, it wasn't until he came to Boston that his scoring prowess was uncovered. Back in Chicago coach Billy Reay employed him mainly as a policeman, a role he perfected when the Big Bad Bruins began their raucous climb to prominence in the late sixties. He can still mix it up with any of the NHL's big boys, and quite often does. But he's much more than a cop and a second fiddle today. He's a winning hockey player, which pretty much says it all.

WILLIAM "FLASH" HOLLETT

BORN: North Sydney, Nova Scotia, April 13, 1912
POSITION: Defenseman-Forward, Toronto Maple Leafs, 1933–35;
    Boston Bruins, 1936–43; Detroit Red Wings, 1944–46
AWARDS: All-Star (First Team), 1945

Bill "Flash" Hollett, a native of Sydney, Nova Scotia, showed up at the Toronto Maple Leafs' Kingston, Ontario, training camp in 1933, looking for a spot on the Toronto defense. Hollett impressed everyone with one destructive bodycheck that sent King Clancy to the ice. "If they don't sign you to this team," Clancy told the kid later in the dressing room, "look me up, and I'll see that you're placed somewhere in the NHL."

Flash was sent to Buffalo in the minors, only to be recalled after the Shore-Bailey affair, when Red Horner was suspended. Upon Horner's return, Hollett was traded to Ottawa, but he returned to the Maple Leafs the next season. He scored 10 goals and 16 assists for 26 points, best among NHL defensemen. Manager Conn Smythe remained unimpressed, and he dropped Flash back to Syracuse the next fall. Flash played for two weeks and persuaded Smythe that he was dispensable. A week later he was sold to the minor league Boston Cubs, from which he graduated to the Bruins. He played seven splendid seasons for the Bruins. Appropriately, Flash applied the coup de grace to the Maple Leafs in April 1939, when he scored the goal that crushed Toronto and won the Stanley Cup for Boston.

GEORGE REGINALD "RED" HORNER

BORN: Lynden, Ontario, May 29, 1909
POSITION: Defenseman, Toronto Maple Leafs, 1928–40
AWARDS: Hockey Hall of Fame, 1965

George Reginald "Red" Horner, who was signed by Conn Smythe in the fall of 1928, took his basic training in hockey on the Toronto playgrounds, although he was born on his father's farm near Lynden, Ontario.

Just before Christmas, 1928, Horner played for the Toronto Marlboros on a Friday night and for his Broker's League team on the following Saturday afternoon. Conn Smythe was at the Saturday game, and he walked into the dressing room after the game. "Red," Smythe declared, "I was wondering whether you'd be in shape to play still another game tonight—for the Toronto Maple Leafs."

Slightly stunned by the invitation, Horner just barely mumbled something about a great thrill. Smythe replied that he personally would drive Red to the game. That night Horner made his debut as a Maple Leaf at the Mutual Street Arena.

Toronto was playing the Pittsburgh Pirates, and young Horner was starting on defense for the Maple Leafs. The game was less than a minute old when Frank Frederickson, the marvelous Icelandic-Canadian forward, moved the puck into the Toronto zone. Frederickson dropped his head one way and lurched the other way, leaving Horner immobilized like a statue. The shot went wide, and the puck skittered back to Pittsburgh territory, where Frederickson recaptured it and launched another attack.

Once again Frederickson tested the rookie Horner. By then Red had sized up his foe, and he dispatched Frederickson to the ice with an emphatic body check. The referee blew his whistle, and Red was sent to the penalty box with his first two-minute infraction. In his career he would eventually serve 1,254 minutes worth of penalties, a record that went unbroken for many years. Of course, the kid wasn't too sure that Smythe approved, but it didn't take long to find out for sure.

"Penalties," said Smythe, "what do they matter? We just write them off as mistakes. No man ever became a millionaire who didn't make mistakes. Besides, penalties show that we have a fighting team."

Horner made a different kind of mistake in his second NHL game, on Christmas night against the Montreal Maroons. He moved the puck out of his zone and detected what he believed was an opening between Nels Stewart and Jimmy Ward, of Montreal. Red skated for daylight. But the old veterans closed the vise on Horner, and in so doing one of the Maroons rapped Red smartly on the hand with his stick. Red skated to the sidelines with a broken hand and was through for the rest of the season.

Nevertheless, Red already had persuaded Smythe that he was in the NHL to stay, and, as usual, the boss was right. Horner soon became so feared a member of the blue line corps that venerable columnist Ted Reeve, of the Toronto *Telegram*, authored the following parody:

> Our Reginald Horner
> Leaped from his corner
> Full of ambition and fight;
> He broke up the clash with a furious dash
> While the stockholders shrieked with delight!

On the night of December 12, 1933, Horner was on the ice at Boston Garden when Eddie Shore of the Bruins knocked Ace Bailey of the Maple Leafs unconscious—and nearly killed Bailey—with a behind-the-back charge. Shore's seeming callousness infuriated Horner who then hit Shore with a punch on the jaw. It was a right uppercut which stiffened the big defense star like an axed steer and got a suspension for Horner.

Horner maintained such robust play through the thirties. In a playoff game against Chicago in April 1938 Red rapped Chicago forward Doc Romnes across the face with his stick. This time Red's attack was in vain. Chicago went on to win the Stanley Cup. Red continued playing through the 1939–40 season when he finally retired.

MYLES GILBERT (TIM) HORTON

BORN: Cochrane, Ontario, January 12, 1930
DIED: February 21, 1974
POSITION: Defenseman, Toronto Maple Leafs, 1949–70; New York Rangers, 1970–71; Pittsburgh Penguins, 1971–72; Buffalo Sabres, 1972–74
AWARDS: All-Star (First Team), 1964, 1968; (Second Team), 1954, 1963, 1967

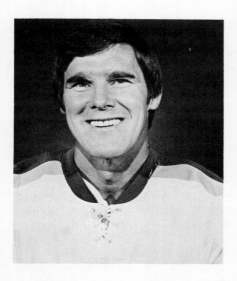

On February 20, 1974 the Buffalo Sabres visited Toronto for a game with the Leafs. Prior to the opening face-off Buffalo trailed Toronto by seven points; a big but not insurmountable gap. A Sabres' win would narrow the margin enough to make the homestretch interesting and coach Joe Crozier planned accordingly. His plan was to start five bruising skaters and disrupt the Maple Leafs with aggressiveness, then beat the supposedly disorganized enemy. The plan looked good on paper but, alas, it failed in practice. Buffalo's big men hit the Leafs, to be sure, but they were handed two early penalties which Toronto immediately converted into power play goals.

After the game, manager Punch Imlach and defenseman Tim Horton took a stroll up Church Street in Toronto, near Maple Leaf Gardens. Tim had a badly bruised jaw and was depressed about the loss. The perennial optimist, Imlach tried to cheer his old pal. "You played only two periods," said Imlach, "and one shift in the third, yet you were picked as a star of the game. If all the guys had played so well, we'd have won going away."

Horton forced a smile. "Well, Punch, there's always tomorrow."

But for Tim Horton there would be no tomorrow. En route to Buffalo in his sports car, Tim died instantly early the next morning when he lost control of his automobile and it crashed on the Queen Elizabeth Way.

The beloved forty-four-year-old defenseman never had a chance, according to police who discovered the wreck. By early morning, news of Horton's tragedy had circulated through the hockey world and resulted in grieving from coast to coast and league to league.

"There were defensemen you had to fear more because they were vicious and would slam you into the boards from behind," said Bobby Hull of the Winnipeg Jets. "But you respected Horton because he didn't need that kind of intimidation. He used his tremendous skill and talent to keep you in check."

Horton had played most of his twenty-two NHL seasons with the Maple Leafs alongside veteran Allan Stanley. "Tim was an All-Star on the ice," said former Leafs' captain George Armstrong, "and a superstar off it."

JOSEPH "BRONCO" HORVATH

BORN: Port Colborne, Ontario, March 12, 1930
POSITION: Right Wing, New York Rangers, 1955–56, 1962; Montreal Canadiens, 1956–57; Boston Bruins, 1957–61; Chicago Black Hawks, 1961–62; Toronto Maple Leafs, 1963; Minnesota North Stars, 1967–68
AWARDS: All-Star (Second Team), 1960

Fortified with a proboscis that would have made Pinocchio proud, Bronco Horvath wasted his first two NHL seasons with the Rangers (1955–56) and Canadiens (1956–57) before finding a productive home in Boston a year later. Teamed with Johnny Bucyk and Vic Stasiuk, Horvath rounded out the highly successful Uke Line, (none were pure Ukrainians). Bronco had a crisp, accurate wrist shot which was at its best during the 1959–60 season when he scored 39 goals and 41 assists for 80 points, a point less than league leader Bobby Hull. Horvath tailed off thereafter and moved on to Chicago in 1961–62, then a split season (1961–62) with the Rangers and Maple Leafs. His final NHL campaign was 1967–68 with the expansion Minnesota North Stars, after which he went into coaching.

REJEAN HOULE

BORN: Rouyn, Quebec, October 25, 1949
POSITION: Right Wing, Montreal Canadiens, 1969–73; Quebec Nordiques (WHA), 1973–

When the Montreal Canadiens defeated the Chicago Black Hawks to capture the Stanley Cup in 1971 and 1973 a young French-Canadian named Rejean Houle was one of the most exuberant and effective Habitant forwards. His job of shadowing superscorer Bobby Hull during the 1971 round is considered a Stanley Cup classic. Following the 1973 triumph, Houle jumped to the WHA's Quebec Nordiques, where he scored 40 goals in 1974–75.

HOUSTON AEROS

The Houston Aeros are an original franchise in the World Hockey Association, and they were located in an area that previously was a graveyard for the sport of professional hockey. The Houston Apollos, the defunct farm club of the

Montreal Canadiens in the old Central Pro League, lasted for little over two years.

The Aeros started their first year of play in the new league on an equal footing with the rest of their division, but were considered not deep enough in talent to make a serious run at the playoffs. But in midseason, the tables turned for the Houston club, and with ex-NHLers Gord Labossiere and Murray Hall leading the way, the Aeros made it into second place, behind the tough Winnipeg Jets and Bobby Hull.

The Aeros pulled the hat trick of the year in securing the all-time great Gordie Howe out of retirement, along with his hockey-playing sons, Marty, a strong young defenseman, and Mark, a wing. Gordie, who left a desk job with his old team, the Detroit Red Wings, was given a huge contract, as were his sons, who still had a year of junior eligibility each.

With the Howes, the Aeros enjoyed a good year (1973–74) at the gate. They constantly outdraw their sports rivals, the Houston Rockets of the National Basketball Association, even though the Aeros played in old Sam Houston Coliseum, and the Rockets play in spanking new Hofheinz Pavilion. The Aeros' new arena opened for the 1975–76 season, seating 16,000 for hockey and with Gordie Howe as the new president of the team.

GARRY ROBERT CHARLES HOWATT

BORN: Grand Center, Alberta, September 26, 1952
POSITION: Left Wing, New York Islanders, 1972–

Garry is probably known more for his pugilistic prowess than his goal-scoring skill, but this has not kept the small (5'9", 170 lbs.) Islander fireplug from delighting the spectators at the Nassau Coliseum. In fact, Islander fans scream in delight when Howatt and an opponent go into the corners with sticks held high.

In his first full season with the Islanders, in 1973–74, Howatt scored only 6 goals and 17 points. But he also set a record of sorts: most penalty minutes without a misconduct—204, as he fought his way through the National Hockey League schedule.

GORDON (GORDIE) HOWE

BORN: Floral, Saskatchewan, March 31, 1928

POSITION: Right Wing, Detroit Red Wings, 1946–71; Houston Aeros (WHA), 1973–75

AWARDS: Hart Trophy, 1952, 1953, 1957, 1958, 1960, 1963; Art Ross Trophy, 1951–54, 1957, 1963; Lester Patrick Trophy, 1967; Gary L. Davidson Trophy, 1974; All-Star (First Team), 1951–54, 1957–58, 1960, 1966, 1968–69, 1970; (Second Team) 1949–50, 1956, 1959, 1961–62, 1964–65, 1967; (WHA First Team), 1974, 1975; Team Canada (WHA), 1974; Hockey Hall of Fame, 1972; WHA Playoff MVP Award in his name, 1975; President, Houston Aeros, 1975–

It was a measure of Gordie Howe's dominant position in hockey that when he finally retired from the NHL prior to the 1971–72 season, he had played in 1,687 regular season games, scored 786 goals, 1,023 assists, 1,809 points, and received 1,643 minutes in penalties—each item a league record.

Between the years of 1946 and 1971, Howe won the Hart Trophy as the most valuable player six times and the Art Ross Trophy as leading scorer six times. His artistry, versatility, and durability, and the fact that he successfully spanned three distinct hockey eras, had marked him unique in sports and at the apex of hockey achievements.

"He was not only the greatest hockey player I've ever seen," says former teammate and Hall-of-Famer Bill Gadsby, "but also the greatest athlete."

Howe was born on March 31, 1928, in Floral, a town on the outskirts of

Saskatoon in Canada's wheat belt. He was the fourth of the nine children of Catherine and Albert Howe. After an unsuccessful try at farming, Albert Howe moved the family to Saskatoon, where he got a job in a garage. It was in Saskatoon where Gordie learned to play hockey. In the winter, temperatures in Saskatoon would drop to 50 below zero. Ten below was considered warm.

"As a kid," Gordie remembered, "the only equipment I had was skates and a stick. I took magazines and mail order catalogues, stuck 'em in my socks, and had shin pads. I tied 'em together with rubber bands made from inner tubes. We played with tennis balls instead of a puck. The ball would get so hard from the cold we'd have to get new ones all the time. A woman next door used to warm them up in an oven for us."

He quit school and got a job with a construction company that was building sidewalks. It was tough work—lugging 85-pound cement bags—but it firmed his muscles. Construction work, though, was just a fill-in between hockey seasons.

"I guess he always knew he'd become a hockey player," Howe's mother once said. "He used to practice at night by the hour under the city lamp on the streets. I put papers on the kitchen floor so he wouldn't have to take his skates off while he ate."

When he was fifteen, Howe packed a shirt, a set of underwear, and toothbrush into a little bag with his skates and took an overnight train to Winnipeg, where the New York Rangers were holding their training camp. He was a big, shy kid and the thought of being away from home among big-league hockey players frightened him. He almost starved because of it.

At meals the veteran players liked to haze the newcomers, and some older pro kept swiping Gordie's plate. During one meal, Alfie Pike, who later was coach of the Rangers, noticed that Howe had nothing but his silverware.

"Drop that plate and let the kid eat," commanded Pike.

Gordie carried his diffidence right into the dressing room. He was especially embarrassed because he had no idea how to adjust the complicated equipment the pros wore.

"I just dropped the gear on the floor in front of me and watched the others," he said. "I found out pretty early that the best way to learn was to keep my mouth shut and my eyes open."

He was only fifteen years old and homesick. Finally, when his roommate left for home, Gordie sulked for two days and then he, too, departed. The next year he was invited to the Detroit camp at Windsor, Ontario. He was signed to a contract by Jack Adams and assigned to the Wings' junior farm team in Galt, Ontario. Because of a Canadian Amateur Hockey Association ruling, he was unable to play for a year. Instead he worked out with the team and played exhibitions.

The Wings wanted him to enroll in the Galt high school. When Gordie saw all the kids clustered in front of the building, he turned around, walked down a railroad track, and applied for a job with Galt Metal Industries as a spot welder.

The next year found him playing with Omaha, and in 1946 he joined the Red Wings. In his first three years he scored 7, 16, and 12 goals. His genius finally surfaced during the playoffs of 1949, when he was high scorer with 8 goals and 11 points.

"I still wasn't so sure I was a star," he said. "When I went home to Saskatoon that summer, I started playing baseball again. One day, a kid came up for my autograph, and while I signed it, he said, 'Mr. Howe, what do you do in the winter?' "

The goals began to come in bunches, and Howe mesmerized both enemy and teammate alike. His stickhandling was so uncanny, Captain Sid Abel felt moved to reprimand young Gordie. "I don't mind this great stickhandling of yours," said Abel, "but why stickhandle around the same player three times?"

Tommy Ivan, who had taken over from Adams as coach of the Red Wings, likened Howe to Charlie Gehringer, one of the finest baseball players to wear a Detroit Tigers' uniform. "Like Gehringer," Ivan explained, "Howe has the ability and the knack for making the difficult plays look easy, routine. You can't miss the skill of a player like Maurice Richard; it's so dramatic! Gordie— you have to know your hockey or you won't appreciate him."

Howe, of course, was the perfect athlete. Taken to a golf course, he outdrove Chick Harbert, then the PGA champion. And Howe was new to the game. When Gordie told former Cleveland Indians' manager Lou Boudreau that he could hit big-league pitching, Boudreau invited him out to the park. The Indians manager fetched one of his best pitchers and told him to throw good and hard at Howe. Gordie proceeded to line the third pitch into the left field bleachers.

As a hockey player, Howe reached the top in 1950–51 when he led the NHL in scoring with 86 points (43 goals, 43 assists); in 1951–52 with 86 points (47 goals, 39 assists); in 1952–53 with a record 95 points (49 goals, 46 assists); and in 1953–54 with 81 points (33 goals, 48 assists). No other player had ever led the league more than two years in a row. Gordie again was at the top of the scoring list in 1956–57 (44 goals, 45 assists), and continued to dominate the game through the late fifties and early sixties.

Dave Keon, who became captain of the Toronto Maple Leafs, once observed, "There are two weak teams in this league and four strong ones. The weak ones are Boston and New York, and the strong ones are Toronto, Montreal, Chicago, and *Gordie Howe!*" Howe remained a major factor in the NHL until his retirement. Then, to everyone's amazement, he surfaced again, this time in 1973 in the World Hockey Association.

Miracles occur in big-league hockey about once a half-century. In 1973–74 there were three: Gordie Howe returned to the ice at age forty-five, and his sons, Marty and Mark, signed to skate alongside Pop with the Houston Aeros. Those add up to a lot of miracles. Then the three Howes led Houston to the AVCO World Cup and the WHA title. And Gordie starred for Team Canada in

1974 against the young Russians, before orchestrating a second AVCO Cup win in 1975.

The Gordie of 1973–75 was not the Howe who won six NHL Hart trophies. He was a stride slower, but a stride wiser. His shot had less whammo and injuries inspired him to put a bit of a curve in his formerly flat stick. He did as much as Phil Esposito did for the Bruins, but he didn't have a Bobby Orr to help.

But King Gordie didn't need help. When he skated at a foe, he was the same Gordie Howe who once pulverized NHL "heavyweight champion" Lou (Rangers) Fontinato and anybody else who dared challenge him.

"Gordie," said defenseman Carl Brewer, who once teamed with Howe on the Red Wings, "is the dirtiest player who ever lived. A great player, but also the dirtiest. He'd gouge your eye out if you gave him a chance, carve you up. He's both big and tough and used his size to intimidate guys. As for his hockey ability, I think he played better in the WHA than in his last couple of seasons in Detroit."

Gordie made his debut with the kids on September 25, 1973, playing in a WHA spectacular at Madison Square Garden. Less than a minute after he stepped on the ice, he scored a goal. He received the standing bravos only he deserved. But the decibel count didn't fool Gordie. His muscles were rusty and his timing off. It was this way during the early weeks of the season. Once, during a practice, he crashed headfirst into the boards and looked like a corpse. But he rebounded, and with each week gained more speed and more points. And when the season had ended the Aeros were champs of the WHA's Western Division, and Gordie had scored 31 goals and 69 assists for 100 points, third best in the WHA.

Howe finished the 1974–75 season with 34 goals and 65 assists for 99 points, and was second only to his son Mark in playoff scoring, with 8 goals and 12 assists. Gordie declared emphatically that he would play his last hockey game in the 1975–76 opener, after having been named club president.

MARK HOWE

BORN: Detroit, Michigan, May 28, 1955
POSITION: Left Wing, Houston Aeros (WHA), 1973–
AWARDS: Lou Kaplan Award (WHA Rookie of the Year), 1974; All-
   Star (Second Team), 1974; Team Canada (WHA), 1974

Regarded as one of the most gifted young forwards in North America, Mark Howe is the second—and youngest—of Gordie Howe's sons to play major league hockey. A native of Detroit, Michigan, Mark first suggested stardom as a member of the 1972 American Olympic team. Like his older brother Marty, Mark was a vital member of the Toronto Marlboros' team in the Ontario

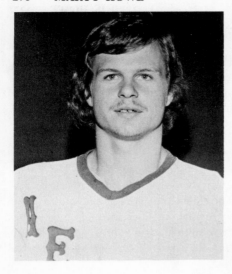

Mark Howe

Hockey Association's Junior A League in 1972–73. Although he was only eighteen years old at the time, Mark was drafted by the Houston Aeros for the 1973–74 season along with Marty. Mark played left wing on a line with father Gordie and Jim Sherrit and scored 38 goals and 41 assists for 79 points in 76 World Hockey Association games. He was named WHA rookie of the year and finished second in Aeros' playoff scoring as Houston won the 1974 AVCO World Cup, emblematic of WHA playoff supremacy. He was similarly effective in the 1974–75 campaign; being high playoff scorer with 22 points, as the Aeros copped the AVCO again in 1975. His dad once said to Mark that he'd try to set the puck up for him to help him score more. "That's okay, Dad," Mark replied, "I'll get my chances. You worry about yours." Most analysts agree that Mark is a born hockey player. "Hockey is all I ever wanted to do," said Mark. "I used to sweep the stands at Detroit Friday night and skate with the Red Wings during Saturday practices. I knew every number, name, and star in the league."

MARTY HOWE

BORN: Detroit, Michigan, February 18, 1954
POSITION: Defenseman, Houston Aeros (WHA), 1973–
AWARDS: Team Canada (WHA), 1974

Like his brother Mark, Marty Howe matured into a bright professional prospect early in the seventies playing for the Toronto Marlboros of the Ontario Hockey Association Junior A League. However, he was not regarded as bright a professional prospect as Mark when the Houston Aeros were scouting the Howes for

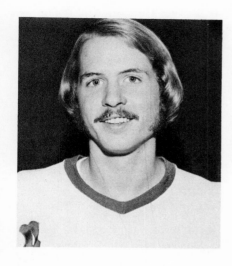

Marty Howe

the 1973–74 season. "We didn't pick Marty until the fourteenth round," said Aeros' coach Bill Dineen. "We were really dumb." Yet Marty played a hard, capable defense in his rookie WHA season, 1973–74, and was good enough to be selected—along with Mark and Gordie—to Team Canada 1974. As an aggressive skater, Marty more suggests his father's style than Mark. "Dad taught us never to immediately rush at somebody who takes a shot at us," said Marty. "Hit 'em when they don't see you coming." Marty is also witty like his dad. "Dad got a little more money than we did for signing with Houston," said Marty, "but we came out ahead because he had to buy a house in Houston." Dad obviously doesn't mind, especially because his sons helped him win the WHA's most valuable player award in 1974. "I was MVP," said Gordie, "simply for siring two very good hockey players. It was the most joyous year of my life."

SYDNEY HARRIS HOWE

BORN: Ottawa, Ontario, September 18, 1911
POSITION: Forward, Ottawa Senators, 1929–30, 1932–34; Philadelphia Quakers, 1930–31; St. Louis Eagles, 1934–35; Detroit Red Wings, 1935–46
AWARDS: All-Star (Second Team), 1945; Hockey Hall of Fame, 1965

The *other* Howe who starred for the Detroit Red Wings, Syd Howe preceded superman Gordie Howe in the Motor City by more than a decade. Like Gordie, Syd Howe was a Red Wings' superscorer and a factor in Detroit's Stanley Cup championships in 1936 and 1937. Syd broke into the NHL with Ottawa in 1929–30. In the following season he skated for the hapless Philadelphia Quakers, followed by two more years with Ottawa. In 1934–35 he skated first for St. Louis and then the Red Wings for whom he played for the remainder of his NHL career which ended after the 1945–46 campaign. Curiously, Gordie Howe made his Red Wings' debut as a rookie the following season, and from that point on Syd Howe's lustre dimmed as Gordie's brightened. By the way, they are not related.

VICTOR STANLEY HOWE

BORN: Saskatoon, Saskatchewan, November 2, 1929
POSITION: Right Wing, New York Rangers, 1950–51, 1953–55

The New York Rangers, the club that originally owned Gordie Howe and then relinquished their rights to him, sought to compensate for this egregious mistake by later signing Gordie's kid brother, Vic. Outwardly, Vic was a reasonable facsimile of Gordie. The younger Howe displayed the same crude strength and skated in the same loping but powerful manner as his older brother. Vic's shot was hard and accurate. In fact, he had everything to become a superstar except a vital intangible that best could be described as drive. Vic played his minor league hockey for the Rangers' Eastern League club, the New York Rovers, and played adequately if not splendidly for them. He was given three different opportunities to make it in the NHL with the Rangers—in 1950–51, 1953–54, and 1954–55—but failed each time. While Gordie continued starring through the midseventies, Vic retired to private life.

HARRY VERNON HOWELL

BORN: Hamilton, Ontario, December 28, 1932
POSITION: Defenseman, New York Rangers, 1952–69; Oakland
    Seals, 1969–70; Los Angeles Kings, 1970–73; New York Raiders/
    Golden Blades/Jersey Knights/San Diego Mariners (WHA),
    1973–74; Player-Coach, San Diego Mariners, 1974–75
AWARDS: Norris Trophy, 1967; All-Star (First Team), 1967

Harry Howell, player-coach for the WHA San Diego Mariners, spent twenty-two years in the NHL; seventeen of those years were spent with the New York Rangers, for whom Howell played more than 1,000 games—a team record. The defenseman began his career with the Guelph (Ontario) Biltmores in the Ontario Junior Hockey Association in 1949 and was called up to the Rangers in 1952. From that time on, Howell established himself as one of the game's best

Harry Howell

defensive defenseman with his subtle—some deprecatingly called it dainty—style of play. Although Howell actually managed to accumulate 101 minutes of penalty time one year, his play was so habitually void of vengefulness that the Madison Square Garden fans took to calling him names such as "Harriet" and "Sonja." But Howell was named to the NHL All-Star squad in 1967, and was the last player to have won the James Norris Trophy (1966–67) as the league's best defenseman before Bobby Orr virtually took possession of that award.

The Rangers sold Howell to Oakland in 1969. After playing two seasons with the Seals, he played three more with the Los Angeles Kings before jumping to the WHA in July 1973. Thirty days into the 1973–74 season he was named player-coach of the New Jersey Knights who moved to San Diego in 1974–75 and reached the playoff semifinals. But the Mariners released him in June 1975.

DENNIS WILLIAM HULL

BORN: Point Anne, Ontario, November 19, 1944
POSITION: Left Wing, Chicago Black Hawks, 1964–
AWARDS: All-Star (Second Team), 1973

Dennis Hull, a powerfully built left winger, didn't come into his own as a recognized NHL star until his more-famous brother, Bobby, opted for the World Hockey Association. Both siblings had been accounting for much of the Chicago Black Hawk offense since 1966 when Dennis established himself as a Hawk regular, joining the already legendary "Golden Jet."

It was a pretty difficult act to follow for the youngster. The elder Hull had already blasted his way to two 50-goal seasons, led the league in scoring three

Dennis Hull

times, and twice won the Hart Trophy as the league's most valuable player. At that point in time, Bobby Hull was the most electrifying player in the game. No one could have been expected to live up to the Golden One's larger-than-life dimensions—not even his own flesh and blood.

But, naturally, the comparisons between the two brothers were endless with Dennis always coming up short. The younger Hull was a more than competent winger and on any other team, said the experts, might have been the number one star of the show. But teamed with Bobby, he just blended in with the supporting cast of characters. Some observers of the hockey scene have dared to suggest that Dennis's intimidating shot was just a mite harder than Bobby's. Once during a Black Hawk practice session at the cavernous Chicago Stadium, Dennis put the screws to a wrist shot that sailed into the second level and splintered one of the seats to kindling wood.

In 1972, when brother Bobby signed with the Winnipeg Jets of the WHA, Dennis seemed to break out of an unseen self-conscious shell. He responded with his best point production ever, and was named to the NHL All-Star team for the first time in his career. Whether Bobby's departure had all that much to do with Dennis's sudden success remains a moot point, but Chicago fans are finally appreciating D. Hull as they never have before.

ROBERT MARVIN (BOBBY) "THE GOLDEN JET" HULL

BORN: Point Anne, Ontario, January 3, 1939

POSITION: Left Wing, Chicago Black Hawks, 1957–72; Left Wing-Coach, Winnipeg Jets (WHA), 1972–

AWARDS: Hart Trophy, 1965, 1966; Art Ross Trophy, 1960, 1962, 1966; Lady Byng Trophy, 1966; Lester Patrick Trophy, 1969; Gary L. Davidson Trophy, 1973, 1975; All-Star (First Team), 1960, 1962, 1964–69, 1972; (Second Team), 1963, 1971; (WHA First Team), 1974, 1975; Team Canada (WHA), 1974

When Bobby Hull executed his sensational leap from the National Hockey League's Chicago Black Hawks to the Winnipeg Jets of the World Hockey Association in the summer of 1972, several hasty predictions were made. Some experts were confident that the Golden Jet would score more than 100 goals against WHA goaltenders. Others ventured that Bobby would certainly guarantee first place and the Avco World Cup for Winnipeg. Then, there were those who believed that Hull's presence would guarantee nothing but standing room crowds at the Winnipeg Arena.

Hardly any of these events took place. For two straight years, Hull missed the WHA scoring title, never nearing the 100-goal mark. True, the Jets finished first in their rookie season, but they were far off the mark in the 1973–74 season and attendance was conspicuously disappointing.

Hull's defection from the National Hockey League was the major reason for the WHA's ability to become the game's second major hockey league overnight.

The Golden Jet had led the NHL in goal-scoring seven times and three times was point leader. He was named to the All-Star team in twelve out of fifteen seasons and he won just about every available award, including the Lady Byng Trophy for good sportsmanship combined with ability. At the age of thirty-four, when he put on the Winnipeg Jets uniform for the first time, Bobby Hull had done just about everything that had been asked of him; but now he was facing the biggest challenge of his life.

Curiously, his first challenge was maintaining his mental stability. In its desperate attempt to kill the WHA, the NHL attempted to bar Hull from playing by using every legal method at its command. A court injunction sidelined him for the first month of the campaign until, finally, that restriction was lifted, And once again the red lights went on when Bobby hit the ice. "I got awfully run down from all the litigation," Bobby admitted. "I lost more than 10 pounds, down from 194 to 180, and since I don't carry any fat, that loss was all in muscle and red meat. I felt just plain unhealthy."

But he never stopped smiling and he never stopped providing the new league with that beautiful, new positive image that it needed so badly at the start. Bobby took an instant pride in the new league, but he is the first to admit he left the Chicago Black Hawks for reasons other than building the WHA.

"If I told you that the big contract had nothing to do with my signing with Winnipeg," Hull smiled, "I'd be telling you a lie. It made the future secure for my family. That was the most important thing. Then there were some things that disenchanted me in the NHL, and the way the Hawks handled their attempts to sign me. They just didn't think I'd consider jumping."

Hull moved his wife, Joanne, and their five children into a fourteen-room $185,000 home in the Winnipeg suburb of Tuxedo. Natives of the Manitoba metropolis appropriately greeted him as a national hero and Bobby repaid them by taking the Jets right up to the top of the WHA's Western Division.

The Jet scored 51 goals and 52 assists in 63 games to finish in a three-way tie for fourth place in the WHA scoring list with Tom Webster of New England and Winnipeg's Norm Beaudin. However, Webster played in 77 games and Beaudin in 78. Bobby's point total was amazing, considering that he frequently was skating at less than top speed.

"I never had many injuries until I joined the WHA," he explained, "but every part of me seemed to hurt after I started skating for the Jets—my elbow, my shoulder, and my knee. It was part of the complete changeover in the schedule. For fifteen years in the NHL we had three games a week with two days off after each game. In the first year of the WHA we had doubleheaders and back-to-back games, which meant that my little injuries never got a chance to heal."

Still, he was able to take Winnipeg all the way to the 1973 finals of the WHA's playoff for the Avco World Cup, before New England defeated the Jets four games to one. People who had never seen him before marveled at the job he had done and extolled his performances despite all the legal problems. During one of Hull's visits to Los Angeles, Bobby dazzled the hometown Sharks with his footwork and stickwork. "When does he ever take a rest?" asked Sharks' goalie George Gardner. "Every time I looked up, there he was."

Winnipeg won the game, 6–5, in sudden-death overtime. The home team had lost, but those who appreciate quality, such as Los Angeles *Times* reporter Dwight Chapin, waxed ecstatic over the Golden Jet.

"Hull did everything," said Chapin. "He scored twice. He added two assists. He was in on power plays. He killed penalties. He talked to his team, and argued moderately with officials." After watching Hull star for Team Canada in 1974, members of the Russian National team echoed the sentiments.

In 1975 Hull scored a record-breaking 77 goals, but missing the WHA scoring title by five points to Andre Lacroix.

FRED HUNT

BORN: Brantford, Ontario, January 17, 1918
POSITION: Forward, New York Americans, 1940–41; New York Rangers, 1944–45

No hockey official has been more closely linked with a city than Fred Hunt has been with Buffalo. A competent minor league winger, Hunt had two big league trials—both with New York teams—in 1940–41 and 1944–45, but spent most of his years, a decade to be exact, with the Buffalo Bisons of the American League. For eighteen years he was general manager and stepped in as Bisons' coach on four separate occasions, following his playing days. When Buffalo entered the National Hockey League, Hunt became the Sabres' assistant general manager and troubleshooter, a job he has held to this day.

JOHN BOWER "BOUSE" HUTTON

BORN: October 24, 1877
DIED: October 27, 1962
POSITION: Goalie, Ottawa Silver Seven (CAHL), 1899–1904
AWARDS: Hockey Hall of Fame, 1962

Hutton was the goalie for the legendary turn of the century Ottawa Silver Seven unit. His stellar netminding brought two Stanley Cups to the Seven in 1903 and 1904.

Despite playing with a stick no bigger than a forward's and pads no wider than a baseball catcher's shinguards, Bouse's career goals-against average is well under 3.00, excellent stats for a goaler of any era. He is a member of hockey's Hall of Fame.

HARRY HYLAND

BORN: Montreal, Quebec, January 2, 1889
DIED: August 8, 1969
POSITION: Right Wing, Montreal Shamrocks (ECHA), 1909–10; Montreal Wanderers (NHA), 1910–12, 1913–17; New Westminster (PCHA), 1912–13; Ottawa Senators, 1917–18
AWARDS: Hockey Hall of Fame, 1962

Harry Hyland, a member of hockey's Hall of Fame, was a small, cricket-quick right winger whose nose for the net and deceptive moves left much larger defenders shaking their heads in disbelief and opposing goalies frustrated to the point of tears.

Little Harry broke into hockey in 1909, the leading scorer on a dismal, last-place Shamrock team. Hyland joined the Wanderers in 1910, a year that saw them capture the Stanley Cup. Harry remained with the Wanderers until they dropped out of the NHA in 1918, but he did venture west in 1912 when the PCHA was formed, helping New Westminster to the first league championship.

When the Wanderers finally left the league, Hyland finished his playing career with Ottawa of the NHL.

GEORGE "PUNCH" IMLACH

BORN: Toronto, Ontario, March 15, 1918
POSITION: Coach, Toronto Maple Leafs, 1958–69; Buffalo Sabres,
1970–71; General Manager, Toronto Maple Leafs, 1958–69; Buffalo Sabres, 1970–

One of the most successful and cantankerous characters in major league hockey
history is George "Punch" Imlach. Imlach's tough-as-nails approach to the

285

game won him four Stanley Cups with the powerhouse Leaf teams of the sixties. Only two other NHL coaches, Toe Blake (Montreal) and Hap Day (Toronto) have ever accounted for more silverware than that.

Before his days as coach of the Leafs, Punch spent eleven years with the minor league Quebec Aces as a player, coach, general manager, and eventually, part owner. Then Imlach joined the Boston Bruin organization as manager/coach of the AHL's Springfield Indians for one year until he took over the coaching duties for the Leafs.

Imlach was named coach and general manager of the Buffalo Sabres in 1970 and built the team into a powerhouse in two seasons, but was forced to step aside from the coaching duties following a massive heart attack during the 1971–72 season. Typically, the attack didn't stop Imlach completely—as one writer observed following a gall bladder operation that Imlach underwent in 1972, "In Imlach's case, they probably removed the bladder and left the gall."

INDIANAPOLIS RACERS

The Indianapolis Racers were the second team in the World Hockey Association's first attempt at expansion. Beginning play in the 1974–75 season, the club did poorly in the standings, but still attracted sizeable crowds—enough to insure the management of the club that the people of central Indiana were hockey fans.

The Racers began playing in the new 16,000-seat Market Square Arena in downtown Indianapolis. Chuck Catto was hired as the club's chief scout and Gerry Moore was named the first coach.

Paul Deneau, a Dayton architect, bought the club from IPS Management, Inc. and proceeded to set up the organization. Deneau was no stranger to the World Hockey Association, having been one of the original owners of the Houston Aeros.

The Racers fared well in the amateur and expansion drafts, getting players like goaltender Andy Brown from the NHL Pittsburgh Penguins; Ed Dyck, who had played goal for the Vancouver Canucks; and strong centerman Joe Hardy, who had played two good seasons for the Cleveland Crusaders and the Chicago Cougars.

Although the Racers struggled with the typical woes of an expansion team, interest in the Indianapolis area was high, and the league looked hopefully to the Racers for a rosier future.

INFRACTIONS

Icing: "Icing" occurs when a team shoots the puck from its own side of the red line over the opponent's goal line (not into the goal, of course). The puck is then brought back for a face-off deep in the zone of the offending team.

There are four conditions when icing is *not* called:

(a) When a team is shorthanded as a result of a penalty it cannot be called for icing (not applicable in the WHA).

(b) When a defending opponent, in the judgment of the officials, could have played the puck before it crossed his own goal line no icing is called.

(c) If the puck cuts across part of the rectangle (called the crease) in front of the goal no icing shall be called.

(d) When a member of the team which ices the puck touches it before the defending opponent, no icing is called and play continues.

Freezing: "Freezing" or pinning the puck occurs when the puck is stopped by the defensive team against the boards by skate or stick. Freezing calls for a face-off, still in the defensive zone, but offers a break in action which can be of benefit to the defensive team.

If the puck is frozen by the player while no one is contesting possession, a penalty for delay of the game can be called.

Offside: A team on the offense is twice restricted in their forward passes up ice. A player in his own zone can pass up to the red line. If he's in the neutral zone, he can pass over the red line but not over the opponent's blue line.

In the WHA, a player may pass the puck from inside his own blue line to a teammate beyond the red center line providing the puck precedes the player across the red line and the receiver takes the puck ahead of his body.

Fans often think they see an offside when a pass is made from the defensive zone to a teammate on the red line or the opponent's blue line. The determining factor is the skates of the player on the receiving end, not his stick or the puck. If just one of the player's skates is not over the line, he is on side.

The puck must always precede the player over the red line and then the attacking blue line. Often you will see a player jam on the brakes and straddle a line until his teammate carries or shoots the puck over the line.

EARL THOMPSON INGARFIELD

BORN: Lethbridge, Alberta, October 25, 1934
POSITION: Center, New York Rangers, 1958–67; Pittsburgh Penguins, 1967–69; California Seals, 1969–71; Coach, New York Islanders, 1973

While the New York Rangers floundered throughout the early sixties, there wasn't much for their few loyal fans to cheer about. However, one player who

Earl Ingarfield

made things just a bit easier for the Blueshirts and their faithful followers was a center-iceman named Earl Thompson Ingarfield.

Ingarfield was not considered a star by most standards, but rather as a journeyman hockey player who did his job well but virtually unnoticed. His five-foot, eleven-inch, and 185-pound frame did not stand out, nor did his graceful, long-stride skating motion. He was an ordinary, unpublicized player who seldom engaged in fisticuffs or ever scored anywhere near 50 goals in a single season. Still, with a booming slapshot, he managed to score 179 goals and 405 points in a career spanning twelve seasons, which was not bad in the preexpansion days.

After completing junior hockey for his hometown Lethbridge Native Sons, Ingarfield turned pro in 1954, playing a mere two games for Vancouver of the Western League. However, three successful years—one with Saskatoon and two with Winnipeg—earned him a trial with the New York Rangers in 1958. For the first two years he saw little action and then in 1960, the mild-mannered Ingarfield made the team permanently and scored 13 goals in 66 games. The following season, he enjoyed his best season as a pro, scoring (26–31–57) and playing the entire seventy-game schedule.

Ingarfield's best nights were those when he centered for Andy Bathgate and Dean Prentice, especially in 1961–62 when the Rangers went up against Toronto in the Stanley Cup semifinals. Earl had been injured early in the series at a point when it appeared that the New Yorkers would upset Toronto. The Rangers desperately needed Ingarfield's productive stick and, as a result, the

New York *Journal-American* ran a six-column headline that immortalized the likeable center. It read: RUSTY RANGERS NEED SHOT OF EARL.

When his playing days were over Ingarfield turned to front office work with the expansionist New York Islanders. He briefly—and successfully—coached the Islanders in the latter part of their first season, 1972–73. However, he refused an offer to return, preferring amateur coaching in his native Alberta.

MICKEY ION

BORN: Paris, Ontario, February 25, 1886
DIED: Seattle, Washington, October 26, 1944
POSITION: Referee, NHL, 1926–43
AWARDS: Hockey Hall of Fame, 1961

Mickey Ion was one of the NHL's foremost officials from the midtwenties into the forties. One night when Ion was refereeing a game in Seattle, he took exception to a front-row fan armed with a large megaphone. Whenever Ion skated by, the fan would assail his ears with an assortment of curses. "Ion finally stopped the game," Lester Patrick recalled, "and demanded that the megaphone or the fan be removed. Ion won the battle this time, but the next time he appeared in Seattle the fans really gave it to him. There were six thousand fans at the game and it seemed that all six thousand of them had brought megaphones."

The moment the megaphones blared, Patrick noticed that Ion had stopped play. He wanted all the megaphones confiscated and removed from the stands. Lester walked down to rinkside and beckoned the referee to the boards.

"For Heaven's sake, Mickey," said Patrick, "you can't get all six thousand megaphones."

"If I don't get the megaphones," said Ion, "the game will end here and now!"

Patrick had no choice but to back his referee, whose decision was made known to the crowd. They were compelled to give up their megaphones. As Lester fondly recalled, the crowd did give Ion the megaphones, although obviously not the way he wanted them. "They threw them at him," said Patrick. "When all the noise had ended, Mickey was standing at center ice, knee-deep in megaphones."

JAMES DICKINSON (DICK) IRVIN

BORN: Limestone Ridge, Ontario, July 19, 1892
DIED: Montreal, Quebec, May 1957
POSITION: Forward, Chicago Black Hawks, 1926–29; Coach, Chicago Black Hawks, 1930–31, 1955–56; Toronto Maple Leafs, 1931–40; Montreal Canadiens, 1940–55
AWARDS: Hockey Hall of Fame, 1958

Dick Irvin had learned the value of hard work as a youngster, when he was employed in the neighborhood butcher shop. He earned enough from that job to buy a pair of ice skates (before that he played in neighborhood games in an old pair of overshoes), and gradually he worked his way up the hockey ladder to the majors, eventually to become one of the most successful players and then coaches with Toronto, Montreal, and Chicago.

A full-fledged NHL star with the Black Hawks, Dick Irvin's career was curtailed when he suffered a fractured skull after being checked by Red Dutton of the Montreal Maroons. It was then that he turned to coaching, first with the Black Hawks and then with the Maple Leafs. Toronto's young crew was well suited to Dick's accent-on-speed philosophy. "As long as they play this game on skates," Irvin would say, "you have to be able to skate to win. Personally, I'll take a young pair of legs over an old head anytime."

Irvin's mind was fertile and quick. Opponents knew that he would go to extreme lengths to make a point for his team. A typical example was an incident during a game against the Rangers on the night of February 18, 1932, at Maple Leaf Gardens. Charlie Conacher and Red Horner of Toronto dressed for the match, but they were unable to play because of injuries. Nevertheless, they remained in uniform and stayed on the bench.

As it turned out, Conacher and Horner acted wisely. Both skaters had accumulated two major penalties in the season, and, according to NHL rules of the day, a third major would result in an automatic one-game suspension. The 1931–32 rulebook also called for a major penalty to any player who took the ice while his team already was at full strength.

Midway in the game Irvin sent Conacher and then Horner on the ice, although the Maple Leafs were already at full strength. Both were given major penalties and suspended for one game, which was perfectly all right with Irvin since injuries would have prevented them from playing in their next game anyway. In that way Dick did away with the suspension, and his Leafs edged the Rangers 5–3.

Irvin's most productive years were in the forties and early fifties, coaching the Montreal Canadiens, paced by Maurice "Rocket" Richard. His last coaching stint was in 1955–56 with Chicago. He died in 1957.

EDWARD AMOS (TED) IRVINE

BORN: Winnipeg, Manitoba, December 8, 1944
POSITION: Left Wing, Boston Bruins, 1963–64; Los Angeles Kings, 1967–70; New York Rangers, 1970–75; St. Louis Blues, 1975–

A big (6'2"), occasionally hard-skating forward, Ted Irvine reached the NHL via the Los Angeles Kings (he only played in one game for Boston) and after a couple of undistinguished seasons continued his pursuit of mediocrity with the New York Rangers until he was traded to St. Louis in June 1975. Heavy checking, occasional brawling, and periodic scoring was the most any team could expect from Irvine.

IVAN DUANE "THE TERRIBLE" IRWIN

BORN: Chicago, Illinois, March 13, 1927
POSITION: Defenseman, Montreal Canadiens, 1952–53; New York Rangers, 1953–58

One of the earliest and most successful creations of New York Rangers' press agent Herb Goren, Ivan Irwin was a tall, balding defenseman who provided the generally weak Blueshirts with a modest amount of respectability. When he reached the Rangers in 1953, Goren detected star quality in Irwin and dubbed him "the Terrible." However, it never was fully determined whether Goren was referring to Irwin's talent or fierce hitting style. When he was "on," Irwin heaved enemies over his hips with sensational bodychecks; but when he was "off," the same opponents exploited his ponderous skating style. Following disagreements with coach Phil Watson, Irwin was dropped to the minors in 1958.

THOMAS N. IVAN

BORN: Toronto, Ontario, January 31, 1911
POSITION: Coach, Detroit Red Wings, 1947–54; Coach, Chicago Black Hawks, 1956–58, General Manager, Chicago Black Hawks, 1954–
AWARDS: Hockey Hall of Fame, 1974

When a severe facial injury ended Tommy Ivan's playing career in junior hockey, his love for the game kept him around as a referee and then as coach of a junior team in Brantford, Ontario.

After serving as a gunnery instructor in the Canadian army during World War II, Ivan began his pro career as a scout in the Detroit Red Wings' organization. In 1945–46 he coached the Omaha Knights of the now defunct United

Tommy Ivan

States Hockey League, and the following year he was promoted to the Indianapolis Capitols of the American Hockey League.

In 1947–48, Ivan made his National Hockey League debut as a coach with the Detroit Red Wings, when Jack Adams relinquished the position to become the Wings' general manager. There, his teams won six straight NHL championships and three Stanley Cups (1949–50, 1951–52, 1953–54) in six years.

While with the Red Wings, Ivan coached in four All-Star games, leading the All-Stars to successive wins over Toronto in 1948 and 1949 with identical 3–1 scores. He then piloted the Wings the next year to a 7–1 win over the Stars, and finally, coached the First Team All-Stars to a 1–1 tie with the Second Team.

In 1954–55 Ivan left the winning Detroit team and took the general manager's job with the Chicago Black Hawks.

From 1959 on, the Black Hawks, with Ivan again solely as general manager, qualified for the playoffs every year but one, and won the Stanley Cup for the first time in twenty-three years in 1960–61. In 1966–67, the Hawks captured their first division title in their forty-year history, added another one three years later, and then won three successive division championships when they moved over to the West Division in 1970–71.

Building an excellent farm system, Ivan is given credit for transforming the floundering and financially troubled Black Hawks into one of the most powerful organizations of the NHL. However, in recent years, Ivan has received criticism for a trade he initiated in 1967, in which he sent Phil Esposito, Ken Hodge, and Fred Stanfield to the Boston Bruins in exchange for Gilles Marotte, Pit Martin, and minor league goalie Jack Norris. Esposito has since broken virtually every scoring record, and Hodge has become one of the premier right wings.

HARVEY "BUSHER" JACKSON

BORN: Toronto, Ontario, January 17, 1911
DIED: June 25, 1966
POSITION: Left Wing, Toronto Maple Leafs, 1929–39; New York
    Americans, 1940–41; Boston Bruins, 1942–44
AWARDS: Art Ross Trophy, 1932; All-Star (First Team), 1932,
    1934–35, 1937, (Second Team), 1933; Hockey Hall of Fame,
    1971

Harvey "Busher" Jackson was the most tragic figure on Toronto's Kid Line of Charlie Conacher, Joe Primeau, and Jackson. Unlike his linemates who acquired fortune after their retirement in the late thirties, Jackson encountered hard times throughout his life. He was even given trouble by the Hall of Fame committee which hesitated for years to nominate him allegedly because of his drinking problems.

A product of Frank Selke's Toronto Junior Marlboros, Jackson turned pro in 1929–30 with the Maple Leafs. According to Selke, Jackson was the "classiest" player he had ever seen. "He could pivot on a dime, stickhandle through an entire team without giving up the puck, and shoot like a bullet from either forehand or backhand. His backhand was the best I ever saw."

Maple Leafs' broadcaster Foster Hewitt called Busher a "brash" youngster. "Fortunately, his ability matched his confidence."

A typical Jackson play occurred on December 24, 1931 in a game against the Canadiens. The score was tied in sudden-death overtime as the clocked ticked off the final seconds. Busher grabbed the puck, skated the length of the rink, and scored a split second before the gong sounded! He was a major factor in the Leafs' first Stanley Cup triumph in 1932. Jackson remained with Toronto until 1938–39 when he was traded to the Americans. In 1941–42 the Amerks dealt him to Boston where he finished his pro career in 1943–44.

WILLIAM (BILL) JENNINGS

From total obscurity in the early sixties, William "Bill" Jennings emerged as one of the most powerful National Hockey League bosses as president of the New York Rangers. An attorney for the New York firm of Simpson, Thatcher and Bartlett, Jennings was leader of the NHL "Young Turks," a group of newer league governors who favored expansion. Jennings spearheaded the leap from six to twelve NHL teams in 1967 and became one of hockey's most influential leaders. He also was one of its most volatile. Following an especially rough game between the Rangers and Boston Bruins, Jennings demanded that a "bounty" be placed on the head of then Bruins' defenseman Ted Green. He later was reprimanded for the outburst by NHL president Clarence Campbell. Jennings was responsible for the creation of the Lester Patrick Trophy, awarded annually to the person who contributes to the growth of hockey in the United States, which he himself was awarded in 1971. Jennings was also elected to the Hockey Hall of Fame in 1975.

ERNIE "MOOSE" JOHNSON

BORN: Montreal, Quebec, 1886
DIED: March 25, 1963
POSITION: Left Wing and Defenseman, Montreal Maroons (CAHL), 1904–05; Montreal Wanderers (ECAHA), 1906–11; New Westminster Patricks (PCHA), 1912–14; Portland Rosebuds (PCHA), 1915–18; Victoria Aristocrats (PCHA), 1919–22
AWARDS: Hockey Hall of Fame, 1952

Ernie Johnson, a nineteen-year veteran of the early hockey wars, was one of the first great defensemen of his day. However, for the first six years of his career, "Moose" was a high-scoring left winger, guiding his Wanderers to three consecutive Stanley Cup wins.

His move back to blue line patrol didn't lessen his value to the club one bit as his long arms and exceptionally long stick made him the most feared poke checker on Canadian ponds. In fact, the very first season that Moose switched to defense, his Wanderers captured their fourth Stanley Cup in five seasons.

Johnson jumped the Wanderers in 1912 to play for the Patricks at New Westminster of the PCHA. He was a fixture of Pacific Coast blue lines for the next eleven years, and although he labored for three different PCHA clubs, he was never traded or sold—a tribute to his consistently outstanding play.

In 1921, near the end of his career, a special "Moose" Johnson night was held in Victoria. He was presented with a trophy from the PCHA which read: "To Moose Johnson as a token of appreciation of his brilliant career as the greatest defence player in the PCHA during the past ten years." A Hall of Famer, Johnson finally retired from hockey in 1922.

IVAN WILFRED "CHING" JOHNSON

BORN: Winnipeg, Manitoba, December 7, 1897
POSITION: Defenseman, New York Rangers, 1926–37; New York Americans, 1937–38
AWARDS: All-Star (First Team), 1932, 1933, (Second Team), 1931, 1934; Hockey Hall of Fame, 1958

There have been few more colorful personalities in sport than Ivan Wilfred "Ching" Johnson, a bald defenseman who skated for the New York Rangers from their original NHL season, 1926–27, through the 1936–37 campaign. He ended his career a year later, skating for the New York Americans.

A native of Winnipeg, Manitoba, Johnson was nicknamed "Ching" because he wore a wide grin on his face whenever he bodychecked an enemy to the ice—which was often—and when he smiled his eyes gave him an Oriental look; therefore Chink or Ching as in Ching-a-ling.

Johnson became an instant hit on Broadway, along with his large defensive sidekick, Taffy Abel. Ching was a buddy of center Frank Boucher who once described the Johnson style:

"Ching loved to deliver a good hoist early in a game because he knew his victim would probably retaliate, and Ching loved body contact. I remember once against the Maroons Ching caught Hooley Smith with a terrific check right at the start of the game. Hooley's stick flew from his hands and disappeared above the rink lights. He was lifted clean off the ice, and seemed to stay suspended five or six feet above the surface for seconds before finally crashing down on his back. No one could accuse Hooley of lacking guts. From then on, whenever he got the puck, he drove straight for Ching, trying to outmatch him, but every time Ching flattened poor Hooley. Afterwards, grinning in the shower, Ching said he couldn't remember a game he'd enjoyed more."

Johnson lost his original partner after three seasons when Abel was traded to the Chicago Black Hawks. But manager Lester Patrick obtained blocky French Canadian Leo Bourgault who became an outstanding defensemate for Ching. Of the three only Johnson is in hockey's Hall of Fame.

THOMAS CHRISTIAN (TOM) JOHNSON

BORN: Baldur, Manitoba, February 18, 1928
POSITION: Defenseman, Montreal Canadiens, 1947–63; Boston Bruins, 1963–65; Coach, Boston Bruins, 1970–73
AWARDS: James Norris Trophy, 1959; All-Star (First Team), 1959, (Second Team) 1956; Hockey Hall of Fame, 1970

When defenseman Tom Johnson was inducted into the Hockey Hall of Fame in June 1970, veteran Hall of Famer Eddie Shore reportedly was so upset that he demanded to buy *back* his own acceptance. Actually Johnson was an unobstrusive, effective defenseman who skated for six Stanley Cup winners with the Montreal Canadiens in fifteen NHL years. Throughout his career, Johnson was overshadowed by the more capable Doug Harvey. Notorious as a dangerous man with his stick, Johnson was lowly regarded as a fighter and once was indicted, along with several players, by the Rangers' Andy Bathgate in an article in *True* magazine as a "spearer."

After his playing career, Johnson became an administrator with the Boston Bruins, coaching the Hub sextet in 1970–71 and 1971–72. "People said," Johnson once remarked, "that I showed no emotion on my face, although that's not quite true. I showed plenty when we won the Stanley Cup at Boston in 1972." A year later Johnson was replaced as coach—he reputedly was too relaxed with the players—by Armand "Bep" Guidolin and given a front office position.

EDWARD JOSEPH (EDDIE) JOHNSTON

BORN: Montreal, Quebec, November 24, 1935
POSITION: Goalie, Boston Bruins, 1962–73; Toronto Maple Leafs,
    1973–74; St. Louis Blues, 1974–

Eddie Johnston, the slightly portly senior member of the St. Louis Blues' net-minding corps, spent the first eleven years of his major league career with the Boston Bruins, guiding them to two Stanley Cups.

E. J., always a popular player with the fans and his teammates, didn't adopt the ever-present goalie mask until late in his career, but it was for good reason.

Johnston suffered the most serious injury of his career during a 1967 pregame warm-up. The peerless Bobby Orr was bearing down on Eddie when suddenly, the bare-faced netminder averted his gaze for a deadly split second. In that instant, Orr snapped off a wicked shot that caught Eddie on the side of his head and knocked him unconscious.

"It knocked me down," Eddie recalled later. "I was in a hospital in Detroit for three days and then they flew me to Massachusetts General in Boston. My weight went from 194 to 155 in that first week. There was a blood clot at the back of my head. They kept taking me to the operating room in case the clot had moved and they had to drill a hole. They never had to, though. When I got back playing I put on a mask—you better believe it."

In 1973 E. J. was traded to the Toronto Maple Leafs where he was part of a three-man netminding rotation with youngsters Doug Favell and Dunc Wilson. When the Leafs decided they needed more scoring punch, it was Eddie who was dispatched to the Blues in return for winger Gary Sabourin.

AUREL JOLIAT

BORN: Ottawa, Ontario, August 29, 1901
POSITION: Left Wing, Montreal Canadiens, 1922–1938
AWARDS: Hart Trophy, 1934; All-Star (First Team), 1931, (Second Team), 1932, 1934, 1935; Hockey Hall of Fame, 1945

Aurel Joliat was a native of Ontario, having grown up in the New Edinburgh district of Ottawa. He learned his hockey on the frozen Rideau River along with Bill and Frank Boucher who also were to achieve enormous fame in the NHL. In time Joliat graduated to a fast league in western Canada and arrived in a Canadiens uniform when manager Leo Dandurand decided to unload the aging Newsy Lalonde.

Aurel weighed 135 pounds, at his heaviest, but his size never bothered him. It apparently motivated him to compensate with a vast repertoire of stickhandling maneuvers and pirouettes. "He transported the world of ballet to the hockey arena," said one admirer. To which Aurel replied, "A fellow *needs* finesse when he weighs only 135 pounds!"

Joliat teamed up with Howie Morenz in the 1923–24 season. The pair jelled perfectly right from the start, although Aurel was to prove that season that he could excel with or without Morenz at his side. The Canadiens had gone up against Calgary in the playoffs and Morenz's shoulder was broken after he was hit successively by Red Dutton and Herb Gardiner. That's when Aurel took over. In the third period he intercepted an enemy pass and circled his own net to gain momentum.

"I traveled through the entire Calgary team," said Joliat, "and faked a shot to the far corner of the net. But even as I let it go I sensed I was covered on the play. So I kept going, rounded the net, and backhanded a shot into the open corner. I tumbled head over heels after that one. We went on to win the Cup and I consider it the best goal I ever scored."

Joliat was a constant source of annoyance to his larger opponents. Once, after Aurel had thoroughly confounded Toronto's Babe Dye with a series of fakes, the distressed Dye skated over to Dandurand at the Canadiens' bench and said: "I'm tired of chasing that shadow of yours—that Frenchman, Joliat. Move him over to center, Leo, hold a mirror to each side of him—you'll have the fastest line in hockey."

HERB JORDAN

BORN: Unknown
POSITION: Center, Quebec (CAHL), 1903–05; Quebec Bulldogs
(ECAHA), 1906–09; Renfrew Creamery Kings (NHA), 1910–11

Herb Jordan, a sharpshooting centerman who owns a career scoring average of better than two goals per game, broke into pro hockey in 1903 with Quebec of the CAHL.

He played with the team for the next seven seasons, leading them in scoring, but unable to single-handedly carry his squad to a championship.

Jordan joined the Renfrew team in 1910, but even this great scorer had to take a back seat to the legendary Newsy Lalonde who was signed in midseason. Jordan's most productive campaign was 1909 when, teamed with linemate Joe Malone, Herb potted 29 goals in 12 games.

WILLIAM (BILL) JUZDA

BORN: Winnipeg, Manitoba, October 29, 1920
POSITION: Defenseman, New York Rangers, 1940–42, 1945–48;
Toronto Maple Leafs, 1948–52

The closest thing to a fireplug on skates, Bill Juzda was a product of the pre-World War II New York Rangers' farm system. A defenseman who played junior hockey for the Kenora (Ontario) Thistles, Juzda spent a season (1940–41) with Philadelphia in the American League before becoming a full-time Ranger the following season. "He was a terrific bodychecker," said Bill Ezinicki, who played both against and with Juzda, "a guy who was capable of wrecking you." After playing for New York's Prince of Wales Trophy winners in 1941–42, Juzda left for the Canadian Armed Forces, returning to the Rangers in 1945–46. He remained in New York until 1948–49 when he was traded to Toronto where he completed his big league career in 1951–52.

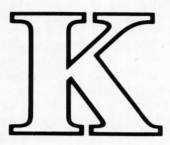

ALEXANDER "KILLER" KALETA

BORN: Canmore, Alberta, November 29, 1919
POSITION: Left Wing, Chicago Black Hawks, 1941–42, 1945–48; New
    York Rangers, 1948–51

A flamboyant skater who could have inspired the line "much ado about nothing," Alex Kaleta launched his big league career with the Black Hawks in
1941–42. After a stint in the Canadian Armed Forces, Kaleta returned to the
NHL in 1945–46 with Chicago where he remained until 1948–49 when he was
traded to the Rangers. New York fans immediately took him to their collective
hearts and named him "Killer" Kaleta because Alex would hurt neither beast,
man, nor enemy hockey player. His last NHL season was 1950–51 with the
Rangers.

RUDOLPH "BINGO" KAMPMAN

BORN: Kitchener, Ontario, March 12, 1914
POSITION: Defenseman, Toronto Maple Leafs, 1937–42

Not many NHL defensemen were better nicknamed than Rudolph Kampman,
who played for the Toronto Maple Leafs from 1937–38 through 1941–42, when
the Leafs captured the Stanley Cup. When Kampman bodychecked an opponent
a "bingo" resounded off the rafters; and for good reason. Kampman was built
along the generous dimensions of a Clydesdale stallion and offered various
ways of demonstrating his Promethean powers. Off the ice, one of his favorite
routines was lifting a heavy table by clenching its top in his teeth.

KANSAS CITY SCOUTS

Big league hockey came to Kansas City in 1974–75 largely through the efforts of the new franchise president Edwin G. Thompson, a real estate mogul who overcame bulbar polio in his youth to set a Catholic high school scoring record in basketball.

Former Detroit Red Wing star and captain Sid Abel was dubbed general manager of the franchise almost a year before the team even existed on ice. Abel had coached the Detroit Red Wings to nine playoff berths, coached the Wings in the years of their decline, and struggled in St. Louis as general manager of a disintegrating Blues' team.

The Scouts happened upon their coach late, for it wasn't until May 1974 that Armand "Bep" Guidolin got the message from the Boston Bruins—no fat, multiple-year contract, and walked in a huff straight into the open arms of Kansas City. Guidolin got his multiple-year contract and no doubt some serious headaches.

The team, for the most part, was drafted from the older clubs' unprotected lists or minor league rosters, and read like a Who's Who of traded journeymen, several having been on the starting rosters of earlier expansion teams.

The two biggest names were thirty-three-year-old Simon Nolet, drafted from the Philadelphia Flyers,and Michel Plasse, a goaltender drafted from the Montreal Canadiens. Following that duo Dave Hudson (center, from the New York Islanders), Gary Croteau (left wing, California Seals), Randy Rota (left wing, Los Angeles Kings), Brent Hughes (defense, Detroit Red Wings), Lynn Powis (center, Chicago Black Hawks), and centerman John Wright (drafted from St. Louis Blues) offered most of the remaining NHL experience, and it wasn't much.

In the amateur draft, Kansas City acquired right wing Wilf Paiement, "the highest paid amateur to enter the NHL," according to his attorney, Alan Eagleson. Second round pick was westerner Glen Burdon, a center from the Regina Pats. Both were talented, but it would take precious time for the rookies to mature into either good goal scorers or two-way players, with the motley crew they joined.

Plasse was seconded in the nets by Peter McDuffe, once a Ranger property. McDuffe had been touted as promising, but had never made the Blueshirt roster. It was somewhat ironic that Plasse should end up in Kansas City, for it was there that he, a minor leaguer, had become one of the very few goaltenders to score a goal. The Scouts could have used a replay of that feat!

The Scouts' first game was a model for what was to follow that first season— they lost 6–2 to the Toronto Maple Leafs, one of the worst Leaf teams in an eon. The two goals were scored by veterans, while the rookies skated very fast, shot like mad, and did zilch. Butch Deadmarsh on defense was a commentary on the ineffectiveness of the team near its own net, while Bart Crashley and

Bryan Lefley echoed the team's defensive weaknesses. The single biggest commentary on the Scouts' lack of experience was their penalty record—too many, too cheap, and their ten penalties in that first game led to three Toronto power play goals—and Toronto had no power play to speak of!

By December 1974 Guidolin was talking trade, managing to acquire Guy Charron and Claude Houde from Detroit for Bart Crashley, Ted Snell, and Larry Giroux. The team had won one game—against the equally nascent Washington Capitals. But the Scouts came on stronger than the Capitals and finished with a record of 15 wins, 54 losses, and 11 ties.

MICHAEL (MIKE) KARAKAS

BORN: Aurora, Minnesota, December 12, 1911
POSITION: Goalie, Chicago Black Hawks, 1935–39, 1943–46; Montreal Maroons, 1939–40
AWARDS: Calder Trophy, 1936; All-Star (Second Team), 1945

For years prior to World War II, the best American hockey products were goaltenders; among them Moe Roberts from Waterbury, Connecticut, and Frankie Brimsek of Eveleth, Minnesota. Not to be overlooked was Mike Karakas, a nimble goalie from Aurora, Minnesota, who starred for the Chicago Black Hawks from 1935–36, when he compiled a neat 1.91 goals-against average, through 1945–46, his last year in the Windy City. Mike had a brief stopover in 1939–40 with the Montreal Maroons before returning to the Hawks. His finest hours occurred during the 1938 Stanley Cup playoffs when he played in eight games, allowed but 15 goals and came off with a 1.87 goals-against average. Not surprisingly, the Hawks won the Stanley Cup.

GORDON "DUKE" KEATS

BORN: Montreal, Quebec, March 1, 1895
POSITION: Center, Toronto Arenas (NHAO), 1916–17; Edmonton Eskimos (WCHL), 1922–26; Boston Bruins, 1926–27; Detroit Cougars, 1927–28; Chicago Black Hawks, 1929

Quick-witted Duke Keats was one of hockey's first bonafide superstars, yet he will always be recalled as the fellow who almost played for two teams at once!

At the mere age of sixteen Keats came to Toronto to play for the Arenas. He also enlisted in the 228th Sportmen's Battalion, which iced a team in the NHA in 1916–17.

"Instead of playing for the Battalion," recalled Babe Donnelly, ex-defenseman, "Keats decided it would be more profitable to skate for the

Arenas. After all, they were paying him a salary; the Battalion boys were playing for nothing."

Keats was thrown into the guardhouse for his sins, but the Battalion released him on the night of a game, since the Toronto newspapers had printed Duke's whereabouts. The Battalion, fearing a rabid reaction from the fans who expected to see their star, gave him "endless latrine duty" instead, according to Donnelly.

While with the Toronto team, Keats centered for the Denneny brothers, Corbett and Cy, and Frank Patrick recalled seeing him make "thirty perfect passes to his wingmates one night."

After the 228th Battalion returned from World War I, Duke joined Edmonton of the WCHL, captaining the Eskimo team for five seasons and leading them in scoring. After guiding the Eskimos to a league championship in 1923, Keats finished his playing days in three seasons—joining Boston, Chicago, and Detroit for one campaign each.

MELVILLE SIDNEY "BUTCH" KEELING

BORN: Owen Sound, Ontario, August 10, 1905
POSITION: Left Wing, Toronto Maple Leafs, 1926–28; New York
    Rangers, 1928–38; Referee (NHL), 1947–50

There have been few sturdier forwards in the NHL than Melville Sidney "Butch" Keeling of Owen Sound, Ontario. Although his NHL career began in 1926–27 with the Toronto Maple Leafs, Butch spent only two years there. In 1928–29 he was dealt to the Rangers where he played continuously through the 1937–38 season. Butch later became an NHL referee and remained one of the most likeable men in hockey.

Despite his many exploits on ice for the Rangers, Keeling is most affectionately remembered for an incident that took place on the club's Pullman car in the early thirties, following a game in Ottawa. The Rangers won the game, 9–1, and were to return to the Pullman which was parked on a siding at Ottawa terminal.

Keeling and his teammates realized that manager-coach Lester Patrick had expected them back on the Pullman reasonably soon after the match. But the Rangers went to a party that lasted until 3 A.M. They then made their way back to the railway station and headed for the Pullman, knowing that (a) manager Patrick was asleep and (b) they had better not awaken him if they wanted to avert heavy fines. Their leader, Frank Boucher, warned them to be quiet as mice as they made their way to the Pullman berths.

Apparently every one of the Rangers was quiet to a fault—except the rather well-juiced Keeling, who in his haste to find a urinal, stumbled in the dark right into Lester Patrick's compartment.

"The door to my compartment opened," Patrick recalled, "and there stood Keeling—wearing one of those silly undershirts that barely reaches his navel. As I came awake and stared incredulously at him, he began to urinate on my floor. I called out to him, 'Butch, Butch, what the devil are you doing?'

"Butch put his finger to his lips and said, *'Shhhhhhhhhh, don't wake Lester!'* "

Keeling is still revered on Broadway for delivering a rinkwide pass to Bill Cook in the 1933 Stanley Cup final game against the Maple Leafs. Cook beat goalie Lorne Chabot with that sudden-death shot and the Rangers won their second Stanley Cup.

RICK THOMAS KEHOE

BORN: Windsor, Ontario, July 15, 1951
POSITION: Right Wing, Toronto Maple Leafs, 1971–74; Pittsburgh
    Penguins, 1974–

A perplexing young right winger, Rick Kehoe seemed destined for a major role with the Toronto Maple Leafs in the seventies. Toronto's first choice (twenty-second overall) in the 1971 amateur draft, Kehoe played thirty-eight NHL games for the Leafs in 1971–72 and two full seasons thereafter. His 33 goals in 1972–73 underlined his excellent potential, but he slipped to 18 the following year and then stunned the club with the announcement that he would no longer play hockey for the Leafs. He demanded to be traded—anywhere. Kehoe was suitably vague about his disenchantment with Toronto, but hinted strongly that as long as Red Kelly was Leafs' coach, he, Kehoe, could not play in Toronto. The Leafs ultimately dealt Rick to the Pittsburgh Penguins for Pittsburgh's 1973 first round amateur draft choice, Blaine Stoughton. Kehoe almost regained his 1972–73 form with the Pens, scoring 32 goals and 63 points in 1974–75.

JOHN ROBERT "BATTLESHIP" KELLY

BORN: Fort William, Ontario, June 6, 1946
POSITION: Left Wing, St. Louis Blues, 1973–74; Pittsburgh
    Penguins, 1974–

Bob "Battleship" Kelly should not be confused with Bob "Hound" Kelly, even though both are left wings with fighting prowess for Pennsylvania teams in the National Hockey League. While "Hound" supplies rough stuff, and some goals for the Philadelphia Flyers, "Battleship" is busy in Pittsburgh playing two-way hockey, scoring goals and improving his all-around game.

"Battleship" entered the NHL with a reputation for hard hitting and harder

Bob Kelly

punching. The St. Louis Blues dealt him to Pittsburgh, in January 1974, and Bob provided protection for the Penguins' prolific scorers. But he started off 1974–75 on a scoring tear and was rated one of the most improved performers in the league.

LEONARD PATRICK "RED" KELLY

BORN: Simcoe, Ontario, July 9, 1927
POSITION: Defenseman, Detroit Red Wings, 1947–59; Toronto Maple Leafs, 1959–67; Coach, Los Angeles Kings, 1967–69; Pittsburgh Penguins, 1970–73; Toronto Maple Leafs, 1973–
AWARDS: Norris Trophy, 1954; Lady Byng Trophy, 1951, 1953, 1954, 1961; All-Star (First Team), 1951, 1952, 1953, 1954, 1955, 1957; (Second Team), 1950, 1956; Hockey Hall of Fame, 1969

One of the most versatile and talented members of the big league hockey community is Red Kelly, the coach of the Toronto Maple Leafs. Kelly broke into the NHL in the midforties with the Detroit Red Wings after a distinguished playing career with the St. Michael's College junior team. The big defenseman became somewhat of an institution in the Motor City where he was a member of eight championship squads and four Stanley Cup winners as well as being named to eight All-Star teams. Among the many honors bestowed on the artful Kelly were four Lady Byng Memorial trophies and the Norris Trophy as the league's top defender.

Kelly was "reborn" in 1960 when he was traded to the Toronto Maple Leafs. At an age when most players are considering retirement, Kelly switched to forward line duty where he helped guide the Leafs to one championship and four Stanley Cup wins. While manning a full-time pivot position with Toronto, Kelly somehow found time to serve a term as a member of Canada's Parliament. The Redhead bowed out of the political arena in 1965 when he found his dual career too strenuous to continue.

Kelly finally retired as a player after the Maple Leafs' stunning 1967 Stanley Cup win and accepted the coaching post for the fledgling Los Angeles Kings. After two seasons with L.A., the Redhead moved on to serve as coach and general manager of the Pittsburgh Penguins.

In 1973, when John McLellan was forced to step aside as coach of the Maple Leafs, a call was hastily put in to Kelly who promptly led the young Leafs to a playoff berth.

In 1974 when Harold Ballard of the Leaf front office suggested that Kelly was too nice a guy to be an effective head coach, the Redhead showed up for the next contest brandishing an imposing bullwhip.

ROBERT JAMES "HOUND" KELLY

BORN: Oakville, Ontario, November 25, 1950
POSITION: Left Wing, Philadelphia Flyers, 1970–

Bob "Hound" Kelly debuted in the NHL at the tender age of nineteen. There is nothing tender about Bob, however. In 1972–73, Kelly collected 238 minutes in the sin bin, second on the Broad Street Bullies. Kelly scored the winning goal in the sixth and final game of the 1975 Stanley Cup finals against Buffalo.

THEODORE (TED) "TEEDER" KENNEDY

BORN: Humberstone, Ontario, December 12, 1925
POSITION: Center, Toronto Maple Leafs, 1942–56
AWARDS: Hart Memorial Trophy, 1955; All-Star (Second Team), 1950–51, 1954; Hockey Hall of Fame, 1966

One of the most tenacious forecheckers in modern hockey, Ted "Teeder" Kennedy became captain of the Toronto Maple Leafs in 1948 upon the retirement of Syl Apps. Kennedy centered the second Toronto Kid Line (the first featured Charlie Conacher, Joe Primeau, and Harvey Jackson in the early thirties) with Howie Meeker and Vic Lynn. Kennedy not only made the most of limited abilities (he was a notoriously poor skater), but generated tremendous leadership qualities and led the Leafs to Stanley Cup wins in 1949 and 1951. As a face-off man, he was peerless. "Kennedy," said Philadelphia Flyers' coach Fred Shero, "seldom lost an important face-off and was never beaten. I remember one night when I was playing for the Rangers. We had the Leafs 2–1 with less than a minute to play and the face-off was in our zone. Edgar Laprade, our center, said: 'I don't want to face that Kennedy in this spot, you take him.' I did, Kennedy won the face-off, and hit the goal post. I turned to Edgar and said: 'Like I told you, it was a cinch. I knew Kennedy would hit the post.' " Few opponents ever were so sure, or so successful against Teeder Kennedy.

DAVID MICHAEL KEON

BORN: Noranda, Quebec, March 22, 1940
POSITION: Center, Toronto Maple Leafs, 1960–
AWARDS: Calder Trophy, 1961; Lady Byng Trophy, 1962, 1963;
    Conn Smythe Trophy, 1967; All-Star (Second Team), 1962, 1971

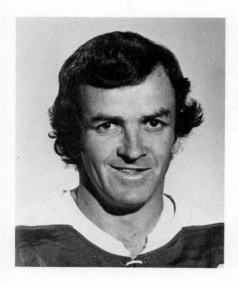

Dave Keon, the hard-working leprechaun, joined the Toronto sextet in 1960 directly from the St. Michael's College junior club. The rookie scored 20 goals in his maiden campaign, no small accomplishment in pre-expansion days, and was awarded the Calder Trophy as the NHL's rookie of the year.

Combining diligent, two-way hockey with his gentlemanly play, Keon twice won the Lady Byng Memorial Trophy and is a bona fide candidate for the bauble each and every season. Testimony to Keon's clean style of play is the fact that in 1973–74, his fourteenth year in the NHL, Keon was slapped with the first major penalty of his entire career.

A distinguished member of four Stanley Cup winning squads, Keon was named the recipient of the Conn Smythe Trophy in 1967 as the most valuable performer in the Cup playoffs.

With better than 800 total points under his belt, Dave Keon ranks as the all-time leading Maple Leaf scorer.

ALBERT "DUBBIE" KERR

BORN: Brackville, Ontario
POSITION: Left Wing, Toronto Maple Leafs (OPHL), 1909; Ottawa Senators (ECHA), 1909; Ottawa Senators (NHA), 1910–12; Victoria Aristocrats (PCHA), 1914–16; 1919–20; Spokane Canaries (PCHA), 1917

Albert "Dubbie" Kerr was a high-scoring left wing who, after three games with the 1909 Toronto club, jumped onto the Ottawa Senator bandwagon and promply helped them to the Stanley Cup.

The line of Kerr, Billy Gilmour, and center Marty Walsh was the most powerful scoring unit in the league, but Kerr's line of 1911 is by far the better remembered of the two. When right winger Bruce Ridpath displaced Gilmour on the Walsh line, the trio exploded for a whopping 91 goals among them and powered Ottawa to its second Cup in three years.

Dubbie Kerr spent one more season with the Senators before jumping to Victoria of the PCHA. He played five years with the Aristocrats and one with Spokane before retiring in 1920.

DAVID ALEXANDER (DAVEY) KERR

BORN: Toronto, Ontario, January 11, 1910
POSITION: Goalie, Montreal Maroons, 1930–31, 1932–34; New York Americans, 1931–32; New York Rangers, 1934–41
AWARDS: Vezina Trophy, 1940; All-Star (First Team), 1940; (Second Team), 1938

A solidly built fellow, Davey Kerr gained fame when he joined the Rangers in 1934 and became one of the NHL's finest goaltenders until his retirement after the 1940–41 season.

Davey Kerr

Kerr won the Vezina Trophy in 1940 when the Rangers finished first. Agile as a ballet dancer, Kerr could do the splits with one skate firmly anchored against one goal post and the other skate stretching right across the goal mouth to the other post.

One of Davey's favorite practice maneuvers was to lay his stick across the goal mouth in front of the goal line. Then, he'd prop his left skate against the right post, thus spreadeagling his body across much of the net. This would leave his two hands free to catch the puck, and his stick to deflect pucks along the ice. Kerr then would dare his teammates to beat him. According to center Frank Boucher, they never did. Boucher, who later coached the Rangers, studied the goalie's style carefully, both on and off the ice and once offered this analysis of the NHL ace:

"Kerr was gifted with an excellent right hand that picked off shots like Bill Terry playing first base for the Giants. He was deliberate and methodical in everything he did. Davey retired long before his time, when he was at his peak and only thirty years old. In a commanding way, Davey was able to shout at his defensemen, giving them guidance without offending them, and getting them to do the job he wanted done in front of him, talking continually when the puck was in our end. I don't ever remember Dave accusing a defense player for a mistake when a goal was scored against him. He always assumed the blame."

EUGENE (GENE) KINASEWICH

One of hockey's rare scholar-athletes, Eugene "Gene" Kinasewich graduated from the outdoor rinks in Edmonton, Alberta, to Harvard University and ultimately the presidency of the old Western Hockey League in 1969. He remained president for three years after which Kinasewich resigned to resume doctoral studies in education at Harvard.

OREST KINDRACHUK

BORN: Nanton, Alberta, September 14, 1950
POSITION: Center, Philadelphia Flyers, 1972–

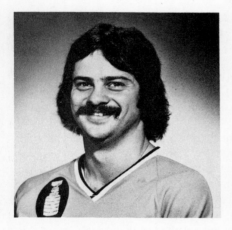

One of the most successful free agent signings in professional hockey was Orest Kindrachuk, the versatile center nabbed by the Philadelphia Flyers in 1972. Kindrachuk registered 41 points in 1973–74, his freshman year. Orest scored two goals in his first Stanley Cup outing against Atlanta in the 1974 playoffs and finished even more powerfully in the Cup finals, won by Philadelphia, against the Boston Bruins. Kindrachuk's five goals and four assists was a major surprise of the 1974 playoffs. Injuries slowed his progress in the 1974–75 season. Kindrachuk finished his optometry school studies between hockey semesters.

JOSEPH FRANCIS KLUKAY

BORN: Sault Ste. Marie, Ontario, November 6, 1922
POSITION: Forward, Toronto Maple Leafs, 1946–52, 1954–56; Boston Bruins, 1952–54

Joe Klukay and his Toronto Maple Leafs' partner, Nick Metz, are known as the two best penalty killers in NHL history. Klukay became a Leaf in 1946–47 and by no coincidence the Leafs won the Stanley Cup that year, the year after that, *and* the year after that! Klukay, who frequently worked with Max Bentley on the best third line in NHL annals, played on another Stanley Cup winner in 1951. In 1952–53 he was traded to the Bruins and played capably for them until the middle of the 1954–55 campaign when he was returned to Toronto. He completed his NHL career a season later.

GERALD JOSEPH (JERRY) KORAB

BORN: Sault Ste. Marie, Ontario, September 15, 1948
POSITION: Left Wing/Defenseman, Chicago Black Hawks, 1970–73; Vancouver Canucks, 1973; Buffalo Sabres, 1973–

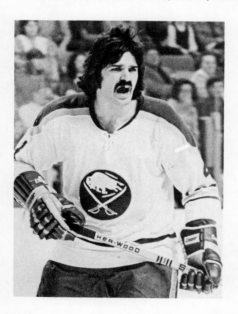

When Jerry Korab was a swingman defenseman-left wing with Chicago from 1970 through 1972–73, he showed little more than an ability to garner senseless penalties at inopportune times. Korab was sent to Vancouver in May 1973, then on to Buffalo on Christmas Eve, 1973, where he developed into a solid rearguard. Always one to mix it up when challenged, Jerry learned to control his temper, and it improved his game immeasurably.

CLIFFORD EUGENE KOROLL

BORN: Canora, Saskatchewan, October 1, 1946
POSITION: Right Wing, Chicago Black Hawks, 1969–

A quiet, articulate man off the ice, Cliff Koroll is that rare player, the product of college hockey in the United States. Koroll came with teammate Keith Magnuson, from Denver University to join the Chicago Black Hawks in 1969–70.

Koroll is fast and can handle the puck, but is an inobtrusive sort of fellow, garnering few headlines while he cruises right wing. Since the 1971–72 season, he has averaged more than twenty goals.

EDWARD GEORGE (ED) KULLMAN

BORN: Winnipeg, Manitoba, December 12, 1923
POSITION: Forward, New York Rangers, 1947–54

Eddie Kullman played his amateur hockey for the Portland Eagles, turning pro in 1947–48 with the NHL Rangers. A right winger, Kullman was described by teammate Glen Sonmor as "the most diligent checking forward I've ever played with. Kullman never would think about scoring; just trail his check wherever the guy went.'' As a result Kullman infuriated the likes of Hall of Famers Maurice Richard and Gordie Howe, particularly since Eddie mastered the art of grabbing his foe hard enough to stop him while remaining out of the referee's line of vision. Once, Richard simply hit Kullman over the head with his stick, poleaxe-style, in Madison Square Garden and nearly killed him. The ever-resilient Kullman returned to the fray wearing a helmet. Howe once waited until all eyes in the rink were on a teammate's breakaway and then kayoed Kullman with a roundhouse right.

Kullman finished his big league career with New York in 1953–54.

ORLAND JOHN KURTENBACH

BORN: Cudworth, Saskatchewan, September 7, 1936
POSITION: Center, New York Rangers, 1960–61, 1966–70; Boston Bruins, 1961–62, 1963–65; Toronto Maple Leafs, 1965–66; Vancouver Canucks, 1970–74

As a junior ace in Western Canada, Orland Kurtenbach was labeled ''the million-dollar prospect'' in 1955. Whoever was responsible for that surely was dealing in Monopoly money. As a big-leaguer, Kurtenbach was a tall flub. His skating was slothful, his scoring light, and his promise unfulfilled. An excellent fighter, however, ''Kurt,'' was involved in two classics with then Montreal Canadiens defenseman Ted Harris. Each took one decision. Fans were spared Kurtenbach's strained style in 1974 when he retired to become coach of the Seattle Totems.

WALTER LAWRENCE "GUS" KYLE

BORN: Dysart, Saskatchewan, September 11, 1923
POSITION: Defenseman, New York Rangers, 1949–51; Boston Bruins, 1951–52

Frank Boucher was the first member of the Royal Canadian Mounted Police to leave the Mounties to join the NHL's New York Rangers and Gus Kyle was the last (1949). An exceptionally rugged defenseman, Kyle later was traded to the Boston Bruins (1951). In time he became a coach and more recently a commentator for St. Louis Blues' hockey games.

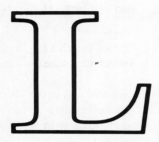

LEO GERALD LABINE

BORN: Haileybury, Ontario, July 22, 1931
POSITION: Right Wing, Boston Bruins, 1951–60; Detroit Red Wings,
   1961–62

Opponents never could make up their minds whether Leo Labine was more to be feared as a scorer or a bodychecker. A member of the Boston Bruins from 1951–52 through 1960, Labine terrorized the enemy while patrolling right wing on a line with Real Chevrefils and whoever else the Bruins could find as third man. Labine was traded to Detroit in 1960–61 and finished his career in a Detroit uniform a season later, but he is really remembered as a Bruin.

In 1956–57, when he scored 18 goals and 29 assists for 47 points in 67 games, Leo's boss, Lynn Patrick, compared Labine with the great Jean Beliveau. Actually, Leo was more a needler than a scorer. During a playoff match with Montreal, Labine nearly killed Maurice Richard with a vicious bodycheck, yet he could also be terribly amusing. Once, when the Bruins were playing an exhibition game against the Rangers at New Haven, Leo decided that he would use the early September fog on the ice as a "smokescreen." After the play shifted from the New York to the Boston end, Labine hid behind the Rangers' net. Soon, he began laughing. Rangers' goalie Lorne Worsley heard him, turned around, saw Leo, and called to referee Red Storey who, himself laughing, ordered the linesman to blow an offside. By this time everyone in the rink, including Worsley, was laughing at Leo's jape.

ELMER JAMES LACH

BORN: Nokomis, Saskatchewan, January 22, 1918
POSITION: Center, Montreal Canadiens, 1940–54
AWARDS: Hart Trophy, 1945; Art Ross Trophy, 1945, 1948; All-Star
(First Team), 1945, 1948, 1952, (Second Team), 1944, 1946;
Hockey Hall of Fame, 1966

Elmer Lach, the center on the Montreal Canadiens' fabled Punch Line, broke in with the Habs in 1940–41, promptly helping the Frenchmen squeeze into the Stanley Cup playoffs.

The following season, the infamous Lach injury jinx that was to earn him the handle of "Elmer the Unlucky" began to surface. In the opening game of the 1941–42 season, Lach crashed into the boards, breaking his arm in two places. He was sidelined for the entire season, but it was only the first in a long line of painful injuries for the big guy.

After his year of convalescence, Lach was elevated to first-line status, where the aggressive forward took a regular shift, skated on the power play, and killed penalties as well.

In 1943–44, the legendary Rocket Richard joined the Habs' forward line, and along with Lach and Toe Blake completed the Punch Line. With that kind of firepower behind them, the Canadiens steamrolled to their first Stanley Cup in thirteen years.

In all, Lach labored for thirteen seasons wearing the *bleu, blanc, et rouge*—a stretch that saw the Frenchmen win three Stanley Cups and finish first in the league four consecutive times. Lach finished his career in 1954, having scored 215 goals and 623 points, and an endless number of stitches for the Canadiens.

ANDRE JOSEPH LACROIX

BORN: Lauzon, Quebec, June 5, 1945
POSITION: Center, Philadelphia Flyers, 1967–71; Chicago Black
Hawks, 1971–72; Philadelphia Blazers (WHA), 1972–73; New
York Golden Blades/New Jersey Knights (WHA), 1973–74; San
Diego Mariners (WHA), 1974–
AWARDS: W. D. Hunter Trophy (WHA Scoring Leader), 1973, 1975;
All-Star (WHA First Team), 1973, 1974, 1975; WHA Team Canada,
1974

After its first year of existence, the WHA scoring leader was Andre Lacroix. He was the league scoring leader in 1972–73 with 50 goals and 74 assists for the Philadelphia Blazers. The following year, with the New Jersey Knights (now the San Diego Mariners), Lacroix was second with 31 goals and 80 assists. Then in 1975 his 147 points won the scoring title again.

Andre Lacroix

Lacroix is a small and very quick centerman who displayed his considerable playmaking abilities on a line with Bobby Hull during the 1974 Team Canada–Russia series. Excellent at winning face-offs, Lacroix was also named to the WHA All-Star squads in 1973, 1974 and 1975.

Before coming to the WHA, Lacroix labored for the Philadelphia Flyers from 1967–71, getting more than 20 goals in each of his last three seasons there. Inexplicably, he scored only 11 points in 51 games for the Chicago Black Hawks when traded there for the 1971–72 season. But in the WHA he is widely recognized as the league's top centerman—and one of the best in the game. Originally a product of the Montreal Canadien organization, Lacroix slipped through their fingers in the first expansion draft in 1967 when the Flyers picked him as one of their top choices.

GUY DAMIEN LAFLEUR

BORN: Thurso, Quebec, September 20, 1951
POSITION: Right Wing and Center, Montreal Canadiens, 1971–
AWARDS: All-Star (First Team), 1975

Until the 1974–75 campaign, when he was among the league leaders in scoring, Guy Lafleur hadn't really caught fire in the NHL. Playing both right wing and center, "point" on the power plays, and killing penalties, Guy was far from the French-Canadian star of the Habs, much less the entire league.

But in 1974, Guy began to earn his tricouleurs. No one has ever doubted his skating ability, shooting, or stickhandling, but he was far from aggressive. Perhaps when Lafleur shed his helmet people began to realize a change was in the works.

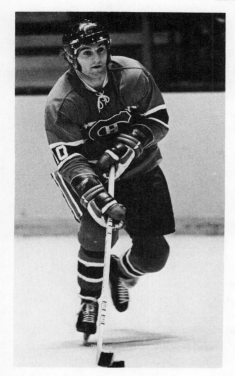

Guy Lafleur

Lafleur is now a full-fledged Canadiens star, the dream of any Quebecois boy.

EDOUARD "NEWSY" LALONDE

BORN: Cornwall, Ontario, October 31, 1887
DIED: Montreal, Quebec, November 21, 1970
POSITION: Defenseman and Forward, Montreal Canadiens, 1910–22; Coach, New York Americans, 1926–27; Montreal Canadiens, 1932–34
AWARDS: Art Ross Trophy, 1919, 1921; Hockey Hall of Fame, 1950

Edouard "Newsy" Lalonde was one of the toughest and most controversial figures to skate in pro hockey. He was a member of the original Montreal Canadiens' team and a legend in his time.

Lalonde, nicknamed "Newsy" during a brief stint working in a newsprint plant, broke into pro hockey with Sault Ste. Marie when he was only eighteen.

In his first game against Pittsburgh he discovered that the defensemen had a habit of backhanding the puck into the air when they wanted to clear the puck from their zone. "Once I figured that out," Newsy revealed, "I made a point of getting in front of them and then, suddenly, swerving around so that I actually had my back to the defensemen."

Lalonde soon proved there was a method to his madness. The next time a Pittsburgh player attempted to clear the puck, Lalonde executed his pirouette. The puck struck him in the back and slipped through his baggy hockey pants to the ice directly behind him. He then deftly spun around, captured the puck, and skimmed it into the net. Newsy executed this maneuver twice in the same game, and Sault Ste. Marie came out on top, 3–1. "After that," he said, "I was in pro hockey for good."

With Newsy leading the team in scoring with 16 goals in sixteen games, Les Canadiens finished second in their second season.

Newsy earned a reputation as one of the roughest players in the game. His clashes with "Bad" Joe Hall, who later became a teammate on Les Canadiens, were studies in jungle brutality, but Newsy didn't reserve his venom for Hall. On December 22, 1912, the Canadiens played their hometown rivals, the Wanderers, in an exhibition game to unveil the new Toronto hockey rink. Midway into the game Lalonde dispatched Odie Cleghorn of the Wanderers into the boards with such force that Odie's teammate and brother, Sprague, charged across the rink and smashed Newsy across the forehead with his stick. The blow just barely missed Lalonde's eye and he required twelve stitches to close the gaping wound.

The episode didn't go unnoticed officially and a constable served a summons on Cleghorn. Sprague turned up in a Toronto court and was fined fifty dollars for his efforts, and an additional fifty-dollar fine was slapped on him by NHA president Emmett Quinn. Cleghorn was also suspended for four weeks, but such was the laissez faire atmosphere of pro hockey at the time that Sprague absented himself from only one game and then returned to the Wanderers' lineup with impunity.

Lalonde, despite his chronic warlike behavior, remained a Canadiens' star through the 1921–22 season. Once he began aging, Lalonde became trade bait and Canadiens' boss Leo Dandurand finally dealt thirty-six-year-old Newsy to the Saskatoon (Saskatchewan) Sheiks for tiny Aurel Joliat prior to the 1922–23 season. Lalonde never returned to the NHL as a player, but he did return as a coach after scoring 29 goals in 26 games as a player-coach of the Saskatoon Sheiks. In the fall of 1926, New York Americans' manager Tommy Gorman hired Lalonde to coach the NHL Amerks. Some of the Americans' players such as Jakie Forbes were a bit disturbed by the move. "Lalonde," said Forbes, "was the dirtiest sonofabitch I ever played against."

Tough as he was, Lalonde couldn't handle the boisterous Americans. Newsy once barged into the hotel room where the players were partying after a loss and berated the drunken skaters. One of the players, Alex McKinnon, told Newsy he was a lousy coach whereupon Lalonde knocked him out with one punch. Lalonde turned to the others and demanded: "Anybody else?" Nobody responded. Still, Newsy quit after a year of coaching the Americans.

Newsy later coached his alma mater, Les Canadiens, from 1932 to 1934 but, once again, suffered player problems. During the 1932–33 season ace forward Johnny Gagnon charged that the Canadiens couldn't get along with Lalonde. The Montrealers finished third in the Canadian Division in his first year behind the bench and second in his final year. Throughout his life, Newsy remained controversial and tough and will go down in history as one of the best hockey and lacrosse players ever produced in Canada.

MYLES J. LANE

BORN: Melrose, Massachusetts, October 2, 1905
POSITION: Defenseman, New York Rangers, 1928–29; Boston Bruins, 1929–30, 1933–34

Among the graduates of the National Hockey League, some of whom have traveled from the ice to the Canadian Parliament, New York State Supreme Court judge Myles Lane ranks as one of the most distinguished. He began wearing the black robes on January 1, 1969. Before that he was a member of the New York State Commission of Investigation, a team of top-level gang-busters which he joined after working as a United States attorney.

Lane was also the first American ever to play on a Stanley Cup team—the Boston Bruins of 1929. Hockey had helped Lane become a lawyer. He worked his way through law school by playing the game—first for the Rangers, then for the Bruins—and by managing the Boston Cubs, a Bruin farm team.

Lane was a competent player, if not a star. And as one of the first Americans in the big league, he had tremendous curiosity value at the box office. This was not always to his advantage, though.

In a locker room interview after his first Ranger game, a sportswriter mis-quoted Lane as saying that "this game is a cinch compared to college hockey." When the Rangers arrived in Montreal the following Saturday night, the news-papers were exhorting the populace to come out and see the wise guy and the arena was packed. The Montreal Maroons were out to get the American college boy who scoffed at the Canadian professionals.

Lane's first rush down ice ended with a bone-crushing bodycheck and a charging penalty for his overanxious opponent. His next rush ended the same way and so did the third.

Emotions were running high and the game grew rougher. Lane escaped unhurt, but by the time the game was over there were two major casualties. Taffy Abel needed twelve stitches in his foot and the great Ching Johnson broke his leg, an injury from which he never fully recovered.

Lane thought of Johnson as his big brother and mentor, but as for the greatest player he ever saw, Lane gives the award to Eddie Shore of the Bruins. He was not alone in his admiration. When Lane was with the Rangers, the New York club tried to set up a deal with the Bruins that would have involved trading Myles Lane for Eddie Shore. The Boston reply was quick and to the point: "You're so many Myles from Shore, you need a life preserver!"

Within his first year in the league, though, Lane was sold to Boston, where he became Shore's teammate. There he performed ably until an automobile accident forced him to hang up his skates and turn to managing the Boston Cubs.

PETER (PETE) LANGELLE

BORN: Winnipeg, Manitoba, November 4, 1917
POSITION: Forward, Toronto Maple Leafs, 1938–42

Although Pete Langelle played only three full seasons with the Toronto Maple Leafs, he achieved a permanent niche in hockey history as the forward who scored the winning goal in the 1942 Stanley Cup final between Detroit and Toronto. In that series the Red Wings took a 3–0 lead in games before the Maple Leafs tied the series at three games apiece. With the score tied, 1–1, in the seventh and final game at Maple Leaf Gardens on April 18, 1942, Langelle beat goalie Johnny Mowers, banging home a rebound from a shot by linemate Johnny McCreedy. It turned out to be Langelle's finest hour and final game; he soon left for the Canadian armed forces and never played big-league hockey again.

ALBERT "JUNIOR" LANGLOIS

BORN: Magog, Quebec, November 6, 1934
POSITION: Defenseman, Montreal Canadiens, 1957–61; New York
    Rangers, 1961–64; Detroit Red Wings, 1964–65; Boston Bruins,
    1965–66

It was Al Langlois's grand good fortune to play defense alongside Doug Harvey for three seasons (1958–59, 1959–60, 1960–61) with the Montreal Canadiens and then again with Harvey on the New York Rangers for another two and a half seasons. As Harvey's play deteriorated, so did Langlois's, and "Junior," as the latter was nicknamed, was finally traded to Detroit in 1963–64 and on to Boston for the 1965–66 season where he ended his NHL career. A mediocre-to-solid defenseman, Langlois excelled when he had someone strong beside him; which helps explain why he skated for three Stanley Cup winners at Montreal; of course, playing alongside the inimitable Harvey.

JOSEPH JACQUES HUGHES LAPERRIERE

BORN: Rouyn, Quebec, November 22, 1941
POSITION: Defenseman, Montreal Canadiens, 1962–75
AWARDS: Calder Memorial Trophy, 1964; James Norris Memorial Trophy, 1966; All-Star (First Team), 1965–66, (Second Team), 1964, 1970

When All-Star defenseman Doug Harvey was traded by the Montreal Canadiens to the New York Rangers in 1961, the Montreal brass scoured their farm system for a good, young replacement. In time they found beanstalk Jacques Laperriere, a native of Rouyn, Quebec, who honed his skills to sharpness with the Montreal Junior Canadiens. Laperriere played six games with the Canadiens in 1962–63 and became a regular the following season. He easily won the National Hockey League rookie-of-the-year award and emerged as one of the best of contemporary defensemen. His size (6–2, 190 pounds) enabled him to use the poke check to great advantage. Jacques played a hard but clean game and remained a Montreal ace through the 1972–73 season when he was hospitalized with a leg injury. Although he played part of the 1973–74 season, the leg still bothered Laperriere so badly that he failed to start the 1974–75 campaign and retired in July 1975 to become coach of the Montreal Juniors, an amateur team.

GUY GERARD LAPOINTE

BORN: Montreal, Quebec, March 18, 1948
POSITION: Defenseman, Montreal Canadiens, 1968–
AWARDS: All-Star (First Team), 1973, (Second Team), 1975

In the spring of 1973 Guy Lapointe, the Montreal Canadiens' agile defense-man, was named to the NHL's First All-Star Team, and not coincidentally the Canadiens won their eighteenth Stanley Cup championship. Combining bruis-ing bodychecks with nimble puck-carrying, Guy quarterbacked the Canadiens' attack. In a typical attack Guy would circle the net driving his legs like pistons en route to the enemy goal. The opposing team was confounded by Lapointe's versatile activities, particularly his hard shot from the point or his radar-sharp passes that bear the Canadiens' "head-man-the-puck" trademark.

Until the 1972–73 season, Lapointe had been known as a defenseman with modest offensive abilities. He scored 15 and 11 goals in the 1970–71 and 1971–72 seasons, respectively, before bursting out with 19 goals in 1972–73. It was then that coach Scotty Bowman decided to place Guy on the potent Mon-treal power play. The result—the Canadiens improved their scoring on the man-advantage situation after Guy began sharpshooting from the blue line.

The Canadiens, who had been searching for a bouncer since the retirement of John Ferguson following the 1970 season, happily discovered that Guy also reveled in physical play.

Guy won a spot on the Canadiens during the last, hectic, unfortunate days of the 1969–70 season, after skating for the Canadiens' Montreal Voyageurs' farm club. On the season's final night Montreal was eliminated from a playoff berth and the Forum was shrouded in gloom. It was the first time that the proud Habitants had failed to make the playoffs in thirty years!

Although the team was down Lapointe was on the way up, and nobody could stop him. On the ice the Canadiens looked like a brand new team as the ebullient Lapointe orchestrated defense and offense en route to the 1971 Stan-ley Cup championship. Lapointe's 107 penalty minutes correctly suggest that the Canadiens boast a stickhandler who isn't afraid to battle yet is prudent enough not to fight at the drop of a puck.

A fractured cheekbone ruined the 1971–72 season for Lapointe. Even after it had healed, Guy appeared hesitant and hardly the musketeer of old.

But by 1972–73 his health was A-1 again and so were the Canadiens. The point was demonstrated most vividly in the third game of the Stanley Cup quar-terfinal series with the pesky Buffalo Sabres. Trailing 2–0, the Frenchmen ap-peared grounded after one period of action. Guy, who has developed into a for-midable leader, tongue-lashed his teammates during the intermission. The Canadiens responded to Lapointe's bilingual blast and went from a collection of Clark Kents to Supermen. They disposed of Buffalo, then Philadelphia, and Chicago en route to their eighteenth Stanley Cup triumph.

Lapointe, thus, is following a long and distinguished tradition set by All-Star Montreal defensemen Doug Harvey, Tom Johnson, Butch Bouchard, and Lapointe's older teammate Jacques Laperriere. None of those, however, combined the strongest elements of offense with defense in the manner of Guy Lapointe. It was no surprise that Lapointe surpassed his personal points record in 1974–75 with 28 goals and 47 assists, nor that the Canadiens were the NHL powerhouse of the regular season.

EDGAR LOUIS LAPRADE

BORN: Mine Center, Ontario, October 10, 1919
POSITION: Center, New York Rangers, 1945–55
AWARDS: Calder Trophy, 1946; Lady Byng Trophy, 1950

Edgar Laprade played ten seasons for the Rangers, beginning with 1945–46, when he won the Calder Trophy as the National Hockey League's top rookie.

A smooth skater and an expert stickhandler, Laprade betrayed one shortcoming—a terribly weak shot. He frequently would find himself in scoring position only to shoot ineffectively; either weakly or wide of the mark. Yet, Laprade's playmaking emerged as one of the jewels of a relatively lackluster New York team. "I've always felt that he missed the general acclaim he deserved," said Rangers' manager Frank Boucher, "because it was his misfortune never to be cast with a winner." Laprade starred for the Rangers in their vain try for the Stanley Cup in 1950, scoring three goals and five assists in twelve Stanley Cup games. He retired following the 1954–55 season and returned to Thunder Bay, Ontario, where he became a sporting goods dealer and village alderman.

CLAUDE DAVID LAROSE

BORN: Hearst, Ontario, March 2, 1942
POSITION: Right Wing, Montreal Canadiens, 1962–68, 1970–74; Minnesota North Stars, 1968–70; St. Louis Blues, 1974–

Claude Larose helped the Montreal Canadiens to quite a few championships in the sixties, but was used sparingly with the club, a victim of too much talent on the Canadiens. He was traded to the Minnesota North Stars along with Danny Grant in June 1968 and scored 25 and 24 goals in the two years he played in the north country. The Canadiens got him back in 1970, giving up Bobby Rousseau, and he played on and off, primarily as a defensive forward for the next four years.

Claude was traded by the Canadiens for the second time, in the winter of 1974, to the St. Louis Blues for future considerations.

JACK LAVIOLETTE

BORN: Belleville, Ontario, July 19, 1879
DIED: Montreal, Quebec, January 9, 1960
POSITION: Defenseman/Forward, Montreal Canadiens, 1910–18
AWARDS: Hockey Hall of Fame, 1962

Although he was a splendid defenseman and forward, Jack Laviolette made his niche as a manager who helped organize the first Montreal Canadiens hockey team in the National Hockey Association (predecessor to the NHL) in December 1909. Laviolette zeroed in on the best French-Canadian talent available. His first coup was the signing of Edouard ''Newsy'' Lalonde, one of the toughest and most adept players available. Next he finagled Didier Pitre away from the rival Canadian Hockey Association. Laviolette soon signed Joe Cattarinich, Ed Decarie, and Art Bernier and Les Canadiens, the original Flying Frenchmen, were in business—thanks to Jack Laviolette. Meanwhile Jack continued as a player and skated for Les Canadiens up to their first season in the newly created NHL (1917–18) in which he scored two goals in eighteen games. That was the year that the Canadiens journeyed to Seattle to play for the Stanley Cup. With the series tied at two apiece the Cup finals were called off because of the flu epidemic. Laviolette retired from NHL play after that season.

DANIEL MICHAEL (DANNY) LAWSON

BORN: Toronto, Ontario, October 30, 1947
POSITION: Right Wing, Detroit Red Wings, 1967–69; Minnesota North Stars, 1969–71; Buffalo Sabres, 1971–72; Philadelphia/Vancouver Blazers/Calgary Cowboys (WHA), 1972–
AWARDS: All-Star (WHA, First Team), 1973

Danny Lawson never quite fulfilled the promise that the Detroit Red Wings set for him when they drafted him from the Hamilton Red Wings of the Ontario Hockey Association.

Lawson bounced around with the Red Wings, Minnesota North Stars, and Buffalo Sabres before he decided to jump to the World Hockey Association when the new league was formed in 1972.

Playing for the Philadelphia/Vancouver Blazers/Calgary Cowboys, Lawson became one of their leading scorers and finished second on the club in scoring in 1973–74, next to Bryan Campbell.

HAROLD RICHARDSON (HAL) LAYCOE

BORN: Sutherland, Saskatchewan, June 23, 1922
POSITION: Defenseman, New York Rangers, 1945–47; Montreal Canadiens, 1947–51; Boston Bruins, 1951–56; Coach, Los Angeles Kings, 1969; Vancover Canucks, 1970–72

One of the few bespectacled defensemen in National Hockey League history, Hal Laycoe was nurtured to the majors in the New York Rangers' farm system originally starring for the Eastern League's New York Rovers. He made his NHL debut, playing seventeen games in 1945–46 with the Rangers and became a regular in the following season. Laycoe was more a thinker than a hitter and was dealt to Montreal prior to the 1947–48 season. After three and a half seasons with the Canadiens, Laycoe was dealt to the Boston Bruins in 1950–51, and finished his career in Boston following the 1955–56 season. Although Laycoe was not considered an especially belligerent type, he is regarded as the catalyst for what became the biggest riot in hockey, the March 1955 eruption in Montreal after Maurice "Rocket" Richard was suspended for the remainder of the 1954–55 season and the playoffs. It was Laycoe who originally struck Richard in a Bruin-Canadien game that inspired the Rocket to retaliate. When linesman Cliff Thompson intervened, Richard hit Thompson. It was that blow which led to Richard's suspension; but it was Laycoe who originally hit Richard. Laycoe briefly coached Los Angeles and Vancouver of the NHL— and not too well.

REGINALD JOSEPH "THE CHIEF" LEACH

BORN: Riverton, Manitoba, April 23, 1950
POSITION: Right Wing, Boston Bruins, 1970–72; California Golden Seals, 1972–74; Philadelphia Flyers, 1974–

A junior teammate of Bobby Clarke at Flin Flon, Reggie Leach is now a senior linemate with Clarke in Philly. Nicknamed "the Chief" for his Indian ancestry, Leach was the third man chosen in the 1970 amateur selections, just ahead of Rick MacLeish. Both were chosen by the Bruins and are now integral parts of the Philadelphia attack.

Clarke urged the Flyers to acquire Leach for the 1974–75 season although there had been reports that Reg would be more a hindrance than a help to the Philadelphia club. Leach responded by scoring 46 goals for the Flyers and appeared destined for a long career in Philadelphia. His major weapon is a devastating shot that overwhelms any stickhandling deficiencies.

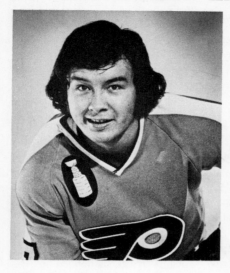

Reggie Leach

ALBERT "BATTLESHIP" LEDUC

BORN: Valleyfield, Quebec, July 31, 1901
POSITION: Defenseman, Montreal Canadiens, 1925–33, 1934–35;
    New York Rangers, 1933–34; Ottawa Senators, 1934

Defensemen such as Albert "Battleship" Leduc infused the Montreal Cana-
diens with the kind of pzazz that earned them the label of hockey's most colorful team. Except for a brief exile in 1933–34, when he played for both the New
York Rangers and Ottawa Senators, Leduc skated exclusively for the Flying
Frenchmen from 1925 through his NHL finale in 1934–35. Leduc frequently
was overshadowed by his defense partners, Sylvio Mantha and Herb Gardiner.
But Leduc, according to former Canadiens' managing director Frank Selke,
Sr., was "a typical Habitant." As Selke described Leduc, "Battleship had a
highly excitable temperament. On the ice he made all of his moves at top
speed. He could score on his long end-to-end rushes but, more than all else, he
handed out a bodycheck which, in his day, was the most important attribute of
any defenseman."

HUGH LEHMAN

BORN: Pembroke, Ontario, October 27, 1885
DIED: Toronto, Ontario, April 8, 1961
POSITION: Goalie, Vancouver Millionaires (PCHA), 1915–26; Chicago Black Hawks, 1926–28
AWARDS: Hockey Hall of Fame, 1958

Hugh Lehman, a Hall of Fame goaltender, broke into hockey in 1909 with Berlin (now Kitchener) of the OPHL. After shuttling around between Berlin, Galt, and New Westminster, Hugh settled down with Vancouver of the PCHA where he minded their nets for the next twelve seasons.

Lehman was on eight championship squads over his twenty-year pro career, but only one Cup winner—the 1915 Millionaires. Hugh moved east in 1927, spending the last two seasons of his career with the Chicago Black Hawks of the NHL.

JACQUES GERARD LEMAIRE

BORN: La Salle, Quebec, September 7, 1945
POSITION: Center, Montreal Canadiens, 1967–

Speedy Jacques Lemaire has never really fulfilled the expectations that the Montreal Canadiens set for him, despite scoring 44 goals in 1972–73. Jacques is known for his potent slapshot, which he is not afraid to use, whether it is from within 60 feet or 6 feet.

It was Jacques's 80-footer, which sailed by Chicago goalie Tony Esposito, that tied the seventh game of the 1970–71 Stanley Cup finals and eventually the Canadiens went on to win their sixteenth Stanley Cup. Jacques picked up 9 goals and 10 assists in that playoff.

Jacques was hot again in 1974–75, tallying 36 goals and 56 assists for 92 points in the regular season.

Jacques Lemaire

ALFRED "PIT" LEPINE

BORN: St. Anne de Bellevue, Quebec, July 30, 1901
DIED: August 2, 1955
POSITION: Center, Montreal Canadiens, 1925–38

A native of St. Anne de Bellevue, Quebec, Pit Lepine epitomized the French-Canadian hockey player who gave his all for Les Canadiens, the sporting symbol of French Canada. Every National Hockey League game that the center Lepine played from his rookie year, 1925–26, through his retirement after the 1937–38 season he played for Montreal's Canadiens. If Lepine had a problem it was the fact that he was chronically overshadowed by the Canadiens' superstar of the late twenties and early thirties, Howie Morenz. "Lepine brought to the game a polish seldom seen before," said former Canadiens' managing director Frank Selke, Sr. "On any other team Pit would have been a blazing meteor, but he was doomed to play all of his hockey in the shadow of the truculent Morenz who, at that time, was the fiercest competitor in hockey."

PERCY LeSUEUR

BORN: Quebec City, Quebec, November 18, 1882
DIED: Hamilton, Ontario, January 28, 1962
POSITION: Forward and Goalie, Ottawa Senators, 1906–14; Montreal
    Shamrocks, 1914–15; Toronto Arenas, 1915–16
AWARDS: Hockey Hall of Fame, 1961

Percy LeSueur, a solid but unspectacular goalkeeper, minded the nets for the old Ottawa Senators until the arrival of the legendary Clint Benedict. LeSueur's statistics were never nearly as impressive as Benedict's, but he did help guide Ottawa to two Stanley Cups in 1909 and 1911. Percy was dealt to the Shamrocks in 1915 and finished out his career with Toronto the following season.

ANTHONY JOSEPH (TONY) LESWICK

BORN: Humboldt, Saskatchewan, March 17, 1923
POSITION: Left Wing, New York Rangers, 1945–51; Detroit Red
    Wings, 1951–55, 1957–58; Chicago Black Hawks, 1955–56
AWARDS: All-Star (Second Team), 1950

In 1946 it was clear to Frank Boucher, who had taken over the helm of the Rangers, that new blood was needed to replace the prewar heroes, who had lost their spark and their style. One of the first of the "finds" was a small, bulldog-type forward named Tony Leswick. Within two years "Tough Tony," as he was known on Broadway, became the team's leading scorer.

The turnabout for the Rangers from chronic losers to consistent winners didn't happen overnight, but Leswick went a long way to pumping fighting blood into the postwar team. He not only led them in scoring during the 1946–47 campaign but was just as useful as the supreme needler of the opposition and "shadow" of its leading scorers, until traded to Detroit in 1951–52.

More than anyone else, the fabulous "Rocket" Richard of the Montreal Canadiens had the life annoyed out of him by Leswick. Once, at the Montreal Forum, Leswick needled the Rocket, and Richard swung his stick at Leswick. The referee sent Richard to the penalty box with a two-minute minor. Leswick

Tony Leswick

didn't stop there and pestered the Rocket throughout the match. With just a minute remaining, Richard blew up again, and again the referee sent him to the penalty box.

At game's end, Richard bolted from the penalty box and charged Leswick, whereupon the two of them brawled for several minutes while teammates and officials attempted to separate the pair. The Richard-Leswick feud continued for several years.

Of course Richard wasn't Leswick's only target. Once, in a playoff game against the Detroit Red Wings, he was given a two-minute penalty, followed closely by a two-minute penalty to teammate Nick Mickoski. The timekeeper, whose duty it was to wave inmates back onto the ice when their penalty time had expired, became Leswick's target.

"Tony chattered and argued about the time he was to return to the ice," said Rangers' publicist Stan Saplin, "and so confused the timekeeper that he was allowed back in the game long before his penalty time was up."

ALEXANDER "KINGFISH" or "MINE BOY" LEVINSKY

BORN: Syracuse, New York, February 2, 1910
POSITION: Defenseman, Toronto Maple Leafs, 1930–34; New York
    Rangers, 1934–35; Chicago Black Hawks, 1935–39

Signed by the Maple Leafs in 1930–31, Alex Levinsky helped Conn Smythe's
club to a Stanley Cup a season later. He played for Toronto through the
1933–34 season, once actually playing goal when Lorne Chabot, the regular
Toronto goalie, was penalized. In 1934–35 he was traded to the Rangers before
joining the Black Hawks the same season. Ironically, Alex was on the Chicago
defense in 1937–38 when the Hawks upset the favored Leafs to win the Stanley
Cup in 1938. Levinsky completed his major league career in 1938–39 with the
Hawks. Levinsky came by his nicknames, "Kingfish" and "Mine Boy," for
his ability to "dig" in the corners and come up with "gold" in the form of the
puck.

RICHARD NORMAN (RICK) LEY

BORN: Orillia, Ontario, November 2, 1948
POSITION: Defenseman, Toronto Maple Leafs, 1968–72; New Eng-
    land Whalers (WHA), 1972–
AWARDS: Team Canada (WHA), 1974

Originally a member of the Toronto Maple Leafs "Kiddie Korps" on defense, along with Jim Dorey and Brad Selwood, Rick Ley joined the New England Whalers in 1972. Only five feet, nine inches tall, Ley is built like a fireplug and is impossible to get around when he's on the ice and fired up. Although he doesn't appear to be, Ley is a thinking defenseman and seldom makes dumb moves. Better defensively than offensively, Ley was chosen for the 1974 Team Canada–Russia series in which he unfortunately distinguished himself by gratuitously thrashing Russian forward ace Valery Kharlamov seconds after the game ended in a loss for Team Canada. He later apologized, but the Canadians lost the series, anyway. He was named Whalers' captain in 1975.

BERT LINDSAY

BORN: Unknown

POSITION: Goalie, Renfrew Creamery Kings (NHA), 1909–11; Victoria Aristocrats (PCHA), 1911–15; Montreal Wanderers (NHA), 1915–16; Toronto Arenas, 1918–19

Bert Lindsay is perhaps best known as the father of "Terrible Ted" Lindsay, Hall of Fame winger for the Detroit Red Wings. But Bert was a fine hockey player in his own right. He was a goaltender for the Montreal Wanderers and at Renfrew, where he teamed up with the likes of Frank and Lester Patrick, Cyclone Taylor, and Newsy Lalonde with the NHA Creamery Kings.

One of Bert's lesser-known contributions to the sport was his invention of the collapsible net. Many skaters of the Eastern Hockey League were crashing into posts and injuring legs and limbs. Lindsay felt that a goal post which would give when crashed into would save on hospital bills, so he designed a net that would bend at the corners with the force of the blow.

What Lindsay neglected to alert officials and forwards to was a distinct advantage built into these cages. If a netminder wished to cut down the angle of the shooter bearing in on him, all he needed do was strategically touch the net, which bent, and thereby cut down the angle. As an ex-goaltender, Lindsay must have enjoyed this little prank.

ROBERT BLAKE THEODORE (TED) LINDSAY

BORN: Renfrew, Ontario, July 29, 1925
POSITION: Left Wing, Detroit Red Wings, 1944–57, 1964–65; Chicago Black Hawks, 1957–60
AWARDS: Art Ross Trophy, 1950; All-Star (First Team), 1948, 1950–54, 1956–57; (Second Team), 1949; Hockey Hall of Fame, 1966

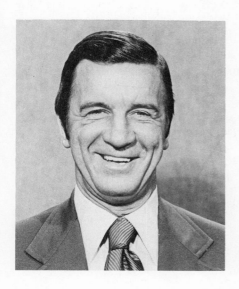

One of the most determined and fearsome skaters in National Hockey League history, "Terrible Ted" Lindsay is best remembered as the left winger on the Detroit Red Wings' "Production Line" with center Sid Abel and right winger Gordie Howe.

The son of Bert Lindsay, himself a splendid player and later the inventor of the collapsible hockey net, Ted skated in the NHL for seventeen years, most of the time with the Red Wings. Lindsay was not especially big (5'8", 163 lbs.), but he was regarded as totally tough. "By my definition," said Lindsay, "there's one helluva lot more to being a tough guy than getting in a few phony fights where no real punches are tossed. To me being tough includes wanting to win so badly that you give it all you've got every shift, going into corners without phoning ahead to see who's there, backing up your mates if they're in trouble and stepping into guys, even if they're bigger than you."

One of Lindsay's most devastating bouts involved the Bruins' "Wild Bill" Ezinicki. The fight, at Olympia Stadium in Detroit, took place on January 25, 1951. When it was over Ezinicki had lost a tooth, had acquired two black eyes, a broken nose and nineteen stitches. Lindsay needed only five stitches above his eye, but was treated for badly scarred and swollen knuckles on his right hand.

It was episodes such as that which caused Lindsay to become the all-time NHL penalty leader with 1,808 minutes in seventeen seasons with Detroit and later Chicago. He could score, too, and finished his career with 379 career goals, was named All-Star left wing nine times, and also made "trouble" in areas outside the rink itself.

Lindsay was a leader in the formation of an NHL players' union in the mid-fifties. When Red Wings' manager Jack Adams discovered Lindsay's role with the proposed union, he had the left winger traded to the Chicago Black Hawks prior to the 1957–58 season. "The concept we had for the players' association," said Lindsay, "was not the creation of one household for all the players in the NHL. What we were aiming for was to benefit the game of hockey, not just the players."

Curiously, Lindsay finished his NHL career with the Red Wings in 1964–65, but remained in the hockey limelight. He was hired as color commentator for the NBC-TV network "Game of the Week" in 1972 and never hesitated to speak out on controversial issues. Lindsay was especially critical of the NHL Players' Association and its director, Alan Eagleson. "The Players' Association," said Lindsay, "has encouraged familiarity among the players. They're one big, happy family now. The coaches have no way of pushing players. They can't send them to the minors; they can't fine them because the Players' Association will raise hell."

Lindsay's comments so enraged Eagleson that in January 1975 Eagleson dispatched a letter to each NHL team urging the players not to cooperate with Lindsay.

HARRY CARLYLE (CARL) LISCOMBE

BORN: Perth, Ontario, May 17, 1915
POSITION: Left Wing, Detroit Red Wings, 1937–46

Before Gordie Howe became a household word in Detroit, skaters such as Carl Liscombe were the Motor City hockey heroes. A left wing from Perth, Ontario, Liscombe came to Detroit from the Hamilton, Ontario, Tigers and turned regular in the 1937–38 season. In the 1943 Stanley Cup round, Carl was the leading goal scorer with 6 and pointmaker with 14 as the Red Wings won the Stanley Cup. Up until 1951 Liscombe held the NHL record for fastest three goals—1:04—and in the 1942–43 season he scored 3 goals and 4 assists against the Rangers for a new league record. He remained with Detroit through the 1945–46 season. A year later Carl was terrorizing American League goaltenders. In 1947–48, playing for Providence, Liscombe led the league in scoring with 50 goals and 68 assists for 118 points in 68 games. The following season Carl scored 55 goals in 68 games for Providence, but he never returned to the bigs.

EDWARD C. J. (EDDIE) LITZENBERGER

BORN: Neudorf, Saskatchewan, July 15, 1932
POSITION: Center, Montreal Canadiens, 1952–55; Chicago Black Hawks, 1955–61; Detroit Red Wings, 1961–62; Toronto Maple Leafs, 1962–64
AWARDS: Calder Trophy, 1955; All-Star (Second Team), 1957

A tall, awkward-looking forward, Ed Litzenberger seemed to be destined for a long career with the Montreal Canadiens when he reached the NHL to stay in 1954–55. But the Black Hawks' franchise was close to folding at the time and the league governors agreed to help Chicago whenever possible. The Canadiens therefore donated Litzenberger to the Black Hawks and Ed became a star in the Windy City. In 1961, he helped the Hawks to a Stanley Cup championship. After being dealt to the Maple Leafs in 1962, Ed orchestrated the Leafs in three straight Cup victories—1962, 1963, and 1964. He left the majors after the 1964 win.

DAVID ROSS LONSBERRY

BORN: Humboldt, Saskatchewan, February 7, 1947
POSITION: Left Wing, Boston Bruins, 1966–69; Los Angeles Kings, 1969–72; Philadelphia Flyers, 1972–

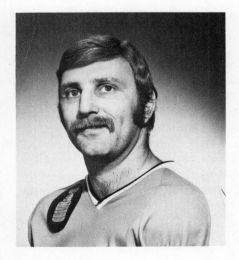

Ex-Bruin Ross Lonsberry was dubbed the Philadelphia Flyers' most valuable player by coach Fred Shero in 1973–74. Lonsberry tallied thirty-two times that glorious year, but his best point producing campaign was 1970–71 with Los Angeles (25–28–53). In addition to his high point total in the 1973–74 Stanley Cup season, Lonsberry provided some of the best forechecking, backchecking, and penalty killing on the Vezina Trophy and Stanley Cup winners.

PETER (PETE) LoPRESTI

BORN: Virginia, Minnesota, May 23, 1954
POSITION: Goalie, Minnesota North Stars, 1974–

The son of Black Hawks' goalie Sam LoPresti, Pete LoPresti was a third round draft choice of the Minnesota North Stars in 1974 and broke in with the NHL club in 1974–75.

Before joining the North Stars, Pete played on the Denver University team. One night after a gruelling series against Michigan Tech, Pete returned home obviously depressed. When his father asked what was the matter, Pete replied, "Goaltending is too much, sometimes. Do you realize I had to make more than 50 saves the other night?" Sam LoPresti smiled and recalled his beleaguered nights with the Black Hawks. "Yes, I know," Sam replied. "I almost made that many saves *in one period!*"

SAM LoPRESTI

BORN: Eveleth, Minnesota, January 30, 1917
POSITION: Goalie, Chicago Black Hawks, 1940–42

A native of Eveleth, Minnesota, Sam LoPresti was the Chicago Black Hawks' goalie in 1940–41 and 1941–42. More than that, he was in the nets on March 4, 1941, the night that more shots were fired at an NHL goalie than ever before—or since. It happened at Boston Garden and the total was 83 shots—of which 80 were saves. The Bruins won the game, 3–2, but LoPresti won the acclaim, for life! "The Bruins didn't get the winning goal until near the end of the game," LoPresti, now an Eveleth tavern owner, recalled. "Eddie Wiseman got it on a rebound. But we couldn't do anything right from the opening face-off; just couldn't get the puck out of our zone. They were shooting from every angle and I didn't see half the shots. They were bouncing off my pads, my chest protector, my arms, my shoulders. I didn't even know where they were coming from. At the other end, Boston's goalie Frankie Brimsek (also of Eveleth) had to make only 18 saves all night. In between periods they had to clean off only one end of the ice—my end. I lost between eight and ten pounds that night." After his second big-league season, Sam joined the United States Navy on the theory that it was safer to face Nazi U-boats in the North Atlantic than vulcanized rubber in Boston Garden.

JAMES PETER (JIM) LORENTZ

BORN: Waterloo, Ontario, May 1, 1947
POSITION: Center, Boston Bruins, 1968–70; St. Louis Blues, 1970–72; New York Rangers, 1971–72; Buffalo Sabres, 1972–

Jim Lorentz was given a regular chance to play after being traded from the St. Louis Blues to the Buffalo Sabres, via New York. The 6-0, 180-pound forward has made the most of his opportunities by increasing his scoring totals drastically since those bygone days.

Lorentz also saw action with the Boston Bruins and played on their Stanley Cup champion team in 1969–70. He spent two seasons with the Blues in 1970–71 and 1971–72, and was then involved in a bizarre three-way deal that also saw Gene Carr come to the Rangers. Lorentz played only five games for the Blueshirts, and was then dealt to the Sabres. Lorentz has payed the Rangers back dearly for the trade—he has been one of the Sabres' leading scorers against their downstate rivals ever since.

Jim Lorentz

LOS ANGELES KINGS

When the Los Angeles Kings first skated into the NHL in the fall of 1967, they were the butt of every kind of joke, and were figured to mop up in the West Division basement. Their biggest claim to fame was thirty-seven-year-old goaltender Terry Sawchuk, at the very end of a brilliant career.

It was the behind-the-scenes set-up of the Kings which was most underrated, however. Multimillionaire Jack Kent Cooke had surprised everyone by outbidding four other groups for the franchise. When Cooke had difficulty in obtaining rights to play in the Sports Arena, he built his own Forum. Perhaps best of all, he hired two fighting Irishmen to key positions—Larry Regan as head scout and Leonard Patrick "Red" Kelly as coach.

Regan had been all over the hockey world: a twenty-six-year-old rookie of the year, in 1956–57, center with Boston and Toronto, player/coach of the AHL Pittsburgh club, manager of the Innsbruck, Austria, hockey team, and aged player with the Baltimore Clippers in 1965–66.

The draft itself was a battle between Cooke and Toronto mogul Stafford Smythe. Cooke understood that Toronto would leave Red Kelly unprotected until the eighteenth round, when Los Angeles would draft him as player-coach. But Cooke and Smythe, both men with sizeable egos, began name-calling instead. Smythe placed Kelly back on the protected list and Cooke cried "foul" to league president Clarence Campbell.

The matter was finally settled when the Kings traded their seventeenth round pick, Ken Block, for Kelly. Kelly had been an All-Star defenseman with Detroit in his early career, and a three-time 20-goal scoring center with Toronto in his later years. Soft-spoken, Kelly was nonetheless tough enough to win the respect and cooperation of his fledgling Kings, taking them further than anyone expected.

In a surprise move, Cooke purchased the entire Springfield Indians of the AHL, supplying Kelly with a unified team to go along with the motley group he had drafted.

Although without a home rink, the Kings began their first season with a scoring burst—four goals in one period against Chicago, four goals in 10 minutes in Detroit, and three tallies in six minutes against the Seals. Cooke chortled when his Kings beat Toronto, 4–1, on two scores by fast Eddie Joyal, a draftee from the Leafs.

When the going got tough, players were brought up from Springfield. One of these was Bill White, a tall and talented defenseman with a marvelously accurate shot. Tiny winger Howie Menard came up to help out, as well as defensemen Jim Murray, Brent Hughes, and Davey Amadio.

Unknowns began to blossom: Brawny Ted Irvine and fast Bill "Cowboy" Flett came right out of the Central League and scored 18 and 26 goals, respectively. In 1967–68 the Kings held the best win record against the established clubs with a total of ten winning games.

The Kings completely flummoxed their critics by finishing second in the West Division their first season, and they took the quarterfinal series against the Minnesota North Stars to the full seven games, before losing, 9–4, in the final bout. It was the last time Terry Sawchuk would play for Los Angeles; the shutout king was traded to his former team, Detroit, for a young forward, Jimmy Peters, son of a former Sawchuk teammate on the 1951 Wings!

The Kings were fourth in the West their sophomore year, but managed to make it to the semifinal round before folding. But by this time things had gone sour in the Los Angeles Forum. They were then out of the playoffs for four years straight, until they once again lost the quarterfinal round to Chicago in 1974, a performance they repeated in 1975 against Toronto.

Cooke was proving to be more of a problem than a blessing. With his flaming style behind the scenes, he turned off the NHL board of governors, none of whom would do him any favors in the draft, or anywhere else. Kelly quit the scene to coach in Pittsburgh, and Regan took over the job, none too successfully. Attendance in the resplendent new Forum sagged terribly after the first season.

In 1971–72 Regan was replaced by Fred Glover, who had just been fired by the Seals. The result was the Kings worst finish ever, a mere 49 points, 11 less than the sickly Seals.

There were major changes made the next year: Veteran center Bob Pulford was retired behind the bench. The defense was perked by ex-Canadien Terry

Harper and former Black Hawk beefy Gilles Marotte, until Marotte was traded to the Rangers in 1973. Blond streak Juha Widing began scoring goals and the Kings' goals-against record was cut. By 1974–75 the team had once again improved enough to make the playoffs. With Rogatien Vachon in goal, the Kings were a powerhouse until fading to second in the Norris Division in April. After acquiring Marcel Dionne in June 1975, they looked to be better yet.

DONALD HAROLD (DON) LUCE

BORN: London, Ontario, October 2, 1948
POSITION: Center, New York Rangers, 1969–70; Detroit Red Wings, 1970–71; Buffalo Sabres, 1971–
AWARDS: Bill Masterton Trophy, 1975

A study in clean living—he neither drinks nor smokes—Don Luce reached the high point in his NHL career on May 21, 1975, when the Buffalo Sabres' center received the annual Bill Masterton Trophy. The award, plus $1,000, is presented annually by the Professional Hockey Writers' Association for "the NHL player who best exemplifies the qualities of perserverance, sportsmanship, and dedication to hockey." A former New York Ranger, Luce turned star when he improved his checking and scoring. In 1974–75 he had his best season with 33 goals and 76 points. He also has won the Sabres' Unsung Hero and Most Improved Player awards, Charlie Barton Silver Stick to the "player who most exemplifies love of the game," and Buffalo's Most Valuable Player Award.

HARRY "APPLE CHEEKS" LUMLEY

BORN: Owen Sound, Ontario, November 11, 1926
POSITION: Goalie, Detroit Red Wings, 1943, 1944–50; New York
  Rangers, 1944; Chicago Black Hawks, 1950–52; Toronto Maple
  Leafs, 1952–56; Boston Bruins, 1957–61
AWARDS: Vezina Trophy, 1954; All-Star (First Team), 1954, 1955

Harry Lumley, an outstanding goalkeeper who labored for sixteen years in professional hockey as one of the stingiest netminders around, had an inauspicious
NHL debut in a two-game trial with the Detroit Red Wings, allowing thirteen
pucks to elude his flailing limbs.

Looking back on that embarrassing goal splurge, one can forgive Lumley if
he was a bit awed by it all since the netminder was only seventeen years old at
the time. This was the 1943–44 season and World War II had decimated the
ranks of the NHL, necessitating Lumley's adolescent awakening to the harsh
realities of big-league shinny.

Harry matured, though, into one of the NHL's most proficient puck stoppers.
He remained with the Wings for six more seasons, guiding them into the
playoffs each year and sipping Stanley Cup champagne in 1949–50, his last
campaign with the Wings.

At the end of that season the Red Wings came up with another whiskerless
wonder in the twenty-year-old Terry Sawchuk, and Lumley was dispatched to a
hapless Chicago Black Hawk team where he spent two frustrating seasons. In
1952, Harry hit the road once more, this time to his home province of Ontario
and the blue and white of the Toronto Maple Leafs. It was in Toronto that
Lumley enjoyed his best years as a pro, leading the NHL in shutouts for two
consecutive seasons and copping the Vezina Trophy in 1953–54 with an amazing 1.85 goals-against average in 69 games.

Nearing the end of his career, Lumley had a three-year stint with the Boston
Bruins and then played in the minor leagues until his retirement in 1960–61.

LARRY LUND

BORN: Penticton, British Columbia, September 9, 1940
POSITION: Center, Houston Aeros (WHA), 1972–

A clumsy skater with extraordinary determination, Larry Lund cracked the big
time more than a decade after he had broken into professional hockey in 1961
with the Muskegon Zephyrs of the International League. Lund was signed by
the World Hockey Association Houston Aeros in 1972. His commanding play
earned Lund the team captaincy, and in 1974–75 he became the team scoring
leader and was rewarded with a new, long-term contract.

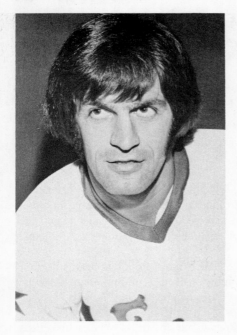

Larry Lund

PENTTI LUND

BORN: Helsinki, Finland, December 6, 1925
POSITION: Left Wing, New York Rangers, 1948–51; Boston Bruins,
    1951–53
AWARDS: Calder Trophy, 1949

A native of Helsinki, Finland, Pentti Lund briefly attained stardom in the 1950 Stanley Cup playoffs, playing left wing for the New York Rangers. Lund played opposite the immortal Maurice "Rocket" Richard, the Montreal Canadiens' high-powered scorer, in the semifinal round. While Richard's stick was muzzled Lund stunned the Canadiens with an outburst of goals that led the Rangers to a four-games-to-one victory in the series. The Rangers reached the seventh game of the Cup finals against Detroit before losing. In twelve Cup games Lund scored six goals and five assists. However, his play sagged in 1950–51 and the Rangers traded him to Boston a year later. He completed his NHL career in 1952–53, scoring only eight goals in fifty-four regular season games and neither a goal nor an assist in two playoff matches. He later turned to journalism and became sports editor of the Thunder Bay (Ontario) *Times*.

VICTOR IVAN (VIC) LYNN

BORN: Saskatoon, Saskatchewan, January 26, 1925
POSITION: Defenseman-Forward, Detroit Red Wings, 1943–44; Montreal Canadiens, 1945–46; Toronto Maple Leafs, 1946–50; Boston Bruins, 1950–52; Chicago Black Hawks, 1952–54

Rabbit McVeigh, a star with the old New York Americans, noticed a burly left winger skating for Buffalo in the American League named Vic Lynn and advised Toronto Maple Leafs' manager Conn Smythe to sign the energetic skater. Lynn had received brief trials with Detroit (1943–44) and the Canadiens (1945–46), but failed on both counts. Smythe, however, took McVeigh's advice and signed Lynn for the 1946–47 season, put him on a line with center Ted "Teeder" Kennedy and Howie Meeker and the Maple Leafs' second "Kid Line" was born. Lynn was not an especially heavy scorer, but he was big and rough and he hit hard. He complemented his linemates perfectly and the trio gave Toronto the spark to win three consecutive Stanley Cup championships (1947, 1948, 1949). Following the 1949–50 season, Lynn was traded to Boston. In 1952–53 he was acquired by the Chicago Black Hawks and completed his NHL career in the Windy City in 1953–54.

Tom Lysiak

THOMAS JAMES (TOM) LYSIAK

BORN: High Prairie, Alberta, April 22, 1953
POSITION: Center, Atlanta Flames, 1973–

Tom Lysiak is one of the most highly rated youngsters to come along in the NHL in a long time. He was the second pick in the 1973 amateur draft behind that year's Calder Trophy winner, Denis Potvin of the New York Islanders.

Although scoring only 19 goals in his rookie season, Lysiak assisted on 45 tallies, and was instrumental in the Flames' surge to the playoffs in only their second season.

Lysiak has been somewhat of a free spirit since getting to know the city of Atlanta, and is quite outspoken in his criticisms of the voting which made him lose out to Potvin in the Calder balloting by a slim margin.

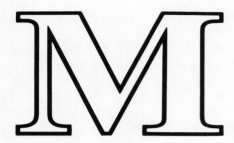

KENNETH LESLIE "TUBBY" McAULEY

BORN: Edmonton, Alberta, January 9, 1921
POSITION: Goalie, New York Rangers, 1943–45

A never-ending debate during the World War II years, when the Rangers held up the bottom of the NHL, was whether the New York skaters were *that* bad or goalie Ken "Tubby" McAuley was really the problem. McAuley was in the New York nets on the night of January 23, 1944, the Rangers' night of infamy. With McAuley supposedly stopping the pucks, the Rangers were bombed, 15–0, by the Red Wings at Detroit's Olympia Stadium. It was the most one-sided score in league history, and, to this day, remains in the NHL record book.

According to the Rangers' coach at the time, Frank Boucher, the problem was less McAuley's than that of his inferior team in front of him. "Ken," said Boucher, "should have been awarded the Croix de Guerre if not the Victoria Cross for all the heroics he put up with in those years. Bless his heart, McAuley very rarely complained against the fates that had deposited him in our goal."

During the 1943–44 season, McAuley played in all 50 Rangers games, allowing 310 goals ("Only a fraction," said Boucher, "belonged to him; *all* of us should share his glory.") for a 6.20 goals-against average. He played 46 games in the following season, this time trimming his average to 4.94. By 1945–46 the two Ranger regular goalies, Chuck Rayner and Jim Henry, were back from the War and McAuley left the NHL for good.

JOHN WILLIAM (JACK) McCARTAN

BORN: St. Paul, Minnesota, August 5, 1935
POSITION: Goalie, New York Rangers, 1959–61; Minnesota Fighting
   Saints (WHA), 1972–73

Jack McCartan played part of two NHL seasons, replacing New York Ranger Al Rollins after McCartan starred for the American entry in the 1960 Olympics. As a big leaguer, McCartan failed miserably after an impressive early start. The Rangers demoted him to the minors after he played seven and one-third games in 1960–61 for a 4.91 goals-against average. In time McCartan became a WHA goalie for the Minnesota Fighting Saints and then an assistant coach for the same team. Still, he is best remembered for guiding the United States Olympic team to one of the biggest upsets in international sports, defeating heavily favored Canada, Russia, and finally Czechoslovakia.

FRANK McCOOL

BORN: Calgary, Alberta, October 27, 1918
POSITION: Goalie, Toronto Maple Leafs, 1944–46
AWARDS: Calder Trophy, 1945

As the 1944–45 season began, Toronto scouts raced all over Canada in search of a goaltender. The ultimate choice was Frank McCool, a tall, skinny Albertan who appeared eminently suited for the job of librarian or bank clerk, but not goaltender. Not only was McCool nervous but he was assailed by a chronic case of ulcers. "Every game was a life-and-death struggle for Frank," Ed Fitkin remembered. "He sipped milk in the dressing room between periods to calm his fluttering stomach. There were times when he took sick during a game—but one thing about him, he'd never quit." Nevertheless, it was believed that Toronto's Achilles' heel would be goaltending. "Ulcers" McCool had finished the season with a mediocre 3.22 goals-against average, although he did win the Calder Trophy.

VERNON KEITH McCREARY

BORN: Sundridge, Ontario, June 19, 1940
POSITION: Left Wing, Montreal Canadiens, 1961–62, 1964–65; Pittsburgh Penguins, 1967–72; Atlanta Flames, 1972–75

A nonscoring left winger in the Montreal Canadiens' system before being rescued by the 1967 expansion, Keith McCreary is a steady two-way hockey player whose defensive diligence offsets his low goal-scoring totals.

After serving as captain of the Pittsburgh Penguins for five seasons, Keith was selected by the Atlanta Flames in the 1972 expansion draft as their "designated captain." He became a free agent in June 1975.

ALVIN BRIAN "AB" McDONALD

BORN: Winnipeg, Manitoba, February 18, 1936
POSITION: Left Wing, Montreal Canadiens, 1957–60; Chicago Black
Hawks, 1960–64; Boston Bruins, 1964–65; Detroit Red Wings,
1965–67, 1971–72; Pittsburgh Penguins, 1967–68; St. Louis
Blues, 1968–71; Winnipeg Jets (WHA), 1972–73

The Montreal Canadiens had hoped in 1958–59 that Winnipeg-born Ab McDonald would be the ideal replacement on left wing for Bert Olmstead, one of the NHL's most effective forecheckers and playmakers. But the tall, gawky McDonald was discarded by the Flying Frenchmen in 1960–61 to Chicago partly on the grounds that he appeared too clumsy to be effective and partly because Forum fans had unmercifully booed him. They suggested that he resembled a skating rhinoceros. But the Black Hawks' brain trust had other ideas. They put Ab on a line with crafty Stan Mikita and speedy Ken Wharram, dubbed them "the Scooter Line," and let them at the enemy goaltenders. The results were a delight to Windy City fans and led directly to Chicago's Stanley Cup win in April 1961.

Ex-Hawk ace Johnny Gottselig was impressed with McDonald's shooting ability. "McDonald's shot doesn't compare with those of Charlie Conacher or Dit Clapper," said Gottselig, "or Boom-Boom Geoffrion, who were the big guns on great lines. But it is good enough. Ab controls it well, keeps it low, is accurate and hard, and uses the quick wrist shot."

Ab was dealt to Boston in 1964–65 and then to Detroit in 1965–66. He appeared on the downgrade when he went to Pittsburgh in 1967–68, but he rallied with the Penguins and then spent two productive years in St. Louis before leaving the NHL after 1971–72. A short WHA stint followed before he retired.

JACK McDONALD

BORN: Unknown
DIED: January 24, 1958
POSITION: Left Wing, Quebec Bulldogs (ECAHA and NHA), 1906–09,
1911–12, 1915–17, 1920; Waterloo (OPHL), 1910; Vancouver Millionaires (PCHA), 1913; Montreal Wanderers, 1918; Montreal
Canadiens, 1918–19, 1921–22; Toronto Arenas, 1921
AWARDS: Scoring Leader, 1912 (prior to NHL's Art Ross Trophy)

Jack McDonald was a restless left winger who, over the course of his seventeen-year playing career, changed teams an amazing fourteen times. He was a powerful, high-scoring winger who held his own with such superstars of the day as Joe Malone and Newsy Lalonde.

McDonald teamed with Malone and Eddie Oatman in 1912 and the dynamic threesome brought Quebec its first Stanley Cup. The awesome scoring unit remained intact for two seasons (a longevity record for McDonald) until Mac got that old itch again and pulled up stakes for Vancouver.

McDonald continued his road act until the very end of his career, but by this time he had lost his scoring magic. He finished out his career with Toronto and the Canadiens of the NHL as a substitute.

LANNY KING McDONALD

BORN: Hanna, Alberta, February 16, 1953
POSITION: Right Wing, Toronto Maple Leafs, 1973–

A strapping Alberta farm boy, Lanny McDonald was the first round draft choice of the Toronto Maple Leafs in the 1973 amateur player pool.

McDonald's impressive junior career with the Medicine Hat Tigers was capped by the 1972–73 Western Canada championship. McDonald scored 62 goals and 77 assists that season, often seeing 40 minutes of ice time per game.

The Leafs picked Lanny fourth overall and he was immediately tabbed a ''can't-miss'' prospect. But a series of painful injuries limited McDonald's effectiveness during his rookie campaign, and he scored only 14 goals and 16 assists in 70 games. The youngster's tough luck continued into the postseason as a shoulder injury prevented him from playing in the 1974 Stanley Cup playoffs.

WILFRED KENNEDY "BUCKO" McDONALD

BORN: Fergus, Ontario, October 31, 1911
POSITION: Defenseman, Detroit Red Wings, 1934–39; Toronto Maple Leafs, 1939–43; New York Rangers, 1944–45
AWARDS: All-Star (Second Team), 1942

Wilfred Kennedy "Bucko" McDonald was an exceptionally fine lacrosse player who had a go with the 1932 professional indoor "box" lacrosse league. When the loop folded after only one year of operation, McDonald was beside himself. In a desperate move, he went to Frank Selke of the Toronto Maple Leafs to inquire about a career in pro hockey.

"Can you skate?" asked Selke, trying to sound sympathetic.

"Oh," replied "Mac," trying *his* best to sound confident. "I can skate a little."

Selke advised Bucko to practice his skating which he did faithfully for the next three years. After a stint with the minor league Buffalo club, McDonald caught on with the 1935 Detroit Red Wings. The awkward McDonald became an instant favorite with the Olympia fans and led the Wings to two successive Stanley Cups. He later starred in Toronto and New York.

JAMES ALEXANDER (JIMMY) McFADDEN

BORN: Belfast, Northern Ireland, April 15, 1920
POSITION: Center, Detroit Red Wings, 1947–51; Chicago Black Hawks, 1951–54
AWARDS: Calder Trophy, 1948

Jimmy McFadden was the first—and last—native of Belfast, Northern Ireland, to win the Calder Memorial Trophy (1947–48) as the NHL rookie of the year. Since McFadden was twenty-seven years old at the time of the honor it was considered terribly unique and McFadden was hailed as a senior *wunderkind*. A chunky, little (5-7, 178 lbs.) guy, McFadden had played some of his best hockey for the Ottawa Senators in the Quebec Senior League. Although he never quite duplicated the excellence of his rookie year (60 games, 24 goals, 24 assists for 48 points), McFadden played capably for Detroit, helping them win the Stanley Cup in 1950. He was traded to Chicago in 1951–52 and starred for the Black Hawks' surprise layoff team in 1952–53, who nearly upset the favored Canadiens in the Stanley Cup semifinals. Jimmy rounded out his big-league career in 1953–54.

FRANK McGEE

BORN: 1880s
DIED: France, September 16, 1916
POSITION: Center and Rover, Ottawa Silver Seven (CAHL, FAHL, and ECAHA), 1903–06
AWARDS: Scoring Leader, 1905 (prior to NHL's Art Ross Trophy); Hockey Hall of Fame, 1945

There are those who still insist that Frank McGee, star of the legendary Ottawa Silver Seven, was the greatest player of all time. It's a pretty good argument. A center and rover (rover was the seventh position), McGee was a lightning-fast skater who could stickhandle and shoot with the very best of them. Testimony to McGee's greatness is the fact that the Silver Seven copped three consecutive Stanley Cups during Frank's brief career while staving off a host of wide-eyed challengers for the mug.

McGee scored better than three goals per game in the twenty-three regular season contests he appeared in, but even more incredible are his Stanley Cup statistics. In twenty-two Cup games, Frank scored 63 goals, including an amazing 14-goal game against Dawson City in 1905! An equally dazzling footnote to these astronomical numbers is the fact that Frank had lost an eye prior to his playing days with Ottawa!

But just as his handicap didn't prevent Frank's hockey heroics, neither did it deter him from military service when World War I broke out in Europe. McGee enlisted for overseas action and was killed in France in 1916. Deservedly, he is a member of the Hockey Hall of Fame.

JACK McGILL

BORN: Ottawa, Ontario, November 3, 1910
POSITION: Forward, Montreal Canadiens, 1934–37

The first of three Jack McGills to make a name for himself in pro hockey was an Ottawa, Ontario, native who played forward for the Montreal Canadiens from the 1934–35 through the 1936–37 seasons. He was not very good.

JOHN EDWARD "LITTLE JACK" McGILL

BORN: Saskatoon, Saskatchewan, June 12, 1923
POSITION: Goaltender, New York Rovers (EAHL), 1941–43; St. Paul Saints (USHL), 1945–51

The second of the Jack McGills was John Edward McGill of Saskatoon, Saskatchewan. Since he weighed in at only 5-10, 155 pounds, he inevitably became "Little Jack." An excellent minor league goaltender, "Little Jack" broke in with the New York Rovers at the start of World War II and distinguished himself as the only pro goalie to play every single game with a white towel wrapped around his neck. After the war, he starred for St. Paul in the United States League.

JOHN GEORGE "BIG JACK" McGILL

BORN: Edmonton, Alberta, September 19, 1921
POSITION: Center, Boston Bruins, 1942–43, 1945–47

The third of the big-time Jack McGills was John George McGill, alias "Big Jack," who was 6-1, 180 pounds and played center for the Boston Bruins briefly during the World War II years and 1945 through 1947. His scoring was modest and he finished his career alternating between the American and United States Hockey leagues. He was, however, quite effective during the 1945 Stanley Cup playoffs, scoring three goals and three assists in seven games.

BRUCE CAMERON MacGREGOR

BORN: Edmonton, Alberta, April 26, 1941
POSITION: Right Wing, Detroit Red Wings, 1960–71; New York
   Rangers, 1971–74; Edmonton Oilers (WHA), 1974–
AWARDS: Team Canada (WHA), 1974

After fourteen years of yeoman's duty in the NHL, Bruce MacGregor's career has gone full circle, back to his hometown of Edmonton, Alberta.

MacGregor broke into the big leagues as a nineteen-year-old hustler with the Detroit Red Wings. Throughout his more than a decade of service, he still hasn't slowed down a bit. It was MacGregor who, in the 1974 Stanley Cup quarterfinals, personally neutralized Montreal's Yvan "Roadrunner" Cournoyer as Mac's New York Rangers took that opening series four games to two.

Bruce was enticed back to his old stomping grounds in Alberta the following season, signing with the Edmonton Oilers of the World Hockey Association. He was a member of Team Canada '74 in their series against the Soviet national team.

Never a spectacular scorer, Mac's credentials included expert penalty killing, tireless backchecking, and cricket-quick moves.

JOHN ARCHIBALD (JACK) MacINTYRE

BORN: Brussels, Ontario, September 8, 1930
POSITION: Left Wing, Boston Bruins, 1949–53; Chicago Black
    Hawks, 1953–57; Detroit Red Wings, 1958–60

Jack MacIntyre holds the NHL record for having his name misspelled for the longest period of time before correction. He became a Bruin in 1949–50 and starred for Boston in the 1953 Stanley Cup semifinal round. It was then, three years after he had entered the NHL, that the misspelling was corrected. Until then, writers spelled Jack's name McIntyre. However, with the Detroit-Boston series tied at one game apiece, Jack came through with a goal in the twelfth minute of sudden-death overtime to give Boston a lead in the series. In the postgame news conference, Jack called for time-out and informed the press that they had better spell his name correctly. "It's MacIntyre," he insisted. "Capital m, small a, small c; not McIntyre like you've been writing!"

Jack was traded to Chicago in the following season and then to Detroit in 1957–58 where he finished his NHL career in 1959–60. To his dismay, writers kept spelling his name *McIntyre*, big goals or not.

DUNCAN (MICKEY) MacKAY

BORN: Chesley, Ontario, May 21, 1894
DIED: May 21, 1943
POSITION: Center and Rover, Vancouver Millionaires (PCHA and
    WCHL), 1915–26; Chicago Black Hawks, 1927–28; Pittsburgh
    Pirates, 1928–29; Boston Bruins, 1929–30
AWARDS: Scoring Leader (prior to NHL's Art Ross Trophy), 1915;
    Hockey Hall of Fame, 1952

Duncan (Mickey) MacKay broke into hockey in 1915 with the Vancouver Millionaires, a squad that went on to win the Stanley Cup. Mickey played on one more Cup winner in his sixteen-year career—that championship coming when he skated for Boston at the twilight of his playing days.

In his rookie campaign, Mickey led the PCHA in scoring and twice repeated that feat over his eleven-year stint with the Millionaires. During MacKay's tour of duty with Vancouver, the Mills glided to six league championships and as many Stanley Cup series.

A clean, law-abiding player, Mickey missed the entire 1920 season due to injuries he received courtesy of Cully Wilson in 1919.

A Hall of Famer, MacKay retired in 1930 after playing with Chicago, Boston, and Pittsburgh of the NHL.

FLEMING DAVID MACKELL

BORN: Montreal, Quebec, April 30, 1929
POSITION: Forward, Toronto Maple Leafs, 1947–52; Boston Bruins, 1952–60

One of the speediest skaters ever to grace the National Hockey League, Fleming Mackell immediately attained notoriety as one of the few players to have lost all his teeth before turning pro with the Toronto Maple Leafs in 1947–48. Mackell skated for two Maple Leafs' Stanley Cup champions (1949 and 1951) before being traded to the Boston Bruins during the 1951–52 season. Mackell's halcyon days were spent in Boston where he concluded his NHL career in the 1959–60 season. In 1957–58 Mackell reached a personal point high with 20 goals and 40 assists for 60 points in 70 NHL games and then totalled 5 goals and 14 assists for 19 points in only 12 Stanley Cup playoff games.

DONALD HAMILTON McKENNEY

BORN: Smith Falls, Ontario, April 30, 1934
POSITION: Center and Left Wing, Boston Bruins, 1954–62; New York Rangers, 1962–64; Toronto Maple Leafs, 1964–65; Detroit Red Wings, 1965–66; St. Louis Blues, 1967–68
AWARDS: Lady Byng Trophy, 1960

In the late fifties and early sixties Don McKenney was regarded as an ''untouchable'' forward on the Boston Bruins. A center who also could play left wing, Don was a mild-mannered skater who graduated to the pros after skating for the Barrie (Ontario) Flyers. His efficiency as a Bruin deteriorated in 1962 and he was traded to the New York Rangers. In February 1964 McKenney was involved in one of hockey's most important trades, going to Toronto with Andy Bathgate for Bill Collins, Rod Seiling, Arnie Brown, Dick Duff, and Bob Nevin. McKenney played superbly in the 1964 Stanley Cup playoffs, scoring 4 goals and 8 assists for 12 points as Toronto won the Cup. However, he was dealt to Detroit for the 1965–66 season and ended his NHL career in 1967–68 with the St. Louis Blues. More recently he has operated hockey schools in the Boston area.

JAMES CLAUDE (JIM) McKENNY

BORN: Ottawa, Ontario, December 1, 1946
POSITION: Defenseman, Toronto Maple Leafs, 1965–

One of the NHL's best offensive-minded defensemen, Toronto Maple Leaf Jim McKenny is the senior statesman of the Leaf blue line corps.

Jim McKenny

Toronto's third selection in the 1963 amateur draft, McKenny bounced around the Leafs' minor league system before becoming firmly established as a regular in 1969.

Teaming beautifully with his oft-injured rearguard partner Brian Glennie, McKenny's rink-length rushes have made him one of the most feared sharp-shooting defensemen in the NHL.

JOHN ALBERT "PIE" McKENZIE

BORN: High River, Alberta, December 12, 1937
POSITION: Right Wing, Chicago Black Hawks, 1958–59, 1963–65; Detroit Red Wings, 1959–61; New York Rangers/Boston Bruins, 1965–66; Boston Bruins, 1966–72; Player-Coach, Philadelphia/ Vancouver Blazers/Calgary Cowboys (WHA),1972–
AWARDS: All-Star (WHA, Second Team), 1970

One of the peskiest skaters ever to skate in the NHL, Johnny McKenzie quit the Boston Bruins and jumped to the Philadelphia Blazers in 1972 as player-coach. The move was slightly disastrous. McKenzie argued with his aide, Phil Watson, through most of the season and the Blazers floundered. A year later the team and McKenzie moved to Vancouver where they continued as the Blazers and continued to stay near the depths of the league standings.

McKenzie remained a Blazer in 1974–75, but remained a shade of his former

NHL self—a player who constantly made headlines and inevitably angered opponents such as Brad Park of the Rangers and anyone else who happened to be in his way. As a Bruin, there was virtually no stopping the impish forward.

In 1970 McKenzie was voted the Most Popular Player on the Bruins. He came a long way from his doldrum days in Buffalo (American Hockey League) in 1963. "That's where I got the 'Pie' nickname," said McKenzie. "A guy named Gerry Melnyk gave it to me. He was on Buffalo too, and I guess he figured my round face looked like a pie so I've been Pie ever since."

In the 1969 Stanley Cup playoff between Boston and Montreal the then Canadiens' coach Claude Ruel fumed over McKenzie's roughhouse style and denounced him to the press as "yellow." That was neither the first nor last blast leveled at the Bruin. Brad Park, the Rangers' gifted young defenseman, verbally tarred and feathered McKenzie in Park's book, *Play the Man*.

Said Brad of Pie: "McKenzie's bag is running at people *from behind*. No player really objects to getting hit straight on, but when a guy rams you from behind that's bad news."

Like him or not, McKenzie comes by his toughness naturally. For years he spent the off-season as a rodeo rider in his native Alberta. "The most I ever won," said Pie, "was $150 in a wild-cow milking contest. I never did make $500 in a season, which would have qualified me for the Cowboys' Protective Association. But I did get to believe that rodeo cowboys are the best conditioned athletes in all sports."

KEN McKENZIE

Ken McKenzie, "the Godfather of hockey publishing," is responsible for the *Hockey News,* the durable weekly often criticized for promulgating something less than good journalism.

McKenzie's publishing empire includes the monthly *Hockey World* and *Hockey Pictorial,* published with the financial assistance of Whitney Communications. Whitney owns 80 percent of the stock, but McKenzie remains the editor, publisher, and chief policymaker.

McKenzie first published the *Hockey News* as an NHL publicist back in 1947. With Clarence Campbell's approval, McKenzie printed weekly circulars, then got the weekly *Hockey News* off the presses and into circulation within a year. By the time pro hockey expanded from six to twelve teams in 1967, the *Hockey News* had turned into a gold mine.

McKenzie has enjoyed a virtual lock on the hockey periodical business. Only two publications have mildly concerned McKenzie as possible competition: the *Hockey Spectator,* published by former World Hockey Association publicist Lee Meade, and the *Hockey Journal,* which made a shaky move to compete in 1974. The *Spectator* folded in 1973 and the *Journal* folded in 1974.

"The guys who ran the *Hockey Spectator* were stupid," says McKenzie, "because they were doing too many other things and not concentrating on the paper. I've given every ounce of energy and blood, sweat, and tears ever since I started *Hockey News,* and I still sell $40,000 worth of advertising each month. As for *Hockey Journal*," he continued, "there were two mistakes—the guy came out monthly instead of weekly and he was underfinanced."

But critics continue to lambaste McKenzie and his newspaper. "It's a publishing atrocity," says Dick Beddoes of the Toronto *Globe and Mail.* "The writing is lamentably mediocre compared to what it could be."

Toronto *Sun* columnist Trent Frayne adds, "The establishment is always right in the *Hockey News.* The stories read like pablum. As for objectivity, it's nothing but a house organ [for the NHL]."

Montreal *Star* columnist Red Fisher has words of admiration for McKenzie. "He shrugged off the raps," said Fisher, "all valid—with a laugh and a wink. I wouldn't say he's thick-skinned but the elephant gun has not yet been invented that can bring him down."

MAJOR FREDERIC McLAUGHLIN

A coffee baron, whose eccentric moves as president of the Chicago Black Hawks suggested that he was a victim of caffeine nerves, Major Frederic McLaughlin went through coaches the way Macy's goes through salesladies. The revolving door of Chicago coaches got so hectic during the late twenties that Black Hawks' veterans would telephone each other in the morning and ask: "Have you heard who's coaching us today?"

Nevertheless, it was Major McLaughlin's team, and he did as he damned pleased with it. In fact, the team's name came from McLaughlin's World War I Battalion, of which he had been a hero.

In the 1927–28 season, Barney Stanley, who was coach, got a good line on the Major's thinking during a prolonged slump. Stanley walked into McLaughlin's office one day and moaned, "For the life of me, I don't know what's the matter with this team."

The Major stared down his coach and snapped, "If you really want to find out quick, just take a look in the first mirror you come to!"

Many McLaughlin-watchers insist that he wasn't really all that tough. When Dick Irvin coached the Hawks, they played pitifully, yet the Major attended every game. "Why do you keep coming to see us play?" Irvin finally asked his boss.

The Major winked: "One of these nights you're going to win a game and I want to be here to see you do it."

HUGH McLEAN

BORN: Unknown
POSITION: Referee, NHL, 1949–51

Early in March 1951, Rocket Richard was incensed over what he believed was poor refereeing in a 2–1 loss to Detroit. The following evening the Canadiens were scheduled to play the Rangers in New York. Richard remained furious over the previous night's episode and found it difficult to sleep en route to New York or at the hotel in Manhattan. He told friends how Sid Abel, of Detroit, had grabbed him by the chin and ditched him into the goal post where he was cut. When he pointed out the infraction to referee Hugh McLean, the official supposedly laughed in his face.

"I skated away," noted the Rocket, "saying, 'This is the damnedest thing I ever saw.'"

McLean immediately gave him a ten-minute misconduct. In the penalty box Richard was needled by Detroit defenseman Leo Reise. He punched Reise and then shoved linesman Jim Primeau. For this he was handed a match penalty and an automatic $50 fine. It was while stewing over these incidents that Richard became involved in one of his most curious difficulties.

Prior to the game with the Rangers he was standing in front of New York's Picadilly Hotel and was next seen heading into the lobby. Canadian Press reported the following: "In the lobby he saw McLean and grabbed the official by the neck. He was ready to pour on some punches when two members of the Montreal Forum staff restrained him. Meantime, linesman Primeau hovered on the scene and attempted to get in a lick or two at Richard, but was held off." Clarence Campbell's response was a $500 fine for the Rocket "for conduct prejudicial to the welfare of hockey."

RICHARD GEORGE (RICK) MacLEISH

BORN: Lindsay, Ontario, January 3, 1950
POSITION: Center, Philadelphia Flyers, 1970–

It was March 8, 1974, a day after the Philadelphia Flyers routed the Detroit Red Wings, 6–1, at the Spectrum. Dominating the first page of the Philadelphia *Bulletin* sports section was a photo of twenty-four-year-old center Rick Mac-Leish, his stick high in the air, signaling a goal. Adjoining the photo were big, bold headlines which seemed improbable to the point of fantastic at the time: NHL CUP HERE? IT MAY HAPPEN!

It did happen. And one reason why it happened was because of the deft shooting, stickhandling, and playmaking of the 5–11, 175-pound MacLeish. Time and again as the Flyers annexed first place in the NHL's West Division and marched along the trail to the 1974 Stanley Cup, the wrist-shooting native

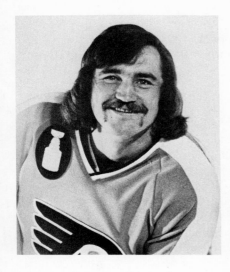

Rick MacLeish

of Lindsay, Ontario, provided Philadelphia with essential goals. Significantly, MacLeish applied himself most diligently against the two tough challengers who confronted Philadelphia en route to the championship—the New York Rangers and Boston Bruins.

When the Cup was a reality and he was offered some victory champagne, he politely declined. "Beer is best," he replied in a husky voice. "Champagne's too rich for my taste. I'm a small town boy; just give me a beer and I'm happy." But no happier than the Flyers who never would have reached such heights if MacLeish had not supplied 13 goals and 9 assists for 22 playoff-leading points. MacLeish was equally invaluable in helping the expansion Flyers to an unprecedented second Stanley Cup in 1975.

JOHN McLELLAN

BORN: South Porcupine, Ontario, August 6, 1928
POSITION: Forward, Toronto Maple Leafs, 1951–52; Coach, Toronto
    Maple Leafs, 1969–73

John McLellan, the assistant general manager of the Toronto Maple Leafs, served as coach of the Leaf sextet for four seasons from 1969 to 1973. John was acclaimed as the NHL's Coach of the Year in 1970–71, which is amusing, since the team was seventh, out of the playoffs. A chronic ulcer condition forced him to retire from the post two seasons later.

A distinguished amateur and minor leaguer during his playing days, McLellan's chores now include overseeing the Maple Leaf developmental clubs, which they need, in the worst way.

MAX McNAB

BORN: Watson, Saskatchewan, June 21, 1924
POSITION: Center, Detroit Red Wings, 1947–50; President, Central
  Hockey League, 1974–

Max McNab, frequently called the nicest guy in hockey (and not without valid-
ity) never quite made it in the big time the way the Detroit Red Wings had
hoped in the late forties. A product of the Saskatoon Elks' senior club, Max was
groomed as the heir apparent center to Sid Abel, who was the aging pivot on
the Ted Lindsay-Gordie Howe Production Line. McNab led the United States
League in goal-scoring in 1947–48 with Omaha, ringing up 44 goals in 44
games. That same season he was given a 12-game trial with the Red Wings and
scored two goals and two assists. A year later he played 51 NHL games in Detroit, this time scoring 10 goals and 13 assists. This encouraged Red Wings'
manager Jack Adams to keep Abel on the big line and, of course, Abel came
through handsomely. The Wings gave him one more shot in 1949–50. Max
very simply failed with only four goals and four assists in 65 games. Injuries
manacled his rise and McNab drifted to the minors. After his playing days he
became one of the game's foremost executives, helping develop San Diego into
a hot hockey city. In 1974 Max was named president of the Central League.

PETER McNAB

BORN: Vancouver, British Columbia, May 8, 1952
POSITION: Center, Buffalo Sabres, 1973–

A replica of his father Max, a former Red Wing, Peter McNab is big (6'3", 210 pounds), dedicated, and likeable. He also is a solid forward who made his NHL impact in 1974–75, scoring 22 goals and 21 assists for the Buffalo Sabres in their march to first place in the Adams Division. He is regarded as one of the more promising centers in the majors.

GEORGE AND HOWARD McNAMARA

GEORGE:
BORN: Penetang, Ontario, 1886
DIED: March 10, 1952
POSITION: Defenseman, Montreal Shamrocks (ECAHA), 1908–09; Waterloo Indians (OPHL), 1911–12; London Tecumsehs (NHA), 1913; Toronto Ontarios (NHA), 1914; Montreal Shamrocks (NHA), 1915; Toronto Arenas (NHA), 1916; Toronto 228th Bttn. (NHA), 1917
AWARDS: Hockey Hall of Fame, 1958

HOWARD:
BORN: Unknown
POSITION: Defenseman, Montreal Shamrocks (ECHA), 1909; Cobalt Canadiens (NHA), 1910; Berlin Dutchmen (OPHL), 1910; Waterloo Indians (OPHL), 1911; London Tecumsehs (NHA), 1913; Toronto Ontarios (NHA), 1914; Montreal Shamrocks (NHA), 1915; Montreal Canadiens (NHA), 1916; Toronto 228th Bttn. (NHA), 1917; Montreal Canadiens, 1920

In order to make the Toronto Ontarios' club in 1914, a young skater had to undergo a unique test. Manager Eddie Livingston had devised a sure-fire manner of determining the toughness of prospective Ontarios.

Livingston had the "Dynamite Twins," George and Howard McNamara (not twins by birth), give the rookies a "workout" in practice sessions. The brothers McNamara each weighed well over 200 pounds, and they would take every opportunity to slam down the kids, smashing them into the boards, and generally playing havoc with their young bodies.

If the brothers felt their prey too weak or timid, they would report this to Livingston. If their judgment was favorable, the rookie made the team.

George, who was inducted into the Hockey Hall of Fame after his death in 1952, was the better known and more talented of the two. He first appeared, shortly after the turn of the century, with the Michigan Soo. McNamara then went east to play with the Halifax Crescents and finally turned professional with the London Tecumsehs in 1913. They won the Stanley Cup the following year.

George McNamara even played hockey during World War I, with the 228th Sportsman's Battalion, until he went overseas. After the war, he returned to the

Sault Ste. Marie area and began coaching. In 1924, he led the famous Greyhounds to the Allan Cup championship.

ALLISTER WENCES (AL) MacNEIL

BORN: Sydney, Nova Scotia, September 27, 1935
POSITION: Defenseman, Toronto Maple Leafs, 1955–60; Montreal Canadiens, 1961–62; Chicago Black Hawks, 1962–66; New York Rangers, 1966–67; Pittsburgh Penguins, 1967–68; Coach, Montreal Canadiens, 1970–71

Is it possible for a terrible coach to guide a team to a Stanley Cup championship? Henri Richard, who captained the Canadiens, believed it was and indicted former Montreal coach Al MacNeil as that man. MacNeil coached the Canadiens during the 1970–71 season; a year in which Montreal finished third in the East Division. Somehow, the Canadiens upset Boston in the opening round and relentlessly advanced to the finals against Chicago. It was then that the dissension erupted. Richard blasted MacNeil as an incompetent coach, telling reporters that Al was the worst coach he'd ever played for. Still, the Canadiens won the Cup—with Richard the chief orchestrator—and MacNeil was behind the bench. But by next season he was in the minors coaching the Nova Scotia (Halifax) Voyageurs. "I was sorry I said MacNeil was the worst," Richard says in retrospect, "but it was true!"

Curiously, MacNeil *was* one of the worst regular defensemen to skate in the NHL, having played for Toronto, Montreal, Chicago, the Rangers, and Pittsburgh from 1955–56 through 1967–68. In his debut at Madison Square Garden in October 1967, he leaped over the boards for a pregame skate and fell flat on his face. Alas, Al MacNeil had forgotten to remove the rubber scabbards from his skates.

GERARD GEORGE (GERRY) McNEIL

BORN: Quebec City, Quebec, April 17, 1926
POSITION: Goalie, Montreal Canadiens, 1947–48, 1949–54, 1956–57
AWARDS: All-Star (Second Team), 1953

Gerry McNeil played goal for the Montreal Canadiens in the early 1950s, filling the void between Bill Durnan's retirement and the later emergence of the spectacular Jacques Plante.

The playoffs of 1954 found the youngster Plante between the Hab pipes as McNeil was coming off a painful midseason injury. Jake the Snake was erratic in the Cup finals, however, and after the Detroit Red Wings had downed the Habs in three of the first four games, McNeil took over.

Gerry was fantastic in goal as Montreal pulled even at three games apiece and then battled the Wings to sudden-death overtime in the seventh and final game. Tony Leswick, a Montreal nemesis all series long, broke into his offensive zone with Montreal's All-Star defenseman Doug Harvey the only object between goaltender McNeil and him. Leswick fired a lazy long shot that McNeil had lined up until suddenly, Harvey stuck out a gloved paw in an attempt to deflect the puck out of harm's way.

Deflect it he did—right over McNeil's shoulder and into the cords to end the series and Montreal's hopes for the Cup. Needless to say, McNeil had nightmares about that shot all summer long. Finally deciding it wasn't worth the aggravation, McNeil retired from hockey for one season, but he returned briefly to the Canadiens in 1956–57.

KEITH ARLEN MAGNUSON

BORN: Saskatoon, Saskatchewan, April 27, 1947
POSITION: Defenseman, Chicago Black Hawks, 1969–

Keith Magnuson often looks like an angry carrot on the Chicago Black Hawk defense. Carrot, because he has bright red hair and because he's tall (six feet); and angry because Magnuson has this thing about psyching himself up for games so that he always seems to be in a fit of pique.

Magnuson came to Chicago by way of Denver University and perhaps because he had to overcome the college boy image and his slight physique, he took boxing lessons to toughen his fighting style if not his defensive style. He made his mark in the NHL the first couple of years by going after anyone in sight and usually losing! He set annual penalty-minute highs in his first two years—1969–70 and 1970–71—but has calmed down recently, hitting an all-career low in 1974 with 105. His defensive play improved also, though he still tends to check wildly and ineffectively at times.

FRANCIS WILLIAM (FRANK) MAHOVLICH

BORN: Timmins, Ontario, January 10, 1938
POSITION: Left Wing, Toronto Maple Leafs, 1956–68; Detroit Red Wings, 1968–71; Montreal Canadiens, 1971–74; Toronto Toros (WHA), 1974–
AWARDS: Calder Memorial Trophy, 1958; All-Star (First Team), 1961, 1963, 1973; All-Star (Second Team), 1962, 1964, 1965, 1966, 1969, 1970; Team Canada (NHL), 1972; Team Canada (WHA), 1974

Perhaps the most misunderstood man in professional hockey is Frank Mahovlich, the one-time skating behemoth of the NHL, who has weathered two nervous breakdowns in his successful quest for superstardom. The "Big M" reached high and low points in his career with the Toronto Maple Leafs before being freed to join, first the Detroit Red Wings, then the Canadiens.

As a young dashing left winger with the Maple Leafs, Frank achieved a high-water mark during the 1960–61 season, when he scored 48 goals and almost matched Maurice "Rocket" Richard's record 50-goal plateau. For Mahovlich, it was too much, too soon.

The demanding fans expected the huge, gifted skater to surpass his 48 goals the following year. But the new pressure cooker atmosphere in the NHL did not suit Frank's psyche and the more he pressed, the more he worried.

"I've always taken the game seriously," said Mahovlich. "When I first came to the NHL nobody gave me a chance to develop. They said I was supposed to be a superstar. If I didn't play like one, then I was no good. But I'm the kind who likes to study my moves and see what mistakes I'm making. I needed a lot of time. I'd watch the game movies and see what I did wrong. I don't think that's moodiness, which is what I was accused of. After all, I scored 61 goals in my first three years. Gordie Howe got only 35 in his first three."

Such comments did little to placate the horde of Mahovlich-watchers who were supported in their criticism by the Maple Leafs' fiery general manager-coach Punch Imlach. The Mahovlich-Imlach relationship plummeted as Frank's scoring diminished.

A stubborn martinet, Imlach always held to the hope that he could mold Mahovlich into his kind of player. The arithmetic said otherwise. Frank's goal-scoring dropped from the high of 48 to an abysmal 18 in 1967.

"It reached a point," said Mahovlich, "where I felt I was beating my head against a wall. If I had to play in Toronto one more year I would've probably retired, although I like hockey and wouldn't want to leave it."

By now, Imlach was ready to consider any reasonable trade offer for Mahovlich. He finally received one from Detroit. On March 3, 1968, one of hockey's biggest deals was consummated by the Red Wings and Maple Leafs.

Mahovlich was dealt to Detroit with Peter Stemkowski, Garry Unger, and the rights to Carl Brewer for Paul Henderson, Norm Ullman, Floyd Smith, and Doug Barrie. Those who knew Frank best were convinced that the change of scene would improve his game. "Detroit," said Frank's brother Peter, "is a different hockey city. Frank will be treated differently by the Red Wings."

He was and it showed immediately. Within a month, Frank scored seven goals and closed the season with the clear suggestion that better things were to come. "I'll be tickled," said then Detroit coach Bill Gadsby, "if Frank scored 35 goals in his first full season with us."

Mahovlich obliged with 49 goals, the most he had ever scored in twelve NHL seasons. It was the most goals for a Red Wings' player since Gordie Howe had scored the same amount in 1952–53. Frank was also voted the number one star in the 1969 All-Star game in Montreal.

Skating on a line with Howe and Alex "Fats" Delvecchio, Mahovlich was a new man. With 118 goals the line broke the 105 record set in 1943–44 by the famed Montreal Punch Line of Maurice Richard, Toe Blake, and Elmer Lach. The line's 264 points smashed the 223-point mark set in 1956–57 by Detroit's Production Line of Gordie Howe, Ted Lindsay, and Norm Ullman.

The grand game once expected of Mahovlich was now on magnificent display at Olympia Stadium. In the 1969–70 season Frank scored 38 goals and 32 assists for 70 points and was a prime catalyst in pushing the Red Wings into a playoff berth for the first time in four years.

Still, there was a gray cloud hanging over Mahovlich's future in Detroit. His brother Peter, an enormously gifted center, had fallen into disfavor with the Red Wings' front office and was traded to Montreal. In addition the Red Wings now had a new coach, Ned Harkness, who had new ideas.

Harkness failed as coach, but was elevated to the managership. Meanwhile, Frank played as if he was skating in mud. A trade was inevitable, and on January 13, 1971, Mahovlich was dealt to the Canadiens in exchange for Mickey Redmond, Guy Charron, and Bill Collins.

For the fourth time in his big-league career Frank was being asked to make a major comeback. He produced better than ever.

The Canadiens' fans immediately took Frank to their collective hearts and he responded by helping Montreal win the 1971 Stanley Cup as he broke the playoff goal scoring record with fourteen big red lights. Manager Sam Pollock acknowledged Frank's leadership qualities by naming him an alternate captain. Mahovlich was touched by the honor. "It's the first time I've ever been chosen for anything," he said. "The Canadiens' management showed that they respected me. It's a nice feeling."

In 1971–72, his first full year in Montreal, he scored 96 points in 76 games and followed that with 93 points in 78 contests during 1972–73. Once again he was a tower of power as Montreal marched to the Prince of Wales Trophy and the Stanley Cup in 1973.

It was a remarkable accomplishment for a misunderstood athlete who had thrice been written off as a superstar. Nothing emphasizes the value of Frank Mahovlich more than his ability, which enabled him to surpass the 500-goal mark and finish the 1972–73 campaign with an all-time goal total of 502.

In his final NHL season, Mahovlich scored 31 goals and 49 assists to lift his all-time NHL totals to 1,182 games played, 533 goals, 570 assists, 1,103 points, and 1,056 penalty minutes. He jumped from the Canadiens to the WHA's Toronto Toros during the off-season and was named team captain. In his first WHA game, against the New England Whalers, Mahovlich scored a hat trick, and led the Toros to a second-place finish in the league's Canadian Division, with a respectable 82 points.

PETER JOSEPH (PETE) MAHOVLICH

BORN: Timmins, Ontario, October 10, 1946
POSITION: Center/Left Wing, Detroit Red Wings, 1965–69; Montreal
Canadiens, 1969–

Peter Mahovlich is the kind of younger brother anyone would like to have. At 6–4, 210 pounds, Pete is the youthful sibling of hockey great Frank Mahovlich, one of the game's outstanding left wingers.

Pete doesn't feel his size is always an asset. "When I have a bad game, it's really bad," "Little M" states. "Because of my size, I stick out more."

The Canadiens obtained him in 1969 from Detroit, where he was seldom used. A year later, Les Habitants dealt for brother Frank, and the two helped Montreal to a pair of Stanley Cups.

Peter is a fine penalty killer and backchecker, but his offensive prowess was unknown until he joined Montreal. In his first four seasons at the Forum, Pete tallied 127 goals, just two less than big brother. He has also been instrumental in the development of Guy Lafleur into a top-notch right wing, as witnessed by the fact that Pete was second in team scoring in 1975, with 117 points, only 2 points behind Guy.

RONALD PATRICK "CHICO" MAKI

BORN: Sault Ste. Marie, Ontario, August 17, 1939
POSITION: Right Wing, Chicago Black Hawks, 1961–75

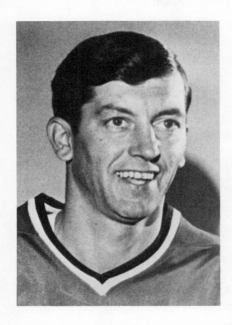

Chico Maki has the distinction of being one of the few Chicago Black
Hawks who saw that town cop a Stanley Cup. It was 1961, Maki's first year,
and the last time the Hawks won it all.

Maki was originally a center, but was switched to right wing. He retired
during the 1974–75 season.

WAYNE MAKI

BORN: Sault Ste. Marie, Ontario, November 10, 1944
DIED: Vancouver, British Columbia, 1974
POSITION: Left Wing, Chicago, 1967–69; St. Louis Blues, 1969–70;
    Vancouver Canucks, 1970–74

The most famous stick-swinging duel in modern hockey took place during, of
all things, a meaningless exhibition game between the St. Louis Blues and Boston Bruins in 1969. The antagonists were Boston's Terrible Ted Green and the
Blues' Wayne Maki.

Wayne, the younger brother of Chico, slashed Green. The Boston defenseman shoved Maki, who went down. As Green skated away, Maki speared him. Green, incensed by this action, hit Maki below the shoulders with his stick.

Things were already out of hand when Maki applied a terrifying chop with his stick atop Green's head. Green crumpled to the ice and Maki was challenged by a number of Bruins.

Green suffered a partially crushed skull. Miraculously, he not only recovered from near-death but he played again. As for Maki, he eventually wound up with the Vancouver Canucks, where he scored 47 goals in two seasons. In tragic irony, Maki was forced to retire in 1972 because of a brain tumor discovered late that year. He died in the spring of 1974.

MAURICE JOSEPH (JOE) MALONE

BORN: Quebec City, Quebec, February 28, 1890
DIED: May 15, 1969
POSITION: Forward, Quebec Bulldogs, 1909–17, 1919–20; Montreal Canadiens, 1917–19, 1920–21, 1922–24; Hamilton Tigers, 1921–22
AWARDS: Art Ross Trophy, 1918, 1920; Hockey Hall of Fame, 1950

Many respected observers regard Joe Malone as the greatest all-around scorer who ever laced on a pair of skates. "He might have been the most prolific scorer of all time if they had played more games in those days," says Frank J. Selke, the former Canadiens' managing director who remembers Malone as a young professional. "It was amazing the way Joe used to get himself in position to score. In that respect his style was similar to Gordie Howe's. Joe was no Howie Morenz as far as speed was concerned. But he was a clean player like Dave Keon and Frank Boucher. On the other hand, though, Joe never took a backward step from anybody."

The handsome native of Quebec City played his early hockey for teams in Ontario before being signed by the Quebec Bulldogs. His acquisition by the Canadiens for the 1917–18 season was considered a coup of major proportions. A centerman, Malone was the Jean Beliveau of his day.

Malone's most notable achievement was his record-breaking seven goals in a game scored on the night of January 31, 1920, in Quebec City. Three of the goals were scored within two minutes of the third period. Unfortunately, the game was played on a night when the temperature hovered around twenty-five below zero and only a handful of spectators turned up at the rink.

RANDY NEAL MANERY

BORN: Leamington, Ontario, January 10, 1949
POSITION: Defenseman, Detroit Red Wings, 1970–72; Atlanta Flames, 1972–

Before the 1972 expansion grab bag, Randy Manery had appeared in only three NHL contests with the defensively deficient Red Wings. For some strange reason, the Wings failed to protect the promising young backliner, and the Flames plucked him and plunked him onto their blue line corps. Manery hasn't missed an Atlanta game since. He is their top offensive defenseman, plays the point on power plays, and yet many consider him to be the best defensively oriented member of the team.

CESARE MANIAGO

BORN: Trail, British Columbia, January 13, 1939
POSITION: Goalie, Toronto Maple Leafs, 1960–61; Montreal Canadiens, 1962–63; New York Rangers, 1965–67; Minnesota North Stars, 1967–

When he flops to the ice to block a shot, he looks like a whooping crane *in extremis,* and when he removes his mask he carries the long-faced look of a man who has just lost his dog or his best friend. It could only be Cesare Maniago, veteran cager of the Minnesota North Stars.

Cesare Maniago

For many years Maniago had good reason for the long face; he was always playing second fiddle behind a hotter goalie. Maniago came up to the NHL in 1960–61 with the Leafs. He played seven games and posted a perfectly respectable 2.57 goals-against average. But Johnny Bower won the Vezina that year. Exit to the minors.

In 1961 Maniago was drafted by Montreal from Toronto, but played the next year in Hull-Ottawa because Habs' ace Jacques Plante was in the process of winning both the Vezina and the Hart trophies. Semipermanent residence in the minors.

Then, in 1965, Maniago was traded by Montreal to the Rangers with Garry Peters, for Earl Ingarfield, Noel Price, Gord Labossiere, and Dave McComb. So what, Ed Giacomin was ruling the Blueshirt net!

Maniago played thirty-four games for the Rangers, in two seasons, and then his luck changed: He was drafted by the expansionist Minnesota North Stars in June 1967. He saw constant action for three seasons and finally proved he was something more than a sub goalie.

But he wasn't able to carry the Stars by himself. Enter Lorne "Gump" Worsley, the aging, tubby pixie from Montreal. Maniago and Worsley shared the duties then, through 1973–74, when Gumper wasn't retiring, quitting, or generally stealing the limelight from the virtually mute Maniago. Cesare wasn't exactly second fiddle anymore, but he certainly couldn't pull the notices like Worsley. For awhile it was even a troika scene in Minnesota, when the North Stars began to groom talented Gilles Gilbert (now starring in Boston).

Finally, in 1974–75, Maniago was *the* goalie again—but he was also in his midthirties and laboring behind a weak North Star roster. Heading toward mid-season, Maniago was playing badly one night when a cheap goal went past his pads. Swiftly he skated off the ice and, before stunned teammates, he stripped off his pads and disappeared—for almost two weeks. Maniago returned to share the nets with Pete LoPresti and Fern Rivard.

SYLVIO MANTHA

BORN: Montreal, Quebec, April 14, 1902
DIED: August 1974
POSITION: Defenseman, Montreal Canadiens, 1923–36; Boston Bruins, 1936–37
AWARDS: All-Star (Second Team), 1931–32; Hockey Hall of Fame, 1960

When the Montreal Canadiens were called to training camp for the 1924–25 NHL season, one of the new faces in the lineup was Sylvio Mantha. A native of Montreal, Mantha played defense and, as such, was obscured by the more exciting young forwards in camp, especially Howie Morenz. Like Morenz, Mantha was to play a vital part in the Canadiens' future success. He played on the Canadiens' Stanley Cup winners in 1930 and 1931 and remained with Montreal until 1936 when he was traded to Boston where he finished his NHL career in 1936–37. He was inducted into the Hockey Hall of Fame in 1960.

HAROLD "MUSH" MARCH

BORN: Silton, Saskatchewan, October 18, 1908
POSITION: Right Wing, Chicago Black Hawks, 1928–45

The Chicago Black Hawks' successes in their early National Hockey League years can in large part be credited to Harold "Mush" March who played exclusively for the Hawks from the 1928–29 season to his concluding year in the majors, 1944–45. March was at his best in the thirties, working on a line with Tommy Cook at center and Paul Thompson on the other wing. On April 10, 1934, March scored the Stanley Cup-winning goal against Red Wings' goalie Wilf Cude in double overtime to give the Windy City its first NHL championship club. Not surprisingly March also was in on the Hawks' second Stanley Cup championship in April 1938, scoring a key goal in the fifth and final game of the series against the Toronto Maple Leafs. Although March never played on another Chicago Cup winner, he sparked the Hawks in the 1941 playoffs with two goals and three assists.

It has been said that one of big league hockey's funniest sights was March, a smallish skater, hiding behind huge Taffy Abel, a Chicago defenseman, as

Abel carried the puck into enemy territory. With March obscured, Abel would then drop his teammate the puck and allow Mush to shoot it between his opened legs.

DONALD MICHEL (DON) MARCOTTE

BORN: Asbestos, Quebec, April 15, 1947
POSITION: Left Wing, Boston Bruins, 1965–

Teddy Roosevelt would have spotted Don Marcotte right away, because no Bruin has spoken softer or carried a larger stick than this patient left winger who endured more than his share of frustration while working his way to the big time.

"I laugh when I hear people calling Donnie an overnight sensation," trainer Dan Canney once said. "He's more like Flip Wilson, who worked all those years in dingy night clubs before hitting the big money. This kid has been a hard worker from the beginning. That's how he made it. And that's why it's so good to see him finally coming into stardom."

Marcotte hits people with all the subtlety of a pile driver, yet he picks up relatively few penalties because his checks are as clean as they are jolting. Until recently, when he finally got a regular job, Don filled in on all three Boston lines and worked well with strange partners. In addition, he was an excellent penalty killer.

So why did he have to wait until he was twenty-five to become a regular?

He scored 31 goals in Hershey in 1967–68 and 35 more the next year. Then the Bruins brought him up. But Boston had just assembled the team which would eventually win two Stanley Cups. It was no time for experimenting, so Marcotte, who was never really given a shot, was shipped back to Hershey where he released his emotions by scoring 28 goals in 35 games. The Bruins brought him back in 1970–71 and kept him as a utility man. He gave them 15 goals and they rewarded him with a regular job in 1971–72, but, alas, a back injury required surgery and Marcotte was once again forced to wait for his chance. In 1972–73 he finally got it. And his record (33 goals in 1975) shows he made the most of it. Why hadn't he demanded to be traded years ago?

"I wanted to make it with the Bruins," he replied.

JOHN "MAROOSH" MARIUCCI

BORN: Eveleth, Minnesota, May 8, 1916
POSITION: Defenseman, Chicago Black Hawks, 1940–42, 1945–48

One of the toughest hombres ever to glide over a big league hockey rink, Johnny Mariucci was a fearsome football player as well. After playing end for

Bernie Bierman's super Minnesota Gopher teams of the late thirties, Mariucci made his NHL debut with Chicago in the 1940–41 season. As one newsman put it, it was a sports parlay without precedent. It still is.

Now assistant general manager of the contemporary North Stars, "Maroosh," as he was known, turned to hockey from a promising National Football League career because of money. The most a good blocking lineman could make in pro football in 1940 was $150 per game or $1,500 per season. The Black Hawks signed him for $3,000.

"Besides," says Mariucci, "I preferred to play hockey. Football is nothing but hard work. Hockey is fun." Mariucci enlisted in the United States Coast Guard during World War II and played defense for the Cutters' sextet. Following the war, he played three more seasons in Chicago before retiring.

JEAN GILLES "CAPTAIN CRUNCH" MAROTTE

BORN: Montreal, Quebec, June 7, 1945
POSITION: Defenseman, Boston Bruins, 1965–67; Chicago Black Hawks, 1967–70; Los Angeles Kings, 1970–73; New York Rangers, 1973–

A classic "defensive-defenseman," Gilles "Captain Crunch" Marotte is a devout believer in a defenseman using his body, as his nickname implies. A squat, muscular blue liner who seems as wide as he is tall, Marotte is an expert bodychecker and shot blocker who usually leaves the scoring chores to his forwards and mops up any one who dares venture into his defensive zone.

Possessing a dangerous low shot from the point, Marotte's career goal-scoring high came in 1972–73 when, skating for the Los Angeles Kings, he notched 10 goals. In 1973 he was traded to the New York Rangers.

ALBERT LEROY (BERT) MARSHALL

BORN: Kamloops, British Columbia, November 22, 1943
POSITION: Defenseman, Detroit Red Wings, 1965–68; California Seals, 1968–73; New York Rangers, 1973; New York Islanders, 1973–

Never known for his scoring, Bert Marshall is a defensive defenseman who broke into the major leagues with the Detroit Red Wings. After a five-year purge with the Oakland/California Seals, Bert's defensive savvy was needed by the New York Rangers in the abortive 1973 rush to the Stanley Cup. The following season saw Bert on the move again, even if it was only crosstown to the New York Islanders where he settled in as a regular fixture on the Isles' defensive rotation.

JACK MARSHALL

BORN: St. Vallier, Quebec, 1877
DIED: August 7, 1965
POSITION: Forward and Defenseman, Montreal Victorias (CAHL),
    1902–03; Montreal Wanderers (FAHL), 1904–05, 1907, 1910–12,
    1916–17; Montagnards (FAHL), 1907; Montreal Shamrocks
    (ECAHA), 1908–09; Toronto Arenas (NHA), 1913–15
AWARDS: Scoring Leader, 1904, 1905 (prior to NHL's Art Ross Tro-
    phy); Hockey Hall of Fame, 1965

A Hall of Famer, Jack Marshall's accomplishments over his sixteen-year playing career could fill volumes and volumes of hockey lore. Laboring for six different teams as a forward and defenseman, Jack played on six championship
teams, five Stanley Cup winners, and twice led his loop in scoring.

In 1910, the first year he made the switch back to the blue line, his Wanderers rolled to the NHA championship and the Stanley Cup. Marshall suffered
a serious eye injury the following season and saw only limited action over the
next two campaigns.

In 1913 Marshall was hired as a playing manager for the new Toronto club
of the NHA. It took just one season for Marshall to meld his unit into Stanley
Cup winners. Jack, at the age of thirty-seven, took a full turn on defense and
starred in the playoffs.

Marshall remained with Toronto for one more season before returning to the
Wanderers to finish out his playing career.

MICHAEL (MIKE) MARSON

BORN: Toronto, Ontario, July 24, 1955
POSITION: Left Wing, Washington Capitals, 1974–

Mike Marson skates well, is fairly tough, has a tendency to be overweight, and
plays for the newest NHL addition, the Washington, D.C., Capitals. Perfectly
ordinary journeyman, right?

So why does he feel as though there's a spotlight on him every time he takes
a turn at left wing? Weeeel, there's just one weensy thing different about
Marson—he's the only black playing major league hockey today.

There have been others—Willie O'Ree in the late fifties and Alton White in
the WHA until 1974—but damn few.

Mike was the Caps' second draft pick, and with the team's initial dearth of
talent, was assured a starting berth if he could shave off a few extra pounds he
sported in training camp. He sloughed off the fat (from 220 to 200 pounds) and
took a regular turn, although he wasn't setting any NHL rookie scoring records.

Mike Marson

HUBERT JACQUES "PIT" MARTIN

BORN: Noranda, Quebec, December 9, 1943
POSITION: Center, Detroit Red Wings, 1961–62, 1963–65; Boston
    Bruins, 1965–67; Chicago Black Hawks, 1967–
AWARDS: Bill Masterton Trophy, 1970

Hubert "Pit" Martin has been around the NHL for quite a while, always doing a superior job in the center position. He began with Detroit in 1961, but couldn't secure a slot with the Wings. After several seasons of scooting back and forth between Detroit and Pittsburgh of the AHL, he was traded to Boston for Parker MacDonald in 1965, where he stayed for only a season and a half.

In 1967 Martin was traded by Boston with Gilles Marotte and goalie Jack Norris for Phil Esposito, Ken Hodge, and Fred Stanfield, and you all know what happened. Esposito went on to break practically every scoring record there is, with Hodge not far behind, and naturally everyone thinks that Chicago got robbed. That may be, but Pit Martin is still a damn competent, but small, centerman. He also flies his own plane, which cannot be said of Phil Esposito.

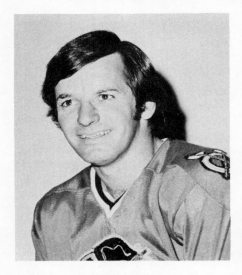

Pit Martin

RICHARD LIONEL (RICK) MARTIN

BORN: Verdun, Quebec, July 26, 1951
POSITION: Left Wing, Buffalo Sabres, 1971–
AWARDS: All-Star (First Team), 1974, 1975

The fastest gun in the National Hockey League? In the fifties it was Maurice "Rocket" Richard. In the sixties, Bobby "Golden Jet" Hull. In the seventies a significant number of goaltenders will point at Richard Martin, the Buffalo Sabres' left wing who scored 52 goals in 78 NHL games in the 1973–74 season, as a member of the "French Connection Line" with Gil Perreault and Rene Robert.

"He's the greatest natural scorer I've ever coached," said Sabres' boss Punch Imlach, who had coached for a long, long time.

Fans at Buffalo's Memorial Auditorium have watched Martin since the 1971–72 campaign, when he scored 44 goals, a rookie record, and helped provide the Sabres with instant respectability.

Students of offensive hockey long have wondered what qualities have made Martin such an accurate shooter. "It's because I depend on the wrist shot 75 percent of the time," Martin explained. "I use the slapshot only from the blue line when a traffic jam looms ahead. The wrist shot is more accurate and you have a quickness edge on the goaler who hasn't as much chance to get set. Also, I try to stick to positional hockey, riding my left lane, but once across the blue line, I try to go into goal on a straight line. In that way I have balance for shooting."

Many of the expert scorers insist that they aim for a general area of the net rather than a specific part of the goal. By contrast, Martin aims for a specific spot. "The trick there," he said, "is to stick with your decision about the spot. "It's amazing how hard it is not to change one's mind. I have to discipline myself particularly when I run into a stretch of goaltender trouble. But it pays off; the alternative is built-in uncertainty."

Martin's critics have had little to carp about except for one incident: The time he walked out on Team Canada in September 1972 when Vic Hadfield, Josh Guevremont, and Gil Perreault also left the team in the midst of its series with the Soviet National squad. Martin argued that he had been overlooked by Team Canada coach Harry Sinden and that his abilities were rusting in Russia when they would have been better honed to sharpness in Canada.

"If I had played in one game," Martin explained, "nothing would have made me leave the team, but I knew my timing was off and I was facing my second year in the NHL, where my career lies. I needed the Sabres' training camp badly. Team Canada wasn't short of cheerleaders and I felt I wasn't going to be any help on the ice. I went to coach Sinden and asked if there was any chance of my playing. He seemed dubious. When I explained my problem he said, 'I think you are conscientious.' If he had asked me to stay I wouldn't have left."

But that's all in the past. The question now is whether Martin's hot stick can break any records. If maturity has anything to do with it, the answer will be in the affirmative.

WILLIAM "BAT" MASTERTON

BORN: Winnipeg, Manitoba, August 16, 1938
DIED: January 15, 1968
POSITION: Forward, Minnesota North Stars, 1967–1968
AWARDS: An award to "the National Hockey League player who
best exemplifies the qualities of perseverance, sportsmanship,
and dedication to hockey" is given annually (starting 1968) by
the National Hockey League Writers' Association in his honor.

Bill Masterton was not a hockey star in the Bobby Hull-Gordie Howe sense of the word. In fact, he'd never played regularly in the National Hockey League until the 1967–68 season. In 1962–63 he scored 82 points for the Cleveland Barons of the American League, but decided to quit pro hockey when none of the NHL teams drafted him. He went to Denver University and obtained a master's degree in finance. After graduation he accepted a job with the Honeywell Company in Minneapolis. For all intents and purposes, his pro hockey career was over.

But, when the NHL expanded to twelve teams, the Minnesota North Stars expressed an interest in Masterton. Although Bill was satisfied with his new job, he couldn't resist the temptation of trying out with an NHL team. He reported to the North Stars' training camp and impressed general manager-coach Wren Blair enough to win a berth on the team. The twenty-nine-year-old center had finally realized his lifetime ambition.

On January 13, 1968, the North Stars played the Oakland Seals at the Metropolitan Sports Center in Bloomington, Minnesota. In the first period of the game Masterton led a North Star rush into Oakland territory. The Seals' defensemen, Larry Cahan and Ron Harris, braced for the attack just inside their blue line. According to Blair, Masterton was checked by the two players after passing the puck in the Oakland zone.

Both Cahan and Harris total more than 400 pounds. Their combined check was described by observers as hard but clean. A split second after Masterton was hit, the North Stars' center flipped backwards, hitting his head on the ice. "It was a momentary check," said Blair, "and they [Cahan and Harris] skated right on after the puck. Masterton hit [the ice] so hard that I'm sure he was unconscious before he fell. I've never seen anybody go down that way. We heard him crash to the ice from the bench."

NHL president Clarence Campbell was not at the game, but received a report from referee Wally Harris who did not impose a penalty when Masterton fell to the ice. "I got it secondhand from the referee," said Campbell, "the same as everybody else. There was no suggestion of anything but a routine accident. His feet went out from under him and he landed on the back of his head. He had dumped the puck into the attacking zone and was chasing it."

Bill Masterton never regained consciousness. He was removed to a Minneapolis hospital where a team of five doctors was prevented from performing surgery by the seriousness of the injury. For thirty hours they managed to keep Masterton alive by use of a respirator, but the massive internal brain injury was too severe. Early on the morning of January 15 Bill Masterton died. He was the first NHL player to die as a result of injuries suffered in league play in the fifty-two-year history of the league and, as nearly as can be ascertained, the first professional player to be killed since Owen McCourt in 1907, ten years before the NHL was formed.

Dr. John Coe, the medical examiner said: "The actual injury was not as marked as we expected but occurred in a very critical area [the pons] within the brain. So it is not difficult to account for death. It has not been determined whether the massive hemorrhaging which occurred was of primary or secondary nature. . . . There was no preexisting injury or disease which was a factor in death."

Following the tragedy, league governors, in cooperation with the National Hockey League Writers' Association, created a Bill Masterton Memorial Trophy to go to a player who demonstrates the qualities exemplified by the late North Stars' center.

GODFREY MATHESON

BORN: Unknown
POSITION: Coach, Chicago Black Hawks, 1932

In 1931 the Black Hawks acquired a respected coach in Dick Irvin, and his orchestration of the Chicago players gave every indication that better things were to come. But this was too much to expect from the Black Hawk franchise. Irvin left the team during the summer to accept a similar job with the Maple Leafs. It was also too much to expect Major McLaughlin to follow Irvin with an equally competent coach. Instead, the Major chose a chap named Godfrey Matheson who had absolutely no big-league hockey coaching experience.

The Major was captivated by Matheson's unique game strategy. But the more experienced players immediately sensed that they had acquired a loser. Defenseman Teddy Graham once cited some of Matheson's foibles:

"Matheson had coached only kid teams that had just one shift of players— one front line, one set of defensemen, and a goalie. He simply had no experience in changing lines."

When the players reported to their new mentor for game plans, Matheson informed them that only six of them would participate in the regular season's action and the rest would be able-bodied reserves. That left about twenty players with nothing to do but watch. The nucleus of the team consisted of Chuck

Gardiner in goal, Taffy Abel and Helge Bostrum on defense, and Tommy Cook at center flanked by Paul Thompson and "Mush" March.

The extras were informed that they were to pay close attention to the big team just in case they had to substitute for any of the regulars. "It was," said Graham, "enough to make a nut house out of any hockey camp."

Matheson added to the improbable situation by referring to each of his hard-bitten pros as "mister." The nonplaying players had to be content with an occasional spin on the ice before and after the special six conducted their practices. The Major had left the preseason training in Matheson's hands, and the weird arrangement would very likely have remained the same had it not been for Bill Tobin, the business manager of the Hawks. Word had filtered back to Tobin's Chicago office about Matheson's unprecedented plans, and at first Tobin considered the reports as amusing balderdash. It wasn't until he arrived at the training base that he learned the truth.

"We got in touch with Tobin as soon as he arrived," said defenseman Graham, "and let him know what was going on. It was for our good and welfare as much as his."

Confronted by Tobin, Matheson promptly turned in his resignation, and disappeared into the oblivion from whence he had come!

EDWARD JOSEPH "SPIDER" MAZUR

BORN: Winnipeg, Manitoba, July 25, 1929
POSITION: Forward, Montreal Canadiens, 1951–55; Chicago Black
    Hawks, 1956–57

The "Spider" of hockey was a tall, gangly, Winnipeg-born forward named Eddie Mazur who appeared to have several extra arms at his side when he stickhandled up the ice for the Montreal Canadiens from 1951 through 1955, occasionally spending time in the minors. Although Mazur had few brushes with stardom, he helped save the Canadiens from Stanley Cup elimination during the 1952 opening playoff round against the Boston Bruins. In that series Montreal won the opening match but lost the next three to the underdog Hub sextet. In the sixth game Boston virtually completed the upset, scoring twice in the first period. When the Canadiens skated out on the ice for the second period, they desperately needed a goal to spark their comeback. The Spider provided the score, shooting the puck past goalie Jim Henry at 4:53. The Canadiens rallied to win the game and the series. Mazur returned to the minors after the 1954–55 season and briefly reappeared with Chicago in 1956–57 before his final *tour de force* in the American League.

HOWARD WILLIAM (HOWIE) MEEKER

BORN: Kitchener, Ontario, November 4, 1924
POSITION: Right Wing, Toronto Maple Leafs, 1946–54; Coach, Toronto Maple Leafs, 1956–57
AWARDS: Calder Trophy, 1947

When Conn Smythe returned to Toronto after serving in Europe during World War II and began rebuilding his Maple Leaf hockey club, he emphasized a policy of hard-nosed play. "Nobody," said Smythe, "pops anybody on this club without getting popped back. I'm not interested in hockey players who don't play to win. You can take penalties, but you gotta play to win." Then, Smythe went about the business of finding youngsters who fulfilled his requirements.

One of those kids was Howie Meeker, a fighter of the Smythe mold. During World War II a grenade blew up in Meeker's face, and doctors said he'd never play hockey again. But there he was, a rookie on the 1946–47 Leafs. Meeker was fast and tough, and he loved to fight with Gordie Howe of Detroit and Tony Leswick of the Rangers. Al Nickleson of the Toronto *Daily Star* described a bout with Leswick: "The two started shoving and the action ended when Meeker picked Leswick up in a crotch-hold, threw him on the ice with a body slam, and with Meeker atop, Leswick's head hit the ice, leaving him a groggy fellow." In April 1947 Meeker was voted NHL rookie of the year.

Meeker was part of the famed second generation "Kid Line," along with Vic Lynn and Teeder Kennedy. Lynn was not an especially heavy scorer, but he was big and rough and he hit hard. Kennedy couldn't skate very well, but he seemed to have the puck all the time. As a unit they meshed perfectly, and they reached their collective peak early on in the 1947–48 season.

Complemented by two other strong lines, the Kid Line steered the Leafs to another Stanley Cup win in 1948 and still another in 1949. Toronto missed in 1950, but in 1951 the Leafs reached the Cup finals against Montreal's Canadiens. With Toronto leading the series three games to one and the fifth game in sudden-death overtime, Meeker helped create the Cup-winning goal by teammate Bill Barilko. Howie outsped several pursuing Montreal players early in the overtime, captured the puck, and set up teammate Harry Watson who, in turn, got the puck to Barilko who shot the rubber over goalie Gerry McNeil.

The quality of Meeker's play ebbed after that grand moment, and he retired after playing only five games for the Leafs in 1953–54. Meeker was named coach of the Leafs in 1956–57 (who finished out of the playoffs) and by season's end gave way to Billy Reay. However, he had been promoted to manager and remained in that position until Stafford Smythe became chairman of a new Maple Leafs' hockey committee. Smythe promptly fired Meeker. "Howie," said Smythe, "was too inexperienced." In recent years, Meeker has become a popular television "color" commentator for hockey as well as author of how-to-play manuals.

JACK MEHLENBACHER

BORN: Unknown
POSITION: Referee, NHL, 1951–56

Respected for his efficiency and no-nonsense brand of refereeing, Jack Mehlenbacher officiated in the NHL from 1951 through 1956. Like some of his colleagues, including Eddie Powers and Dalton McArthur, Mehlenbacher took exception to the lack of support referees then received from the NHL office. ''The big wheels of the NHL,'' said Mehlenbacher, ''figure they have to have blood to fill the arenas. During my years in the league that was all they were interested in.'' Such anti-establishment remarks earned Mehlenbacher the displeasure of NHL bosses and helped shorten his officiating career despite his excellence with the whistle.

GILLES MELOCHE

BORN: Montreal, Quebec, July 12, 1950
POSITION: Goalie, Chicago Black Hawks, 1970–71; California Golden Seals, 1971–

You have to feel sorry for California's Gilles Meloche. One of the top netminders in the NHL, Meloche has been tending goal behind the most porous of defenses for most of his career. In 1973–74 he was forced to miss seven weeks when a teammate skated over his hand in practice.

Through all this, Meloche has shown a catlike quickness and great savvy in the nets. Though his goals-against average has never been among the best in the league, he is generally regarded as one of hockey's outstanding goaltenders, and many an NHL contender would like to have him guarding their cage.

MEMORIAL CUP

Emblematic of the Junior (A Division) hockey championship of Canada, the Memorial Cup has been in competition since 1919. It was donated by the Ontario Hockey Association in memory of all professional and amateur Canadian hockey players who were killed in World War I, and currently is supervised by the Canadian Amateur Hockey Association.

In the past, winners from the Eastern provinces would skate against champions of the West for the Memorial Cup. However, the format was altered in 1972. Presently, the Cup winner is decided as a result of a round robin elimination playoff between the best teams in Western Canada, Quebec, and Ontario. The Toronto Marlboros won the Memorial Cup in 1975, defeating the New Westminster (British Columbia) Bruins, 7–3. Previously, they had defeated the

Sherbrooke (Quebec) Beavers, 10–4. It marked the Marlies' second Memorial Cup in three years and their sixth in the history of the national junior hockey championship.

DONALD MAURICE (DON) METZ

BORN: Wilcox, Saskatchewan, January 10, 1916
POSITION: Forward, Toronto Maple Leafs, 1939–49

A product of the Wilcox, Saskatchewan, wheat fields, Don Metz played occasionally for the Toronto Maple Leafs from 1939–40 through the 1948–49 season, but is best remembered for two episodes that contributed to two Stanley Cup victories. In 1942, with the Leafs trailing the Red Wings three games to none in the Cup finals, Metz replaced high-scoring Gordie Drillon. Don popped in four goals and three assists—every one of them vital—and orchestrated the Toronto Cup championship. In the 1947 Cup semifinals with Montreal, Don bowled over the Canadiens' crack center Elmer Lach, sidelining him for the series. Montreal coach Dick Irvin insisted that if it was, in fact, a deliberate attempt to injure, God would see to it that the Leafs lost. Toronto, with Don contributing an important two goals and three assists, won the Stanley Cup.

NICHOLAS J. METZ

BORN: Wilcox, Saskatchewan, February 16, 1914
POSITION: Forward, Toronto Maple Leafs, 1934–48

Older than brother Don by two years, Nick Metz along with teammate Joe Klukay developed the best penalty-killing combination the NHL has known. Nick became a Leaf in 1934–35 and remained with the Toronto club through the 1947–48 campaign when the Leafs finished first and won the Stanley Cup. He was regarded as one of the most versatile forwards of all time.

NICHOLAS (NICK) MICKOSKI

BORN: Winnipeg, Manitoba, December 7, 1927
POSITION: Forward, New York Rangers, 1948–54; Chicago Black Hawks, 1954–57; Detroit Red Wings, 1957–59; Boston Bruins, 1959–60; Ass't. Coach, Winnipeg Jets (WHA), 1972–

BASHFUL NICK–READY TO CLICK!
So read the headline in the New York Rangers' program magazine over a story about Nick Mickoski, one of the most beloved but star-crossed Blueshirts.

True, Nick was bashful. And, in a sense, he did click—during the 1950 playoffs he tallied six points in twelve games and scored 20 goals a season later. But the big fellow never quite reached the plateau expected of him when he became a Ranger in 1948–49 after stints with the Rovers and New Haven Ramblers, both Rangers' farm clubs. During the 1950 playoffs, Nick had a chance to win the Cup for New York during the sudden-death overtime of the seventh and final game; but his shot hit the goal post behind Detroit goalie Harry Lumley and bounded out. Occasionally, Madison Square Garden fans would twit Nick about his shot which sailed over the protective screen at the endboards and, finally, he was traded to Chicago in November 1954. He remained with the Hawks until 1957–58 when the Red Wings obtained him. His last NHL campaign was 1959–60 with the Bruins. By now Nick was less bashful, but he really hadn't clicked.

STAN MIKITA

BORN: Sokolce, Czechoslovakia, May 20, 1940
POSITION: Center, Chicago Black Hawks, 1958–
AWARDS: Hart Trophy, 1967, 1968; Art Ross Trophy, 1964, 1965, 1967, 1968; Lady Byng Trophy, 1967, 1968; All-Star (First Team), 1962, 1963, 1964, 1966, 1967, 1968, (Second Team), 1965, 1970

If any single player can be described as the guts of a hockey team, Stan Mikita, the shifty Chicago Black Hawk center, is precisely that man. More than any

National Hockey League club, the Black Hawks were decimated by World Hockey Association raids. First, Bobby Hull, the Golden Jet, jumped to Winnipeg. Then in 1973 the Black Hawks lost first-string defenseman Pat Stapleton and reliable center Ralph Backstrom to the Chicago Cougars. They were quality players that a team could ill afford to lose, unless it possessed a very strong backbone. Which is where Stan Mikita comes in. His combined excellence as a leader and an artistic scorer enabled coach Billy Reay's team to weather the storm.

Chicago finished first in the West Division in 1972–73, following Hull's exit, and Stan scored 27 goals and 56 assists for 83 points. His guidance for the younger players enabled the Black Hawks to reach the Stanley Cup finals before the Canadiens eliminated them in six games. The Black Hawks had more trouble in 1973–74 with Stapleton and Backstrom gone and the Philadelphia Flyers coming on strong. Chicago, nonetheless, finished a strong second while Mikita led the team in scoring with 30 goals and 50 assists for 80 points.

To purists, Mikita is the total hockey player. Coach Reay once said that Stan has Rocket Richard's accuracy as a shooter, Gordie Howe's defensive mastery, Bobby Hull's speed and shot, and Jean Beliveau's stickhandling ability. "Mikita," added Reay, "does more with everything he's got than any player I've seen."

In February 1974 Chicagoans displayed their appreciation for Mikita by throwing a "night" in his honor at the Black Hawks' Stadium. At first Stan was reluctant to participate, but told the promoters he would agree to the fete on one condition: He didn't need or want any gifts such as the cars which were donated to previous Black Hawks' aces. He appreciated the thought behind the ceremony, but he wanted the money channeled into a scholarship fund at Elmhurst College in Illinois. "Then," said Mikita, "I'll have the satisfaction of knowing some kids will get educations that otherwise would be out of reach."

Stan is especially sensitive about education since he, himself, was a highschool dropout in St. Catherine's, Ontario, his adopted hometown. Stan was born in Czechoslovakia, but his aunt and uncle, both Canadians, adopted him and moved the lad to their Ontario home. It was in St. Catherine's that he learned his hockey. A superior intellect, Mikita no doubt would have gone on to university honors had he not forsaken school for professional hockey. But he remained an avid reader and he even received an honorary doctorate from Brock University in St. Catherine's.

If hockey doctorates were awarded, Stan would be first in line, judging by his cerebral play. "He automatically makes the right play," said Black Hawks' manager Tommy Ivan, "and is already thinking about where the next one will develop, and heads in that direction." For vintage Mikita, one merely has to flash back to the 1974 semifinal playoff round between Chicago and Boston. With the series tied one game apiece and the third game at Chicago Stadium, the Black Hawks rallied from a 1–3 deficit to pull within a goal of the Bruins with a minute to play.

Coach Billy Reay then yanked goalie Tony Esposito in favor of a sixth attacker. Chicago won control of the puck as defenseman Phil Russell led the Black Hawks' attack against goalie Gilles Gilbert. Russell barely missed a tip-in shot as Gilbert sprawled to make the save. Meanwhile, Mikita moved toward the action. "Germain Gagnon got a good shot which I thought was in," said Mikita. "Then I saw the puck loose and took a shot. It bounced back to me. I played a lot of pool as a kid so I figured it had to angle in. I bounced the puck off the goalie's rear and it went in." That tied the match at 3–3 with 42 seconds left in regulation time. The Black Hawks won the contest on Jim Pappin's goal in sudden-death overtime.

The Black Hawks didn't win the Cup, but they gave Boston a good run and, as always, Mikita distinguished himself this time without Bobby Hull, Pat Stapleton, or Ralph Backstrom at his side. He had rejected offers to jump to the WHA and decided he was going to be a Black Hawk for life. The Black Hawks want the feeling to be mutual.

"Unless a man believes in himself, makes a total commitment to his career, and puts everything he has into it," Mikita concluded, "he will never be successful in anything he undertakes."

MILDRED THE GOOSE

For the most part the presidency of the National Hockey League has been a position surrounded by an aura of dignity. During the long reign of Frank Calder from 1917 to 1943 there was little levity associated with the NHL's highest office. The same might be said about the years following World War II when Clarence Campbell, former referee, Rhodes Scholar, and prosecutor at the Nuremberg war crimes trials, was the NHL president.

But in the short period between the death of Frank Calder in 1943 and the nomination of Clarence Campbell in 1946, there was a rare lightheartedness combined with the efficiency and dedication usually associated with the office. The cause for the change was the personality of Mervyn "Red" Dutton, who was designated president following the death of Frank Calder.

Unlike Calder and Campbell, Dutton, who played for and subsequently ran the New York Americans, was a rollicking type. His good-natured manner, the cockeyed behavior of the Americans, and the generally nutsy world of hockey in New York in the thirties had inured Red to frolicsome behavior. So while he was league president it was not surprising that he became the prime mover in an adventure that involved two newsmen and a very active piece of poultry named Mildred.

Mildred was a pure white goose with a distinctive red beak who, in March

1943, accomplished what no player, manager, or owner could—she scared the living daylights out of the chief executives of the National and American Hockey leagues in one night.

The leading characters in what since has become known as "The Case of the Loose Goose" were Red Dutton, John Digby Chick (vice-president of the American Hockey League), and two Toronto sportswriters, Vern DeGeer and Jim Coleman. Oh, yes, and Mildred.

Dutton, an extrovert given to great bursts of enthusiasm, had promised to deliver a dozen ducks to his newspaper admirers after a hunting expedition in western Canada. "Red never delivered," said DeGeer, the late columnist for the Montreal *Gazette,* "so we needled him about the ducks whenever we saw him."

The goading of Dutton became more intense when the Stanley Cup semifinals series between the Toronto Maple Leafs and the Detroit Red Wings opened in Detroit on March 21. By the time the series switched to Toronto, the exasperated Dutton had decided to fulfill his promise.

"He smuggled a dead duck into my suitcase," DeGeer recalled. "When I got home and opened my valise, there was this terrible-looking bird that smelled to high heaven. I thought it was a funny sight, but my wife was madder than a hornet when she saw it. I knew it was Dutton's work so I decided to get even."

Accompanied by Toronto *Globe and Mail* sportswriter Jim Coleman, DeGeer went shopping for another duck at Wasserman's Poultry Market. "I wish to buy a well-plucked duck," DeGeer advised Wasserman.

"I'll tell you what I'm going to do," Wasserman replied. "I'm fresh out of well-plucked ducks, but as a special favor I'm going to let you have a goose. This is an exceptional goose, named Mildred, and I do not wish to kill her. Take her home and she'll outtalk your wife."

Aware that Dutton had checked into the Royal York Hotel, the writers decided to sneak Mildred into the president's suite. "We had Wasserman wrap Mildred up in paper," says DeGeer. "When he got finished, she looked more like a bouquet of flowers than a goose."

Having determined that Dutton was not in his room, Coleman persuaded the assistant manager to give him the NHL president's room key. Meanwhile, Mildred remained silent in her wrapping. "She was perfectly behaved until we got into the elevator," says Coleman, now a columnist for the Southam newspaper chain in Canada. "But the elevator was crowded and, once it started, she stuck out her beak and nudged a stout lady standing directly in front of DeGeer."

The embarrassed DeGeer stuttered an apology, but he was mute when Mildred gave the unsuspecting woman a second nudge and this time accompanied it with a long, low hiss. "The lady turned and gave DeGeer a searching look," says Coleman. "Then she smiled faintly. I attributed the smile to the wartime manpower shortage in Toronto."

When the elevator reached the eleventh floor, DeGeer, perspiring profusely, trotted to Dutton's suite, where he deposited Mildred in the bathtub. He filled the tub with water, drew the shower curtain, and retreated with Coleman to a hiding place in the room closet.

A few hours later, Dutton returned to freshen himself up for the third playoff game that night. "I was half-naked when I walked into the bathroom," says Dutton. "As soon as I started shaving, I heard this strange hissing noise from the bathtub. I pulled aside the curtain and this crazy goose flies at me and out of the room. I was dumbfounded at first, but then I went after it."

There were two doors to the presidential suite, and Mildred chose the one conveniently left open by Coleman and DeGeer. Out flew Mildred, then Dutton, then Coleman and DeGeer. The incredible sight of a red-haired man, clad only in shorts, chasing a goose down the eleventh-floor corridor of the Royal York Hotel, with two men alternately sprinting and howling in pursuit, proved too bewildering for a chambermaid who was walking the other way.

"She became hysterical," DeGeer remembered, "and started screaming. Meanwhile, Dutton was yelling, 'The goose is loose, the goose is loose.' We were afraid of the noise so we gave the chambermaid a dollar and convinced her to be quiet. Finally, Dutton got tired of chasing Mildred and went back to his room."

Within minutes, DeGeer and Coleman recovered Mildred and this time carried her to the room of the late John Digby Chick, a portly gentleman who had left for the Stanley Cup match at the Maple Leaf Gardens. Once again, the writers placed Mildred in a bathtub, provided her with water, and drew the curtain to give her some privacy.

After the game, Chick indulged in a few drinks and returned to his room. "He was feeling very little pain," says Coleman. "After getting into his pajamas, he decided to have a nightcap. He poured a short one and went into the bathroom to add some water."

As he turned on the faucet, Chick felt a pinching sensation on his right thigh. He looked down and observed Mildred leaning out from behind the shower curtain. He stared at her for several seconds, walked back into the bedroom, and stared at the label on his bottle. Assured that it was his regular brand, Chick picked up the telephone and asked for room service. "Please send the house detective to my room," Chick implored. "There's a goose in my bathtub."

The call was transferred to the assistant manager, who was accustomed to dealing with inebriated guests. In a soothing manner, he urged Chick to be calm. "Now, Mr. Chick," he said, "you just climb into bed and you'll find the goose is gone when you wake up in the morning."

The assistant manager's prescription failed to calm Chick. "Either get rid of the goose or me," he demanded. "There'd be three house detectives up here if I had a girl in my bathtub. Get that man up here before I go out in the corridor and start screaming."

Flanked by three house detectives, the assistant manager went up to Chick's room and, sure enough, found Mildred phlegmatically floating in the bathtub. She was removed, amid profuse apologies to Chick, and held in custody overnight at the hotel.

The following day, Mildred was punished for the traumas she had inflicted on the hockey executives. The assistant manager and the house detectives had Mildred for dinner—"but not as a guest," says Coleman. "Chick and Dutton profanely declined an invitation to the banquet."

But Mildred managed to get even with her oppressors, even if she had to do it posthumously. "The assistant manager told me she was the toughest, worst-tasting goose he ever had," says Coleman. "But you couldn't beat her for laughs."

JAKE MILFORD

Jake Milford, general manager of the Los Angeles Kings, played minor league hockey in Springfield, Mass., and had his experiences under the mercurial Eddie Shore.

Not the least unusual was being traded for a couple of hockey nets! Milford recalls the incident this way: "Eddie called me in one day to tell me he'd sold me to Buffalo," remembers Milford. "As I stepped off the train my eye caught a headline in the Buffalo paper—MILFORD ACQUIRED FOR TWO HOCKEY NETS; I wasn't surprised, but Shore complained later that the Buffalo team had led him to believe they'd be *new* nets. Apparently the ones they had sent him were used."

Shore, therefore, retains the unique distinction of being the only owner to ever have traded one of his players for two nets and later to have complained that he got a raw deal.

JOSEPH MILLER

BORN: Morrisburg, Ontario, October 6, 1900
DIED: August 1963
POSITION: Goalie, New York Rangers and Americans, 1927–29;
   Pittsburgh Pirates, 1929–30; Philadelphia Quakers, 1930–31

As one might expect, Joe Miller emerged as something of a joke around NHL circles in the late twenties despite some rather competent goaltending. Miller broke into the majors with the New York Americans in 1927–28. At the time the Amerks were the lowest-scoring team in the league, which didn't help Joe very much although he had the ninth worst goals-against average in the ten-team league. Inevitably, Madison Square Garden fans dubbed him "Red Light" Miller and he was kidded throughout the league.

But Joe's moment of glory was soon to come. During the 1928 Stanley Cup playoff between the Montreal Maroons and New York Rangers, regular New York goalie Lorne Chabot was seriously injured in the second game of the series. Manager Lester Patrick substituted for Chabot during the game in which his regular goaltender was hurt and led the Rangers to victory. But Lester had no intentions of playing any more and Chabot was still shelved. It was then that Miller stepped in—with the permission of the Maroons—and took the nets for the Rangers for the rest of the series.

In Miller's first game as a Ranger—the series was tied one apiece in the best-of-five playoff—the Maroons won, 2–0, although Joe played very well. But in the fourth game the Rangers managed a goal and Miller blanked the Maroons, tying the finals at two games each.

Miller was sensational again in the finale, allowing only one Montreal score. The Rangers had scored twice and captured their first Stanley Cup with a 2–1 triumph and a 3–2 victory in games. "Joe Miller," wrote Lou Marsh in *The Toronto Star,* "the substitute goalie, was the hero."

Despite his heroics, Miller found himself dealt to Pittsburgh in 1929. He played two full seasons with the Pirates and then was dealt to the Philadelphia Quakers where he ended his major league career in 1930–31. Ironically, Joe Miller's only NHL playoff adventure took place with the Rangers, the team that didn't even own him—and that's no joke!

MINNESOTA FIGHTING SAINTS

An original member of the World Hockey Association when it began operation in 1972–73, the Minnesota Fighting Saints were based in St. Paul and automatically became competitors for the fan dollar with the NHL's Minnesota North Stars, based in nearby Bloomington. The Saints were molded by its first manager Glen Sonmor, a former NHL player who had become the hockey coach at the University of Minnesota. Sonmor believed that he could build a winner by mixing seasoned pros with a number of collegians. He blended former NHL aces such as Wayne Connelly, Ted Hampson, and Mike McMahon with youngsters such as Mike Antonovich, Mike Curran, Len Lilyholm, and Keith Christiansen. On January 1, 1973, the Saints moved into the new St. Paul Civic Center and beat Houston, 4–3, before a crowd of 11,700.

The Saints' first regular season found them in a dead heat with the Edmonton Oilers. In a playoff for fourth place, the Saints won, 4–2, to qualify for the WHA playoff series against Winnipeg. But the Jets easily whipped the Fighting Saints in five games and Sonmor went hunting for more talent.

He signed former Boston Bruins' ace Mike Walton as well as other NHL skaters such as Rick Smith and Steve Cardwell. The acquisition of Walton was a pivotal move. Mike led the WHA in scoring and helped the Saints to a solid second-place finish in the Western Division. In the playoffs Minnesota ousted

Edmonton in the opening round only to be beaten by Houston, four games to two, in the semifinals.

To the surprise of some observers the Saints failed to improve immeasurably during the regular 1974–75 season. They finished third in the strong Western Division, behind San Diego and first place Houston, and went up against New England in the first round of the playoffs. Defeating the Whalers in six games, the Saints then lost to Quebec in the semifinals, also in six games.

MINNESOTA NORTH STARS

Prior to the formation of the North Stars in 1967, Minnesota had been represented in the old United States League by the Minneapolis Millers and the St. Paul Saints, and in the Central League when the Boston Bruins worked with Minneapolis and the New York Rangers were aligned with St. Paul.

In order to compete in the NHL, Minnesota had to produce a suitable arena. This was accomplished in less than a year, the time required to erect the magnificent Metropolitan Sports Center in Bloomington, which was completed just prior to the opening of the 1967–68 season.

With such eminent sportsmen as Gordon Ritz, Walter Bush, W. John Driscoll, Robert McNulty, Robert Ridder, and Harry McNeely, Jr., as members of the North Stars' board backing the new entry, success was virtually guaranteed. Wren Blair, a veteran hockey organizer and the man who discovered superstar Bobby Orr, was named general manager, and the building of the North Stars was underway.

The first game of the first season was held on October 21, 1967, at Bloomington, and the score was Minnesota North Stars 3, California Seals 1. But the building process was not easy. Some players who had been expected to lead the Minnesota sextet in that first season were complete disappointments. Defenseman Elmer "Moose" Vasko, a ten-year Black Hawk veteran, never regained his old-time form, and Parker MacDonald, an uneven player with Toronto, Detroit, Boston, and New York for fifteen years, apparently had come to the end of his line as a productive scorer. The most stunning blow was the death of twenty-nine-year-old Bill Masterton in the early morning hours of January 15, 1968, following a brain injury sustained in a game against Oakland two days earlier.

The North Stars finished fourth in the West Division, reaching the NHL playoffs in their rookie season. They eliminated the Los Angeles Kings in a rugged, seven-game, first round series, fighting back from 2–0 and 3–2 positions. Milan Marcetta won the sixth game with an overtime goal, and then the Stars routed the Kings in Los Angeles, 9–4. In the semifinals, Minnesota went up against the St. Louis Blues and carried the foe to seven games before losing 2–1 in double sudden-death overtime.

The North Stars finished out of the playoffs, in sixth place, in their second season, but a complete housecleaning by Blair turned things around and Minnesota moved up to third in 1969–70. Still, there was something missing, a stabilizing factor behind the bench to relieve Blair and provide the North Stars with the coaching guidance necessary for bigger wins.

Blair finally found his man in 1970 when he appointed Jack Gordon to the bench post. Blair also infused the playing roster with significant names. One of them was defenseman Ted Harris, a hardrock ex-Canadien who became the team captain; not to mention veterans such as Doug Mohns and Gump Worsley and youngsters Jude Drouin and Barry Gibbs.

Despite a fourth place finish in 1970–71, the North Stars played mightily in the Stanley Cup competition, defeating the heavily favored St. Louis Blues in the first round. Eventually they were eliminated by the Stanley Cup-winning Montreal Canadiens, but not until they took the Flying Frenchmen to six hard-fought games.

The Minnesotans obtained another measure of glory in the 1971–72 season, challenging Chicago for first place in the West before settling for a strong second place position. Their eventual defeat by the Blues in the seventh game of the opening Cup round has gone down as a Stanley Cup classic and enhanced the North Stars' appeal both at home and on the road.

What better proof is there than in the computations of Metropolitan Sports Center? The North Stars' average attendance was 11,800 fans in their first NHL season for a rink with a seating capacity of 15,095. By the third season the average had jumped to 14,351, and in the 1971–72 season it was next to impossible to find an empty seat in the building at any time.

In 1974–75 the North Stars fell apart, finishing a weak fourth in the Conn Smythe Division, and a major reworking of the franchise was in order.

WILLIAM CARL (BILL) MOE

BORN: Danvers, Massachusetts, October 2, 1916
POSITION: Defenseman, New York Rangers, 1944–49

As a defenseman, in the pure sense of the term, Bill Moe of Danvers, Massachusetts, was singularly ordinary. But in the photogenic sense, he was literally spectacular. A Ranger from 1944–45 through 1948–49, Moe perfected a submarine hip check that delivered the enemy up and over his back, plunging the foe in an upside-down position to the ice. So unusual were Moe checks that Madison Square Garden photographers would zero in on him and him alone in the hopes of obtaining such rare displays of bodyblocking. The best such photo was taken by Andy Lopez of Acme Newspictures. In the picture Moe has checked Toronto Maple Leaf forward Gaye Stewart at Madison Square Garden during the 1947–48 season. Stewart is perfectly upside-down in the photo. Moe continued his devastating checking in Hershey of the American League after leaving the Rangers in 1949.

DOUGLAS ALLEN "DIESEL" MOHNS

BORN: Capreol, Ontario, December 13, 1933
POSITION: Defenseman, Boston Bruins, 1953–64; Chicago Black Hawks, 1964–71; Minnesota North Stars, 1971–74; Washington Capitals, 1974–

Apart from being the only NHL player nicknamed "Diesel" (he used to skate fast), Doug Mohns achieved latter-day fame as one of the first NHL players to wear a toupee. "It makes me look younger," Mohns said. "I wish it made me feel younger."

The first time Mohns wore the rug, Stan Mikita of the Black Hawks introduced him to Al Eagleson, executive director of the NHL Players' Association, with the explanation: "This is one of our new men." The Eagle was expressing his pleasure before he realized he was being taken.

"I went to the Black Hawks in exchange for Reggie Fleming and Ab McDonald, after eleven seasons in Boston," Mohns recalled. "I've outlasted those two guys and I've outlasted all the guys who were with me on the old Barrie Memorial Cup teams."

He began his NHL career with the Bruins in 1953, before some of his 1974–75 Washington Capitals teammates were born. Among his credentials are being only the second defenseman to score 20 goals in an NHL season (although some of the goals were scored while he was at left wing) in 1959–60; a lifetime total of some 250 goals and 450 assists, and a streak of twenty-one consecutive NHL seasons before joining Washington in 1974.

MONTREAL CANADIENS

The Montreal Canadiens, more than any other team, have over the years personified all that is beautiful about the game of ice hockey. Organized in 1909, eight years before the National Hockey League came into existence, the Canadiens have always been the personification of Gallic flamboyance, of the French love of style and speed.

Montreal's "French connection" was due to the historical fact that most of the Canadien players have been natives of Canada's Quebec province, where the earliest French immigrants had originally settled.

From their very inception, the Canadiens displayed exceptional speed and *élan,* and soon they were dubbed "the Flying Frenchmen." And almost from the very start they captured the imagination of critics, fans, and even casual sports followers on both sides of the border.

"In truth," wrote sports historian Herbert Warren Wind, "it is difficult to think of any team in any sport—be it the New York Yankees or the old New York Giants or the Brooklyn Dodgers in baseball, the Green Bay Packers or the Chicago Bears in football, or the original Celtics or the Harlem Globetrotters in basketball—that has managed to establish a more vivid or a more enduringly attractive public personality than the Montreal Canadiens."

Hero-hungry French-Canadian fans lavished affection on their beloved hockey team from the very start. Fortunately, there were heroes aplenty on the club that proudly wore the *bleu, blanc, et rouge* uniform of Montreal. For typecasting purposes, the team's first captain and manager, Jean Baptiste "Jack" Laviolette, epitomized what was most appealing about the Montreal sextet. A speedy, lyrical skater, Laviolette had what one observer described as "a mane of theatrically long black hair, which streamed behind him when he came swooping down the ice to set up shots on goal for Edouard 'Newsy' Lalonde and Didier 'Pit' Pitre."

By the time World War I had ended, the Canadiens already had captured the first of what eventually would be a record-breaking number of Stanley Cups, emblematic of professional hockey's world championship. Their manager and coach, Leo Dandurand, emerged as one of the most adroit talent-finders in hockey, and by the early twenties he had molded a team whose competitive fire and aesthetic appeal were enormous. *"Les Canadiens sont synonyme de la vi-*

tesse'' (The Canadiens are synonymous with speed) boasted Montrealers. Obviously, there were many great players on this dynasty in the making, yet they were a diverse group in the most interesting ways.

The Canadiens' goaltender, Georges Vezina (after whom the NHL goaltending trophy is named), was given to writing poetry and other inspirational messages. Howie Morenz, "the Stratford Streak," became the most exciting player of the late twenties and early thirties. Vezina, also known as "the Chicoutimi Cucumber," died on March 27, 1926, but was replaced by George Hainsworth who, himself, developed into a superior goalie.

Managed and coached by Cecil Hart, the Canadiens won the Stanley Cup two years in a row, 1930 and 1931, before sinking to the lower depths of the NHL in the midthirties. The death of Morenz in 1937 symbolized the plight of the once-mighty club, but a rebuilding program was underway that eventually would reap dividends.

From November 29, 1924 on, the Canadiens played their home games at the Forum, which eventually was expanded with a roof-lifting in 1968. On March 11, 1937, Howie Morenz's funeral was held in the Forum before 12,000 admirers.

With Morenz's passing, the Canadiens looked to new, young players for their rejuvenation. One of them was left winger Hector "Toe" Blake, who developed into a scoring ace in the late thirties, and another was goalie Bill Durnan, who was bypassed by the Toronto Maple Leafs only to become a Canadiens' ace in the early forties. Thanks to the astute manager Tommy Gorman, the Canadiens melded into a championship team during the 1943–44 season. Gorman had acquired Maurice "Rocket" Richard to play right wing alongside Blake and center Elmer Lach to comprise "the Punch Line" and iced a formidable defense in front of Durnan, headed by Emile "Butch" Bouchard. With Gorman managing and Dick Irvin behind the bench, the Canadiens won the Stanley Cup in 1944 and 1946. By that time Richard had developed into hockey's most exciting goal scorer and on March 23, 1944, he scored all five goals—Blake got five assists—as the Canadiens defeated the Maple Leafs, 5–1.

A new Canadiens' era began in 1946 when Frank Selke, Sr., switched from the Maple Leafs' front office to become managing director of the Canadiens, succeeding Gorman. Selke immediately began developing a farm system which would pay dividends by the early fifties when such stars as Dickie Moore, Bernie Geoffrion, and Jacques Plante would lead the Canadiens.

Selke's prize acquisition was big Jean Beliveau, a center of immense promise who first played for the junior Quebec Citadelles and then the Quebec Aces of the professional Quebec League. Beliveau made his pro debut with the Canadiens on October 3, 1953, playing five games for the Canadiens. In his fourth game for Montreal Beliveau scored a hat trick against goalie Chuck Rayner of the Rangers although Jean was only twenty years old at the time.

With Maurice Richard pacing the attack and the inscrutable Doug Harvey anchoring the defense, Montreal won the Stanley Cup in 1953 before Beliveau became a full-fledged regular on the Canadiens' front line. When he did, there was no stopping the Montrealers. Toe Blake replaced Dick Irvin as coach for the 1955–56 season and the Canadiens went on to win the Stanley Cup five years in a row.

Maurice Richard retired after the 1960 Stanley Cup win, but his younger brother, Henri, had become a star with the Montrealers in his own right and the Canadiens continued as a power all during Blake's coach tenure. They won the Cup for Toe again in 1965, 1966, and 1968.

When Blake retired at the conclusion of the 1967–68 season, he was replaced by pudgy Claude Ruel who lacked his predecessor's domineering personality. Yet the Canadiens won the championship again in 1969 with Ruel in command, but sagged badly the following year and Ruel eventually made way for Al Mac-Neil. Late in the 1970–71 season MacNeil promoted former Cornell University All-American goalie Ken Dryden from the farm system and decided to start Dryden in the Stanley Cup playoffs against the Boston Bruins. Dryden was so impressive right at the start that he played in all twenty Canadiens playoff games as Montreal scored a major upset Stanley Cup triumph in May 1971. But like Ruel, MacNeil had little control over his team and soon gave way to Scotty Bowman, who previously had coached the St. Louis Blues. Bowman helped maintain the glorious Canadiens' tradition with a Stanley Cup championship in 1973.

Behind the Canadiens' numerous accomplishments in the sixties and seventies was the crafty hand of manager Sammy Pollock, who maintained the excellent farm system originally developed by Selke. Pollock's prize catch for the seventies was Guy Lafleur, another French Canadian who, like Beliveau, had played his junior hockey in Quebec City. After a rather unimpressive start, Lafleur blossomed as a star in 1974–75 when the Canadiens finished first in the James Norris Division of the NHL and Guy scored 53 goals to join Maurice Richard and Bernie Geoffrion in the Canadiens' 50-goal club. A magnificent stickhandler with a blazing shot, Lafleur underlined Montreal's theme: *"Les Canadiens sont synonyme de la vitesse."*

MONTREAL MAROONS

Now but a distant memory to only the oldest hockey fans, the Montreal Maroons once reigned as one of the most competent and most colorful teams in the National Hockey League. In Montreal, the English-speaking Maroons provided the perfect counterpoint to the French-speaking Canadiens, although the Maroons were created long after the Canadiens had intruded on the NHL scene.

The Maroons came into being in 1924, when Canadiens' boss Leo Dandurand sold half of the Canadiens' territorial rights in Montreal to the owners of the Canadian Arena Company, who owned the new Montreal Forum. Dandurand's asking price was $15,000. Dandurand later admitted that his generosity in permitting the Maroons to become NHL members wasn't as altruistic as it appeared on paper. "I figured that having an English team to compete with the French Canadians would make for a great rivalry," he said later, "and I was proven right."

The most crowd-pleasing unit on the Maroons comprised the big "Three S Line" of Nels Stewart, Babe Siebert, and Hooley Smith, a unit that had a collective butcher's touch. Once, in a game against the Boston Bruins the trio broke Boston defenseman Eddie Shore's nose, slashed his face, and detached him from his front teeth.

Another time, in a game at the Forum against the Canadiens, Newsy Lalonde of the Canadiens attempted to behead Hooley Smith, the Maroons' captain, with his stick. At the same time Canadiens' president Dandurand connected with a few well-placed jabs at Smith while referee Mike Rodden tried to haul the Maroon out of danger. The French-English rivalry was sustained into the thirties with the bigger Maroons having the edge in the fighting if not always the scoring. But the newer English-speaking club displayed quality and won the Stanley Cup in 1926 with Eddie Gerard coaching and managing the club. In 1935 the Maroons won the Stanley Cup again, this time with Tommy Gorman managing and coaching.

The Maroons failed to win any more trophies after that, but they continued to make news. On March 24, 1936, they met the Detroit Red Wings at the Forum in what developed into the longest NHL game ever played—Mud Bruneteau of the Red Wings scored the game's only goal at 2:25 A.M. Eastern Standard Time at 16:30 of the sixth overtime period. The Maroons' goalie was Lorne Chabot who fell to the ice as Bruneteau drove the puck into the net. Some three hours after the winning goal Chabot showed up at Bruneteau's room to deliver him the game-winning puck. "Maybe you'd like to have this souvenir of the goal you scored," said the Maroons' goalie.

Few were as kind to the Maroons as Chabot was to Bruneteau. The depression had cut sharply into the Maroons' bankroll. Competition for the fans' dollar with the Canadiens became keener and keener and soon it became apparent that one or the other Montreal team would have to fold. Since more than 70 percent of Montreal's population is French-speaking, the Canadiens prevailed and the Maroons went out of business in 1938.

MONTREAL WANDERERS

Organized in December 1903, the Montreal Wanderers played a pivotal part in the formation of the National Hockey Association and, in turn, the National Hockey League. The Wanderers were an especially tough club in their early years. Once, the Wanderers and a team from Ottawa engaged in a near massacre in a game at Montreal that had editorial writers running to their typewriters in indignation. A *Montreal Star* story complained: "They [the players] should get six months in jail is the opinion as to Saturday's brutality. . . . Old players say it was the worst exhibition of butchery they ever saw . . ."

At the time the team played in the Eastern Canada Hockey Association, the major league of its time. Officials of the Association, however, angered the Wanderers by selecting the Westmount Arena in Montreal as the site of its games. The Wanderers were the property of the Jubilee Rink which had natural ice—and Wanderers' backers immediately perceived they were being victimized by a hockey squeeze play.

The question perplexing the ECHA high command was how to outfeint the Wanderers. The ultimate strategy was an example of front office chicanery that hasn't yet been matched by today's high-pressure moguls. On November 25, 1909, the ECHA simply dissolved itself and then reincarnated the league with the sobriquet "Canadian Hockey Association."

To create an aura of legality it went through the motions of "granting" franchises to Ottawa, the Montreal Shamrocks, Quebec, the Nationals, and All-Montreal. Each team paid an initiation fee of $30 with an annual upkeep fee of $25.

Naturally, the Wanderers applied for membership. There was nothing particularly unusual about it other than the fact that the application was rejected, along with that of the Renfrew (Ontario) Creamery Kings, headed by mining executive J. Ambrose O'Brien. Minutes after their rejection was delivered, O'Brien met Jimmy Gardner, an official of the Wanderers. The two losers-of-the-moment were exchanging condolences when they suddenly realized they ought to combine their efforts against the CHA—which they did. They formed their own league. For starters they had the Wanderers, a respected and established outfit. O'Brien, himself, owned teams in Cobalt and Haileybury, Ontario, and his pals, the Barnett brothers, had title to the Renfrew club. That made four teams, which was a good start, but not good enough for the ingenious O'Brien and Gardner. They agreed that a metropolis such as Montreal could support still another team, but not another team dominated by English-speaking players, as the Wanderers were.

"It was Gardner who suggested that a French team should go well in Montreal," O'Brien explained. Thus, the first steps toward the formation of the Montreal Canadiens, the NHL's most distinguished team over the years, were taken. Representatives from Renfrew, Cobalt (Ontario), Haileybury, and the Wanderers convened in Montreal on December 2, 1909. In a "secret" conclave, they formally organized the National Hockey Association of Canada which ultimately became the National Hockey League.

Fred Strachan of the Wanderers, the Association's first president, immediately sanctioned franchises in the original four cities. On December 4 the NHA convened again and announced that a fifth team, the Canadiens, had applied for membership and that T. C. Hare of Cobalt, Ontario, would put up security for the franchise with a special proviso that the club be transferred to French-Canadian owners at the earliest possible date.

The new NHA proved more vital than many observers expected. On January 15, 1910, both Ottawa and the Montreal Shamrocks jumped the CHA for the new NHA. It was the beginning of the end for the CHA. As for the Wanderers, they finished that first season with an 11–1 record and went on to win the Stanley Cup. But more important by taking a firm stand in their original dispute with the ECHA, the Wanderers helped in the formation of two key hockey bodies—the Montreal Canadiens and the National Hockey Association, which later became the National Hockey League!

ALFRED ERNEST (ALFIE) MOORE

BORN: Toronto, Ontario, (year unknown)
POSITION: Goalie, New York Americans, 1936–37, 1938–39; Chicago
  Black Hawks, 1938; Detroit Red Wings, 1939–40

In April 1938 the Chicago Black Hawks, coached by the American-born Bill Stewart, who doubled as a major-league baseball umpire in the off-season, encountered the Leafs in a best-of-five-games round for the Stanley Cup. The Black Hawks were given no more chance of winning the Stanley Cup than a walrus has of crossing the Sahara Desert. Toronto had finished in first place with 57 points. Chicago was a woefully weak third in the American division with 37 points—20 fewer than the Maple Leafs. Besides, Chicago had "those American players," considered singularly inept for the NHL by their Canadian counterparts; and the upstart Stewart wasn't considered any bargain either!

With two strikes already against them, the Black Hawks appeared to take a third whiff when it was learned that their regular goalie, Mike Karakas, had suffered a broken toe in his final game against the Americans. Karakas didn't realize the extent of the damage until he tried to lace on his skates for the Toronto game. He couldn't make it, and the Hawks suddenly became desperate for a goalie.

"I'd like permission to use Davey Kerr of the Rangers," Stewart requested of Conn Smythe before the game.

Smythe turned livid. "You certainly will *not*," Conn snapped.

Stewart's temper boiled over. "Why, you sonofabitch!" In a trice the two were grappling, shouting, and generally disturbing the peace until their heads cooled. When it was over, Stewart appreciated that while he may have won the battle, he had lost the right to use Kerr.

At that point the Chicago coach was willing to use *anybody,* as long as he'd be willing to strap on the bulky goal pads. "How about Alfie Moore?" someone suggested. "He's available."

A minor league goalkeeper who had had a brief stint with the New York Americans, Moore, according to NHL legend, was quaffing some liquid refreshment in a local tavern a few hours before game time. Whether this was true or not turned out to be irrelevant to Moore's performance in the Chicago nets. If anything, Smythe had erred in causing a rumpus over Stewart's original request for Davey Kerr.

Once the Chicago coach told his players about Smythe's lack of hospitality, the Black Hawks stormed out of their dressing room determined to support Alfie Moore and exact revenge against Smythe. Only Gordie Drillon seemed capable of stopping them. He scored for Toronto early in the game, but then the Black Hawks' defense of Bill McKenzie and ex-Leaf Alex Levinsky threw up a wall in front of their net, and the Chicago attack took over. Johnny Gottselig scored twice, and Paul Thompson got the third Black Hawks' goal. Alfie Moore had done the impossible, stopping Toronto at Maple Leaf Gardens.

Stewart could hardly contain his joy, and immediately he announced that Alfie would start in the second game, April 7, 1938, also at Maple Leaf Gardens. But this time Smythe objected to Moore, and NHL president Frank Calder ruled that the Black Hawks would have to employ their minor league goaltender, Paul Goodman. Goodman had never played an NHL game before, and when he played the second game, he lacked Alfie's poise. The Maple Leafs won the second game, 5–1.

But Alfie's single game was enough to provide a catalyst for the Black Hawks, who went on to win the Stanley Cup. As for Moore, he surfaced briefly during the 1938–39 season, playing two games for the Americans. He allowed 14 goals for a 7.00 goals-against average. His swan song in the NHL was with Detroit in 1939–40 when he played a single game and allowed three goals.

RICHARD WINSTON (DICKIE) MOORE

BORN: Montreal, Quebec, January 6, 1931
POSITION: Left Wing, Montreal Canadiens, 1951–63; Toronto Maple
    Leafs, 1964–65; St. Louis Blues, 1967–68
AWARDS: Art Ross Trophy, 1958, 1959; All-Star (First Team),
    1958–59, (Second Team), 1961; Hockey Hall of Fame, 1974

When the Montreal Canadiens were building one of the best hockey clubs of all time during the early fifties, Richard Winston (Dickie) Moore was among the most gifted young players signed by the Montreal brass. Brash to a fault,

Moore was at first believed to be uncontrollable, but the combination of tough coach Dick Irvin—later the equally tough Toe Blake—and veterans such as Maurice Richard and Doug Harvey settled Dickie into a calmer, more manageable position. The results were sensational. Along with Boom-Boom Geoffrion, Jean Beliveau, and Claude Provost, Moore became one of the most significant of the Canadiens. So significant that out-of-town newspapermen soon took notice of his talents.

"We like Moore," said Jim Vipond in his Toronto *Globe and Mail* column. "He's a chippy operator who mixes with the toughest and still knows how to stickhandle and skate his way to the opposition net. He's not unmindful of Milt Schmidt as he leans far forward in gaining top speed. These Montreal kids are making the customers forget Maurice Richard."

Well, not quite. Dickie was placed on a line with young Henri Richard at center and Maurice Richard on right wing and it became one of the best the NHL has known. Dickie won the scoring championship in 1958 and 1959. He was lionized for playing the second half of the 1958–59 season while wearing a cast to protect a broken hand, yet he still managed to capture the scoring title.

Moore remained with the Canadiens until the 1962–63 season when he temporarily retired. However, Toronto Maple Leafs' manager-coach Punch Imlach coaxed Moore out of retirement for the 1964–65 campaign. Injuries forced him to "quit" again, but only temporarily. In 1967–68 he was signed by the then brand-new St. Louis Blues. He played in only twenty-seven regular-season games alongside his old-time Canadien crony, Doug Harvey, and helped steer the Blues into the playoffs. Moore was absolutely stupendous in the playoffs, old legs and all. He scored seven goals and seven assists in 18 games and was as important as any St. Louis player in the Blues' march to the Stanley Cup finals, and this in their first season. Moore retired once and for all after the 1967–68 season. In June 1974 Dickie Moore was inducted into the Hockey Hall of Fame.

BRIAN MORENZ

BORN: Brampton, Ontario, September 28, 1948
POSITION: Center, New York Raiders/Golden Blades/New Jersey
     Knights (WHA), 1972–74; San Diego Mariners (WHA), 1974–

A nephew of immortal Howie Morenz, centerman Brian Morenz scored 50 points for the New Jersey Knights (now the San Diego Mariners) in the 1973–74 campaign. It was his second year in the WHA, coming off four high-scoring years on the squad of Denver University. A blood clot on the brain and a shattered skull suffered in the 1972–73 season have not prevented Morenz from continuing his career.

HOWARTH WILLIAM (HOWIE) MORENZ

BORN: Mitchell, Ontario, September 21, 1902
DIED: March 8, 1937
POSITION: Forward, Montreal Canadiens, 1923–34, 1936–37; Chicago Black Hawks, 1934–35; New York Rangers, 1935–36
AWARDS: Hart Trophy, 1931–32; Art Ross Trophy, 1928, 1931; All-Star (First Team), 1928, 1931–32, (Second Team), 1933; Hockey Hall of Fame, 1945

The son of a railroad man, Howie Morenz was born in Mitchell, Ontario, a hamlet about thirteen miles from Stratford, in 1902. A little fellow, the young Morenz was often severely beaten by the older boys with whom he played hockey in the neighborhood games. From time to time he'd return home so badly cut and bruised he'd often consider quitting the game; but his love for hockey was so passionate he'd inevitably return to the rink. Soon he was the star of the Stratford team which journeyed to Montreal for a playoff game. Canadiens' owner Leo Dandurand happened to be in the stands on the night that Morenz dipsy-doodled around the hometown defensemen from the start to the finish of the game. Leo conferred with his aide, Cecil Hart, and both agreed it would be prudent to sign Morenz before the Maroons, Hamilton, Ottawa, or Toronto beat them to it.

Raw speed was Howie's forte as he gained a varsity center ice berth on Les Canadiens. Within weeks he was dubbed "the Stratford Streak," "the Mitchell Meteor," and assorted other appellations that almost but never quite described his presence on the ice. "The kid's *too fast,*" said one observer. "He'll burn himself out."

Morenz was a superstar in his second year of big-league play. He finished second in scoring to Cecil "Babe" Dye of Toronto and was doing things with the puck that astonished even such skeptics as Conn Smythe, founder of the Maple Leaf empire and the venerable dean of hockey in Toronto.

"The trouble is," said Smythe, "that writers are always talking about what a great scorer Morenz is. Which is true enough. But they overlook the fact that he's a great two-way player."

Many respected hockey observers claim that Morenz was singly responsible for the successful expansion of the NHL into the United States in the 1920s. It was no secret that New York promoter Tex Rickard became a hockey fan the moment he spied Morenz in action. Not long afterward Rickard introduced the Rangers to New York.

"There isn't a team in the league that has not in some way been affected by some aspect of Montreal hockey," wrote Peter Gzowski, "even if the link is as tenuous as the Detroit Red Wings' crest, which is based on the old Montreal Athletic Association's winged wheel."

But Gzowski was quick to point out that Morenz was the leader of "the most exciting team in hockey from the mid-1920s to the mid-1930s." He adds. "While most fans remember Morenz mainly for his blistering speed and his headlong rushes on goal, he also provided one of the most remarkable examples of the passionate dedication to the game—to winning—that has been another characteristic of Canadien teams. Many people say, of course, that Morenz's fierce involvement in hockey, and in the Canadiens, led to his untimely death, although Morenz's dedication is not unique in the annals of the Montreal team."

It was easy enough for Montreal players and writers to wax ecstatic about Morenz and it was not uncommon for opponents to do likewise. But when the opponent happened to be Eddie Shore, the fiercest defenseman in the game, *then* Morenz knew he had arrived!

"He's the hardest player in the league to stop," Shore admitted. "Howie comes at you with such speed that it's almost impossible to block him with a bodycheck. When he hits you he usually comes off a lot better than the defenseman. Another thing that bothers us is his shift. He has a knack of swerving at the last minute that can completely fool you. Everybody likes Howie. He's one player who doesn't deserve any rough treatment."

Howie's scoring abilities began eroding in 1933–34 when he finished forty-eighth on the NHL scoring list. Even worse, Morenz was booed several times by his formerly loyal Forum supporters. He was thirty-three years old at the time and appeared at the end of the line. Just prior to the 1934–35 season Howie was traded to the Chicago Black Hawks. Morenz scored only eight goals for the Hawks and, a season later, he was dealt to the New York Rangers, but he was a shadow of his former self and New York's Lester Patrick was happy to return him to the Canadiens for the 1936–37 season.

Wearing the *bleu, blanc, et rouge* once more proved to be a tonic for Morenz. True, he had lost his old getaway power, but he was reunited with his old buddies, Gagnon and Joliat, and every so often he'd bring the Forum crowd to its feet with one of the exquisite Morenz rushes.

He was doing just that on the night of January 28, 1937, at the Forum when a Chicago defenseman caught him with a bodycheck, sending Morenz hurtling feet first into the endboards. It wasn't a normal spill and Howie had lost all control as he skidded toward the boards. When his skate rammed into the wood, a snap could be heard around the rink and Morenz crumpled in excruciating pain.

Howie was rushed to the hospital with a badly broken leg, and there was some doubt that he would recover in time to return for another season of play. Once in the hospital, the thirty-six-year-old Morenz began brooding about his fate. Instead of recuperating, he suffered a nervous breakdown. Then he developed heart trouble.

Nobody is quite sure what transpired in the hospital to bring about the utter deterioration of Howie's condition. One theory has it that he was overwhelmed by well-intentioned friends who filled his room with flowers, books, and candy. "The hospital," said one visitor, "looked like Times Square on a Saturday night. The continual stream of visitors tired him."

Perhaps too late, hospital officials forbade all but Howie's immediate family from visiting him. Then, early on March 8, 1937, Morenz was given a complete checkup. It appeared he was rallying. It was a deceptive analysis. A few hours later, Howie Morenz was dead.

The funeral service for Morenz was held at center ice of the Forum where thousands filed silently past his bier. Andy O'Brien, of *Weekend Magazine,* was there at the time and recalls the scene as thousands of hockey fans lined up outside the rink that Morenz had made famous:

"Outside," said O'Brien, "the crowd was so great, we of the press had to enter through the boiler room on Closse Street. As I walked below the north end, profound silence left an impression of emptiness, but at the promenade I stopped in breathless awe. The rink was jammed to the rafters with fans standing motionless with heads bared."

The NHL paid an official league tribute to Morenz on November 7, 1937, by sanctioning an All-Star game at the Forum. In it the Canadiens and Maroons combined forces to challenge a select squad of NHL stars, including Frank Boucher, Charlie Conacher, Eddie Shore, et al. The All-Stars won, 6–5, before some 8,683 fans who contributed $11,447 to a fund for the Morenz family. Howie's uniform was presented to his son, Howie Morenz, Jr.

JAMES ANGUS GERALD (GUS) MORTSON

BORN: New Liskeard, Ontario, January 24, 1925
POSITION: Defenseman, Toronto Maple Leafs, 1946–52; Chicago
    Black Hawks, 1952–58; Detroit Red Wings, 1958–59
AWARDS: All-Star (First Team), 1950

In the autumn of 1946 Toronto manager Conn Smythe took one of pro hockey's biggest gambles. He dropped many of his veterans and imported a bunch of raw kids, including a pair of defensemen, Jim Thomson and Gus Mortson. The pair was teamed together and named "the Gold Dust Twins."

A native of Kirkland Lake, Ontario, Mortson was a splendid skater and fearless checker. Immediately, the Gold Dust Twins hit it off perfectly and the Leafs began the first year of a three-consecutive-year Stanley Cup reign. Fans in foreign rinks were infuriated by Mortson's robust style. One night a Detroit fan hurled a chair at him, but Mortson was nonchalant. The Leafs won four Stanley Cups with Gus on the backline. He was traded to Chicago in 1952–53 and was a significant asset as the Black Hawks won a playoff berth. His last NHL season was 1958–59 with the Detroit Red Wings.

KENNETH (KEN) MOSDELL

BORN: Montreal, Quebec, July 13, 1922
POSITION: Center, Brooklyn Americans, 1941–42; Montreal Cana-
    diens, 1944–56, 1957–58; Chicago Black Hawks, 1956–57
AWARDS: All-Star (First Team), 1954; (Second Team), 1955

Maurice "Rocket" Richard has said that the most underrated center he ever played with was Ken Mosdell. A tall, speedy forward, Mosdell broke into the NHL with the Americans in 1941–42. After two years in the Canadian armed forces, Ken joined the Canadiens in 1944–45 and remained with them through 1955–56. He spent the 1956–57 season with Chicago and finished his lengthy career in 1957–58 with Montreal.

WILLIAM (BILL) MOSIENKO

BORN: Winnipeg, Manitoba, November 2, 1921
POSITION: Right Wing, Chicago Black Hawks, 1941–55
AWARDS: Lady Byng Trophy, 1945; All-Star (Second Team), 1945,
    1946; Hockey Hall of Fame, 1965

Bill Mosienko was an integral part of Chicago's renowned "Pony Line" with Max and Doug Bentley. A speedy winger, Mosienko carved his niche in the

Bill Mosienko

Hall of Fame on March 23, 1952, when he scored *three goals in 21 seconds* against the Rangers at Madison Square Garden. "Like they say," Mosienko observed, "I caught lightning in a beer bottle."

Actually, Mosienko's lightninglike moves were evident before and after that memorable game. He came to the Black Hawks at training camp for the 1940–41 season, a nineteen-year-old who appeared too fragile for the NHL. At first Mosienko was farmed out to Providence and then Kansas City, but eventually he was returned to Chicago where he was put on a line with the Bentleys. Dubbed "the Pony Line" because of the small, coltish moves of the three skaters, the unit ultimately became one of the most exciting in Chicago's history. Mosienko remained a Black Hawk from 1941–42 until his retirement following the 1954–55 season. He never played on a Stanley Cup winner nor a first-place team, but he scored a creditable 258 goals, 282 assists, for 540 points in 711 NHL games. And it is likely his three goals in 21 seconds will remain a record never to be equalled in the NHL.

HARRY MUMMERY

BORN: Unknown
POSITION: Defenseman/Goalie, Quebec Bulldogs (NHA), 1913–16;
Montreal Canadiens (NHA), 1917, 1920–21; Toronto Arenas,
1918–19; Quebec Bulldogs, 1919–20; Hamilton Tigers, 1922–23

Harry Mummery was a gentle giant who patrolled NHA and NHL blue lines for eleven seasons and even found the time to tend a little goal as well.

Harry got his start in pro hockey with the 1913 Quebec team, a unit that went on to win the Stanley Cup. He played three years with "Bad Joe" Hall as his defense partner, and the duo were the scourge of the league.

In 1917 big Mum was traded to the Canadiens and immediately helped the Habs to the NHA championship. Harry found himself in Toronto the following season and the huge good-luck charm had a hand in the Ontarians copping the Stanley Cup.

In 1920 Harry was skating for the Quebec sextet and for the last two games of the season Mum was pressed into service as an emergency goaltender. Harry's first game between the pipes was a forgettable affair that saw every Ottawa Senator in sight sneak the puck past the giant backstop as Quebec was swamped, 11–6. But two days later Harry evened his record as he allowed just four tallies in a 10–4 Quebec win. Harry had one more year with the Canadiens, a season that saw him score 15 goals—his career high.

He also set an NHL record for eating which may well stand today! Mummery was known to consume as many as six meals a day, and weighing in at 258 pounds, it was remarkable he could play hockey.

Mummery would always be present at the pregame meal usually served a few hours before game time. Yet he was always starved before face-off hour had arrived. The legend goes, that Mum would buy a large steak or two, broil it in the rink's furnace room, and help himself to a tasty pre- or postgame snack.

He once handed Canadiens' owner George Kennedy a tab for more than $100 in food bills acquired during a short trip from Manitoba east. Kennedy refused to pay such a hefty sum until Mummery threatened to go out and have "a really big meal," again on the club. Kennedy paid.

Mummery played for two more seasons, with Hamilton and Saskatoon, before hanging up his oversized skates in 1923.

JOHN MURRAY MURDOCH

BORN: Lucknow, Ontario, May 19, 1904
POSITION: Left Wing, New York Rangers, 1926–37
AWARDS: Lester Patrick Trophy, 1974

One of the earliest NHL iron men, Murray Murdoch broke in to the majors in 1926–27 with the Rangers and remained with the big club until his retirement at the conclusion of the 1936–37 season. During that span, Murdoch *completed eleven seasons without missing a game.* He played a total of 508 consecutive games and played in every one of the Rangers' fifty-five Stanley Cup playoff games during that span.

Murdoch retired at the age of thirty-three to become head hockey coach at Yale University where he became something of a collegiate hockey legend. His regular season total was 84 goals and 108 assists for 192 points. In playoff matches he scored a total of 9 goals and 12 assists for 21 points. The figures, however, are deceptive. Murdoch was a solid player, a member of the original Rangers and one of the reasons the New Yorkers won Stanley Cup championships in 1928 and 1933.

ROBERT RONALD (RON) MURPHY

BORN: Hamilton, Ontario, April 10, 1933
POSITION: Left Wing, New York Rangers, 1952–57; Chicago Black
    Hawks, 1957–64; Detroit Red Wings, 1964–65; Boston Bruins,
    1966–70

According to the New York Rangers' script, Ron Murphy should have been one of the highest scorers in NHL history, just as he was in the Ontario Hockey Association's Junior A League with the Guelph Biltmores. Instead, Murphy became somewhat less than a living legend for two reasons—he was defenseman Harry Howell's brother-in-law, and he was the player Bernie Geoffrion clubbed during an infamous bloodbath on Madison Square Garden ice in 1953–54. Murphy's problem was that he was elevated to the Rangers too soon (1952–53) in his young career, right out of the junior league. When Geoffrion bopped him on the head with the full force of a hockey stick swing and nearly killed him, Murphy's progress was halted. Although he fully recovered from the conk, Murphy never was a threat as scorer until his twilight NHL years with the Boston Bruins, playing alongside the likes of Bobby Orr and Phil Esposito. Under the circumstances, anybody would have been a threat. Murphy finally retired in 1969–70.

LOUIS PHILIPPE (PHIL) MYRE

BORN: Ste.-Anne-de-Bellevue, Quebec, November 1, 1948
POSITION: Goalie, Montreal Canadiens, 1969–72; Atlanta Flames,
   1972–

In three seasons with Montreal, Phil Myre appeared in only forty-nine contests. He played in forty-six his first season in Atlanta, posting a 3.03 goals-against and two shutouts. Phil didn't waste his time on the Canadiens' bench while Ken Dryden and Rogie Vachon guarded the goal. Myre learned how to control rebounds as well as any netminder in the game, to cut down angles, and to clear the puck deftly. His quickness helps Atlanta's mobile defensemen, and his know-how has been a big factor in his—and partner Dan Bouchard's—progress.

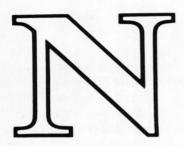

LOUIS VINCENT (LOU) NANNE

BORN: Sault Ste. Marie, Ontario, June 2, 1941
POSITION: Defenseman/Right Wing, Minnesota North Stars, 1968–

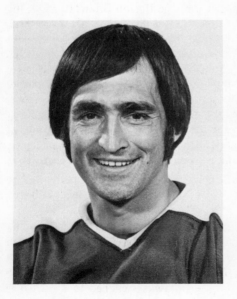

Lou Nanne is one of the more versatile North Stars, alternately playing defense and right wing according to the needs of the team. Before joining the North

Stars, Nanne captained the 1968 U.S. Olympic squad. Since then he has been voted North Star Defenseman of the Year and Most Popular Player. As a youngster in Sault Ste. Marie, Nanne starred on a team that included the brothers Esposito.

NATIONAL HOCKEY LEAGUE

The National Hockey League, the oldest pro-hockey major league in existence today, has undergone myriad changes over the years. The original league, created in 1917, consisted of five teams; the Montreal Wanderers and Canadiens, the Quebec Bulldogs (not playing in 1917), the Ottawa Senators, and the Toronto Arenas. The following season the Wanderers dropped from the league after the burning of their arena, and in 1919 Toronto changed its name to St. Pats.

Until the midtwenties the NHL was but one of three leagues that vied for the Stanley Cup, the other two being the Pacific Coast Hockey League (begun in 1911), run by Frank and Lester Patrick, and the Western Canada Hockey League (organized in 1922). The PCHL folded in 1924 and two years later the WCHL foundered and became the WHL, a minor league compared to the NHL.

The first American team to join the NHL was the Boston Bruins in 1924, the same season in which the Montreal Maroons joined the league. By 1926 three new American teams had joined the NHL and it became a ten-club circuit with a Canadian Division encompassing Toronto Maple Leafs (changed from St. Pats), Ottawa Senators, Montreal Canadiens, Montreal Maroons, and New York Americans. The American Division included the Bruins, the brand new New York Rangers, Chicago Black Hawks, Detroit Cougars, and the second-year Pittsburgh Pirates. The schedule had doubled from twenty-two games to forty-four. Between 1926 and 1942 the Pittsburgh franchise was transferred to Philadelphia (Quakers), then dropped from the league; Detroit changed its name from Cougars to Falcons to Red Wings; Ottawa and the Montreal Maroons disappeared; and the Americans' franchise expired in 1942. The league then remained a six-team unit until the era of modern expansion began in 1967.

At that time the league doubled to twelve teams, adding the Oakland Seals, Los Angeles Kings, Minnesota North Stars, Philadelphia Flyers, Pittsburgh Penguins, and St. Louis Blues, all in the new West Division. Further expansion took place in 1970 with the addition of the Vancouver Canucks and Buffalo Sabres in the East Division, while the Black Hawks switched to the weaker West Division to provide more balance. In 1972 the NHL added the Atlanta Flames in the West and the New York Islanders in the East; and in 1974 the league inflated to eighteen teams and four new divisions with the addition of the Kansas City Scouts and Washington, D.C., Capitals. The schedule was extended to eighty games per team, the playoff system was completely altered, and the All-Star game, once a contest between the previous year's Stanley Cup winners and a chosen few from the other five teams, became an annual showpiece of not-so-spectacular names and faces chosen from the Clarence Campbell Conference and Prince of Wales Conference respectively, played in late January of each season.

The original symbol of first place in the National Hockey league was the Prince of Wales Trophy, first presented in 1924 to the winner of the American Division. When the League expanded in 1967 and created the West Division, the Clarence Campbell Bowl was made the winner's emblem of the West. Today, the Lester Patrick Division (New York Islanders, New York Rangers, Atlanta, and Philadelphia) and Conn Smythe Division (Chicago, Kansas City, Minnesota, St. Louis, and Vancouver) comprise the Clarence Campbell Conference while the James Norris Division (Detroit, Los Angeles, Montreal, Pittsburgh, and Washington) and Charles F. Adams Division (Boston, Buffalo, California, and Toronto) make up the Prince of Wales Conference.

In 1972 the NHL was confronted with its first serious competition in nearly five decades, when the World Hockey Association was formed. Salaries became astronomical, and with the world financial crisis of 1974, several weak franchises, such as Pittsburgh and California, began to founder, and expansion for 1975 was postponed.

VACLAV NEDOMANSKY

BORN: Czechoslovakia, 1944
POSITION: Center, Toronto Toros (WHA), 1974–

Until 1974 there was but one successful Czechoslovakian player in professional hockey—Stan Mikita. But recent developments have brought two more Czechs to North America.

Vaclav (Vatz-lav) Nedomansky and Richard Farda were enjoying summer vacations with their families in Switzerland when they jumped leagues, moving from the established Czechoslovakian National Team to the three-year-old WHA.

Of the two, Nedomansky is the prize. Formerly captain of the Czech team, big Ned has assumed a large role in Toronto's success. He centers the Toros' top line, flanked by Frank Mahovlich and Tony Featherstone. (Farda is only the fourth line center.) As a rookie he scored 41 goals and 40 assists for 81 points, placing him among the top twenty WHA scorers.

GREG NEELD. See THE TRUSHINSKI (NHL) BYLAW.

JAMES ANTHONY "CHIEF" NEILSON

BORN: Big River, Saskatchewan, November 28, 1940
POSITION: Defenseman, New York Rangers, 1962–74; California
 Golden Seals, 1974–
AWARDS: All-Star (Second Team), 1968

Big Jim Neilson, a husky, half-Cree Indian, patrolled blue lines for the New York Rangers for twelve seasons before falling victim to the 1974 Blueshirt purge. By way of a three-cornered deal that saw hockey's dead-end kid, Derek Sanderson, come to the New Yorkers, "Chief" Neilson was dispatched to the NHL's version of Siberia—the California Seals.

Always a gentlemanly defenseman, despite his imposing 6'2'', 200-pound frame, Neilson's finesse with his stick was often overlooked by the more collision-conscious New Yorks fans. When the New Yorkers fell victim to the Philadelphia Flyers' bully-boy tactics in the 1973–74 playoffs, it was Neilson who unfairly received a major brunt of the blame. Less than three months later, he was traded.

An unselfish hockey player who often skated with painful injuries that would have kept lesser men on the sidelines, Neilson was an All-Star selection in 1967–68.

FRANCIS NELSON

Back in the good old days of hockey, it was not considered a conflict of interest to go from writing about the game, to being an executive in the sport, and Francis Nelson, a former sports editor of the Toronto *Globe,* was only one of many writers who became organizational men. Nelson was vice-president of the OHA from 1903 through 1905 when he became an OHA governor to the Amateur Athletic Union of Canada.

He was elected to the Hockey Hall of Fame. Nelson died in 1932.

ERIC PAUL NESTERENKO

BORN: Flin Flon, Manitoba, October 31, 1933
POSITION: Right Wing, Toronto Maple Leafs, 1951–56; Chicago
    Black Hawks, 1956–72; Chicago Cougars (WHA), 1973–74

An intelligent player who never fulfilled his early notices, Eric Nesterenko gained acclaim as the only hockey player mentioned in Studs Terkel's best seller *Working*. In the book, Nesterenko provided insight into what it was like playing forward for the Toronto Maple Leafs and Chicago Black Hawks over a twenty-year period. Nesterenko put it this way:

"I haven't kept many photographs of myself, but I found one where I'm in full flight. I'm leaning into a turn. You pick up the centrifugal forces and you lay into it. For a few seconds, like a gyroscope, they support you. I'm concentrating on something and I'm grinning. That's the way I like to picture myself. I'm something else there. I'm on another level of existence, just being in pure motion. Going wherever I want to. That's nice, you know."

ROBERT FRANK (BOB) NEVIN

BORN: South Porcupine, Ontario, March 18, 1938
POSITION: Right Wing, Toronto Maple Leafs, 1957–64; New York Rangers, 1964–71; Minnesota North Stars, 1971–73; Los Angeles Kings, 1973–

Bob Nevin once objected when a reporter described his skating style as "comatose." Nevin was an efficient checking forward who played on a line with Frank Mahovlich and Red Kelly for the Maple Leafs starting in the 1960–61 season. He was dealt to the Rangers in February 1964 where he was team captain from 1965 to 1971 and even scored 31 goals in 1968–69; then to Minnesota in 1971; and finally in 1973 to Los Angeles where he refound old skills.

NEW ENGLAND WHALERS

The seeds of the New England Whalers were planted in October 1971 by a pair of young sportsmen, Howard Baldwin and John Coburn, Jr., who had originally planned to build a small hockey arena near Cape Cod. Out of this blueprint emerged one of the most powerful teams in the World Hockey Association.

Having obtained backers for the proposed WHA team, Baldwin and Coburn flew to the league meeting in Miami and obtained a green light from the new league's bosses, Gary Davidson and Dennis Murphy. With the franchise in hand, Baldwin, a former business manager of the Jersey Devils of the old Eastern Hockey League, hired Jack Kelley, the Boston University coach, to manage and coach the Whalers. Kelley immediately hired Ron Ryan as assistant coach and director of player personnel. Former Montreal Canadiens' center Larry Pleau of Lynn, Massachusetts, was the first Whaler signed by Kelley, followed by NHL regulars Brad Selwood, Rick Ley, and Jim Dorey, all former Toronto Maple Leafs, and Tim Sheehy of Boston College.

On July 27, 1972, the Whalers signed former Boston Bruins defenseman Ted Green as captain and then signed other NHL aces such as Tom Webster, Al Smith, and Tom Williams. On October, 12, 1972, the Whalers played their first home game at Boston Garden before a crowd of 14,442, defeating the

Philadelphia Blazers, 4–3. A well-balanced unit, the Whalers went on to finish first and win the Avco World Cup.

However, the Whalers encountered financial problems because of competition from the NHL Boston Bruins who featured Bobby Orr and Phil Esposito. Attendance remained less than satisfactory in the second season of operation, 1973–74, at Boston Garden. Kelley had assigned Ron Ryan the head coaching position and once again the Whalers moved to the top of the East Division. Because of the weak crowds, Baldwin began entertaining offers from other cities which coveted the franchise. He finally selected Hartford which was building a new arena in the Connecticut city's civic center. A group of Hartford's leading businesses invested $1.5 million in the Whalers with a limited partnership, including a group of Boston investors. The companies included, among others, Aetna Life and Casualty, Connecticut Bank and Trust Company, United Aircraft, the Hartford Courant, and the Greater Hartford Chamber of Commerce.

Instead of waiting until the end of the 1973–74 season, the Whalers moved their "home" games to the Eastern States Coliseum in Springfield, Mass., because their new home in Hartford had yet to be completed. Playing their final games in Springfield late in the 1973–74 season had a negative effect on the Whalers. Although they finished first in their division, the Whalers were eliminated from the playoffs in a first-round, seven-game upset by the Chicago Cougars.

The Whalers continued to excel during the 1974–75 campaign which was launched in Springfield and was continued in Hartford late in the season upon completion of the 10,400-seat Civic Center arena. Once again they finished first in their division, but not without problems. En route to a match in Toronto on March 30 coach Ryan collapsed and was rushed to a hospital. He was replaced behind the bench by Kelley. On the plus side the Whalers became an instant hit in Hartford, frequently selling out in the new building. It appeared that the Whalers, at last, had found a comfortable home although they were eliminated by Minnesota in the opening round of the 1975 playoffs in six games.

NEW YORK AMERICANS

A case could be made for the New York Americans as the most colorful hockey team to have passed from our midst. They were organized by a newspaperman, bankrolled by a bootlegger, and murdered by their landlord.

The Americans' owner was William "Big Bill" Dwyer, a very large, very important bootlegger. Brought up within rock-throwing distance of the old Madison Square Garden, he became a prominent peddler of illegal alcohol during the zany Prohibition days of the twenties.

The fact that Big Bill served a couple of years in Sing Sing prison didn't seem to matter. Everybody—cops, cronies, customers—thought he was an unusual chap. And he was. Big Bill had never heard of ice hockey when sportswriter Bill McBeth told him he ought to buy a team and play it out of New York, but Dwyer wrote a check for $75,000 and bought the entire Hamilton, Ontario, Tigers' franchise.

The year was 1925, and for the following decade it was better than even money that wherever the Americans were, on or off the ice, all hell would be breaking loose. Tall Thomas Patrick "Tommy" Gorman was the first manager of the "Amerks," as they were nicknamed, and a more ideal personality could not have been found for the job. He knew his hockey and he loved a good gag, and there was a surplus of both in the Americans.

As for the hockey, it was abundantly competent, if not sensational. The team consisted of the Green brothers, Shorty and Red, who flanked center Billy Burch, giving the Amerks a line of extraordinary ability; forward "Bullet" Joe Simpson, who had a shot as good as Bobby Orr's; and defensemen "Big Leo" Reise (whose son was later to play for the Rangers), Alec McKinnon, and Lionel "Big Train" Conacher, voted Canada's Athlete of the Half-Century. As netminder, the Amerks had Roy "Shrimp" Worters, who emerged as one of the better diminutive goaltenders of the time.

In those days money was a piddling matter to the Americans. Even though Dwyer was taking a modest loss on his hockey team, he was raking in so much on his bootlegging business that he couldn't spend it fast enough. What's more, hockey was catching on in New York and the instant success of the Americans inspired Madison Square Garden to go out and form a second New York team, the Rangers.

The Amerks forced tough Newsy Lalonde to quit as coach after the 1926–27 season when the club did not reach the playoffs in its division. Shorty Green took over as bench manager the next year and lasted exactly one season. They finished second in their division, the best they would ever do, but were eliminated in the first round of the playoffs by the Rangers.

Nevertheless, manager Tommy Gorman decided to take the club on a postseason exhibition trip that eventually brought them to Portland, Oregon, for a game with the local team. By this time, all the players knew that Dwyer, a first-class bootlegger, also had a first-class mob, and it was not unusual for some of his all-star gangsters to show up at hockey games.

Unknown to the Amerks, the Portland management had a unique way of announcing that a period of play had ended. At the end of the first period, a loud gunshot that sounded like a cannon blast went off, and the Americans reacted appropriately. Gorman remembered it well:

"Johnny Sheppard and Tex White fell right off the bench, while Roy Worters and Lionel Conacher raced like a Mutt and Jeff team from the vicinity of our net to the nearest boards and scrambled right over them. A couple of our other players on the ice were so startled that they lost their balance and fell flat on their pants."

Maybe that last fact was symbolic. The Americans finished fifth the next season and eventually Big Bill Dwyer was arrested and convicted as a bootlegger. While Dwyer was in the penitentiary the club's debts began mounting. By the time he got out in 1935, the bills were enormous and Dwyer was broke. The team needed a multimillionaire to bail it out. Fortunately, the father of the Americans' superb defenseman, Mervyn "Red" Dutton, just happened to be a multimillionaire. The senior Mr. Dutton's contracting business in western Canada was doing so well that Red could have played hockey for nothing if he had wanted to. The wealthy Duttons provided the money to keep the team going and continued to do so even after the infamous Dwyer passed out of the picture the next season.

But the New York hockey fans weren't blind to the growing inadequacies of the Americans. Even though they had developed some outstanding young players like "Bonnie Prince Charlie" Rayner, a goaltender of amazing courage, and "Boxcar" Egan, a defenseman with great color and sock, it was the Rangers, not the Amerks, who were winning Stanley Cups. The Amerks began to grow desperate. They tried to bolster their forces by signing such aging stars as Eddie Shore, but it didn't work. To stimulate attendance, Dutton had the club's name changed to the Brooklyn Americans in the 1941–42 season, but that didn't help either. Even worse, World War II had arrived and the best of the players were leaving for the Canadian armed forces.

The staggering personnel losses and the equally alarming bills were too much for even the redoubtable Red Dutton. The Americans were finally forced to fold in the spring of 1942. But New York's first hockey team will never really be forgotten. For men like Bill Dwyer, Bill McBeth, Shrimp Worters, Lionel Conacher, and Red Dutton are what hockey is all about, and their spirit remains. Bill McBeth and his faith in hockey are particularly remembered each year when the McBeth Trophy is awarded to the outstanding Ranger in the playoffs. The spirit of the Americans abounds whenever stick hits puck and the crowd roars. They were the boys who started New York's undying love affair with hockey.

NEW YORK ISLANDERS

It was June 6, 1972, and for the first time in thirty years, the New York City Metropolitan area had two NHL teams . . . in name at least. In fact, there were the established New York Rangers who had not won the Stanley Cup in thirty-two years, and the brand new Islanders, who began the 1972–73 season looking as though they might never win a game!

The Islanders' problems began at the top and ran all the way to the bottom: Owner Roy Boe, who also owned the New York Nets basketball team, knew enough about hockey to hire Bill Torrey as general manager. But Torrey, once executive vice-president of the California Golden Seals, made some horrendous mistakes that first year.

Torrey ignored the newborn WHA and paid for it dearly, as half his team jumped leagues, among them veteran forwards Norm Ferguson, Ted Hampson, and Garry Peters. Torrey topped this fiasco by hiring former Canadien/Ranger/Sabre Phil Goyette as coach. Goyette was best known for skating with that Montreal-induced finesse and wearing pointed shoes off-ice. In other words, Phil was a nice guy but he had zero coaching experience. It didn't work.

When hockey came to Long Island's new Nassau Veterans Coliseum in October 1972, it was a joke. The Islanders played their rival newborn, the Atlanta Flames, and lost, 3–2. It looked like two teams trying hard not to play hockey, with the Islanders far superior in not playing!

From there the Islanders sank to new lows. They had drafted a right wing whose style was so awkward they had to give him skating lessons. Defenseman Neil Nicholson played one whole game in the wrong color helmet, which, had the other team complained, would have meant an automatic penalty.

But to the fans, none of this mattered. Baseball's New York Mets had played ridiculous ball for years to massive and happy crowds. The tradition well-established, these hordes gleefully turned out in the Colisuem, cheering the Islanders on to defeat after defeat. The team finished the season by setting a new NHL record of sixty losses.

Contrary to appearances, however, the Islanders didn't do everything wrong. They drafted talented rookie Billy Harris their first season, and although the kid slumped badly in midyear, he took the strain of rookiedom and being the mainstay of the new club remarkably well. Ed Westfall, a steady veteran of the Boston Bruins, was also drafted and made team captain. It was a good choice in picking veteran guidance for what was to become a very young team.

Unlike many previous expansion clubs Torrey clung to the advantage of his basement position—first round draft picks, instead of trading them away for bodies. In their sophomore round, Denis Potvin, the most highly touted rookie defenseman since Bobby Orr, was drafted and the club began to bolster its defense. Potvin performed even better than his advance press, setting NHL records for first-year defensemen with most goals (17) and most points (54). Potvin was voted rookie of the year, after playing the second half of the 1973–74 season with a broken ankle.

Continuing to compensate for earlier mistakes, Torrey signed their next first round draft choice, Clark Gillies in 1974. By this time he had also enhanced the club with tiny but tough Garry Howatt at left wing and the much-improved Bob Nystrom at right wing.

On the coaching side, Goyette was replaced in midseason of the first year by Earl Ingarfield, originally an Islanders' scout. Ingarfield's relationship with his players was better, but performance wasn't. In June 1973 Alger J. "Al" Arbour, former coach of the St. Louis Blues, replaced Ingarfield.

Although the Islanders were nowhere near the playoffs after their second year, they had set another NHL season record, by trimming 100 goals off their goals-against total. This was a clear indication of improved defense and adequate goaltending, although after two seasons of being shellshocked in the Islanders' nets, Gerry Desjardins fled the scene to the WHA. By this time goaltender Billy Smith had improved enough to carry the number one spot behind the Islander defense.

The most interesting change in the Islanders as they began their third season, 1974–75, by climbing into an early lead in the Lester Patrick Division, was their metamorphosis into "tough guys." Modeling themselves after the ferocious Philadelphia Flyers who had just become the first expansion club to cop the big Cup, they began pummeling opponents into submission, while also playing decent hockey. The Islanders made the playoffs and shocked the hockey world by beating the Rangers in an opening three-game play-down. More astonishingly, they then became the first team since Toronto, in 1942, to come back from a three-game deficit, winning the quarterfinals against the Penguins. In the semifinals the "miracle" Islanders almost duplicated that remarkable feat against the Cup-winning Flyers. First, they dropped three games, then they won the next three. But they succumbed in the seventh.

NEW YORK RANGERS

The New York Rangers were born in the midtwenties, in response to a philosophical truism—namely, that "nature abhors a vacuum."

Tex Rickard, a rambunctious fight promoter, had noticed in 1920 that an insurance company was foreclosing the mortgage on the old Madison Square Garden at Twenty-fourth Street. Together with friends, whom he called the 600 millionaires, he formed a corporation to build a new Garden at Eighth Avenue and Fiftieth Street. The "new" Garden was long on space, but short on events for its spectators.

Colonel John S. Hammond, a friend of Rickard's and a business advisor, suggested hockey for one of the sports events. Hammond had visited the old Mount Royal Arena in Montreal and returned sold on the idea that hockey could enthusiastically be supported by New Yorkers. Tex was skeptical, but agreed to lease his Garden to the New York Americans (who had been the Hamilton Tigers).

Rickard became so intrigued with the sport that he yearned for a bigger and better team to play on his ice. He retained Conn Smythe, a young Canadian who was then successfully managing hockey teams in Toronto, to organize another team for New York. It was a foregone conclusion that the name of the team should be "Tex's Rangers" after Rickard's homestate police. And Rangers it was and is.

Smythe, on the payroll a month, couldn't abide the front-office flak, so he left his position by mutual agreement. He was replaced by Lester "the Silver

Fox'' Patrick, a formidable ex-player who had become a hockey promoter. Lester started building a club with such outstanding players as Frank Boucher, a center who went on to win the Lady Byng Trophy for sportsmanship so many times that it was retired and given to him; and the Cook brothers, Bun on left wing and Bill on right wing. The team also included goaltender Lorne Chabot and defensemen Ching Johnson and Taffy Abel.

The Rangers, with a boost from a 1–0 victory over the Montreal Maroons in their opening game on Garden ice, went on to finish first in the American Division of the newly expanded National Hockey League in 1926–27. But they were wiped out in the quarterfinals of the 1927 playoffs.

The 1927–28 season, the Rangers' second in the league, was most interesting. The team had endeared itself to New York fans and had finished second to the Boston Bruins in the American Division. They defeated Pittsburgh in the opening round of the playoffs, then eliminated Boston for a shot at the Montreal Maroons in the Stanley Cup finals. Center Frank Boucher, who later coached the Rangers, recalled the odd circumstances under which the series was played: "We couldn't play the games at home in the finals because the Garden was booked with another attraction [the circus]. We had to play every game at the Montreal Forum,'' Boucher remembered. Well, it was hard enough getting past the Pirates and the Bruins, and now this. No ice! What next?

New York was down one game to none after absorbing a 2–0 defeat from the Maroons. The teams were scoreless in the second period of the game when Nels Stewart, a Maroon center and one of the supreme scorers of his era, took a shot that crashed into Rangers' goalie Lorne Chabot's left eye.

Chabot fell to the ice unconscious, blood dripping from his eye. Now Patrick was without a goaltender—teams didn't carry a replacement in those days. There were two adequate goalies watching the game from the stands: Alex Connell, the goaltender of the Ottawa Senators, and Hughie McCormick, a minor league goaltender.

But Eddie Gerard, the Montreal manager, refused to give the Rangers permission to use either. Time was running short. Finally, center Frank Boucher approached his silver-haired coach. "How about you playing goal?'' Patrick was asked. Although forty-five years old, Lester Patrick, who had some goaltending experience, agreed to strap on the pads for the cause. Before he went out on the ice, "the Silver Fox'' said very simply, "Boys, I'm going to play goal. Check as you've never checked before, fellows, and protect an old man!''

The Rangers, inspired by the courage of their coach, did check as they never had before, held the Maroons off and took a 1–0 lead into the third period. But with six minutes left in the period, Montreal tied it up on a goal by the shifty Nels Stewart, and the game went into overtime.

Montreal came on in waves in the extra session. Patrick held them off. Then Frank Boucher grabbed the puck, skated in alone on the Montreal goalie and scored after 7:05 of the overtime period.

After Patrick had been mobbed by his team, the Rangers tried to settle down and win their first Stanley Cup. They lost the next game, despite the use of a first-rate goaltender, Joe Miller, and were one game away from elimination. Frank Boucher wasn't going to waste the performance Patrick had turned in earlier in the series. He scored the only goal of the next game and both New York goals in the fifth game to lead the Rangers to a 2–1 victory over Montreal for the first New York Stanley Cup.

Cup wins were scarce around the Garden until the 1932–33 season. The Cook brothers and Boucher were anxious for another taste of champagne from the Stanley Cup before they would have to hang up their skates for good. Ironically, the second New York Cup came at the expense of Conn Smythe, the man once hired to organize the Rangers. He had taken a job with the Maple Leafs. This Cup-winning New York team is regarded as one of the finest of all time.

Patrick realized that the Cooks, Boucher, Ching Johnson, and Chabot wouldn't last forever, so he organized a farm system that produced such quality players as Davey Kerr in goal, defensemen Art Coulter, Ott Heller, Babe Pratt, Murray "Muzz" Patrick (one of Lester's sons), and forwards Alex Shibicky and the Colville brothers, Neil and Mac. These players would help lead the Rangers to their third Stanley Cup in the 1939–40 season after Frank Boucher had taken over as coach.

With Boucher behind the bench, the Rangers innovated hockey styles that remain in vogue today. One idea was the box defense. When a team is short-handed due to a penalty, the four remaining skaters arrange themselves in a box in front of the goaltender. The box defense was an obvious help to Davey Kerr, who in 1939–40 won the Vezina Trophy.

Another Rangers' innovation was the practice of removing the goaltender from the ice in favor of a sixth skater in the final minute of a game when a goal was desperately needed.

Near the halfway point of the 1939–40 season, New York was behind, 1–0, going into the third period of a game in Chicago. The Rangers were riding a nineteen-game unbeaten streak at the time and needed a goal to keep it going. Normally, the goalie, if he was removed from the ice at all, was removed during a face-off. But removing him at that time gives the other team a chance to adjust to the strategy. Boucher decided to surprise the Black Hawks and remove Davey Kerr while play was going on.

"We had decided," he explained, "that it would be better to pull the goalie without making it obvious."

The Boucher ploy took everybody by surprise—everybody including Lester Patrick. Patrick was sitting with the official timekeeper between the Chicago and New York benches. When he saw the extra skater on the ice he became alarmed and ran to the Ranger bench to beseech Boucher to remove him before the referee called a penalty on the Rangers for having too many men on the ice.

Patrick hadn't realized that Kerr was already sitting on the bench and that the Rangers had the correct number of men on the ice. Patrick was so vehement in his pleas to Boucher that Black Hawks' coach Paul Thompson heard him and screamed for a penalty. The referee looked around and blew his whistle, but then realized that Kerr was on the bench and that no penalty should be called. But it was too late. Chicago won, 1–0. The nonlosing string had come to an end, but the Rangers still were not going to be denied that season.

At the peak of World War II an end was brought to the New York dynasty. The Rangers finished sixth four years in a row, and managed an ignominious twenty-five-game nonwinning streak in 1944. (The Americans, by this time, had lost players to the army and fans to the Rangers. They finally dropped out of sight in 1942.)

The end of the war marked the end of the Rangers' congenial mediocrity. The team achieved a new respectability with Charlie "Prince Charles" Rayner in goal, forwards Pentti Lund, Tony Leswick, and Edgar Laprade, and a defense including Gus Kyle, Pat Egan, and Allan Stanley.

New York launched another serious assault on the Stanley Cup in the spring of 1950. The Blueshirts again were at a disadvantage because the spring season, along with its flowers and showers, meant that the lions and tigers of the Ringling Brothers Circus would be pitching camp on the Madison Square Garden floor.

So, robbed of any home-ice advantage, the Rangers struggled against the Red Wings, in the finals. The Wings took first blood with a 4–1 verdict at Olympia Stadium, then the series shifted to "neutral" Maple Leaf Gardens where the Rangers scored, 3–1. The Wings came back with a 4–0 shutout, then succumbed to New York in a 4–3 overtime game. The teams exchanged victories again, setting the stage for a seventh game at the Olympia.

The Rangers squandered a 2–0 lead when Detroit nullified early goals by Allan Stanley and Tony Leswick. Buddy O'Connor put New York back in the lead almost halfway through the middle session. Then Jim McFadden captured the puck from Stanley, beat Charlie Rayner with an impossibly angled shot and it was time for overtime again.

Although the Rangers appeared to be running out of steam, they held the Red Wings off during the first overtime. Charlie Rayner just managed to stop George Gee on a clear breakaway early in the second overtime and set up the face-off deep in the Rangers' end.

It was Gee against O'Connor on the vital draw. Gee got the puck to Pete Babando to the left of the net. Babando caught the puck on his backhand and let fly through a screen of players including Stanley, Gee, and Couture. The New York goalie next saw the puck two feet behind him in the nets. That was that. The Wings took the Cup.

The letdown was painful for the Blueshirts. They had to wait through the early fifties before they were to make the playoffs again—under coach Phil

Watson in the 1955–56, 1956–57, and 1957–58 seasons, only to be eliminated each time in the semifinal rounds. Meanwhile, the farm system produced such young players as Andy Bathgate, Harry Howell, Dean Prentice, Aldo Guidolin, Ron Murphy, and Lou Fontinato. When Doug Harvey became player-coach in 1961–62, the Rangers gained another playoff berth but lost in the semis again.

Four more years of frustration followed with the name "Rangers" synonymous with "fifth place."

A major turnabout began with the replacement of manager Muzz Patrick by Emile Francis in October 1964. Since then it has been an uphill fight complete with many frustrations, the most important of which has been the elusiveness of the Stanley Cup despite the fact that the Blueshirts achieved a playoff berth every year since 1966. Ron Stewart, an ex-NHLer, took over the Ranger bench in October 1975.

NEW YORK ROVERS

(Left to Right) Murdo McKay, Walter "Whitey" Rimstead, Lloyd Ailsby, Albert "Ab" Collings

The New York Rangers for years maintained a productive farm club right in their own building, Madison Square Garden. The club, the Rovers, played in the Eastern Hockey League starting in the late thirties. Directed by Tom Lockhart, the manager, the Rovers won the National Senior Open (U.S.) championship in 1939, developing such future Rangers as Alf Pike, Lloyd Ailsby, and Gus Kyle, among others. By the midforties the Rovers' games were so popular at the Garden they frequently filled the arena, and once actually outdrew the parent Rangers. Such colorful characters as Larry "King" Kwong, Hank D'Amore, and the Atomic Line (Cal Gardner, Church Russell, Rene Trudell) skated for the Redshirts. Attendance tailed off in the early fifties and the club eventually was disbanded.

FRANK "DUTCH" NIGHBOR

BORN: Pembroke, Ontario, January 26, 1893
DIED: April 13, 1966
POSITION: Center, Toronto Arenas (NHA), 1913; Vancouver Millionaires (PCHA), 1914–15; Ottawa Senators (NHA and NHL), 1916–17, 1918–30; Toronto Maple Leafs, 1930
AWARDS: Hart Trophy, 1924; Lady Byng Trophy, 1925, 1926; Hockey Hall of Fame, 1945

When old-timers get together to reminisce about the great two-way players of all time, Hall of Famer Frank Nighbor's name invariably pops up. Never a rough or dirty player, Dutch was a model of controlled, artistic hockey whether playing offense or backchecking on defense.

Frank started his career with Toronto of the NHA and then spent two seasons with Vancouver of the PCHA, helping the Millionaires to the Stanley Cup in 1915.

But Dutch Nighbor is best remembered for his long and distinguished career with the Ottawa Senators. Nighbor spent thirteen years with the Senators, playing on four Stanley Cup winners and helping to earn his team the nickname of "the Super Six."

Frank was the very first recipient of the Hart Trophy, awarded annually to the league's most valuable player. He also was a two-time winner of the Lady Byng for combining sportsmanship and playing excellence.

EDWARD REGINALD (REG) NOBLE

BORN: Collingwood, Ontario, June 23, 1895
DIED: January 19, 1962
POSITION: Left Wing, Center, and Defenseman, Montreal Canadiens, 1917; Toronto Arenas, 1917, 1918–19; Toronto St. Pats,
1919–25; Montreal Maroons, 1925–27, 1932–33; Detroit Cougars
and Falcons, 1927–32
AWARDS: Hockey Hall of Fame, 1962

Reg Noble, a versatile, colorful player, spent thirteen seasons in the pro hockey wars and was a member of three Stanley Cup squads.

Reg's first shot at the Cup came while skating for the Montreal Canadiens during the 1917 playoffs. Reg had started the season with Toronto of the NHA, but finished up with the Habs when the Ontarians became the 228th Battalion and were shipped overseas. Noble chipped in a solid playoff series against Ottawa, but Seattle balked when the adopted left winger was slated to see action against them in the Cup finals.

Noble bided his time, however, and upon his return to Toronto the following season, found himself on the 1918 Stanley Cup team. This began a bizarre seven-year love-hate relationship between Noble and the Toronto management. Reggie was a darling with the fans, but his star status led him into a few training regulation hassles with the St. Pat front office.

Dealt to the Montreal Maroons in 1925, Reg was tried at center and later, defenseman. Blue liner Noble helped guide Montreal to his third Stanley Cup in 1926. Reg spent one more season in La Belle Province before moving on to Detroit where he performed nobly for five and a half more years. Noble finally closed out his career in 1933.

BRUCE NORRIS

Under the benevolent despotism of James Norris, Sr., hockey survived and thrived in Detroit during the thirties. Big Jim, the wheat magnate, passed his love of hockey on to his sons, James, Jr., who eventually became president of the Black Hawks, and Bruce, who took over the Red Wings as well as Olympia Stadium in Detroit. In time Bruce Norris became one of the most powerful NHL governors. However, his numerous business interests frequently diverted his attention from the Red Wings and, as a result, the Detroit club began plummeting down toward the bottom of the standings. Norris's most significant blunder was turning the stewardship of the Red Wings over to a troika, headed by former Cornell University coach Ned Harkness, former lacrosse promoter Jim Bishop, and any one of a handful of inept coaches imported by Harkness. Harkness and Bishop finally were cleared out of Olympia by the 1974–75 season, but the Red Wings were almost beyond salvaging. Compounding Norris's woes was a serious auto accident which hospitalized him in the fall of 1974 in Florida.

JAMES NORRIS, SR.

A wealthy grain broker from St. Catharines, Ontario, James Norris once played for the Montreal Victorias. He began his hockey dynasty by purchasing the Chicago Shamrocks of the AHA in 1930.

Three years later he popped up in Detroit where he bought the Detroit Olympia arena and the Detroit NHL franchise, whereupon he promptly changed their name from the Falcons to the Red Wings.

Just as the saying goes, "money breeds money," one might well say that "power breeds power," for within two years Norris had himself a Stanley Cup (1935–36), and for the better part of three decades the Wings were a steady contender.

Norris, a member of the Hall of Fame, also purchased the moldy Chicago Stadium. At one time before his death in 1952 he even owned a majority interest in Madison Square Garden. How's that for power!

The James Norris Memorial Trophy, awarded annually to the best defenseman in the league, was first presented to the league in 1953 by the four children of James Norris, Sr., in his honor.

JAMES D. NORRIS

James D. Norris was co-owner of the Detroit Red Wings with his father, James. Then, in 1946, he and partner Arthur Wirtz became owners of the Chicago Black Hawks. He was elected to the Hockey Hall of Fame—probably out of gratitude for leaving a couple of teams to other people!

MARGUERITE NORRIS

Marguerite Norris Rilke took over the presidency of the Red Wings upon her father James Norris's death in 1952, and held that office until 1955, making her the only woman to ever be actively involved in NHL power politics.

NORTH AMERICAN HOCKEY LEAGUE

Founded on May 1, 1973, in New York City, the North American Hockey League succeeded the old Eastern Hockey League as charter memberships were granted to Mohawk Valley, Cape Cod, Binghamton, and Johnstown. Maine, Long Island, and Syracuse joined them shortly thereafter, and Philadelphia became the first expansion franchise in the summer of 1974.

The Lockhart Cup, emblematic of NAHL supremacy, honors veteran hockey administrator Tom Lockhart, who organized and ran the EHL in several of these locations over a span of nearly four decades.

WILLIAM M. NORTHEY

It was William Northey who prevailed upon Sir Montague Allan to present his silver cup as the new emblem of amateur hockey supremacy, when the Stanley Cup became the professional award.

For years the managing director of the Montreal Forum, Northey supervised construction of that venerable arena, and for his years of supporting the development of hockey, he was elected a member of the Hall of Fame.

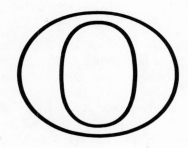

HERBERT WILLIAM "BUDDY" O'CONNOR

BORN: Montreal, Quebec, June 21, 1916
POSITION: Center, Montreal Canadiens, 1941–47; New York
    Rangers, 1947–51
AWARDS: Hart Trophy, 1948; Lady Byng Trophy, 1948; All-Star (Second Team), 1948

Buddy O'Connor, a tiny, wisplike centerman, broke into pro hockey with the 1941–42 Montreal Canadiens, pivoting a line of mighty mites known as "the Razzle-Dazzle Line." This fulfilled a boyhood ambition of Buddy's that began on the frozen ponds of his suburban Montreal home.

But it was easy for the diminutive forward to get lost in the shuffle of the Canadien's awesome firepower. So after six successful but anonymous seasons with the Habitants, Buddy was peddled to the New York Rangers in 1947 for the paltry sum of $6,500.

O'Connor was welcomed to New York with open arms, and it was there that he truly began to find himself. He finished out the 1947–48 campaign in grand style, missing out on the NHL scoring crown by a single point, but copping both the Hart Trophy, as the league's most valuable player, and the Lady Byng for sportsmanship.

An automobile accident forced Buddy to miss much of the following season, a mishap that Ranger manager Frank Boucher pointed to as the only reason the Rangers failed to make the playoffs.

Buddy played two more seasons with the Rangers before finally retiring as a player at the end of the 1950–51 campaign

DONALD EDWIN "NIPPER" O'HEARN

BORN: Halifax, Nova Scotia, February 14, 1928
POSITION: Goalie, Ft. Worth (USHL), 1948–49; Springfield Indians
    (AHL),   1948–49;   Oakland/Springfield,   1949–50;   Spring-
    field/Portland (PCHL), 1950–51; Syracuse (AHL), 1951–52;
    Springfield Indians, 1953–54.

Don "Nipper" O'Hearn was an unfortunate minor-league goalie who had the experience of toiling for the renowned Eddie Shore from 1948 to 1957 in places like New Haven, Fort Worth, Oakland, Vancouver, San Diego, Fresno, Springfield, Syracuse, Troy, and Halifax.

If anything, playing for the great Shore was a nerve-shattering life-style. One year, Shore paid O'Hearn the great total of $3,300 for an entire season between the pipes. That was when he was playing. When he wasn't, well, Shore had this system.

Those fellows on the Awkward Squad, or the Black Aces, as the bench-warmers were called, were expected to work for Shore in some other manner—like selling peanuts in the stands or blowing up balloons for the coming Ice Capades show.

"We blew 'em up in the dressing room," O'Hearn remembers. "We had that room floor to ceiling in balloons. You could open the door, stand way back in the corridor, and then run and jump feet first into so many balloons that you'd bounce right back on your ass in the corridor."

Working in *games* for Shore had its moments, too. Once, O'Hearn whipped the Buffalo Bisons, 2–1, in what he regarded as the best game he had ever played. Shore didn't think so.

"You'd have had a shutout," he rasped afterwards, "if you'd have stayed on your feet."

HAROLD (HARRY) OLIVER

BORN: Selkirk, Manitoba, October 26, 1898
POSITION: Forward, Calgary Tigers (WCHL), 1922–26; Boston
    Bruins, 1927–34; New York Americans, 1934–37
AWARDS: Hockey Hall of Fame, 1967

Mild-mannered Harry Oliver was a veteran of sixteen professional hockey seasons, eleven Stanley Cup playoffs, and one Cup championship. He broke in with Calgary of the old WCHL and led them in scoring over his five-year stay there.

Oliver moved east in 1927 and was welcomed with open arms by the NHL's Boston Bruins. Harry responded nicely to the Bs' hospitality, leading them in scoring and right into the playoffs. Harry O was a star of the 1927 playoffs for the Beantowners, almost singlehandedly pulling off an upset over the strong Ottawa Senators in the Cup finals.

Oliver led the Bruins in scoring again, during that championship season of 1929. Boston steamrollered to the Cup, flattening the New York Rangers and Harry, once again, was outstanding in the finals.

Ollie spent five more seasons with Boston before being sold to the New York Americans in 1934. He skated with the Amerks for three campaigns before retiring in 1937. Harry Oliver is a member of the Hockey Hall of Fame.

MURRAY CLIFFORD OLIVER

BORN: Hamilton, Ontario, November 14, 1937
POSITION: Center, Detroit Red Wings, 1957–58, 1959–61; Boston
     Bruins, 1961–67; Toronto Maple Leafs, 1967–70; Minnesota
     North Stars, 1970–

Murray Oliver made his first appearance in an NHL game with Detroit back in 1958. Since then he has played in over 1,000 contests, scored more than 250 goals, and become renowned as a premier penalty killer. Oliver was Minnesota's MVP in the North Stars' greatest season, 1970–71. Oliver's reputation as a clean, gentlemanly performer was punctuated by his 1973–74 campaign in which he appeared in all 78 Star games and collected only four penalty minutes.

MURRAY BERT OLMSTEAD

BORN: Scepter, Saskatchewan, September 4, 1926
POSITION: Left Wing, Chicago Black Hawks, 1948–51; Montreal
     Canadiens, 1951–58; Toronto Maple Leafs, 1958–62
AWARDS: All-Star (Second Team), 1953, 1956

Known around the NHL as "Dirty Bertie," Montreal's Bert Olmstead gained the reputation as one of the best left wingers in the sport. Rarely would he get involved in fistfights, although he started many of them by provoking his opponent.

Olmstead's most famous bouts were with Lou Fontinato of the Rangers. "Dirty Bertie" had moved on to Toronto by 1959 when the two assailed each other following a high stick by the Maple Leaf. Fontinato blackened Olmstead's eye with one punch.

As the pair attempted to leave the penalty box following their banishments, Olmstead jumped in front of Fontinato in an effort to get on ice first. Lou simply opened the door to the box, knocking Bertie down, then proceeded to beat up on his rival.

"If he didn't block the door," Louie revealed, "nothing would have happened."

The battle continued later in the season before a sellout crowd in Madison Square Garden. Fontinato skated from the face-off circle toward Olmstead and hurled himself, nearly parallel to the ice, at Bertie. "I don't know how Olmstead got up," related Camille Henry, who was on the ice at the time and nearly served as an unwary roadblock to Fontinato, the Flying Ranger. "Louie broke his stick on Olmstead's face, put his knee in his ribs, and threw him into the glass. It was the dirtiest check I've ever seen."

WILLIAM ELDON (WILLIE) O'REE

BORN: Fredericton, New Brunswick, October 15, 1935
POSITION: Right Wing, Boston Bruins, 1957–58, 1960–61

The first black to skate in the NHL, Willie O'Ree was hardly the Jackie Robinson of hockey in terms of ability. He played two games without scoring for the Boston Bruins in 1957–58. The Bruins gave O'Ree another chance in 1960–61. This time the native of Fredericton, New Brunswick, scored 4 goals and 10 assists in 43 games and was dispatched to the minors where he remained. Opponents said that while O'Ree was speedy, he was easily knocked off the puck and shied away from the heavier, rough play.

JOSEPH JAMES TERENCE (TERRY) O'REILLY

BORN: Niagara Falls, Ontario, June 7, 1951
POSITION: Right Wing, Boston Bruins, 1971–

For youngsters like Terry O'Reilly, the Boston Bruins' 1972 loss of key players to the WHA was a blessing. O'Reilly, a stocky right winger with a reddish blond mane to match his Irish name, spent the 1971–72 season with the Boston Braves, an American Hockey League affiliate of the Bruins. Although he scored a paltry 9 goals in 60 games, the six-foot, 180-pounder earned a reputation as a rough 'n' ready roisterer who was not adverse to doing his opponents bodily harm. He spent 165 minutes in the penalty box repenting for such transgressions.

The Niagara Falls, Ontario, native was placed on a line with rookie center Gregg Sheppard and three-year man Don Marcotte. Christened "the Kid Line" despite Marcotte's veteran standing, the trio hustled, dug, and battled their way into the hearts of the Bruins' fans and, even more important, Bruins' management. Rarely a game went by when the line wasn't responsible for either scoring goals or preventing their opponents from mounting a consistent offense.

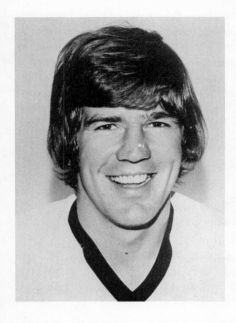

Terry O'Reilly

O'Reilly personally contributed 5 goals and 22 assists to the line's output, while logging 109 minutes in the sin bin.

O'Reilly and then teammate Derek Sanderson staged a bloody brawl in the Bruins' dressing room at Oakland in 1973–74. As a result, Sanderson eventually was traded to the Rangers.

JAMES (JIMMY) ORLANDO

BORN: Montreal, Quebec, February 27, 1916
POSITION: Defenseman, Detroit Red Wings, 1936–38, 1939–43

Sometimes it pays to shave before a hockey game. At least that might have averted a major fight for Detroit defenseman Jimmy Orlando in 1942–43 when Orlando had become the swarthy terror of the ice lanes. The Red Wings were playing the Toronto Maple Leafs on this night when Orlando rattled Toronto rookie Gaye Stewart with a bodycheck. Jimmy had been doing this ever since the 1936–37 season for Detroit and usually his enemies took it quietly, but not Stewart.

"Why don't you get yourself a shave," Stewart told the heavy-bearded Detroiter.

Orlando leaned back and hurled one of his most devastating punches at Stewart who hit the ice in what looked like a permanent KO. When Gaye recovered, he returned to the bench and soon had enough energy to take his regular turn as a forward. Minutes later he took the puck for a ride down left wing where Orlando once again awaited him. This time Stewart forsook the puck and took a home run-cut with his stick at Jimmy's head. He connected and it's considered a miracle that Orlando managed to keep his head from rolling down the ice. "The only time I saw more blood," said reporter Jim Coleman, "was the day I was taken on a tour of the cattle-killing floor of an abattoir." Orlando recovered, finished the season with Detroit, but never played in the NHL after the 1942–43 campaign.

ROBERT GORDON (BOBBY) ORR

BORN: Parry Sound, Ontario, March 20, 1948
POSITION: Defenseman, Boston Bruins, 1966–
AWARDS: Hart Trophy, 1970–72; Calder Trophy, 1967; Norris Trophy, 1968–75; Art Ross Trophy, 1970, 1975; Conn Smythe Trophy, 1970, 1972; All-Star (First Team), 1968–75, (Second Team), 1967

It has been said with some justification that Bobby Orr is the most accomplished contemporary hockey player and, perhaps, the best of all time. Although he plays defense for the Boston Bruins, Orr has led the National Hockey League in scoring twice (1970, 1975). He won the Hart Trophy as the

NHL's most valuable player three years in a row (1970, 1971, 1972) and won the James Norris (best defenseman) Trophy a record eight years in a row, from 1968 through 1975. He won the Calder (rookie) Trophy and has been a First Team All-Star defenseman since 1968.

Some historians insist that Bruins' defenseman Eddie Shore, Canadiens' center Howie Morenz, Red Wings' right wing Gordie Howe, and Black Hawks' left wing Bobby Hull were better players than Orr. But only Hull and Howe were contemporaries of Orr and many experts give the nod to Orr.

"Howe could do everything but not at top speed," said Bruins' managing director Harry Sinden. "Hull went at top speed but couldn't do everything. Orr can do everything, and do it at top speed."

Whatever the critics' opinions, one fact is indisputable: Before Orr became a Bruin, the Boston franchise was buried at the bottom of the NHL. When he arrived, he helped turn it into a contending and eventually a Stanley Cup champion team. This was hardly surprising considering that major league scouts had touted him as a thoroughly unique skater and stickhandler before he had ever reached high school age in his native Parry Sound, a summer fishing resort town some three hours north of Toronto.

Orr was discovered by hockey professionals as a twelve-year-old playing in a midget hockey game in the Ontario town of Gananoque. At that time a professional team could gain control of a twelve-year-old simply by putting his name on a protected list.

Several Bruin officials were sitting in on the game at Gananoque, scouting two other players, but whenever they looked up, towheaded Bobby had control of the puck. The Bruins immediately drafted plans to keep young Orr within their system, and when he was fourteen he was signed to play for the Oshawa (Ontario) Generals of the strong Ontario Hockey Association's Junior A League. Although Orr was skating against older and stronger players, he was an almost immediate hit. By the time he was sixteen, his picture had appeared on the cover of *Maclean's,* the national magazine of Canada. It was already clear that Bobby Orr was the most remarkable young player to come along since Gordie Howe.

At the time, the Bruins were in last place. In order to soothe their disappointed fans, Boston officials began promoting Bobby. When he comes up, they said, the Bruins would be great again. He finally arrived at the Boston training camp in the autumn of 1966 when he was barely seventeen. "I was scared stiff," said Bobby. "I didn't know whether I could play in the NHL. And I was alone."

There was only one threat to Bobby's prospect of becoming the greatest hockey player ever. A seemingly insignificant knee injury became aggravated, and after two NHL seasons he underwent two operations. "It was the cartilage the first time," said Orr. "Then I think I came back a little too soon and the two bone surfaces rubbed together and the knee went all hairy on me. I don't think there's too much you can do to prevent it. I think everyone will say the same thing. If you get hit, there's nothing you can do.''

The second operation was completed before the 1968–69 season, and there was serious concern in Boston that Orr might never be fit to skate normally again. When he arrived in training camp, the knee bothered him so much that he was ordered off the ice. In time, however, he returned, and with each week the knee grew stronger and stronger. It was so strong in the 1969–70 season that Orr was able to play the entire seventy-six-game schedule, as well as the lengthy playoffs, without missing a game.

Orr's popularity has never been equalled by any other hockey star. Boston writers said he had become the most popular athlete in the city's history, far outdistancing Ted Williams. His fan mail was staggering. Some days he received over 300 letters.

From time to time thoughtful hockey writers attempt to put Orr in perspective by comparing him with immortals from other sports. The easiest analogy is Babe Ruth, but Robert Markus, the Chicago *Tribune* columnist, argues that Orr isn't a home-run hitter in the Ruthian tradition, but more like Joe DiMaggio. "Orr," said Markus, "is a stylish, graceful athlete who does everything extremely well, much in the manner of DiMaggio."

Some observers insist that for all Orr's superhuman efforts he has received special treatment from referees throughout the league. Chicago Black Hawks' coach Billy Reay, for one, has said that officials have been giving Orr too much credit for his "Academy Award performances."

According to Reay's theory, Orr frequently takes "dives" to inspire referees to whistle penalties against the opposition. "It's brutal what Orr gets away with," said Reay. "One of my players will hardly touch him and Orr will go down."

Although Orr continued to dominate the NHL scene through the 1974–75 season because of his offensive contributions, his weaknesses defensively and in the area of public relations became dramatized. Despite Orr and his high-scoring teammate, Phil Esposito, the Bruins were unable to overtake the Buffalo Sabres in the regular season race for first in the NHL Adams Division. And in the playoffs a weaker Chicago Black Hawks' club wiped out the Bruins in the opening round. Orr himself admitted that his much-operated-upon knees had braked his skating ability and there was considerable question just how long he could last as the dominant athlete in big-league hockey.

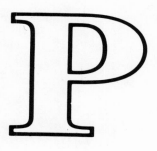

WILFRED (WILF) PAIEMENT

BORN: Earlton, Ontario, October 16, 1955
POSITION: Right Wing, Kansas City Scouts, 1974–

The first selection of the Scouts in the 1974 amateur draft was eighteen-year-old Wilf Paiement. A younger brother of former NHLer Rosaire Paiement, Wilf was "the highest paid amateur to enter the NHL," according to his attorney, Alan Eagleson. The right wing scored 50 goals and added 73 assists in his final junior season before becoming a star with Kansas City. Paiement finished his rookie year in Kansas City (1974–75) with a respectable 26 goals and 13 assists.

JAMES JOSEPH (JIM) PAPPIN

BORN: Sudbury, Ontario, September 10, 1939
POSITION: Right Wing, Toronto Maple Leafs, 1963–68; Chicago Black Hawks, 1968–75; California Seals, 1975–

Jim Pappin is big and startlingly fast and took a long time to come into full-blown maturity. He turned pro in 1959–60, bounced for years between Toronto and the minors, and was traded to Chicago in 1968 for Pierre Pilote.

Eventually Pappin was put on right wing with Pit Martin at center and Dennis Hull in the left slot and the trio clicked beautifully—witness Pappin goal totals of 41 and 32 in 1973 and 1974, respectively.

Pappin is quiet, even gruff, around the press, so he enjoys very little comment on his prowess, and whenever he can, he flies his own plane away from the critical eye of the media. He was traded to California in June 1975.

Jim Pappin

BERNARD MARCEL (BERNIE) PARENT

BORN: Montreal, Quebec, April 3, 1945
POSITION: Goalie, Boston Bruins, 1965–67; Philadelphia Flyers, 1967–71, 1973– ; Toronto Maple Leafs, 1971–72; Philadelphia Blazers (WHA), 1972–73
AWARDS: Vezina Trophy, 1974 (shared with Chicago's Tony Esposito), 1975; Conn Smythe Trophy, 1974, 1975; All-Star (Second Team), 1969, (First Team), 1974, 1975; (WHA, Second Team), 1973

He crouches slightly at the waist. The hamlike trapper's mitt hangs off his left hand, expectantly ready to snare the flying chunk of black rubber flak. Behind the white perforated mask, his eyes are riveted to the puck. Rarely do they ever lose sight of it, even at speeds of up to 130 miles per hour.

The human rubber radar machine is none other than Bernie Parent of the Philadelphia Flyers, who has climbed to the top rung as one of the best goaltenders in the National Hockey League, if not the world. Thanks to the French Canadian from Montreal, the Flyers finished first in the West Division in 1974, first in the Lester Patrick Division in 1975, and then marched triumphantly to the Stanley Cup both years.

"Bernie," said Flyers' captain Bobby Clarke, "is the most valuable player in all of hockey."

Nobody in Pennsylvania will deny that. Playing in 73 out of 78 regular season games in 1973–74—more than any other NHL goalie—Parent produced a dazzling 1.89 goals-against average, best in the league. Unfortunately for Bernie, the Vezina Trophy is a team award and both the Flyers and Chicago Black Hawks finished with identical 2.10 goals-against averages (Bobby Taylor

Bernie Parent

played seven games for Philadelphia and compiled a 4.26 average). Consequently, there was a Vezina tie.

Parent made up for that in the 1974 playoffs. While Chicago's Tony Esposito and his Black Hawks were bombed out of the semifinals by Boston, Bernie was virtually flawless in the Flyers' goal.

In the sixth and final game of the last round against Boston, Parent shut out the high-scoring Bruins, 1–0, and won the Conn Smythe Trophy as the most valuable player in the Stanley Cup playoffs. It was a remarkable comeback, considering that only a year earlier Parent had been playing for the World Hockey Association's Philadelphia Blazers and quit that club during the playoffs because of contract problems. The Blazers eventually moved to Vancouver while Bernie returned to the NHL and the Flyers, for whom he had played previously. Only this time he had a new coach in Fred Shero and fans who weren't exactly sure, at first, about welcoming him back.

"I really didn't know how good Bernie was," said Shero. "I only coached against him six or seven times in the Central League and I'd seen him on TV a few times. Whenever I had played against him, my team always beat him pretty badly. But I wanted to get a reading on him, you know, to feel him out. So I invited him over to the house and we spoke."

Shero told him: "The thing you've got to remember is that you live here now, and you'll have a lot of extra pressure. You're going to have some games when they're going to boo you. But if you're good, you don't have to worry about that for long."

The decisive moment occurred on opening night in October 1973 against the

Toronto Maple Leafs at Philadelphia's Spectrum. Parent had also played for Toronto and openly criticized the city at the time. Now the Maple Leafs were out for revenge. However, they didn't accomplish much. Nothing, in fact. The Flyers scored twice and Parent shut out the Leafs. "I had no choice," Bernie recalled. "I knew I had to produce real early to take off the pressure. That shutout took 500 pounds off my shoulders."

If it were possible, Parent improved as the season progressed. He compiled twelve shutouts, just three shy of a league record, and displayed the dexterity that reminded seasoned observers of the goaltending master, Jacques Plante. This was less than surprising since it was the very same Plante who had taken Bernie under his wing when they alternated in goal for the Maple Leafs.

"We had pretty much the same styles," said Parent. "But, gee, Plante was forty-four years old. I watched him play and I watched everything he did, how he handled himself on shots. And whatever he was doing, I tried to do."

Bernie also developed a sense of humor. After leading the Flyers to four straight victories, including the opening night shutout and another whitewashing, he told a writer: "I'm really mad. My average is all the way up to 1.00!" And when Parent was asked about his gray hair, he shot back: "Hell, what do you think, I've been married five years, you know."

Bernie's biggest smile, of course, was reserved for that moment on May 19, 1974 when the final buzzer sounded at the Spectrum and the Flyers had beaten Boston four games to two for the Cup, a feat duplicated in 1975 against the Buffalo Sabres. "When I was a boy," Parent remembered, "I used to watch so many great Montreal teams win the Cup. In my mind I would try to figure out what the feeling would be like to win it."

Bernie finally got his chance when he and Flyers' captain Clarke cradled the ancient silver mug in their arms during the traditional postgame rites.

"Winning the Cup is not like I thought it would be," Parent explained. "It is better than I thought it would be. It's a feeling you can't describe. I'll never forget this feeling; it will always be with me. So many guys play hockey and never win the Cup. I feel sorry for anyone who never experiences what I'm feeling."

That good feeling is shared by Philadelphians who summed up their reaction to their favorite goalie by buying thousands of bumper stickers with the apt description: ONLY THE LORD SAVES MORE THAN BERNIE PARENT!

JEAN-PAUL PARISE

BORN: Smooth Rock Falls, Ontario, December 11, 1941
POSITION: Left Wing, Boston Bruins, 1965–67; Toronto Maple Leafs, 1967; Minnesota North Stars, 1967–75; New York Islanders, 1975–
AWARDS: Team Canada (NHL), 1972

In 1967 J. P. Parise became a well-traveled gentleman without moving a muscle. Drafted by the nascent Oakland Seals from the Boston Bruins in the expansion draft, he was sold to the Maple Leafs as the season started and, after one game in the Queen City, he was sold to the new Minnesota North Stars, where he became an important fixture on left wing for seven years.

Parise is a digger, keeping the puck alive in the corners and working it to his mates in front of the net. These scrambling abilities earned Parise a berth on the 1972 Team Canada.

In January 1975, Parise again proved that he was good trade bait, when the North Stars shipped him off to the New York Islanders with Jude Drouin, for Ernie Hicke and Doug Rombough. Parise and Drouin were instrumental in gaining the Isles their first playoff shot in a mere three years of existence, with J. P. collecting 23 goals and 32 assists during the regular season. And it was Parise and Drouin again who sparked the team astoundingly into the semifinals against the Flyers, where they went the full seven games before succumbing.

DOUGLAS BRADFORD (BRAD) PARK

BORN: Toronto, Ontario, July 6, 1948
POSITION: Defenseman, New York Rangers, 1968–
AWARDS: All-Star (First Team), 1970, 1972, 1974; (Second Team),
1971, 1973

Brad Park plays the game precisely the way it was meant to be played—hard but clean. He has perfected the "submarine bodycheck," with which he thrusts his hip into the path of onrushing opponents and catapults them upside down to the hard ice. The check, rare in contemporary hockey, is a throwback to the days when the game was slower and defensemen had considerably more time to plan such devastating, yet clean maneuvers.

Park's submarine checks are not feared more than his fists. When suitably provoked, he has retaliated with a barrage of lefts and rights that usually guarantees him no less than a draw and often a victory over his enemies. During the 1971–72 season, when the Boston Bruins were intimidating most of the Rangers, it was Park who virtually single-handedly took on the bruising Bruins, whipping Ted Green and Johnny McKenzie and fighting awesome Bobby Orr to a draw.

Park made it to the NHL in 1968 with the New York Rangers. It was then that his toughness received its supreme test from the greatest hockey player of them all, Gordie Howe.

During a game late in the 1968–69 season at Olympia Stadium in Detroit, Howe tried to circle around Park in the Rangers' zone. Brad crouched low and crunched his six feet and 190 pounds into the Detroit player's stomach. "I was told to go low on the man,'' said Park, ''because if I went high I might get the stick in the mouth.''

It was a textbook bodycheck, hard but clean, and Howe was deftly removed from the play. Unfortunately for Park, he still was young and naive about the ways and means of the NHL jungle. He assumed that Howe would respect a clever body block and quietly congratulate Park for his talent.

Brad innocently watched the puck move out of his zone and conspicuously failed to notice Howe rise from his fallen state and skate back toward the action. Suddenly, with the ease a tribesman might use in felling an animal with a machete, Howe deposited Park on the ice with his stick. ''He hit Brad so fast and so hard,'' said Win Elliot, who was handling the Rangers' telecast that night, ''that hardly anybody knew what had happened and who had done it.''

The Rangers knew. And once Park was revived with trainer Frank Paice's smelling salts, he realized what had happened. ''Howe,'' Park later related, ''got me in the neck. *Pfwoop!* Like that, with his stick.'' At that point most rookies would have left well enough alone and given the menacing Howe a wide berth. But Park is tough. He took a direct line to the Detroit ace. ''One more move like that,'' Park snapped, ''and I'll shove this stick down your throat.''

The Park vs. Boston war lasted through the 1972 Ranger-Bruin Stanley Cup final. Whenever possible such heavyweight Bruins as Wayne Cashman, Ken Hodge, and Carol Vadnais singled Brad out for punishment. He took it well and dished it out, too, once even fighting Bobby Orr to a draw at center ice. But Brad couldn't do it alone, and the Bruins overwhelmed him and the Rangers to sweep the 1972 Cup series in six games.

It was regarded as one of the most intensely bitter series ever played. Yet only seconds after the final buzzer had sounded, the man leading the Rangers' handshaking parade to the Bruins was none other than the skater Boston hated the most, Brad Park.

Heading the handshaking lineup was, perhaps, one of the most difficult moves of his life. He was torn between his natural urge as a hard-but-clean sportsman and his withering hatred for the team which had just beaten him. ''I said what I thought about the Bruins in my book,'' Park concluded, ''but you can't spit on them because they won!''

During the 1973–74 season Park led all the Rangers in scoring, but they finished third in the NHL's East Division and were wiped out of the Stanley Cup semifinal round after a brutal series with the Philadelphia Flyers. Philadelphia's Mean Machine singled out Park for considerable punishment. Leading the Flyers' assault was the superaggressive Dave Schultz, who dealt Brad several lumps—not all of them legal. Park fought back nobly but, when the series had ended, he stuck by his philosophy that hockey can be played tough but clean. ''The way to stop Schultz is simple,'' Brad concluded. ''Take one swing with your stick and take his head off.

"I thought about it a couple of times and I made a decision. I decided that if I have to maim somebody to win the Stanley Cup, I don't want to win it!"

In the summer of 1974 Park was named captain of the Rangers.

GEORGE PARSONS. See TRUSHINSKI BYLAW.

FRANK PATRICK

BORN: Ottawa, Ontario, December 21, 1885
DIED: June 29, 1960
POSITION: Defenseman, Montreal Victorias (CAHL), 1904; Westmount (CAHL), 1905; Montreal Victorias (ECAHA), 1908; Renfrew Millionaires (NHA), 1910; Vancouver Millionaires (PCHA), 1912–18; Vancouver Millionaires (WCHL), 1925; Coach, Boston Bruins, 1934–36
AWARDS: Hockey Hall of Fame, 1958

Less publicized than his brother, Lester "the Silver Fox" Patrick, Frank was nonetheless as influential in his way. There are twenty-two pieces of legislation in the NHL Rule Book which Frank proposed, including the origination of the blue line.

Frank Patrick was an excellent defenseman, starring first with McGill University and later for the Renfrew Millionaires with brother Lester.

The Patricks moved West to Nelson, British Columbia, where they began their own league and built arenas for all the teams—how's that for starting from the ground up? They were so successful that they bagged the Stanley Cup in 1915, but they later sold their players to the NHL.

A Hall of Famer, Frank Patrick later coached Boston and managed the Canadiens prior to his death in 1960.

FREDERICK MURRAY "MUZZ" PATRICK

BORN: Victoria, British Columbia, June 28, 1916
POSITION: Defenseman, New York Rangers, 1937–41, 1945–46; Coach, New York Rangers, 1954–55; General Manager, New York Rangers, 1955–64

One of the two hockey-playing sons of former Rangers' manager Lester Patrick, "Muzz" was an exceptional athlete who at one time was a six-day bike racer, basketball star, a heavyweight boxer of repute, not to mention the first NHL player to enlist in the armed forces at the start of World War II. Like his older brother, Lynn, Muzz was under heavy pressure when his father promoted him to the NHL club late in the 1937–38 season. He was twenty-two years old, huge, but clumsier on skates than Lynn.

Muzz was paired with Art Coulter and the two gave the Rangers one of the game's toughest backline corps. Patrick soon refined his style and also acted as the team's policeman. His classic bout on ice was against Boston Bruins' badman Eddie Shore. It happened when Shore had picked on Rangers' center Phil Watson one night at Madison Square Garden. Muzz came to the rescue and wasted Shore with a flurry of punches.

After World War II, Muzz turned to managing hockey clubs in the minors and also coaching. He returned to New York as coach in 1954–55 and then manager, 1955–56, succeeding Frank Boucher. He remained manager until October 1964 when he was pushed "upstairs" at the Garden to make way for Emile Francis, Muzz's former assistant.

LESTER "THE SILVER FOX" PATRICK

BORN: Drummondville, Quebec, December 30, 1883
DIED: June 1, 1960
POSITION: Rover, Defenseman, and Goalie, Westmount (CAHL), 1905; Montreal Wanderers (ECAHA), 1906–07; Renfrew Millionaires (NHA), 1910; Victoria Aristocrats (PCHA), 1912–16, 1919–26; Spokane (PCHA), 1917; Seattle Metropolitans (PCHA), 1918; New York Rangers, 1927–28; Coach, New York Rangers, 1926–39
AWARDS: All-Star Coach, 1931–36, 1938; Hockey Hall of Fame, 1945; trophy for outstanding service to hockey in United States named in his honor in 1966; division of NHL named in his honor, 1974

No single individual contributed more to the improvement of professional hockey on every level—playing, coaching, managing, and operating—than Lester Patrick. Dubbed "the Silver Fox" because of his shock of gray hair and his uncanny foxiness in dealing with opponents, Lester was born in Drummondville, Quebec. He and his brother Frank moved to Montreal when Lester was ten years old, and it was there that the Silver Fox mastered the game.

Lester could play any position from goalie to defenseman to rover. The latter position was an integral part of the seven-man game of hockey. A rover could play forward or defense, and Lester did both with equal agility. A natural athlete, he eventually played for the McGill University team in Montreal.

Frank and Lester were both competent enough to move on to the professional ranks. They skated for such respected teams as Westmount, Montreal, and Brandon, each season enhancing their reputations as high-grade pros. When the Canadian millionaire Martin J. O'Brien decided to place a National Hockey

Association team in Renfrew, Ontario, O'Brien offered the Patricks $3,000 apiece to skate for the new club and they accepted.

Even then, while playing professionally and making a good living, Lester concentrated on the administrative end of the game. His ambition was to operate his own team and his own league, while continuing to play. His dream was realized in 1911 when his father, Joseph Patrick, a millionaire lumberman, retired. With their father's financial support, Lester and Frank organized the Pacific Coast Hockey League.

Their base of operation was Victoria, British Columbia, the most British of all of Canada's cities. Lester had his cake and ate it, too. He not only helped run the PCHL but also played for Victoria, and later Spokane and Seattle before returning to play, coach, and manage in Victoria again, while also operating the league and overseeing its growth.

Cyclone Taylor, Maurice Richard, and Lester Patrick

His goals were manifold. He believed that it was necessary to erect new arenas that offered artificial ice plants. He realized that it was necessary, if the PCHL was to gain major league recognition, to have his champions compete for the Stanley Cup with the Eastern representatives and he knew that it was necessary for him to continue playing as long as he maintained a high standard of ability and continued to lure people to his rinks. Thus, Lester was at once player, developer, and entrepreneur through the start of the Roarin' Twenties. His earliest successes, however, were in Victoria where he and Frank built Canada's first artificial ice rink.

They soon built another rink in Vancouver and put franchises in Seattle, Spokane, Portland, Victoria, and Vancouver. By 1914 an East-West playoff for the Stanley Cup had begun, and the Patricks had reached the pinnacle in big-league hockey.

In 1924, at the age of forty-two, Lester coached and managed the Victoria Cougars to a Stanley Cup triumph over the Montreal Canadiens, three games to one. In the same year NHL franchises were awarded to the Montreal Maroons and the Boston Bruins, and a year later to the Pittsburgh Pirates and New York Americans. Patrick realized he couldn't match the salaries the big-time eastern moguls were offering players. He knew that the time of the Pacific Coast League had ended, so he sold his entire roster to the new owners in the East and planned to retire and move to California.

After nineteen consecutive years managing and frequently playing hockey, Lester Patrick was ready to take a vacation. Then Conn Smythe walked out on the Rangers and Lester was called. He took the first available train east, and the new era in hockey for New York City had begun.

Patrick labored for thirteen seasons behind the Ranger bench, dominating the annual balloting for coach of the year. In fact, from the time that honor was first started in 1930, Patrick was named to the prestigious post seven of the first eight years.

"There's more to coaching a hockey club than standing behind the bench," Patrick would say. "That's almost the least important phase of the job— watching your men when a game is in progress. It is incumbent upon you initially to build up their morale and then maintain it, and before you can do that you must have acquired their confidence in your judgment and you must know the man.

"When it comes to teaching hockey to my young men," Patrick continued, "I say as little as possible and avoid blackboards and diagrams. I've seen a lot of players in this league who've been blackboarded half to death so that when they go on the ice they're completely befuddled and the simplest plays hold terrors for them."

Lester proceded to illustrate. "Once I had a fellow on this club who made a simple play wrong for three years," he recalled.

"One night in a tight game he made it right and it won the game for us. Afterwards, in the dressing room he said to me: 'Now I've got it. I wouldn't have believed that anybody could be as stupid as I've been.'

" 'Never mind about that,' I said. 'Now that you know how to make the play, keep making it that way.' "

But without a doubt, Patrick's finest hour as a coach came during the 1928 Stanley Cup playoffs when the Rangers were facing the powerhouse Montreal Maroons in the final round. The Montrealers were highly favored in the series and to make matters worse, Madison Square Garden was unavailable to the Blueshirts because of the annual New York appearance of the circus. All the games of the best-of-five series were to be played in the unfriendly Montreal Forum.

The Maroons won the first game, 2–0, and all of Montreal was expecting a workmanlike, three-game Maroon sweep. Undaunted, the Rangers skated out to meet the Maroons in the second game. Early in the second period, with no score on the board, Nels Stewart, a dangerous Maroon forward, broke into the clear and unleashed a whizzing shot that caught the Ranger netminder, Lorne Chabot, squarely in the left eye.

With Chabot out of the game, surely now the Rangers were sunk. With no spare goaltender and the gloating Maroons refusing the Blueshirts the services of a major league netminder who was watching the game from the stands, all hope seemed to be lost. But in typical Patrick fashion, the forty-four-year-old Silver Fox stepped forward and strapped on the pads.

With the Rangers backchecking like fiends to protect their aging leader, Patrick preserved a 1–1 tie as the game went into sudden-death overtime. After seven nail-biting minutes of the extra frame, Ranger defenseman Ching Johnson, whipped a pass to Frank Boucher who put the puck past the Maroon goalie to win the game and tie the series at one game apiece.

Patrick's heroics in goal became an instant legend as the inspired Rangers rallied to win the Stanley Cup. Jim Burchard, a journalist with the New York *World-Telegram,* was so moved by Lester's heroics, he took pen in hand and inked the following commemorative poem:

> Twas in the spring of twenty-eight
> A golden Ranger page,
> That Lester got a summons
> To guard the Blueshirt cage.
>
> Chabot had stopped a fast one,
> A bad break for our lads,
> The Cup at stake—and no one
> To don the Ranger pads.
>
> "We're cooked," lamented Patrick,
> "This crisis I had feared."
> He leaned upon his newest crutch
> And wept inside his beard.
>
> Then suddenly he came to life,
> No longer halt or lame.
> "Give me the pads," he bellowed,
> "I used to play this game."
>
> Then how the Rangers shouted.
> How Patrick was acclaimed.
> Maroons stood sneering, gloating,
> They should have been ashamed.
>
> The final score was two to one.
> Old Lester met the test.
> The Rangers finally won the Cup,
> But Les has since confessed.
>
> "I just spoke up to cheer the boys,
> I must have been delirious.

But now, in reminiscence,
I'm glad they took me serious.''

With his goaltending days behind him, Patrick continued behind the Ranger bench until 1939 when he was succeeded by Frank Boucher. Patrick remained very much a part of hockey, staying on as general manager of the Rangers until 1946. He died in 1960.

LYNN PATRICK

BORN: Victoria, British Columbia, February 3, 1912
POSITION: Forward, New York Rangers, 1934–46; Coach, New York
   Rangers, 1949–50; Boston Bruins, 1950–54; Coach/General
   Manager, Boston Bruins, 1955–65; St. Louis Blues, 1966–67; St.
   Louis Blues, Executive Vice President, 1967–
AWARDS: All-Star (First Team), 1942; (Second Team), 1943

No hockey player ever faced more pressure in his major-league debut than Lynn Patrick, the eldest son of hockey patriarch Lester Patrick, manager of the New York Rangers. Lester had managed the Blueshirts ever since the team's inception, but never faced a more difficult decision than during training camp in the fall of 1934, when Lynn seemed good enough to make the big team. Lester sensed that his twenty-two-year-old son was good enough to play left wing in the NHL, but he was anxious about charges of nepotism. Before making his decision, Lester consulted with two of the Rangers' older players, Bill Cook and Frank Boucher.

"We'd watched Lynn," Boucher recalled, "and told Lester his son had a lot to learn but we believed he'd eventually help us."

Lynn's start was modest—nine goals and 13 assists in 48 games—during his rookie year, but he showed noticeable improvement every season thereafter. In the 1937–38 season Lynn played left wing on a line with center Phil Watson and Bryan Hextall, comprising what was to be one of the best lines in NHL history. During the 1941–42 season Lynn was named First Team All-Star left winger and helped the Rangers win the Stanley Cup in 1940.

His last big season was 1942–43 before a stint in the armed forces. He returned to the Rangers in 1945–46, but lacked the speed and finally decided to retire. Like his brother Muzz, Lynn turned to coaching and in 1949–50 he directed the Rangers to the Stanley Cup finals, losing to the Red Wings in the second sudden-death overtime period of the seventh game.

A season later, Lynn "jumped" to the Bruins where he continued his success behind the bench. In time he became manager and eventually moved to the administrative chambers of the St. Louis Blues where he has remained since 1967–68, the first year of NHL expansion.

MARTIN NICHOLAS (MARTY) "BLACKIE" PAVELICH

BORN: Sault Ste. Marie, Ontario, November 6, 1927
POSITION: Forward, Detroit Red Wings, 1947–57

When the Red Wings' juggernaut ran over the opposition during the early fifties, Ted Lindsay and Gordie Howe captured most of the headlines among the Detroit forwards. But just as vital was defensive forward Marty Pavelich. Wings' manager Jack Adams knew it all the time. "Pavelich," said Adams, "was one of the four key men around whom we built our hockey club."

Marty came to Detroit via the Red Wings' junior affiliate in Galt, Ontario. He played 41 games during the 1947–48 NHL season and remained a Red Wing regular through his final year, 1956–57. During that period Pavelich played on four Stanley Cup winners. "His scoring records never stood out," said Adams, "but he always had the toughest jobs—checking the great scoring right wings such as Maurice Richard. We practically had to put handcuffs on him to keep him off the ice." Pavelich, otherwise known as "Blackie," later became a business partner in Detroit with former teammate Ted Lindsay. "Pavelich," Adams concluded, "was a real man and a real hockey player, one of the most popular ever to play in Detroit."

MARCEL PELLETIER

BORN: Drummondville, Quebec, December 6, 1927
POSITION: Goalie, Chicago Black Hawks, 1950–51; New York Rangers, 1962–63

Drummondville, Quebec's contribution to high-grade hockey humor and medium-grade goaltending is Marcel Pelletier who graduated from the Kitchener-Waterloo Flying Dutchmen senior team to the pros in 1949 and has been titillating hockey people and fans ever since. Pelletier never was a very good goalie, but he never was bad and generally played a competent game; good enough to win two big-league trials. The Black Hawks had him up for six games in 1950–51 when Chicago had a lamentable team. He gave up 29 goals for a 4.83 average and returned to the minors. By 1962 he had moved to the Rangers' sphere of influence and was imported for two games during the 1962–63 campaign. Marcel allowed but four goals for a handsome 2.00 average.

The Rangers, unfortunately, had no room for him so Marcel returned to the minors, but also acted the gregarious big-leaguer in every other respect. His monologues, sprinkled with a French accent, made Pelletier a veritable hockey troubadour. He became the Philadelphia Flyers' scout and goaltending advisor in 1967 and has been with them ever since.

PENALTIES

There are five classifications: (a) minor penalties, (b) bench minor penalties, (c) misconduct penalties, (d) match penalties, (e) penalty shot.

(a) A minor penalty calls for the guilty party(ies) to serve two minutes' playing time in the sin bin and can be called on any player or players, including the goalie. (However, if a goalie is called, a substitute may sit out his penalty.)

The most common minor penalties are checking into the boards, charging, high-sticking, holding, hooking, interference, kneeing, and, most common of all, tripping.

The following are less common but more vicious fouls for which a minor penalty is served:

Butt-ending. The art of unobtrusively jamming the blunt top of one's stick through one's glove opening and into an opponent's ribs. It is especially effective in close combat along the boards.

Cross-checking. An obvious blow—usually to the head—delivered with both hands about a foot apart on the stick, and no part of the stick on the ice.

Elbowing. The most useful jawbreaker, delivered with a hammerlike sideways thrust of the elbow to the face. It is most frequently and easily executed along the boards.

Pitchforking. A faked backhand shot during which the shooter deliberately misses the puck in order to follow through and "accidentally" clout his foe anywhere from the groin to the forehead. It can be fatal.

Skate-kicking. The most subtle and agonizing maneuver, delivered along the boards by pulling an enemy's skates out from under him, thereby rendering him horizontal on the ice.

Slashing. A two-handed swing, although one-handed variations also exist. In extreme cases it resembles a baseball swing for the fences, against an opponent's head. It is also used against shoulders, hips, legs, and ankles.

Spearing. The act of digging one's stick into an opponent's midsection. Due to the offensiveness of this foul, the referee can inflict either a minor (two minutes), a major (five), or even a match penalty on the guilty party.

(b) A bench minor penalty involves removal from the ice of a player of the team called for the penalty for a period of two minutes.

If, while a team is shorthanded by one or more minor or bench minor penalties, the opposing team scores, the first of such penalties shall automatically terminate. There is no exception. If a shorthanded team incurs a penalty shot against it, and the penalty shot succeeds, a player is sprung from the penalty box.

(c) A misconduct penalty is a 10-minute penalty, generally called against a player who becomes abusive in language or gesture. It puts him out for 10 minutes, but does not leave his team shorthanded. It is also accompanied by an automatic $25 fine against the offender.

(d) A match penalty means ejection from the game. It's levied for (a) deliberate attempt to injure, wherein a sub can be used after five minutes, or (b) deliberate injury to an opponent, calling for 10 minutes without replacement plus an automatic $100 fine.

(e) The penalty shot, seldom invoked, gives a player a clear shot at goal with only the goalie to defend. It's called chiefly when a player who has crossed the opposition's red line is fouled from behind (not from a side swipe), when he has a clear path to the goal. (See also **PENALTY SHOT.**)

At no time is a team asked to play shorthanded by more than two men, even if its penalty box is jammed to overflowing. There are, of course, separate penalty boxes for each side.

PENALTY KILLING

Penalty killing has recently become an art in the NHL and WHA. Blunting an opponent's power play has taken on added importance in these days of booming slapshots and artful tip-ins. Many people feel that neutralizing a team's man advantage situation leads directly to beating that club.

The most widely accepted manner in which a penalty is killed comes by use of "the box." Each of four men defensing the power play guards an area in a box formation in their zone. This helps negate the manpower edge. So does forcing the opponent into numerous passes without being able to work the puck closer to the goal.

A favorite tactic used by squads with excellent skaters and stickhandlers killing the penalty is the method of "ragging the puck." If able to control the disc some time during the penalty, the shorthanded team will give it to their best skater on ice, or will play "keepaway" by just holding the puck and skating in circles. Bobby Orr, Bobby Clarke, Walt Tkaczuk, and Peter Mahovlich are the masters of this technique.

PENALTY SHOT

Hockey's most exciting play is undoubtedly the penalty shot. A shot may be called for a variety of reasons, but mainly when one of the following occur:

1. The puck carrier is past the opposition's red line, clearly free, and moving in on the goaltender when he is hooked from directly behind and brought down without being allowed to complete the play.

2. Someone other than the goaltender falls on the puck in the goal crease.

3. The goaltender intentionally throws his stick at the puck.

Penalty shots are rarely called by the referees, basically because most officials feel it is too drastic a measure that puts the goaltender at an unfair advantage. But recent statistics show that it is the netminder who holds the advantage.

In 1972–73, only two of eight shots were successful. The following season, just five of thirteen made their way into the net. Whether a penalty shot is successful or not, the two minutes assessed to the offender are not served. So it is just the shooter against the goalie, and since the man with the puck is allowed to skate only towards the goal, he must decide quickly his plan of attack and then take the one shot awarded him.

GILBERT PERREAULT

BORN: Victoriaville, Quebec, November 13, 1950
POSITION: Center, Buffalo Sabres, 1970–
AWARDS: Calder Trophy, 1971; Lady Byng Trophy, 1973

Hockey is far more than just a sport in the French-speaking province of Quebec, Canada. It is more like a religion. Stars such as Maurice "the Rocket" Richard, Jean Beliveau, and Bernie "Boom-Boom" Geoffrion have been worshipped as folk heroes.

Now, another name has been added to the list—Gilbert Perreault, the lyrical skater for the NHL's Buffalo Sabres and a man who has the most credentials to fill Beliveau's distinguished skates.

Obviously, it would not be easy for the 6–0, 195-pound Perreault. To join such ranks one must be more than merely a point-getter. Nobody knows that better than Beliveau himself. "Among French Canadians," said Beliveau, "there is a lot of pride in our hockey playing. That has been our game. Now many eyes are turning to Perreault. There's no doubt that he can become a great leader and everybody in our province will be proud."

In only four NHL seasons, Perreault has won both the Calder and Lady Byng trophies and almost immediately took over as leader of Buffalo's hockey club. He is an example of what scoring finesse is all about. "He's always tempting you to go for the puck," said Boston superman Bobby Orr. "His head and shoulders will be going one way and his legs are going the other way and the puck is doing something else."

In that sense, Perreault most resembles Beliveau when Jean was having his finest years with the Montreal Canadiens. "Like Beliveau," said Rangers' general manager Emile Francis, "Gil has all the moves and great range. There's no way to stop him if he's coming at you one-on-one."

Gil Perreault

Curiously, Perreault *was* stopped during the 1973–74 season, but by one of his own teammates. In a game against the New York Islanders at Buffalo's Auditorium, defenseman Mike Robitaille fell on Perreault and fractured Gil's left ankle. As a result, Perreault missed twenty-three games and finished the season with a rather modest 18 goals and 33 assists for 51 points. Fortunately, his recovery was complete and he seemed the same or better in 1974–75 when he had his best season, with 39 goals and 57 assists for 96 points.

PHILADELPHIA FLYERS

Although hockey had proven a guaranteed moneymaker during the six-team NHL era nobody was absolutely certain how fans in the six new expansion cities would react to the ice sport. The trick, of course, was to produce a winner. So in 1967 the Philadelphia Flyers' hierarchy went about the business of putting together a first-rate front office with which to build a winning team.

Bill Putnam, vice-president of Morgan Guaranty Trust Company, became president of the hockey club. Putnam hired Norman ''Bud'' Poile, a veteran minor league manager, to manage the Flyers. The burly, often outspoken Poile, designated slick-haired Keith Allen, a long-time minor league coach, to run the Flyers behind the bench.

Edward M. Snider, by this time the Flyers' majority stockholder, and Bill Putnam jetted to Montreal in June 1967 for the draft. They returned with two first-rate young goaltenders, Bernie Parent and Doug Favell, and a defensive and offensive roster that appeared as good as or better than any of the other expansion clubs.

Philadelphians had an opportunity to see the Flyers in person for the first time on October 19, 1967. There were 7,812 spectators in the Spectrum, not exactly a capacity crowd in the 14,558-seat arena.

The Flyers made the night a success by defeating the Pittsburgh Penguins, 1–0. After becoming playoff contenders their first season, the Flyers fell into limbo until the 1972–73 season.

Then, in a matter of two years the Philadelphia Flyers enjoyed one of sportdom's rare metamorphoses. Once the patsies of big league hockey, the Flyers suddenly have emerged as (a) the most controversial; (b) the most hated; (c) the most respected; and (d) the most colorful team since the Big Bad Bruins of 1970, and maybe even more so.

Stanley Cup winners in 1974—the first expansion club to do it—and 1975, the Flyers were amazing, from owner Ed Snider to their iconoclastic coach, Fred Shero, to their diabetic superstar, captain Bobby Clarke. More than anything, though, the Flyers, reputation has been built on sock. "If you keep the opposition on their behinds," said Shero, "they don't score goals."

During the 1973–74 campaign, the Flyers spent a staggering 1,750 minutes in the penalty box, which is astonishing, considering that no other team ever topped 1,400 minutes. Unbelievably they topped themselves in 1975, with 1,951 minutes, or almost 40 percent of a season in the penalty box. Fortunately, the Flyers have been able to succeed in spite of their extreme zeal and penchant for penalties because they also own the very best goaltender in hockey—Bernie Parent, 1975 winner of the Conn Smythe Trophy as top playoff performer.

TOM PHILLIPS

BORN: Kenora, Ontario, May 22, 1880
DIED: December 5, 1923
POSITION: Left Wing, Montreal Victorias (CAHL), 1903; Toronto Marlboros (OHA), 1904; Rat Portage Thistles (OHA), 1905; Kenora Thistles (MHL), 1907; Ottawa Senators (ECAHA), 1908; Vancouver Millionaires (PCHA), 1912
AWARDS: Hockey Hall of Fame, 1945

Tom Phillips, a talented left winger who finished his career scoring almost two goals per game, played in six Stanley Cup series over his spotty, six-season tour of duty.

A restless, nomadic-type player, Tom saw action with seven different teams.

He was in the right place at the right time in 1907, though, as his Kenora squad wrested the Stanley Cup from the Wanderers. Tom saw action in six playoff games that season, lighting the goal lamp thirteen times.

He dropped out of hockey after the 1908 season, but came back for one last hurrah with the 1912 Vancouver team. He is a member of the Hockey Hall of Fame.

PHOENIX ROADRUNNERS

When the World Hockey Association decided to expand following the 1973–74 season, one of the logical places to go was Phoenix, Arizona. The Phoenix hockey fans had been entertained by the Western Hockey League Roadrunners, and had built up strong fan support, so WHA officials figured that the city would be able to support a major league franchise.

Club president William McFarland, a past player, coach, and manager, as well as a past president of the Western Hockey League, went on a coast-to-coast safari searching for the best players available for the club. Many of them were holdovers from the old WHL team, like forwards Bob Barlow, Michel Cormier, Murray Keogan, and Howie Young. In addition, the Runners were able to draft youngsters from the colleges and amateur ranks like highly touted Cam Connor and Dennis Sobchuk.

With Gary Kurt and Jack Norris, both former NHLers, sharing the goaltending chores, Phoenix ran surprisingly well in their first season (1974–75) in the World Hockey Association.

ALLAN W. PICKARD

One of the builders of hockey in Western Canada, Allan Pickard was originally from Exeter, Ontario, where he played his hockey.

In Regina, Saskatchewan, Pickard helped start the ''Aces,'' a senior club of which he was later coach and president. He later presided over the Saskatchewan Amateur Hockey Association, where he watched the likes of Elmer Lach and the Bentley brothers on their way to the NHL; and played the same role for the CAHA in 1947, 1948, and 1949. He was elected to the Hockey Hall of Fame.

NICHOLAS (NICK) PIDSODNY

BORN: Hamilton, Ontario, February 9, 1926
POSITION: Goalie, Buffalo (AHL), 1944–45; Dallas (USHL), 1945–46,
    1946–48; Oakland (PCHL), 1945–46; Houston (USHL), 1948–49

Colorful was an understatement for goalie Nick Pidsodny, a native of Hamilton, Ontario, who starred for several minor league teams in the post-World War II era. Earlier he had been especially brilliant with the Eastern (Amateur) League Baltimore Blades, and later with the New Haven Blades Nick enjoyed wandering far from his cage even when play threatened his goal.

ALFRED (ALF) PIKE

BORN: Winnipeg, Manitoba, September 15, 1917
POSITION: Forward, New York Rangers, 1939–47; Coach, New York
    Rangers, 1959–60

Not many major leaguers spend an entire career with a single team, but Alf Pike was one of them. The Winnipeg-born forward became a Ranger in 1939–40 and played every one of his eight seasons in Manhattan. He skated for the New York club that won the Prince of Wales Trophy (first place) in 1942 and was a key member of the Rangers' Stanley Cup-winning sextet in 1940.

Pike played his last season in 1946–47 and then turned to coaching where he was to help the Rangers even more as a molder of young hockey talent. As coach of the Guelph Biltmores in the Ontario Hockey Association Junior A League, Pike won the Memorial Cup in 1952, symbolic of the junior championship of all Canada. His products include Andy Bathgate, Harry Howell, Lou Fontinato, Ron Murphy, and Aldo Guidolin, to name a few.

Curiously, none of this would have happened had Pike not outwitted Rangers' manager Lester Patrick in the fall of 1939—with the complicity of then coach Frank Boucher. According to Boucher, this is what happened:

"He'd been an outstanding junior player in Winnipeg. I remember that a few days after he reported to training camp in the fall of 1939 he and Lester got bogged down on contract negotiations. When Alf told me that the difference was $500 I told him that if Lester didn't give it to him, I would. I was making $4500 then, but I was determined to succeed and was convinced Pike would help us. And so Alf went to Lester and told him he'd decided to sign. Lester was puzzled, naturally enough, and probed Pike to find out why the boy who'd been so stubborn had suddenly relented, and finally Alf admitted I'd said I'd give him the $500. Lester bawled the hell out of me for being soft, but my gamble—for it really had been that, I suppose—paid off; Lester came up with the five hundred."

PIERRE PAUL PILOTE

BORN: Kenogami, Quebec, December 11, 1931
POSITION: Defenseman, Chicago Black Hawks 1955–68; Toronto
    Maple Leafs, 1968–69
AWARDS: James Norris Trophy, 1963–65; All-Star (First Team),
    1963–67; (Second Team), 1960–62; Hockey Hall of Fame, 1975

When the Chicago Black Hawks began their ascent from the depths, in the fifties, to respectability in the sixties, smallish defenseman Pierre Pilote was in a large part responsible, although teammates Bobby Hull, Stan Mikita, and Glenn Hall received most of the credit.

Pilote was effective defensively and offensively; he could hit and hurt and he could skate well and score. Before retiring after the 1968–69 season Pilote amassed 80 goals and 418 assists for 498 points in 890 games.

Pierre's credentials include First All-Star Team (five times), Second All-Star Team (three times), Norris Trophy (three), as well as the captaincy of the Black Hawks when they won the Stanley Cup in April 1961.

During Pilote's later years a bit of friction developed between the captain and outspoken stars such as Mikita. One of Pierre's dilemmas was that, as captain, he frequently had to deal with management and was unfairly labeled by some teammates "a company man." In June 1975 he was elected to the Hall of Fame.

DIDIER "CANNONBALL" PITRE

BORN: Sault Ste. Marie, Ontario, 1884
DIED: July 29, 1934
POSITION: Defenseman, Rover, and Right Wing, Ottawa Nationals
    (FAHL), 1904–05; Montreal Shamrocks (ECAHA), 1908; Montreal
    Canadiens (NHA), 1910–13, 1915–17; Vancouver Millionaires
    (PCHA), 1914; Montreal Canadiens, 1918–23
AWARDS: Hockey Hall of Fame, 1962

To the uninformed hockey fan, the Montreal Canadiens might have earned their flamboyant nickname of "the Flying Frenchmen" due to the heroics of the likes of Rocket Richard, Yvan Cournoyer, or Jacques Lemaire. And while this trio most assuredly qualifies as speedburners par excellence, the Habs first earned their illustrious handle back in 1910, thanks to the efforts of Didier Pitre and company.

Pitre, originally a defenseman in his first four seasons of big league hockey, was shifted to right wing when he joined his friend, Jack Laviolette, on the NHA's new entry, the Montreal Canadiens. Didier's eye-blurring rushes and booming wrist shots immediately earned him the nickname of "Cannonball" with the fans. And when the two speedsters teamed up on the same forward line—"Flying Frenchmen" was the only way to describe them. Obviously, the name stuck with that proud tradition still being lived up to today.

Pitre labored for thirteen seasons wearing the *bleu, blanc, et rouge,* taking one year off with the Vancouver Millionaires where he was used as a rover. In all, the speedy Didier saw action with three championship teams. He took part in four Stanley Cup playoffs and was on one Cup-winning squad.

In 1923, with his weight ballooning and his scoring coming on pure instinct, Pitre hung up his skates for good. He scored 240 goals over his long and illustrious career and is a member of the Hockey Hall of Fame. He was truly the original Flying Frenchman.

PITTSBURGH PENGUINS

Before the blue, black, and white jerseys of the 1967–68 NHL expansion team, the Pittsburgh Penguins, puffed laboriously on to the ice (the average age was thirty-two!), hockey was not an unknown quantity in that coal- and steel-producing metropolis.

The arrival of the NHL in Pittsburgh had, in fact, killed the AHL Hornets, who had just won the AHL title and the Calder Cup in 1966–67. The city wasn't happy with the name "Penguin" nor impressed with the prospect of seeing a bad team play the likes of Gordie Howe and Bobby Hull.

"I can see it now," expostulated then Penguin coach Red Sullivan. "The day after we play a bad game the sportswriters will say, 'They skated like a bunch of nuns.' " But the name stuck.

This wasn't the first arrival of the NHL in Pittsburgh, either. From the fall of 1925 through the 1929–30 season, the Pirates (the name taken from the National League baseball team) held forth, evolving in that short time from a playoff contender (1926 and 1928) to a basement dweller. Then in 1930–31 they were the Philadelphia Quakers and even more inept.

It is somewhat surprising that the Pirates performed as badly as they did, considering the talent they iced: Hall of Famer Roy "Shrimp" Worters in goal, Hib Milks, Harold Darragh, Lionel Conacher, Harold "Baldy" Cotton, Duke McCurry, Gerald Lowrey, Herb Drury, Tex White, Jesse Spring, and Odie Cleghorn as coach. Cleghorn was the first man to use three forward lines on short shifts, a procedure used to this day.

In the expansion draft of 1966–67, coach Sullivan and general manager Jack Riley went after experience, which resulted in the oldest club in the league, but Pittsburgh's hockey history explains their reasoning. "We won the Calder Cup last year," explained Riley, referring to the AHL Hornets. "Our fans don't want a building program; they're used to winners. We felt we had to put a quality product on the ice immediately. I am aware of some of the potential problems, but we tried to select players with pride—good competitors who will go all out.''

Three crucial draftees were Earl Ingarfield, Ken Schinkel, and former All-Star Andy Bathgate. They had all been Rangers, where Sullivan himself had played and coached. Incredibly, the Penguin team ended up looking like a geriatric clinic for ex-Rangers: defensemen Al MacNeil, Noel Price, and Dunc McCallum; forwards Val Fonteyne, Mel Pearson, Billy Dea, Art Stratton, Paul Andrea, and George Konik had also been, or were until traded for, Rangers. To this Blueshirt refugee camp were added wingers Ab McDonald, Bob Dillabough, and Keith McCreary from Detroit, Boston, and Montreal, and defenseman Leo Boivin from Detroit.

Pittsburgh had already made some acquisitions from the minor league Cleveland Barons: Ted Lanyon, Dick Mattiussi, and Bill Speer on defense and Les Binkley in goal. In the first training camp a four-way battle developed for netminder honors between Binkley, a former trainer who started goaltending at the late age of twenty-five; rookie Joe Daley; ex-Hornet Hank Bassen; and Marv Edwards out of the amateur ranks. Binkley, seconded by Bassen, took over the nets.

Pittsburgh's first season was streaky, and they finished out of the playoffs. Major changes took place before the team's sophomore season: Ab McDonald was traded, veteran Lou Angotti was acquired; two forwards from Oakland—Charlie Burns and Wally Boyer—arrived. They even tried to balance all that age with young minor leaguers Jean Pronovost (forward) and defenseman John Arbour. Then, in training camp, Hank Bassen announced his retirement and Bathgate, who had staged a remarkable comeback with the Penguins, walked out. It wasn't until 1970 that Pittsburgh earned its first playoff berth, when they lasted until the semifinal round against St. Louis.

While fans gradually came around and began to fill more of those yawning seats in the Civic Arena, there were rumors that the franchise would be sold to the backers of the Atlanta Braves' baseball team and moved, or even to Avon cosmetics and moved. Instead, a group of Michigan investors took over the Penguins, retaining Jack E. McGregor, a young Pennsylvania state senator, as president. McGregor, along with attorney Peter Block, had originally assembled the local group of backers. Most important, the franchise would stay in Pittsburgh. In the 1970s, Peter Block was to return, forming a group which bought the franchise back from the failing Michigan outfit. None of these behind-the-scenes machinations helped the stability of the team nor the response of the fans, of course.

Considering the uneasy ownership and inability to gain a playoff berth, the managing and coaching positions went much as you might expect—in circles. Riley lasted a long while as general manager, until he was kicked into scouting in 1974–75. Coach Red Sullivan was replaced by Red Kelly, who, in 1972, was fired and replaced by player Ken Schinkel. Schinkel was replaced by Marc Boileau in 1974–75. Assistant general manager Jack Button became general manager when Riley was put to pasture.

On the ice the Penguins tried to replace age with youth in the forms of Syl Apps, Jr., Bryan Hextall, Jr., Greg Polis, and Rich Kehoe. They also continued their penchant for Rangers—first trading for oldie defenseman Tim Horton (who later went to Buffalo before being killed in a tragic automobile accident), and in 1974, they sent defenseman Nick Beverley to New York for one-time 50-goal scorer Vic Hadfield.

Perhaps the saddest event in the history of the Penguins involved their rookie White Hope, Michel Briere. The team had made the playoffs the season before, and looked forward to Briere scoring heavily in 1970–71. Before the season began, however, Briere was seriously injured in an automobile accident, and the youth never recovered. After months of coma and slow convalescence, Brier died in 1971.

While the Penguins improved sufficiently in 1975 to gain the quarterfinal playoffs against the New York Islanders (who defeated them in seven games), rumors of their move and/or demise persisted.

BARCLAY GRAHAM PLAGER

BORN: Kirkland Lake, Ontario, March 26, 1941
POSITION: Defenseman, St. Louis Blues, 1967–

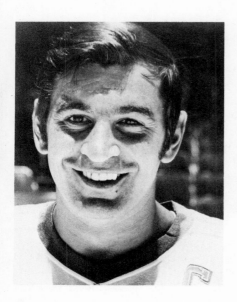

St. Louis Blues' captain Barclay Plager is the guts of the team's defense. Since beginning his NHL tenure with the Blues, Barclay, eldest of three flamboyant Plager brothers, has been the leading shotblocker, body crusher, and scorer of the blue line corps.

ROBERT BRYANT (BOB) PLAGER

BORN: Kirkland Lake, Ontario, March 11, 1943
POSITION: Defenseman, New York Rangers, 1964–67; St. Louis
    Blues, 1967–

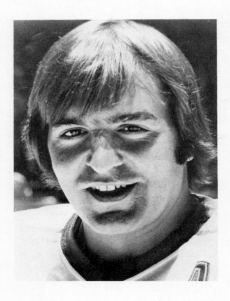

Although Bob Plager was unable to crack the New York Rangers' defensive line, when he was traded to St. Louis in 1967, his NHL career flowered. A tough competitor and mean hitter, Bob is also injury-prone, and it wasn't until 1972–73 that he managed to play a full season—his best year, with 33 points.

WILLIAM RONALD (BILL) PLAGER

BORN: Kirkland Lake, Ontario, July 6, 1945
POSITION: Defenseman, Minnesota North Stars, 1967–68, 1973; St.
    Louis Blues, 1968–72; Atlanta Flames, 1972–73

Bill Plager is the youngest, nicest, and least talented of the trio of defense-minded brothers, and after bouncing around the NHL for years, he was last seen disappearing into the minors from the reserve lists of the Minnesota North Stars.

JACQUES "JAKE THE SNAKE" PLANTE

BORN: Shawinigan Falls, Quebec, January 17, 1929
POSITION: Goalie, Montreal Canadiens, 1952–63; New York Rangers, 1963–65; St. Louis Blues, 1968–70; Toronto Maple Leafs, 1970–73; Boston Bruins, 1973; Edmonton Oilers (WHA), 1974–   ; Coach, Quebec Nordiques (WHA), 1973–74
AWARDS: Hart Trophy, 1962; Vezina Trophy, 1956–60, 1962, 1969 (shared with Glenn Hall); All-Star (First Team), 1956, 1959, 1962, (Second Team), 1957, 1958, 1960, 1971

The most remarkable of the modern goaltenders, Jacques Plante pioneered the use of a goalie mask after a near fatal injury at Madison Square Garden on November 1, 1959. Plante was struck in the face by a hard shot fired from the stick of the Rangers' Andy Bathgate. Jacques, who had been experimenting with the mask in practice scrimmages, donned the protector and reappeared on the ice after his wounds were dressed. From then on he always wore the mask, and soon more and more goalies began using the device to the point where today hardly any maskless goalies remain.

Nicknamed "Jake the Snake," Plante broke into the NHL with the Canadiens in 1952–53 and starred for Montreal in a critical semifinal playoff round with Chicago in which the Canadiens triumphed. He soon was hailed as a superb goalie and an innovative one at that. A superior skater, Plante frequently would wander from his net to field pucks and relay them to teammates. He starred for the Canadiens until 1963 when he was dealt to the Rangers. In 1968–69 he was traded to St. Louis. He was a Maple Leaf for two seasons (1970–71 and 1971–72) and two-thirds, being traded to Boston late in the 1972–73 season.

Plante was extremely gifted, but also troublesome in many ways. He was an excellent tutor and helped refine the style of Flyers' goalie Bernie Parent when he and Parent played for the Maple Leafs. On the other hand, Plante was notorious as a clubhouse lawyer. This is believed to be the reason he was dealt by Montreal, New York, and St. Louis.

Following a weak playoff performance for Boston in April 1973, Plante signed as general manager-coach of the WHA's Quebec Nordiques. He held that position during the 1973–74 season and saw his team finish out of the playoffs. At the age of forty-five, Jacques returned to active play with the Edmonton Oilers in 1974–75 and appeared to have lost little of the ability that enabled him to be classified as one of the best goaltenders in hockey history.

In 1962 Plante won the Hart (MVP) Trophy and three times was named to the First All-Star Team. He was also a seven-time winner of the Vezina Trophy.

MICHEL PLASSE

BORN: Montreal, Quebec, June 1, 1948
POSITION: Goalie, St. Louis Blues, 1970–71; Montreal Canadiens, 1972–74; Kansas City Scouts, 1974–75; Pittsburgh Penguins, 1975–

With one minute left to play in a February 21, 1971 Central League game between Kansas City (a St. Louis Blues' farm club) and Oklahoma City (a Bostom affiliate), Kansas City goaltender Michel Plasse was justifiably concerned. "We were ahead 2–1," the Montreal native recalls, "and we got a penalty. Oklahoma City pulled out its goalie and put on an extra forward. They were really putting it to us, believe me."

So Michel decided it was time to take matters into his own hands. "They [Oklahoma City] threw the puck into our end from center, and when it came right to me, I skated out a bit—maybe ten feet—and flipped it down the ice. It went up over the Oklahoma City players and straight into the enemy net—not slow, either, but quick. It was a hell of a shot.

"Was I planning it? No, I was just trying to clear the puck out of there."

And that is how Michel Plasse became an immortal—the only modern goal-tender to score a goal in professional hockey. To score a goal is not exactly the average netminder's dream, but you can be sure that they've all tried it at one time or another. (In fact, Chuck Rayner once skated across the red line and scored a goal when playing for an unofficial World War II Canadian army team, and Ottawa Senator goalie Clint Benedict recalled once scoring a goal in an exhibition game.)

Plasse came to the NHL by way of St. Louis and the Canadiens, but was left unprotected in the 1974 draft (because Ken Dryden was returning), and, ironically, Michel ended up back in Kansas City with the freshman Scouts. In January 1975, Plasse was traded to the Pittsburgh Penguins, but missed the playoffs due to injury.

PLAYERS' STRIKE

The only major players' strike in National Hockey League history occurred in 1925. The result was drastic. The players were suspended and fined and the NHL left Hamilton for New York. What's more, the strike and resulting league action deprived the Tigers of a chance to play for the Stanley Cup.

One of those involved was Wilfred Thomas (Shorty) Green, the Tigers' captain. Although his Hockey Hall of Fame biography describes him as spokesman for the strikers, that role was played by Redvers (Red) Green, a top scorer and one of three players who had scored five goals in one game in the 1924–25 season.

With extension of the schedule, the playoff format was changed. The second- and third-place teams—Montreal Canadiens and Toronto St. Patricks—were to play off and the winner would meet the Tigers, who had finished first. The survivor would then play the Western Canada champions for the Cup.

Red Green drew attention to the fact he had signed a two-year contract the previous season calling for a 24-game schedule. Noting he had already played 30 games and was being asked to play more, he and his teammates demanded an extra $200 each.

Frank Calder, the NHL president, refused to give in to the strikers and ruled that the semifinal winner would represent the league in the Cup final.

The Canadiens defeated Toronto 3–2 and 2–0 and advanced against the Victoria Cougars. Led by Jack Walker and Frank Frederickson, the Cougars won their best-of-five series three games to one and captured the Stanley Cup.

The Tigers were suspended in April and fined $200 each. Then the team was sold to a New York group headed by gambler Bill Dwyer for $75,000 and appeared in 1925–26 as the Americans. They opened in the new Madison Square Garden before a crowd of 17,000.

Among Tiger players who were reinstated and made the jump to the Americans, besides the two Greens, were Billy Burch, the 1924–25 Hart Trophy winner as most valuable player in the NHL, Ken Randall, Alec McKinnon, Charlie Langlois, Mickey Roach, Edmond Bouchard, and goalie Vernon "Jumping Jake" Forbes. In addition the Americans obtained "Bullet Joe" Simpson from the Edmonton Eskimos and Earl Campbell from the Ottawa Senators.

The team finished fourth beating out Toronto and the Canadiens. What's more, the schedule was again extended—to 36 games—but there was no more strike talk.

LARRY PLEAU

BORN: Lynn, Massachusetts, June 29, 1947
POSITION: Center, Montreal Canadiens, 1969–72; New England
    Whalers (WHA), 1972–

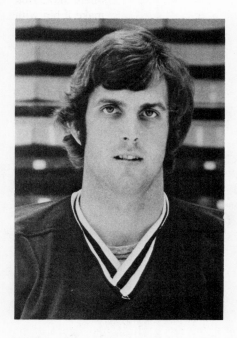

One of those rarities, an American-born player, Larry Pleau was so superior to his Boston-area teammates that he went to Quebec at the age of fifteen and subsequently came up through the Montreal Canadiens' organization. The background shows in his style, which is classic stickhandling and finesse. Ironically, this cousin of Montreal's great center Jean Beliveau was never able to excel with Les Habitants who were overloaded with superior talent at center. After four seasons with Montreal (1969–72), Pleau jumped leagues to the New England Whalers where he has shone, tying the club record for goals in 1972–73 with 39.

Although big (6-1, 190 pounds) Larry is fast, à la Frank Mahovlich, and a whiz at setting up plays.

NORMAN ROBERT "BUD" POILE

BORN: Fort William, Ontario, February 10, 1924
POSITION: Center, Toronto Maple Leafs, 1942–44, 1945–47; Chicago Black Hawks, 1947–49; Detroit Red Wings, 1949; New York Rangers, 1949–50; Boston Bruins, 1950; General Manager, Philadelphia Flyers, 1967–69; Vancouver Canucks, 1970–74; Vice President, WHA, 1974–

Feared by National Hockey League goaltenders because of his hard shot, Bud Poile was one of three players from Fort William, Ontario, to make it big with the Toronto Maple Leafs in the midforties. Along with Gus Bodnar and Gaye Stewart, Poile led "the Flying Fort" line in Toronto's march to the Stanley Cup in 1947. However, in the middle of the following season, Poile and his linemates were dealt to the Chicago Black Hawks, along with defenseman Ernie Dickens and Bob Goldham for Max Bentley and Cy Thomas. Within a year, Poile was dispatched to the Detroit Red Wings, and in 1949–50 moved to the New York Rangers and, finally, the Boston Bruins. His NHL playing career ended in Boston in 1950.

Poile turned to managing and coaching in the minors with considerable success. In sixteen years Bud's teams missed making the playoffs only twice. When the Philadelphia Flyers were admitted to the NHL in 1967 Poile was named general manager of the new club and remained in that position until he was replaced by Keith Allen in December 1969. Poile soon became manager of the Vancouver Canucks, but relinquished the position in 1974 and moved to the World Hockey Association where he was named vice-president and director of hockey operations.

GREGORY LINN (GREG) POLIS

BORN: Westlock, Alberta, August 8, 1950
POSITION: Left Wing, Pittsburgh Penguins, 1970–74; St. Louis Blues, 1974; New York Rangers, 1974–

Greg Polis was a first-round draft choice of the Pittsburgh Penguins in 1970 and he cracked the parent club in his first try. An extremely fast skater on the left wing, Polis couldn't break the 20-goal mark his rookie season, but he made up for it in 1971–72 with 30 goals.

Polis was traded by Pittsburgh to St. Louis in the middle of the 1973–74 season. In August 1974 New York Ranger coach and general manager Emile Francis made a deal with the Blues, and Polis became a Ranger in trade for Larry Sacharuk and a Ranger draft choice.

Polis was immediately placed on the Ratelle-Gilbert line, substituting for the overpriced Vic Hadfield, who had been traded to Pittsburgh. Polis had some difficulty adjusting to Ratelle's slower style at center, and he wasted half the 1974–75 season committing a multitude of icings. He also forgot at times that part of the game was passing, as he made beautiful rushes into nowhere, with great speed and little effect.

SAM POLLOCK

Succeeding Frank Selke, Sr., as Canadiens' manager in 1964 was thirty-eight-year-old Sam Pollock, who had been director of the Canadiens' farm system since 1958 and thus became the youngest club manager in the NHL. Pollock's credentials were quite sound. He had devoted nineteen of his years to hockey management, seventeen of them as a full-time employee of the Forum. He was instrumental in developing the Junior Canadiens and led them to the Memorial Cup, emblematic of national supremacy, in 1950. In more recent years Pollock took a more active role in the actual manipulating of players on the NHL Canadiens and helped negotiate the famed Worsley-Plante deal.

Pollock knew what he wanted, and he was going to run Les Canadiens his way. Thus, having Selke around would soon prove to be an embarrassment and an irrelevancy until the elder statesman finally moved gracefully to the background. Pollock peddled off enough fringe talent to enable Les Canadiens to retain the nucleus of a future winner and they entered the 1967–68 season as strong as possible under the circumstances. The North Stars' manager, Wren Blair, did a low bow in the direction of Montreal to honor Pollock. Pollock was appreciative. "I'm glad to see the teams we dealt with got their money's worth," he said.

In a matter of four years, Pollock, at forty-three, had completely overshadowed his predecessor, Selke. The former managing director was forgotten as Pollock accepted the compliments as big-league hockey's presiding genius. "Sam," wrote Dick Beddoes in the *Globe and Mail,* "is the smartest man now connected with hockey in any front-office job."

Sam Pollock is generally hailed as the most successful manager in modern hockey. Actually his predecessor, Frank Selke, Sr., was the brainier boss and better builder, while Pollock mainly inherited the system and techniques of Selke's genius.

DENIS POTVIN

BORN: Hull, Quebec, October 29, 1953
POSITION: Defenseman, New York Islanders, 1973–
AWARDS: Calder Trophy, 1974; All-Star (First Team), 1975

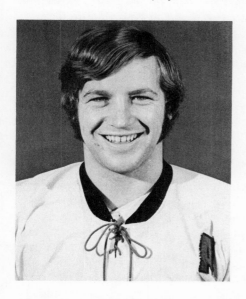

New York Islanders' defenseman Denis Potvin did a lot of growing up in 1973–74, his rookie big-league season. He may have started the year as a highly touted, wealthy nineteen-year-old, but he certainly finished like a mature veteran. He made mistakes and suffered at least one major humiliation en route to the Calder Trophy as the National Hockey League's rookie of the year.

Bobby Orr, in 1966–67, had been the last defenseman to win the Calder Trophy. And Orr was the man with whom Denis has been most often compared. Orr's records as an amateur defenseman in the Ontario Hockey Association's Junior A League had been obliterated by Potvin, a bilingual backliner from Hull, Quebec, just across the river from Ottawa. Potvin would be earning four times as much as Orr did in his rookie season. And the nineteen-year-old with the ferocious slapshot had built a reputation as a fighter with the Ottawa 67's Junior A team in the Ontario Hockey Association. It was still an intimidating set of circumstances because of young Potvin's ballyhoo. But Denis was modest about his press notices heralding him as another Orr. "I'm not Bobby Orr and I know it," he said. "You can't compare us anyway because our styles are different. I can't skate as well as Bobby, but I feel there are a couple of other things I do better—like hitting. That's a big part of my game. I just hope I can accomplish some of the things Bobby has done, but in a different way.''

Potvin's sunny raves were temporarily obliterated by a black cloud of embarrassment on December 16, 1973. The Islanders were to play the Philadelphia Flyers that night at the Spectrum. Denis overslept, missed a 10 A.M. team bus from the Nassau Coliseum, and instead of trying to find alternate means of transportation, drove home. He was hit with a token fine, but stung by the resultant bad press. The incident made him realize it is not just what you do, but who you are, especially when you're a rookie making well over $100,000 a year.

EDWARD (EDDIE) POWERS

BORN: Toronto, Ontario, August 24, 1917
POSITION: Referee, NHL, 1956–63

One of the most respected and forceful referees the National Hockey League has known, Eddie Powers officiated in the majors from 1956 to 1963 when he quit following a long history of conflict with his bosses, the owners. Powers objected to interference from referee-in-chief Carl Voss who would relay messages from NHL president Clarence Campbell. ''A referee would call a game in a certain way in the first period,'' complained Powers, ''and then the next thing that would happen is he'd get a visit in the dressing room and be told he's calling it too close. Another time he'd let everything go and be told he's not calling it close enough.'' Because of his forthright position, Powers was unofficially blackballed by several major league officials. He returned to private life in Toronto, respected by those who recalled his courage and ability, but ignored by the league which he helped so much by his presence.

WALTER "BABE" PRATT

BORN: Stony Mountain, Manitoba, January 7, 1916
POSITION: Defenseman, New York Rangers, 1935–42; Toronto
    Maple Leafs, 1942–46; Boston Bruins, 1946–47
AWARDS: Hart Trophy, 1944; All-Star (First Team), 1944, (Second
    Team), 1945; Hockey Hall of Fame, 1966

The ideal successor to Ranger Ching Johnson when the original defense workhorse had reached the end of his career, Babe Pratt had a lovable disposition when he wasn't flattening the foe. He replaced Ching during the 1937 playoffs against Toronto and made headlines by scoring the winning goal in the deciding game. Babe remained a Ranger for seven years, starring on the 1940 Cup winners and for the 1942 winners of the Prince of Wales Trophy. The next year he was dealt to Toronto, where he continued to excel and, as a result, was elected to the Hall of Fame.

Pratt always was good for a laugh, whether he was on the giving or receiving end of a joke, and the Rangers' scene was that much richer for the Babe being a part of it. When Babe reported to training camp in September 1940 he was full of ginger, and he didn't slow down as the Rangers embarked on their usual exhibition tour. One night he checked into the team's Pullman car at 3 A.M., only to discover that Lester Patrick was waiting. "Babe," said Patrick, "I'm fining you $1,000. But if you don't take another drink for the rest of the campaign, I'll refund your money at the end of the season."

Pratt went on the wagon and the Rangers went on a long, long losing streak. Patrick was worried and, one day, suggested to Babe that maybe a drink wouldn't hurt after all. "No, no," said Pratt, "my word is my bond." Word of the Patrick-Pratt meeting leaked to the players. They figured that if Babe didn't get off the wagon the club would really be in trouble. They told Pratt they would chip in and raise $1,000 if only he would have an occasional drink or two. But Pratt was adamant. The Rangers wound up in fourth place and were knocked out of the playoffs by Detroit. "There's a moral to that story," Pratt said years later, "but I've been trying for thirty years and still haven't been able to figure it out."

The Babe and Lester didn't always get along, especially when money was the subject. According to Pratt, Patrick wasn't tight with money, "he was adjacent to it!" Lester finally traded Babe to Toronto in 1942, and to Pratt's astonishment he was paid more by the Leafs than Lester ever paid him. As a result he began to play even better. When Lester found out about Pratt's good fortune, he asked Babe about it. "Lester," Pratt explained, "now I'm being paid enough to eat on. I'm finally getting the wrinkles out of my belly!"

In time, he became a spokesman for the NHL's Vancouver Canucks and a popular after-dinner speaker. Pratt once asked for questions from the audience after addressing a banquet.

"How many goals a season would Cyclone Taylor score in today's watered-down NHL?" somebody asked.

"Seven or eight," Pratt replied.

"How can you say that?" the man cried. "Taylor was one of the greatest players who ever lived."

"Certainly," Pratt said, "but you must remember the man is ninety years old."

DEAN SUTHERLAND PRENTICE

BORN: Schumacher, Ontario, October 5, 1932
POSITION: Left Wing, New York Rangers, 1952–62; Boston Bruins, 1962–66; Detroit Red Wings, 1966–69; Pittsburgh Penguins, 1969–71; Minnesota North Stars, 1971–74
AWARDS: All-Star (Second Team), 1960

One of the most underrated skaters in modern National Hockey League history, Dean Prentice broke in with the Rangers in 1952–53 and skated for five NHL teams until his retirement after the 1973–74 season. Dean's best years were spent in New York in the late fifties, working left wing on a line with center Larry Popein—later Earl Ingarfield—and right winger Andy Bathgate. Prior to the 1962–63 season Prentice was dealt to the Boston Bruins and remained in Beantown through the 1965–66 campaign. For the next four seasons he skated for the Detroit Red Wings and split his final years between the Pittsburgh Penguins and the Minnesota North Stars. Prentice, who never spent a minute in the minors as a player, became coach of the American League New Haven Nighthawks in 1974–75. Under his baton, the Nighthawks finished last in the North Division. An active member of the Federation of Christian Athletes, Prentice spends considerable time addressing church groups.

A. JOSEPH (JOE) PRIMEAU

BORN: Lindsay, Ontario, January 29, 1906
POSITION: Center, Toronto Maple Leafs, 1928–36
AWARDS: Lady Byng Trophy, 1932; All-Star (Second Team), 1934;
    Hockey Hall of Fame, 1963

Few opponents ever got the better of Montreal immortal Howie Morenz when Howie was in his prime, although Joe Primeau, the crack Toronto center, did just that one night when Les Canadiens and the Maple Leafs were locked in a Christmas Eve match. The teams were tied, 1–1, after regulation time and nobody scored in overtime. When the siren sounded to end the game, both clubs headed for the dressing room until they were halted by the referee. Apparently the timekeeper had erred by ten seconds and the referee ordered the players back to the ice to play out the remaining unused time.

This act of recall nettled Morenz who was anxious to get home to his family. Before the referee dropped the puck, Howie urged Primeau not to touch it after it hit the ice; that way the ten seconds would be squandered and everybody could quit for the night. Primeau understood Howie's point, but had no intentions of complying. Once the puck hit the ice the Leaf center slapped it to the left side, where his winger, Busher Jackson, gathered it in and roared toward the Montreal goal. His shot fooled goalie George Hainsworth and Toronto won the game, 2–1.

This necessitated another face-off and now Morenz was furious. He glared at Primeau as they went through the ritual of the last face-off and then told him in no uncertain terms that he would get even, which he did less than a week later when the teams clashed again. Nobody could touch Howie for the three periods of regulation time, but he, in turn, couldn't get the puck past the Leaf goalie.

At last the teams went into overtime and Morenz took possession of the puck immediately after the opening face-off. Bobbing and weaving through the Leaf defense, Howie worked his way right up to the goal mouth before depositing the puck where it belonged. Primeau, who was known as "Gentleman Joe," recalled that Morenz never said a word to him after scoring. "He had promised to get his revenge," said Primeau, "and he did. There was nothing more to say." Primeau remained the ace center on Toronto's Kid Line with Busher Jackson and Charlie Conacher.

GEORGE "GOLDIE" PRODGERS

BORN: 1892

POSITION: Forward and Defenseman, Waterloo Indians (OPHL), 1911; Quebec Bulldogs (NHA), 1912, 1914; Victoria Aristocrats (PCHA), 1913; Montreal Wanderers (NHA), 1915; Montreal Canadiens (NHA), 1916; Montreal 228th Battn. (NHA), 1917; Toronto St. Pats, 1920; Hamilton Tigers, 1921–25

Goldie Prodgers, an unknown strapping redhead with a thirst for violent body contact, broke into hockey in 1911 with Waterloo of the OPHL. His obvious aptitude for blue line duty was forsaken for his swift skating however, and he found himself manning a forward position where he scored 9 goals in 16 games with Waterloo.

The Quebec Bulldogs of the NHA had other plans for Goldie when he joined their squad the following season. Teamed with "Bad Joe" Hall on defense, Prodgers quickly helped Quebec to the NHA championship and the 1912 Stanley Cup.

The next five seasons saw Goldie wearing five different team sweaters as he checkerboarded his way across Canada's frozen ponds. Usually, Goldie's presence meant a successful season for his squad. The big redhead saw duty on two more championship teams and another Cup winner—that being the 1916 Canadiens.

World War I interrupted Goldie's string of triumphs and he didn't return to the ice until 1920 when, over the protests of the Bulldogs, he inked a pact with the Toronto club.

Hamilton entered the loop the following season and Goldie soon found himself traveling west as part of an "expansion pool" to stock the new franchise with talent. The hapless Hamiltonians shuttled Prodgers back and forth from defense to forward for the next four seasons, but to no avail—the club went nowhere. In the 1925 season, after appearing in only one game, Goldie Prodgers retired from hockey.

RENE MARCEL PRONOVOST

BORN: Lac la Tortue, Quebec, June 15, 1930
POSITION: Defenseman, Detroit Red Wings, 1950–65; Toronto Maple
    Leafs, 1965–70
AWARDS: All-Star (First Team), 1960–61, (Second Team), 1958–59

Of all modern hockey players, Marcel Pronovost has the most claim to the unofficial trophy for the most injured man in hockey. Episodes of Marcel's derring-do are legend around NHL rinks. He broke into big-league hockey with Detroit in the Stanley Cup playoffs of 1950 and was around to play a few games for the Toronto Maple Leafs in the 1969–70 season. In between, he collected hundreds of stitches and innumerable broken bones. Once, in a game against the Chicago Black Hawks, Marcel sped across the blue line as two husky Chicago defensemen dug their skates into the ice, awaiting his arrival. They dared Pronovost to pass. "I decided there was only one move," said Marcel. "Bust through the middle." Even the most ironfisted hockey players shudder at the thought of crashing a defense, but Pronovost wasn't thinking about getting hurt. He never did. He eyed the two-foot space between the Hawks, boldly pushed the puck ahead, and leaped at the opening.

Too late. The crouched defenseman slammed the gate, hurling Pronovost headfirst over their shoulders. In that split second of imminent danger—when even the strongest of men would automatically have shut their eyes—Marcel looked down and saw the puck below him. He swiped at it, missed, and had to settle for a three-point landing on his left eyebrow, nose, and cheek.

A few minutes later the doctor was applying ice packs to Pronovost's forehead as he lay on the dressing room table. Marcel's skull looked as if it had been the loser in a bout with a bulldozer. His nose was broken and listed heavily toward starboard. His eyebrow required twenty-five stitches. "And my cheekbones," Marcel recalled in his deep tone, "felt as if they were pulverized." He was right, they were cracked like little pieces of china.

"What hurt most," says Pronovost, whose face became as craggy as an apline peak, "was that I had to miss the next two games. As for the injuries, I didn't think twice about them." Marcel always regarded his misfortunes casually. "To me," he says, "accidents are as common as lacing on skates. One of the prizes of my collection of injuries is a break of the fourth dorsal vertebra." In 1959, after Pronovost had broken his beak for the thirteenth time, he examined it with the air of a true connoisseur and said, "Frankly, I was disappointed. After a few towels were put on I could see out of both eyes. The first time I broke my nose in a hockey game, my eyes were swollen shut for three days.''

CLAUDE PROVOST

BORN: Montreal, Quebec, September 17, 1933
POSITION: Right Wing, Montreal Canadiens, 1955–69
AWARDS: Bill Masterton Trophy, 1968; All-Star (First Team), 1965

One of two ''lantern-jawed'' skaters in big-league hockey (the other being Jack Evans), Claude Provost skated for years in the shadows of more famous Montreal Canadiens while doing key legwork as a checker and penalty killer. In many ways Provost was as vital to the Montreal machine during his career as were Maurice Richard and Jean Beliveau. Provost shadowed aces such as Bobby Hull, but did it with a gentility and efficiency that bespoke the ultimate in fair play. A genial sort, he once was ribbed as ''the ugliest man in the NHL,'' and culminated his career by winning the Bill Masterton Trophy in 1968 for good sportsmanship. During his 1,005 games, he scored 254 goals, 335 assists, and 589 points while accumulating only 469 minutes in penalties. His other unique quality was his legs-wide-apart skating style which led one observer to note that, ''when Provost skates he looks like a drunken sailor walking the deck during a hurricane.''

HARVEY PULFORD

BORN: Toronto, Ontario, 1875
DIED: October 31, 1940
POSITION: Defenseman, Ottawa Silver Seven (AHA, CAHL, ECAHA),
    1894–1908
AWARDS: Hockey Hall of Fame, 1945

Harvey Pulford, a Hall of Famer who labored for Ottawa's ice men for his entire fourteen-year career, has got to be considered *the* defensive defenseman of all time.

Although we have only faded, yellowing newspaper accounts of the day to determine what style of player Pulford was, his career statistics illustrate that he considered himself a pure defender who left the scoring chores to the forwards and rarely ventured past his opponent's blue line.

Not surprisingly, it took Harvey seven full seasons before registering his first big-league goal. His lack of scoring punch didn't seem to bother his Ottawa squad though, because Pulford was a regular throughout most of his career. In fact, he captained the great turn-of-the-century Silver Seven teams to three consecutive Stanley Cups.

In the twilight of Pulford's career he was paired on defense with a brash youngster named Fred "Cyclone" Taylor. Taylor earned his nickname via his whirlwind, rink-length rushes—the exact opposite of his blue line mate's conservative play. A dramatic illustration of the two contrasting defensive philosophies came in Taylor's rookie campaign when he scored 8 goals, equaling Pulford's entire career output.

ROBERT JESSE (BOB) PULFORD

BORN: Newton Robinson, Ontario, March 31, 1936
POSITION: Center, Toronto Maple Leafs, 1956–70; Los Angeles Kings, 1971–72; Coach, Los Angeles Kings, 1972–

Bob Pulford, a classy, two-way centerman, labored for sixteen seasons in the National Hockey League with the Toronto Maple Leafs and later the Los Angeles Kings. Never a flamboyant player in the "superstar" category, Pulford quietly and efficiently got the job done, taking a regular shift, skating on the power play, and killing penalties.

Pulford finished his active playing career in 1972, retiring as the Kings' captain and stepping right into their coaching post. Since Bob took over the Kings' reins, the Beverly Hills squad developed into one of the finest defensive units in the league and made themselves serious contenders.

JEAN BAPTISTE PUSIE

BORN: Montreal, Quebec, October 15, 1910
DIED: April 23, 1956
POSITION: Defenseman, Montreal Canadiens, 1931–32, 1935–36;
    New York Rangers, 1933–34; Boston Bruins, 1934–35

A husky French-Canadian defenseman with an immense ego and a low-comedy accent, Pusie made his debut in the autumn of 1930 at the Montreal Canadiens' training camp.

Coach Cecil Hart was startled when the twenty-year-old rookie entered his office, introduced himself, vigorously pumped his hand, and declared: "Meestair 'art. Pewsee weel be zee greatess. Heet's 'ockey playairs like me dat weel make dis game pop-u-lair.''

Hart admired the youngster's office exuberance, but he detected two serious flaws in his playing technique. Pusie's heavy shot worked only when he had ample time to lower his head for a protracted windup, and when Jean Baptiste skated, his eyes remained dangerously and blindly glued to the puck.

Hart was unimpressed; thus Pusie was depressed when he joined the London (Ontario) Tecumsehs of the International League, but confident that he would yet be an NHL star. "I weel show dem,'' he assured coach Clem Loughlin. "Dey make beeg mistake.''

In his first home game Pusie was fed a lead pass and broke into the clear. This was a perfect opportunity for Jean Baptiste to fire his unusual shot. He wound up in the classic style and hit the puck so hard it yanked the goalie's mitt from his hand. Both puck and glove sailed into the net.

Before the goalie could move, Pusie dived into the cage, retrieved the glove and presented it to the goaltender with a low bow. He held his opponent's bare hand up to the crowd, carefully counted the fingers and said: "Dey are all dere. You are luck-y.'' He replaced the glove and patted the goalie on the back.

Pusie went on to ever greater shenanigans, but never cracked the majors, gaining trials with the New York Rangers, Boston Bruins, and the Canadiens, but failing to produce more than startled laughter at his crazed antics.

The rather sad end of Jean Baptiste Pusie was symbolized one night as he played for St. Louis in the American Association. Pusie found himself stranded on the blue line, the lone defenseman confronted by a four-man rush. He looked pleadingly at the crowd, gazed at the onrushing skaters, and executed a play which had never been seen in hockey before.

"He dropped his stick,'' recalled Jack Riley, now an executive with the Pittsburgh Penguins, "lifted his hands in surrender, and fell to his knees. When the skaters had almost reached him, he buried his face in his gloves.'' The opponents skated easily past the ostrichlike form of Pusie and scored.

Pusie retired from hockey in 1942 and died of a heart attack in Montreal on April 23, 1956.

HUBERT GEORGE (BILL) QUACKENBUSH

BORN: Toronto, Ontario, March 2, 1922
POSITION: Defenseman, Detroit Red Wings, 1942–49; Boston
  Bruins, 1949–56
AWARDS: Lady Byng Trophy, 1949; All-Star (First Team), 1948, 1949,
  1951, (Second Team), 1947, 1953

In the late 1940s and early 1950s Bill Quackenbush was one of the best defensemen in the National Hockey League, first with the Detroit Red Wings (1942–49), then the Boston Bruins (1949–56).

Quackenbush was always in the thick of the action—sometimes on the wrong side. In the 1952 Stanley Cup opening round, when Rocket Richard scored the winning goal in the seventh game against the Bruins at the Montreal Forum, Bill Quackenbush was the defenseman that the Rocket circled to make the score possible. It broke a 1–1 tie and won the series for Montreal.

Quackenbush played on some of the best Detroit Red Wing teams in history. "Ted Lindsay, Gordie Howe, Sid Abel—every forward on that great line backchecked," Quackenbush recalls. "It made it a hell of a lot easier on me. They took a lot of the defensive pressure off the defenseman. There aren't too many players like the guys who were on that Production Line anymore."

A classic defensive-defenseman, Quackenbush was a cautious and remarkably clean-playing soul who won the Lady Byng Trophy in 1949.

QUEBEC ACES

One of the most highly regarded senior amateur—later minor professional—Canadian teams, the Aces sent innumerable stars to the National Hockey League, including Jean Beliveau. The name Aces is derived from the Anglo-Canadian Pulp and Paper Company based in Quebec City. ACE represented "Anglo-Canadian employe."

The paper company sponsored the team in 1945 when it was a member of the highly rated Quebec Senior Hockey League and boasted such stars as George "Punch" Imlach, a balding defenseman who later was to become coach of the Toronto Maple Leafs. Imlach learned coaching in Quebec and tutored the likes of Larry Zeidel, Gordie Heale, and Rags Raglan, not to mention the superb Jean Beliveau.

In 1953 the Quebec League went professional at a time when Beliveau was its biggest drawing card. But when Beliveau signed with the NHL's Montreal Canadiens the Aces and the league were doomed. Beliveau's successor on the Aces was skinny Camille Henry, a stickhandling virtuoso who later became NHL rookie of the year with the New York Rangers. Although the Aces never again enjoyed the glory years of Beliveau the club survived in one way or another until the Quebec Nordiques of the World Hockey Association supplanted the Aces in 1972.

QUEBEC NORDIQUES

The Quebec Nordiques have been from inception one of the World Hockey Association's strongest franchises at the gate. Although missing the playoffs the first two years, finishing three points out of fourth place in 1972–73, and a single point out of the money the following year, the club has drawn very well, pulling in an attendance of over half a million for its first two years of operation in the Quebec Coliseum.

The Nordiques went for fan appeal right from the start when they commissioned the great Maurice "Rocket" Richard to be the first coach. The Rocket, however, succumbed to the pressures behind the bench, and did not last out the first season, one in which the Nordiques were last or next to last throughout.

The following year another French-Canadian great, goalie Jacques Plante, took over for interim coach Maurice Filion and alternated between the bench and the nets. Plante couldn't cut it either, and the club finished fifth.

The Nordiques' brass finally realized that names weren't enough, and Jean Guy Gendron became the third coach of the club in 1974–75. Gendron had played for the Rangers, Bruins, Canadiens, and Flyers in the National Hockey League and the Nordiques in 1972–73 and 1973–74.

With the help of such fine players as defenseman J. C. Tremblay and right wings Rejean Houle and Serge Bernier, the Nordiques fared better in 1974–75, staying atop the new Canadian Division of the WHA, and gaining the playoff finals where they were demolished in four straight games by Houston.

JOHN BRIAN PATRICK (PAT) QUINN

BORN: Hamilton, Ontario, January 29, 1943
POSITION: Defenseman, Toronto Maple Leafs, 1968–70; Vancouver
    Canucks, 1970–72; Atlanta Flames, 1972–

Pat Quinn began his NHL life with Toronto, continued on to Vancouver, and then Atlanta. In each city Pat was the policeman, "the Irish Enforcer." Perhaps he is best remembered for a playoff brawl with practically the entire Boston Bruins' club after he smashed Bobby Orr into the boards. It went this way:

When the Leafs and Bruins were paired in the 1969 playoffs Quinn was in action for the opening game and all hell broke loose. A major fuse was planted in the second period by Quinn and detonated by the Boston fans. It happened at 18:03 of the middle period, seconds after Bobby Orr had picked up speed for a rush along the right boards. "Bobby had his head down," Boston coach Harry Sinden admitted after the contest, "and when you have your head down you have to take your lumps."

Quinn, who had been playing defense in a very one-sided game in the Bruins' favor, detected Orr on his radar. The Leaf rookie rushed Orr from almost a right angle and deposited him on the ice with a devastating check. It remains questionable whether there was anything illegal about the check. Even subjective viewers such as Sinden allow that, at the very worst, Quinn was guilty of charging.

Orr fell backward on his right hip after the blow and then lay motionless on the ice, face down. Trainer Dan Canney rushed to the scene and, almost immediately, summoned Dr. Ronald Adams, the team physician. At this point referee John Ashley announced that Quinn would receive a five-minute major penalty for elbowing, instead of the traditional two-minute minor.

In terms of its influence on the game, the penalty was totally irrelevant. Boston held a commanding 6–0 lead and was coasting to victory. Perhaps the award of a major rather than minor penalty may have suggested to the enraged crowd of 14,659 that Quinn was guilty of hyper-ruthlessness. On the other hand it's conceivable that a few bloodthirsty Boston fans merely wanted a pound of Quinn's flesh and would have started an uprising no matter what the penalty.

Seconds after the Leaf player took his seat in the penalty box some fans crowded around him. The police were conspicuous by their lack of protection for the visiting player. One fan clouted Quinn on the head with his fist while another bounced a hard object off Quinn's skull.

An intelligent young man, Quinn realized that his life was in grave and imminent peril, and he sought to protect himself as much as possible. The crowd wasn't satisfied and began a crescendolike chant that reached deafening proportions. "Get Quinn! Get Quinn! GET QUINN!!!"—who eventually was forced to seek sanctuary in the Toronto dressing room.

Orr was taken to Massachusetts General Hospital for overnight observation with a slight concussion and a slight whiplash in the neck. X-rays taken at the hospital proved negative, a factor that was unknown to the audience which remained disturbed as the third period progressed.

They wanted more Leaf scalps and got them late in the period when another brawl erupted, involving Forbes Kennedy of Toronto and several other players. "Fans leaned over the glass to pound Kennedy," reported Red Burnett in the Toronto *Daily Star,* "while Bruins' goalie Ed Johnston had him in a bear hug. . . . There were times when it appeared as if some of the kookier members of the roaring crowd would invade the ice after the Leafs."

All three Toronto papers agreed that the scene was shameful. The Boston *Globe* on April 4 not only carried a lead editorial about the foofaraw but also ran an editorial cartoon depicting Bruins and Leafs players fighting on the ice while a fan tosses beer at Quinn in the penalty box. A plainclothes investigator stands aside and remarks: "Excuse me gentlemen . . . I'm from the commission to study violence in America."

In 1972, Quinn was obtained by the Atlanta Flames and his improvement as a backliner became obvious. During 1973–74, Pat collected a total of 32 points, indicating his growing confidence as a puck carrier and playmaker, rather than a simple mayhem producer.

JAMES DONALD "BONES" RALEIGH

BORN: Kenora, Ontario, June 27, 1926
POSITION: Center, New York Rangers, 1943–44, 1947–56

The 1950 Stanley Cup finals had been a particularly grueling series for center Don Raleigh. Nicknamed ''Bones'' by his teammates for his conspicuous lack of flesh, Raleigh was ''mod'' twenty years before his time. He lived alone on the remote New York borough of Staten Island; wrote poetry; grew a moustache; and always gave the impression that one more turn on the ice would be his last.

But Raleigh was on the ice as the clock passed the eight-minute mark of the first sudden death in the fourth game of the finals which the Rangers trailed Detroit two games to one. He took a pass from bulky linemate El Slowinski and, as he was falling, swiped the puck past a beaten goalie, Harry Lumley. The Rangers had tied the series at two apiece.

Now the Red Wings were reeling. They fell behind, 1–0, in the fifth game and appeared to be doomed to a Chuck Rayner shutout when Ted Lindsay tied the score with less than two minutes remaining in the third period. Once again it was time for sudden death—and Bones Raleigh.

An unlikely hero if ever there was one, Raleigh wasted little time in his second dramatic sudden-death effort. Only a minute and a half had elapsed when he took a pass from teammate Eddie Slowinski and beat Lumley with a ten-foot drive. But it was all to no avail, as the Rangers lost the finals in the seventh game.

FRANK RANKIN

BORN: Stratford, Ontario, April 1, 1889
DIED: Unknown
POSITION: Rover and Defenseman, career at amateur level, 1906–14; Toronto Arenas/St. Pats, 1917–23; Hamilton Tigers, 1923–25; New York Americans, 1925–26; Coach, Toronto Granites Olympic Team, 1924
AWARDS: Hockey Hall of Fame, 1961

From a family full of talented hockey players—Charlie, Gordon, Ramsay, and Hall of Famer Frank—came some of the finest hockey played in the early decades of this century.

Frank Rankin began his winning ways as a junior with the Stratford (Ontario) team, winning the OHA championships for three years in a row, 1906 through 1909. He moved on to senior hockey with the Eaton Athletic Association of Toronto and two more championships in 1911 and 1912.

In those days of seven-man hockey, Rankin played rover, switching from offense (they were known, even then, for their "garbage goals") to defense as the action demanded. Rankin later coached and piloted the 1924 Toronto Granites Olympic team.

JOSEPH GILBERT YVON JEAN RATELLE

BORN: Lac St. Jean, Quebec, October 3, 1940
POSITION: Center, New York Rangers, 1960–
AWARDS: Lady Byng Memorial Trophy, 1972; Bill Masterton Memorial Trophy, 1971; All-Star (Second Team), 1972; Team Canada, 1972

It was a curious sensation. Jean Ratelle could feel streams of pain coursing through his long lean body. The gifted young New York Rangers' center felt the shock waves near the end of the 1965–66 season.

The end of a bright career loomed for the French-Canadian ace. He was taken to a doctor who diagnosed chronic lower spinal deterioration and prescribed delicate spinal fusion surgery. It was a tricky operation, involving bone grafts. Normally, the chances of complete recovery for a hockey player who bounces around the ice as if he were caught in a crazed pinball machine are not bright.

There seemed no way that Jean could repeat his performance of a season earlier when he had scored 21 goals, and the Rangers' new coach, Emile Francis, was predicting stardom for the lanky kid from Lac St. Jean, Quebec. In his last year of junior hockey Ratelle had been called to the big club for a three-game tryout. He impressed Madison Square Garden critics by scoring two goals in

Jean Ratelle

three games. In 1961–62, a season later, Ratelle started the year with the Rangers, but after playing a few games rather dismally, he was demoted to Kitchener of the old Eastern Pro League.

When the next Rangers' training camp opened, Ratelle returned and flopped for the second year in a row. He was then dispatched to Baltimore where he enjoyed a good season. He believed he was now ready to stick with the Rangers, but manager Muzz Patrick offered him a bush-league salary, so Ratelle returned to Montreal. Patrick, however, was dismissed and replaced by Emile Francis who persuaded Ratelle to return.

Ratelle rejoined the Rangers—for good! He played fifty-four games for the New Yorkers and scored 14 goals. Coach Red Sullivan put him on a line with Lou Angotti on the right and Vic Hadfield, a turbulent young draftee, on the left. It looked like the start of something big for Jean.

In 1965–66 Ratelle had a good year scoring 21 goals until his back pains demolished the joy. The spinal fusion operation was followed by a black cloud of fear. Jean was plagued with doubts as he journeyed to Kitchener, Ontario, for the Ranger training camp in September 1966. Could he make a comeback?

Hampered by his injuries, Ratelle played only forty-one games and scored a disillusioning six goals. Ratelle had hit the bottom of the trough. Some Ratelle-watchers believed that the trouble was in the coaching. When Francis fired Sullivan and took over the coaching duties in 1966–67, he immediately inserted Ratelle on a line with Hadfield and Jean's boyhood chum, Rod Gilbert. The gears meshed neatly and the Rangers made the playoffs for the first time in five years. The Ratelle-Hadfield-Gilbert trio—later to be nicknamed the GAG Line—emerged as the Rangers' most consistent unit. Ratelle scored 28 goals and finally seemed ready to fulfill his promise.

Employing a crisp wrist shot, Jean embarked on a string of three consecutive 32-goal seasons. He was the club's leading scorer throughout those campaigns and commanded the respect of teammates and opponents alike as a quiet, efficient centerman. His forte was not power, but grace. His skates glided lyrically across the glistening ice surface as he put beautiful syncopated passes right smack on the sticks of his wings, setting them up for perfect scores. But, somehow, the hockey world failed to take full notice of Ratelle until the 1971–72 season.

Ratelle, Hadfield, and Gilbert were together again as the Rangers' number one forward line, but only after Francis stunned Jean and Rod by replacing Hadfield with Jack Egers, the blond left winger with a booming slapshot. The Egers experiment went the way of the *Titanic* and in 1971–72 Ratelle, Gilbert, and Hadfield once again made beautiful music together.

They scored and scored. The New York press renamed them the G-A-G Line since they managed to provide a goal a game. Although it was Ratelle who was doing much of the scoring, one of Francis' chief complaints about Jean was "I wish he'd shoot more." Ratelle took the coach's advice. By midseason, he was the NHL's leading scorer, outpointing even the fabulous Phil Esposito of Boston's Bruins for the $500 that goes with the honor.

With the Rangers in first place, and Ratelle's line setting all kinds of scoring marks, Ranger fans were flying high. One of the loudest and longest ovations we heard on February 27, 1972, when Jean became the first Ranger in history to score 100 points in a single season. Ratelle briefly and modestly acknowledged the cascading applause and, looking embarrassed, skated back to the bench.

Less than a week later disaster struck. Shooting against the California Golden Seals, defenseman Dale Rolfe fired the puck at a maze of players in front of the net. The shot careened goalward and struck Ratelle on the right ankle. Jean's ankle was fractured. He was disabled for the rest of the regular season.

He had accumulated 109 points. With fifteen games left, he had scored 46 goals. Fifty was clearly in sight, but it was not to be. His value was underscored as the Rangers faltered without number 19 in the lineup. They fell to second place and barely finished ahead of the onrushing Canadiens.

Ratelle briefly returned for the Stanley Cup finals against Boston, but clearly was not the same Ratelle. As a result, the Rangers were outclassed by the powerful Bruins in six games.

Nevertheless, Ratelle led his club in scoring, and finished third in the league, behind Esposito and Bobby Orr. For his efforts, and for his sportsmanship on the ice, Jean was awarded the Lady Byng Trophy. He thus became the first Ranger to win a major NHL trophy since Harry Howell had captured the Norris Trophy in 1964.

Ratelle received another honor in the summer of 1972 when he was named to the roster for the Team Canada series against the Soviet national team. Ratelle was named the captain for that historic first game in the Montreal Forum. He played six of the eight games as Canada beat the Soviets four games to three with one tie.

CLAUDE EARL (CHUCK) "BONNIE PRINCE CHARLIE" RAYNER

BORN: Sutherland, Saskatchewan, August 11, 1920
POSITION: Goalie, New York/Brooklyn Americans, 1940–42; New
    York Rangers, 1945–53
AWARDS: Hart Trophy, 1950; All-Star (Second Team), 1949–51;
    Hockey Hall of Fame, 1973

A classic example of a superb goaltender yoked to a mediocre hockey club was the New York Rangers' Charlie Rayner. "Bonnie Prince Charlie," a bushy-browed, acrobatic netminder, broke into the professional ice wars with the old New York Americans before donning the red, white, and blue Ranger sweater in 1945.

Laboring for a Ranger team that never finished higher than fourth place, Charlie almost single-handedly guided the Rangers to the final round of the 1950 playoffs, only to see his Blueshirts fall to the mighty Detroit Red Wings in the final game—a heart-stopping, double overtime affair.

The Wings' Pete Babando was the culprit who burst Rayner's magical bubble, whipping a screened shot past the helpless netminder with a little more than eight minutes gone in the second overtime frame. The phantom puck, whistling unseen out of a tangle of bodies, served only to punctuate Charlie's definition of his chosen craft. "Goaltending," the beleaguered Rayner had once said, "is like walking down a dark alley and never knowing when some-one is going to chop you down."

Lynn Patrick, the Ranger coach during that Cinderella season of 1949–50, remembered Rayner's inspiring heroics with the defenseless Blueshirts. "Rayner never had great protection," recalled Patrick, "yet he always came up with a better-than-average record and very often with a sensational perfor-mance."

Chuck was the overwhelming choice for the 1950 Hart Trophy as the NHL's most valuable player—it was only the first time since 1929 that the honor was bestowed upon a backstop. A courageous netminder who constantly played with a painful assortment of injuries that would have kept lesser men on the sidelines, Rayner was in such agony near the end of his career that he literally had to be lifted off the ice by his teammates and propped up against the goal cage after making a save.

In addition to his illustrious netminding career, Chuck Rayner has the distinction of being the only goaltender in big-league hockey to dash the length of the ice and score a goal against an opposing goalie. It happened during World War II when Charlie was minding the nets for an All-Star Royal Canadian Army team. A wild scramble for a loose puck saw all five opposing skaters charge behind Charlie's net. Somehow, the lozenge squirted out in front of Chuck's crease with nothing but wide open spaces between Rayner and the opposing netminder.

With a ten-stride lead on his opponents, Charlie cradled the puck on his oversized goalie's lumber and set off toward the enemy net. While all ten skaters stopped and stared in amazement, Rayner barreled into the offensive zone and nudged the puck past his shocked opposite number.

Clint Benedict, a netminder with the old pre-NHL Ottawa Senators, and Michel Plasse, goalie for the Pittsburgh Penguins, are on record for scoring goals into their opponent's vacated goal cages from behind their own blue lines. (Benedict in an exhibition game, Plasse in a minor league.) But Rayner stands alone as the only netminder in history to skate across the red line and put the puck past an opposing goaltender.

KENNETH JOSEPH REARDON

BORN: Winnipeg, Manitoba, April 1, 1921
POSITION: Defenseman, Montreal Canadiens, 1940–43, 1945–50
AWARDS: All-Star (First Team), 1947, 1950, (Second Team), 1946, 1948–49; Hockey Hall of Fame, 1966

Kenny Reardon, a tough defenseman for the powerhouse clubs of the Montreal Canadiens, was not exactly the type of skater one associates with the flamboyant Flying Frenchmen. A lumbering, straight-ahead blue liner, Reardon's punishing bodychecks and deft stickwork more than earned him his keep on the star-studded Habitant roster.

One of the quickest men in hockey with his fists, Reardon is credited with starting one of the bloodiest brawls in modern hockey history even though Kenny himself missed much of the fun 'n' games.

On March 16, 1947, the Canadiens were playing the hosting New York Rangers in Madison Square Garden. As Kenny lugged the rubber disc out of his defensive zone, New York's Bryan Hextall loomed in wait at the blue line. Hex delivered a crunching check on the Canadien rearguard and sent him caroming into the razorsharp stick blade of the Rangers' Cal Gardner.

With his upper lip resembling raw chopped liver, Reardon was escorted to the tunnel leading to the trainer's room when all hell broke loose. A slightly inebriated Ranger fan lunged at Reardon as the bloodied warrior passed the first row of seats, causing the startled Hab to swing his stick in self-defense. Immediately, Reardon was pounced on by several burly Garden cops. This hubbub caused the entire Ranger bench to stand up for an innocent look-see.

Meanwhile, back at the Canadien bench, the scuffle caused the Habs to think that the entire Ranger reserve corps was beating up on their wounded comrade. In an instant, the entire Montreal bench had emptied and they streaked across the rink to come to Reardon's aid. Pairing off with every Ranger they could latch on to, the outraged Montrealers chopped away for twenty solid minutes before the Pier Sixer finally ended and order was restored.

And Reardon? Well, throughout all this mayhem, Kenny was in the trainer's room where he belonged having his shredded lip attended to.

"I was the guy who started the damn fight," Reardon later recalled, "but believe it or not, I never saw it. Right after the cop knocked me down I got up and walked to the clinic. Sorta burns me up. I coulda had a great time!"

WILLIAM T. (BILLY) REAY

BORN: Winnipeg, Manitoba, August 21, 1918
POSITION: Forward, Detroit Red Wings, 1943–45; Montreal Canadiens, 1945–53; Coach, Chicago Black Hawks, 1963–
AWARDS: Prince of Wales Trophy, 1967; Clarence Campbell Bowl, 1971–73 (as coach)

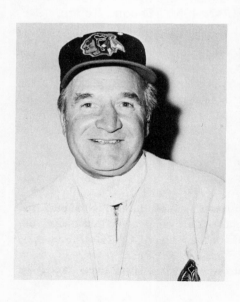

In the fall of 1974 Bill Reay became the longest tenured coach in the NHL, and the only one, besides Scotty Bowman of Montreal, to have won both the Prince of Wales Trophy (East Division league winner) and the Clarence Campbell Bowl (West Division trophy). Reay took over the bench of the Chicago Black Hawks in 1963–64, two years after they won their last Stanley Cup, and his single greatest burden is the fact that, although the Hawks are perennial Cup contenders, he has not brought that ultimate glory back to Chicago Stadium.

Reay is basically a quiet man who does not enjoy a pleasant relationship with the press—in fact his press conferences have gained some notoriety for being either sparring matches with writers, or non-press conferences all together.

MICHAEL EDWARD (MICKEY) REDMOND

BORN: Kirkland Lake, Ontario, December 27, 1947
POSITION: Right Wing, Montreal Canadiens, 1967–71; Detroit Red
    Wings, 1971–
AWARDS: All-Star (First Team), 1973, (Second Team), 1974

In a sense the 1973–74 season was a banner year for Mickey Redmond, the dashing twenty-six-year-old Detroit right wing. For the second campaign in a row, he scored more than 50 goals and was runner-up to Marcel Dionne as leading scorer of the Red Wings.

But Mickey was less than exultant about those results. Even though he collected 51 goals and 26 assists for 77 points, the total represented a drop of 16 from his mark the previous year.

Even worse, the Detroit sextet once again missed the playoffs while Mickey's kid brother, defenseman Dick, enjoyed the playoffs skating for Chicago. "I don't like packing my bags at the beginning of April," said Mickey. "When I played for the Canadiens, I got a taste of the playoff feeling and I can tell you, there's just nothing like it."

Redmond, 5-11, 185 pounds, also got "the feeling" years earlier as an offensive prodigy playing his hockey on outdoor rinks in frigid northern Ontario. He was nurtured early in the whys and wherefores of shooting a puck and learned his lessons well. When Mickey was growing up in the city of Kirkland Lake, he and brother Dick would disdain the usual childhood pastimes to sharpen their puck-shooting skills in the compact "Redmond Arena"—otherwise known as the basement in Mickey's house. "Dick and I used to shoot by the hour in the cellar—when we weren't on the ice somewhere," the Red Wings' star right winger reminisced recently.

"Sometimes we'd rig something in the shape of a goal, but most of the time we'd shoot at targets—usually bottles our mother would give us. I guess she cleaned up a few tons of broken glass. What I remember best was laying a cardboard box on its side and then putting a bottle right at the back of it," he continued. "Dick and I would have a contest to see who could break it first. It was quite a trick to drive the puck into the box hard enough, and at the same time, there wouldn't be any fragments to clean up because it would all be in the box."

Now the older Redmond prefers breaking other things—records, for instance. His 52 goals during the 1972–73 National Hockey League campaign set an all-time Detroit mark for most tallies in a single season. Considering that the record was formerly held by the legendary Gordie Howe, Mickey's milestone is all the more impressive. He joins such luminaries as Maurice Richard, Bernie Geoffrion, Bobby Hull, Phil Esposito, Johnny Bucyk, Rick Martin, Rick MacLeish, Guy Lafleur, Danny Grant, and Vic Hadfield—all of whom have netted 50 goals or more in just one season.

Redmond's forte is his overpowering shot, which has been known to cause opposing goaltenders great distress. The superstar Redmond claims he acquired the shot by practicing with a metal puck while playing Junior A hockey for the Peterborough Petes. "It was too heavy to slap," he said. "You had to push it with a wrist shot. But when I'd get out on the ice with a real rubber puck, it used to feel like I was shooting a twenty-five-cent piece."

Unfortunately, Redmond did not acquire the kind of leadership skills in Junior hockey which some coaches would have preferred. Bep Guidolin, who coached in the Ontario Hockey Association when Redmond was playing for Peterborough, said that Mickey lacked a leadership temperament. "He's no Gordie Howe," said Guidolin, "nor a Phil Esposito or Bobby Orr. Don't look for

Mickey to grab a player, like Espo might do, and tell him, 'Look, you're not carrying your weight, so get with it.' Redmond's not that kind of guy.'' But he can score goals. And as long as he does that in abundance, Mickey Redmond will rate as an exceptional hockey player.

RICHARD (DICK) REDMOND

BORN: Kirkland Lake, Ontario, August 14, 1949
POSITION: Defenseman, Minnesota North Stars, 1969–71; California
    Golden Seals, 1971–72; Chicago Black Hawks, 1972–

Dick Redmond is one of today's many offensive-minded defensemen, which means in simplest form that he carries the puck out, tries to score, gets caught up ice, and leaves a lot of the more mundane defensive blue line work to more conventional rearguard types.

He is the brother of high-scoring Red Wing Mickey Redmond, and the product of the old Black Hawk junior system St. Catharines' team. When he came up to the NHL, however, he began with the Minnesota North Stars, in 1969–70. He was sent down after seven games to Iowa and later Cleveland in the minors, until he popped up in Minnesota again in 1971, in time to be traded to the Seals with Tom Williams for Ted Hampson and Wayne Muloin. He came to Chicago in 1972 for Darryl Maggs.

LAWRENCE EMMETT (LARRY) REGAN

BORN: North Bay, Ontario, August 9, 1930
POSITION: Center, Boston Bruins, 1956–59; Toronto Maple Leafs, 1959–61; Coach/Manager, Los Angeles Kings, 1967–74
AWARDS: Calder Trophy, 1957

As stickhandlers and playmakers go, Larry Regan was among the better members of the breed during the late fifties, spent first with Boston and then Toronto. His most significant contribution occurred on March 22, 1959, when he scored two critical goals against the Red Wings as the Leafs beat the Rangers for a playoff berth on the final night of the season. Just as important, Regan set up Dick Duff for what proved to be the fifth goal of the match; and the winner in a 6–4 decision. Prior to the decisive play, Regan told Duff: "Dick, you're goin' to get the winner. I'm goin' to give it to you. Just be there." Regan won the face-off and eventually delivered a needlepoint pass to Duff who shot the puck past goalie Terry Sawchuk.

After his playing days had ended, Regan turned to front office work. He coached and managed the Los Angeles Kings rather unsuccessfully. In 1974 he moved to Montreal where he became a coach on the junior level, quitting in May 1975.

LEO CHARLES REISE, JR.

BORN: Stoney Creek, Ontario, June 7, 1922
POSITION: Defenseman, Chicago Black Hawks, 1945–46; Detroit Red Wings, 1946–52; New York Rangers, 1952–54
AWARDS: All-Star (Second Team), 1950–51

There are not many chips-off-the-old-block who are so identical in style and ability than Leo Reise, Sr. and Junior. The younger Reise also was a defenseman, and a much-feared one at that. Although Leo, Jr., broke in with the Black Hawks in 1945–46, he was dealt to Detroit the next year and played his best hockey for the Red Wings through the 1951–52 season. His most memorable play was a sudden-death goal in the seventh game of the bitter 1950 Stanley Cup semifinal against Toronto. In 1952–53 he became a Ranger and, like his dad, finished his big-league tenure on Broadway (1953–54). Although Gordie Howe, Ted Lindsay, and Red Kelly received much of the attention it was Leo Reise, Jr., who did much of the unheralded spade work for the champion Red Wing teams in 1950 and 1951 when they won the Prince of Wales Trophy.

LEO CHARLES REISE, SR.

BORN: Pembroke, Ontario, June 1, 1892
DIED: July 8, 1975
POSITION: Defenseman, Hamilton Tigers, 1920–24; New York Americans, 1926–29; New York Rangers, 1929–30

A defenseman out of Pembroke, Ontario, Leo Reise, Sr., was an effective defenseman who played for Hamilton in the NHL from 1920–21 through 1923–24. When the Hamilton franchise was transferred to New York and became the Americans, Reise continued playing his steady game. He remained with the Amerks through the 1928–29 season and closed out his major league career on Broadway with the Rangers in 1929–30.

JACQUES RICHARD

BORN: Quebec City, Quebec, October 7, 1952
POSITION: Left Wing, Atlanta Flames, 1972–

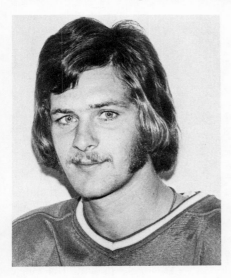

The best way to tell how a young player is reacting to life in the NHL is by the way he speaks. French-Canadian-born Jacques Richard rarely spoke to anyone in his rookie season, a disappointing campaign that resulted in but 13 goals and 18 assists. But Jacques was absolutely effervescent in his sophomore year, much of his flowing verbiage attributable to center Tom Lysiak, who helped Jacques to 27 goals. Richard was the second man chosen in the 1972 amateur grab bag, mainly because of his 227 goals as an amateur.

JOSEPH HENRI "POCKET ROCKET" RICHARD

BORN: Montreal, Quebec, February 29, 1936
POSITION: Center, Montreal Canadiens, 1955–75
AWARDS: Bill Masterton Memorial Trophy, 1974; All-Star (First
Team), 1958; (Second Team), 1959, 1961, 1963

Henri and Maurice Richard began drifting apart as the kid brother came into his own around the NHL. If the Rocket was the home-run hitter, the Pocket was more the base stealer and opposite-field hitter on the Montreal Canadiens.

The Pocket Rocket was an essential cog in Frank Selke's rebuilding plan, and he was an asset to Sam Pollock, in Sam's first years in Montreal. Les Canadiens finished first in 1965–66, breezed past Toronto in the first round of the playoffs with four straight wins, and appeared capable of disposing of the Detroit Red Wings at will in the Cup finals, especially since the series opened with two games at the Forum. But Detroit's hot hand, goalie Roger Crozier, was sizzling, and the Red Wings upset Les Canadiens in the first two games. They became favorites as the series shifted to Olympia Stadium. But Blake rallied his crew and Montreal didn't lose again. The Cup-winning goal was scored by the Pocket Rocket in sudden-death overtime as he slid feet-first toward the net. Crozier appeared to have the puck in hand, but both the puck and the Pocket got past him. Richard crashed into the end boards and the puck slid into the goal.

In a sense Jean Beliveau fulfilled the most realistic hopes of management when he was named captain. His calm assurances proved to be a balm to the younger Canadiens and his deportment on ice was a tacit encouragement to the team as a whole. But the volcanic essence of the Rocket was nowhere to be found in Beliveau, so the natural reaction was to turn to the other Richard for fire and brimstone. Henri resented these demands as much as Beliveau.

"What do they expect from me?" the Pocket said. "I am me, not my brother. Maurice is the best hockey player of all time. I do not try to imitate him. I just try to do my best. All I can say is that I try to play my best."

Henri's best was quite good. Within five seasons of big league hockey he had helped win five Stanley Cups; he made the All-Star team; led the league in assists; he finished second in scoring; and he was called the fastest skater of all time. "The Pocket," said Blake, "became a better all-around player than Rocket was. But it's asking an awful lot of any man to be the scorer that Rocket was. He was the greatest scorer under pressure that I've ever seen."

Others defined their differences in another but equally cogent way: "Henri is mechanically better than Rocket was. But he doesn't have the killer instinct to be the great scorer that Rocket was."

Henri himself once elaborated on that theme. "My brother's biggest thrills came when he scored many goals. I am most satisfied when I play in a close game and do not have any goals scored against me. Sometimes people have asked me whether it helped or hurt having Maurice as an older brother.

"Sometimes it was not easy, because many people expected me to be as spectacular as Maurice. But I believe it helped me more than it hurt me. Don't forget, Maurice was a great scorer, and he could get goals that many other players could not get. That helped my passing because I knew that he would always be near the net awaiting for a shot. But Maurice never gave me any advice. I never asked him for it and he never offered it. Except for a few fundamentals, it is hard to teach anyone how to play hockey. It is a game that you must learn yourself." Henri retired at the end of the 1974–75 season.

MAURICE "ROCKET" RICHARD

BORN: Montreal, Quebec, August 4, 1921
POSITION: Right Wing, Montreal Canadiens, 1942–60
AWARDS: Hart Trophy, 1947; All-Star (First Team), 1945–50, 1955–56, (Second Team), 1944, 1951–54, 1957; Hockey Hall of Fame, 1961

"Maurice Richard," summed up a writer for a Canadian magazine, "was the most exciting athlete I have ever seen. So much has been written about Richard that for me to offer a flood of new praise would be roughly equivalent to a Ph.D. candidate announcing he is going to prove *Hamlet* is an interesting play."

In the beginning, though, there was no suggestion that fourteen thousand Forum fans would someday be chanting *"vas-y* Maurice" whenever Richard would boom along the boards in a wide-eyed rush. The elder son of Onesime Lucien Richard preferred baseball to hockey, although when winter arrived in Montreal, he would lace on his skates and play shinny on the treacherous Rivière des Prairies (the Back River) near his home in Bordeaux in the northern section of town.

Some of his neighborhood chums suspected that Maurice would make a better boxer than either a baseball or hockey player. At one point in his teens Richard entered the Golden Gloves tournament in Montreal, and, according to one report, handled himself quite well. It was a portent of things to come on the ice.

(Left to Right) Rocket Richard, Gump Worsley, Ivan Irwin

Richard's interest in hockey intensified while he attended St. François de Laval School in Bordeaux and continued after he graduated to Montreal Technical High school. In summer he would play ball in the fast Provincial League and in winter he'd play hockey for the Paquette Club of Montreal's Intermediate Hockey League. Four men who were to play a significant role in Richard's future entered his life at this time.

His manager was sports commentator Paul Stuart, who immediately detected the spark of a supercompetitor in Richard and began touting him to coaches around the city. Georges Norchet, the trainer, would soon become Richard's father-in-law. It was while Richard skated for the Paquette Club that Aurel Joliat, the former Canadiens' ace, and Arthur Therrien recommended Maurice as a candidate for the Verdun Maple Leafs, one of Montreal's most distinguished junior teams.

While admiring Richard most hockey scouts agreed that it was much too soon to determine whether or not he had the capabilities to cut the ice with the professionals. His physique had not completely filled out when as a nineteen-year-old he was promoted to the Montreal Canadiens of the crack Quebec Senior Hockey League. And there was some doubt whether or not he could handle the more severe bodychecking and assorted illegalities of minor-league hockey. The suspicions were almost immediately confirmed in his first game with the Senior sextet when he crashed heavily into the boards and broke his left ankle. Maurice was finished for the season and possibly forever.

Fortunately, his injury healed perfectly and he returned to the Senior Canadiens for the next season. This time, after about twenty games, he was careening down the ice in one of his headlong dashes that were later to characterize his NHL style, when he tripped and slid headfirst into the steel upright of the goal cage. He was able to thrust his arm in front of his face before striking the net, but his human bumper, while protecting his head, absorbed too much of the blow and he was carried off the ice with a broken left arm.

That was all the bird dogs had to see. Word soon filtered up and down the hockey grapevine that Richard was too brittle to get anywhere in the pros. Several scouts who had expressed a keen interest in the kid turned attentions to more substantial types.

Significantly, Richard's recovery came about a lot sooner than it had the first time he was injured and he was welcomed back to the lineup at playoff time. His response was six goals in a four-game series and an invitation from Dick Irvin to attend the Canadiens' autumn training camp.

Irvin inserted Richard on a line with the veteran Tony Demers and young center Elmer Lach. The line clicked immediately and Demers scored two goals as the Canadiens won their opening game from Boston, 3–2. The result was especially appealing to one of the game's linesmen—Aurel Joliat.

On November 8, 1942, Richard played his third NHL game. Montreal's opponents in the Forum that night were the Rangers who had beaten them on the previous night in New York. This time Les Canadiens were the winners by a score of 10–4. The highlight of the game was a pulsating end-to-end rush by Richard who made his way through the Ranger defense like a pinball bouncing its way past the obstacles to the goal. Richard's shot beat goalie Steve Buzinski, and even so critical an analyst as Newsy Lalonde raved about the rookie.

After fifteen games Richard had played commendably, if not always spectacularly. His record was 5 goals and 6 assists for 11 points, and the Canadiens, as a team, appeared refreshed by his vitality. Then, in the sixteenth game, it happened again. The Canadiens were skating against the Bruins when Jack Crawford, a big but clean defenseman, collided with Richard and sent Maurice sprawling to the ice in pain. He had suffered a clean break just above his right ankle and was finished once again for the season.

But Richard came back again. "Not only will he be a star," Irvin predicted at the start of the 1943–44 season, "but he'll be the biggest star in hockey!"

Irvin had theorized that Lach was the ideal center for Richard, but he wasn't so sure about the present left winger. He finally decided that Toe Blake would be worthy of an experiment on the unit, and in no time the line was made—for keeps. The trio, soon to be named "the Punch Line," finished one-two-three (Lach, Blake, Richard) in scoring on the team with Richard collecting 32 goals and 22 assists for 54 points in 46 games.

Oddly enough the reaction to Richard's accomplishments was not totally enthusiastic. Some viewers suggested that the "injury jinx" would soon catch up with him again. Others predicted that he would burn himself out. "He won't last" was a familiar cry whenever Richard was discussed. "Let's see what he'll do *next* year" was another.

When "next year" arrived, Les Canadiens iced virtually the same team they had when they won the Stanley Cup in April with only a few exceptions. The Punch Line remained intact and launched the season with the same syncopated attack that had stirred the fans in 1943–44. Richard seemed particularly bolstered by a full season under his belt without serious injury and he broke from the post like an overzealous thoroughbred. His scoring was becoming so prolific that opposing coaches began mapping specific strategies to stop Maurice alone, on the theory that if you could blockade Richard you could beat Les Canadiens. These stratagems took on many variations as they would over the years. One of the favorites was simply to goad Maurice into a fight. This was not exactly difficult since the brooding French Canadian still couldn't speak English and was rather sensitive and self-conscious about his language barrier.

One of the most effective methods for inciting Richard to riot was for an opposing coach to select one of his less-effective hatchet men to pester Maurice with an assortment of words, elbows, high sticks, and butt ends until Richard retaliated. Both players would then likely be penalized, but at least Richard would be off the ice. The Rangers tried this ploy in Madison Square Garden on December 17, 1944.

Midway in the second period Bob "Killer" Dill, a young Ranger defenseman, challenged Richard a few seconds after Chuck Scherza of the Rangers and Leo Lamoureux of the Canadiens had started their own private war. Up until then Dill's chief claim to fame was the fact that he was a nephew of Mike and Tom Gibbons of fistic fame. From that night on, however, Dill became renowned as the man who lost two knockouts to Maurice in one period!

In the first bout, Richard disposed of Dill with a hefty right to the jaw. When the Ranger recovered, referee King Clancy sent him to the penalty box with a major penalty for fighting and doled out the same sentence to Richard. In those days the penalty benches were constructed without a barrier separating players of opposing teams, so it was not unusual for the combatants to exchange insults while they awaited their release.

Still smarting from his knockout, Dill challenged Richard to a return bout. Maurice didn't quite understand Bob's English, but there was no mistaking his sign language. Dill tossed the first punch and the two were off and swinging on the dry wood of the penalty box. Richard KO'd Dill a second time!

Later in the season, Les Canadiens, snug in first place, invaded Madison Square Garden and routed the Rangers, 11–5. Banging two shots past goalie Ken McAuley, Richard lifted his goal-scoring mark to an astonishing 48 in only 47 games. "McAuley," observed a reporter, "acted shell-shocked."

Maurice seemed to rise above the smog of blather and cruised speedily along at a goal-a-game pace. He had surpassed Joe Malone's goal-scoring record, for which he received a standing ovation at the Forum, and the pressing question remaining was whether or not Richard would reach the hitherto unattainable plateau of fifty goals.

He scored number forty-nine on March 15 with only two games remaining on the schedule. In the next-to-last game, against the Black Hawks on Forum ice, Les Canadiens triumphed, but somehow Maurice was thoroughly blanked. That left only one more match, the final game of the season at Boston Garden. This time Richard came through in a 4–2 win over the Bruins and he finished the season with 50 goals in 50 games, a modern hockey average that has never been and will likely never be equaled.

Richard's histrionics had already become too numerous for most fans to remember. Some rooters preferred to recall the goals he scored. Others remembered the fights, and still others pointed to the obscure episodes that marked Maurice so unique.

"The impact Richard had on the Canadiens," said Peter Gzowski, "and through them on the rest of the league, seems to be beautifully summed up in one incident that occurred in Toronto. It was the time that, soaring head over heels as the result of an artful Maple Leaf check, Richard shattered the 'unbreakable' Herculite glass that had just been installed in Maple Leaf Gardens around the top of the boards. No one had nicked it before, and only Eddie Shack has broken it since, which was unfair, since Shack hit a faulty piece. Richard put the *heel of his skate* through it, and there was something perfect about its being the Rocket, the epitome of recklessness, of untrammeled fire and fury and abandon on the ice, who did it."

Few players ever upstaged Richard. One of those who did was Gordie Howe, and the Red Wing immortal managed to pull the surprise on "Maurice Richard Night" at the Forum. As the presentation was coming to an end, Richard headed for the sideboards when Howe called out, "Hey, Rocket!" As Richard turned, Howe pulled off his leather gauntlet and extended his hand. For a brief second the Forum crowd hushed as the two archfoes shook hands at center ice. "It was a sort of genuinely unrehearsed spontaneous gesture that caught the big crowd completely by surprise," said Elmer Ferguson, a Montreal columnist.

The crowd remained silent for another moment and then burst into a thunderous ovation that gave veteran press-box viewers a case of goosepimples. Howe then went out and scored a big goal for the Red Wings.

GEORGE TAYLOR RICHARDSON

BORN: Kingston, Ontario, 1880s
DIED: February 9, 1916
POSITION: Unknown, played only as amateur from 1909 until death in 1916, for Queen's University of OHA and 14th Regiment, Kingston
AWARDS: Hockey Hall of Fame, 1950

At the turn of the century Kingston, Ontario—"the Limestone City"—was a major hockey center, and George Richardson, who never turned professional, was one of the top players in the game.

He was a member of such championship teams as the 14th Regiment of Kingston, which won the senior hockey title in 1908. In 1909 Richardson played with Queen's University and helped his team to the Allan Cup.

Richardson went overseas in World War I and was killed in action in 1916. Elected posthumously to the Hall of Fame, he also has a stadium erected in his honor at Queen's University.

THE RINK

All rinks are not standardized. And even if they were, they would not be identical because some boards which surround a rink are lively, others dull; some stiff, some resilient. And some ice surfaces are slicker than others.

As nearly as possible, a rink should be 200 feet long, 85 feet wide. For example, the Spectrum rink in Philadelphia (as all new NHL arenas) is 200 feet by 85 feet. Where it is shorter than some is in the center or neutral zone, since the blue lines which divide the rink into three zones should be drawn 60 feet from the goal lines.

The red line which splits the neutral zone is 12 inches wide. It came into being in 1943–44. The purpose: to speed up the game, make it possible to pass forward half the length of the rink without being offside, that is, from one's own defense zone to the red line.

The texture of ice itself varies from rink to rink. The Spectrum surface is about five-eighths of an inch thick and is considered fast. In those arenas where ice is kept on longer, it is usually thicker and slower.

Each rink has similar ice markings, spots, and circles. Most face-offs take place on the spots. The circles are at center ice, and one to either side of each goal. Four other spots are in the neutral zone. The circles are 30 feet in diameter, and only the two players facing off are permitted within the circles.

JOHN ROSS ROACH

BORN: Fort Perry, Ontario, June 23, 1900
POSITION: Goalie, Toronto St. Pats, 1921–26; Toronto Maple Leafs, 1926–28; New York Rangers, 1928–32; Detroit Falcons, 1932–33; Detroit Red Wings, 1933–35
AWARDS: All-Star (First Team), 1933

John Ross Roach was one of the smallest (5'5", 130 lbs.) and most exciting goaltenders of all time. He labored for four different clubs over his fourteen-year major league career, seeing action with the Toronto St. Pats, New York Rangers, Detroit Red Wings, and Toronto Maple Leafs.

In his rookie year with the Pats, 1922, Roach guided his club to the Stanley Cup—the only Cup of his entire career. Roach came close on several other occasions—but he could never recapture the silverware.

During his first season with the New York Rangers, Roach racked up an incredible three consecutive playoff shutouts before the Blueshirts were finally eliminated. All was not a bed of roses with the New Yorkers though. Two seasons later John allowed six goals in each of his three playoff appearances against Toronto and was sold to the Red Wings the following season.

At Detroit he came his closest to winning the Vezina Trophy, missing by only fractions of a percentage point, but he was named to the First All-Star Team. Roach finished up his career with the Maple Leafs, seeing action in only one game before hanging his pads up for good.

RENE PAUL ROBERT

BORN: Trois-Rivières, Quebec, December 31, 1948
POSITION: Center and Right Wing, Toronto Maple Leafs, 1970–71; Pittsburgh Penguins, 1971–72; Buffalo Sabres, 1972–
AWARDS: All-Star (Second Team), 1975

After kicking around the NHL with Pittsburgh and Toronto for a couple of years, René Robert found a home on the right wing of the Buffalo Sabres' prolific French Connection Line, where he blended perfectly with Gil Perreault and Rick Martin. After years of relative mediocrity, Robert burst forth with 40 goals and 43 assists in 1972–73, but his production slackened in 1973–74 while

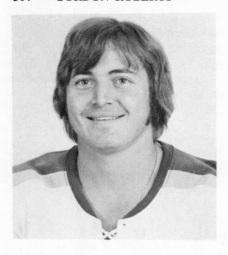

René Robert

centerman Perreault missed a third of the season with an injury. But the French Line had recovered by 1974–75, and Robert connected so well that he led the club in scoring, with 40 goals and 60 assists to break into the 100-point club during the regular season. Robert also performed outstandingly in the 1975 Stanley Cup playoffs, until the Sabres were defeated in the finals by Philadelphia.

GORDON ROBERTS

BORN: (Place Unknown), September 5, 1891
DIED: September 2, 1966
POSITION: Left Wing, Ottawa Senators (NHA), 1910; Montreal Wanderers (NHA), 1911–16; Vancouver Millionaires (PCHA), 1917, 1920; Seattle Metropolitans (PCHA), 1918
AWARDS: Hockey Hall of Fame, 1971

Gordon Roberts ranks as one of the greatest left wingers of all time. Although never skating on a Cup winner over his entire ten-year career, he scored better than a goal per game and was one of the most feared shooters of his day. All of these heroics came, by the way, while Roberts was studying and/or practicing medicine.

After playing one year for Ottawa, Roberts joined the Wanderer squad in order to be near McGill University where he was a medical student. He played with the Wanderers for six seasons until his graduation from McGill.

Roberts moved to the West Coast to begin his practice in 1917, and while he was in the neighborhood, he signed with the Vancouver Millionaires of the

PCHA. Between house calls, Roberts found time to establish an all-time PCHA scoring record, lighting the lamp 43 times in 23 games.

Dr. Roberts's medical obligations brought him to Seattle in 1918 where he played for the Mets and led them into the playoffs, only to see them fall to Vancouver. Roberts sat out the 1919 season, but returned to Vancouver in 1920 to have one last go at it before retiring.

CLAUDE C. ROBINSON

BORN: Harriston, Ontario, December 17, 1881
POSITION: Forward, Winnipeg (years uncertain); Coach, Canadian 1932 Olympic Team
AWARDS: Hockey Hall of Fame, 1945

A firm believer in the dictum "Go West, Young Man!" this Ontario native moved to Winnipeg in 1881 where he later became involved with hockey as a player and as an executive.

Claude Robinson played with the Winnipeg Victorias and the team won both the Stanley Cup and the Allan Cup while he was associated with them.

This Hall of Famer suggested the idea of a national association which later became the Canadian Amateur Hockey Association. Robinson served as the CAHA's first secretary and in 1932 he managed the Canadian winter team for the Olympic games.

DALE ROLAND CARL ROLFE

BORN: Timmins, Ontario, April 30, 1940
POSITION: Defenseman, Boston Bruins, 1959–60; Los Angeles Kings, 1967–70; Detroit Red Wings, 1970–71; New York Rangers, 1971–

One of the biggest (6–4, 205) skaters in the contemporary National Hockey League, defenseman Dale Rolfe played most of his early professional career in the minors. He had a brief fling in Boston with the Bruins in 1959–60, returning to the NHL after expansion with the Los Angeles Kings. Alternately nicknamed "Goat," "Reindeer," and "Turkey" because of his elongated neck and herky-jerk motion, Rolfe was dealt to Detroit in 1970 and then to the Rangers in 1971. Upon his arrival in New York, Rolfe matured as a big-leaguer and played the best defense of his life. His skating ability enabled him to lead many a dangerous rush and his long reach enhanced Rolfe's defensive capabilities. His career with New York was pockmarked with injuries, the most serious being a severe compound fracture of his left ankle late in the 1974–75 campaign. The injury was, at the time, believed to be a threat to his playing future.

ELWIN IRA (AL) ROLLINS

BORN: Vanguard, Saskatchewan, October 9, 1926
POSITION: Goalie, Toronto Maple Leafs, 1949–52; Chicago Black
    Hawks, 1952–57; New York Rangers, 1959–60.
AWARDS: Hart Trophy, 1954; Vezina Trophy, 1951

A case could be made for Al Rollins as the most underrated superb goalie in NHL history. As understudy for Toronto's legendary Turk Broda in 1949–50, Rollins consistently came up with the good game, but was always over-shadowed by his more colorful partner. In 1950–51, Rollins played forty games for the Leafs, gaining the Vezina Trophy. Rollins's goals-against average was an impeccable 1.75. Better still was his playoff work—only six goals allowed in four games for a 1.50 average. Needless to say the Leafs won the Stanley Cup that year. Rollins played one more season in Toronto and again was superb, ending up with a 2.20 average. However, he slipped during the playoffs and was traded to Chicago before the 1952–53 campaign.

The Black Hawks had been a consistent non-playoff club until Rollins came along. He made miracles for the patchwork Chicago sextet and helped them into the playoffs. In turn he won the Hart Trophy as the NHL's most valuable player. Rollins performed gallantly in the playoffs against the powerful Cana-diens as Chicago took a three-games-to-two lead. But Montreal rebounded to win the semifinal round. In 1959–60 Rollins was acquired by the Rangers and he finished his major league career in New York where he played excellent hockey. But typically, he was overshadowed; the Rangers had obtained 1960 Olympic hero Jack McCartan and Rollins was shunted aside.

ELWIN "DOC" ROMNES

BORN: White Bear, Minnesota, January 1, 1909
POSITION: Center, Chicago Black Hawks, 1930–38; Toronto Maple
    Leafs, 1939; New York Americans, 1939–40
AWARDS: Lady Byng Memorial Trophy, 1936

One of the classiest American-born players to skate in the National Hockey League, Doc Romnes was an offensive star for the Chicago Black Hawks in two (1934, 1938) of Chicago's three Stanley Cup triumphs. Lionel Conacher, Canada's athlete of the half-century, called Romnes one of the best centers he ever skated with, a statement that has never been disputed. Doc scored the win-ning goal in the 1938 semifinal series against the New York Americans, and scored a pivotal goal in the finals against the Toronto Maple Leafs. He origi-nally broke in with the Black Hawks in 1930–31 and played in the Windy City until 1938–39 when he was traded to the Toronto Maple Leafs. He concluded his big-league career in 1939–40 with the New York Americans.

ERSKINE "SKENE" RONAN

BORN: Unknown
POSITION: Defenseman and Center, Toronto Maple Leafs (OPHL), 1909; Haileybury (NHA), 1910; Renfrew Creamery Kings (NHA), 1911; Ottawa Senators (NHA), 1912–14; Montreal Shamrocks (NHA), 1915; Toronto Arenas/Montreal Canadiens, 1916; Ottawa Senators, 1919
AWARDS: Scoring Leader, 1913 (prior to NHL's Art Ross Trophy)

Erskine Ronan was an artistic, high-scoring centerman who, for his first three years in pro hockey, labored in relative obscurity as a journeyman defenseman. Skene was rescued in 1912 when Ottawa picked up his contract from the defunct Renfrew club. Ottawa's star center, Marty Walsh, was approaching middle age so Ronan was given a shot at filling the pivot position between Jack Darragh and Dubbie Kerr. And fill it he did—when the smoke had cleared Ronan was the league's leading scorer and top centerman.

Ronan had two more solid seasons with Ottawa and then was sold to the Shamrocks where he starred for one season before moving on again. Skene split time between the Toronto Arenas and Montreal Canadiens during the 1916 campaign, winding up on the Hab's Stanley Cup-winning squad.

That was Ronan's only Stanley Cup and his last year as an effective scorer. He tried a comeback three years later with Ottawa but it had all left him by then.

PAUL RONTY

BORN: Toronto, Ontario, July 12, 1928
POSITION: Center, Boston Bruins, 1947–51; New York Rangers, 1951–55; Montreal Canadiens, 1955

Paul Ronty, a blond, clean-playing center, spent his eight-year National Hockey League career skating for also-rans. A product of the Boston Bruins' farm system, Ronty graduated to the big club in 1947–48, playing on a line with Ken Smith and Johnny Peirson. The youngsters helped the Bruins to three straight playoff berths, but never a Stanley Cup. Ronty was traded to the New York Rangers prior to the 1951–52 season and skated well on a nonplayoff club for three years, although he excelled at playmaking for high-scoring right winger Wally Hergesheimer. Ronty closed his NHL career in 1954–55 with a Montreal Canadiens team that was eliminated in the Stanley Cup finals by the Detroit Red Wings.

Paul Ronty

ARTHUR HOWEY (ART) ROSS

BORN: Naughton, Ontario, January 13, 1886
DIED: August 5, 1964
POSITION: Defenseman, Westmount (CAHL), 1905; Brandon (MHL), 1907; Kenora Thistles (MHL), 1907; Montreal Wanderers (ECAHA), 1908–09; Haileybury (NHA), 1910; Montreal Wanderers (NHA), 1911–14, 1917; Ottawa Senators (NHA), 1915–16; Montreal Wanderers, 1917–18
AWARDS: Art Ross puck, net, and trophy (begun 1947) in his name; Hockey Hall of Fame, 1945

The official NHL puck, "the Art Ross puck" and the official goal net, "the Art Ross net," were not named after the former Boston Bruins' manager for nothing. One of the more creative minds in hockey, Ross redesigned the rubber puck—which formerly had sharp edges that caused painful cuts—had the edges bevelled, and improved the game. Pre-Ross nets were simple devices with sloping flat rear sections that frequently inspired pucks to bounce out of the twine

Art Ross

as fast as they went in. Ross's improvement became today's net with a double half-moon interior built to retain pucks that are shot into the webbing.

But Ross did considerably more than that. His major accomplishment was building the Boston Bruins into a dynasty in the late twenties and constantly rebuilding the Bruins so that they remained the class of the NHL for most of Art's life. He developed such aces as Eddie Shore, Frankie Brimsek, the Kraut Line, Bill Cowley and Dit Clapper. He also was a cantankerous sort who frequently feuded with his managerial colleagues but especially Conn Smythe of the Maple Leafs.

Smythe claims the feud started because Ross screwed him first. It happened when Smythe had bought the Toronto franchise in the late twenties and was on the lookout for talent. Ross recommended a player named Jimmy "Sailor" Herberts. Smythe bit, paid $18,000 for Herberts, and then learned that he had purchased a dud.

According to Smythe, Ross's chief goal in life was making a fool of Smythe. "Once," said Smythe, "Ross stationed two longshoremen near our bench in Boston Garden and their instructions were to goad me into a fight. Ross wanted to have me put in jail."

Sure enough the longshoremen pushed and shoved Smythe as he was heading for the dressing room after the game. Smythe snarled at them and then noticed Ross in the background, apparently ready to charge at Smythe. "My assistant, a little guy named Frank Selke, saw Ross coming and dove at him with a flying block that knocked Ross down," Smythe recalled. "We got out of there fast, but not before I yelled at the longshoremen, 'When your boss gets up tell him I can't waste my time with anybody that a man as small as Selke can lick.' '' All Smythe had done was pour gasoline on the flames of his feud with Ross. Each man eagerly awaited the opportunity to go one up—or two or three up, if possible—on the other.

During a Bruins' slump, Smythe bought four columns of space in all of the Boston newspapers. Addressed to the fans, the ad read: ''If you're tired of what you've been looking at, come out tonight and see a decent team, the Toronto Maple Leafs, play hockey.''

Livid, Ross demanded that league president Frank Calder fine Smythe $3,000 for conduct detrimental to the NHL. He snapped that Smythe was nothing more than ''the big wind from Lake Ontario.''

Ross didn't get his way and subsequently Smythe went at him again. This time, when the Leafs returned to Boston, Conn rented a tuxedo and pranced haughtily around Boston Garden, tipping his hat and waving to the Bruins' fans as if he was the city's official greeter. A bouquet of roses were dispatched to Ross as the added fillip.

Smythe always respected Ross's hockey ability and following World War II they patched up their feud. According to the Toronto boss, it was *his* idea, based on Ross's sons' participation in the armed forces. ''His two sons served overseas,'' Smythe explained, ''and had excellent records. I figured anybody who could rear two boys like that must be all right!''

JOSEPH JEAN-PAUL ROBERT (BOBBY) ROUSSEAU

BORN: Montreal, Quebec, July 26, 1940
POSITION: Right Wing, Montreal Canadiens, 1960–70; Minnesota
    North Stars, 1970–71; New York Rangers, 1971–
AWARDS: Calder Memorial Trophy, 1962; All-Star (Second Team),
    1966

A slick playmaker equally adept at center or on the wing, Bobby Rousseau played ten glorious seasons with the power-packed Montreal Canadiens. Twice a 30-goal man for the Habs, Bobby was on four Stanley Cup-winning squads before being traded to the Minnesota North Stars in 1970.

After a wasted season with the Stars, Rousseau was bartered to the New York Rangers where he gained quite a reputation as a favorite of the Madison Square Garden gallery. A chronic back ailment and spinal fusion surgery shelved Rousseau early in the 1974–75 season with many observers doubtful he would ever make it back to the ice wars.

DONALD V. (DON) RUCK

When the National Hockey League decided to expand from six to twelve teams in 1967 it also expanded its front office, opening a base in New York City. The NHL's Manhattan mogul was Don Ruck, a former Connecticut newspaperman who later handled public relations and advertising for Blue Cross in that state. Dynamic and efficient, Ruck eventually made his way up the hockey ladder and became NHL vice-president and the man supervising the league's commerical arm—NHL Services Inc. By 1975 his office was staffed by fifteen employees and handled everything from public relations to filmmaking.

CLAUDE RUEL

Claude Ruel, a Montreal coach, had no big league coaching experience and unlike Dick Irvin or Toe Blake had never played a game in the NHL. He was short (5′5″), fat (223 pounds), crew-cut, and so Santa Clauslike that he often made the onlooker feel jolly, whether Claude was or not! Before he lost the sight of one eye in a hockey accident, Ruel had been one of the best junior defensemen in Canada. He later coached the Junior Canadiens and, in time, became the director of player development for the NHL club. Perhaps more important, Ruel was what Blake wasn't; he was Sam Pollock's handpicked choice to coach Les Canadiens in 1968. ''Claude is the coach—the best man we had for the job," said Pollock in defending his choice against critics who charged that Sam would do the coaching from the sidelines.

Succeeding Blake and Irvin was about as easy as a team of trained seals following Frank Sinatra and Barbra Streisand in Las Vegas. "Me, I can only go down," said Claude in his fractured English.

Montreal slipped and there were rumblings that Ruel wasn't getting through to his men the way Blake had. "I like the fundamentals of hockey," Ruel insisted in his defense. "Skate, play position, and move that puck ahead. You've got to be tough and honest for success." Ruel prevailed in his rookie season. The Candiens finished first and won the Stanley Cup. Instead of winning acclaim, Ruel was virtually ignored; until the following season when Montreal actually *missed* a playoff berth. "Ruel failed," wrote John Robertson of the Montreal *Star*, "because it was just not in him to lead."

Ironically, Ruel was replaced by Al MacNeil who also won a Stanley Cup and then found himself exiled to the minors. Pudgy Claude was placed in a superscouting position with the Canadiens and, with the pressure gone, he seemed to have found his niche.

ERNIE RUSSELL

BORN: Montreal, Quebec, October 21, 1883
DIED: February 23, 1963
POSITION: Rover and Center, Montreal Winged Wheelers (CAHL), 1905; Montreal Wanderers (ECAHA and NHA), 1906–14
AWARDS: Scoring Leader, 1907, 1912 (prior to NHL's Art Ross Trophy); Hockey Hall of Fame, 1965

Ernie Russell was a tiny 140-pounder, but his size didn't prevent him from becoming one of the most proficient scorers hockey has ever seen. After one year of amateur shinny, Ernie was snapped up by the professional Wanderers in 1906 as a rover/center.

Ernie virtually dominated the game for the next three years, leading his Wanderers to three successive Stanley Cups and scoring an amazing 84 goals in 24 games.

Russell sat out the 1909 season, but returned the following year and promptly guided his team to yet another Cup. Russell was embroiled in a fierce neck-and-neck race for the scoring lead with Newsy Lalonde that season, but lost out when Lalonde erupted for a nine-goal game on the very last day of the campaign.

Ernie Russell played four more seasons with the Wanderers, closing out his career as a sub in 1914. He is a member of the Hockey Hall of Fame.

PHILLIP DOUGLAS (PHIL) RUSSELL

BORN: Edmonton, Alberta, July 21, 1952
POSITION: Defenseman, Chicago Black Hawks, 1972–

The Chicago Black Hawks' first choice in the 1972 amateur draft, Phil Russell moved comfortably into the NHL after playing defense for the Edmonton Oil Kings. He proved a capable puck carrier and puncher while scoring a healthy amount of points—29 in 80 games in 1974–75—for a backliner. He clocked 260 penalty minutes that season, his personal high.

RUSSIAN HOCKEY

The Russians, who previously had considered soccer their number one sport, became attracted to ice hockey after World War II. The Soviet Union was as far north and as cold as Canada. For millions there it was as natural to ice-skate as to walk. Since the long, cold winters provided thousands of natural ice-skating rinks from Leningrad to Vladivostok, the shift to hockey was natural and easy.

The Soviets made the first splash in 1954. The top Soviet team entered the world (amateur) hockey championships in Stockholm, Sweden, and played so well they reached the finals against a Canadian team comprised of the best nonprofessionals in North America. Although the Canadian amateurs were hardly of NHL quality, they *were* Canadians and therefore considered capable of beating anybody.

The Russians won, 7–2, and the first chip had been delivered against Canada's image of worldwide hockey superiority. But this was only the beginning. Using unique training techniques and developing their own style, the Russians got better while the Canadian amateurs remained static. And this was reflected in the results.

By 1962, the Russians, coached by Anatoli Tarasov and Arkadi Cherneshev, began a rampage of championship victories that was unparalleled in amateur hockey competition. From 1962 through 1972 the Soviets won twelve out of a possible thirteen championships in Olympic and world hockey play.

As Canadian hockey critic Jock Carroll pointed out, Canada was left clinging to the idea that its *professional* players were still the best in the world. And even as the 1970s dawned, most hockey experts agreed that NHL players would make short work of the Soviet National team—if they should ever get the chance. The Russians, encouraged by international amateur hockey officials, still refused to meet professional opponents.

But then Soviet coach Tarasov startled the hockey world by revealing that the Russians would, in fact, be willing to play an NHL team. "I wouldn't care if we got beaten 15–0," said Tarasov. "The score won't matter. What will matter is to determine how our hockey players stand up to the best professionals in North America."

The machinery was set in motion to arrange the game, and after considerable haggling, officials of the NHL and the Soviet Ice Hockey Federation arranged for an eight-game series in September 1972. The first four games would be played in Canada and the final set would be played on Russian ice.

"We used to listen to stories about Canadian hockey as if they were fairy tales," said Tarasov. "That the Canadians were invincible, that the skill of the founders of this game was truly fantastic." Now, thought the Canadians, the Russians would have a chance to see for themselves.

The Russians went about their business with extreme thoroughness. They had spent years scouting the NHL teams, filming the big league games and learning the best of the professional game while discarding the worst. They prepared carefully and thoroughly for their four games in Canada.

Team Canada, on the other hand, treated the Russians with a casualness bordering on contempt. Scouts were sent to analyze the Russian brand of hockey, but they took the most cursory glance at the Soviet sextet. They returned fully confident that Canada would win, reporting that the Russians' most glaring weakness was in the net. Soviet goaltender Vladislav Tretiak was inferior, they said.

The boasts and predictions finally would be put to the test on September 2, 1972, when the opening face-off would take place in Montreal. By that day all of Canada was in a frenzy, thirsting for the kill, awaiting the big victory of Team Canada, "the best hockey team in the game's history," according to Frank Orr of the Toronto *Star*.

After the eight games, Team Canada skated off the ice with a series victory—four games won, three games lost, and one tied.

But when the excitement died down, observers agreed that the Soviets had proven themselves equal to the best professionals in North America.

The Team Canada–Russian series had reverberations which will be heard for years to come. It set big league and amateur coaches to examining the Soviet style of play and conditioning techniques. The excitement created by the series brought new popularity for hockey particularly in Europe, and a European Professional League was organized with the backing of Detroit Red Wings' owner Bruce Norris.

Some experts argued that the Canadians were the real losers because they had been favored to win eight straight games and were fortunate to squeeze out a last-minute triumph in the final game.

Perhaps the most accurate appraisal of all was made by Canadian author Henk W. Hoppener, who wrote when it was over: "We won the games. We lost a legend."

The Russians, however, had not had their fill of the North American professional game. In the spring of 1974 Soviet hockey leaders arranged another series, this time with All-Stars from the World Hockey Association. Once again the first four games would be played in Canada and the final four in Moscow.

Unlike Team Canada I, the new group of Canadian pros fully anticipated problems from the Russian skaters at the outset and trained accordingly. Instead of being swept off the ice in game one as Team Canada I was in 1972, the 1974 WHA sextet held the Russians to a 3–3 tie in the opening game at Quebec City. Even more startling, the WHA club, coached by Billy Harris, won the secnd match, 4–1, in Toronto. The Russians rebounded for a 8–5 victory in Winnipeg. In the decisive fourth game, at Vancouver, the Russians overcame a three-goal deficit to pull out a tie, 5–5.

The Vancouver debacle completely deflated the Canadians. Although they boasted such aces as Gordie Howe, Bobby Hull, J. C. Tremblay, and Gerry Cheevers, Team Canada II simply couldn't cope with the Russians on Soviet ice. Powerful and confident, the Red icemen won three out of the last four games to capture the series. Although the WHA club failed to win as many games as Team Canada I, they were hailed for their gallant effort with special accolades to Gordie Howe, who, at age forty-six, skated with the best of the Russians.

ST. LOUIS BLUES

Although St. Louis had a rich hockey heritage as a minor league city it was not considered a favorite to gain entry to the National Hockey League when, in 1965, the league finally voted to expand from six to twelve teams. The franchise price was $2 million, and twenty-four groups representing twelve cities bid for the honor of having a major league hockey team.

Within a year, five cities were admitted—Los Angeles, Minneapolis-St. Paul, Pittsburgh, Philadelphia, and Oakland. Still out in the cold, St. Louis, if it hoped to gain entry, would have to outbid Vancouver, Buffalo, and Baltimore, among others.

When the final decision had to be made, St. Louis was able to present some overwhelming assets. It had a completed arena that fulfilled the NHL's requirement that there be at least 12,500 seats; it had the support of the Chicago Black Hawks, who owned the St. Louis Arena; and it had a purchasing group with the highest credentials, headed by Sidney Salomon, Jr. and his son, Sidney Salomon III.

On April 6, 1966, the NHL Board of Governors granted St. Louis the franchise. In no time at all the team was nicknamed "the Blues." Then the Arena was purchased from Arthur Wirtz, owner of the Chicago Black Hawks, for $4 million.

The Salomons were responsible for several monumental improvements in the St. Louis sports scene, but none compare with the multimillion-dollar renaissance of the Arena. In a matter of months the classic building received a complete face-lifting, including an increased seating capacity to 14,500. By

516

opening night it was superior in both design and construction to the other ultra-modern structures that house the NHL teams.

But producing a winning team had top priority. To do so, the Salomons hired Lynn Patrick, a man who had long experience as an NHL player, coach, and manager. He was appointed manager-coach, and Scotty Bowman became assistant manager and coach. Thanks to the league draft, they obtained Glenn Hall from Chicago—otherwise known as "Mister Goalie"—first and built a team around him. Veterans such as Ron Stewart, Jim Roberts, Don McKenney, and Al Arbour were signed as well as a large sprinkling of youngsters such as Terry Crisp, Gary Sabourin, Tim Ecclestone, and Frank St. Marseille.

The Salomons required all the courage they could muster in the first half of the 1967–68 campaign. Crowds thinned out after the opening game, and although Glenn Hall performed weekly miracles in goal by November 22 the Blues were in the West Division cellar, and Patrick turned the coaching reins over to Bowman. On November 26, St. Louis lost its seventh straight game, and concern was rampant throughout the front office.

The Blues visited Madison Square Garden on November 26 and were beaten 1–0 by the Rangers. More important than that, however, was a meeting between New York manager-coach Emile Francis and the Blues' high command. Francis had been unhappy with the performance of center Gordon "Red" Berenson and dispatched him to St. Louis on November 27 along with Barclay Plager in return for Ron Stewart, who had been the Blues' leading scorer, and Ron Attwell. It turned out to be one of the most one-sided trades in hockey history. With the Blues, Berenson scored 22 goals and was voted West Division Player of the Year by *The Sporting News*.

Suddenly every move made by the Salomons and their staff seemed to have the magic touch. Sparked by Berenson's scoring punch and Hall's craftmanship in the nets the Blues vacated the NHL's West Division cellar and barged into the Stanley Cup playoffs. St. Louis's first round opponents were the division leaders, the Philadelphia Flyers. In a bitterly fought series that went the full seven games, St. Louis knocked off the Western champs and then went on to dispose of the Minnesota North Stars in the exact same fashion. In their first year of existence the fledgling Blues suddenly found themselves in the Stanley Cup finals against the tradition-rich Montreal Canadiens.

Most observers of the pro shinny scene described this final round pairing as the biggest mismatch since Custer's Last Stand. Not only were Les Habitants expected to sweep the series, four games to none, but it was predicted they would outscore the Blues by as many as twenty goals.

As it turned out, the Habs did win the series in four games, but the feisty Blues twice forced the Frenchmen into overtime and were outscored only eleven to seven. St. Louis received inspired goalkeeping from Glenn Hall who was voted the Conn Smythe Trophy as the most valuable player in the Cup round.

With Hall in the nets—later to alternate with another super veteran, Jacques Plante—the Blues climbed to the top of the West Division, finishing first in 1969 and 1970, but each time they were wiped out in the Stanley Cup finals.

More important, the Salomons had made hockey the prestige sport in St. Louis. The Arena's seating capacity was increased to 18,008 and nearly every game from 1970 on was a guaranteed sellout. Unfortunately, the Blues' lost some of their early thrust and began slipping in the standings, finishing sixth in the West Division in the 1973–74 season. They rebounded a year later and landed in second place in the newly formed Conn Smythe Division. However, they were eliminated from the playoffs in two straight games by the Pittsburgh Penguins.

DONALD SALESKI

BORN: Moose Jaw, Saskatchewan, November 10, 1949
POSITION: Right Wing, Philadelphia Flyers, 1971–

Affectionately known as "the Big Bird," 6–2, 200-pound Don Saleski captivated Philadelphia Flyers' fans with his swooping skating style and frequent lust for combat. The hulking right wing became a National Hockey League regular in 1972–73, scoring 21 points—12 goals, 9 assists—in 78 games, but also totalling 205 penalty minutes. In 1973–74 he lifted his points total to 15 goals, 25 assists, and 40 points. When the Flyers made their successful march to the Stanley Cup in May 1974 Saleski contributed two goals and nine assists in seventeen playoff games. However, his play tapered off terribly the following year—only 28 points in 63 games—and the Big Bird no longer was revered on Broad Street.

BORJE SALMING

BORN: Kiruna, Sweden, April 17, 1951
POSITION: Defenseman, Toronto Maple Leafs, 1973–
AWARDS: All-Star (Second Team), 1975

One of the best European hockey players to make the trip across the Atlantic, Borje Salming was the steadiest defenseman on the struggling Maple Leafs during the 1974–75 season and was rewarded with a selection to the NHL's Second All-Star Team.

Formerly a member of the Swedish National Team with Maple Leaf teammate Inge Hammarstrom, Salming was so impressive in his rookie season (1973–74) that he finished third in the balloting for the Calder Trophy. A defensive defenseman, Salming nonetheless scored 76 points in his first two campaigns with the Leafs.

DEREK MICHAEL SANDERSON

BORN: Niagara Falls, Ontario, June 16, 1946
POSITION: Center/Left Wing, Boston Bruins, 1965–72, 1973–74; Philadelphia Blazers (WHA), 1972; New York Rangers, 1974–
AWARDS: Calder Trophy, 1968

If media coverage could be translated into talent, Derek Sanderson would have been the most gifted player ever to lace on a pair of skates. Combining a lusty sex appeal with considerable talent and a penchant for saying outrageous things to the press, Sanderson was featured in such publications as *Esquire, Life,* and *Sports Illustrated* while more talented teammates were overlooked.

Sanderson was five years old when his father, Harold, first put skates on him. Derek has frequently mentioned how strong an influence his dad was in developing his philosophy toward life, toward hockey, and toward just plain toughness. The fittest survive, and Derek made it plain in his autobiography, *I've Got to Be Me,* that that was precisely what his father had meant.

"If it's worth fighting over," Harold Sanderson told his son, "the fight is worth winning. So, if the other fellow is bigger than you, use something—a stick, a pipe, anything you want. Just make sure you beat him."

Not long after receiving the fatherly lecture, Derek played a game of hockey and was soundly licked in a fight on the ice. After the game Harold Sanderson took his son aside and said, "If you let a guy do that to you again, I won't talk to you."

The art of toughness as practiced by the Sanderson clan involved the development of an immunity to pain. Harold Sanderson began teaching his son when

Derek was eight years old. One day after a puck slammed into Derek's head, opening a large, bloody wound, the kid skated to the sidelines expecting first-aid treatment from a doctor and commiseration from his dad. He got neither. "You're all right, for Christ's sake," said Harold Sanderson. "Get back out there. The blood will dry. Shake it off."

Derek bled for the entire workout. An hour elapsed before his father took him to the hospital, where three stitches were required to close the wound. Before the week was up, Derek returned to the doctor to have the stitches removed. "Let me have them," said Harold Sanderson. The surprised doctor handed the stitches over to Mr. Sanderson while his son looked on in amazement, wondering what his father had in mind. "When we got home," Derek recalled, "he put them in a little plastic box. He saved every one of my first 100 stitches and, pretty soon, I started to become proud of them. I'd come home after a tough game and say, 'Hi, Dad, eight more!' "

Derek is the first to admit that toughness was not the only thing Harold taught him ("He was a bug on scientific hockey"), but it seemed to be the main thing as Derek's ice career unfolded.

He climbed up the amateur hockey ladder, ultimately landing with the Niagara Falls Flyers, a powerful club in the Ontario Hockey Association, Junior A Division. In September 1967, a *tour de force* of the Boston Bruins' training camp convinced everyone that Sanderson was good enough for the NHL, and tough enough, too.

The Bruins knew that Sanderson had a surplus of guts when he ran at defenseman Ted Green, the Boston jawbreaker. Derek hit Green once, twice. *Whop!* Green's stick slashed at Sanderson's head. Undaunted, Sanderson slashed back. Green's thin, slitlike eyes seemed to be trying to bore through Derek like laser beams. "Listen, kid," snapped the veteran defenseman. "I hit you. But you don't hit me. You got that straight? You don't ever hit me or you won't be playing in this league very long."

Normally, Green would wither a rookie with such a knifelike assertion. Sanderson stared right back at the Bruins' bully. "The next time you do that," said Derek, "I'm gonna crush your face."

An unspoken armistice had been declared, but it was clear that Sanderson had won something few others have from Green. Not long after the episode, Green approached Derek. "Y'know, kid," he said, "I like you. You've got guts."

Most of the time Derek could take care of himself. He fought the best boxers in the NHL, including Ted Harris and Orland Kurtenbach. "I'm giving you an A-plus for effort," said his mentor, Green. And he fought some more. Noel Picard, Terry Harper, Reg Fleming. Sanderson had more than fulfilled his advance notices. The word had gone out all over the league. "Settle down," Green advised. "By now everybody knows you'll fight anybody."

It is doubtful whether the Bruins would have given Sanderson a full turn at center in his rookie season if he couldn't play his position as well as he could handle his dukes. But he was a superb center, scored 24 goals, and also was voted the Calder Trophy as NHL rookie of the year.

Derek was sentenced to ninety-eight minutes in penalties during his rookie season. A year later the figure climbed to 146 penalty minutes, and his reputation as a ruthless skater spread from New York to Los Angeles. If a newspaperman warned him about the possibilities of retribution, he dismissed them from his mind.

As wild as he was, Derek remained perennially talented. He helped the Bruins to a Stanley Cup victory in 1970 and again in 1972. He single-handedly ignited riots in Philadelphia and St. Louis with the spectators and aroused patrons at Madison Square Garden so that they unfurled an assortment of anti-Sanderson signs: "Kill Derek" . . . "Skin the Hairy Fairy" . . . "Sanderson Is a Flake . . ."

There are some critics who believe Sanderson was nearly finished when he said good-by to the Bruins in the summer of 1972 and signed what was reported to be a ten-year $2.5 million contract with the Philadelphia Blazers of the World Hockey Association. "I might just buy myself the whole damn city," said Sanderson when he jetted to Philadelphia and signed his contract. The Blazers expected him to be the captain, sex symbol, and first-class fighter. When president Jim Cooper mentioned the fighting aspect to Derek, the suddenly rich young man seemed unhappy. "Fighting," Derek replied. "I don't know about that. That was my image when I was twenty-three, twenty-two, twenty-one. But I'm getting older, you know. I'm twenty-six now. I'm getting too old for that kind of nonsense."

Sanderson's failure to lead, score, or fight for the Blazers has gone down as one of the singular disappointments of professional sports. Not to mention one of the biggest heists, because Sanderson was paid something like $1 million *not* to play for Philadelphia.

He returned to the Bruins and seemed to have lost none of the inner mustard of yesteryear. In no time at all, the team began winning big and Derek was in the forefront, antagonizing and shocking the world.

Then, in midseason, all hell broke loose. During a game in Oakland against the California Golden Seals, Sanderson and tough teammate Terry O'Reilly engaged in a bitter fist fight. Clubhouse battles have erupted before but this time there was no peacemaking. Sanderson missed the team plane back to Boston and was suspended by manager Harry Sinden.

Coach Bep Guidolin said he wanted no part of Derek on the Bruins, as long as he, Guidolin, was coach. Sanderson eventually came out of hiding and blamed Guidolin for his troubles. "I'd play for the Bruins again," said Derek, "but not as long as Guidolin is coach."

The Bruins fired Guidolin in May 1974 and Derek, the flake, was soon traded to the Rangers. Sanderson made Brad Park a prophet when the Ranger said: "At any given time you don't know what Derek is going to do." Ranger players feared Sanderson would be a disruptive force, but actually he developed into an effective performer in 1974–75, scoring 25 goals, 25 assists, 50 points, and 106 penalty minutes. More significantly, he kept a low profile and appeared more a team player than ever before in his life.

SAN DIEGO MARINERS

Born as the New York Raiders, the San Diego Mariners were also the New York Golden Blades and the New Jersey Knights before establishing themselves as one of the World Hockey Association's strongest franchises.

Given the New York franchise in 1972, original owners Richard I. (Dick) Wood and Seymour (Sy) Siegel got themselves into trouble by signing a ridiculous lease with Madison Square Garden that called for exhorbitant rents. The rent, and the inability to draw fans, forced Siegel and Wood to sell out to a group led by Ralph Brent, who renamed the club the New York Golden Blades.

The Raiders/Blades came up with a surprising group of forwards who could score—Bobby Sheehan, whom they wrested from the California Golden Seals; Garry Peters, who had once led the American Hockey League in scoring; Norm Ferguson, one of the Seals' former mainstays; Wayne Rivers, a good AHL forward who had somehow never made it to the NHL; and a guy by the name of Ron Ward, once a nobody in the Vancouver Canucks' organization, who finished second to Andre Lacroix of Philadelphia in the WHA scoring race in 1972–73.

Poor goaltending and a spotty defense were their bane, however, eliminating the Raiders from the 1973 playoff contention. The following year, under new management, the situation got even worse. The club was never in the race, and as a result, fans were hardly ever in the building. The owners moved the club to Cherry Hill, New Jersey, where they played out the season. Club ownership reverted to the league.

After the league assumed control of the Knights, Joseph Schwartz, a Baltimore shipping magnate, bought it up, and in April 1974 moved the club to San Diego, renaming it the Mariners.

The roster contained few of the original names that had been on the Raider roster. Andre Lacroix had been obtained for Ron Ward in 1973 and Harry Howell, an NHLer for eons, had replaced the first coach of the team, Camille Henry. Howell was dropped in June 1975 and was replaced by Ron Ingram who managed the team as well.

Under new ownership, with a new atmosphere, and a strong following among San Diego hockey fans, the Mariners were in the thick of the playoff battle in their first season on the West Coast.

ANDRE SAVARD

BORN: Temiscamingue, Quebec, September 2, 1953
POSITION: Center, Boston Bruins, 1973–

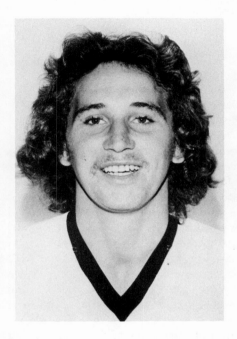

Andre Savard at 6-1, 184 pounds, was the Bruins' top choice in the 1974 junior amateur draft after he had scored an impressive 67 goals and 84 assists for 151 points with the Quebec Remparts.

The suspension of unpredictable center Derek Sanderson late in the 1973–74 season meant that Savard contributed more ice time and even moved into Sanderson's spot. Andre wound up centering for Terry O'Reilly and Don Marcotte, each of whom played his respective opponent to a standstill when on the ice. More than anything it was Savard's offensive thrusts against Philadelphia Flyers' goalie Bernie Parent and his stouthearted ability to fend off their body blows that lifted Andre up to a starry level during the 1974 Stanley Cup finals. However, he slumped in 1974–75.

SERGE A. SAVARD

BORN: Montreal, Quebec, January 22, 1946
POSITION: Defenseman, Montreal Canadiens, 1966–
AWARDS: Conn Smythe Trophy, 1969

One of the Canadiens' brightest prospects, Serge Savard has had to fight his way through a number of crippling injuries, which might have ended the careers of other athletes.

As an example, Savard missed most of 1965–66 with the Montreal Junior Canadiens due to torn ligaments in his right knee. After a brilliant rookie season in 1968–69, when he was the recipient of the Conn Smythe Trophy for the most valuable player in the Stanley Cup playoffs, Savard missed the final weeks of the following season with a fractured left leg. That injury also caused him to sit out parts of the next two years as well, as he refractured the leg, and complications set in.

Since 1972–73, however, Serge has been healthy, and once again is an integral part of the Habs' defense corps.

TERRANCE GORDON (TERRY) SAWCHUK

BORN: Winnipeg, Manitoba, December 28, 1929
DIED: New York, May 31, 1970
POSITION: Goalie, Detroit Red Wings, 1950–55, 1957–64, 1968–69;
   Boston Bruins, 1955–57; Toronto Maple Leafs, 1964–67; Los
   Angeles Kings, 1967–68; New York Rangers, 1969–70
AWARDS: Calder Trophy, 1951; Vezina Trophy, 1952, 1953, 1955,
   1965 (shared with J. Bower); Lester Patrick Trophy, 1971; All-
   Star (First Team), 1951, 1952, 1953, (Second Team), 1954, 1955,
   1959, 1963; Hockey Hall of Fame, 1971

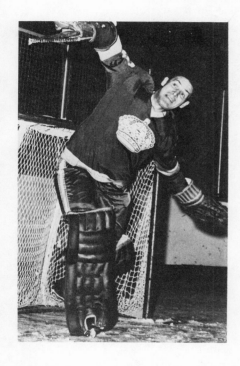

One of the greatest and most tragic players ever to grace a major league hockey
rink, was Terry Sawchuk. Quite possibly, Terry was the best goaltender ever to
strap on the tools of ignorance, but he was a moody, brooding figure who was a
physical and mental wreck of a man when he met his untimely death in 1970.

His twenty-year career in big-league hockey included tours of duty with the
Detroit Red Wings, Boston Bruins, Toronto Maple Leafs, Los Angeles Kings,
and New York Rangers. Terry broke into the majors with the Wings, making

First Team All-Star during his maiden season and copping the Calder Trophy as the NHL's rookie of the year.

Incredibly, his goals-against average never topped 2.00 during his first five years with Detroit, a stretch that saw him rack up 56 shutouts. He finished his up and down career with an amazing 103 career shutouts, 65 more than his then closest challenger, Glenn Hall (by 1975 Jacques Plante had posted 83 shutouts).

Sawchuk's early years were great ones, but he insisted that the finest moment of his career came with the 1966–67 Toronto Maple Leafs, when he dramatically guided the Leafs to an upset Stanley Cup victory.

It was said of Terry Sawchuk that he wasn't a whole man, rather, he was stitched together—held in place by catgut and surgical tape. He suffered a painful shoulder injury early in his career that for the rest of his playing days restricted his lifting his stick hand any higher than chest level. A full-page photo of Terry once appeared in a national magazine illustrating each stitch he had taken in his ruined face. The shocking picture could easily have passed for a horror movie's publicity shot.

An enigmatic, bitter man to the end, Terry died as a result of injuries received in a scuffle with teammate Ron Stewart on the lawn of his home.

KENNETH (KEN) CALVIN SCHINKEL

BORN: Jansen, Saskatchewan, November 27, 1932
POSITION: Right Wing, New York Rangers, 1959–64, 1966–67; Pittsburgh Penguins, 1967–73; Coach, Pittsburgh Penguins, 1973–74

A workmanlike forward with little flourish who played in the National Hockey League for ten seasons, Ken Schinkel broke in with the Rangers in 1959–60 and remained with the New York sextet through the 1966–67 season. He was acquired by the Pittsburgh Penguins in the first year of NHL expansion and played capably for the expansion team through the 1972–73 campaign. His last season was his best in many ways. Ken scored a personal NHL high of 20 goals during the regular season and added four goals and one assist in ten playoff games. Schinkel was named Penguins' coach in January 1973 and held the job until February 1974 when he was replaced by Marc Boileau whereupon Ken became a scout for the Penguins.

ROBERT JAMES (BOBBY) SCHMAUTZ

BORN: Saskatoon, Saskatchewan, March 28, 1945
POSITION: Right Wing, Chicago Black Hawks, 1967–69; Vancouver Canucks, 1970–74; Boston Bruins, 1974–

In New York City Bobby Schmautz will be forever known as "that bleeping nobody who shot a long one past that bleeping goalie Ed Giacomin in the 1968

Stanley Cup playoffs.'' Of course, the Rangers really managed to lose on their own quite nicely, but Schmautz will always be blamed. That was about the first and last thing anybody can remember about Bobby Schmautz, until February 1974.

Schmautz disappeared into the minors after the 1968–69 season with Chicago, and reemerged with the birth of the Vancouver Canucks in 1970, where he played three seasons, performing his best in 1972–73 with 38 goals and 33 assists for 71 points. In February 1974 he was traded to Boston for Chris Oddleifson and Fred O'Donnell.

Oddleifson became a mainstay of the rejuvenated Canucks, while in 1974–75 the somewhat small Schmautz began having trouble making a third-line slot on right wing with the Bruins.

MILT SCHMIDT

BORN: Kitchener, Ontario, March 5, 1918
POSITION: Center, Boston Bruins, 1937–42, 1945–55; Coach, Boston Bruins, 1955–62, 1963–66; General Manager, Boston Bruins, 1967–73; General Manager, Washington Capitals, 1974– ; Coach, Washington Capitals, 1975–
AWARDS: Hart Trophy, 1951; Art Ross Trophy, 1940; All-Star (First Team), 1940, 1947, 1951, (Second Team), 1952; Hockey Hall of Fame, 1961

Milt Schmidt is best known as the center for the famed ''Kraut Line'' of the Boston Bruins in the thirties. Schmidt played the pivot for Woody Dumart and Bobby Bauer, and was a prime force in the Bruins' Stanley Cup championships of 1939 and 1941. In 1940 Schmidt won the Art Ross Trophy as the NHL's leading scorer and became the policeman of the Bruins' forward corps.

Although Schmidt's career began unfortunately with a broken jaw, keeping him out for four weeks in 1938, and a painful ankle injury, keeping him on the sidelines again for the 1939 season, he recovered to lead the Bruins in playoff scoring.

In 1955 Schmidt resigned from active duty and was given the coaching reins of a struggling Boston hockey club. He stayed on until 1962–63, when Phil Watson was called in to take charge. But Watson could not rejuvenate the Bruins, and Schmidt took over again in the middle of the 1962–1963 season.

He stayed atop the Bruin organization as general manager from 1966 until 1973 and saw his club win two Stanley Cups with help from trades which he masterminded.

Perhaps the greatest coup of Schmidt's managerial career was engineering that famous—or infamous—trade between the Bruins and Black Hawks in which Chicago got goalie Jack Norris, defenseman Gilles Marotte, and center

Milt Schmidt

Pit Martin in return for forwards Ken Hodge, Fred Stanfield, and Phil Esposito. Hodge, Stanfield, and Esposito formed the backbone of the feared Bruins' power play that enabled them to walk away with the Stanley Cup in 1970 and again in 1972.

When the National Hockey League expanded in 1974 to eighteen teams, Schmidt accepted the position of general manager of the new Washington Capitals. Beset by a lack of talent due mostly to the slim pickings in the expansion draft, the Caps finished with the worst record in National Hockey League history, leaving Schmidt the unenviable task of trying to build a contending hockey club from the ashes of a disaster. Furthermore, in his first season, Schmidt exhausted three coaches—Jimmy Anderson followed by Red Sullivan, and finally, himself! He returned as manager-coach in 1975–76.

RONALD (RON) LAWRENCE SCHOCK

BORN: Chapleau, Ontario, December 19, 1943
POSITION: Center, Boston Bruins, 1963–67; St. Louis Blues, 1967–69; Pittsburgh Penguins, 1969–

Slow to mature as an offensive threat, Ron Schock made it big with the Pittsburgh Penguins during the 1974–75 season when he led the team in scoring—23 goals, 63 assists, 86 points—and guided the Penguins to a playoff berth. Originally a Boston Bruins' farmhand, Schock made his NHL debut in 1963–64 in the Hub, but failed after several tries with the Bruins. When the NHL expanded in 1967 Schock was drafted by the St. Louis Blues and played for St. Louis through the 1968–69 season when he was traded to Pittsburgh. A frequent penalty killer, Schock was named Penguins' captain in 1973–74 and that year was named the club's unsung hero, for which he received the Bill McCracken Unsung Hero Award.

DAVID "SWEENEY" SCHRINER

BORN: Calgary, Alberta, November 30, 1911
POSITION: Left Wing, New York Americans, 1934–39; Toronto Maple Leafs, 1939–43, 1944–46
AWARDS: Calder Trophy, 1935; Art Ross Trophy, 1936, 1937; All-Star (First Team), 1936, 1941, (Second Team), 1937; Hockey Hall of Fame, 1962

There have been few more exciting forwards in NHL history than Dave 'Sweeney" Schriner who broke in with the New York Americans in 1934–35 when he was named rookie of the year. A season later Schriner led the NHL in scoring and repeated the feat a year after that. After five seasons with the Amerks, the left winger was traded to the Maple Leafs in 1939–40.

Sweeney continued to shine and played a pivotal role in the Leafs' comeback in the 1942 Stanley Cup finals with the Red Wings when they trailed three games to none. Prior to the fourth game, Schriner was especially moved by a letter written to the Toronto club by a fourteen-year-old-girl. Before taking the ice, Sweeney rose in the dressing room, looked over at coach Hap Day and shouted, "Don't worry about this one, Skipper. We'll win this one for the little girl!" The Leafs, thanks to Schriner's scoring, won the next four straight games. With Toronto behind, 1–0, in the seventh and final game, Schriner tied the score. Pete Langelle put Toronto ahead, 2–1, and then Sweeney scored the clincher as the Leafs won, 3–1. He starred again in April 1945 when the Leafs again whipped the Red Wings in seven games. Schriner ended his NHL career a year later with the Leafs.

DAVID "THE HAMMER" SCHULTZ

BORN: Waldheim, Saskatchewan, October 14, 1949
POSITION: Left Wing, Philadelphia Flyers, 1971–

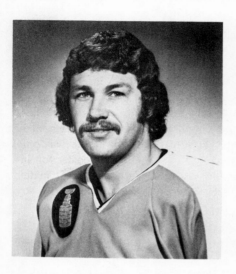

No athlete ever received more media attention for less talent than Dave Schultz, a pugnacious forward who burst onto the NHL scene in 1971–72 for one game and became a regular a season later. A key member of the ferocious Philadelphia Flyers, Schultz has worked hard to earn his nickname—"the Hammer."

He led the NHL in penalty minutes during the 1972–73, 1973–74, and 1974–75 seasons (garnering an astronomical record-breaking 472 minutes in 1974–75), and in his eight years as a pro, he has spent the equivalent of fifty-seven games in the penalty box. "I fought my way into the NHL and that's something I can't forget," the big left winger explained.

Schultz is certainly tough. On Philadelphia's "Mean Machine," he is the "baddest of the bad." He has also developed some skill—and that makes him twice as dangerous. He reached the 20-goal mark in 1973–74, and scored some key goals in the Flyers' successful 1974 Stanley Cup crusade. At one point, his "plus-minus" rating (team goals for and against while on the ice) was the best of all West Division forwards.

Still, Schultz is primarily an intimidator. "I would never have made it without fighting," he admitted, "but I don't go out there just to fight. If you check rough, they give you a little more room to shoot, or they may not crowd you in the corners. It helps." Because of his truculence, Schultz has frequently been censured and occasionally suspended by NHL president Clarence Campbell. Although he, at first, had been a darling in Philadelphia, Schultz lost considerable favor in 1974–75, while his goal-scoring also dropped to a meager nine.

JAMES ENIO SCLISIZZI

BORN: Milton, Ontario, August 1, 1925
POSITION: Forward, Detroit Red Wings, 1947–50; 1951–52; Chicago
   Black Hawks, 1952–53

Enio played forward for the Detroit Red Wings beginning in the 1947–48 season and ending in the 1951–52 season, none of which were terribly impressive. By 1952–53, he had been dealt to the Chicago Black Hawks with whom he continued his record of nonproductivity. However, with the Hawks nobody knew the difference. Sclisizzi did achieve fame in another area; he was only one of two NHL players to have his name changed to make life easier for announcers. Thus, Enio Sclisizzi became Jim Enio. But it really didn't matter because by 1954 Enio was out of the majors, proving that a Sclisizzi by any other name couldn't flash the red light.

RODNEY ALBERT (ROD) SEILING

BORN: Elmira, Ontario, November 14, 1944
POSITION: Defenseman, Toronto Maple Leafs, 1962–63, 1974– ;
   New York Rangers, 1963–74; Washington Capitals, 1974

Mild-mannered Rod Seiling, a gentlemanly defenseman whose prowess at stickchecking and positional play usually went unnoticed by many of New York's (unsophisticated) spectators, labored for eleven solid seasons with the Rangers from 1963–74.

Usually quiet and unassuming, Seiling finally blasted Madison Square Garden's leather-lunged boobirds in the local tabloids as "know-nothings." Soon the gallery was screaming for Seiling's head. Each time he touched the puck or stepped on the Garden ice, a shower of taunts, insults, and an occasional rotten egg rained down upon him from the paying customers.

Soon, in much the same manner that former Rangers Allan Stanley and Bob Nevin were purged from the Big Apple, Seiling received his walking papers and was peddled to the lowly expansionist Washington Capitals. But Seiling's painful odyssey wasn't over yet. Five short days later, Rod was on the move again—this time he was traded to the Toronto Maple Leafs, where he began his pro hockey career in 1962. Ironically, in the Leaf's first meeting with Rod's old teammates, Seiling was checked from behind and was disabled for several weeks with a knee injury.

Always a purely defensive player, Rod's point totals were far from impres-

Rod Seiling

sive, but in the all-important plus-minus tabulations that NHL coaches hold so dear, Seiling consistently rated among the best in the league.

ROBERT BRITON (BRIT) SELBY

BORN: Kingston, Ontario, March 27, 1945
POSITION: Left Wing, Toronto Maple Leafs, 1964–67, 1969–70; Philadelphia Flyers, 1967–69; St. Louis Blues, 1970–72; Quebec Nordiques (WHA), 1972; Philadelphia Blazers (WHA), 1972; New England Whalers (WHA), 1972–73; Toronto Toros (WHA), 1973–75; Baltimore Blades (WHA), 1975
AWARDS: Calder Memorial Trophy, 1966

A seemingly gifted forward, Selby won the rookie-of-the-year award in 1965–66 with the Toronto Maple Leafs and appeared destined for bigger and better things. Instead, he got worse and worse. Selby was traded to the Philadelphia Flyers in 1967–68, but returned to Toronto the following year. He then bounced to the St. Louis Blues (1970–72), but jumped to the WHA's Quebec Nordiques in 1972–73. He failed in Quebec and wound up with the New England Whalers who, in turn, dealt Brit to the Toronto Toros. The reason for Selby's letdown? Former Toro Carl Brewer said that Selby's rookie year under Punch Imlach thoroughly disenchanted him and he gradually lost the desire to be a hockey professional. Whatever the case, Selby's saga is one of the saddest in contemporary hockey. Late in the 1974–75 season Selby was traded to the WHA Baltimore Blades, while injured, and the team folded at season's end.

FRANK SELKE, SR.

Few men have been more steeped in hockey lore than Frank Selke, Sr., the little man from Berlin (now Kitchener), Ontario. Selke broke into the hockey business like most Canadians, as a player. Until hockey permanently intruded, Frank was an electrician. But he became more and more enamored of the game, and when old-time Montreal Wanderers' star Hod Stuart presented him with a gift stick at the end of a game in Berlin, young Selke was hooked for keeps. By 1912 he was managing City League teams and he continued climbing the hockey ladder while working at non-ice jobs on the side.

He eventually made his way to Toronto where it was inevitable that he would come into contact with Conn Smythe. In time Smythe appointed Selke his aide-de-camp, a decision that proved rather fortuitous for Smythe, Selke, and the Toronto Maple Leafs. When Smythe went overseas to serve with the Canadian Armed Forces in World War II, it was Selke who ably filled the breach and guided the roster-riddled Toronto sextet. However, one of Selke's smartest moves in Toronto led to his downfall as a member of the Leaf hierarchy and his "deportation" to Montreal.

The *coup de grace* was rooted in a decision Selke made in 1944 while Smythe was overseas. At the time the Leafs had signed Frankie Eddolls, a young defenseman who had learned his hockey in Verdun, not far from where Rocket Richard had played his junior games. Montreal coach Dick Irvin had seen Eddolls play and liked what he had seen. Since Dick was on speaking terms with Selke, he mentioned that he wouldn't mind having the Montreal lad in the Canadiens' system.

Selke's mind was turning. He knew that Les Canadiens had the rights to a tenacious center playing in nearby Port Colborne, Ontario. "We'll let you have Eddolls," said Selke, "if you give up Ted Kennedy."

The proposal was both intriguing and perplexing to both sides and very nearly foundered on the rocks of uncertainty. At last, the parties agreed to the swap and Ted Kennedy put on the royal blue and white uniform of the Maple Leafs. In time, young "Teeder" would become the darling of Toronto hockey fans, one of the most proficient centers in NHL history, and the captain of the Leafs.

There was only one thing wrong. In his haste to complete the deal Selke neglected to obtain the green light from Smythe who happened to be in war-torn France at the time. When the vitriolic Smythe finally learned about the trade, he made nearly as much noise as the cannons that were booming around him.

He promptly cabled Maple Leaf Gardens demanding that the deal be erased and Eddolls return to the Toronto fold. This, of course, could not be arranged, and when Smythe was so advised he blasted off again to no avail.

"The deal spelled finis to my usefulness as assistant to Conn Smythe," Selke later reflected in his autobiography, *Behind the Cheering*.

The wisdom of Selke's decision would be underlined in years to come. Eddolls eventually became a member of the Canadiens, but only as a mediocre defenseman soon traded to the Rangers. Kennedy was eventually voted into the Hockey Hall of Fame.

Smythe's return to Toronto at war's end generated open warfare at Maple Leaf Gardens. He publicly roasted Selke for the Leafs' demise in the 1945–46 season, overlooking the fact that Toronto had annexed the Stanley Cup in the previous season. Smythe still rankled over the Kennedy deal, and the Major, a stern advocate of discipline, inspired Selke to resign from the Maple Leaf organization in May 1946. By autumn, Selke had obtained a job with the Montreal sextet.

In his first months as managing director of Les Canadiens, Selke had little to worry about. Montreal opened the 1946–47 season at home with a 3–0 triumph over the Rangers and continued to play splendidly.

In time, Selke became the architect of the great Canadiens' dynasties of the late forties, through the fifties, and the early sixties. The Canadiens won nine Stanley Cups from 1950 to 1966, including five in a row from 1956 to 1960.

Selke developed such stars as "Boom-Boom" Geoffrion, Dickie Moore, Jean Beliveau, Doug Harvey, Jacques Plante, and Henri Richard, among many others. He retired in the early sixties.

BRADLEY WAYNE (BRAD) SELWOOD

BORN: Leamington, Ontario, March 18, 1948
POSITION: Defenseman, Toronto Maple Leafs, 1970–72; New England Whalers (WHA), 1972–
AWARDS: WHA Team Canada, 1974

Selwood turned pro in 1968 with Tulsa of the Central League, then spent the 1969–70 season with Vancouver of the WHL, where he earned rookie-of-the-year honors.

The Toronto Maple Leafs were impressed with Selwood, bringing him up to the NHL at the beginning of the 1970–71 season. There he won a starting berth which he held until he collided with a goal post in Montreal in November 1970. After his recovery Selwood and the Leafs never again seemed to get along too well, and in 1972 he signed with the New England Whalers.

Brad has played All-Star quality defense with the Whalers and was chosen for the 1974 Team Canada series. He plays a steady yet inconspicuous game, but is known to be a practical joker off-ice.

EDWARD STEVEN PHILLIP (EDDIE) SHACK

BORN: Sudbury, Ontario, February 11, 1937
POSITION: Left Wing, New York Rangers, 1958–60; Toronto Maple
   Leafs, 1960–67, 1973–75; Boston Bruins, 1967–69; Los Angeles
   Kings, 1969–70; Buffalo Sabres, 1970–72; Pittsburgh Penguins,
   1972–73

"Clear the track—here comes Shack!" That used to be Eddie "the Enter-tainer" Shack's calling card when he started to come into his own as a player with the Toronto Maple Leafs during the midsixties. Eddie, a left winger by trade, is known for his mad dashes up, down, and across hockey rinks when-ever the mood happens to seize him.

Shack broke into the NHL in 1958 with the New York Rangers and played for five other NHL clubs before being bought by the Toronto Maple Leafs in 1973.

Apart from his immense physical strength that enabled him to trade body-checks with the biggest foe, Shack possessed a hard shot and a delightful sense of humor. Point-wise, his most successful season was 1972–73, when he scored 25 goals and 20 assists for 45 points in 74 games with the Pittsburgh Penguins. Once the hero of Toronto fandom, Shack became a benchwarmer in 1974–75 with the Maple Leafs, playing in only twenty-six games, and he was placed on unconditional release by June 1975.

GREGORY WAYNE (GREGG) SHEPPARD

BORN: Battleford, Saskatchewan, April 23, 1949
POSITION: Left Wing, Boston Bruins, 1972–

Playing on a line with Don Marcotte and Terry O'Reilly, 5' 8", 160-pound Gregg Sheppard has made the most of his scoring opportunities since joining the Bruins in late October 1972. In only his second game with the parent club, Sheppard scored a three-goal hat trick to lead the team to a 9–1 rout of the hapless New York Islanders.

Everyone knew that Gregg could score in the minors. He compiled a total of 98 goals and 141 assists in three full seasons with the Oklahoma City Blazers of the Central League. But there was always some doubt as to whether his size, or lack of it, would neutralize his scoring knack in the big leagues. When the Bruins ran into trouble at the beginning of the 1972–73 season, winning only three of their first nine games, the Boston brass decided to take a chance on the highly touted Sheppard, who had started the season with the Braves, Boston's American Hockey League entry and a Bruins' affiliate.

When the opportunity presented itself, Sheppard didn't waste it. He tallied 24 goals and assisted on 26 others during the 1972–73 season. He also took up the slack left by defensive specialist Derek Sanderson after Derek moved to greener pastures in WHA country. When Sanderson returned to Boston later in the season, Sheppard had already secured the third line center position, and Sanderson was relegated to spot duty. At the end of the season, Gregg was voted the most popular Bruin by the Boston fans.

FRED ALEXANDER SHERO

BORN: Winnipeg, Manitoba, October 23, 1925
POSITION: Defenseman, New York Rangers, 1947–50; Coach, Philadelphia Flyers, 1971–

Called everything from the Casey Stengel of hockey to a latter-day W. C. Fields, Shero is a mystery to Philadelphia sports writers, his players, and even his family. Shero is an emotional man, although his sentiments are almost always locked deep inside. Even after great wins, Shero likes to sit by himself, perhaps concentrating, and conquering his emotions so they won't be visible to the outside world. Shero often expresses himself with a personal note placed in a player's locker or a handwritten quote on the locker room blackboard. After his Flyers came back from a 4–1 deficit to defeat the New York Rangers, Shero scribbled the score in the locker room with a sign reading: "This game will never be forgotten by me. Money doesn't live forever. But great moments do."

At the beginning of each month and during special moments in the season, Shero uses the blackboard to write "meaningful" notes to his players. One day during the season, he wrote: "Those who live on past glories will have only the glories of the past to live on." His players watch, listen to, and love the man.

Bernie Parent, the Flyers' amazing goalie, was named the 1974 Stanley Cup's most valuable player, after Captain Bobby Clarke, the other prime contender, announced that no one but Parent deserved the award. At the official presentation, Parent took the key to the car which went along with the prize, said he needed twenty-three more for his teammates, and handed it to his mentor, Fred Shero. That morning, Shero did show emotion allowing more tears to flow than perhaps ever before during his reign in the city.

The Flyers have responded to their perfectionist coach with dogged determinism, tough drive, and two consecutive Stanley Cups. The team has become a strong unit, labeled by some as a "hockey family." Shero has explained that he teaches his players "to live, love, and labor together—not necessarily in that order." Shero has a strict policy never to criticize a player openly; if a player is loafing, he'll find out what the coach thinks, but in Shero's way.

For thirteen years, starting in 1957, Shero coached minor league teams in St. Paul, Omaha, and Buffalo. Prior to that time he had played for the New York Rangers. As a coach he led six teams to first-place finishes and five to playoff championships. Surprisingly, Shero was ignored by NHL teams like the North Stars and the Sabres, which had opportunities to assess his value.

Finally, in 1971, Ed Snider gave Shero a group of loosely organized men who just hadn't made it with the big boy teams. Equipped with a system based on the discipline of Russia's national team, Shero began to build.

Shero has had The Cup, a hefty raise, and a city at his feet, but he won't even stop to enjoy it. He'll continue that never ending search for new ways, new ideas, new techniques; he'll keep reaching for perfection.

ALEXANDER (ALEX) SHIBICKY

BORN: Winnipeg, Manitoba, May 19, 1914
POSITION: Center, New York Rangers, 1935–42, 1945–46

Among the lesser but nonetheless superb lines of pre-World War II NHL hockey, the Rangers' unit of Neil Colville, Mac Colville, and Alex Shibicky ranks in the unsung category. "The line," according to then coach Frank Boucher, "patterned themselves on our old Cook-Boucher-Cook line, each knowing his routine perfectly, the three swooping over the ice with the precision of a flying circus."

Of the three, Shibicky, a native of Winnipeg, was the talker and the hardest shooter. He became a Ranger in 1935–36 and played on Broadway until 1946, with a three-year interruption for wartime duties with the Canadian Armed Forces.

A strong skater who played a vital part on the Rangers' 1940 Stanley Cup championship team, Shibicky betrayed one quasiserious flaw; he'd often hold on to the puck too long when he had a grand opportunity for a shot on goal. He thereby created a humorous response from the Rangers' bench as his frustrated teammates watched him in agony. As Alex waited and waited, the response went: "Shoot, Shibicky . . . Shoot Shibicky . . . Ah, *shit,* Shibicky!"

EDWARD W. (EDDIE) SHORE

BORN: St. Qu'Appelle-Cupar, Saskatchewan, November 25, 1902
POSITION: Defenseman, Boston Bruins, 1926–40; New York Americans, 1940
AWARDS: Hart Trophy, 1933, 1935, 1936, 1938; Lester Patrick Trophy, 1970; All-Star (First Team), 1931–33, 1935, 1936, 1938–39, (Second Team), 1934; Hockey Hall of Fame, 1945

The old Pacific Coast Hockey League, directed by Frank and Lester Patrick, had run aground in 1925 and the Patricks were auctioning off some excellent players at reduced prices, including Eddie Shore, Harry Oliver, and Perk Galbraith. Adams, the Bruin owner, had the money, and for $50,000 he purchased Shore, Duke Keats, and Frank Boucher in a seven-man package. Boucher, in turn, was sold to the newly organized Rangers. Others were dealt to the new Detroit team that had also joined the league.

Nobody really knew it that summer, but the first Boston hockey dynasty had begun to form, and Eddie Shore was to be its general. Until Shore came along the Bruins lacked a definitive image. They were both amusing and pathetic, effervescent and fumbling, but if you tried to find an adjective that would adequately describe them, you wound up with nothing.

Shore changed that! From the moment he tugged on the gold, white, and black jersey the Bruin adjective was "tough." With very rare exceptions it was to remain the most singular characteristic of the team, even in the days when it appeared to be loaded with lightweights. And, obviously, it is true today.

Ironically, manager Art Ross wasn't convinced that Shore belonged on the

Bruins when Eddie reported to training camp in the autumn of 1926. This was surprising because Shore, at twenty-four, had already created a Bunyanesque aura about himself in western Canada. Sure, Eddie had demonstrated his toughness in the minor leagues out West, but Ross wasn't so sure the big fellow with the slicked-back hair could make it with the big leaguers. The answer was supplied in a training-camp scrimmage. The Bruins had a hard-hitting veteran named Billy Coutu who wasn't particularly enamored of Shore's behavior. During practice one day Coutu punched Shore in the mouth. The rookie returned the blow, and it seemed a truce was declared. A few minutes later Coutu lumbered along the ice like a rhinoceros, picking up speed with every step. Everybody in the rink knew he was bearing down on Shore, and not because he wanted to score a goal; he was after Eddie's head.

Shore instinctively realized that Coutu had him lined up for a pulverizing bodycheck so he dug his skates into the ice and crouched for the blow. Coutu hit him amidships, but Shore was the immovable object this time. He held his ground as the veteran crashed to the ice, stunned and embarrassed. When Shore returned to the bench, he discovered that he hadn't escaped without injury. His ear was soaked with blood and hanging loose as if it had been sliced with a razor. The Bruins' trainer rushed Shore to a physician, who stopped the bleeding and stopped Shore—the ear would have to be amputated! Eddie, who had accumulated a wealth of questionable medical "knowledge," challenged the diagnosis. "I want to see another doctor," he demanded. And persist he did until he at last discovered a doctor who would stitch the ear together.

Shore was brash beyond belief and just as mayhem-oriented. In his second NHL season Shore set a league penalty record with 166 minutes worth of fouls. The boisterousness that personified Shore was immediately translated to the Boston crowd, until it was impossible to determine which was the catalyst for mania, the frenetic Bruins' audience or the player, Shore.

As if the general air of exuberance generated by Boston fans wasn't enough, Shore was also galvanized to fury by Ross's machinations. "He played up the villain in Shore by various stunts," wrote author Al Silverman.

One of the best—or worst, depending on one's sense of the dramatic—kept Eddie off the ice when his teammates appeared for the opening face-off. When the ploy was first executed fans wondered if Shore had been injured, so they wouldn't get their money's worth for the night. Precisely at that moment, the band would break into a chorus of "Hail to the Chief," and Shore would trot out in a matador's cloak, followed by a valet, who would remove Eddie's outer garment, allowing him to play.

Shore's continual clashes with the Montreal Maroons were legendary. Several of the Montreal players had decided that Shore was too liberal in his manhandling of them. During one game, one of them tore open Eddie's cheek with his stick blade, and another sliced his chin. With trip-hammer consistency, the Maroons clobbered Shore, and in the waning minutes of the game Shore was felled by a clout in the mouth tossed by a Maroon which removed several teeth and knocked him so cold he had to be carried from the rink after lying un-conscious on the ice for fourteen minutes. In that one game Shore had ac-cumulated wounds that many players avoid in a lifetime. He had a broken nose, three broken teeth, two black eyes, a gashed cheekbone, and a two-inch cut over the left eye.

He returned to action in the next Bruin game. And when friends tried to commiserate with him, he dismissed their platitudes abruptly. "This is all part of hockey," he replied. "I'll pay off."

His high-speed collision with a goal post at Madison Square Garden left the steel upright intact, but cost Shore three broken ribs. The damage was so severe the Bruins left Shore in the care of a physician and entrained for a game in Montreal. The doctor eventually escorted Eddie to a nearby hotel and left momentarily to register Shore at a hospital. "Now, Eddie," the doctor cau-tioned, "I want you to stay in your room until I can come back and take you over to the hospital."

The doctor, who should have known better, assumed that Shore's lack of response indicated compliance. He left the hotel, signed up for a hospital room, and returned to Shore's room to escort the wounded player to the infirmary. But he found the door wide open and no trace of the player or his baggage. Eddie had stumbled to the lobby and had hailed a cab for Grand Central Station, where he purchased a ticket for the late train to Montreal. He arrived in time for the game with the Canadiens and scored two goals and an assist. Such exploits did much to erase Eddie's image as a ruthless, insensitive player.

Ross, on the other hand, was never one to permit sentimentality to stand in the way of a good deal. He realized by 1939 that Shore had only a couple of years left, and despite what Eddie had done for the Boston franchise, Ross was prepared to trade him to any high bidder. The New York Americans indicated they would make a handsome offer, and Ross seemed interested when they sug-gested a $25,000 tab.

While Ross was mulling this over, Shore was doing some business of his own and finally announced he had purchased the Springfield Indians of the In-ternational-American League for $42,000. Shore was fascinated by the prospect of running his own club and made no bones about the fact that he was moving his family to Springfield.

Ross was livid when he learned of Shore's purchase. He attempted to humili-ate his star before local newsmen with the plaintive but hollow question, "Where do the Bruins come in?"

The answer was second fiddle from now on. Ross and Shore finally agreed that Eddie would play with the Bruins after December 15, 1939, in case of emergency, but he would continue playing for and managing the Springfield sextet also. Ross tried to circumvent the deal by wooing Shore to the Bruins' lineup before December 15 on the grounds that the club was already confronted with an "emergency."

Eddie played in three games and scored his final goal as a Bruin on December 5, 1939. By the time the December 15 deadline arrived Shore was fed up with Ross and his chicanery. He revealed that he would no longer play for Boston because the club wouldn't permit him to fulfill his playing obligations in Springfield. Ross wasn't about to quit. It took the stubborn Scot a month to realize he no longer could dominate the man who had made hockey in Boston. At last, on January 14, 1940, Ross called a press conference and made the following announcement: "Shore has a heavy investment with his Springfield club and we want to give him a hand." Within two weeks of this altruistic declaration, Ross had traded Shore to the New York Americans for Eddie Wiseman and cash, thus ending the Shore era in Boston.

SAM HAMILTON "HAMBY" SHORE

BORN: Ottawa, Ontario, 1886
DIED: October 14, 1918
POSITION: Left Wing, Defenseman, Ottawa Silver Seven (FAHL,
    ECAHA), 1905, 1907; Strathmore and Winnipeg (MHL), 1908; Ottawa (NHA), 1910–17; Ottawa Senators, 1917–18

Hamby Shore was a restless, two-way hockey player who broke in as a forward in 1905 with the Stanley Cup winners, the Ottawa Silver Seven. Several teams and leagues later, Hamby finally settled down in 1910 with Ottawa of the NHA He was a stalwart on defense for the Senators and helped them to the 1911 Stanley Cup. Shore had four more very successful seasons with the Senators, but then his relations with Alf Smith, the Ottawa coach, began to strain. Hamby wanted desperately to move to the new West Coast league, but Ottawa refused to give him his release. An unhappy Shore remained with the Senators until 1918 when he met his untimely death, a victim of a deadly influenza epidemic.

ALBERT CHARLES "BABE" SIEBERT

BORN: Plattsville, Ontario, January 14, 1904
DIED: August 25, 1939
POSITION: Left Wing, Defenseman, Montreal Maroons, 1925–32;
    New York Rangers, 1932–34; Boston Bruins, 1934–36; Montreal Canadiens, 1936–39
AWARDS: Hart Trophy, 1937; All-Star (First Team), 1937–38; Hockey Hall of Fame, 1964

Albert "Babe" Siebert broke into the professional hockey wars in 1925 with the Montreal Maroons. He was a high-scoring left winger during his rookie season and promptly helped the Maroons storm to the Stanley Cup.

Babe's thirst for body contact was instantly appreciated by Eddie Gerard, the Maroons' coach, and soon the strapping Siebert was shuttling back and forth from defense to the forward line. In 1930, Babe moved up as a permanent portsider with the formation of the "Big S Line." Skating with Nels Stewart and Hooley Smith, this unholy trio was the scourge of the league, averaging well over 200 penalty minutes for the next three seasons.

Sold to the New York Rangers in 1932, Siebert was moved back to defense where he was paired with the great Ching Johnson. This defensive duo decimated opposing wingers and once again Siebert found himself on a Cup-winning squad.

The following season found Babe on the move again. This time he was off to Boston where he was hastily pressed into service as a replacement for Eddie Shore. Shore had been suspended by the league following a brutal encounter with Ace Bailey. After Shore's reinstatement, he and Siebert formed one of the most feared blue line patrols in the entire league.

Babe was traded to the Montreal Canadiens in 1936–37, where he collected the Hart Trophy as the league's most valuable player. Siebert played two more seasons with the Habs, captaining the 1939 squad. He was named coach of the Frenchmen for the coming season, but that was never to be. Tragically, Babe Siebert died in a drowning mishap that very summer.

DON SIMMONS

BORN: Port Colborne, Ontario, September 13, 1931
POSITION: Goalie, Boston Bruins, 1956–61; Toronto Maple Leafs, 1961–64; New York Rangers, 1965–69

Don Simmons played considerable goal for the Boston Bruins (1956–57 through 1960–61) and later part-time for the Toronto Maple Leafs and New York Rangers. But his most memorable moments occurred when he was in the nets for Hall of Famer Eddie Shore's Springfield Indians of the American League in the early fifties.

Simmons nearly suffered a nervous breakdown in one tense game between Cleveland and Springfield. Referee Frank Udvari had called a penalty against the Indians that so enraged Shore he ordered his entire team off the ice with the exception of Simmons. Udvari pulled out his watch. "You got ten seconds to ice a team," the referee said, "or I drop the puck." Shore ignored the threat.

Udvari dropped the puck, and five Cleveland players charged at Simmons. So amazed were the attackers at this unheard-of scoring opportunity, they fought among themselves over who should take the shot. Finally, Bo Elik of Cleveland shot and missed. Three succeeding shots went wild, and Simmons fell on the puck, stopping play. Finally, Shore sent his team back on the ice.

HARRY SINDEN

Harry Sinden was the right man in the right place at the right time when the Boston Bruins handed him its coaching reins at the start of the 1966–67 campaign. The Bruins had finished dead last five times in the previous six seasons and the city was hungry for a winner. It didn't happen immediately. The Bruins finished sixth in Harry's first year on the job, but a hotshot rookie named Bobby Orr provided plenty of consolation. A year later Derek Sanderson arrived, along with Phil Esposito, Kenny Hodge, and Fred Stanfield, and suddenly nobody laughed at the Bruins anymore. For the first time in eight years they made the playoffs, and two seasons later they captured Boston's first Stanley Cup in twenty-nine years.

The whole town was just wild about Harry. In the midst of that grand celebration, Sinden abruptly quit Boston—publicly charging the brass with underpaying him—and began a new career in the modular home industry. But at the start of the 1972–73 season, the firm he was working for went into bankruptcy. Meanwhile the Bruins, who had added another Stanley Cup in his absence, were rapidly coming apart at the seams. Defections to the upstart World Hockey Association, injuries to veterans, and below par performances by formerly dependable players all took a toll on the Bruins. In September 1972 Sinden coached Team Canada to its stirring victory over the Soviet national team. When a new owner bought the Bruins, the first move was to bring Sinden back, hoping he was the man to put Humpty Dumpty together again in 1972–73.

Just three years after he had left town as a conquering hero of sorts, Harry returned to a less than heartwarming welcome. He was introduced as the team's managing director, a strange title which did not hide the fact that he was actually replacing one of the most popular personalities on the Boston sports front, Milt Schmidt.

Schmidt, who had been general manager during Harry's successful coaching stint, was given the new title of executive director, but everybody knew Milt had been relegated to mere window-dressing in the front office. Sinden caught the full force of backlash from the sympathy extended to Schmidt by both the press and the public. Understandably, Harry was slow to assert himself.

Except for replacing coach Tom Johnson with Bep Guidolin, Harry walked softly through his first year at the post. "I intend to get a lot closer to the players in the future," he said. "I'm going to try opening up our lines of communications." He rolled up his sleeves and went to work. After the 1974 playoff loss to Philadelphia, Sinden dropped Guidolin and hired Don Cherry as coach. But, as manager, Sinden still has not proven he is as competent as he was as coach. His Bruins were rapidly wiped out of the playoffs in 1975.

DARRYL GLEN SITTLER

BORN: Kitchener, Ontario, September 18, 1950
POSITION: Center, Toronto Maple Leafs, 1970–

From the moment the Toronto Maple Leafs were born, their hallmark has been an abundance of quality centermen. Check the Hockey Hall of Fame: Joe Primeau, Syl Apps, Sr., Ted Kennedy, and Max Bentley. Each of them contributed to former Leafs' boss Conn Smythe's theory that the secret of winning hockey teams is "strength through the center." During Toronto's last spate of Stanley Cup-winning years under Punch Imlach, the key Leaf pivots were George Armstrong, Bob Pulford, and Dave Keon. All but Keon are retired and now the Leafs are looking to Darryl Sittler as their superstar center of the immediate future.

In his first three National Hockey League seasons, Sittler's point total climbed from 18 (in 1970–71) to 32 to 77. His team-leading 84 points—38 goals, 46 assists—in the 1973–74 season, was his best of all and confirmed the Toronto organization's faith in the 6–0, 190-pound farm boy.

Sittler was drafted by the Leafs in 1970. When his contract ran out in 1972–73, the Maple Leafs, satisfied with Sittler's production, prepared a new pact. However, the WHA Toronto Toros also wanted Sittler and were prepared to unload something like $1 million to prove their sincerity. Sittler chose to stay with the Leafs.

Toronto finished fourth in 1973–74 after lodging in sixth the previous year, and Darryl clearly was the top center on the club. He finished 15 points ahead of veteran pivot Norm Ullman and an embarrassing—but not for Darryl—31 points ahead of onetime ace center Keon.

ALF SKINNER

BORN: Unknown
DIED: April 1961
POSITION: Right Wing, Montreal Shamrocks (NHA) 1915; Toronto
    Arenas (NHA), 1916–17, 1917–19; Montreal Wanderers (NHA),
    1917; Vancouver Millionaires (PCHL), 1920–24; Boston Bruins,
    1924; Montreal Maroons, 1925; Pittsburgh Pirates, 1925–26

Alf Skinner was a small, quick right winger who broke into hockey in 1915 with the Shamrocks. Alf joined the Toronto Arenas the following season and quickly emerged as one of their top scoring threats. Skinner was the star of the 1918 Stanley Cup playoffs, scoring eight goals in seven games and leading the Arenas to the championship.

Alf journeyed west to Vancouver in 1920 where he saw action in the playoffs for the next five seasons. He never again drank victory champagne from the Cup though, and finally finished out his career as a sub for Boston, Montreal, and Pittsburgh of the NHL.

ART SKOV

BORN: Wheatley, Ontario, September 2, 1928
POSITION: Referee, NHL, 1957–

The brother of former Detroit Red Wings' defensive forward Glen Skov, Art developed into the National Hockey League's most respected referee during the early and midseventies. During the 1974–75 season Skov wore the official's number one on his referee jersey, emblematic of his stature among the league whistleblowers. Like many of the better officials, Skov suffered criticism from detractors. During the 1974 Stanley Cup finals between the Bruins and Flyers, Skov was accused by Boston managing director Harry Sinden of favoring the Philadelphia skaters. Indignant over the insult, Skov threatened to retire, but was persuaded to continue as referee. Sinden was fined for his gesture of ill will.

ALOYSIUS MARTIN (TOD) SLOAN

BORN: Vinton, Quebec, November 30, 1927
POSITION: Forward, Toronto Maple Leafs, 1947–58; Chicago Black
    Hawks, 1958–61
AWARDS: All-Star (Second Team), 1956

By November 2, 1950, the Maple Leafs sat securely in first place and had gone through nine games without a loss. The kids were coming through as Toronto boss Conn Smythe had hoped. The best surprise of all was the acquisition of an Irish-Canadian forward named Tod Sloan. The Leafs had twice before rejected him because of his small size, but he had given up smoking and gained fifteen pounds.

"Tod is his own boss," Smythe said. "He does what he likes with the puck. It took us a few years to discover that the best way to handle him is to leave him alone."

Smythe favored Sloan not merely because he could put the puck in the net but also because Tod was tough. One night he crashed headlong into the boards during a game against the Red Wings and appeared to have broken his collarbone. Rink attendants unfolded a stretcher and dashed across the rink to take Sloan to the hospital. Just as they arrived at Tod's side, the young Leaf flipped himself over on his stomach and got to his knees. He shooed away the stretcherbearers and skated, rubber-legged, toward the bench. When it came time for his line to take its next turn, Sloan was out there, apparently as fresh as a flower.

Another time, in Montreal, he was hit in the mouth by a flying stick. Tod tapped teammate Harry Watson on the shoulder. "I'm not complaining," said Tod, "but I think your stick knocked out all my front teeth."

Watson peered momentarily at the ice and then at Sloan. "Quit beefing," said the veteran, "you only lost four."

EDWARD STANLEY SLOWINSKI

BORN: Winnipeg, Manitoba, November 18, 1922
POSITION: Right Wing, Detroit Red Wings, 1947; New York Rangers, 1948–53

A Red Wing in his rookie (1947–48) season, Ed Slowinski was almost immediately traded to the Rangers for whom he played the rest of his NHL hockey through the 1952–53 season. Slowinski was a huge broth of a boy whose finest hours occurred during the 1950 Stanley Cup playoffs, when he played on a line with center Don Raleigh and left winger Pentti Lund. Together, they helped lift the underdog New Yorkers to the seventh game of the Cup finals before losing in double sudden-death to the Detroiters.

J. COOPER SMEATON

BORN: Carleton Place, Ontario, 1890
POSITION: Referee, NHA, 1913–16; General Manager, Philadelphia Quakers, 1930–31; Referee in Chief, NHL, 1931–37
AWARDS: Hockey Hall of Fame, 1961

J. Cooper Smeaton moved to Montreal as a young lad and became involved in several sports—baseball, football, hockey, and basketball. His hockey ability was such that he twice refused offers to turn professional.

But it is for refereeing the game that Smeaton has gained immortality as a member of the Hockey Hall of Fame. He began officiating in the amateur leagues before being appointed to the National Hockey Association by Frank Calder in 1913. He called the shots for several Stanley and Allan Cup series.

Smeaton tried his hand at managing with the Philadelphia Quakers of the NHL in 1930–31, but returned to refereeing the following season after the Philadelphia franchise folded. He was then made referee in chief of the league until his retirement in 1937.

Smeaton, a World War I winner of the Military Medal, was appointed a trustee of the Stanley Cup in 1946.

AL "SMITTY" SMITH

BORN: Toronto, Ontario, November 10, 1945
POSITION: Goalie, Toronto Maple Leafs, 1965–67, 1968–69; Pittsburgh Penguins, 1969–71; Detroit Red Wings, 1971–72; New England Whalers (WHA), 1973–

Al Smith came up through the Toronto Maple Leaf organization just prior to the initial expansion of the NHL. He was barely able to break into the game, with the likes of Johnny Bower, Glenn Hall, Jacques Plante, and Terry Sawchuk still tending the nets in their twilight years.

After bouncing up and down from 1965 through 1970, Al finally found a permanent berth with the Pittsburgh Penguins, where he usually suffered from shell shock behind a weak team. In 1971 he was traded to Detroit which was in equally bad shape, but by this time Smith had begun to show talent, in the old stand-up style which has become a rarity.

In 1972 Smith was one of the first NHL'ers to jump to the new WHA, with the New England Whalers, where he has settled down to being one of the half-dozen best netminders in all of professional hockey today. He has lightning-fast reflexes and an exceptional glove hand—and would you believe he writes poetry!

ALFRED E. (ALF) SMITH

BORN: Ottawa, Ontario, June 3, 1873
DIED: August 21, 1953
POSITION: Right Wing, Ottawa Senators (AHA, CAHL, FAHL, ECAHA), 1895–97, 1904–07, 1908; Kenora Thistles (MHL), 1907
AWARDS: Hockey Hall of Fame, 1962

Alf Smith, nastiest of the seven hockey playing Smith brothers, spent his entire career with Ottawa, twice winning the Stanley Cup, and leading the league in scoring for the 1897 season. Mysteriously, the pugnacious right winger dropped out of hockey following his league-leading performance and did not reappear until 1904.

Alf was thirty years old at this time and to most observers, age had not mellowed the ruffian one bit. Despite his impressive abilities around the opponent's net, Smith was constantly criticized for his dirty play. In 1907, after a particularly vicious stick duel with the Montreal Wanderers, Smith was arrested, fined, and warned that any further incidents might mean his lifetime banishment from hockey. This brush with the law seemed to temper Smith's outbursts, and after one more year with Ottawa, he retired to become coach of the squad.

DALLAS EARL SMITH

BORN: Hamiota, Manitoba, October 10, 1941
POSITION: Defensemen, Boston Bruins, 1959–62, 1965–

Dallas Who?, fans around the NHL circuit have asked for more than a decade. It's true Dallas Smith isn't exactly a household name, but in Boston he has been considered a bulwark of the Bruins' defense. He may also be the strongest man on the club, although his 180-pound frame looks deceptively frail.

Smith played in the first NHL game he ever saw. That was back in 1959. He would later spend seven more seasons in the minors, but on this occasion the Bruins needed help on defense. Since they had nobody outstanding in their farm system, they brought Dallas right into Boston Garden from Junior A hockey. The first team he faced was Chicago. He was eighteen at the time. "Bobby Hull came streaking down on left wing," veteran Hub hockey writer Leo Monahan remembered, "and Dallas just took him right into the corner effortlessly. I don't think he even knew who Hull was. He just knew Bobby was the guy with the puck."

That's still the Smith style: cool, plain, and consistent. Typical of Dallas's charisma is his nickname. Teammates call him Half-Ton, after his tractor, of all things. The veteran is still a farm boy at heart. He owns a wheat farm in his

Dallas Smith

native Hamiota, Manitoba, and spends his off-seasons working the land he loves.

FLOYD SMITH

BORN: Perth, Ontario, May 16, 1935
POSITION: Forward, Boston Bruins, 1954–57; New York Rangers, 1960–61; Detroit Red Wings, 1962–68; Toronto Maple Leafs, 1968–70; Buffalo Sabres, 1970–72; Coach, Buffalo Sabres, 1974–

Throughout his eleven-year NHL career, Floyd Smith was a model of the steady, unspectacular defensive forward.

A bit more dramatic, however, was the manner in which he was introduced to the harsh world of NHL coaching. While Smith was in the twilight of his active playing days with the Buffalo Sabres, the regular Sabre mentor, Punch Imlach, suddenly was taken ill, forcing Smith behind the bench. The new coach's debut saw the Sabres lose a heartbreaker, 2–1, to the Toronto Maple Leafs and the very next day, Smith was the regular coach of the Sabres' AHL Cincinnati Swords.

Smith steered the Cincinnati sextet for the next two seasons, guiding them to one AHL Calder Cup and missing by an eyelash in his second attempt. Named again to the Sabres' bench post in May 1974, the heavy-browed Smith has seen

Floyd Smith

his club become one of the strongest units in the National Hockey League, reaching the 1975 Stanley Cup finals before bowing out in six games to the Philadelphia Flyers.

GARY EDWARD SMITH

BORN: Ottawa, Ontario, February 4, 1944
POSITION: Goalie, Toronto Maple Leafs, 1965–67; Oakland/California Golden Seals, 1967–71; Chicago Black Hawks, 1971–73; Vancouver Canucks, 1973–
AWARDS: Vezina Trophy (shared with Tony Esposito), 1972

The son of former NHL defenseman (Maroons, Canadiens, Black Hawks, Bruins) Des Smith, tall (6-4, 215 pounds) goalie Gary Smith achieved eminence during the 1974–75 season with the Vancouver Canucks. Thanks to the tall netminder, the Canucks finished first in the Conn Smythe Division, upsetting the Chicago Black Hawks and St. Louis Blues. Prior to his Vancouver experience, Smith goaled for the Toronto Maple Leafs (1965–66, 1966–67), Oakland Seals (1967–68 through 1970–71), and then two seasons in Chicago as understudy for Tony Esposito. "I played so seldom for the Hawks," said Smith, "I felt like an outsider. I wasn't contributing as I have been in Vancouver." He played adequately for the Canucks in 1973–74 when the team was torn by internal problems and an overhauling in the front office. When calm was restored Smith really excelled.

HARRY SMITH

BORN: Unknown

POSITION: Left Wing and Center, Ottawa Victorias (ECAHA), 1906, 1907; Montreal Wanderers (ECHA), 1909; Haileybury (NHA), 1910; Waterloo Indians (OPHL), 1911; Toronto Tecumsehs (NHA), 1913; Ottawa Senators (NHA), 1914

Harry Smith, a brilliant but erratic forward, could have been one of the greats of all time if not for his extremely volatile temper. Like his brother Alf, Harry was a pugnacious left wing/center who appeared to draw as much satisfaction from a good Pier Six brawl as he did from scoring an important goal. Between trips to the sin bin, Harry did manage to finish his seven-year career with an even two-goals-per-game average—pretty good numbers for an "inconsistent" player.

The high point of Harry's career came in 1906 when, after leading the league in scoring over the regular season, he almost single-handedly overcame an eight-goal Wanderer lead in a two-game, total goals series for the Stanley Cup. Harry scored five goals in the second game, only to see his Ottawa squad lose the Cup by two goals.

After stints with the Wanderers, Haileybury, Waterloo, and the Tecumsehs, Harry returned to Ottawa in 1914 where he finished out his career as a sub.

REGINALD JOSEPH "HOOLEY" SMITH

BORN: Toronto, Ontario, January 7, 1903

DIED: Montreal, Quebec, August 24, 1963

POSITION: Center/Right Wing, Ottawa Senators, 1925–27; Montreal Maroons, 1927–36; Boston Bruins, 1936–37; New York Americans, 1937–41

AWARDS: All-Star (First Team), 1936, (Second Team), 1932; Hockey Hall of Fame, 1972

A Hall of Famer, Hooley Smith played both forward and defense, starring first for the Ottawa Senators, then the Montreal Maroons, Boston Bruins, and finally the New York Americans. He was nicknamed Hooley by his father after the then popular comics character Happy Hooligan. Beside his hockey talents, Smith also excelled as an oarsman, rugby player, and boxer. Hooley's best years were spent with the Maroons who obtained him from Ottawa in 1927 for Punch Broadbent and $22,500. His final NHL season, with the Americans, was 1940—41 when he scored two goals and seven assists.

SIDNEY JAMES (SID) SMITH

BORN: Toronto, Ontario, July 11, 1925
POSITION: Forward, Toronto Maple Leafs, 1946–58
AWARDS: Lady Byng Trophy, 1952, 1955

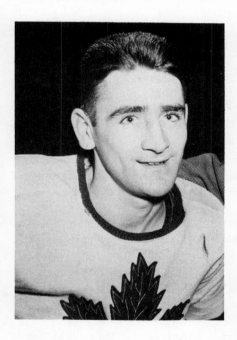

The smilingest forward on the Toronto Maple Leafs during their golden era of
the late forties and early fifties was Sid Smith. Smith had a lot to smile about.
After a fourteen-game trial with the Leafs in 1946–47, Sid bounced up and
down between the Leafs' Pittsburgh farm club in the American League and the
big club. He played on the 1948 and 1949 Stanley Cup winners, but really
came into his own as a goal mouth terror in 1951 when the Leafs again captured the championship. In eleven playoff games, Smith scored 7 goals and 3
assists for 10 points.

Inevitably, Smith treated the game with rare good humor. One night, after a
game in which the Leafs defeated Montreal at Maple Leaf Gardens, both the
Toronto club and Montreal were traveling on the same train. It so happened
that Smith had kept Maurice Richard from scoring during the game and the
next morning they wound up sitting next to each other in the diner. Richard got
up and left long before Sid was finished, prompting a teammate to remark,
"Rocket didn't take much notice of you, Smitty, did he?"

Smith grinned. "He didn't, eh? He knocked over my bowl of cereal as he went by!"

Smith remained a Maple Leaf until his retirement following the 1957–58 campaign.

THOMAS J. (TOMMY) SMITH

BORN: Ottawa, Ontario, September 27, 1885
DIED: August 1, 1966
POSITION: Left Wing, Center, Ottawa Victorias (FAHL, ECAHA), 1906; Brantford (OPHL), 1909–10; Cobalt (NHA), 1910; Galt (OPHL), 1911; Moncton, 1912; Quebec Bulldogs (NHA), 1913–16; Montreal Canadiens (NHA), 1917; Quebec Bulldogs, 1920
AWARDS: Hockey Hall of Fame, 1973

Tommy Smith was the youngest of the hockey-playing Smith brothers and was also the best of the lot. He wasn't nearly as pugilistic as his brother Alf, but he did have the same itch to keep moving that saw brother Harry switch teams almost annually.

Tommy was the highest scorer of the family, three times leading his loop in goal-getting. In fact, his first league-leading year, 1909, saw him miss the final two games of the season when he ventured north to play in the Mines League. By that time, Smith was so far ahead of his nearest competitor, he felt the last two contests wouldn't make a difference. He was right, and finished the campaign with 33 goals in 13 games.

Smith signed with the Quebec Bulldogs in 1913 and promptly helped guide them to a Stanley Cup. Teamed with the legendary Joe Malone, Smith was a scoring sensation for Quebec for the next three years and the pair constantly swapped first place in the league's scoring race.

Over his eleven-year career, Tommy Smith was on four championship squads and one Cup winner. He finished his playing days with well over a goal per game average.

CONSTANTINE FALKLAND KERRYS (CONN) SMYTHE

One of the most influential and colorful characters associated with the National Hockey League, Conn Smythe first gained notice in the months following the start of World War I. At the time Smythe played center and captained the University of Toronto's varsity hockey club while majoring in engineering. Smythe's team did the unprecedented when they won the Ontario Hockey Association's Junior championship. After that hockey players enlisted *en masse* in the Canadian Armed Forces, and Smythe was sent overseas where he served with distinction.

Upon his return from the war, Smythe headed straight for the university, where he obtained his degree in applied science and continued to stay in close touch with the varsity hockey team as unofficial manager, promoter, and all-round rah-rah leader. In time this association would be the catalyst for Smythe's success in the professional hockey ranks.

The much-decorated veteran of World War I gained acclaim in college hockey circles for his superb stewardship of the University of Toronto hockey clubs. Each year Smythe would shepherd his varsity sextet to Boston, where the Toronto skaters wowed Beantown fans on the ice while young Smythe impressed newspaper editors with his flamboyant prose and knack for headline-grabbing, a trait he refined with age. Charles F. Adams, owner of the Bruins, was fascinated by Smythe's deportment and remembered him when Colonel John Hammond, president of the Rangers, asked for a recommendation for a man to organize a group of players to be Hammond's NHL entry. "Conn Smythe is your man," said Adams. "You won't find any better."

With customary vigor Smythe spent the summer of 1926 signing players for the rookie Rangers' franchise. His selections were impeccably sharp, and before the season had begun, Smythe had signed such stickhandlers as Frank Boucher, Bill and Bun Cook, Ching Johnson, Murray Murdoch, and Bill Boyd.

When the players gathered at a Toronto hotel for preseason training, Smythe felt content. His team, he believed, with good reason, would be indomitable. One night, after convening at the training hotel, Smythe chose to take the night off to go to a movie with his wife. It was a reasonable plan, so Smythe was flabbergasted when Colonel Hammond accosted him in the lobby upon his return. "Where have you been?,' Colonel Hammond demanded.

When Smythe revealed that he and his wife had enjoyed a leisurely dinner and a good movie, Colonel Hammond bristled with anger: "Well, that night out has just cost us one of the greatest players in the game. St. Pats just sold Babe Dye to Chicago. We could have had him for $14,000."

Smythe was unimpressed, and he told Colonel Hammond so. "I wouldn't want Babe Dye on my team, no matter what the price," snapped Smythe with the brand of finality that either convinces an employer or causes a man to lose his job. "He's not the type of player we need."

Smythe was not about to be fired on the spot; the Colonel wanted more evidence, and for a one-dollar phone call he got it. Hammond phoned Barney Stanley, coach of the Black Hawks, and pointedly mentioned young Smythe's opinion of Dye. Stanley's guffaws could be heard across the continent. When he stopped laughing, the Black Hawks' coach sputtered: "Smythe wouldn't want Dye on his team? Why that man must be crazy. It only proves how little he knows about hockey players. I can't understand, Colonel, why you keep a man like that when there's an outstanding hockey man like Lester Patrick loose and ready to be signed.''

The Colonel didn't understand it either. Smythe was promptly summoned to the Colonel's office and given his discharge papers before the season even began.

''Unwittingly,'' wrote former Toronto hockey publicist Ed Fitkin, ''Babe Dye was mainly responsible for the formation of the Toronto Maple Leafs, because Smythe, angered by the Rangers' rebuff, decided he'd get into pro hockey or bust. Within a year he was back in the NHL, this time to stay.''

Conn went about the business of trying to purchase the Toronto St. Patricks so that he could proudly reenter the NHL. It required one year from the time the Rangers had fired him for Conn to come through the front door of the major league again. The momentous day in Toronto hockey history was February 27, 1927, when an NHL governor's meeting was held in Toronto. Querrie resigned as governor, and Smythe was elected to be his replacement. The name St. Patricks was officially dropped. From then on the team would be known as the Toronto Maple Leafs.

It was too late to salvage the 1926–27 season, and Smythe realized that only a five-year plan to build a new hockey empire would be realistic. To do so he would have to wheel and deal as never before in league history. ''From 1927 to 1930,'' said Fitkin, ''Smythe engineered so many trades in an effort to put together a winning combination that he was nicknamed 'the David Harum of hockey.' He promised fans a fast-skating young team, and, in time, he produced just what he had promised.''

Smythe decided to build his team around a couple of young aces with rare promise. One of them was Hap Day, a forward who was converted to defense on the night the newly christened Maple Leafs won their first game, and Joe Primeau. Frank Selke had discovered Primeau when Joe first tried out for—and was rejected by—the St. Cecilia's Bantam squad, which Selke then was managing.

But Primeau worked at his game and improved enough to gain a berth on Selke's St. Mary's squad, which later became the Marlboros. ''Few coaches or players thought much of Primeau's chances,'' said author Ron McAllister, ''for the simple reason that Joe seemed much too quiet and methodical to ever make a living at a sport that required a maximum amount of showmanship.''

Tipped off about Primeau by Selke, Smythe originally had planned to sign him for the Rangers. Young Joe was ready and eager to make the move. When Colonel Hammond fired Smythe, the young center said he would have no part of the New York organization; despite the fact that he was rejecting a rare opportunity to play in the NHL, he remained loyal to Smythe and rejected the Rangers' offer.

Primeau and Day would not be enough for a winning team, and Smythe knew it. After the club finished last in the Canadian Division in 1926–27, Smythe suffered what Selke described as one of Conn's severest depressions about the Maple Leafs' outlook. It was then that Selke saved the day, if not the franchise.

"Conn," said Selke, "what you have to do is get rid of the old veterans on the Leafs and get some good youngsters, like the kids I have on the Marlboros." Selke vividly remembered that Smythe's response was one of incredulity lightly distilled with scorn. "There are times," Smythe sputtered, "when I think there's something wrong with your head."

Nevertheless, Smythe accepted Selke's advice and it proved to be one of his wisest moves. Fortified with the Marlboros' youngsters and some wily veterans, Smythe built a dynasty in Toronto to coincide with the opening of his hockey palace, Maple Leaf Gardens, in November 1931. His deals—especially the one that brought colorful defenseman King Clancy to Toronto—usually had a touch of genius, and in 1932 the Maple Leafs won their first Stanley Cup for Smythe.

His club was regarded as the Gashouse Gang of the NHL because of such robust characters as Charlie Conacher, Red Horner, Hap Day, Baldy Cotton, Busher Jackson, Joe Primeau, and the irrepressible Clancy. Always, though, Smythe was the leader and with each season he managed to gain more importance within the NHL hierarchy itself. When his Gashouse Gang sagged in the midthirties, Conn built a new empire around gifted center Syl Apps and goalie Turk Broda. They won the Stanley Cup in April 1942 in a seven-game series with Detroit in which the Maple Leafs fell behind, three games to none, and then won the next four straight matches—a feat unprecedented then in NHL history.

While Smythe was overseas serving in the Canadian Armed Forces in World War II, his Leafs won another Cup in 1945 with Selke presiding while Conn was away. When his club disintegrated during the following season, Smythe returned from Europe and engineered a complete rebuilding of the club. Accenting youth, he made daring changes and produced what were the best Maple Leaf clubs in history. With Hap Day coaching, the Leafs won the Stanley Cup in 1947, 1948, and 1949, a three-straight sweep that had never before been accomplished. They missed in 1950, but with new coach Joe Primeau behind the bench in 1951 they won the Cup again. By this time his interests began moving away from hockey toward thoroughbred racing. Although he had been president and managing director of Maple Leaf Gardens he became less active on the hockey front and finally retired in 1961 while his son, Stafford, moved into many of the key NHL roles once occupied by Conn himself.

The elder Smythe, however, continued to remain in the news, frequently orating on some subject that would create headlines. In June 1971 he did just that, resigning from the NHL Hall of Fame Committee in protest over the selection of one of his own Cup-winning stalwarts of the 1932 Leafs, Busher Jackson. To this day he frequently surfaces to lambast the commercialism of today's game and has remained as colorful and quotable as ever.

C. STAFFORD "STAFF" SMYTHE

One of the most colorful and, at once, tragic figures in modern professional hockey, Staff Smythe often was regarded as a chip off the old block—father Conn Smythe. Like his dad, Staff was groomed in the hockey wars at an early age, learning the stickhandling business at Maple Leaf Gardens before he was out of knickers. But Stafford had a tough act to follow although follow it he did. He was bombastic like Conn and equally as quotable. It was considered inevitable that Staff eventually would move into a position of NHL power as soon as his father would permit such a move.

At the age of sixty, Conn Smythe retired as the manager of the Maple Leafs in favor of former coach Hap Day, but Conn retained the presidency of the team. Bereft of ability, the Toronto brass turned to slogans. With King Clancy coaching the team in 1955–56, Day promised a team with "guts, goals, and glamour." They had only a smidgen of each, however, and they dropped from fourth to fifth with Howie Meeker doing the coaching. Amid all this confusion a power struggle developed for control of Maple Leaf Gardens and the hockey club. A group led by Stafford spearheaded the revolution, and soon Conn's "little boy" was running the show.

A coach and manager as an eleven-year-old while playing minor hockey, a coach and manager during student days at the University of Toronto, and a manager with the Marlboro Juniors, Stafford alternately lauded and fought his father.

"My dad gave me lots of rope and lots to do," said Stafford. "When I was thirty I was ten years ahead of everybody, and at forty I was ten years behind everybody." Stafford meant that after his father allowed him to learn so much so soon, Conn continued to regard him as an employee and refused to permit him to make significant decisions even when he had reached the age of forty. As a result, Stafford decided he had to challenge his father, no matter what the reaction, public or private.

"The people my father respects," said Stafford, "are those who stand up to him and fight. After I learned to do this, he respected me, but we had plenty of scraps."

In 1957, during the Maple Leafs' depression, Conn Smythe decided to pump new blood into the organization. He appointed Stafford chairman of a new Maple Leafs' hockey committee. He fired Howie Meeker, who had become general manager. "Meeker," Stafford said, "was too inexperienced."

Stafford Smythe gradually laid the groundwork for a revitalization of the

Maple Leafs' machine, in much the way his father had done so thirty years earlier.

On November 23, 1961, Stafford—along with Harold Ballard and John Bassett—bought Conn Smythe's stock at $40 a share with a $2 million bank loan
that was repaid in four years.

Stafford and Harold Ballard, his friend and business associate of twenty-five
years, were arrested on June 17, 1971. Smythe was charged with defrauding
Maple Leaf Gardens of $249,000 and stealing $146,000 in cash and securities
from the Gardens. Ballard was charged with defrauding Maple Leaf Gardens of
$83,000 and stealing $146,000 in cash and securities. Smythe was also charged
under the Canadian Income Tax Act with evading taxes on income of $289,372
and Ballard, on income of $134,000.

On October 31, 1971, just twelve days before he was scheduled for trial on
the tax charges, Stafford Smythe died of complications arising from bleeding
stomach ulcers. He was fifty years old. The news sent Toronto into a state of
shock. "No," wrote Toronto *Star* sports columnist Milt Dunnell, "it wouldn't
be in order to break out the orchids for Stafford Smythe now that he is dead.
Maybe he didn't deserve orchids. At any rate, he didn't want them. One thing
is sure: he got more nettles than he deserved—but he didn't seem to mind that
either."

ED SNIDER

Ed Snider is the chairman of the board of the Philadelphia Flyers and was one
of the original people who spearheaded a drive to bring big-league hockey to
the Philadelphia area.

He is one of the more dynamic owners in the NHL, and according to the
people who know him, is as much a fan as an owner. In 1974, when the Flyers
became the first expansion team to win the Stanley Cup, Snider said it was the
"thrill of a lifetime." He said it again in 1975.

Besides serving as the chief of the Flyers, Snider is also a co-owner of the
Spectrum, chairman of National Hockey League Services, and a member of the
NHL's Finance Committee.

Snider has been praised by his colleagues as one of the NHL's most progres-
sive owners, and has been one of the main reasons why the Flyers are a loyal,
close-knit organization.

FREDERIC WILLIAM (FRED) STANFIELD

BORN: Toronto, Ontario, May 4, 1944
POSITION: Center, Chicago Black Hawks, 1964–67; Boston Bruins,
    1967–73; Minnesota North Stars, 1973–74; Buffalo Sabres, 1974–

Unfortunately, Fred Stanfield's most famous accomplishment may well be his inclusion in hockey's greatest steal. Stanfield was the third member of the Phil Esposito-Ken Hodge heist pulled off by the Boston Bruins in 1967.

While Stanfield's status as a Bruin was far less auspicious than Espo or Hodge, he was no slouch in Boston. He scored 125 times for the Bruins and manned the "other" point on the power play (Bobby Orr owned the right point, as well as most of the rest of the ice). Fred was dealt to Minnesota after six seasons as Boston's number two center and subsequently to the Buffalo Sabres, where he regained his Boston form.

ALLAN HERBERT STANLEY

BORN: Timmins, Ontario, March 1, 1926
POSITION: Defenseman, New York Rangers, 1948–54; Chicago
    Black Hawks, 1954–56; Boston Bruins, 1956–58; Toronto Maple
    Leafs, 1958–68; Philadelphia Flyers, 1968–69
AWARDS: All-Star (Second Team), 1960–61, 1966

Mocked for his languid play in New York and Chicago, Allan Stanley later was revered in Boston and Toronto where he crystallized into one of the most accomplished defensive defensemen in the National Hockey League from 1956 through 1967. Stanley originally climbed to the NHL via the Providence Reds of the American League. The Rangers spent what then was regarded as a staggering amount ($80,000) for the husky defenseman who made his debut in 1948–49. Harsh Madison Square Garden fans took a dislike to his non-belligerent tortoiselike movements and ironically dubbed him "Sonja" as in Sonja Henie. Stanley's manager, Frank Boucher, appreciated his defenseman's play, but ultimately responded to the fans' criticism by trading Stanley to Chicago in November 1954. Allan was less than successful in the Windy City and was traded to Boston in 1956–57. There, Stanley flourished for two years, but he was dealt to Toronto in 1958–59 and played on four Stanley Cup champions under manager-coach Punch Imlach. His last NHL season was spent with Philadelphia in 1968–69.

THE STANLEY CUP

Professional hockey's most revered possession is the Stanley Cup, emblematic of the world's championship. Curiously, though, the Stanley Cup wasn't origi-

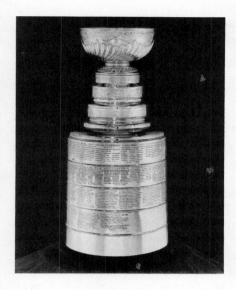

Stanley Cup

nally meant to be awarded to the champions of professional hockey. It was intended to be presented to the leading amateurs of Canada.

Even more ironic, the man after whom it was named—Lord Stanley of Preston, Canada's governor general—really didn't give a damn about hockey. His son, Arthur Stanley, was the hockey buff in the family and he, along with his aide, Lord Kilcoursie, and Ottawa publisher P. D. Ross, persuaded Lord Stanley to purchase the silver mug in 1893 and award it to the leading amateur team. The Cup, valued then at $48.67, was first won by the Montreal Amateur Athletic Association. It remained in the amateur ranks until 1912, when it was captured by a professional team, the Quebec Bulldogs.

With a few exceptions, the Stanley Cup playoffs have been held regularly since Lord Stanley of Preston donated the prized trophy. Nature often intervened to impair the quality of the ice in the 1890s and early 1900s before the advent of artificial ice rinks.

Death intervened in 1919 when a continent-wide epidemic of the black flu infected some of the Montreal Canadiens, who were playing the Seattle Metropolitans in Washington. The series was canceled after five games had been played—each team had won two games and one had ended in a draw—and "Bad" Joe Hall of the Montrealers had died of the disease.

If Sir Arthur Conan Doyle had spent his writing years in Canada, there's good reason to believe he'd have penned a few adventures of Sherlock Holmes and the Stanley Cup. One of the earliest and best Cup stories occurred in 1905 after the Ottawa Silver Seven had won the Cup.

Jubilant Ottawa fans had presented their champs with a gala victory dinner that sent many of the victors well into the grape. Finally, the party ended and the Ottawa skaters stumbled home in the bitter cold of the night. As refreshing as the Arctic air may have been, it wasn't enough to clear the mind of Harry Smith, a stalwart of the Silver Seven. Through Harry's somewhat distorted eyes, the revered Cup took on all the aspects of a football. He grabbed the trophy and delivered a perfect place-kick that sent the Stanley Cup arching into the Rideau Canal.

Since the other troops were no more sober than Smith, the Cup remained in the Rideau and the Silver Seven headed home. The next morning, Harry Smith began to suspect that he had been guilty of a rather rash place-kick. He dressed quickly, dashed back to the Rideau Canal, and there he found the Cup, nestled in the bone-dry bed.

The dents that Harry's boot had put in the Cup weren't to be its last. A year later, the Montreal Wanderers captured the championship and proudly, and somewhat more soberly, hauled the Cup to the studio of a photographer named Jimmy Rice. There they proudly lined up for the traditional victory portrait with the Stanley Cup standing before the victorious Wanderers.

When Jimmy Rice gave the final click of the shutter, the Wanderers gleefully filed out of the studio for the nearest pub. Perhaps the visions of malt hops were dancing in their heads. Whatever it was, the Wanderers jubilantly departed and never gave a thought to the trophy. In fact, nobody but a charwoman was concerned about the Cup. When the last of the Wanderers had left the studio, the cleaning lady noticed the interesting silver cup sitting on the floor. "My," she must have said, "but this would make a lovely flower pot." So she took the Stanley Cup home.

Several months later, the Wanderers' management thought it would be a noble gesture if the Stanley Cup were placed on display in the victors' arena. But, alas, where was the trophy? The last place anyone remembered seeing it was at Jimmy Rice's studio. Jimmy was contacted. He called his charwoman, who explained that the Stanley Cup was on her mantel—literally in full bloom.

As the Cup grew older, it grew proportionately in size. In order to inscribe the names of each new winner on the trophy, it became necessary to enlarge the base of the cup again and again until it more than quadrupled its original size. And as the trophy grew, greater and greater security measures were taken to protect it from thieves and players with short memories. Even so the Cup managed to get away.

During the playoffs of April 1962, the Cup resided in a huge glass case right in the midst of the Chicago Stadium lobby for all to see. The Black Hawks had won the world championship the previous year and were now engaged in another furious battle for the trophy.

A Montreal fan by the name of Ken Kilander took a dim view of the Stanley Cup's residing in Chicago. He studied the silver mug and the glass case with the intensity of a safecracker about to launch a great heist. The temptation proved too much for him so he did it. He opened the glass case and when, to his supreme amazement, neither gongs nor sirens nor any form of warning buzzer sounded, he gingerly reached in and plucked the Cup off its stand. Still not a sound. There was just one thing to do. Leave. And that he did. Nursing the Cup with affection, Kilander sauntered through the lobby of Chicago Stadium and headed for the exit doors. It was almost too good to be true.

Kilander was just a few yards from freedom when a cop spotted him and asked why he happened to be carrying the Stanley Cup out of Chicago Stadium. "I want to take it back where it belongs," he explained. "To Montreal."

Being a Chicagoan, the cop disagreed. He returned the Cup to the glass case where it belonged, and Kilander was urged to permit Cup movements to be decided on the ice.

RUSSELL "BARNEY" STANLEY

BORN: Paisley, Ontario, January 1, 1893
DIED: May 16, 1971
POSITION: Right Wing, Vancouver Millionaires (PCHL), 1915–19; Calgary (WCHL), 1922; Regina (WCHL), 1923–24; Edmonton (WCHL, WHL), 1925, 1926
AWARDS: Hockey Hall of Fame, 1962

Barney Stanley, a ten-year veteran of the western hockey wars, was a solid right winger whose best years were with Vancouver of the PCHA. Barney joined the Millionaires in 1915, just in time to help them win their first PCHA Stanley Cup. He was the clutch star of that series, scoring four goals in the third and final game.

Stanley was traded to Calgary in 1920, but did not play again until the 1922 season. Despite bagging 26 goals in 24 games with Calgary, Stanley was traded to Regina the following year. He finished up his career at Edmonton where he was paired on defense with the legendary Eddie Shore.

PATRICK JAMES (PAT) "WHITEY" STAPLETON

BORN: Sarnia, Ontario, July 4, 1940
POSITION: Defenseman, Boston Bruins, 1961–63; Chicago Black Hawks, 1965–73; Defenseman/Coach, Chicago Cougars (WHA), 1973–75; Indianapolis Racers (WHA), 1975–
AWARDS: Dennis A. Murphy Award (Best Defenseman WHA), 1974; All-Star (Second Team), 1966, 1971, 1972, (WHA First Team), 1974; WHA Team Canada, 1974

There were only two people who believed that the Chicago Cougars could rise from the 1973 ashes and become 1974 playoff contenders. One of them was

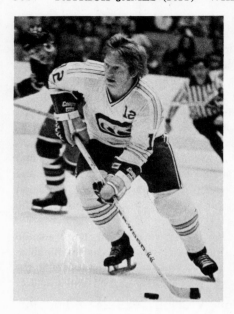

Pat Stapleton

brilliant center Ralph Backstrom and the other was his pal, Pat Stapleton. By no small coincidence, Backstrom and Stapleton both left the Chicago Black Hawks during the summer of 1973, took the subway crosstown and signed long-term contracts with the Cougars. Stapleton not only would take his position on defense but also would coach the WHA sextet.

For the jovial Stapleton it was an onerous challenge. In their rookie season (1972–73), the Cougars finished sixth in the Western Division with a 26–50–2 record, worst in the WHA. With Pat behind the bench—and playing—in 1973–74 the Cougars gained 27 points, finishing with 38 wins, 35 losses, and 5 ties. To a man, the players attributed the upbeat change to Stapleton and his style. "Pat," said Backstrom, "is the kind of guy you want to work for and these guys really worked."

They upset the New England Whalers in a thrilling seven-game playoff, winning the final match on enemy ice. Then, with Stapleton leading the charge, the Cougars knocked off the favored Toronto Toros in another seven-game set, again capturing the seventh game on foreign ice.

One good reason for this victory was Pat's record on ice as well as behind the bench. He led all WHA defensemen in assists with 52, while old pal Backstrom had 33 goals and 50 assists.

Hard work had also guaranteed Pat ten NHL seasons and a league-leading 15 assists in the 1973 Stanley Cup playoffs with the Black Hawks, just weeks before he decided to head for the Cougars. "My decision to join the WHA wasn't that difficult," he said. "When Bobby Hull went, I knew it was for real." Like Hull, Stapleton frequently was frazzled by the dual player-coach role. During the seventh game of the Cougar-Whaler series he was given a game misconduct by referee Bill Friday for giving the official the "choke" sign following a Chicago penalty.

Instead of faltering, however, the Cougars rallied and took a come-from-behind victory, 3–2. "When we saw Pat go off with the game misconduct," said Backstrom, "we all decided that we had to try twice as hard in order to win the game for him. And we did."

Pat ran out of miracles in the 1974 playoff finals against Gordie Howe and the Houston Aeros. The Cougars lost the first two games on their own ice and then were wiped out in Houston, dropping the series in four straight. Stapleton had nothing to be ashamed of, not when one considers the reclamation job he did on the once impotent Cougars.

In December 1974, it appeared that the Cougars would fold, but Stapleton and teammates Ralph Backstrom and Dave Dryden saved the team by purchasing it from Jordan and Walter Kaiser. Thus, Pat became the first player in the history of big-league hockey to at once play, coach, manage, and own a hockey team. But the Cougars folded in 1975 and Pat moved to Indianapolis.

VICTOR JOHN STASIUK

BORN: Lethbridge, Alberta, May 23, 1929
POSITION: Left Wing, Chicago Black Hawks, 1949–50; Detroit Red
    Wings, 1951–55, 1961–63; Boston Bruins, 1956–60; Coach, Phil-
    adelphia Flyers, 1969–71; California Seals, 1972; Vancouver
    Canucks, 1972–73

Vic Stasiuk, a hulking left winger who liked to use his body in heavy checking, began his career in Chicago (1949–50), but his best hockey was played in Detroit (1951–52 through 1954–55) and Boston (1955–56 through 1959–60). He played his last three NHL seasons back in Detroit, finishing his big-league career in 1962–63.

Stasiuk could be intimidating, as he was against the Rangers in the 1958 Stanley Cup playoffs. In that series Stasiuk skated the width of the ice to smash the Rangers' Red Sullivan with an elbow and break his jaw. Vic was credited with turning the series in Boston's favor with the blow. However, he got his retribution when the Rangers' Andy Bathgate wasted Stasiuk twice in fights during a later match. In time Vic turned to coaching and handled the Philadelphia Flyers. During the 1970–71 season Stasiuk feuded with several players who opposed his directive ordering the Coke machine removed from the dressing room. In June 1971 Stasiuk was replaced by Fred Shero. However, he has remained in hockey in various capacities.

PETER DAVID (PETE) STEMKOWSKI

BORN: Winnipeg, Manitoba, August 25, 1943
POSITION: Center, Toronto Maple Leafs, 1963–68; Detroit Red
    Wings, 1968–70; New York Rangers, 1970–

He's known as the Polish Prince, the Kilbassa Kid, the Clown Prince of the
NHL. Peter Stemkowski, who's been compared to comedian Rich Little for his
hilarious impressions, Jimmy Durante for his protruding proboscis, and the
Goodyear blimp for his awesome girth, has been conducting his center-ice business in the NHL at a laugh-a-line pace since 1963.

It was Stemmer's devil-may-care attitude that sent him packing from the
floundering Detroit Red Wings in 1970. The hapless Wings were going nowhere fast, and ex-Cornell coach Ned Harkness was using some of his tried 'n
true Ivy League disciplinary tactics to whip his Motor City sextet into shape.
But, in the solemn depths of the Detroit dressing room lurked the impish Peter
Stemkowski.

After a particularly nauseating rah-rah practice session, Stemmer had somehow impounded Harkness's beloved Cornell windbreaker and baseball cap.
Emerging from the coach's office decked out in full Cornell regalia, Stemmer
proceded to entertain the weary troops with his patented Harkness imitation.

"Okay guys, gimme a C," Pete gleefully ordered.

The howling Red Wings responded with a booming "C!!"

"Gimme an O," continued Stemmer. "Gimme an R!"

Suddenly, the Red Wing dressing room fell silent. Looming behind Stemkowski was a not-at-all-amused Ned Harkness.

Without missing a beat, Stemkowski removed the coach's beloved outfit and handed it over. "Okay coach, take over," he said soberly, "I've got 'em warmed up for you."

Needless to say, Stemmer's days at Detroit were numbered after that cheerleading incident. Traded to the New York Rangers, Stemkowski settled in as the regular checking line center, penalty killer, and emergency left winger.

Although a notoriously slow starter during the regular season, Stemmer has proved himself to be a valuable clutch performer for the Rangers, usually saving his best efforts for the Stanley Cup playoffs. Other than his fertile wit, Stemmer will probably be best remembered for his dramatic sudden-death goal in the third overtime period of the 1971 Stanley Cup semifinals against the Chicago Black Hawks.

JOHN SHERRATT "BLACK JACK" STEWART

BORN: Pilot Mound, Manitoba, May 6, 1917
POSITION: Defenseman, Detroit Red Wings, 1938–43, 1945–50; Chicago Black Hawks, 1950–52
AWARDS: All-Star (First Team), 1943, 1948, 1949, (Second Team), 1947; Hockey Hall of Fame, 1964

If John Sherratt "Black Jack" Stewart is a name that gives you goose pimples, you can imagine what this husky, surly-looking defenseman did to opponents from 1938 through 1952 in the National Hockey League. A Detroit Red Wing for most of his career, Stewart accumulated fifty scars and 220 stitches, but never missed a minute because of it during his first ten years in the bigs. "Sew fast, Doc," Stewart would tell the medics who were repairing his injuries, "I'm due back on the ice."

Stewart was as brave as any pro and once played an entire season with a broken hand. A special device attached to his stick and wrist enabled him to firm up his grip. Red Wings' manager Jack Adams called him "one of the strongest guys I've ever seen in a hockey uniform."

Like the Rangers' Ching Johnson, Stewart took a joyous delight in bodychecking. "He was a mean individual," said ex-Wing Ted Lindsay, "but when he was mean he had a big smile on his face. When he had that smile, it was time for the opposition to look out. Once Gordie Howe and I decided we'd take this old guy into the corner during practice and rough him up. Jack took his left arm and pinned me across the chest against the screen and then he lifted Howe off the ice by the shirt. Then, he just smiled at both of us." One of Stewart's toughest battles was with Johnny Mariucci, the brawling Chicago defenseman. They battled for 15 minutes on the ice and in the penalty box. At the very worst, it was a draw for Stewart who rarely lost a fight.

NELSON (NELS) "OLD POISON" STEWART

BORN: Montreal, Quebec, December 29, 1902
DIED: August 3, 1957
POSITION: Center, Montreal Maroons, 1925–32; Boston Bruins, 1932–35, 1936; New York Americans, 1935–36, 1937–40
AWARDS: Hart Trophy, 1926, 1930; Art Ross Trophy, 1926; Hockey Hall of Fame, 1962

Nels Stewart, a strapping centerman, broke into the NHL with the Montreal Maroons in his typically dynamic fashion. During Nels's maiden season, he led the league in scoring and copped the Hart Trophy as the league's most valuable player while leading the Maroons to the coveted Stanley Cup.

A big, rough player with a deadly accurate shot, Stewart was the pivot man for the Maroons' infamous "Big S Line" with Hooley Smith and Babe Siebert. As a unit they were the roughest 'n readiest forward line in the entire league. Stewart often would chew tobacco, produce juice and then spit it, blindingly, in the enemy goalie's eyes before shooting and scoring.

After seven seasons with the Maroons, Nels was sold to Boston where he centered a line with Dit Clapper and Red Beattie. He continued his scoring heroics in Beantown, picking up his 200th career goal as well as maintaining his bully boy image. In 1935 he was suspended for fighting just before being peddled to the New York Americans.

Stewart played five years with the Americans, collecting his 300th career goal in 1938 and finally retiring from hockey in 1940.

JOHN EDWARD (JACK) STODDARD

BORN: Stony Creek, Ontario, September 26, 1926
POSITION: Forward, New York Rangers, 1951–53

If Jack Stoddard had been able to play as well as he looked he might have been in the NHL for a long time. The Rangers obtained the tall, handsome forward from Providence of the American League in 1951–52 amid considerable fanfare. It was a measure of Stoddard's ineffectiveness that his only claim to fame was his number—13. In 1952–53 Jack played a full sixty-game schedule, scoring 12 goals and 13 assists for 25 points. It was his last experience in the big time.

GEORGE JAMES "RED" SULLIVAN

BORN: Peterborough, Ontario, December 24, 1929
POSITION: Forward, Boston Bruins, 1949–53; Chicago Black Hawks, 1954–56; New York Rangers, 1956–61; Coach, New York Rangers, 1962–65; Pittsburgh Penguins, 1967–69; Washington Capitals, 1975

A tenacious forechecker and garrulous needler of the enemy, Red Sullivan lacked the basic skills of a hard-shooting and adroit stickhandler to become a superior offensive center. He did, however, excite the fans in Boston (1949–50 through 1952–53) and Chicago (1954–55 and 1955–56) before coming to New York where he became a hero with the Rangers. Red's most productive year was 1958–59 when he totalled 63 points on 21 goals and 42 assists, but, significantly, the Rangers missed the playoffs. Sullivan's truculence resulted in several significant clashes with the opposition. He frequently took runs at Montreal Canadiens' wandering goalie, Jacques Plante, and duelled with Canadiens' defenseman Doug Harvey. Sullivan once so antagonized Harvey that the Montrealer responded by spearing Red in the stomach and rupturing his spleen. Sullivan received last rites of the Catholic Church in the hospital, but recovered to play again. He retired following the 1960–61 season and coached the Rangers from December 1962 through December 1965.

Sullivan later worked for the Boston Bruins as a scout and, when the Washington Capitals were admitted to the NHL in 1974–75 he became a scout under manager Milt Schmidt. Late in the season Schmidt asked Sullivan to relieve coach Jim Anderson behind the bench. He did so for a few weeks, but ill health forced him to relinquish the coaching and return to scouting.

CAPT. JAMES T. SUTHERLAND

Sometimes referred to as "the father of hockey," this member of the Hockey Hall of Fame made Kingston, Ontario, a hotbed of the game prior to World War I.

Sutherland coached the Kingston Frontenac Juniors to several championships and later became president of the OHA from 1915 to 1917. Returning from the war, he became president of the CAHA for two years, in 1919. He died in 1955.

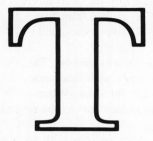

MICHAEL DALE TALLON

BORN: Noranda, Quebec, October 19, 1950
POSITION: Defenseman, Left Wing, Vancouver Canucks, 1970–73;
    Chicago Black Hawks, 1973–

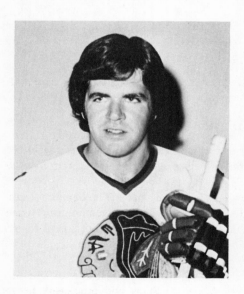

Dale Tallon is a native of Noranda, Quebec, where he grew up in the shadow of such NHL talent as Dave Keon, Pit Martin, Jacques Laperriere and Wayne Connelly.

570

Tallon played his first games of junior hockey for the Oshawa Generals, where he was constantly compared to another Oshawa graduate, Bobby Orr. The comparison didn't stop there: Tallon played defense, most of the time, shared Alan Eagleson as a lawyer, and when he was drafted by the Vancouver Canucks, was expected to be the Great White Hope of that nascent franchise. Tallon, still a junior, was traded to the Toronto Marlboros for five bodies, and the comparisons went on.

Through all of this, and the continuing rivalry with Bobby, Tallon took on the NHL in Vancouver, competing simultaneously with that season's number one draft choice (Tallon was number two), Gil Perreault. When he began to play center, which he now does for the Chicago Black Hawks, he naturally was constantly compared to Perreault.

Dale was traded to Chicago in 1973 after three seasons with the Canucks. The Black Hawks hailed his arrival with considerable fanfare. At a press conference the team announced that Tallon would receive Bobby Hull's revered number nine jersey. However, public reaction was so negative Tallon requested, and received, another number. It was a wise move considering his ineffective play. During the 1973–74 season Dale scored 15 goals and 19 assists for 34 points in 65 games. A year later he flopped altogether with 5 goals and 10 assists for 15 points in 35 games. The Great White Hope at times looked hopeless.

MARC TARDIF

BORN: Granby, Quebec, June 12, 1949
POSITION: Left Wing, Montreal Canadiens, 1969–73; Los Angeles
    Sharks (WHA), 1973–74; Michigan Stags (WHA), 1974; Quebec–
    Nordiques (WHA), 1974–
AWARDS: WHA All-Star (Second Team), 1975

A left winger, Marc Tardif came up to the Montreal Canadiens from the Junior Canadiens in 1969–70. He didn't click at first and was sent down to the minor league Voyageurs to shape up, which he did.

Tardif was never completely satisfied in Montreal, and felt he deserved more ice time. There were rumors he didn't get along with management, and when the WHA arrived, word went out that they would surely woo Tardif to the Quebec Nordiques. In 1973–74, he did go to the WHA, but to the Los Angeles Sharks.

He was high scorer for the Sharks, with 40 goals and 30 assists for 70 points, but in 1974–75 the team became the Michigan Stags and proceeded to go broke. The new Stags' coach, Johnny Wilson, wanted Tardif to play defense, but the rangy six-footer balked, and in December 1974 Tardif and his high salary were unloaded on the Quebec Nordiques for three players. Tardif was back

Marc Tardif

home in Quebec and the Stags had rid themselves of their biggest financial burden. The Stags departed but Tardif starred in Quebec.

FRED "CYCLONE" TAYLOR

BORN: Tara, Ontario, June 23, 1883
POSITION: Defenseman, Rover, Center, Ottawa Senators (ECAHA, ECHA), 1908–09; Renfrew Millionaires (NHA), 1910–11; Vancouver Millionaires (PCHL), 1913–21, 1923
AWARDS: Hockey Hall of Fame, 1945

Cyclone Taylor was a talented, high-scoring rover/centerman who played for nine successful seasons with the Vancouver Millionaires of the PCHA. His reputation as a scorer, however, as well as his flamboyant nickname, was earned back east where he broke into hockey as one of the game's earliest rushing defensemen.

Fred Taylor earned the handle "Cyclone" with the 1908 and 1909 Ottawa squads, scoring 17 goals in 21 games and helping his team to the 1909 Stanley Cup. The following year saw the newly formed Renfrew club vying for Taylor's services and, after much heated discussion and threats about legal litigation, Taylor had found a new home.

This began one of the fiercest rivalries in big league hockey history and also started Taylor on the road to becoming a Canadian folklore legend. Quite naturally, contests between Renfrew and Ottawa took on warlike dimensions with Taylor being scorned as a turncoat and traitor in his old hometown. It didn't help matters much when, on a bet, Cyclone brashly announced that in the two teams' first meeting, he would skate backwards through the entire Ottawa squad and score a goal.

Fact and legend become muddled at this point, but it is on record that Taylor did in fact, skate backwards for "about five yards" before lifting a blistering backhander into the Ottawa cage. The fact that Renfrew lost the game was beside the point—soon Cyclone Taylor stories abounded all the way to Medicine Hat and back.

Renfrew's franchise floundered after two seasons and Cyclone made his way west to Vancouver where he remained until his retirement in 1921. The old warrior couldn't get the game out of his blood that easily, however, and returned for one last game in 1923.

CECIL "TINY" THOMPSON

BORN: Sandon, British Columbia, May 31, 1905
POSITION: Goalie, Boston Bruins, 1928–38; Detroit Red Wings, 1938–40
AWARDS: Vezina Trophy, 1930, 1933, 1936, 1938; All-Star (First Team), 1936, 1938, (Second Team), 1931, 1935; Hockey Hall of Fame, 1959

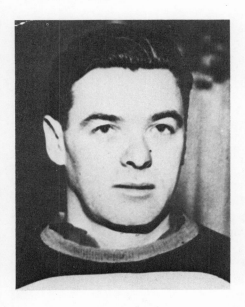

One of the National Hockey League's most accomplished goaltenders, Tiny Thompson won the Vezina Trophy four times in twelve NHL seasons. His rookie year, 1928–29, saw him produce an astonishing 1.18 goals-against average with the Boston Bruins and twelve shutouts. Boston also won the Stanley Cup that season. With Tiny in the nets, Boston finished first, winning the Prince of Wales Trophy in 1929, 1930, 1931, 1933, 1935, and 1938. Thompson was prepared to continue in the Bruins' goal, but Boston had discovered sensational young Frankie Brimsek and decided to trade Tiny to the Detroit Red Wings. Thompson completed his NHL career after the 1939–40 season in Detroit. He later became the chief scout of western Canada for the Chicago Black Hawks, a position he has maintained until the present. He is a member of the Hockey Hall of Fame.

JIM THOMSON

BORN: Winnipeg, Manitoba, February 23, 1927
POSITION: Defenseman, Toronto Maple Leafs, 1945–57; Chicago
    Black Hawks, 1957–58

Along with his sidekick, Gus Mortson, Jim Thomson was one of the two kid defensemen broken into the NHL by Maple Leafs' manager Conn Smythe in 1946–47 for one of the biggest gambles a tactician ever took. Both Thomson and Mortson—"the Gold Dust Twins"—played a robust game in keeping with the Leafs' style of the times.

Thomson skated for Toronto Stanley Cup winners in 1947, 1948, 1949, and 1951. When Thomson, along with Ted Lindsay, Tod Sloan, Doug Harvey, and others, attempted to organize an NHL Players' Association, he was exiled by Smythe to the Chicago Black Hawks where he completed his NHL career.

WALTER ROBERT TKACZUK

BORN: Emstedetten, Germany, September 29, 1947
POSITION: Center, New York Rangers, 1967–

Possessing an iron constitution and an alphabet-soup surname, Walt Tkaczuk has been generally acknowledged around the NHL as one of hockey's most underrated players. Never a consistently high-point man, Ranger opponents point to the big native of Emstedetten, Germany, as an effective forward but cannot explain his mediocre point total.

Practically immovable when skating under a full head of steam, Walt's brute strength suggested better scoring in the future.

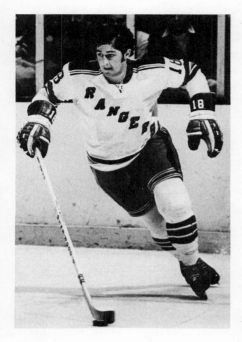

Walt Tkaczuk

TORONTO ARENAS

Long before the Toronto Maple Leafs became the national team of Canada, the Toronto Arenas represented Canada's Queen City in professional competition. The name derived from Arena Gardens, which opened in 1912 as the first artificial ice rink in Ontario. The Arenas gained strength prior to the 1916 season when the club merged with the Montreal Shamrocks. Aces such as George McNamara, Duke Keats, the brothers Corbett and Cy Denneny starred for the Arenas, who won the Stanley Cup in 1918 with Charlie Querrie managing and Dick Carroll coaching.

Considering the wealth of talent on the Arenas, Querrie escaped with rock-bottom prices for his stars. The *entire* payroll came to $6,250, or less than one-third of the contract of the lowest paid player on the contemporary Maple Leafs. Jack Adams and Harry Cameron topped the scale, earning $900 apiece, while goaltender Hap Holmes and forward Reg Noble each commanded $700.

After the Arenas won the Stanley Cup in 1918 the club took a nosedive, both artistically and financially. At the end of the 1918–19 season Toronto's pro crowds were depressingly small, and the owners of the Arenas decided to sell the club to the first buyer. However, purchasers made themselves so scarce that when a group of Toronto sportsmen collected a grand total of $2,000, the

Arenas' directors leaped at the bid. They gave the new owners rights to the club name and goodwill and tossed in sticks, sweaters, ice privileges, and a dozen athletic supporters. They then obtained an NHL franchise for $5,000—to be paid off in time—and a new era was ushered in for Toronto hockey. The name Arenas was replaced by St. Patricks. In time, the name St. Patricks would give way to the Maple Leafs.

TORONTO MAPLE LEAFS

The roots of the Toronto Maple Leafs—and of hockey in Toronto—date back to 1887 when a Montrealer, T. L. Patton, visited Toronto and described the game that had become so popular in his hometown. Torontonians were so enraptured by Patton's tales of hockey play that they demanded he import some hockey equipment to the Queen City of Canada. Patton did just that and, quickly, teams sprouted all over town, the most prominent being the Toronto Athletic Club, the Granites, and St. Georges. The Wellingtons became Toronto's first team to compete for the Stanley Cup. That happened in 1902 when the Winnipeg Victorias won the two-game series by 5–3 scores.

The first authentic superstar to wear a professional uniform in Toronto was French-Canadian Edouard "Newsy" Lalonde who played center for the Maple Leafs, a team then competing in the Ontario Professional League. The Leafs soon folded and were replaced on the popularity scale by the Tecumsehs and the Torontos and then the Arenas.

However, the direct descendents of the contemporary Maple Leafs were a collection of hard-bitten pros who made their debut at the start of the Roarin' Twenties. The Toronto Arenas became the Toronto St. Patricks and the St. Pats immediately made their presence felt in the then young National Hockey League. The St. Pats' biggest sharpshooter was Cecil "Babe" Dye who, in 1921–22 scored 30 goals in 24 games. Dye then powered St. Pats to a Stanley Cup victory over Vancouver Millionaires. It was the first and last Stanley Cup championship for the St. Pats although they frequently sported excellent skaters, some of whom would eventually star for the Maple Leafs. One of them was Clarence "Hap" Day, a defenseman who ultimately would become one of the most proficient NHL backliners and one of the best coaches in history.

But Day couldn't help the St. Pats much in 1925–26 when they fell to sixth place in a seven-team league, and dead last a year later. The gloom enshrouding the Toronto hockey scene was soon to be cleared by one of the most insightful and entertaining men in all sport—Constantine Falkland Kerrys (Conn) Smythe.

Backed by some sports-minded friends, Smythe organized a syndicate that bought the St. Patricks for $165,000 and changed the name to Maple Leafs. He then set about the business of erecting a hockey palace suitable for the new club. It was the nadir of the depression when the fabulous Maple Leaf Gardens opened.

Smythe's timing could have been disastrous in view of the economic crisis, but he stocked his team with such young stars as Frank "King" Clancy, Harvey "Busher" Jackson, Joe Primeau, and Charlie Conacher, and Maple Leaf Gardens was usually filled to capacity.

The Leafs won the Stanley Cup in 1931–32 and continued to thrill National Hockey League audiences with their Gashouse Gang style until the outbreak of World War II, when Smythe joined the armed forces. In 1942, exactly ten years after the Leafs' first Stanley Cup win, Toronto captured the Cup again. Coached by Clarence "Hap" Day, the Maple Leafs defeated the Detroit Red Wings in a seven-game Stanley Cup final that is regarded as the most thrilling in hockey history.

Toronto lost the first three games of the series and appeared to be on the brink of defeat. Coach Day, in a daring but desperate move, benched both his leading scorer, Gordie Drillon, and ace defenseman, Bucko McDonald, and inserted utility forward Don Metz and rookie defenseman Ernie Dickens for them. Toronto did what had never been done before. Down 0–3, the Leafs won four straight playoff games and the Stanley Cup. While Smythe was overseas the Leafs won the Cup again. However, when he returned, his Toronto sextet was floundering near the bottom of the NHL. Smythe decided to rebuild the club with a massive infusion of youth in that first season after World War II.

Cherubic Turk Broda returned from the army to play goal for the Leafs. In front of him the Leafs recruited two juniors from St. Michael's College, Jim Thomson and Gus Mortson, later known as "the Gold Dust Twins."

Garth Boesch, a big moustachioed defenseman, returned from the army to play defense and, later in the year, Bill Barilko, a brash, rollicking rookie was to be imported from the Hollywood Wolves to pair with Boesch.

Howie Meeker, wounded overseas when a grenade blew up in his face and told by doctors that he would never play hockey again, was on right wing with Ted Kennedy and another upstart rookie, Vic Lynn. The club was further augmented by "Wild Bill" Ezinicki, a right winger with castiron hips who was to be the policeman on the line with Syl Apps, later Ontario's commissioner of sports, and Harry Watson.

The club was rounded out by the Metz brothers, Don and Nick, Bud Poile, Gus Bodnar, Gaye Stewart, and Bob Goldham.

When his Leafs won the Cup in 1946–47, the youngest club ever to do so, Smythe was as surprised as anyone, but he sensed greatness now. Before the 1947–48 season he told reporters, "If this team finishes first and wins the Cup again it will be the greatest club the Toronto organization has ever had."

Coached by Hap Day, the Leafs started the season in first gear and remained in a state of slow motion until the beginning of November. This, and the fact that Smythe still itched for one more superstar, irked the Leafs' boss. He opened negotiations with the Chicago Black Hawks for either Max or Doug Bentley. "I offered Chicago five players for one of the Bentleys," Smythe admitted. "Since I can't tell the brothers apart I told Day to pick the man I wanted."

On November 3, 1947, Smythe completed the biggest deal in hockey history, trading five players—including a complete high-scoring front line—for Max Bentley. The Leafs gave up their "Flying Fort Line" of Stewart, Bodnar, and Poile, as well as defenseman Goldham and Ernie Dickens. "Conn has given Chicago almost a complete team," said Day.

But Smythe was unperturbed. "Strength through center is the key to scoring strength," Smythe explained. "I made a gamble but I think it's worth it. I got the league-leading scorer for center-ice duties."

In 1948–49 coach Hap Day guided the Leafs to an unprecedented third consecutive Stanley Cup. Led by Turk Broda, who was approaching the end of a long and colorful NHL career, the Leafs took care of the Boston Bruins in five games, then swept past the Detroit Red Wings in four. In the nine games, old Turk allowed just 15 goals for a 1.67 per-game average.

The Red Wings, however, were determined to put a stop to Toronto's playoff domination. In 1949–50, Detroit was strengthened by the "Production Line" of Gordie Howe, Sid Abel, and Ted Lindsay, who combined for 92 goals and 215 points in preparation for what was to be an exciting Stanley Cup showdown with the Maple Leafs.

In one of the most bitter series ever played, the Red Wings prevailed, four games to three, winning the finale on a sudden-death goal by defenseman Leo Reise, Jr. Earlier in the series young Detroit ace Gordie Howe collided with Toronto captain Ted Kennedy. Howe crashed headfirst into the boards and was removed to a hospital where his life was considered in danger for several days.

The injury stirred charges and countercharges. Detroit players insisted that Kennedy deliberately butt-ended Howe and sought revenge. A bloody series followed, ending in the Detroit conquest.

The Leafs rebounded to win the sacred bowl in the 1950–51 season. They had no problems with Boston. They then outdueled the Montreal Canadiens in four of the five overtime contests. At that point the dynasty came to a tragic end. Toronto lost defenseman Bill Barilko in a plane crash. It had been Barilko's shot in game five that had clinched the Cup for the Leafs in the spring of 1951. Not until 1958–59 did Toronto again make it into the Stanley Cup finals. By then the Leafs' front office realized it was time for a shakeup.

Toronto invited George "Punch" Imlach, player-personnel director for the Bruins, to join the Leafs' organization. In time, Imlach became coach and general manager of the team.

Punch's first move as general manager was to fire coach Billy Reay. Imlach looked around for the best possible successor until he realized that *he* was the man most likely to succeed. He began to rebuild the team. Punch first made the somewhat unlikely acquisition of thirty-three-year-old goalie Johnny Bower, a Ranger reject who had been playing with Cleveland of the American Hockey League.

In the 1958–59 season, Toronto played sluggish hockey and the Leafs were in last place until the tail end of the season. They finished by winning five in a row, and passed a sinking New York Ranger team to reach fourth place and the playoffs on the final night of the season. It was one of sports' most remarkable comebacks. Toronto then managed to beat Boston in five games in the semifinals, but lost to Montreal, the team that broke the Leafs' own record by winning their fourth consecutive Stanley Cup.

Toronto now had the makings of a very strong team. Bower was in goal; in front of him were defensemen Marcel Pronovost, Tim Horton, and Carl Brewer; the forwards were Frank Mahovlich, George Armstrong, and Bob Pulford. They comprised the nucleus of the team that returned the Stanley Cup to Toronto for three consecutive years starting with 1961–62.

On February 22, 1964, Imlach traded five players, Arnie Brown, Rod Seiling, Bob Nevin, Dick Duff, and Billy Collins to the New York Rangers for Andy Bathgate and Don McKenney.

The deal was not greatly appreciated either by New York or Toronto fans, but in the long run it paid off for both clubs. Bathgate and McKenney combined for 21 points for their new teammates in the maximum fourteen games it took to eliminate Montreal and Detroit and win the Stanley Cup. Brown, Seiling, and Nevin helped turn the Rangers from the NHL pushovers into a formidable hockey club.

Punch was subject to some ridicule because he was the coach of a team with an average age of thirty-plus years. The fans thought a winning coach should put the emphasis on youth. Johnny Bower was forty years old. He shared the Toronto nets with Terry Sawchuk, thirty-eight. Defenseman Tim Horton and Allan Stanley were thirty-seven and forty, respectively. How could a bunch of "grandfathers" win a Stanley Cup? They had finished third in the league and were up against a young Montreal team in the final series of the 1966–67 playoffs. It would be a great surprise if the old-timers could keep it up for a few more games.

Punch was smiling to himself. He knew that this was the finest team in hockey that year. The Canadiens were just upstart kids. Montreal got away with a 6–3 victory in the opening game, but John Bower's netminding shut out Les Canadiens, 3–0, in the next. The Leafs took the third game in sudden-death overtime and went on to win the Cup.

That, however, was the beginning of the end for the grand Leaf teams. Imlach's influence on his players began to ebb and he ultimately was fired by club president Stafford Smythe after the 1968–69 season. Smythe hired Jim Gregory as manager and Johnny McLellan as coach, but the results remained negative.

On October 13, 1971, Stafford Smythe died of complications arising from bleeding stomach ulcers. He was fifty years old. Harold Ballard took over control of the Leafs and, despite an occasional sensational move, achieved little positive with the team. His appointment of Red Kelly as coach was hailed as a significant move at the start of the 1973–74 season, but Kelly failed to stir the Leafs either in his rookie year or the 1974–75 campaign when Toronto gained a playoff berth, but was eliminated in four straight games of the Stanley Cup second round by the Philadelphia Flyers.

TORONTO TOROS

Although the Ottawa Nationals made it into the 1972–73 WHA playoffs, hockey fans did not turn out in droves to the Ottawa Civic Center, and the club died after the its fledgling season.

A Toronto businessman by the name of John Bassett took over the Nationals, brought them to Toronto—the seat of National Hockey League power itself—and laid down a challenge to the Maple Leafs.

In their first year in the Queen City, the club, renamed the Toros, finished a strong second in the Eastern Division, only four points behind the New England Whalers. Billy Harris, a former NHL player, coached the Toros to their finish and was rewarded with the WHA's coach of the year honor.

Despite their early nomadic existence, the Toros have stayed pat with their roster. Les Binkley and Gilles Gratton shared the netminding chores throughout the first three years. Forwards Wayne Carleton, Gavin Kirk, and rookie Wayne Dillon supplied much of the scoring punch on a team mostly comprised of youngsters looking to make it in the majors. Carleton was traded to the New England Whalers in 1974 for Jim Dorey who improved the Toro rearguard corps after the retirement of veteran Carl Brewer.

In 1974–75 the Toros stayed close to the top of the new Canadian Division for most of the campaign. But attendance in Maple Leaf Gardens was not enough to ensure a lengthy tenure in Toronto, despite the fact that Frank Mahovlich and Paul Henderson were in the lineup.

BILL TORREY

Never a pro iceman himself, Bill Torrey, general manager of the New York Islanders, has been actively involved in the world of shinny since his collegiate playing days at St. Lawrence University, New York.

Torrey's climb up hockey's corporate ladder began with the AHL's Pittsburgh Hornets in 1960 where he served for five years as that club's publicity director and business manager.

In 1968 Torrey moved out west as executive vice-president of the Oakland Seals. Four years later he was appointed general manager of the Islanders. After a weak start, the Islanders made the playoffs in 1975 and upset the Rangers and Penguins. Torrey was voted Manager of the Year by *The Sporting News*.

JEAN CLAUDE (J. C.) TREMBLAY

BORN: Bagotville, Quebec, January 22, 1939
POSITION: Defenseman, Montreal Canadiens, 1959–72; Quebec Nordiques (WHA), 1972–
AWARDS: All-Star (First Team), 1971; (Second Team), 1968; (WHA First Team), 1973; (WHA Second Team), 1974, 1975; Dennis A. Murphy Award (Best Defenseman, WHA), 1973

J. C. Tremblay was the most sought-after player when the Quebec Nordiques were formed in 1972. The popular Canadiens' defenseman was often referred to as "J. C. Superstar," after the Broadway show of the same name.

J. C. was one of the highest scoring defensemen in the NHL during the 1970–71 and 1971–72 seasons, and won a berth on the First All-Star Team in 1971. After a brilliant season in his first WHA campaign, when he scored 89 points, Tremblay suffered an injury, and only played 68 games the following season, collecting a still-respectable 54 points.

With J. C. in good health in 1974–75, the Nordiques enjoyed a fine year, finishing in the playoffs for the first time in their history.

HARRY TRIHEY

BORN: Montreal, Quebec, December 25, 1877
DIED: December 9, 1942
POSITION: Center, Montreal Shamrocks (AHC, CAHL), 1897–1901
AWARDS: Hockey Hall of Fame, 1952

Harry Trihey was the captain of the great Stanley Cup Montreal Shamrock teams of 1899 and 1900. Trihey, a high-scoring pivot man, holds the pre-NHL record of scoring 10 goals in a regular season game. Despite a painful, nagging hand injury, Trihey played the entire 1901 season, scoring seven goals in as many games, but failing to bring the Shamrocks a third consecutive Cup.

THE TRUSHINSKI (NHL) BYLAW

Bylaw 12:6 of the National Hockey League forbids players who are sightless in one eye from playing in the NHL. It states that players with one eye, or 3/60ths of normal vision shall not be eligible to play for a member club. Loss of 75 percent of sight in an eye is required for insurance to take effect.

This regulation became known as "the Trushinski Bylaw" because of a major leaguer named Frank "Snoozer" Trushinski who played right defense for the Kitchener (Ontario) Greenshirts. According to NHL officials at the time, Trushinski lost sight in one eye playing hockey and came back and lost most of the sight in his other eye from another accident. The NHL didn't want that to happen again so it passed Bylaw 12:6.

Mrs. Trushinski once recalled her husband's problems several years after he died: "A year or so before he lost his eye, his skull was fractured in a game against the Toronto Granites hockey team. He got along seeing, but not too well.

"All his life he had a film on his left eye, so he really had trouble after the puck hit his right eye; that was during a game in 1921 when a puck hit the eye. He never saw out of it again. He was able to work a long time, though, for Schneider's, a meat company in Kitchener, Ontario."

The Trushinski Bylaw became important in March 1939 when Toronto Maple Leafs left winger George Parsons lost his left eye in an injury during an NHL game at Maple Leaf Gardens against the Chicago Black Hawks.

"NHL President Frank Calder told me that I couldn't play in the NHL again," said Parsons. "Calder said that the NHL governors wouldn't allow one-eyed players in the league because of the Trushinski precedent. Calder said the NHL didn't want that happening again."

The ruling was challenged in June 1975 when forward Greg Neeld was drafted by the Buffalo Sabres of the NHL. Neeld had lost sight in one eye while playing amateur hockey in 1973. Neeld's lawyer Roy McMurtry threatened to sue the NHL when Neeld was kept out of the league because of the Trushinski Bylaw in a June 1975 ruling.

LLOYD TURNER

Lloyd Turner was almost single-handedly responsible for making hockey popular in Alberta, particularly Calgary. He installed ice in the old Calgary Sherman rink, organized a team, then a league, and by 1914 won the Alberta title. In 1918 he installed ice in the Calgary horse show building and began the Western Canada League.

Turner was responsible for Calgary being the host for the Allan Cup championships in the thirties, and was inducted into the Hockey Hall of Fame for his development of the game in Western Canada.

TWO-GOALIE SYSTEM

Newcomers to hockey find it hard to believe that as recently as the early sixties it was commonplace for goaltenders to play an entire season without substitution and without using a protective face mask. In time Jacques Plante made the face mask a fundamental part of a goaltender's equipment and, eventually, the two-goalie system was employed by every big-league team.

Curiously, the two-goalie system dates back to the fall of 1945 when Charlie Rayner and Sugar Jim Henry, both Ranger goalies, showed up at training camp after serving in the Canadian Armed Forces. Rayner originally had belonged to the New York Americans, but when that club disbanded he was acquired by the Rangers.

Suddenly, Rangers' coach Frank Boucher found himself with an embarrassment of goaltending riches at training camp. It was Boucher who created the two-goalie system and here, in his own words, is how it happened:

"There was little to choose between them at training camp and I decided to keep them both until I acquired a clearer picture of their relative skills. Through our first twenty games I alternated them, partly because I still hadn't decided who was better and partly because a new philosophy toward goaltending was creeping into my mind. It was true that the six NHL teams had adjusted to the center red line, that they'd learned to compensate for the advantages the line gave to the offense, but it was also true that goaltenders were being subjected to a much more difficult assignment than they'd ever known before. Power plays, deflected shots, and pile-ups in front of them that blocked their vision were presenting them with tensions and obstacles and injuries almost unknown five years earlier.

"Anyway, it was in this fashion that the two-goaltender system, now commonplace, found its way into hockey. Essentially it was because Henry and Rayner were so evenly matched; the refinement came when I realized that the practice of alternating them made sense. On a few occasions I switched them every few minutes in the same manner as I switched defensemen, but neither liked the idea and it didn't seem to offer any particular advantage, so I jettisoned it. We employed Rayner and Henry over parts of three seasons, but had to abandon the scheme each year for two reasons: our New Haven farm team in the American Hockey League was hard-pressed for good goaltending, and we were so weak offensively, so desperate for people who could put the puck in the net, that we simply couldn't afford the luxury of two goaltenders.''

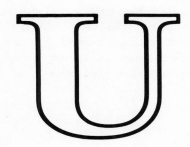

FRANK JOSEPH UDVARI

BORN: Yugoslavia, 1924
POSITION: Referee, NHL, 1951–66
AWARDS: Hockey Hall of Fame, 1973

One of the few referees ever inducted into the Hockey Hall of Fame, Frank Udvari was a less effective official than his Hall of Fame induction would indicate. However, unlike some of his more outspoken contemporaries of the late fifties and early sixties, Udvari was more of an establishment official who, unlike Dalt MacArthur, Eddie Powers, or Red Storey, rarely criticized NHL management. An inferior referee when he began his career, Udvari did mature into a competent whistleblower. He was rewarded for his efforts after retirement when the NHL named him one of the league's supervisors of officials.

NORMAN VICTOR ALEXANDER (NORM) ULLMAN

BORN: Provost, Alberta, December 26, 1935
POSITION: Center, Detroit Red Wings, 1955–68; Toronto Maple
    Leafs, 1968–75
AWARDS: All-Star (First Team), 1965, (Second Team), 1967

While high-priced National Hockey League rookies and superscoring centers captured the headlines, taciturn veteran Norm Ullman quietly did a steady job at center. Overshadowed by his flashier Toronto teammates, Ullman, nevertheless, consistently outscored them.

585

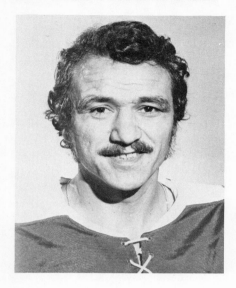

Norm Ullman

When the Maple Leafs released him in 1975, Ullman had scored 490 NHL goals, putting him in exalted status with Gordie Howe, Alex Delvecchio, Jean Beliveau, and other major point producers.

Originally a member of great Detroit Red Wing teams, Ullman never played on a Stanley Cup championship team. Or, perhaps it isn't so shocking, when you examine Norm's dossier. He came to the Detroit Red Wings as a rookie in 1955, the year after they had won the Cup. The Wings traded him to the Maple Leafs in the middle of the 1967–68 season, the year after the Leafs had won the Cup.

GARRY DOUGLAS UNGER

BORN: Edmonton, Alberta, December 7, 1947
POSITION: Center, Toronto Maple Leafs, 1967–68; Detroit Red Wings, 1968–71; St. Louis Blues, 1971–

Blond and beautiful, Garry Unger stands out as the example of a stickhandler who was overcome with publicity—too much, too soon. He was groomed in the Maple Leafs' system and reached the NHL in 1967–68 with Toronto, but was almost immediately dealt to Detroit. Unger's messianic notices failed to materialize, and Wings' manager Ned Harkness objected to Unger's long hair. He sent Garry to a barber. The barber cut Unger's locks, but not enough to suit Harkness. Garry was ordered back to the barber shop. This time Gary got the

Garry Unger

notion he didn't want to play for Harkness. In February 1971 Garry was traded to St. Louis. There he was told he could let his hair grow down to his ankles, if he wanted, as long as he scored goals. He did score goals, although not at record-breaking levels.

UNITED STATES HOCKEY HALL OF FAME

America has a Hockey Hall of Fame all its own in Eveleth, a small Minnesota mining town sixty miles northwest of Duluth and 100 miles south of Canada. The Hall opened in 1973. Unlike its larger counterpart in Toronto, which includes players from many nations, the United States Hall of Fame devotes itself almost entirely to American natives. Only three of the thirty-four inductees were born outside United States boundaries, and they moved to America before or during their stints in the NHL.

The "Great Hall" has a $1,300, 10-foot Plexiglas pylon devoted to each of the players. Within each pylon is a picture of the subject and his career biography. Other displays include paraphernalia of years gone by: old skates, uniforms worn by some of the players, and the like.

Roger Godin, the Hall's executive director, says it must charge admission fees ranging from 75 ¢ for children to $1.50 for adults to help make up a yearly operating cost of $75,000 and a $140,000 museum debt.

Few hockey fans would remember many of the inductees. The most prominent include Frankie Brimsek, Mike Karakas, Moose Goheen, and Hobey Baker.

Another notable is Sam LoPresti, Black Hawk goalie in the early forties. LoPresti holds the NHL record for most saves in one game: on March 4, 1941, Boston shot 83 times on the Chicago net, and LoPresti made 80 stops. Unfortunately, the Hawks only scored twice that night and lost, 3–2.

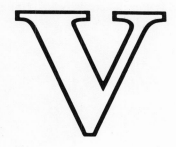

ROGATIEN ROSAIRE (ROGGIE) VACHON

BORN: Palmarolle, Quebec, September 8, 1945
POSITION: Goalie, Montreal Canadiens, 1966–71; Los Angeles
 Kings, 1971–
AWARDS: Vezina Trophy (shared with Lorne Worsley), 1968; All-Star
 (Second Team), 1975

After having a hand in three Montreal Canadien Stanley Cup seasons, ''Rogo''
Vachon was traded to the Los Angeles Kings in 1971. With the number one job
in goal his for the taking, Vachon settled into his sunny new surroundings by
becoming one of the most exciting goaltenders in the NHL.

A tiny netminder at 5'7", 160 pounds, Vachon is a superb reflex goalie who
uses his catlike reactions to offset his lack of bulk.

Vachon had no trouble adjusting to the West Coast's balmy weather and free
'n' easy life-style. Soon after he joined the Beverly Hills sextet, Vachon
sprouted a droopy Fu-Manchu moustache and an even woolier pair of mut-
tonchop sideburns. Asked about his new-found tonsorial tastes, the free-spirit
backstop responded, ''Zee sideburns, zey are good for zee balance.''

CAROL MARCEL VADNAIS

BORN: Montreal, Quebec, September 25, 1945
POSITION: Left Wing and Defenseman, Montreal Canadiens,
 1966–68; California Seals, 1968–72; Boston Bruins, 1972–

Boston Bruins' officials predicted big things for Carol Vadnais when they
acquired him from California midway through the 1971–72 season, because,

589

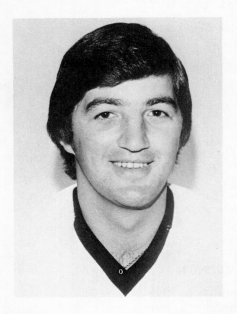

Carol Vadnais

after all, he had been selected to the NHL's West Division midyear All-Star team in each of the three previous seasons. They paid a steep price to get this high-scoring defenseman, and that was the beginning of Carol's problems. Popular spare defenseman Rick Smith, brawling Bob Stewart, and top draft pick Reggie Leach were all dispatched to the Golden Seals as payment for Vadnais. The hotly partisan Boston fans were incensed, especially since Smith and Stewart had become crowd favorites. To make matters worse, Vadnais replaced longtime Bruins' star Teddy Green, perhaps the best-loved of all the Boston skaters.

It was an uncomfortable situation, compounded by the fact that Vadnais had no chance to learn the Bruins' system before playing in front of the Boston audience. Predictably, he was roasted. He was not as good as Boston fans thought he would be—but he certainly wasn't as bad as they claimed he was. Fellow teammates, sizing up the situation, offered moral support. "Every time someone scored, they'd all skate past me and tap me with their sticks, like I had done something to help them," he smiled. "I couldn't wait to contribute."

He scored four goals in Boston's last sixteen games and added three more in their march to the 1972 Stanley Cup, gradually winning the fans to his side. By the 1972–73 season, he was a bona fide Bruin, playing steady—though unspectacular—defense and doing his bit to keep the offense rolling. It had taken longer than he expected, but he finally felt at home in Boston Garden.

ERIC DOUGLAS VAIL

BORN: Timmins, Ontario, September 16, 1953
POSITION: Left Wing, Atlanta Flames, 1974–
AWARDS: Calder Trophy, 1975

The Atlanta Flames' second round draft choice in 1973, Eric Vail became a National Hockey League ace in his first full year of big-league play, 1974–75. The 6-1, 210-pound left winger finished third in scoring on the Flames with 39 goals and 21 assists for 60 points in 72 games. He played part of the 1973–74 season with Omaha of the Central League before his elevation to the Flames on January 31, 1974. A fractured back slowed his progress and he played only 23 games as a rookie. His progress suggests stardom within four years of his NHL debut. He was named NHL rookie of the year in 1975.

VANCOUVER BLAZERS

The Vancouver (née Philadelphia) Blazers were making waves in the WHA before the team even stepped onto the ice. After New Jersey businessmen James L. Cooper and Bernard Brown bought the WHA's eleventh franchise, they took over the contract of their NHL supergoalie, Bernie Parent, who had originally signed with the league's stillborn Miami Screaming Eagle franchise. The pair made headlines again when they signed John McKenzie of the Boston Bruins to be the Blazers' playing coach. But the biggest news was the signing of Bruin badboy Derek Sanderson to a ten-year contract alleged to be $2.65 million.

Despite the presence of the three stars, the Blazers got off to a rocky start. First, McKenzie broke his arm in training camp. Then Sanderson, injured in preseason play, decided he was unhappy with the club. He played only eight games all season. To top it off, the team's first two games had to be postponed, as the ice in Philadelphia's Civic Center cracked under the weight of the ice-making machine.

The club's problems didn't end there. After playing the first game of the Blazers' playoff series against the Cleveland Crusaders, goalie Parent deserted the team. The Blazers promptly lost four straight to the Crusaders. Parent later rejoined his old team, the Philadelphia Flyers of the NHL.

The Blazers had a new look for the 1973–74 season. Canadian industrialist Jim Pattison bought the franchise in May 1973, and moved the team to Vancouver. In a dubious move, center Andre Lacroix, an All-Star and the league's leading scorer, was traded to the New Jersey Knights for Ron Ward, the league's second highest scorer. With a nucleus of center Bryan Campbell and Danny Lawson, the team finished fifth and out of the playoffs.

The Blazers next signed highly touted junior stars Pat Price and Ron Chipperfield before the 1974–75 season, but they flopped. In June 1975 the franchise was transferred to Calgary and renamed the Cowboys.

VANCOUVER CANUCKS

When Vancouver entered the NHL in the fall of 1970 everything seemed to augur well. It was time the league let another Canadian team into its own sport, and Vancouver, in beautiful western British Columbia, was one of the largest cities in the Dominion, with a long and rich history of good hockey.

It was peculiar, then, that the club ended up being owned by an American Minnesota-based group called Medicor. The group was headed by Thomas K. Scallen and Lyman D. Walters, and these two gentlemen picked Norman "Bud" Poile to manage the development of the team. Poile, a former NHL star with Toronto, New York, and Chicago, had managed the Flyers when they entered the NHL in 1967–68. After winning the West Division championship in its first season, the Flyers had then slowly slipped for several years and Poile thought he knew why: "They didn't concentrate on centers. Centers are the key to hockey success and without good ones, you don't stand a chance."

So it was not surprising that Poile picked up centers from wherever he could—big Orland Kurtenbach, one of the best fighters in the league, from the New York Rangers; and Ray Cullen, a fair-to-middling veteran of the North Stars. In the amateur draft Poile chose Dale Tallon, a center, of course, from the OHA's Toronto Marlboros.

The Canucks also acquired fifty-two players from their own Western League club and several from the AHL Rochester Americans. Even if there was little talent among all those bodies, they supplied depth and could simply plug holes if the team became injury-laden. They also had size, with Kurtenbach up front and veterans Pat Quinn and John Arbour in the rearguard.

Thus it came as no great surprise that the Canucks were a contender through much of their first season, though they finally settled for sixth in the East Division. The crowds were enormous and rookie Tallon did well. In the next amateur draft Poile copped Jocelyn Guevremont, a strapping French-Canadian defenseman, and Bobby Lalonde, a small winger with good scoring potential.

But the sophomore slump hit in 1971–72 and the Canucks finished in the basement. Coach Hal Laycoe, a former NHL defenseman and coach of the Los Angeles Kings, was kicked upstairs and replaced by feisty Vic Stasiuk, who had been fired by the Flyers and the California Seals. There were more stories about behind-the-scenes battles between management and unhappy players than there were about the games themselves.

As though they didn't have troubles enough, the WHA arrived in the summer of 1972 and robbed the Canucks of Rosaire Paiement (Chicago Cougars) and goalie George Gardner (Los Angeles Sharks). Poile put Dunc Wilson between the pipes and crossed his fingers.

But Wilson and Stasiuk didn't get along—at all. In fact, Stasiuk didn't get along with most of the team, a problem he had had in Philadelphia also. Tallon, who had been moved from center to defense and back again, made it clear he wanted out of Vancouver; Wayne Maki suffered a brain tumor in mid-season and was hospitalized; and captain Orland Kurtenbach was out with stomach problems. The Canucks decorated the basement for a second year and Stasiuk was replaced by Bill McCreary, a pleasant ex-NHL player.

Then everything seemed to come unraveled. Poile was hospitalized and told to give up managing the team, although he remained as a vice-president. In April 1973 Tom Scallen, Canucks' president, was sentenced to four years in prison for transferring $3 million from one corporation to another to keep Medicor from collapsing.

While the crowds continued to fill Pacific Coliseum, the Canucks were out of the playoffs for the fourth straight year in four seasons of existence. But all was not lost, because there were major changes begun in the last half of the 1973–74 season, and even more in the fall of 1974, which has transformed Vancouver, at last, into a contender.

Scallen went to jail, but before he did, he sold the Canucks to a local group, and the team was at last in Canadian hands. Phil Maloney, a former NHL center, was made general manager-coach during the 1973–74 season, and although the team finished out of the playoffs, they played .500 hockey.

In the amateur draft they had obtained defenseman Bob Dailey and wings Dennis Ververgaert and Paulin Bordeleau. During that fateful 1973–74 season they traded for big goaltender Gary Smith, who was languishing with the Chicago Black Hawks. In other trades they got defenseman Tracy Pratt (his father, a former NHL All-Star, had been a part of the Canucks' organization since its inception) and forwards John Gould and Chris Oddleifson.

That was only the beginning. The 1974–75 season had barely gotten underway, when Maloney bought Ken Lockett from Baltimore to give Smith support in goal, purchased veteran forward Leon Rochefort from Atlanta; traded defenseman Josh Guevremont and winger Bryan McSheffrey to Buffalo for rearguard Mike Robitaille and centerman Gerry Meehan; traded wing Dave Dunn to Toronto for defenseman John Grisdale and wing Garry Monahan; then traded defenseman Barry Wilkins to Pittsburgh for lanky defenseman Ab De-Marco.

By the middle of Vancouver's fifth season in the NHL there were new owners in the driver's seat, fresh faces in the front office, a new general manager-coach, and only six of the bodies on the whole squad who had started with the Canucks in 1970.

There was something else new—the Vancouver Canucks in 1975 finished on top of the Conn Smythe Division.

EDWARD CHARLES (ED) VAN IMPE

BORN: Saskatoon, Saskatchewan, May 27, 1940
POSITION: Defenseman, Chicago Black Hawks, 1966–67; Philadelphia Flyers, 1967–

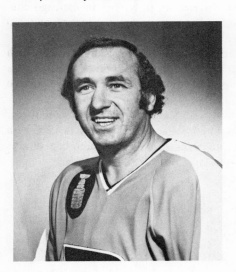

Superficially, it would seem that Ed Van Impe has enjoyed a particularly normal hockey career. After a long minor league apprenticeship, Van Impe reached the NHL in 1966–67 with the Black Hawks. He moved on to Philadelphia the following season and played on a Stanley Cup winner in 1974 at the age of thirty-four and another Cup winner in 1975.

However, Van Impe *is* unique. He remains the one and only NHL player to be asked by a society matron to relinquish his jockstrap to her. No other defenseman—or forward or goalie, for that matter—can make that statement.

As a player, Van Impe has been one of the most underrated defensive defensemen in the NHL. During the 1974–75 season, for example, he scored only one goal in seventy-eight games, but his value behind the blue line was one of the major reasons Philadelphia finished with the best record in the NHL and goalie Bernie Parent won the Vezina Trophy for having the lowest goals-against average. Van Impe rarely takes a gamble in the enemy's offensive zone and concentrates on the foe within his own defensive perimeter. He can deal out thudding bodychecks and has not been averse to using his stick blade to occasionally prod the opposition. In this regard former teammate Larry Zeidel describes Van Impe as "the master surgeon."

ELMER "MOOSE" VASKO

BORN: Duparquet, Quebec, December 11, 1935
POSITION: Defenseman, Chicago Black Hawks, 1956–66; Minnesota
    North Stars, 1967–70
AWARDS: All-Star (Second Team), 1963–64

It was the perfect Mutt and Jeff combination for a decade in Chicago Stadium—the hulking "Moose" Vasko teaming his six feet, three inches, and 210 pounds with the petit Pierre Pilote on the Black Hawk blue line.

Vasko performed his defensive skills with an even-tempered geniality which belied his size, and the nickname "Ferdinand the Bull" would have been more appropriate than "Moooooooooooose" which bounced around the arena each time he took the ice.

As a rookie, Vasko was expected to be the defenseman for the coming era, but his basically gentle heart was his downfall. He finished quietly in 1970 with the expansion Minnesota North Stars, then disappeared into suburban Illinois where he took to coaching a bantam team and selling hockey sticks.

GEORGES VEZINA

BORN: Chicoutimi, Quebec, January 1887
DIED: March 24, 1926
POSITION: Goalie, Montreal Canadiens, 1917–26
AWARDS: Vezina Trophy named in his honor; Hockey Hall of Fame,
    1945

Georges Vezina, "the Chicoutimi Cucumber," as well as being a superb goalie, was the acme of gentility on the ice. He also had a philosophic nature and once penned a short essay called "Sport, Creator of Unity."

Few were aware of Vezina's capacity for philosophy. The fans cared about only one thing, whether or not he was a good goaltender, and through the early twenties there was no doubt about his excellence. He proved his mettle in the 1922–23 season in several episodes, some of which were defaced with blood.

During a game at Hamilton his former teammate Bert Corbeau smashed into Vezina with such force that the goaltender's head was cut open and his nose was broken. Vezina continued playing despite the wounds and continued to excel. A few games later he led the Canadiens to a win over Ottawa, allowing the Senators only one goal, although seventy-nine shots were hurled at him.

"After the game," wrote Canadian author Ron McAllister, "he left the rink a solemn, plodding figure, in sharp contrast to the wild hilarity of his teammates, who were already celebrating the victory that Vezina had won for them."

Another reporter observed, "Georges has a calmness not of this world." The commentary was more prophetic than the writer had realized, for Georges Vezina's body was being tortured by the early symptoms of tuberculosis. Whether or not Vezina himself was aware of the gravity of his condition is debatable. One thing is certain, and that was his determination to continue in the nets for Les Canadiens. There was no outward suggestion that Vezina was faltering.

Although the Canadiens finished second to Ottawa in the 1923–24 season, Vezina allowed only 48 goals in 24 games, including three shutouts, for a goals-against average of 2.00. He then blanked Ottawa, 1–0, in the NHL playoff opener and sparkled as Les Canadiens swept the series, 4–2, in the second game, thus qualifying to meet a representative from one of the two western professional leagues.

A squabble between officials of the Western Canada Hockey League and the Pacific Coast Hockey Association resulted in a bizarre turn of events. Instead of one team coming east to challenge Montreal for the Stanley Cup, both Calgary and Vancouver showed up. Les Canadiens really weren't overly extended. They first dispatched Vancouver by scores of 3–2 and 2–1 and routed Calgary, 6–1 and 3–0. The final game was switched to Ottawa because of poor ice conditions in Montreal, but Vezina was never better. His Stanley Cup record was six goals against in six games for a perfect 1.00 average.

Proof that Vezina was outfighting his ailment was provided by his uncanny performance in the 1924–25 season. Les Canadiens finished in third place behind Hamilton and Toronto, but Georges's 1.90 goals-against average was easily the best in the league. His teammates rallied behind him in the first round of the playoffs to oust Toronto, 3–2 and 2–0, but Vezina enjoyed only one good game—a 4–2 win—at Victoria as the western champs dispatched Les Canadiens by scores of 5–2, 3–1, and 6–1 to win the Stanley Cup, the last time for a western professional team. The Pacific Coast League folded and the Stanley Cup was competed for by NHL teams only since 1926.

The 1925–26 season was truly momentous for the National Hockey League. It had expanded into the United States, first accepting Boston the previous year, and now embracing New York and Pittsburgh as well. A second team, the Maroons, had been added to Montreal to provide an English-speaking club as the natural rivals for the Canadiens. Needless to say, the outstanding attraction in the American cities among Montreal players was the redoubtable Vezina. But Vezina was beginning to betray signs of fatigue.

Pittsburgh, one of the new entries, provided the opposition for Les Canadiens in the season opener on November 28, 1925, at Mount Royal Arena. There were six thousand spectators in the stands on that rainy night who had come to see the great Vezina, ignorant of the fact that the lean goalie was suffering enormous discomfort as he took the ice for the opening faceoff.

"No one knew," wrote McAllister, "that the great goaltender had struggled to the arena in spite of a temperature of 105 degrees. A deathlike chill settled over him; but with Pittsburgh forcing the play from the face-off, Vezina functioned throughout the entire first period with his usual dexterous ease, deflecting shot after shot. In the dressing room he suffered a severe arterial hemorrhage, but the opening of the second period found him at his accustomed place in goal."

Fighting desperately against the fatigue and fever that completely throttled his body, the great Vezina could no longer see the puck as it was skimmed from one side of the rink to the other. Suddenly, a collective gasp engulfed the arena. Vezina had collapsed in his goal crease! "In the stricken arena," said one observer, "all was silent as the limp form of the greatest of goalies was carried slowly from the ice."

It was the end of the trail for Georges and he knew it. At his request he was taken home to his native Chicoutimi where doctors diagnosed his case as advanced tuberculosis. On March 24, 1926, a week after the Canadiens had been eliminated from a playoff berth, Georges Vezina passed away.

An enormous funeral, held in the old cathedral at Chicoutimi, saw players and fans from all parts of the country deliver their final tribute to the gallant goaltender. A year later, the Canadiens' owners donated a trophy in his honor which is now given to the goaltender with the best goals-against average in the NHL.

VEZINA TROPHY

Leo Dandurand, Louis Letourneau, and Joe Cattarinich, former owners of the Montreal Canadiens, presented a trophy to the National Hockey League in 1926–27 in memory of Georges Vezina, the Canadiens' outstanding goaltender who collapsed during an NHL game on November 28, 1925 and died of tuberculosis a few months later. The first winner was George Hainsworth of the

Canadiens, Vezina's successor, who won the trophy three years in a row—1927, 1928, and 1929. Another Canadiens' ace, Bill Durnan, won the Vezina four years in a row from 1944 through 1947. Durnan also won the prize in 1949 and 1950. Still another Montreal goaltender, Jacques Plante, set a record, winning the Vezina in five consecutive seasons from 1956 through 1960; and again in 1962. Plante shared the Vezina with teammate Glenn Hall of St. Louis in 1969.

The trophy now is regarded as an annual award "to the goalkeeper(s) having played a minimum twenty-five games for the team with the fewest goals scored against it." The winner is selected on regular season's play. In 1973–74, for the first time in forty-eight years, there was a tie for the Vezina as Philadelphia and Chicago each had surrendered 164 goals. Because goalies Bernie Parent (Philadelphia) and Tony Esposito (Chicago) played a majority of their teams' games, only their names are inscribed on the trophy.

Actually Parent had the best *personal* average—1.89 goals-against—and Esposito was next with 2.04. A year later Parent and the Flyers won the Vezina without having to share it with anyone.

STEPHEN JAMES (STEVE) VICKERS

BORN: Toronto, Ontario, April 21, 1951
POSITION: Right Wing, New York Rangers, 1972–
AWARDS: Calder Memorial Trophy, 1973; All-Star (Second Team), 1975

By the end of 1972–73, his first year in the NHL, Steve Vickers had quietly proven to the rest of the league that he was a tough man to beat. He doesn't look for fights, but he'll never back away from one. During that first season, Steve was involved in five major brawls and never lost a single decision. In his sophomore year, 1973–74, he scored 34 goals in 75 games, the second best goal-scoring mark on the Rangers. Despite his awesome arsenal, few opponents dared challenge him as they often do to other high scorers.

Vickers played with the Toronto Marlboros in Ontario Hockey Association Junior A League and in his last season, in addition to scoring 43 goals and 107 points, he made his mark by demolishing his opponents like so many tenpins. In the amateur league as in the pros, he was not one to start a skirmish, but was always, *always* around at the finish.

In the second game of the five-game series for the 1973 Stanley Cup, Boston took an early 1–0 lead. Steve tied it up later in the first period, taking a pass from Bill Fairbairn in front of the net. The Rangers went on to win 4–2 and Vickers was instrumental in setting up linemate Walt Tkaczuk's final goal.

Vickers scored another goal in the fourth game, but saved the *coup de grace* for game five. At the thirty-five-second mark, Fairbairn passed the puck across the crease from the right side, and all Steve had to do was poke it in the net.

Steve Vickers

Later in that same period, with New York trailing 2–1, Vickers blasted one from about thirty feet out, putting it past goalie Ross Brooks. And with two minutes remaining in the game, Steve scored a three-goal hat trick, taking another pass from Fairbairn while standing in front of the net. When the season was over, Vickers was named rookie of the year.

Competence and confidence accounted for Vickers' instant success. He missed sixteen games with a knee injury, yet set a Ranger goal-scoring record for rookies with thirty and wound up with fifty-three points in sixty games. He scored on 23 percent of his shots, tops on the club, and had the best plus-minus statistics as well. In 1974–75 he was even better.

Vickers developed a penchant for positioning himself in front of the enemy net. He became an immovable object in front of the foe's goalie, working with Jean Ratelle and Rod Gilbert.

GILLES VILLEMURE

BORN: Trois-Rivieres, Quebec, May 30, 1940
POSITION: Goalie, New York Rangers, 1963–64, 1967–69, 1970–
AWARDS: Vezina Trophy (shared with Ed Giacomin), 1971

Gilles Villemure was an excellent minor league goalie who saw isolated action with the New York Rangers throughout the sixties. While Villemure had been a pro for several years, playing for Baltimore and Buffalo in the American Hockey League and Vancouver in the Western League, the NHL was still far away.

Then in 1970–71 Villemure was once again in training camp for the Rangers, but for the first time, the Blueshirts were going to the two-goalie system.

Eddie Giacomin had played practically every one of the Rangers' games in 1969–70, but he faded somewhat in the playoffs that season, and the Rangers were eliminated by Boston. So a change was in the offing.

Villemure responded beautifully, compiling a 2.29 goals-against average and he and Giacomin split the Vezina Trophy. Villemure and Giacomin have alternated in the Ranger nets since that year. Villemure's lifetime NHL average is a splendid 2.45.

In recent years Villemure's playing time has been reduced due to a variety of injuries.

CARL POTTER VOSS

BORN: Chelsea, Massachusetts, January 6, 1907
POSITION: Forward, New York Rangers/Detroit Falcons 1932–33; Detroit Red Wings/Ottawa Senators, 1933–34; St. Louis Eagles, 1934–35; New York Americans, 1935–36; Montreal Maroons, 1936–37; Chicago Black Hawks, 1937–38
AWARDS: Calder Trophy, 1933; Hockey Hall of Fame, 1974

There have been few more accomplished American-born players in the NHL than Carl Voss who broke into the majors with the Rangers (1932–33), was immediately dealt to Detroit, then Ottawa (1933–34), St. Louis (1934–35), the Americans (1935–36), the Montreal Maroons (1936–37), and finally the Black Hawks where he gained most of his fame. Coach (and major league baseball umpire) Bill Stewart of the Black Hawks overruled club owner Major Frederic McLaughlin over Voss. The Major insisted Voss be cut from the squad as an obvious loser. Stewart was adamant. Voss would stay. He not only stayed but played a vital part in Chicago's most stirring hockey triumph, winning the Stanley Cup in 1938. In ten playoff games, Voss scored three big goals and two assists. Yet, he left the majors after that season and gained renown later in life as referee in chief of the NHL under President Clarence Campbell. In that position, Voss was frequently criticized as a puppet of the clubowners. He eventually retired and was replaced by Scotty Morrison.

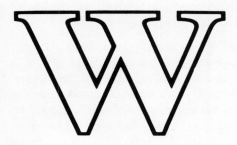

FRED WAGHORNE

BORN: Tunbridge Wells, England, 1866
DIED: 1956
POSITION: Referee, Several leagues prior to NHL
AWARDS: Hockey Hall of Fame, 1961

This Hall of Fame member was a referee for more than fifty years, was one of the founders of the Toronto Hockey League, and introduced several innovations, sometimes in the middle of a game!

Fred Waghorne began the practice of dropping the puck for face-offs rather than placing the puck on the ice between the two sticks. ''Wag'' also introduced the whistle for stoppage of play rather than the bell, which must have lightened the referee's load considerably.

Hockey pucks were originally two pieces of material glued together, and it was Waghorne who ruled ''no goal'' one night when a puck split in two, one piece entering the net and one flying into the boards. Waghorne ruled the legal size had not entered the net.

JACK WALKER

BORN: Silver Mountain, Ontario, November 28, 1888
DIED: February 16, 1950
POSITION: Left Wing and Rover, Port Arthur, 1911; Toronto Arenas, 1913–15; Seattle Metropolitans (PCHA), 1916–24; Victoria Cougars (PCHA), 1925–26; Detroit Falcons, 1926–28
AWARDS: Hockey Hall of Fame, 1960

Jack Walker broke into hockey with Port Arthur in 1911 before moving on to Toronto where he was on the Stanley Cup-winning squad of 1914. This diminutive left wing/rover had perfected the hook check to a fine art, making him one of the most feared defensive forwards in the provinces. Jack could carry his load of the offense as well and displayed a deft scoring touch around his opponent's net.

Moving to Seattle of the PCHA in 1916, Walker settled down for an eleven-year stint on the West Coast before finishing his career with Detroit of the NHL.

Seattle won three championships and one Stanley Cup with Walker manning the port side, where he starred as a fearless backchecker. Walker moved on to Victoria when Seattle dropped out of the league and quickly established himself as their regular left winger. Victoria won the championship in 1925 and a brilliant individual effort by Walker helped defeat the mighty Montreal Canadiens for the Stanley Cup.

In all, this tireless two-way player appeared on seven championship teams and three Cup winners. In 1921 he was named to the PCHA All-Star team.

MARTY WALSH

BORN: Kingston, Ontario, 1883
DIED: Gravenhurst, Ontario, 1915
POSITION: Center, Queen's University, 1906; Ottawa Senators, 1908–12
AWARDS: Leading Scorer (prior to NHL's Art Ross Trophy), 1909–11; Hockey Hall of Fame, 1962

Marty Walsh was a multitalented centerman who impressed even the great Frank McGee with his play while he was still a schoolboy star for Queen's University. The Queen's U squad had unsuccessfully challenged the powerful Ottawa Silver Seven, but Walsh's play for the collegians wasn't quickly forgotten by the sophisticated pros.

Walsh finally joined the Ottawa squad in 1908 and was an immediate success, scoring 28 goals in 9 games. He starred for the Senators for the next four seasons, directing them to two Stanley Cups and picking up an incredible 160 goals in 67 games. These heroics included a ten-goal splurge in a 1911 game against Port Arthur.

MICHAEL ROBERT (MIKE) WALTON

BORN: Kirkland Lake, Ontario, January 3, 1945
POSITION: Center, Toronto Maple Leafs, 1966–71; Boston Bruins, 1971–73; Minnesota Fighting Saints (WHA), 1973–
AWARDS: All-Star (WHA Second Team), 1974; Bill Hunter Trophy (WHA Leading Scorer), 1974; WHA Team Canada, 1974

Walton signed with the Toronto Maple Leafs as a National Hockey League rookie in 1966–67, and became an integral part of the Leafs' family—in more ways than one. He married Candy Hoult, granddaughter of Conn Smythe, Leafs' founder and president, and niece of Stafford Smythe, Conn's son and successor. One would have thought these credentials would cement his relationship with the Leafs, but by February 1969 it was clear this was just not the case. After doing more bench-sitting for Punch Imlach than he believed he deserved, Mike walked out on Toronto in the homestretch of their desperate playoff drive. It took the mediation of Mike's attorney, Al Eagleson, to achieve a truce and return Mike to the team, which then gained a playoff berth.

Still, the Leafs were humiliated in the Stanley Cup round by the Bruins, and in the wake of the four-game defeat, Imlach was fired. But this was not to be the end of Walton's woes. Under coach John McLellan, Walton moved up and down faster than a yo-yo.

By late November 1970 Walton was terribly depressed, and after watching one too many Maple Leafs' victories from the sidelines, he again walked out on the team.

He refused to rejoin the Leafs, and was suspended. In the depths of his despair, and with his livelihood in jeopardy, Mike visited an NHL-sanctioned psychiatrist. The doctor reported that Mike's depressive illness, complicated by his family relationship to the team, would attain serious proportions if he remained with the Leafs.

Finally, on February 1, 1971, Walton was traded to the Philadelphia Flyers, and then to the Bruins as part of a complicated three-way deal. Although Mike skated hesitantly for the Bruins at first, he regained his confidence and a year later helped Boston win the Stanley Cup.

Just when he seemed to be sitting on top of the hockey world, the nomadic center jumped to the WHA's Minnesota Fighting Saints, signing a three-year contract that included, among other provisions, hefty scoring bonuses and an option to return to the NHL after his first WHA season. Not so coincidentally, Mike's kid brother, Rob, also was signed by the Saints, which turned out to be a mixed blessing. Both Waltons played mediocre hockey through December 1973 and the Fighting Saints went nowhere. Then Rob was traded to the Vancouver Blazers, and Mike and the Saints went into orbit. The 5-9, 170-pound Walton sped past the pack—including former WHA scoring pace-setters Andre Lacroix, Gordie Howe, and Wayne Carleton—and finished the season with 117 points on 57 goals and 60 assists, as well as the WHA scoring title.

Walton performed admirably in the Saints' opening playoff round in which they routed Edmonton, and was spectacular in a losing cause against Gordie Howe's Houston Aeros. Then, just as rumors bubbled forth that Walton might skip back to the NHL again, Mike signed a new Saints' contract that purportedly made him one of the three highest paid players in the game, courtesy of Eagleson. Observers estimated it to be a five-year pact worth $800,000 to $1,000,000.

The twenty-nine-year-old Walton evidently found a comfortable home after his psychic and geographical struggles, although he was a keen disappointment skating for Team Canada in the 1974 series against the Russians.

RONALD LEON (RON) WARD

BORN: Cornwall, Ontario, September 12, 1944
POSITION: Center, Toronto Maple Leafs, 1969–70; Vancouver Canucks, 1971–72; New York Raiders (WHA), 1972–73; Vancouver Blazers/Los Angeles Sharks (WHA), 1973; Cleveland Crusaders, 1974–
AWARDS: All-Star (WHA Second Team), 1973

Center Ron Ward is probably the strangest feast-or-famine story in modern hockey. After playing briefly with the Toronto Maple Leafs (no goals scored), and one full season with the Vancouver Canucks (two goals scored), Ward jumped to the New York Raiders, now San Diego Mariners, of the WHA and started making up for lost time.

By season's end, Ron had racked up 51 goals and finished second among league scorers. Yet before the following season ended, Ward had been traded three times, and Ward ultimately wound up in Cleveland.

GRANT DAVID "KNOBBY" WARWICK

BORN: Regina, Saskatchewan, October 11, 1921
POSITION: Forward, New York Rangers, 1941–48; Boston Bruins, 1948–49; Montreal Canadiens, 1949–50

"Knobby" Warwick played a robust and efficient brand of offensive hockey for the Rangers from 1941–42 until he was dealt to Boston in 1947–48. He finished his NHL career in 1949–50 with the Canadiens, but his chief source of fame was yet to come. Knobby received his "amateur" reinstatement and played for the Penticton, British Columbia, V's, a senior division club that won the Allan Cup in 1954. Surrounded by a hard-bitten crew, Knobby, along with his brothers Bill and Dick, skated for Penticton in the World Amateur Hockey championships in 1955 at Krefeld, Germany. The Canadians brought a boisterous, gashouse-gang style of hockey to the championships. Paced by the galvanic Warwick brothers, Penticton reached the finals against a favored Russian sextet and whipped the Soviet club, 5–0. The Warwicks, but particularly Knobby, were hailed as national heroes.

WASHINGTON CAPITALS

The choice of Washington, D.C. as the site of a new NHL franchise in 1974 isn't as bizarre as it looks on the surface. Washington was a member of the old Eastern Amateur Hockey League with the Washington Eagles, who became the Washington Lions near the end of World War II, and reached their acme in the AHL, before dissolving in the fifties.

Next door to Washington, in Baltimore, there is also a long involvement with shinny. At the outset of World War II, with players rapidly disappearing into the services, the Curtis Bay Cutters were formed from a Coast Guard outfit outside Baltimore. After the war Baltimore iced the Blades, and later, in 1962, entered the AHL with the Clippers. Throughout this history, the capital area teams were feeders for the NHL and many a potential star labored below the Mason-Dixon Line before making the bigs.

When Abe Pollin and his consortium of backers won the franchise, they decided to build a new arena, the Capital Centre, complete with huge instant-replay screens above center ice. Pollin, owner of the NBA Bullets basketball team, elected Milt Schmidt to put together a team.

Schmidt, a Hall of Famer and center on the famous Bruin Kraut Line of the late thirties and forties, had retired from playing in 1954 to coach the Bruins, becoming their general manager in 1967. He brought in Lefty McFadden as his assistant general manager, Jimmy Anderson as coach, and Red Sullivan as head scout. McFadden, a former writer, had organized the Dayton (Ohio) Gems of the IHL; Anderson had played in the minors and coached in Springfield, Oklahoma City, and Dayton; Sullivan had been a top NHL player and an indifferent coach with the Rangers and Pittsburgh. There was more talent behind the bench than there would be on it!

Prior to this expansion round the NHL had ruled that no new club could trade away its amateur draft choice numbers for two years. Established teams such as Montreal had bolstered their clubs tremendously by robbing weak new clubs of their first round amateur numbers, depriving the expansion clubs of their opportunity for talented new blood.

The Capitals had also learned from teams like the Islanders that it pays to sign draft choices fast, before they are enticed out of the league by the WHA. Schmidt signed defenseman Greg Joly of the Regina Pats and MVP in the Memorial Cup playoffs. He also signed the number two pick, winger Mike Marson of Sudbury, a chunky black who showed up in training camp more than twenty pounds overweight. (Ironically, in June 1975, the Caps traded away their first-round draft choice to the Stanley Cup-winning Philadelphia Flyers, for veteran Bill Clement, apparently with NHL sanction!)

From the expansion and intraleague drafts Washington garnered the likes of second-rate forwards Denis Dupere, Dave Kryskow, Gord Brooks, Jack Egers, Pete Laframboise, Steve Atkinson, Mike Bloom, and Lew Morrison. On defense they collected Bill Mikkelson, Gord Smith, and Yvon Labre. They drafted Ron Low and Michel Belhumeur for goal and purchased the aged, toupeed Doug Mohns from the Atlanta Flames to be father to the inexperienced defense and Bill Lesuk from the Los Angeles Kings to bolster the offense. Tommy Williams bolted the WHA New England Whalers for the Capitals. Out of this potpourri of mediocrity, only Denis Dupere could be called something other than questionable, and in three seasons with Toronto he had never tallied more than 13 goals in one season.

The season began with Washington scribes clutching for straws in a haystack of futility—they would talk of brilliant rookie play while the team tolled another loss, or "Capitals Defense Sparkles in Defeat." If nothing else, the new team would set records for writers trying to be positive about something hopelessly negative.

Jack Egers, drafted from New York with a bad back, had to undergo surgery. On November 2, 1974, Schmidt picked up veteran defenseman Rod Seiling on waivers from New York, and a day later traded him to Toronto for Tim Ecclestone and defenseman Will Brossart. Schmidt sold Ecclestone to Atlanta and by the end of November Brossart had a broken ankle.

Perhaps the biggest surprise was that the Capitals beat the Chicago Black Hawks and tied the Kings in their first two home games. Washington writers described a Capitals' "streak" in terms of not losing two games in a row!

One night a Washington TV "color" man interviewed Canadiens' captain Henri Richard, and no doubt expecting a phony saccharine reply, he asked Richard if the Capitals' chances lay in the future. Richard replied, "I don't see *any* chances for them." Spoken like a true son of hockey past, but Richard had forgotten that the New York Islanders, the garbage can of the NHL in 1972, were beating everyone in sight by 1974. By the time the Capitals had completed their freshman season, they had set a record for futility with only 8 wins, 67 losses, and 5 ties. They went through three coaches, starting with Jimmy Anderson and ending with general manager Milt Schmidt who ultimately went behind the bench while also running the front office. In between Schmidt asked scout Red Sullivan to coach the Caps after Anderson was fired. Sullivan tried the job for a few weeks until it upset his metabolism so much he relinquished the post and Schmidt took over as coach and manager. Despite their horrendous record, the Caps frequently drew large crowds and showed promise to eventually become one of the most successful franchises in the NHL.

BRYAN JOSEPH "BUGSY" WATSON

BORN: Bancroft, Ontario, November 14, 1942
POSITION: Defenseman, Montreal Canadiens, 1963–65, 1967–68; Detroit Red Wings, 1965–67, 1974– ; Oakland Seals, 1968–69; Pittsburgh Penguins, 1969–74; St. Louis Blues, 1974

Back in 1966, Bobby Hull dubbed Bryan Watson "Superpest" for his role of shadowing the Black Hawks' star whenever he was on ice. The hard-hitting veteran defenseman is nicknamed "Bugsy," and Watson is still dogging the game's big stars. Never one to bypass a set-to, Watson has been bothering opponents (and teammates) in Detroit, Montreal, Oakland, Pittsburgh, St. Louis, and, once again, Detroit. In 1971–72, Bugsy led the NHL in bugging players and referees alike, collecting 212 penalty minutes.

HARRY PERCIVAL WATSON

BORN: Saskatoon, Saskatchewan, May 6, 1923
POSITION: Left Wing, Brooklyn Americans, 1941–42; Detroit Red Wings, 1942–43, 1945–46; Toronto Maple Leafs, 1946–55; Chicago Black Hawks, 1955–57

One of the strongest—and least publicized—lines in NHL history comprised Toronto's Syl Apps, Sr. (center), Bill Ezinicki (right wing), and the least known forward of the trio, left winger Harry Watson. A onetime Brooklyn American, Watson skated powerfully, shot hard and true, and, unknown to most, was one of the kindest yet toughest forwards ever to patrol the majors. Watson, Apps, and Ezinicki powered the Leafs to Stanley Cups in 1947 and 1948. He once broke Boston defenseman Murray Henderson's nose with one punch.

Every NHL skater respected Watson's fighting ability although he frequently was a candidate for the Lady Byng Trophy for sportsmanlike play. Once, during a Leaf-Red Wing Pier Six brawl, Watson found himself confronted by defenseman Bill Quackenbush, himself a Byng candidate. While everyone else was pushing and shoving, Quackenbush grabbed Watson by the shoulder. "Shall we waltz?" he asked, grinning.

"No," Watson grinned back, "let's get in the middle and start shoving a bit. I think they're going to take pictures!"

JIMMY WATSON

BORN: Smithers, British Columbia, August 19, 1952
POSITION: Defenseman, Philadelphia Flyers, 1972–

The junior member of the Watson family on Philadelphia's defense is Jim. Showing the cool for which his sibling Joe is renowned, Jim was played solidly when the Flyers captured the Stanley Cup in 1974 and 1975. "He is one of the best and most underrated defensemen in the NHL," said coach Fred Shero.

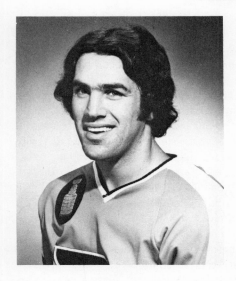

Jimmy Watson

JOSEPH JOHN (JOE) WATSON

BORN: Smithers, British Columbia, July 6, 1943
POSITION: Defenseman, Boston Bruins, 1964–65; Philadelphia Flyers, 1967–

A Flyer from the word go, Joe Watson has been Mr. Steady on the Philadelphia backline. He is also the resident cheerleader, "the only yell guy on the team when I got there," says coach Fred Shero. Watson's finest season coincided with Philadelphia's top semester, and Joe was named to the West Division Mid-Year All-Star squad. He is Jim Watson's older brother.

PHILLIPE HENRI (PHIL) WATSON

BORN: Montreal, Quebec, October 24, 1914
POSITION: Center, New York Rangers, 1935–43, 1944–48; Montreal Canadiens, 1943–44; Coach, New York Rangers, 1955–60; Boston Bruins, 1961–62; Philadelphia Blazers (WHA), 1972–73; Vancouver Blazers, 1973–74
AWARDS: All-Star (Second Team), 1942

Phil Watson was a classy center for the Rangers and was architect for Bryan Hextall on right wing and Lynn Patrick on the left. Together, they comprised the Rangers' top line in the late thirties and early forties until World War II disrupted them.

Watson never served in the armed forces. After the 1942–43 season, he was "loaned" to the Montreal Canadiens. Phil purportedly took a job in a war plant, was exempted from the draft, and was able to play a full season with the Canadiens. He returned to New York in 1944–45 and finished his career with the Rangers in 1947–48.

A battler who rarely won a fight, Watson played his last game as a Ranger in the semifinals of the Stanley Cup playoffs against the Red Wings. Detroit wiped out the Rangers in the series, the final game of which was played at Madison Square Garden. Symbolically, Watson squared off with Jimmy McFadden of the Red Wings, who rarely won a fight. This time McFadden won.

Watson turned to coaching, first with the New York Rovers of the Eastern League and eventually the Rangers in 1955–56. He inherited a team developed by Frank Boucher, his former mentor, and guided it to a playoff berth in his rookie coaching season. His flamboyant style appealed to New York newsmen and he became the darling of the press—until he started losing.

By the 1958–59 season his players had become disenchanted with Watson. Although the Rangers had been playing well, Watson ordered brutal practices. Once, *immediately* after a loss at Madison Square Garden, Watson ordered his skaters *back* onto Garden ice and put them through an energy-sapping workout.

On March 11, 1959, the Rangers had a nine-point lead over fifth-place Toronto. Watson's practices had drained the Rangers and they blew the lead, finishing fifth on the final night of the season in what was the biggest collapse in sports since the 1951 Dodgers folded to the Giants.

Watson's days were numbered in New York. He soon was fired, later surfacing in Boston where he also failed. When the WHA was organized, Watson popped up again this time with the Philadelphia Blazers. When the Blazers moved to Vancouver, Watson went with them. However, he soon left the club and retired from pro hockey.

THOMAS RONALD (TOM) WEBSTER

BORN: Kirkland Lake, Ontario, October 4, 1948
POSITION: Right Wing, Boston Bruins, 1968–70; Detroit Red Wings, 1970–71; California Seals, 1971–72; New England Whalers (WHA), 1972–
AWARDS: All-Star (WHA Second Team), 1972–73

Tom Webster was a highly touted draft choice of the Boston Bruins in 1968, after leading the Junior OHA with 50 goals and 64 assists for 114 points. His NHL career then became largely a history of injuries: He missed part of the 1968–69 season with abdominal surgery, and most of the 1969–70 season with torn cartilage in a knee that also required surgery.

In June 1970 Webster was drafted by the new expansion Buffalo Sabres who promptly traded him to the Detroit Red Wings for goalie Roger Crozier. In

Tom Webster

1970–71 he played his first injury-free season with the Wings, on a line with Alex Delvecchio and Gordie Howe, and finally produced up to expectation, with 30 goals and 37 assists for 67 points.

Traded to the California Seals the next season, Webster then spent most of the year with a spinal injury which also required surgery. In 1972 Tom jumped to the WHA New England Whalers where he began playing in top form, with the records to prove it. His first season with the Whalers, Webster joined the ranks of the 50 goal-scorers, with 53 and 50 assists, to break the 100-point mark. He's fast and makes stickhandling look like a cinch, something he must have picked up from Howe and Delvecchio.

RALPH "COONEY" WEILAND

BORN: Seaforth, Ontario, November 5, 1904
POSITION: Center, Boston Bruins, 1928–32, 1935–39; Ottawa Senators, 1932–34; Detroit Red Wings, 1934–35; Coach, Boston Bruins, 1939–41
AWARDS: Art Ross Trophy, 1930; Lester Patrick Trophy, 1972; All-Star (First Team) as coach, 1941; Hockey Hall of Fame, 1971

"Cooney" Weiland centered "the Dynamite Trio," playing between Dit Clapper and Dutch Gainor when the Boston Bruins won their first Stanley Cup in 1929. He scored 43 times in 44 games that season. Weiland led the Hubmen to another title in 1939, then coached the Bruins to the NHL championship in

Cooney Weiland

1939–40 and the Stanley Cup in 1940–41. A winner of the Lester Patrick Trophy for "outstanding service to hockey in the United States," Weiland coached Harvard's Ivy League powerhouses from 1950–71.

Weiland doesn't approve completely of hockey as it is now played: "Years ago, you could always see great man-to-man showdowns, one-on-one with the goaltender. Now, you are never sure who scored the goal and how it's scored. There are so many people in front of the goaltender, jockeying for position and slapping at the puck.

"There's no bodychecking in hockey today, either," Weiland continues. "They call it bodychecking, but it's really boardchecking, which isn't the same. I'm talking about rocking the guy at mid-ice."

As a coach, Cooney always stressed defensive hockey. "Any championship team has to have a sound defense. They have to know when to play defense and how to check each man, keep his man under control."

EDWIN VERNON (EDDIE) WESTFALL

BORN: Belleville, Ontario, September 19, 1940
POSITION: Right Wing, Boston Bruins, 1961–72; New York Islanders, 1972–

It took eleven seasons, but Eddie Westfall has finally become a team leader—even if it is because of seniority. A spear carrier defensive forward and sometime blue liner with the powerhouse Bruins of the late sixties, it was not until

Eddie was tabbed by the New York Islanders in the 1972 expansion draft that his true worth was realized.

Named the captain of the fledgling sextet, Westie's veteran savvy proved to be a steadying influence on the improving Isles' performance, and within three years of birth the team was making a respectable showing in the playoffs under the aegis of "Captain Eddie," a star in the 1975 cup round.

HARRY "RAT" WESTWICK

BORN: Ottawa, Ontario, April 23, 1876
DIED: April 3, 1957
POSITION: Goaltender/Rover, Ottawa Silver Seven, 1895–1908
AWARDS: Hockey Hall of Fame, 1962

Harry Westwick broke into hockey in 1895 with the legendary Ottawa Silver Seven. "Rat" was a goalie by trade in those days, but after only two games in the nets some insightful observer suggested that he switch to the forward line. It was no sooner said than done and Westwick became the Silver Seven's regular rover for the next twelve seasons, bagging better than a goal per game over his lengthy career.

Harry played on three consecutive Stanley Cup winners with the Seven.

KENNETH MALCOLM (KEN) WHARRAM

BORN: Ferris, Ontario, July 2, 1933
POSITION: Right Wing, Chicago Black Hawks, 1951–70
AWARDS: Lady Byng Trophy, 1964; All-Star (First Team), 1964, 1967

A speedy, intelligent right winger, Ken Wharram was the dynamo on one of the NHL's most productive units—Chicago's Scooter Line, along with center Stan Mikita and left winger Ab McDonald. Wharram actually played his first game as a Black Hawk in 1951–52, but he didn't achieve acclaim until November 1960 when coach Rudy Pilous inserted Wharram with the crafty young Mikita and the galumphing McDonald. Manager Tommy Ivan dubbed them "the Scooter Line." Coach Pilous regarded Mikita as the playmaker and McDonald the positional player who did the heavy checking. "Wharram," said Pilous, "is the real scooter. He's after the puck like a hound dog." Wharram took off as a scorer in 1960–61, the year Chicago won the Stanley Cup.

At the age of thirty-six, apparently at the top of his game, Wharram developed a heart condition. A year later, in September 1970, Wharram officially retired.

ALTON WHITE

BORN: Amherst, Nova Scotia, May 31, 1945
POSITION: Right Wing, New York Raiders (WHA), 1972–73; Los
  Angeles Sharks (WHA), 1972–74; Michigan Stags (WHA), 1974

Alton White is important in the annals of hockey, if not for his playing, for the fact that he is one of a mere handful of blacks who have ever made it even to the minors.

White played minor league hockey for years, until the birth of the World Hockey Association in 1972–73, when he joined the new New York Raiders.

The fact was that White's talents were so minimal (he's a good skater, but poor on checking and shooting) that he was traded to the Los Angeles Sharks in midseason. New York was too needy to carry any dead wood. Even in California White couldn't quite make the team until 1973–74, when he was brought back up from Greensboro by the Sharks, and he moved with the team to Michigan in 1974. Alas, by December 1974 he returned to the minors.

WILLIAM EARL (BILL) WHITE

BORN: Toronto, Ontario, August 26, 1939
POSITION: Defenseman, Los Angeles, 1967–70; Chicago, 1970–
AWARDS: All-Star (Second Team), 1972, 1973, 1974

Bill White had the fortune, or misfortune, depending on how you look at it, of playing in Springfield under Eddie Shore, the ex-Bruin defensive legend. Living with Shore would either teach a player one hell of a lot of hockey, or turn him into a basket case. In White's case, he became a damn good defenseman.

He's long and tall and does his job without fanfare. He can lug the puck out with great speed and élan, but his forte is behind the blue line, thus he is usually low on goals.

White came to the NHL with the birth of expansion and the Los Angeles Kings, who owned the Springfield minor league team. In the middle of the 1969–70 season, White was traded to Chicago with Bryan Campbell and goaltender Gerry Desjardins for Gilles Marotte, Jim Stanfield and goaltender Denis DeJordy. He has been the best defenseman the Black Hawks have had since Pat Stapleton left the NHL.

JUHA MARKKU "WHITEY" WIDING

BORN: Uleaborg, Finland, July 4, 1947
POSITION: Center, New York Rangers, 1969–70; Los Angeles Kings,
   1970–

The first pioneer in the great Scandinavian hockey invasion, Juha Widing (pronounced Yoo-ha Vee-ding) was lured away from the fjords in 1969, when he was a Swedish national hero, having just completed a successful tour of duty with the Swedish national team.

Signed by the New York Rangers, Whitey couldn't crack the Blueshirts' talented lineup and was shipped to the Los Angeles Kings along with Real Lemieux in return for Ted Irvine.

With the Kings, Widing established himself as one of the smoothest skaters in the NHL. He also demonstrated his nose for the net, leading the Kings in scoring for his first three full seasons on the Coast.

THOMAS MARK (TOM) WILLIAMS

BORN: Duluth, Minnesota, April 17, 1940
POSITION: Right Wing, Boston Bruins, 1962–69; Minnesota North
   Stars, 1969–71; California Seals, 1971–72; New England Whalers
   (WHA), 1972–74; Washington Capitals, 1974–

After two seasons in the WHA, Tom Williams returned to the established NHL, where he had performed solidly for Boston, Minnesota, and California. Williams's best pro season was 1969–70, when he accumulated 67 points (15–52) for the North Stars. His most memorable moment came in the 1960 Olympics when he set up the gold-medal winning score for the American team as they upset the world champion Soviets. In 1974–75 he played for the NHL's new Washington team.

CAROL "CULLY" WILSON

BORN: 1893
DIED: Unknown
POSITION: Right Wing, Toronto Arenas (NHA), 1913–16; Seattle Met-
   ropolitans (PCHA), 1916–19; Toronto St. Pats, 1919–20; Montreal
   Canadiens, 1921; Hamilton Tigers, 1921–23; Calgary Tigers
   (PCHL), 1923–26; Chicago Black Hawks, 1926–27

With a handle like Carol, a guy has to be the toughest kid on his block merely to survive. So it's no surprise that Carol "Cully" Wilson, despite his slight, 150-pound frame, was one of the roughest 'n readiest right wingers who ever graced a penalty box.

Despite his mean streak, Cully could score and stickhandle with the very best of them. He scored almost 200 goals over his fifteen-year career and was on two Stanley Cup-winning squads.

While playing for Seattle of the PCHA, Cully crosschecked an opponent so viciously that he was banished from the league for the next five years. Wilson found employment on the eastern Canadian rinks during that time, but was back west with Calgary for the 1924 season. While playing in the 1924 Stanley Cup playoffs, a Cully Wilson check put Montreal star Howie Morenz out cold and out of further action. This check, by the way, was perfectly legal and no penalty was called on the play.

Wilson played two more years with Calgary before moving on to Chicago of the NHL where he retired following the 1927 campaign.

DUNC WILSON

BORN: Toronto, Ontario, March 22, 1948
POSITION: Goalie, Philadelphia Flyers, 1969–70; Vancouver Canucks, 1970–73; Toronto Maple Leafs, 1973–75; New York Rangers, 1975–

Dunc Wilson, an often brilliant but erratic netminder during the Vancouver Canucks' formative years, finally seemed to find himself with the Toronto Maple Leafs. In 1973, after three seasons as resident whipping boy of the frustrated Canuck fans, Dunc was traded to the Leafs where he teamed with flaky Doug Favell and old pro Ed Johnston in Toronto's troika netminding rotation.

Normally a workhorse at Vancouver, a well-rested Wilson played one-third of the 1973–74 schedule, posting the best goals-against average of his career. Johnston was traded to the St. Louis Blues prior to the 1974–75 season, leaving the Leaf goaling to youngsters Wilson and Favell. Then in February 1975, Wilson, reputedly in trouble for missing Leaf team buses, was picked up by Ranger general manager Emile Francis for the $30,000 waiver price.

JOHNNY WILSON

BORN: Kincardine, Ontario, June 14, 1929
POSITION: Left Wing, Detroit Red Wings, 1949–55, 1957–59; Chicago Black Hawks, 1955–57; Toronto Maple Leafs, 1959–61; New York Rangers, 1961–62; Coach, Los Angeles Kings, 1970; Detroit Red Wings, 1972–73; Michigan Stags/Baltimore Blades (WHA), 1974–75; Cleveland Crusaders (WHA), 1975–

Johnny Wilson's eleven-year NHL career included a string of 580 consecutive regular-season games, a record he set in 1960 while playing for the Toronto

Maple Leafs. That record was broken by Andy Hebenton of the Rangers in 1964, and Andy still holds the record with 630 straight games played.

Johnny broke into hockey with his brother Larry, and played alongside him for several campaigns with Detroit and Chicago.

Although never a big scorer, Wilson nonetheless collected 23 goals in 1952–53 and 24 in 1955–56 for the best seasons of his career.

The end of his career was hastened by a broken collarbone suffered in training camp in the fall of 1961.

The Michigan Stags/Baltimore Blades gained his coaching services in 1974. In 1975 he signed to coach the WHA Cleveland Crusaders.

HAROLD LANG (HAL) WINKLER

BORN: Gretna, Manitoba, March 20, 1892
DIED: Unknown
POSITION: Goalie, Edmonton (PCHL), 1922–23; New York Rangers, 1926–27; Boston Bruins 1927–28

Goalie Hal Winkler's problem was that he was born too soon. After a distinguished pro career in Canada during the early twenties, Hal made it to the NHL just when the league was expanding to include more and more American cities. He entered the NHL during the 1926–27 season, playing for the New York Rangers and Boston Bruins. At the age of thirty-six, Winkler played a full forty-four-game schedule for the Bruins the following year. He allowed but 70 goals for a 1.59 average. Better still, Hal had 15 shutouts. By then he was a senior citizen and the Bruins had gifted Tiny Thompson in the wings so it was exit Winkler.

WINNIPEG JETS

The Winnipeg Jets became the cornerstone of the new World Hockey Association when owner Ben Hatskin gave Robert Marvin Hull a million dollars for becoming player-coach of the team.

Led by Hull, the Jets breezed to a first-place finish in the WHA's Western Division before bowing out to the eventual champions, the New England Whalers, in five games in the World Cup finals.

Hull knocked in 51 goals and garnered 103 points as he won the loop's Most Valuable Player Award and was named to the First All-Star Team. The Winnipeg fans came out to see Hull and the new team quite often, and the Jets finished third in the league in attendance.

In 1973–74, however, the league was stronger, and not even the presence of a Bobby Hull was enough to buoy up the Jets as they slumped to fourth place, finishing five games under .500. They were also eliminated in the quarterfinals by the Houston Aeros, who went on to win the Cup under the leadership of Gordie Howe. The City of Winnipeg financially backed the team.

Major changes took place both behind the bench and on the ice. Hull gave up the coaching duties and was replaced by Rudy Pilous. Also, under the WHA's new format, the Jets were placed in the new Canadian Division, with Quebec, Toronto, Vancouver, and Edmonton.

The Jets also went to Europe for talent, and came away with defensemen Heikki Rihiranta and Lars-Erik Sjoberg, forwards Veli Pekka Ketola, Ulf Nilsson and Anders Hedberg (the WHA Rookie-of-the-Year in 1975) and goaltender Curt Larsson. But the influx of troops from the Continent didn't help all that much and the Jets remained at or near the bottom of the Canadian Division for most of the 1974–75 season.

EDWARD RANDALL WISEMAN

BORN: Newcastle, New Brunswick, December 28, 1912
POSITION: Forward, Detroit Falcons, 1932–33; Detroit Red Wings, 1933–35; New York Americans, 1935–40; Boston Bruins, 1940–42

Never an All-Star, not quite a Hall of Famer, Eddie Wiseman remains suspended in the limbo of the accomplished nonsuperstar. That he played ten full NHL seasons speaks for his ability. Eddie broke in with Detroit in 1932–33, played three seasons in the Motor City before being traded to the New York Americans. He remained an Amerk forward until 1939–40 when he was dealt to the Boston Bruins. His career ended following the 1941–42 campaign. He may be forgotten by many but old Boston hockey fans recall the affection the Bruins' 1941 Stanley Cup victory and Wiseman's vital contribution—six goals and two assists.

WORLD HOCKEY ASSOCIATION

The World Hockey Association began in a dream, at least as early as 1967. That was when Dennis Arthur Murphy of Fullerton, California, was planning the formation of the American Basketball Association, and, in the back of his mind, thinking ahead to the WHA. Four years later, it was Murphy, again, who telephoned young California attorney Gary L. Davidson to tell him of his idea to start the World Hockey Association. On July 10, 1971, Articles of Incorporation for the WHA were filed in Delaware and By-Laws were drawn with Davidson, Murphy, and Donald J. Regan, a law partner of Davidson's, as officers.

Gary Davidson startled the hockey world in Chicago on October 20, 1971, by announcing that the WHA would operate without a reserve clause or "any substitute therefore, such as an option clause," in all player contracts.

Following two days of meetings at the Americana Hotel in New York, the World Hockey Association was formally organized on November 1, 1971, with ten franchises: Calgary, Chicago, Dayton, Edmonton, Los Angeles, Miami, New York, St. Paul, San Francisco, and Winnipeg. Two additional franchises were granted in Tampa, Florida, on November 21, to groups from Ontario and New England, bringing membership in the WHA to twelve.

A Chicago hockey writer predicted the WHA's chance of success was bleak because it "lacks three things: players, arenas, and television."

So, armed with Davidson's theory that the reserve clause was illegal, the twelve WHA teams signed more than seventy players from the NHL, giving each of them the only opportunity in their hockey-playing lives to improve their position by considering an alternative contract proposal.

Arenas suddenly became available to the new league. Some were there to be rented. Minnesota's St. Paul Civic Center—a $19 million hockey showplace of the world—was built. Others were renovated and provided with hockey facilities for the first time.

No professional sport has ever achieved success until it has had network television exposure. In the WHA's first year, Davidson negotiated television contracts in two nations—with the Columbia Broadcasting System in the United States and the Canadian Broadcasting Corporation in Canada.

By the first months of 1972 the WHA had begun to acquire the bodies it needed. Vern Buffey became the referee-in-chief for the new league, being the first NHL employee to jump ranks; two partners in a New Jersey law firm purchased the rights to a New York City franchise; and two outstanding coaches, Jack Kelley of Boston University and Glen Sonmor of Minnesota joined the New England Whalers and Minnesota Fighting Saints, respectively, both wearing two hats as coach and general manager. Owners for Quebec and Chicago came forth in February and the first player draft was held.

March and April looked like one of those good news-bad news jokes: United States Olympic goaltender Mike Curran signing for Minnesota, and the first two NHL players, Wayne Connelly and goalie George Gardner, joining Minnesota and Los Angeles, were the good news. The bad news was franchise troubles: Miami and Calgary defaulted and were cancelled. But by June two New Jersey businessmen established the Philadelphia Blazers and Cleveland's Nick Mileti, a baseball and basketball owner who had dearly coveted an NHL franchise, obtained the twelfth franchise for Cleveland, dubbing it the Crusaders.

Former Bruin Johnnie "Pie" McKenzie signed with Philadelphia as player-coach in June 1972 and then the real shocker hit the hockey world. On June 27, 1972, Bobby Hull, "the Golden Jet" and perennial superstar with the NHL

Chicago Black Hawks, signed a contract with the WHA Winnipeg Jets which included $1 million for signing, $250,000 a year for five years as player or player/coach, and another $100,000 a year for five years as a sort of glorified public relations and goodwill figure for the league.

After that the number of players jumping leagues began to look more like a flood than a trickle: Montreal's ace defenseman J. C. Tremblay joined the Quebec Nordiques, Bruin defenseman Ted Green stayed in Boston Garden, but went to the New England Whalers, and Boston playboy Derek Sanderson joined the Philadelphia Blazers for a reputed $2.65 million. The NHL was sufficiently threatened to take the new league to court, lawsuits proliferated rapidly, and the NHL succeeded in preventing Bobby Hull from playing the first fifteen games of the first WHA season before losing their battle. With the new competition, players salaries in both leagues began to take on unreal proportions—anyone negotiating a new contract simply hinted that he was talking to the other league.

Weaknesses began to show as the first season got underway, with the New York Raiders running into immediate financial difficulties and similar problems occurring in Philadelphia. The league took over the New York franchise, but in Philadelphia the Blazers decided that their problems centered around the non-productivity of the flaky Sanderson, and they paid him an alleged $1 million simply to leave the league!

By midseason the strongest franchises were New England, Quebec, Winnipeg, and Cleveland, with Houston and Chicago occasionally pulling in respectable crowds despite weak teams. By April 1, 1973, the WHA had attracted a surprising 2 million fans to its twelve arenas, and soon the New England Whalers became the first team to win the Avco World Trophy, the WHA equivalent of the Stanley Cup.

After the playoffs immediate action was taken to solve the problem of weak franchises: the Blazers were purchased by a group in Vancouver and moved there, the Ottawa Nationals switched to Toronto and became the Toros, and a syndicate purchased the Raiders, leaving them in New York, but changing the name to Golden Blades.

But along with the snags were more blockbusters to come. In the summer of 1973 word spread that the man with more goals scored in hockey than any other, former Detroit Red Wing Gordie Howe, would come out of retirement and sign with the Houston Aeros. More incredible, however, was the fact that Gordie would only sign on the condition that his two oldest boys, defenseman Marty and forward Mark, be signed by Houston also—right out of juniors. Unbelievably, this came to pass and in the fall of 1973 the hockey world first witnessed a father, son, and son act on ice. Another significant but anticlimactic event was the signing of Pat Stapleton as player-coach of the Chicago Cougars, as the veteran left the NHL Chicago Black Hawks.

Almost immediately after the WHA began its sophomore season, the New

York franchise was in trouble again, and the team was soon moved to Cherry Hill, New Jersey, renamed the New Jersey Knights and purchased by Baltimore real estate developer Joseph Schwartz. Shortly after midseason the WHA and NHL settled their differences out of court, with the WHA being reimbursed $1.7 million for legal costs, the reserve clause virtually being eliminated, and the two leagues agreeing to arrange for preseason exhibition games in the fall of 1974.

League founder Gary Davidson resigned (partly under pressure and partly to devote his time to the new World Football League) and was replaced by Dennis A. Murphy, who left his post as president and general manager of the Los Angeles Sharks. Meanwhile, Houston, with the blazing glory of the three Howes, easily won the Avco Trophy, while the foundering Los Angeles Sharks were transferred to Detroit as the Michigan Stags, and the equally sorry New Jersey Knights moved to San Diego to become the Mariners.

The 1974–75 season saw the introduction of two new teams, the Indianapolis Racers and Phoenix Roadrunners, joined by Cincinnati in 1975–76. The league was divided into three divisions, Canadian, East, and West, and the WHA played its first Team Canada series against the Russians, eventually losing the series in Moscow. Superstar Frank Mahovlich jumped from the Montreal Canadiens to the Toronto Toros; the Michigan Stags were in dire difficulties, eventually moving to Baltimore as the Blades, and Nick Mileti was edged out of power in Cleveland.

The Quebec Nordiques achieved the number one slot in the Canadian Division, with New England topping the East and Houston best in the West, heading into the 1975 playoffs. Houston won the Avco World Trophy for the second year in a row in May 1975. Murphy resigned in June 1975 and Hatskin became the league czar although he did not take the title President. Former NHL executive Leo Ornest was lured to the WHA to operate its new office in Toronto. The WHA also added Denver to its roster of teams in 1975, while the Chicago Cougars and Baltimore Blades folded and the Vancouver Blazers became the Calgary Cowboys.

LORNE "GUMP" WORSLEY

BORN: Montreal, Quebec, May 14, 1929
POSITION: Goalie, New York Rangers, 1952–53, 1954–63; Montreal
    Canadiens, 1963–70; Minnesota North Stars, 1970–74
AWARDS: Calder Trophy, 1953; Vezina Trophy, 1966 (shared with
    Charlie Hodge), 1968 (shared with Rogatien Vachon); All-Star
    (First Team), 1968, (Second Team) 1966

Gump Worsley was one of the most colorful, cantakerous, and stubborn characters in modern-day hockey. The nomadic netminder saw duty with ten clubs in five different leagues over his twenty-four-year professional career, leaving a hilarious trail of Worsley anecdotes wherever he parked his pudgy frame.

It took twenty-four years before Gump gave in and agreed to wear a mask while tending goal, and in this age of coast-to-coast competition, he never got over his intense fear of flying. In fact, it was said to be written into Gump's contract that he be allowed to fly in the pilot's cockpit so he could be sure the plane's skipper was paying attention.

Originally the property of the New York Rangers, Gump came up to the NHL with the 1952 Broadway team. Worsley was the diamond in the rough on this conglomeration of underachievers. His fearless performances while facing as many as fifty shots per game earned him the Calder Trophy as the NHL's rookie of the year.

Gump's round, jowled face and watery, hound-dog eyes sometimes gave the impression of intense nonchalance as he flopped around the ice covering up for his teammates' many blunders.

Worsley's comic-strip form became a fixture for New York's hockey community until the summer of 1963. At the annual league meetings in Montreal, Worsley was traded to the Montreal Canadiens.

Gump was thirty-four years old when he was traded to the Habs, and although few knew it at the time, Worsley had been reborn. It wasn't easy at first—Charlie Hodge had inherited the Hab netminding chores so Gump found himself gathering splinters on the Canadien bench or laboring for the minor league Quebec Aces. But the 1964–65 playoffs found Gump carrying the brunt of the Canadien netminding as the Habs rolled to the Stanley Cup. Worsley, supposedly in the twilight of his career, posted a 1.68 goals-against average including two shutouts to lead all playoff netminders.

Gump was a Canadien fixture for the next four seasons, steering them to three more Stanley Cups and twice winning the coveted Vezina Trophy, awarded annually to the loop's top netminder. Midway through the 1969–70 season, Worsley, then almost forty years old, was sold to the expansionist Minnesota North Stars. Teamed with another veteran, Cesare Maniago, this Mutt 'n Jeff pair of backstops proved they still had some good games left as they steered the Stars into the playoffs for the next five consecutive seasons.

After the 1972–73 season had ended, Gump, for the umpteenth time, announced his retirement from pro hockey. He returned to his home to watch the Stanley Cup finals before settling down to a life of leisure. The final round that year pitted his old Montreal Canadiens against the powerful Chicago Black Hawks. The series was being billed as a "battle of the goaltenders" as Hab Ken Dryden and Hawk Tony Esposito reigned as the loop's top two stoppers.

When the smoke had cleared after the highest scoring slugfest of a final round in recent history, Gump showed that his retirement age had not mellowed him one bit. "If those two guys are supposed to be the best," he observed acidly, "then I know I can play at least one more year."

He did just that at the age of forty-five, playing one more season with Minnesota before hanging up his goaler's pads for good.

ROY "SHRIMP" WORTERS

BORN: Toronto, Ontario, October 19, 1900
DIED: November 7, 1957
POSITION: Goalie, Pittsburgh Pirates, 1926–28; Montreal Canadiens, 1930; New York Americans, 1928–29, 1930–37
AWARDS: Hart Trophy, 1929; Vezina Trophy, 1931; All-Star (Second Team), 1932, 1934; Hockey Hall of Fame, 1969

Roy "Shrimp" Worters, one of the tiniest goaltenders in hockey history, broke into pro shinny with the Pittsburgh Yellowjackets of the USAHA. When the Pittsburgh Pirates were granted an NHL franchise in 1926, little Roy was signed as their netminder.

After three steady years with the Bucs, Roy got into a bitter contract dispute with the club's brass and was suspended by league president Frank Calder. The New York Americans, who had finished their season in the NHL's cellar, were in desperate need of a goalie with Roy's credentials. A deal was hastily worked out between the two clubs and in 1929 Roy was decked out in the red, white, and blue spangled jersies of the Amerks.

Worters played so well that first year with the New Yorkers that he lifted his club out of the league basement and into the playoffs. For his heroics, Roy was awarded the Hart Trophy as the league's most valuable player. It was the first time the honor had been bestowed on a backstop.

Shrimp's finest season was 1931 when he racked up a stingy 1.68 goals-against average and won the Vezina Trophy as the loop's top stopper. There was one small problem though—the Americans' forwards sometimes seemed unable to score any goals. Despite Roy's artful acrobatics in goal, the Americans failed to make the playoffs.

Worters played six more years with the punchless Americans, performing admirably, but unable to single-handedly carry his club to the playoffs. He finally retired in 1937.

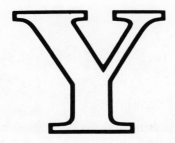

DOUGLAS (DOUG) YOUNG

BORN: Medicine Hat, Alberta, October 1, 1908
POSITION: Defenseman, Detroit Falcons, 1931–33; Detroit Red
    Wings, 1933–39; Montreal Canadiens, 1939–41

Doug Young could have been one of the most discussed players in hockey history, but he missed by an inch. A Detroit Red Wings' defenseman, Young played in the NHL's longest ever game, March 24–25, 1936. Skating against the Montreal Maroons in the Stanley Cup playoffs at the Forum, the Red Wings won the match, 1–0, after 116 minutes and 30 seconds of overtime on Mud Bruneteau's shot—at 2:25 A.M. However, Young had a splendid opportunity to win the match (and be permanently lionized) in the fifth sudden-death period when his shot hit Maroons' defenseman Lionel Conacher's skate and changed direction. The puck slid straight for an empty side of the net. Both Young and Montreal goalie Lorne Chabot appeared to have an equal chance to get to it first. Chabot won the race and that explains why everybody knows Mud Bruneteau while nearly everybody has forgotten Doug Young. Actually, Doug played commendably for Detroit from 1931 through 1939, finishing his major league career with two seasons for the Montreal Canadiens.

HOWARD JOHN EDWARD (HOWIE) YOUNG

BORN: Toronto, Ontario, August 2, 1937
POSITION: Defenseman, Detroit Red Wings, 1960–63, 1966–68; Chicago Black Hawks, 1963–64, 1968–69; Phoenix Roadrunners (WHA), 1974–

At one point (1962–63), defenseman Howie Young was regarded as the wildest, if not the toughest, skater in the NHL. He collected 273 penalty minutes that year, breaking Lou Fontinato's seven-year record and put the fear of God in many a foe. A super skater and hard shot, Young found inflammatory beverages more a challenge than his opponents. He played five seasons for the Detroit Red Wings and two for the Chicago Black Hawks until his unpredictability compelled the Hawks to unload Young to the minors. He eventually reformed while playing minor league hockey and wound up in the majors again in 1974–75 with Phoenix of the WHA.

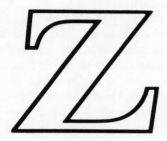

LAWRENCE (LARRY) "THE ROCK" ZEIDEL

BORN: Montreal, Quebec, June 1, 1928
POSITION: Defenseman, Detroit Red Wings, 1951–53; Chicago Black
   Hawks, 1953–54; Philadelphia Flyers, 1967–69

Few sports comebacks have ever been laced with the flair produced by defenseman Larry Zeidel in the summer of 1967. Zeidel was one of the few Jewish
players in professional hockey, and in Yiddish there's a word for what he did—
it's called *chutzpah*.

A rugged type, Zeidel had played briefly in the NHL for Detroit and Chicago before being demoted to the minors in 1954 where he played until 1967 when the National Hockey League expanded from six to twelve teams. In that year Zeidel, aged thirty-nine, compiled a flashy resume complete with a letter from a doctor stating he had the heart of a twenty-two-year-old and sent the brochure to everybody important on each of the twelve NHL teams.

Every club but one said "thanks-but-no-thanks." The Philadelphia Flyers were willing to take a chance. Manager Bud Poile signed Zeidel and started him alongside Joe Watson. The Flyers began winning and Larry appeared to be playing better hockey than he had with the Cup champion Red Wings or the Black Hawks (1953–54).

On November 4, 1967, the Flyers were scheduled to meet tougher competition than they had met in their expansion division—the Montreal Canadiens. That afternoon Bernie Parent, then a young goalie, and Zeidel were in their hotel room where Parent had a bad case of the shakes. But Zeidel encouraged him to think "positive" and to have confidence in his ability.

Five hours later, the game was over, Philadelphia 4, Montreal 1. Bernie Parent had thought "positive." A week later Philadelphia went to Boston and defeated the Bruins. A week after that Philadelphia defeated the Rangers. Zeidel started every game with Watson at his side.

The Flyers finished first, winning the Clarence Campbell Bowl, and Zeidel was among the best players on the club. Although the Flyers were eliminated from the playoffs Zeidel appeared to be a fixture with the Flyers. But he disputed with Poile in the 1968–69 season. Poile wanted Zeidel to play in Quebec of the American League, but Zeidel refused. He retired from hockey in 1969 and went into the investment counseling business.